UNIVERSITIES:
BRITISH, INDIAN, AFRICAN

UNIVERSITIES:
BRITISH, INDIAN, AFRICAN

A Study in the Ecology of Higher Education

ERIC ASHBY

in association with Mary Anderson

WEIDENFELD AND NICOLSON
5 Winsley Street London W1

© 1966 by Eric Ashby

Printed and bound in England by
Hazell Watson & Viney Ltd, Aylesbury, Bucks

CONTENTS

ACKNOWLEDGEMENTS

Without the support of the Carnegie Corporation of New York this book would not have been written. We describe in the introduction how the corporation came to finance the research on which our work is based. Chief among our acknowledgements is our indebtedness to the corporation's trustees and to two of its officers, Alan Pifer and Stephen Stackpole, for their interest and encouragement.

In collecting material we have received generous help from many institutions. We would particularly like to record our gratitude to the University of Ghana for hospitality to one of us (M.A.) and for giving us access to documents and records, especially to Thomas Hodgkin, director of the institute of African studies, also to Graham Irwin, who was head of the history department there at the time of our visit; to W. J. Harris and J. Packman, in the library of the University of Ibadan, for allowing us to borrow microfilms of ten years' issues of the Nigerian press; to Eric Belton of Makerere University College, Uganda, for access to files of the East African press and other records; to the Church Missionary Society for much valuable co-operation and for permission to publish some documents; and to the secretariat of the inter-university council for higher education overseas. The University of London, through the principal, Sir Douglas Logan, has allowed us to read, and to quote from, records concerning the scheme of special relationship. The colonial office has permitted us to reproduce two documents of historical importance from the records of the advisory committee on education in the colonies: the Currie report and the Channon report. Dr Channon himself has allowed us to use his memorandum to the advisory committee which was the turning point in British policy for higher education overseas; also he has given us access to his correspondence with the secretary of state for the colonies shortly before the appointment of the Asquith and Elliot commissions. Mr B. Cheeseman and Mr W. E. F. Ward have helped us to trace sources of information and Mrs Hussey kindly gave us material about the work of her husband. We are grateful to the president and fellows of Harvard University for allowing us to incorporate a few pages of material published in the Godkin Lectures for 1964, and to the association of commonwealth universities and Sir John Mountford for permission to quote from the Commonwealth Universities Yearbook.

A good deal of the material in part three of the book is based on personal visits one of us (E.A.) has made to universities in Africa over the last five years. Hospitality is one of the delightful qualities of African life and it would not be practicable for us to record our thanks to all who have entertained us and patiently explained to us their ideas about higher education. We would, however, like to mention specially Sir Bernard de Bunsen, who was until recently principal at Makerere; Mgr. L. Gillon, the rector of Lovanium University in the Congo; Dr Walter Adams at the university college in Salisbury; Dr Dafalla at the University of Khartoum; Dr Davidson Nicol at Fourah Bay College; and H. E. Lij Kassa Wolde Mariam in the Haile Sellassie I University.

We have had many illuminating conversations with people who have taken part in the founding of university institutions in Africa and, without in any way involving them in our opinions and arguments, we wish to record our gratitude to them: in Britain especially to Sir Christopher Cox, Sir James Duff, Mr Creech Jones, Dr Kenneth Mellanby, Professor Margaret Read, Sir Richard Southwell; and in Africa, among names too numerous to publish in full, Okoi Arikpo, K. Twum-Barima, J. B. Danquah, Sir Leslie M'Carthy, Eni Njoku, and K. A. B. Jones Quartey.

Several people generously consented to read parts of our typescript. They must not be blamed for our opinions or for inaccuracies which doubtless remain in the book, but without their help there would have been more inaccuracies and fewer sound opinions. In particular we record our thanks to Robin Moore, who criticised the whole of the section on India; Edward Shils, whose wise counsel has improved many parts of the book; T. Alty, who read the section on the higher education of Africans in South Africa; and D. Levy, who read the section on higher education in French Africa.

To our sorrow the two people whose advice we would have valued most have died. We would like to pay tribute to their memories. Lillian Penson taught one of us the disciplines of historical research; her energy and determination helped to launch the scheme of special relationship between the University of London and the colonial colleges; her special affection for the University of Khartoum will long be remembered there. John Lockwood frequently accompanied one of us on missions to African colleges. His genius for negotiation and conciliation among warring academics, his lively and youthful mind, his patience with pedants, rightly earned him the title (in a *Times* editorial) of 'one of the architects of the new Commonwealth'. These two people created some of the history which we have recorded.

E.A.

M.A.

April, 1966

INTRODUCTION

To understand the purpose of this book it is necessary to know how it came to be written. For a dozen years one of us (E.A.) has made frequent visits to tropical Africa to give advice on the development of university institutions. Most of these visits have been concerned with the technology of higher education: with finance, building programmes, expansion, administration, the spectrum of studies. Their purpose was to deal with problems of immediate, local, practical, relevance. Advice was given, or decisions were made, within a framework of assumptions which my colleagues and I never had time to examine, still less to question. The elements of the framework were first, assumptions about the history of 'British policy' for the export of universities to the Commonwealth; second, assumptions about the pattern of higher education appropriate for non-European societies; third, assumptions about the attitude of non-European societies to western learning. Our advice was accordingly empirical. We lacked an understanding-in-depth of the problems we were asked to think about; nor did we find books or people to enlighten us.

In 1961 the Carnegie Corporation of New York generously offered to finance a piece of work which would illuminate the historical background of these problems in Africa and which would offer reflections on present policies there. The corporation's grant made possible a partnership between a professional historian and a university administrator who could interpret the historian's findings from his own practical experience. This book is the result of that partnership.

In writing the book our most difficult problem has been to decide what to leave out. The subject sprawls all over the place. It requires some knowledge of history, education, and social anthropology. It could include – unless limits are drawn round it – a consideration of exports of higher education from America to the Philippines, from France to Vietnam, from Britain to Malaya. It could cover not only universities but technical colleges, teacher-training colleges, adult education. It could describe the systems of education existing in non-European societies before they were colonised. Let us therefore state clearly at the outset what this book includes, and what is left out.

U–E.I.A.—1*

The core of the book is a history and analysis of ideas about university education in the English speaking countries of tropical Africa, with special attention to the evolution (for it has been an evolution) of that body of intentions, beliefs, and prejudices which together are recognised as 'British policy'. We describe the influence of the United States on this policy. We discuss concepts of academic freedom and autonomy as they have developed in Britain and as they have fared in Africa. We have comments to make on relations between the university and the state. We try to cut a path through the tangled controversies which surround content of curricula and standards of achievement.

But this material cannot be understood unless it is put into a setting of place and time. To comprehend the university colleges planted in the Gold Coast, Nigeria, and Uganda one has to recollect the pattern of higher education in Britain in the late 1940s, and one has to recollect that in other parts of Africa there are other, and quite different, patterns of higher education. So we devote some space to a summary of ideas about the function and purpose of universities in Britain immediately before and after world war II; and, so that comparisons can be made, we include sketches, all from first hand experience, of the 'Bantu' university colleges in South Africa, and of the university systems in Ethiopia, in the Congo, and in African countries previously attached to France.

This material, in part three of the book, puts the story in a setting of place. As to the setting of time, British strategy for higher education overseas did not begin in Africa, nor did it begin in the twentieth century. Over a century ago universities were planted in Ireland, India and Australia; and in Ireland and India their creation was due to deliberate acts of the metropolitan government. Therefore, in part two of the book, we have written, largely from unpublished records, an account of the evolution of British policy for universities in India up to 1919. In part one we give a brief account, from published material, of university-founding in Ireland and in Australia, and the state of British universities at the time of these foundations, in the 1850s. Finally, since we have all the time been conscious of the ancient lineage of universities, and the part which this descent plays in contemporary thought, we have reminded ourselves, and our readers, how the export of universities has been going on for seven centuries, from France to England, from Italy to Scotland, from Spain to South America, from England to North America. The main theme of our study is merely a recent incident in the unbroken history of a remarkable medieval institution.

So much by way of introduction to the topics included in this book. Now we mention some of the topics we have had to leave out, with notes on where information about them can be found.

In describing commonwealth educational strategy since 1945 we confine ourselves to tropical Africa. We have omitted a great deal of material (which by and large supports our conclusions) from the West Indies, Malaya, Ceylon,

India and Pakistan.[1] Moreover, in order to keep the book within bounds, we have, even within Africa, excluded any consideration of post-secondary technical education.[2] The unlucky history of the colleges of arts, science, and technology (the so-called COCAST colleges) which were intended to offer an alternative to universities, still remains to be told. But it could not be told adequately without an analysis of the state of technical education in Britain, the attitude of the professional engineering institutes toward apprenticeship and the national certificate courses in Africa, and the salary-differentials in Africa between those holding degrees and those holding diplomas. The serious imbalance in many African countries between university and other kinds of further education is due more to economic than to educational reasons.[3] To discuss all this adequately would have made the book too long.

In our treatment of the Indian universities we have confined ourselves almost entirely to the relations between universities and governments. To have included the history of the universities themselves, or the attitude of Indian society toward western learning, or the political climate within which the universities worked, would have involved an enormous extension of the scope of our work. By selecting one aspect only of the history of higher education in India we believe we have provided the background necessary for part three of the book. But we leave untouched the field of the sociology of education in India; in any case scholars of great distinction are already at work in this field.[4]

In discussing the contribution now being made by the United States to higher education overseas we have confined ourselves to tropical Africa. It would give a most misleading impression of the scale of American aid if we did not emphasise here that commitments in Africa are only a small fraction of the massive total effort of the American people to lift the level of higher education in developing countries. Those who wish to put American aid to African higher education in perspective should consult the references and notes to this introduction.[5]

Another omission from our study is consideration of the non-European student who travels abroad for his higher education. It is still true in 1965 that about as many students from tropical Africa are attending universities in Europe and America as are attending universities in their own countries; and it is fair criticism to say that most African students would prefer to go abroad for their higher education than to have it at home. A good deal is known about African students in America, Britain, and France. Student societies, such as the West African Students' Union in London (WASU) and the Fédération des Étudiants d'Afrique Noire in Paris (FEANF), have played a notable part in the agitation for African nationalism. At the same time, Africans who have graduated from European universities are among the most reactionary, when they return home, in resisting adaptations of university systems to the needs and economic capacities of their homelands. A good start has already been made in the systematic study of the African student in

Europe and America, but we have had to omit consideration of it in this book.

We have omitted, too, discussion of the conflicting currents of opinion which surround the idea that Africans should replace expatriates on the staffs of African universities. Insofar as the university is a supra-national institution, this question is irrelevant; it is noteworthy that the University of Sydney, for instance, a century after its foundation, was still filling nearly half its chairs with graduates of British universities. Great universities pride themselves upon their cosmopolitanism. But inasmuch as African universities are inevitably nurseries for nationalism, it is politically important that as many posts as possible should be held by Africans, and it is clearly embarrassing that policies for the higher education of young Africans should be in the hands of their former overlords. We have discussed this dilemma elsewhere and concluded that however loudly the drums for Africanisation may be beaten in the press and in parliament, scholars from overseas are welcome on the faculties of African universities, provided they come as colleagues and not as neo-colonialists, and provided the administrative officers, such as vice-chancellors and registrars, are African.[6]

If African universities are to retain their quality, they will have to rely on support from expatriate teachers for a long time to come. And this means that the indigenous self-sustaining intellectual community, which Edward Shils regards as indispensable for a viable national system of higher education, is not likely to appear in African countries for many years.[7] So long as large numbers of university professors working in Africa look to Europe or America as the centre of gravity of their intellectual life, Africa will remain intellectually a province of Europe or America. The price of premature intellectual independence would be a deterioration in quality. The psychological problem is to persuade African countries to accept this filial position while they establish their own intellectual style and their own techniques, until they reach maturity by becoming not only recipients, but donors, of world knowledge. We see no short-term solution to this problem and we have nothing new to say about it.

Finally we have not attempted, except incidentally in our narrative, to assess the impact of higher education on African communities. On one hand there is no doubt that Africans avidly accept all the western education they can get, and on the whole prefer it as little altered as possible from the patterns of education to be found in Europe. (One reason for this is that the least adapted patterns of higher education lead to the most prestigious posts.) On the other hand there is equally no doubt that western education in Africa did not (except so far as it was concerned with science and technology) fill an intellectual vacuum: it displaced indigenous values deeply rooted in the African character, and some thoughtful Africans (and Europeans familiar with Africa) doubt whether the displacement has been for the better. It was Margery Perham who said that a western money economy and christian education are two acids eating into the healthy cells of family and tribal life.[8]

The process of corrosion is bound to go on. To wish it otherwise – to advocate a sort of atavistic African celtic revival – is of course nostalgic nonsense. Western civilisation is undoubtedly behaving like a dominant character in heredity, concealing the recessive indigenous civilisations. But what is concealed is not necessarily destroyed. Western civilisation, in the very process of exerting its dominance as it flows into the villages of Africa, itself becomes influenced by African values; so do the instruments of western civilisation, of which the university is one.

An exhaustive treatment of our theme would therefore require an analysis of the values transmitted in indigenous African education and their possible effects on the imported values of western education (the western assumption, for example, that 'improvement in living standards' means material improvement). We know already a good deal about these values: the preparation of children to submerge their individuality in that of the family or the tribe; the custom of giving the child at each stage of his development responsibilities commensurate with his maturity; the emphasis on conformity in order to preserve cohesion; the placid disregard for the clock; the tranquillity of human relationships; the vivid continuity between man and nature, and between the living, the dead, and the unborn. What no-one has yet reflected upon very deeply is the effect which these values will have upon imported systems of western education.[9]

Our task is unfinished. We have selected for this book only a few problems in the ecology of higher education. We hope that other scholars, particularly in Africa, will continue the work we have begun.

Part I

THE SETTING*

* In this part of the book the references to sources are assembled in a bibliographical summary at the end (p. 380). In the text the only references given are those to certain quotations.

CHAPTER ONE

HISTORICAL BACKGROUND

I COSMOPOLITANISM IN THE MEDIEVAL UNIVERSITY

An institution is the embodiment of an ideal. In order to survive, an institution must fulfil two conditions: it must be sufficiently stable to sustain the ideal which gave it birth and sufficiently responsive to remain relevant to the society which supports it. The university is a medieval institution which fulfils both these conditions. The ideal – the disinterested pursuit of learning – which drew scholars to Oxford seven centuries ago still unites a guild of scholars in that city, and similar guilds flourish in hundreds of other cities. Yet the university has kept pace with the mutations of society; a college in California is as relevant to modern American society as the *studium generale* in ancient Paris was relevant to church and state in the middle ages.

The first universities fell under the jurisdiction of the catholic church. This was an enormous benefit to them because the authority of the church covered Europe; and so the medieval universities were truly supra-national. Their frontiers were those of the church which, for a European citizen of those times, were the frontiers of the civilised world. Their students spoke the same tongue and knelt before the same Cross. Indeed to be a student was to belong to an international fraternity, coincident with the catholic faith. The wandering scholar, migrating from one university to another, was a common sight on the roads of Europe. The very word 'university' denoted in ancient Bologna the society of foreign students, associating themselves together in 'nations': Ultramontane, Lombard, Tuscan, and Roman. The peoples of Europe were united in an intellectual solidarity they have never since regained.

One consequence of this was an isomorphism among the universities of medieval Europe. There were two templates, as it were, from which new universities were cast: the Bolognese student-university and the Parisian university of masters. For centuries the new foundations, from Uppsala to Lisbon, were formed in one or other of these two moulds. Two circumstances secured this isomorphism: the central control from Rome, for even when, as in Spain and Portugal, the universities were founded by kings, it was the Pope who granted the *ius ubique docendi* which constituted official recognition; and a uniform cultural milieu, inconceivable to a modern European, which surrounded educated men throughout christendom. Aristotle's *Ethics*, Ptolemy's *Almagesta*, the *Topics* of Boethius: these and a score of other books were the common curriculum from Scotland to Spain.

'Nothing', wrote Rashdall, 'can more strikingly illustrate the cosmopolitanism of the medieval university system than the fact that up to the middle of the fourteenth century Germany possessed no university at all'; and it was not until the fifteenth century that universities were founded in Scotland and Scandinavia. Students from these countries (and there were many of them) travelled abroad for their studies, just as students from some tropical African countries do at the present day. When new universities were founded, even though the initiative came from a local prince or bishop, they were given constitutions based on those of Bologna or Paris, they hired teachers from these or other established universities, and they adopted a curriculum and a pattern of faculties which had become standardised wherever the catholic church held sway. Moreover the social purpose of these universities was similar all over Europe. Their scholars concentrated on the official corpus of knowledge of the age. Their graduates, trained as theologians, lawyers, or physicians, occupied positions of responsibility in church and state. They had their moments of ascendancy, when they became immensely influential in forming the ideas and even guiding the politics of their time; indeed there was an occasion in the fifteenth century when the University of Paris became 'a European power'. The universities had moments of lethargy, too, when they became querulous and defensive, obstructing the progress of thought, sheltering mediocrity and bigotry.

At the end of the fifteenth century there were in all seventy universities. Over some million square miles of Europe they constituted an intellectual commonwealth, embodying the same ideal, fulfilling the same function, exchanging teachers, students, and ideas. Their great contribution to society was, as Rashdall said, 'that they placed the administration of human affairs . . . in the hands of educated men'.

With the reformation and the rise of nationalism the channels of communication between the universities of Europe became overgrown and stagnant. The common language decayed; the common religion became fragmented into sects. But, largely under the influence of the scientific revolution, the traffic in ideas revived in Europe; during the nineteenth century the universities incorporated science into their curricula and began to regain a prestige in European life which they had lost since the middle ages. It was a prestige with a difference, for by this time nationalism had arisen as an influence on intellectual life and had destroyed much of the isomorphism of universities. The ancient universities in England, Scotland, Germany, France, and Italy now displayed many diversities. They still embodied the same ideal, but they had responded in different ways to the needs of the societies they served: each of them in its own way had taken on national colours.

Today we live at a time when universities are again in the ascendant. In a new context and with profound differences, the ontogeny of medieval higher education is being repeated. A 'developing' country (it was once Scotland or Germany: it is now Nigeria or Senegal) at first has no university. For generations its students travel abroad to study. Pressure builds up for indigenous higher education. The pressure is fortified by political discontents. A new university is founded as a facsimile of some protoype, imitating its statutes, adopting its curriculum, attracting as founder-professors some of its teachers. And, as in medieval Europe, so in modern Africa and America, the prime contribution of universities to society is still that they place the administration of human affairs in the hands of educated men.

In the cultural climate of the medieval catholic church, these new universities must have taken root easily. Wherever they were planted, they were in a familiar soil. Scotland, Hungary, Spain, Germany; all were nourished by the same waters of christendom. Adaptation to national needs must have played a very minor part. But today, in the cultural climate of the modern state, a new university cannot remain a facsimile of some foreign model. National pressures will force it to adapt or die. This poses a dilemma. For every new university must still fulfil the two conditions for survival: it must – if it is to belong to the commonwealth of universities – remain loyal to the idea which brought the *studium generale* into being seven centuries ago; and it must adapt itself to its own society, whether that society is marxist or capitalist, catholic or muslim, whether it comprises American technocrats or Hamitic nomads. The process of adaptation is the theme of this book.

II DIFFERENTIATION AMONG EUROPEAN UNIVERSITIES IN THE NINETEENTH CENTURY

Before the end of the nineteenth century the universities of Europe had lost much of their isomorphism; they had become differentiated under the influence of the communities they served. Higher education in Italy, splintered into small units as a legacy of the city states, and entangled in an incompetent bureaucracy, had lost its ancient glory. The provincial universities of France, suppressed by Napoleon and replaced by a clumsy central administrative machine (even the word 'university' became synonymous with the whole educational system) were not reconstituted until 1891, and then only as integral parts of a monolithic educational service. They inherited little from the ancient and cosmopolitan universities whose names they acquired; the new streams of thought flowed into the grandes écoles. The universities of Germany and Britain fared better. They too had changed, but the changes were not decay: they were vigorous adaptations to new social conditions. For reasons which were lucidly analysed by Paulsen, the social conditions of nineteenth century Germany introduced a new dimension into the idea of a university: the university as a research institute; the professor surrounded by his disciples;

the almost monomaniacal dedication to *Wissenschaft*. 'The principle has triumphed', Paulsen wrote, 'that the scholars and investigators of the nation shall also be the teachers of its youth.'

In Britain universities took a different path of adaptation. In Oxford and Cambridge the professional faculties of theology, law, and medicine, had long ago been allowed to atrophy, and the colleges concentrated on what in medieval times was simply the prerequisite for professional education: studies in the faculty of arts. During the nineteenth century the standard of these studies improved, and they were throughout associated with the flair for character-training which made these universities nurseries for leadership in church and state; an education (as Milton wrote) 'which fits a man to perform justly, skilfully, and magnanimously all the offices, both private and public, of Peace and War'. Until late into the nineteenth century the emphasis of these two universities was on the all-round education of a privileged class, not on the disinterested pursuit of learning. They were, as Matthew Arnold wrote, 'places where the youth of the upper class prolong to a very great age, and under some very admirable influences, their school education . . . they are in fact still schools'. Within these limitations Oxford and Cambridge devised a good pattern of education. It was relevant to one need, at any rate, in contemporary English society. But it was essentially the activity of a national, not a supra-national, institution. It was unrecognisable as a co-descendant, with the German universities, of the great intellectual power-houses of the middle ages.

Side by side with Oxford and Cambridge, but at that time not closely integrated with them, were the new foundations: exemplified by the Victoria University of Manchester and the colleges associated with the examining machine known as the University of London (it was not a teaching university until 1900). The pattern of these institutions could be summarised as the German mystical idea of a university brought to earth by English utilitarianism. There was a genuine zeal for research not only in science but in the humanities. There was a willingness to include technological subjects which in Germany would have been excluded from universities. Higher education in such cities as Manchester, Birmingham, and Leeds was relevant to another need in contemporary English society, a need among the industrial bourgeoisie of England.

In Scotland there was still another variant of the university, closer to the medieval pattern than any other in Europe. For the Scottish universities retained up to the end of the nineteenth century many of the traditional features they had acquired at their foundation. The arts course was a liberal education suitable for schoolboys; broadly based and, as late as 1895, still including (as Rashdall puts it) 'the old medieval "three philosophies"' (natural, moral, and metaphysical), 'enlarged by the gradual infusion of the Renaissance Greek . . .'. University education was not, as in Oxford, truncated at this stage: every year some students went on to the professional faculties of theology, law, and medicine. There was no effort to superpose character-training on the formal teaching or to cultivate the qualities of leadership: the universities offered learning to the rank and file of the people; they were not finishing schools for gentlemen.

The Scottish university in the nineteenth century was admirably adapted to its social environment. Universities were open to all comers, with no entrance examination and very modest fees. Even if the parents were poor, it was the custom for the cleverest boy in the family to be sent to the university. So many of them were the sons of peasant-farmers that the terms were arranged to fit the agricultural year; boys left their farms after they had harvested the grain and they returned the following spring in time to cut the hay, or often even earlier to sow the grain. Study had to be sandwiched between the annual cycle of crops. They walked from their homes, a hundred miles perhaps, to the university, carrying a sack of oatmeal for food. They lodged in some cheap room in the city. Poverty protected them from temptations. When term was over they walked home in parties, some of them taking three or four days over the journey. Every village they passed through recognised them as scholars, and they could count on hospitality on the way. This is a world away from the Eton schoolboy arriving by coach at Cambridge with his hunting gear and his gun; or from the German aspirant asking shyly whether he may enter the professor's laboratory as a disciple. While Oxford and Cambridge slept, insulated by Anglicanism from influences from abroad, the Scottish universities maintained a constant traffic of ideas, especially with the universities of Holland. This was one cause of their vitality. In philosophy, science, and medicine, they provided an austere but healthy diet; moreover they precipitated the reform of higher education in England, for it was the immoderate animadversions of Sir William Hamilton in the *Edinburgh Review* which helped to stimulate Oxford and Cambridge to adapt themselves to the Victorian age.

Thus the universities of Europe became differentiated under the selective influence of national ideas. In nothing was their differentiation more apparent than in the character of their graduates. The German graduate was the product of a university cult; likely as not he had been steeped in a blend of the meticulous accuracy (so easily deteriorating into pedantry) and earnest dedication to labour on the unmapped frontiers of knowledge, inspired by Ranke, combined with the idealist conception of a university (so easily deteriorating into intellectual arrogance), inspired by Fichte; intense, dogmatic, his mind stocked with footnotes. The English graduate – if he came from Oxford or Cambridge – was a striking contrast: the reasonable man, whose motto was 'in nothing too much'; impregnated with the traditions (so easily deteriorating into fetishes and taboos) of his college; suspicious of intellect disengaged from character; rating duty and conformity high among the virtues. Upon him rested responsibility for sustaining the English national idea of that time: the idea which brought light and order to backward peoples and created an empire upon which the sun never set. The Scottish graduate was more down-to-earth; the university had given him, by example rather than precept, a severe but durable set of moral principles and a respect for learning. Likely as not he would want to devote his life to faithful service in his profession; so he would return to his own folk to practise as a doctor or an advocate; or to be the village dominie; or (highest calling of all) to occupy the manse.

Much more could be said in evidence for the diversification of the university in Europe, and much thought still needs to be given to the analysis of this diversification: how a curriculum and mode of teaching which were once as constant throughout the length and breadth of Europe as the canon of the mass became modified by the pressures of national opinion to suit diverse societies. But enough has been said to introduce the theme of this book. Since the sixteenth century universities have been transplanted from Europe overseas. The transplantations are still going on. To analyse comprehensively the adaptations which universities undergo in these alien environments would be a stupendous task, beyond the capacity of any one man. But a sample analysis can be made, and the remainder of this book is devoted to that end.

III EARLY TRANSPLANTATIONS BEYOND EUROPE

The proliferation of universities in the fifteenth century took place in a uniform cultural climate created by the catholic church. Until the reformation and the sharpening sense of nationalism which followed it, there were no strong pressures for diversification among the universities of Europe. In the sixteenth century a new movement appeared: universities began to be transplanted outside Europe, and the movement goes on to this day; indeed in the twentieth century there has been the greatest wave of transplantations to foreign countries for five hundred years.

The transplantations fall into three categories: those under the aegis of church and king, as in Latin America; those organised by groups of emigrants, as in the seaboard colonies of North America; and those inspired by governments, either metropolitan governments, as in India and some of the English-speaking countries of Africa, or the governments of countries wishing to 'import' western higher education, as in Japan, or colonial governments, as in New South Wales. Most of the earlier transplantations were for the benefit of European expatriates; most of the later ones were intended to bring European higher education to non-European peoples. It has been a vast and fascinating experiment in social biology. In this section we summarise two early transplantations.

The first began in 1551 when the Emperor Charles V founded universities in Mexico and Peru with all 'the privileges, exemptions, and limitations of the University of Salamanca'. Salamanca had at that time one of the largest and most distinguished universities in Europe, with four thousand students, in a society which so respected learning that to be a professor was to be assured of high standing in the city. Doctors of civil law, we are told, when walking abroad in Salamanca, were addressed as 'Knights' or 'Lords of the Law'. For Spaniards at that time the university was 'the absolute prerequisite of an urbane life'. They considered it essential, therefore, that their colonists in America should have the benefits of higher education. Lanning has given us a vivid picture of the origin and growth of one academic society in Latin America, the University of San Carlos in Guatemala. The history of San Carlos, which is astonishingly well documented, may be regarded as typical of the Spanish university in America.

It was a later foundation than the universities in Mexico and Peru and the outcome of a long struggle between jesuits, dominicans, and the local colonial government. In the end it was the local government which successfully petitioned the king of Spain for a university. The statutes of the university had to be approved by the king and confirmed by the Pope. The royal decree prescribed even the subjects to be taught, the number of professorships, and the salaries to be paid. (There were to be seven chairs, in moral theology, scholastic theology, canon law, civil law, medicine, and – surprisingly – two chairs in native languages.) Candidates for chairs had to enter a competitive disputation called '*oposición*', which was held with meticulous ceremony. A child inserted a knife at random between the pages of one of the books in the medieval curriculum: by Peter Lombard, or Gratian, or Aristotle. The candidate opened the book at the page selected by the child, and defended one of the propositions on the page, in Latin, before a committee comprising the bishop, the rector, the dean of the cathedral, one of the professors, and the senior doctor. The successful candidate then had to distribute gratuities to the rector, councillors, secretary, and bedels of the university.

It is fascinating to imagine these courtly academic rites, following to the letter an incredibly intricate procedure, being conducted under the tropical sun of Guatemala three hundred years ago. They are but one example of the formalities of the Salamancan tradition which were exported to the New World. The order of precedence in the academic procession, the exact procedure at examinations and convocations, were matters deemed so important that a special salaried official was appointed to supervise them, even at a time when there was not enough money in the university chest to pay the emoluments of the professors; and on at least one occasion the university had to appeal to the king of Spain to secure a ruling on ceremonial procedure. As for the government of the universities in the Spanish colonies, it was controlled by statutes which (Lanning says) 'while reducing administration to a minimum, also reduced change and flexibility to less than a minimum'. Under the king of Spain, as patron, and the captain general in Guatemala, as vice patron, the university was governed by an academic electorate called the *claustro*, which (like convocation in Oxford) consisted of all graduates of the university living in the community. The *claustro* elected the rector, who was the chief officer of the university. Its day-to-day business was conducted in ways only too familiar to academics: a small executive committee (*claustro ordinario*) met on the first Saturday of every month, alternating with a finance committee (the curators of the university chest). Centuries later a similar mimicry of a European university was to be found in Ghana.

The Spanish colonies required for the priesthood, for the profession of the law, and for the practice of medicine, the same academic prerequisites as were required in Spain. So, as in African universities centuries later, the curriculum in Guatemala was virtually identical with that of the metropolitan country. The one adaptation to local conditions, the provision of chairs for two indigenous languages, failed to materialise, for although a professor was appointed, and was permitted to make his inaugural speech in Cakchiquel instead of in Latin, no students were forthcoming. But there is ample evidence that up to the time of its country's independence (1821) the University of San Carlos was in no sense isolated from the metropolitan universities and unaffected by the great changes in the climate of thought in Europe. Reforms in the University of Salamanca were soon followed by corresponding reforms in the colonial universities. From an analysis of student-theses Lanning has established that the ideas of Descartes, Locke, Newton, and even the experiments of Franklin were as familiar among the scholars of Latin America as among those of Europe. 'By 1785', he says, 'authors from France, England, Scotland, Prussia, Italy, Holland, Spain, and Portugal are likely to figure in any up-to-date library in Madrid, Mexico, Guatemala, or Lima'. The cultural lag between the South American colonies and the Iberian peninsula was no more than the time taken for a ship to cross the ocean.

The universities of Latin America have now fallen far behind those of North America. But their record up to the time of independence from Europe is impressive. Between the conquest and 1821 Spanish universities in the New World conferred 150,000 academic degrees. An inflexible control from the Spanish throne (even the creation of a new chair required the assent of the king-in-council) prevented universities in Latin America from evolving, as their counterparts did evolve in North America, into new patterns; moreover the influence of the church preserved – as it had in Europe during the middle ages – a stable cultural environment from Mexico to Lima. But if Latin American universities had no flexibility for innovation, neither did they have any latitude to lag behind the universities of Spain; the intellectuals of Lima and Guatemala entered the nineteenth century as familiar with contemporary thought as were their colleagues in Salamanca and Madrid.

Since independence the universities of Latin America have lost their vigour and initiative, and today most of them lie, untended gardens of obsolete learning, their curricula stagnant, their statutes and hierarchies of authority persisting as quaint survivals of a vanished age. Here and there are to be found signs of rejuvenation and renewal; but by and large they preserve a medieval isomorphism, for their history has made them resistant to change. Their qualifications confer social status; their graduates belong to a new and exclusive élite – barons (as Atcon puts it) in the new social order. The administrative unit is the faculty, which is composed of past and present members, jealous of their privileges and feudal in their control of appointments.

Moreover there is a tradition, avoided in Guatemala, but to be found in seventeenth century Mexico, of student participation in the government of Latin American universities. In some universities this tradition still survives and the students still hold genuine power. There are universities where half the members of the council are students, and in all universities they take part (not always a very constructive part, if eyewitness accounts are correct) in academic politics. If this were done in the best interests of scholarship, it might be a stimulating, if exhausting, experience for the officers of the university. Atcon concludes that a Latin American university is 'a society in which the young have only rights without obligations'. But it may not always be as bad as this: as recently as 1960 a new law was passed in the University of San Marcos in Lima which gives students one third of the membership of the university assembly, the university council, and the faculty council. Since most of the academic staff are part-time the students play a powerful (and according to an American observer, a constructive) part in academic affairs.

For the theme of this book the significant fact about the transplantation of universities from Spain to the New World is that the colonial universities retained their isomorphism with the universities of Spain, for three reasons: first, that they were for two centuries firmly controlled from Spain; second, that the universities were primarily for Spaniards living in a society jealously Spanish in its codes and traditions; third, that both church and state preserved in Latin America a replica of catholic imperial Spain – a sort of academic greenhouse reproducing the cultural climate of the Iberian peninsula.

Nearly a century after the first Spanish university was founded in Mexico the first transplantation of a university appeared in North America. This time it came from England. The Laws, Liberties, and Orders of Harvard College, drawn up in about 1646, closely resemble the Elizabethan statutes of Cambridge. But the North American colleges, of which Harvard was the first, were from the beginning free from the constraints of European control. Therefore while universities in the South American colonies were bound by law and tradition to a pattern of higher education on the far side of the Atlantic, universities in the North American colonies were free to adopt, but equally free to dissent from, the practices of higher education in Britain.

Of course they were subject to other constraints. Hofstadter and Metzger have vividly described how the puritan fathers, having escaped from the intolerance of England, created their own climate of intolerance in New England. 'Unquestionably', they write, 'Harvard was meant to be the orthodox instrument of the community and its faith'. Indeed this was true of all the colonial colleges established before 1776. William and Mary, Princeton, Yale, Brown, Rutgers (at first called Queen's), and Dartmouth, were all essentially clerical foundations, committed to a stern and uncompromising orthodoxy.

But it was an orthodoxy susceptible to evolution. Liberalism began to wear down intolerance, and by the middle of the eighteenth century (while the University of Guatemala was still pursuing its courtly Salamancan way), adaptations began to appear in the government and curriculum of the American college. The history of these adaptations has been very fully documented and no summary is needed here. But it is appropriate to describe two features, which represent fundamental mutations in the pattern of universities, both of which have parallels in the twentieth century in Africa. One is the government of universities by lay trustees; the other is the democratisation of the curriculum.

The significant feature of lay control in American universities and colleges is that in law sovereignty resides in the trustees, not in the faculty. The faculty members are employees of the trustees. As so commonly happens in university constitutions, the *de jure* position does not represent the *de facto* position. Today the balance of power, in all respectable American universities, is distributed by convention among trustees, faculty members, and the administration. But this balance, in the outcome not very different from the balance to be found in British universities, was reached by a very different path of adaptation from that pursued in Britain.

It appears to have been the initial intention of the founders of the first two colleges in North America, Harvard, and William and Mary, that their institutions should, like those in Oxford and Cambridge, be governed by their own members. William and Mary College was set up as a corporation of president and masters, with a board of visitors; Harvard's charter of 1650 created a corporation of president and fellows, with a board of overseers. But the social structure of the American colonies was such that the visitors and the overseers took control over the teachers. There is a certain homology between this and the pressures for lay control in African universities today; so it is worth while to recapitulate the circumstances.

Two factors, according to Hofstadter and Metzger, brought about trustee-control in the early American colleges. The first was the puritan tradition. The Founding Fathers, having wrested control of the church from the hands of clerics, were predisposed to the idea of lay-control of other social institutions, such as schools and colleges. As in the middle ages, the pattern of university government followed the pattern of church government. It was, therefore, regarded as a logical and enlightened policy to put colleges under the control of the community rather than to follow the English pattern of corporate autonomy for the president and masters. Secondly, the academic staff of these early colleges were young, inexperienced, and migratory. In 1650 the president of Harvard was 40 and the average age of the treasurer and five fellows constituting the corporation was 24. Moreover in a fluid colonial society very few men entered college-teaching as a career for life; they served as tutors for a few years and then were promoted to posts of greater responsibility in church or state. So the board of overseers at Harvard (six magistrates and six ministers) and the visitors at William and Mary (fourteen lay-men and four clergy) regarded the college staff as 'no more than transient employees'. And even when the teaching staff in these colleges became more distinguished and more experienced and more stable in composition, the lay boards, having acquired sweeping powers, would not give them up, 'being, like other parents, unwilling to accept the fact of their own obsolescence'. When, in 1729, a charter granting considerable powers of self-government was given to William and Mary, the teachers, most of whom were Oxford men, put up a spirited resistance to lay control; but they failed to establish their privileges, and the lay visitors remained in control: a crisis which was repeated with a happier outcome by the foundation professors of the University of Sydney some 130 years later.

Harvard, and William and Mary, were conceived as autonomous academic societies. Management in the one was assumed by the overseers, and in the other by the visitors. (When, eventually, the corporation of president and fellows of Harvard acquired power, the fellows were no longer academics: they were predominantly lawyers and businessmen.) Yale and Princeton were, from the beginning, unambiguously under non-academic control. The ten original trustees of Yale were all clergymen; later on some representatives of the state of Connecticut were added. And the pattern of lay-government at Princeton, strongly influenced by presbyterianism, was officially recognised by the British crown when it granted a charter to the college in 1746.

The story of the gradual, sometimes painful, redistribution of power between boards of trustees and teaching staff has been recorded in studies by Hofstadter and Metzger and by MacIver. The power of lay trustees in American and Canadian universities is still strong. An American university president can still talk about 'hiring' professors. He can still nominate the members of committees; for many purposes he does not have to work with elected committees. He has authority to issue directives, though a wise university president does not lightly exercise this authority. His power is the direct outcome of lay-control, for when the laymen are off the campus he acts on their behalf. In a modern African university the circumstances are in some ways analogous. The academic body is largely expatriate and is therefore assumed not to identify itself with national aspirations; and the African staff, which is in a minority, is assumed to be inexperienced in academic government. So it is not surprising, and indeed not unreasonable, that the American hierarchical structure of university government and strong lay-control appeals to some leaders in newly developing countries. Later in this book, we shall hear voices from Africa advocating the supremacy of lay government in universities and emphasising the notion that academics should not be bothered with administration.

The 'democratization of the curriculum' is a phrase attributed to Andrew White, the first president of Cornell University. Of course the *Corpus Academicum*, the body of knowledge deemed worthy of inclusion in university curricula, has been enlarging ever since the middle ages. Greek came with the renaissance; natural science with the enlightenment; technology at the tail-end of the industrial revolution. There has, of course, been opposition: new subjects have had to be forced into the curriculum against the heavy inertia of faculties and senates. Even Tait and Stanley, two leaders of reform in Victorian Oxford, restricted their proposals for diversifying the curriculum to the introduction of a fourth year in science, law, history, or theology without allowing honours to be taken in these subjects. To permit honours to be taken:

in the case of Physical Science, would make it assume the position of a groundwork in liberal education, for which it is totally unfitted, and it would open the doors for a similar intrusion of *tripos* upon *tripos* in every conceivable department of human knowledge. Such a scheme, fully carried out, must end in the ruin of English education.*

Nevertheless, university curricula have for centuries undergone gradual and cautious diversification. But the idea that all knowledge, from genetics to golf, could (as the Americans say) be studied for credit, and that all professions, from medicine to advertising, could look to the university for vocational training, was a novelty. It is condensed into the founder's words, which appear in the motto on the great seal of Cornell University: '*I would found an institution where any person can find instruction in any study*'. At the hands of writers like Flexner and Hutchins this idea has had a bad press. Doubtless mass higher education in America has suffered from a dulling of sensitivity to quality which commonly accompanies any kind of mass production. Doubtless triviality has been tolerated and mediocrity admitted into American universities. But it is a shallow conclusion to assume that mass production inevitably spells the destruction of high standards. There is abundant evidence that quantity and quality can flourish side by side; Rolls-Royce cars have not been driven off the market by mini-minors; E.M. Forster had not been ousted by mushy novelettes. There are American state universities which demonstrate for the academic world what Ford demonstrates for the automobile industry: that diversity and mass production, far from debasing standards, divert the pressure of competition and public opinion away from the high quality product, leaving it free to preserve its tradition of excellence.

So the democratisation of the curriculum deserves to be welcomed as a great innovation in higher education, as necessary in twentieth century Africa as it was in nineteenth century America. The need for it in nineteenth century America was crystal-clear. James Garfield, a future president of the United States, addressed a college audience on the subject in 1867. To get a B.A. at Harvard (which was typical of the colleges of that day) a student had to devote four-sevenths of his time and labour to Greece and Rome. He learnt no American history. English literature was not mentioned in the curriculum.

* Quoted in Geoffrey Faber, *Jowett, a portrait with background* (London, 1957), 195

No wonder, said Garfield, that men are demanding to know how it happens that :

placing in one end of the balance all the mathematical studies, all the physical sciences in their recent rapid developments, all the principles of political economy and social science which underly the commerce and industry, and shape the legislation, of nations, the history of our own nation, the constitution of government, and its great industrial interests, all the literature and history of modern civilization— placing all this, I say, in one end of the balance, they kick the beam when Greece and Rome are placed in the other.*

It was a long time before Garfield's advice was taken. In Yale, even as late as 1875, the only full-time studies offered for the first two years of the under-graduate course were Greek, Latin, and mathematics, and the only part-time studies were rhetoric, Roman history, and a little hygiene. Yet Yale was comparatively enterprising, for it had started in the 1860s a short course in agriculture and eighteen lectures each year for mechanics. Most of the eastern colleges were (as Andrew White tartly said) 'as stagnant as a Spanish convent, and as self-satisfied as a Bourbon duchy'.

In the end it was pressure at the pioneer frontier which precipitated the great mutation in the curricula of American colleges. As American society became stratified these early institutions of higher learning, with their emphasis on training men for ministry in church or chapel, became less and less fitted to the needs of the people. The energy of Americans was concentrated on their western frontier, manned by farmers who were taming the prairies and plains west of the Mississippi. These men were suspicious of education; they were not interested in giving their sons a European schooling in Latin and Greek. Their struggles with a harsh and unfamiliar climate, new patterns of agriculture, an unmapped country without roads or railways, forced them to demand that if there was to be any higher education at all, it should be technical and utilitarian. In the early nineteenth century you could still see in America clumsy ploughs, sickles and flails unchanged for centuries, the grain still trodden out by horses. These primitive techniques were inadequate for pioneer agriculture; the farmers needed a new pattern of education for their rural life. In 1824 the first response to this need appeared: the Rensselaer Polytechnic Institute. Its aim was to prepare teachers who would instruct the sons and daughters of local farmers and craftsmen in the arts of applying science to farming and domestic economy. This interest in utilitarian higher education gathered momentum through the nineteenth century, along with a determination that democratic ideas should pervade universities. Young America had no use for scholarly élites. These social pressures, acting on a system of higher education imported from Britain, culminated in the land grant colleges, which are the unique contribution of the United States to the idea of a university.

* Quoted in Allan Nevins, *The state universities and democracy* (Urbana, 1962), 6

They were founded by act of congress in 1862, amid the anxieties and distractions of civil war. The act put aside 30,000 acres of land in each state; the income from this land was to form a perpetual fund for an institution of higher education in each state. The purpose (to quote from the act) was to endow and maintain:

at least one college where the leading object shall be without excluding other scientific or classical studies, and including military tactics, to teach such branches of learning as are related to agriculture and the mechanic arts, in such manner as the legislatures of the States may respectively prescribe, in order to promote the liberal and practical education of the industrial classes in the several pursuits and professions in life.*

There was, of course, opposition from conservatives. 'We want no fancy farmers', one senator sneered. More serious, there was apathy among the very citizens for whom the colleges were founded. Those who wanted education for their children as a status-symbol (and these were days when status could be achieved without a bachelor's degree) sent them to the eastern seaboard or to Europe. Many of those who wanted their children to learn good farming believed they could learn best as apprentices on the farm, not by going to a cow-college. So for a time the provision for this novel utilitarian college education ran ahead of the demand for it. But when the land grant colleges celebrated their centenary in 1962 there were sixty-nine of them; they enrolled about a third of the college and university students of the nation; their graduate schools had trained about half the nation's Ph.D.s.

The adaptation of the land grant colleges to American society came slowly. At first there was great confusion about curriculum; in Wisconsin, for instance, in the early days there were courses on *How to Plough* and on *Mental and Moral Philosophy*. But a pattern has developed which does indeed fulfil the purpose of the act of 1862. On the one hand there has been no neglect of traditional subjects. History or English or pure mathematics can be studied as effectively in many land grant colleges as in conventional traditional universities. Some of the most distinguished research in the humanities and the natural and social sciences is being done in land grant colleges which have become state universities. Of the world's Nobel prizewinners, eight took their first degrees in the University of California (a land grant college) and eight or nine are on the faculty there. In the University of Michigan (another land grant college) the ratio of graduate to undergraduate students is about two to three. On the other hand dozens of vocational activities developed in the land grant colleges at a time when they were excluded from more conventional universities. Agriculture and veterinary science, and the applications of science to farming had, of course, pride of place. But a rural community needed roads and railways and the telegraph, so engineering was an important ingredient. So were economics and the principles of business and,

* Quoted in Edward Danforth Eddy, Jr., *Colleges for our land and time* (New York, 1956), 33

for the daughters of farmers, domestic science and the art of running a home. The countryside needed good newspapers, so courses in journalism became a feature of some land grant colleges. The first school of journalism, according to Allan Nevins, was founded in Missouri in 1908, after a student-group had been invited to contribute a Sunday section to the St Louis *Post-Dispatch*. Gradually the idea took shape that a university should be a sort of intellectual department store offering courses in an extraordinary range of subjects, from how to dance to how to bury the dead.

Accompanying this democratization of the curriculum there was a democratization of the student body. Land grant colleges do not exist solely to educate the young. They are service stations for the whole community. In the frontier states the prime need of the community was improved farming. And so about sixty years ago the land grant colleges became educational missionaries in their regions; not primarily (as happened in the university extension movement in England) to provide liberal and non-vocational education, but to carry utilitarian knowledge into farms and homesteads. In 1904, for instance, Iowa State College arranged for two trains to run through the farming area to persuade farmers to use better seed-corn. 'Seed Corn Gospel Trains', they were called. The trains carried lecturers, charts, specimens, books, and demonstrations. At every farming community on the railway the trains stopped and there were lectures and discussions. This enterprise spread to twenty-eight states and in its peak year (1911) it reached audiences of nearly a million people. So agricultural extension, which in many countries is a responsibility of the ministry of agriculture, became associated in America with the land grant colleges. This brought the university and the rural community intimately together. It promoted research in the universities which had profound effects on agriculture. Thus when Wisconsin turned from growing wheat to the production of milk, the state university is said to have saved the dairy farmers millions of dollars by the Babcock fat test which its research workers devised. This in turn gave the farming community confidence in academics. 'In Wisconsin,' an observer wrote, 'the university is as close to the intelligent farmer as his pig-pen or his toolbox.' Nor did Wisconsin stop at agricultural extension. Under the formidable presidency of Van Hise, knowledge of all sorts was made available to all who wanted it, whether they could attend the university or not. District centres of extension teaching were planted everywhere. Thousands of people took courses by correspondence, as they still do today. A bureau of general welfare run by the university answered thousands of questions about everything from sanitation to income tax. The university's campus was the whole state; its purpose was not only higher education but social improvement and human welfare. People mattered as much as scholarly standards. At first sight it seems a policy utterly alien to the function of a university as it was conceived in, say, the Oxford of Pusey. But Pusey's preoccupation with the college as a place for 'character-training' was inspired by equally sincere and unacademic motives, and achieved equally useful but unacademic ends, as Van Hise's preoccupation with the college as 'a highly conscious lobe in the common community mind of the people of Wisconsin'. Both Pusey and Van Hise used the university for purposes other than the narrow pursuit of higher learning: the one for the education of gentlemen; the other for the social welfare of the common people. It is not our purpose here to discuss whether either or both of them was right to do so. The relevance of their thought to the theme of this book is simply that both Pusey's ideas and those of Van Hise have been exported to the universities of developing countries. Later on we shall discuss the consequences of these exportations.

It is noteworthy that the two major adaptations of the university to the social climate of North America were responses to public opinion in an immature developing community, materialistic, rural, dependent for its cultural inheritance upon Europe, yet anxious to disengage itself from some of the constraints of Europe. A century later, in Africa, universities were transplanted into a social climate in most respects totally different from that of Abraham Lincoln's America, but nevertheless bearing certain basic resemblances: also materialistic, rural, dependent on European influence and yet anxious to repudiate it. In some African countries people are already asking whether they have not as much to learn from the American pattern of higher education as from the European.

CHAPTER TWO

THE NINETEENTH CENTURY MODEL

The spread of universities into new countries has gone on ever since English scholars were recalled from Paris to Oxford in the twelfth century. But there have been four major waves of this kind of intellectual colonisation: one in the fifteenth century, already alluded to here and fully described by Rashdall; one in the sixteenth and seventeenth centuries which carried higher education across the Atlantic to the New World; one in the nineteenth century, when for the first time universities were founded in non-christian societies supplanting ancient indigenous centres of learning; and one in our own day.

The third of these waves of colonisation reached its peak in the 1850s, with the foundation of universities in Australia and India. But all through the century the movement went on. There were French seminaries (but not universities) in Canada before 1800; and in the maritime provinces colleges in the British tradition received royal charters as early as 1802 (Nova Scotia) and 1828 (New Brunswick). Toward the end of the century university colleges developed in New Zealand (Otago, 1869; Canterbury, 1873; Auckland, 1882; and Wellington, 1897). In 1872, by imperial decree, the ancient *daigaku* of Japan were converted into universities on the French model. In part two of this book we analyse in some detail the evolution of British policy for universities in India. As in the middle ages, so in the nineteenth century, new universities were fashioned in the form of older ones. So, as a necessary background, something must be said about the state of British universities at the time universities were established in India. Also, as part of the background, we describe briefly two other foundations which illuminate British policy for higher education in India, namely the establishment of the Queen's University in Ireland and of the first two universities in Australia.

In the 1960s new countries proposing to found universities are apt to seek advice from international commissions whose members bring experience of several systems of higher education. But this is a recent procedure, and not always a satisfactory one. Since universities lost their isomorphism and became adapted to national cultures they have – even though they pursue the same ends – developed minor incompatibilities toward one another. It is not always practicable to graft scions from one university system on the stock of another. In the 1850s this problem did not arise. The British government did not ask whether German universities, or the centralised and articulated educational system of France, might be more appropriate patterns than the universities of Britain for export to the colonies. It was assumed in 1850 that universities in British possessions overseas should be as far as possible facsimiles of universities at home.

In the 1850s there were five 'genera' of universities in Britain which might have served as prototypes for export to British possessions overseas: Oxford, Cambridge, and Trinity College, Dublin (which, though unlike in many details, belong to the same academic genus); London and the Queen's University of Ireland (also with differences, but belonging to the same genus); Durham; Owen's College, Manchester; and the four universities of Scotland. It is difficult to discern a common social purpose or ideology among these five kinds of universities; nor at that time were there any commonly agreed and clearly enunciated principles of higher education, such as contributed to the foundation of universities in Africa a hundred years later. Although Newman's magnificent *Idea of a university* was published in 1852, his views did not represent common opinion outside Oxford. There was nothing which could be described as official policy over British higher education, for the state had taken practically no part in the organisation or endowment of universities. Apart from training men to be ordained in the anglican church, the English universities (unlike those in Scotland) were not gateways into the professions. Candidates for the legal profession went to the inns of court; candidates for medicine to the medical schools attached to hospitals. Except over theological matters, therefore, the influence of universities as corporate bodies was negligible, and even the impact of their graduates on the intellectual life of Britain was hard to discern: in 1850 only 409 students matriculated at Oxford and 360 at Cambridge. Most of the important intellectual advances of the time were being made outside the universities. Moreover it was a time of bitter controversy and bewildering uncertainty about higher education. No British university really knew what its purpose was or where its future lay. It is interesting to reflect what might have happened if there had been a 'Robbins' committee in the mid-nineteenth century. But there was no such comprehensive enquiry; instead, the problems of the very dissimilar kinds of higher education were dealt with separately and without reference to one another.

Oxford and Cambridge had since the turn of the century been reawakening to their responsibilities. Examinations had been introduced in place of the empty formalities of the eighteenth century; here and there standards of scholarship had been raised. There were pressures for reform both from outside and from inside. From outside Hamilton opened fire in a series of savage essays in the *Edinburgh Review*. His attacks stirred up feeling in the 1830s but he overstated his case and to this extent the defence of the conservatives was strengthened. From inside Oxford there came more effective criticism from Jowett, Stanley, and Mark Pattison. These were men who had seen at first hand the renaissance of learning in Germany. There they found a system of higher education conducted by experts: the professor, a scholar at the growing point of his subject, gave lectures on his specialism and conducted seminars. In Oxford and Cambridge the professors had become a vestigial part of the teaching force; the whole emphasis was on college-based education. There was practically no endowment for the chairs and practically no attendance at the lectures. Teaching was in the hands of college tutors, each tutor covering with his pupils the whole spectrum of knowledge for a degree. This unscholarly and superficial attitude to learning, compared with the intensive cultivation of specialism by German professors, alarmed the men who wanted reform in Oxford. 'We are so far below the level of the German Ocean', wrote Jowett in 1847, 'that I fear one day we shall be utterly deluged.'

But response to the pressures of reform was too slow to satisfy the reformers. The 'organised torpor' of Oxford and Cambridge showed no signs of yielding on the most critical question, which was whether to diminish the power of the colleges and to increase the effectiveness of the university. Accordingly in 1850 two royal commissions were appointed, one for Oxford and one for Cambridge. They reported in 1852, after every conceivable obstacle had been put in their way by the universities and the colleges (though Cambridge was more cordial in its obstructions than Oxford). Gladstone, who was one of Oxford's representatives in parliament, was persuaded by the commissions' reports that some reform was necessary, and he patiently steered two acts through parliament, one for Oxford (1854) and one for Cambridge (1856). Under these acts, statutory commissions were appointed to draw up new legislation for the two universities. The commissioners were given powers which were to remain in force until 1859, or at latest 1860.

The reforms recommended by the commissions covered many things: the curriculum (especially the need to teach science), the strengthening of university teaching vis-à-vis college teaching, the use of college endowments. They did not satisfy either side. Pattison of Oriel – one of the leaders of reform – complained that parliament 'had only touched the ark of our property with half a heart', and he tried, on the encouragement of a few colleagues, to set down on paper, in his *Suggestions on academical organization*, the changes still needed to make Oxford a viable university. Prominent among these changes was a greater emphasis on research. Perhaps one quotation from the pamphleteering of the time will show how wide was the gap between the reformers, drawing their inspiration from Germany, and the die-hards, deeply entrenched in a genteel sort of anti-intellectualism. Pusey – one of the chief opponents of reform in Oxford – wrote two years after the commission reported:

The problem and special work of an University is, not how to advance science, not how to make discoveries . . . not to produce new works in Medicine, Jurisprudence, or even Theology; but to form minds religiously, morally, intellectually . . . Acute and subtle intellects, even though disciplined, are not needed for most offices in the body politic. Acute and subtle intellects, if undisciplined, are destructive both to themselves and to it, in proportion to their very powers. The type of the English intellectual character is sound, solid, steady, thoughtful, well disciplined judgement. It would be a perversion of our institutions to turn the University into a forcing house for intellect.*

The story of these reforms at the two ancient universities is well known and does not need to be repeated here. Clearly Oxford and Cambridge, still in this whirlpool of controversy, were no use as models for new universities overseas. Indeed the commissioners left them no better as models after their reports than they had been before; they were, despite some relaxation of religious tests, still anglican strongholds (for the master's degree, which alone gives full membership of these universities, was reserved for anglicans); and there was no assurance that they were going to offer that education in 'useful knowledge' which was supposed to be appropriate for the kind of students a colonial university would be expected to have. Even a quarter of a century later the singular notion persisted that the content of higher education in Britain should be stratified according to class. When Lyon Playfair – a man who ought to have known better – spoke at a meeting in Leeds to publicise the new Yorkshire College, he said, 'our universities have not yet learned that the stronghold of literature should be built in the upper classes of society, while the stronghold of science should be in the nation's middle class'.† This conviction was deeply embedded in the minds of some of the men who had to express opinions on Britain's policy for universities in her overseas possessions.

It is unlikely that either the University of Durham or Owens College (later to become the Victoria University of Manchester) occurred to anyone in Whitehall as models for export. Durham, obsessively anglican, had made such poor progress since its foundation in 1832 that there was talk in 1857 of closing it down. By 1861 its student numbers had fallen to forty-one, and a commission was appointed by parliament to look into its affairs. Owen's College opened in 1851 with sixty-two students; by 1856 the number had dropped to thirty-three. These figures were not encouraging for the foundation of universities in such remote places as Calcutta and Sydney.

As for the Scottish universities, it is at first sight surprising that they were not selected as models for export. They were universities of the people, excluding neither the poor nor the lowly born. They set no religious tests. They served a rural community of farmers and even peasants. They offered a sound training in the traditional professions of law, medicine, and the

---

* E. B. Pusey, *Collegiate and professorial teaching and discipline* (London, 1854), 215
† Quoted in A. N. Shimmin, *The University of Leeds: the first half-century* (Cambridge, 1954), 15

church; they offered, too, a broadly based liberal education which included science, metaphysics, and logic. They assumed no high level of schooling and accepted boys as young as fourteen. They had no entrance examination. And yet they stood high in prestige throughout Europe; moreover they attracted good students from England; Adam Smith, David Hume, and Joseph Black had adorned chairs there, and the prince consort even sent his son to Edinburgh to learn chemistry from Lyon Playfair.

But all was not well with the Scottish universities. In 1826 a royal commission was appointed to look into their affairs. It reported in 1831 but no bill was introduced in parliament until 1836; then it met with such strong opposition that it was dropped. It was not until 1858 – a year after the establishment of the first three Indian universities – that a university act for Scotland received the royal assent. The chief disqualifications of the Scottish universities as models for export in the 1850s was their mode of government. Glasgow University was in the hands of its professors and had been described as 'a supreme example of self-patronage'; they mismanaged not only academic affairs but the university's property. Edinburgh University was ruled by the city magistrates with the lord provost as rector, and was an egregious example of lay interference in academic affairs; the city fathers quarrelled with the university even over such a technicality as the inclusion of midwifery in the medical curriculum. And despite their high reputation for scholarship, Scottish universities had not modernised their curricula. As late as 1833 the examination for a medical degree in Edinburgh was still in Latin, with a Latin thesis defended publicly in Latin; and their achievement in some subjects (e.g. classics, which became the measure of excellence for civil service examinations in England) fell far below that of the English boy who had studied little else throughout his school and university career. It is for this reason that Scotsmen in the mid-nineteenth century failed to win places in the Indian civil service. The romantic picture of the peasant's son, working on the croft through the summer and attending classes in winter, lost some of its appeal when one discovered that most arts students did not in fact take degrees; they improved themselves by taking isolated courses, but returned home with nothing but a 'class ticket' for diligent study; and even some professional degrees were said to have been 'bought and sold as openly as fish in Billingsgate'.

For reasons such as these, and there were many more, the Scottish universities did not appeal to Englishmen as models to be copied when new universities were founded in Ireland and overseas in the 1850s; though some of their features, such as specialised teaching by professors instead of generalised teaching by tutors (or by regents, as used to be the case in Scotland up to the late eighteenth century) did undoubtedly influence academic opinion in England. Also there were some examples of a direct transplantation of the Scottish tradition, as when in 1841 the Queen's University in Ontario was founded on the model of Edinburgh University and under the sponsorship of the presbyterian church; and later in the century a Scottish influence on universities overseas became more pronounced.

Finally, of the five 'genera' of British universities which might have been used as models for export in the 1850s, there was the University of London and its variant the Queen's University of Ireland. The foundation of a university in London is an often-told story, but parts of it are so relevant to this essay that they must be repeated here.

The university was created in 1836 solely to conduct examinations for students of two rival independent colleges, the 'godless' University College which opened in 1828 and the anglican King's College which opened in 1831, and to award degrees to successful candidates. The university was governed by a senate (the word is significant, for it reappears as the title of the governing bodies of Indian and Australian universities) which did not consist of representatives of the two colleges (they were in fact excluded from membership), but of nominees of the privy council. The examination and graduation fees went to the treasury, which paid the salaries of the university staff, all of whom were administrators or clerks, none of whom were teachers. They had accordingly the status of civil servants and the university was, in all but name, a government department. The treasury made up any deficit or retained any profit. The university premises were maintained by the office of works. If the university wanted a new chair or table it had to send the office of works a requisition. For sixty-four years after its foundation – until the year 1900 – the university did no teaching. But it underwent other changes. In 1849 a supplemental charter was issued which allowed the university to award degrees on examinations taken by students from any institution approved by the privy council provided it was in the British empire or in 'territories under the Government of the East India Company'. It may at first seem surprising that the university had no powers of inspection or control over the 'recognised' colleges; but, in the context of the time, is it surprising? Legislation was in the hands of Oxford and Cambridge men, and at that time if there was one measure more than another which would be anathema to an Oxford or Cambridge man it would be control of colleges by a university. This, too, is significant in the light of subsequent events in India. To throw examinations open to candidates outside London: this was easier to swallow, for it was something consistent with contemporary opinion; it was a free trade in degrees.

The privy council 'recognised' an astonishing variety of colleges, including the University of Oxford and the Protestant Dissenters' College at Rotherham, and medical schools as far abroad as Malta, Montreal, and Ceylon. In 1858 a new charter was granted which 'quietly dispensed with the requirement of attendance at an approved institution and thereafter the university accepted as candidates all who presented themselves for examination, provided of course that they had passed the Matriculation Examination and had paid their fees'.* The charter of 1858 made another change which had

* Douglas Logan, *The University of London, an introduction* (London, 1962), 11

repercussions overseas; it constituted a convocation of all graduates of the university, with the right to elect one quarter of the members of the senate; but the teachers in the London colleges had no such right and remained unrepresented on the governing body of the university.

In the 1850s the idea of a university as a purely examining body would not have seemed out of place. For during the first half of the nineteenth century the universities of Oxford and Cambridge had not been much more than this. 'If you want a University, 'wrote Walter Bagehot', which is trusted without suspicion to decide the result of tuition . . . you must not let it begin to interfere in tuition.' Moreover examinations were becoming a remedy for all sorts of difficulties. In 1853 a commission recommended that entry to the civil service should be by examination, and this was adopted two years later. Oxford started a scheme for the local examination of schoolboys in 1857. Shortly afterwards Robert Lowe, as vice-president of the education department, introduced a grim 'payment by results' scheme for financing schools. The 'results' were measured as attendance and as success in passing examinations in reading, writing and arithmetic.

In such a university as this, all the real educational problems are delegated to the colleges which prepare students for examinations. It is they, not the university, which have to tackle teaching methods, staffing, libraries, laboratories, social amenities and residence for students. It is not surprising, therefore, that the administrative pattern of the University of London should have appeared the most suitable for export to India.

What were the current views in England about the content of higher education, which must have influenced the men who were thinking about founding universities in India? In Cambridge, despite the labours of the commission, the curriculum for the degree remained without much change until some years after the Indian universities were established. There was no entrance examination to the university, and attempts to introduce one were regarded by the colleges as a monstrous interference with their freedom to admit the men they wished to have. Similarly, attempts to diversify the curriculum were resisted because the colleges would not be able to teach new subjects; therefore they would have to be taught by the university, and this again had to be resisted because it would have weakened the autonomy of the colleges. The B.A. degree was awarded after two examinations, one taken in the second year and one in the third. There was no choice of subjects. All candidates sat a 'previous' examination comprising one of the gospels in Greek, a Latin and a Greek classic, Paley's *Evidences of christianity*, the first three books of Euclid, and arithmetic. This was followed by the 'ordinary examination' which Winstanley described as 'little more than a repetition of the Previous on a slightly larger scale'. In 1861 the subjects for the 'ordinary' were the Acts of the Apostles in Greek, a Latin and a Greek classic, the history of the English reformation, the first four books of Euclid and the first six propositions of the sixth book, elementary algebra, mechanics and hydrostatics. An examination in law, leading to an LL.B. degree, was instituted in 1854. A degree examination for medicine was revived by John Haviland, who came to the regius chair in 1817; but a generation later he had to confess to the commissioners that the study of medicine in Cambridge was at a very low ebb. Moral sciences and natural sciences had been admitted as subjects of study in 1848 (the initiative for this had come from the prince consort, who had been elected to the office of chancellor a year earlier), but a degree could not be awarded in either of these subjects until 1860. 'What', the critics asked, 'is the value of knowing that Aristotle defined virtue in this way, and Plato in that . . .?' It was not until the 1870s that subjects like history (separate from law) and oriental languages were recognised as respectable ingredients for a degree; medieval and modern languages had to wait until 1886, mechanical sciences until 1894, and economics until 1905, for recognition as fields of specialisation for degrees.

The degree-structure in Oxford did not offer any more encouragement to diversity of studies. In a pamphlet written in 1839 by two Oxford men (Tait and Stanley) during their visit to Bonn in a long vacation, the idea was canvassed for a fourth year of special study – not to compete with the traditional degree, and certainly not to replace it – in physical science, law, history, or theology. Some of these subjects were introduced over the ensuing decade; but listen to the comment of a fellow of Oriel (a college of advanced views and one of the centres of reform) over the introduction of history. He was writing in 1849.

I can but fear the worst, a majority of fourteen in Convocation voted in favour of a fourth school—namely Modern History. We did indeed by a large majority reject the details of this novelty, but the principle has been admitted . . . rightly or wrongly we have fallen into the weakness of yielding to the spirit of the age.*

Under statutes introduced in 1850, a candidate for a B.A. degree at Oxford was required, after passing moderations (the 'first public examination') to take examinations in two schools, one: classics with divinity; and the other: either mathematics and physics, or natural sciences, or law and modern history. Thus the lawyer, the mathematician, and the scientist, though now their subjects could 'count' for degrees, still had to satisfy the examiners at the final examinations in classics and divinity. It was not until 1865 that a student who had done well enough in classics and divinity in moderations was allowed to choose to specialise in one school at his final examination.

If the curricula at Oxford and Cambridge were deemed unsuitable for export, so, for reasons already given, were the curricula in the Scottish universities. It was not until after the first universities were established in Australia and India that an honours course was introduced in Scotland. Then, under the Universities (Scotland) Act, 1858, the Scottish universities adopted a pattern in some respects similar to that already current in London. There

* Quoted in A. Mansbridge, *The older universities of England* (London 1923), 150

remained as model the curriculum prescribed for degrees in the University of London. Here there were significant points of contrast with the degree courses of the older universities in England: novelty in the curriculum reflected the novel purpose for which the university had been founded. In 1850, the University of London offered degree courses in arts, law and medicine; and for entry to the arts courses a matriculation examination was prescribed. Only two years' study was required for the B.A. degree, and this was awarded on the results of a single examination. A further two years' study was required for the M.A. degree. Both at matriculation and the B.A. examination, successful candidates were able to sit for honours. Two degrees of a higher standard were awarded in each of the professional faculties. Candidates for the LL.B. were required to be arts graduates of a British university who had pursued one year of further study, or graduates of the university's medical faculty. Candidates for the M.B. were required to have pursued four years' professional study at an institution approved by the university after either matriculating at London or graduating in arts at any British university.

In keeping with the non-sectarian character of the university, scriptural subjects were carefully excluded from the degree courses of the arts faculty. But this was not the only distinctive feature of the arts curriculum. In each of the three main courses, but more especially those for matriculation and for the first degree examination, the traditional range of subjects was widened to include new or hitherto neglected branches of study. In the matriculation examination four subjects were prescribed: not only mathematics and classics, but natural philosophy and chemistry; and classics was stretched to cover both the study of English language and the outlines of modern English history and geography. Honours could be taken in one or more of all these subjects (mathematics and natural philosophy as a combined subject); and a further option was offered in natural history (botany or zoology or both). Mathematics and classics still formed the hard core of the examination. For a pass, competence was required in both these subjects and *either* natural philosophy or chemistry. For honours, candidates were confronted with six papers in each of mathematics and natural philosophy, and classics, and only one in each of chemistry and natural history. Five of the six classics papers were still devoted exclusively to Greek and Latin; and it was only on the results of the matriculation honours examination in mathematics and natural philosophy and classics that exhibitions were awarded. The breakaway from the narrowly confined curriculum of the past had nevertheless begun.

In the B.A. examination, competence was required in all four of the branches prescribed: at this level, animal physiology, and logic and moral philosophy, in addition to mathematics and natural philosophy, and classics. Classics again received an extended interpretation, including a compulsory paper in French or German as well as one in English history. There was, however, no follow-up to the paper in English language at matriculation. Honours could be taken in one or more of three of these subjects: mathematics and natural philosophy, classics, and animal physiology; and further options were provided in chemistry and botany. Again there was a new and welcome diversification in the curriculum, but again there was the drag of tradition. It was only on the results of the honours examination in mathematics and natural philosophy, and classics, that exhibitions were awarded; and while six papers were set in each of these subjects (five of the classics papers still devoted to Greek and Latin) only one was provided in each of botany and chemistry, and two in animal physiology. For the M.A. degree, the curriculum was still moderately progressive in the humanities; but in science it was disappointingly thin and conventional. Candidates could be examined in one or more of only three branches: two of them, inevitably, mathematics and natural philosophy, and classics (the latter including here the study of modern European history, yet wholly ignoring the claims of modern European languages) and a third covering the broad and less orthodox field of 'Logic, Moral Philosophy, Philosophy of the Mind, Political Philosophy, Political Economy'.

Apart from minor modifications in the matriculation examination, the arts courses remained unchanged until the end of the decade when new regulations again proclaimed the university a pioneer in curricular reform. In 1859 the B.A. examination was divided into two parts, and, for the first time in a British university, English language, literature and history was prescribed as a separate and *compulsory* branch of study. In 1860 a parallel degree structure was instituted in science, with examinations leading to the two degrees of B.Sc. and D.Sc. But even before the introduction of these radical innovations, the range of studies at the University of London was sufficiently novel, and the standard of its degrees sufficiently well established, for its curriculum to serve as an obvious point of reference for those planning new universities. It was not in fact the curriculum of the University of London that was chiefly responsible for its being selected as a model for India*; and in so far as Sir Charles Wood commended the pattern of its degree courses to the planners there, he did so by reference to the negative argument of the relevance of a curriculum which excluded religious studies. But the broad spread of academic and professional studies embraced in the London curriculum clearly made it an appropriate guide for the comprehensive examination system the Indian universities were designed to supply. And by the time Sir Charles Wood issued his famous despatch, the virtues of the London curriculum had already received recognition in the shaping of two earlier university transplantations.

---

* Both Mouat (see p. 54) and Wood (see p. 59) were attracted to London University as a model for Indian universities on account of its administrative structure rather than its curricular enlightenment. The need, for example, to unite in one system of higher education the scattered colleges of Bengal; the need to save money by avoiding a salary-bill for academic staff; and the opportunity to by-pass the problems of religious education by having non-residential universities: these were the considerations, more than curriculum, which commended London as a model.

II TWO NINETEENTH CENTURY TRANSPLANTATIONS: IRELAND AND AUSTRALIA

Such was the mid-nineteenth century background against which decisions were made to establish universities in India. Before we turn to an analysis of British policy for higher education in India, there are two other episodes to be described which illuminate the theme: they are the establishment of universities in Ireland and Australia.

Dublin has had a university since 1591: a protestant foundation, in the early nineteenth century still firmly attached to the anglican ascendancy; no longer formally excluding catholics and dissenters from its student body, but reserving its fellowships, professorships, and prizes for anglicans. It was, and still is, a university of one large college, displaying in the 1850s many of the agreeable virtues and suffering from some of the stuffy prejudices that were to be found in the colleges of Oxford and Cambridge. This exclusiveness of the University of Dublin was one of the many grounds for political discontent in that unhappy country.

All negotiations between England and Ireland over education are steeped in religious controversy. In 1795 the government sanctioned a college for catholics at Maynooth, primarily to dissuade candidates for the priesthood from attending seminaries in France and becoming tainted with republican and revolutionary ideas. This concession to catholics prompted the presbyterians in the north, who were sending their boys to Glasgow or Edinburgh for a university degree, to ask for a college for candidates for the presbyterian ministry. This, and other appeals for a second Irish university in Ulster, were rejected by the British government.

The pressure for extended opportunities in education was kept up. A remarkable Irishman, Thomas Wyse, a catholic who had entered Trinity College after religious tests were removed, and who had then been one of the first eight catholics to enter the British parliament, devoted his energies and his great eloquence to social reform in Ireland, especially for a comprehensive system of education. Some of his statements made over a century ago might be put into the mouth of an African politician in the 1960s.

The national intellect, waste but fertile, should be brought into cultivation, and another people, truly such and not as they hitherto have been, too frequently a populace, should be raised up, out of the wrecks and lees of the past. England owes us this atonement for her former misrule and spoliation; she it was who made us and kept us ignorant.*

In his comprehensive scheme, Wyse proposed a university on the pattern of London, to consist of provincial colleges which prepared candidates for examinations set by a central body empowered to grant degrees.

* Quoted in T.W. Moody and J.C. Beckett, *Queen's, Belfast, 1845-1949* (London, 1959) I, liv.

For years Wyse worked without result. The indifference of politicians; the complexity of Irish politics; the necessity that any agreement on any project for a university should satisfy both catholics and presbyterians: these were obstacles which even his eloquence could not overcome. Then in 1841 Sir Robert Peel took office as prime minister. Conciliation of Ireland became one of his preoccupations, and by 1844 Wyse had at last persuaded the British government to act. Peel pledged himself to attempt a solution of the Irish university problem, and his home secretary, Graham, turned to the scheme which Wyse had produced six years earlier: a university open to all without distinction of creed and with a curriculum which excluded religion. In the summer of 1844 the British government began its preparations for a bill to put before parliament in the following year. Its chief architect was Graham, but Peel as prime minister and Lord Heytesbury as viceroy in Dublin were drawn into every stage of the preparations. It was the first time a British government had been faced with the problem of founding a teaching university under crown control. Most of the problems which exercised the government ten years later, when it sanctioned the establishment of universities in India, had to be faced in the 1840s. There seems to be no evidence that the architects of the first Indian universities drew upon Irish experience. Yet there are interesting similarities between the two operations. Religious differences bedevilled education in both countries. Both countries wanted universities on a British model in order to train professional men and officials for the higher civil service. For both countries the appropriate model seemed to be the non-sectarian University of London. In a sense, therefore, the principles which led to the establishment of the Queen's University of Ireland constitute a prototype for the export under government auspices of British higher education to an impoverished and subject people overseas.

Clearly there would have to be more than one teaching institution and the most obvious pattern was to have three provincial colleges; one in Ulster, one in Munster, and one in Connaught. Should each of these colleges be a separate university, on the Scottish model? Or should they be affiliated to a central examining and degree-granting body, on the London model? In 1844, in the atmosphere of growing dissatisfaction with the ancient universities and controversy over their future no one would have suggested Oxford or Cambridge as models. In the event, a decision on this was deferred and the first bill simply set up three colleges to teach at university level, drawing on the experience of the universities of Scotland and of University College, London. The colleges were to be non-residential (as in Scotland and London), free from religious tests, and teaching was to be in the hands of professors appointed by the crown. The question of awarding degrees to the students from these three colleges was left to a later bill, but Graham, when moving the adoption of the bill in the house of commons, said he had a preference for a central university of the London type, where 'the youth of Ireland may assemble, and contend, in honourable and honest rivalry' rather than for three independent universities. The bill was passed, not without criticism (Sir Robert Inglis, M.P. for Oxford University, denounced it as a gigantic scheme of godless education, unprecedented in English history). The catholic hierarchy were divided in their reaction; some denounced the scheme as a danger to faith and morals, others sullenly assented provided various safeguards were assured, such as the appointment of a fair proportion of catholic office bearers whose moral character had been certified by their respective bishops. By 1849 college buildings were nearing completion in Belfast, Cork, and Galway; a provisional curriculum had been agreed upon; and the first professors were assembling to meet the first students. Co-ordination between the three colleges had been achieved through a board of the presidents and vice-presidents of the three colleges, which was set up in January 1846 by the lord lieutenant, and which met under the chairmanship of Robert Kane, president-elect of the college at Cork.* But there was still no university to examine or to grant degrees.

The creation of a university could no longer be delayed; so the British government had to face once more the decision as to whether there should be three unitary universities or one federated university, and (if federated) what measure of independence the colleges should have. The board of college presidents and vice-presidents was asked by the lord lieutenant, Clarendon, to give their advice. They were, as academics are apt to be, sharply divided in opinion. It seems that the Belfast members, with their traditional links with Scotland, favoured three independent universities. Others, including Kane, wanted the London pattern, with the control of standards firmly in the hands of one central body. Others wanted a loose association of virtually independent colleges, each conducting its own examinations, and in which policy-making at the centre was dominated by college representatives. Even the prince consort was drawn into the discussion. He was strongly in favour of the London pattern: it would ensure healthy competition between the colleges 'which will keep every one of them to the highest state of efficiency', and he is reported to have been indiscreet enough to say that three colleges, each with its own power to grant degrees, would become 'common nuisances and nests of jobbery and sectarianism'. The Scottish universities, still unreformed despite the royal commission of 1826, were not in favour at Whitehall as models for export.

After a very painstaking assessment of opinions from all sorts of quarters, Clarendon decided to recommend that a royal charter should be granted for a Queen's University in Ireland which should examine and award degrees to candidates who had pursued courses in one or other of the three colleges, and in these alone. In one important respect this pattern differed from that in London, where degrees could be awarded to candidates from a long list of

---

* Kane had a first-rate scientific mind. He was a pioneer in the study of the applications of science to society. At this time he was not only taking part in the establishment of the Queen's Colleges; he was also helping to assuage the agonising tragedy of the Irish famine.

affiliated (but in no way inspected or controlled) institutions. This departure from the London pattern was deliberate, and the reason for it was evident. For one thing, Kane was convinced that in Ireland it would lead to a lowering of standards 'to suit the capacities of the smaller and inferior affiliated bodies' (a consideration which did not weigh with those who founded universities in India ten years later). But the decision rested mainly on political, not educational grounds. The purpose of the non-sectarian Queen's Colleges was to bring together in a common pursuit of learning young people with different sectarian backgrounds, in the hope that this would heal the ancient wounds which divided the Irish people. Therefore it was important to ensure that the three colleges remained the only institutions from which it was possible to get a Queen's University degree. It was known that the Pope and some of the catholic hierarchy were wanting to found a catholic university which would draw catholics away from the Queen's Colleges. The only way to discourage this move was to prevent any such university from having the power to grant degrees. If the contemporary London pattern were to be followed, it would not be feasible to deny affiliation to a college founded by the catholic hierarchy.

The university was to be controlled by a senate of twenty members, together with a chancellor appointed by the crown and a vice-chancellor who had to be approved by the lord lieutenant. Three of the members – the presidents of the three colleges – were *ex-officio*, and the rest were appointed for life by the crown. All professors of the colleges were to be professors of the university. Professors, however, had no seats on the university senate. When a commission looked into the university's affairs in 1857 the professors complained about this and asked for representation. The commissioners were not convinced, and the new charter of 1864 still excluded professorial representation from the senate. The colleges retained a great deal of independence from the university, for the senate was enjoined not to control the colleges 'further than as regards the regulations for qualifications for the several degrees'. In other respects, their independence was very limited. It is true that internally they were self-governing corporations consisting of a president, a vice-president, and the professors, with an executive council comprising the president, vice-president, and four elected deans. But the professors were appointed by the crown and were virtually civil servants (in 1851 one of them, Robert Blakey, was formally dismissed from his chair by the crown, for absenting himself from his college duties). The finances were controlled (sometimes very meticulously controlled) by the government. The board of works was responsible for buildings and furniture.

Each college was allowed to set its own matriculation examination (the content and standards of these examinations differed among the colleges). So the admission of students was solely in the control of the colleges. But the curriculum and the standard of degrees were unambiguously determined by the university. The senate made regulations for degree examinations and for the courses of instruction leading to degrees. It appointed examiners, held examinations, and awarded degrees.

From the outset, the colleges and the university were encouraged not to follow precedent over the curriculum. Graham himself prepared a memorandum for the first meeting of the board of the colleges – in 1846, before the university had been created – first emphasising that the undergraduate course in arts must be the foundation of all the colleges' teaching, and must be worked out before attention was given to professional courses. Graham went on to say that the curriculum in arts must be 'in advance, if possible, of the systems of undergraduate education hitherto and elsewhere adopted'. It should include 'those branches of modern literature and science now essential to be known by every well-educated man'. This enlightenment from a home secretary in 1845, brought up in the prejudices of early Victorian England, a product of Westminster and Christ Church, is perhaps not surprising, for he had already displayed radical views and had helped to draft the first reform bill under Grey's whig administration.

The board of colleges took Graham at his word and produced a draft curriculum for the B.A. degree which no-one could describe as narrow: it included sixteen subjects, as follows:

Year 1	Latin	Botany
	Greek *or* German	Logic
	Mathematics	English composition
Year 2	Latin	Chemistry
	Greek *or* a modern language	Anatomy
	Mathematics	Natural history
Year 3	Natural philosophy	English literature
	Logic and mental philosophy	Any *two* of:
	Geology and physical geography	Classical literature
		Modern foreign literature
		Rural economy

Even Graham questioned the profusion of studies required for the degree and asked whether it was prudent to make Greek optional; and the board subsequently retreated from their position: Greek and Latin were obligatory for the first year, after which both became optional, and the number of subjects was reduced to thirteen. The final course for Queen's College, Belfast, which appeared in the calendar for 1850, was as follows:

> *Year* 1   1 English language (1 term)
>   2 Greek (3 terms)
>   3 Latin (3 terms)
>   4 Mathematics (3 terms)
>   5 French *or* German *or* Italian (3 terms)

Year 2 1 Logic (1 term)
           2 Chemistry (3 terms)
           3 Zoology and botany (3 terms)
           4 Higher mathematics *or* Greek and Latin (3 terms)

Year 3 1 Natural philosophy (3 terms)
           2 History and English literature (2 terms)
           3 Physical geography (1 term)
           4 Metaphysics *or* jurisprudence and political economy (1 term)

In its range of subjects it went considerably beyond what was prescribed for the B.A. pass degree at London where there was no provision for English language, English literature, or Italian, nor for physical geography, chemistry, zoology or botany. But although students were required to pass college sessional examinations in all these subjects, they were able to select from them when they went to Dublin to sit the university degree examination. As first prescribed in 1852, the syllabus for this was as follows:

Part I 1 Greek
        2 Latin
        3 French *or* German *or* Italian
        4 Mathematics

Part II 5 *Any one of:*
           (a) English philology and criticism; logic; and *either* metaphysics *or* jurisprudence and political economy.
           (b) Chemistry and natural philosophy
           (c) Zoology, botany, and physical geography

Whilst the college course was thus more comprehensive than the comparable degree course at London, the university requirements were considerably less so. History did not even figure in the subjects which could be offered at the university examination; and the choice permitted in part II was sufficiently wide to enable a student to graduate without taking any science subjects at all.

By 1847 the government decided not to wait until the arts courses were running before starting professional faculties. Accordingly provision was to be made for the teaching, in one or other of the colleges, of medicine (a four-year course leading to an M.D. degree); law (a three-year course run concurrently with a B.A. course, and leading to a diploma, with a further year for an LL.B.); engineering (a two-year diploma course together with three years of obligatory practical experience); agriculture (a two-year diploma course). Another innovation for the 1840s, and one particularly significant for the theme of this book, was provision for the teaching of Celtic (it is interesting that this provision was made even before the colleges opened, whereas the universities in Nigeria and Ghana had to wait ten years before any African language was included in their curricula).

The arts course was more comprehensive than any other in Britain at that

time. Moreover, as in London, it was made the foundation not only for professional courses (some students took a B.A. even before proceeding to a
medical degree and it was obligatory to graduate in arts before reading for a
law degree) but also for more specialised higher education; candidates who
had satisfactorily passed the examinations for a pass degree could then sit for
honours in any of thirteen special groups, and after a further year's work they
could take an M.A. by examination. The system had obvious drawbacks:
what it gained in surface it lost in depth, particularly as honours students had
only limited opportunities to specialise until after they had completed the pass
course. But it was a far better curriculum than was at that time available from
Oxford or Cambridge; it had the diversity of the London curriculum, with
one added improvement, namely that the Queen's curriculum was arranged
as an orderly sequence of studies, so that third year work could with confidence be built upon first and second year work. Finally it passed the most
convincing pragmatic test: its products found a ready welcome in the market.
In competition with candidates from all the other universities in the
United Kingdom, and especially in the examinations for the Indian civil
service, Queen's College candidates earned distinction. In 1857, for instance,
Belfast candidates took the first, fourth, and tenth of the twelve places offered.

There was an opportunity to review the scheme after seven years, for in
1857 a commission was appointed by Palmerston's government to enquire
into the progress of the Queen's Colleges. The commission prepared a
meticulous and judicial report; they were satisfied with the progress of the
colleges, considering that there were four formidable drags upon their
success: a sense of despondency following the Irish famine; the continued
hostility of sections of the catholic church, the pernicious practice of Trinity
College to allow students to graduate by examination only, without attendance at courses, and the rudimentary state of secondary education in Ireland
at that time. The commissioners proposed no radical changes but the professors in all three colleges took advantage of the occasion to set out their own
criticisms of the curriculum; these criticisms are an interesting commentary
on the impact of this novel pattern of university education upon the Irish people.

There was strong objection to the large number of subjects – fourteen in
all – which had to be studied for a pass B.A. degree. It was undoubtedly a more
exacting examination than had to be taken for degrees at Dublin, Oxford, or
Cambridge. The colleges advocated a reduction to eight or nine subjects for a
degree, though the evidence was still well nigh unanimously in favour of compulsory classics and mathematics. (If the godless colleges were also to become
Greekless, one witness declared, they would find even less favour in the eyes
of the presbyterian church.) Other witnesses, including the celebrated mathematician George Boole, who held the chair at Cork, pressed for earlier
specialisation: a scheme which would enable students after their first year to
concentrate upon literature and history, or mathematics and physical science,
or the natural sciences. The Queen's University (according to another witness)

'belonged to the same genus as the universities of Germany and France but the mistake had been made of modelling its educational system on that of Dublin, Oxford, and Cambridge. The system in these ancient universities was directed towards a general education for the sons of gentlemen; the system in the continental universities, on the other hand, provided specialist courses for students aiming at professional careers.' This argument led to the proposal that general education should be completed at matriculation, and at the university students should concentrate upon one field: literature and philology, or physical science, or natural science. These proposals did not convince the commissioners, nor did the university adopt them in their entirety; though (despite the commissioners' objection to specialisation) the senate did in 1860 improve the opportunities for some measure of specialisation.

In one respect the public attitude of the Irish people to the university differed enormously from the attitude of the public in India and – a century later – in tropical Africa to their universities. The Queen's degree conferred neither social status nor the privilege of voting in a university constituency. Accordingly although there was a satisfactory response in the numbers of students coming to the Queen's Colleges (750 matriculated students in the first five years: a much better rate of growth than there had been over the corresponding period in London) only 208 degrees were awarded to this generation of students. The difference was not due mainly to failures or withdrawals; it was due to the fact that in Ireland – as in Scotland – attending college was regarded as more important than getting a degree, at least a degree with no social status attached to it. And so in the early days many students were deterred (perhaps by money) from the three-week visit to Dublin to sit for Queen's University examinations.

The experience acquired in founding a new university in Ireland undoubtedly influenced the pattern of two universities founded overseas shortly afterwards, namely the University of Sydney (founded in 1850) and – much more directly – the University of Melbourne (founded in 1853). Unlike the universities of Canada, the Australian universities were not influenced by American or French institutions: they are in the direct succession of the British tradition. It is important, therefore, before we turn to India, to give some account of the genesis of these two Australian universities.

In 1849 a select committee was appointed by the legislative council of New South Wales to 'report upon the best means of instituting an University for the promotion of literature and science, to be endowed at public expense'. The committee (its mind must have been made up before it started) reported in fifteen days. It recommended a university 'accessible to all classes', belonging to no religious denomination and requiring no religious test. Eleven days later a bill was introduced into the legislative council 'to incorporate and endow the University of Sydney'. It was introduced by William Charles Wentworth, a Cambridge graduate of advanced academic views; not only did he want the university to provide the opportunity for 'the child of every man, of every class, to become great and useful in the destinies of his country'; he also wanted to ensure that no clergy of any persuasion took part in the government of the university or taught on its staff. This was too much even for the colonists of New South Wales. The churches protested and the bill was withdrawn. Ten months later it was re-introduced, and provision was made for a governing body which included clergy nominated from four denominations.

In pattern of organisation and government the university was clearly modelled on the contemporary University of London. It was intended to be a body which examined and awarded degrees to candidates from approved colleges. It was to be governed by a senate appointed by the legislative council (until there were sufficient graduates to elect some representatives). There was no provision for professors to have seats on the governing body.

A senate was appointed and held its first meeting in 1851.* It duly resolved 'to establish a College in connection with the University' and it invited a committee in London to select three professors for the college, one in classics, one in mathematics, and one in chemistry and experimental physics. The London committee comprised G. B. Airy, Sir John Herschel, Professor Henry Malden – the same Malden who had been consulted ten years earlier about the establishment of universities in India (see p. 54) – and Henry Denison, a fellow of All Souls. The choice of subjects for the first three chairs was symptomatic of the attitude of the senate: although determined not to imitate the pattern of academic self-government in Oxford, nor Oxford's association with church rather than state, the senate could not bring itself to abandon Oxford's curriculum. Classics and mathematics were to be at the foundation of the degree. The traditional professional faculties of law and medicine were not at first to be included (it was in fact forty years before a law school was set up in Sydney, and thirty-three years before chairs in pre-clinical medicine were established). The letter from the senate in Sydney to the selection committee in England was specific about the educational philosophy to which the founders of the university subscribed. 'We consider it most important', the letter ran, 'that the Classical and Mathematical Professors should bring with them the prestige of high Academical distinction at one of the Universities of Oxford or Cambridge. And we hope we shall not inconveniently fetter your choice by confining it to first class men at either University in Classics, and the first ten Wranglers in Mathematics at the University of Cambridge.' The fellows of the senate clearly knew what they were talking about. 'In Experimental Philosophy', they wrote, 'the course adopted by the Plumian Professor at Cambridge would serve as a model for the character of the

* Its membership was impressive, although it was criticised as representing the 'establishment' – the élite of Sydney colonial life. The sixteen fellows of the senate included graduates from Cambridge, Dublin, Edinburgh and Oxford; three queen's counsel, two doctors of medicine, and three clergy; the colonial secretary, the auditor general, and the speaker of the legislative council

lectures; but we think that our Professor must take rather a wider range, so as to include those subjects which belong exclusively to other chairs, such as the Jacksonian at Cambridge.' For chemistry the senate wanted a course similar to that given in Edinburgh or in London. The letter went on to emphasise that the professors would teach in a college of the university: 'as the University is not instituted for tuition, but solely for examination as the test of qualifications for the Degrees which it is empowered to confer, there is clearly no occasion for the nomination of University Professors.'

The first three professors arrived in Sydney in 1852: the Reverend John Woolley, a classicist, formerly fellow of University College, Oxford; Morris Birkbeck Pell, a fellow of St John's College, Cambridge, a mathematician who was senior wrangler in 1849; and John Smith, a lecturer in chemistry from Marischal College, Aberdeen. Woolley was also appointed principal; he was older than the others, and, as a friend of Dean Stanley, he was familiar with the Oxford reformers. The influence of these three men (and of their own educational backgrounds) on the ethos of Sydney University cannot be overestimated. They found themselves to be academic pioneers; free from the constraints of indigenous traditions, expected to turn into a living institution the aspirations and enthusiasms of a handful of colonial administrators and public men. They must have encountered in Sydney conflicting opinions about the purpose of a university: on one hand idealists, themselves educated at Edinburgh, Cambridge, or Dublin, nostalgic for the civilisation they had left, who firmly believed that 'a classical education was the ideal and the colonial interest in practical things a difficulty to be surmounted'; on the other hand the rank-and-file of the colonial community, expecting a university supported by public funds to be able to justify the expense by being useful. (Indeed these two contrary currents of opinion still assailed the professor from England who went to Australia seventy-five years later.) Clearly the 'locals' were prepared to listen to their first three professors, for within a few years of their arrival the professors had implanted in the university three important features which have determined its history ever since. First, they questioned the assumption, adopted from London and from unreformed Oxford and Cambridge, that the university should be a mere examining body and that all teaching should be done by colleges. Within a few weeks of their arrival they asked to be styled 'Professors of the University' and urged that the university should be in charge of teaching and that all matriculated students should be obliged to attend university lectures; a system, they wrote, 'which it is the prominent object of the Royal Commissioners to restore at home – the general teaching of the Professors, supported and enforced individually by College tutors. But if the pupils of the various institutions were educated entirely apart, we cannot hope to escape the ill effects which have resulted in Oxford and Cambridge from the overgrowth of the tutorial system.' The senate concurred (concurrence was made easier because there was no institution in the colony fit to be affiliated as a college), and so, within a year of its foundation, Sydney abandoned the idea of reproducing London University in the antipodes, and became a teaching university based on a professoriate: a reform which had been in the air in England since Jowett and Pattison had observed its virtues in Germany. Woolley, Pell, and Smith became 'Professors of the University'. Colleges were subsequently founded under denominational control (St Paul's, anglican; St John's, Roman catholic; St. Andrew's, presbyterian; and also a women's college) and they did supplement university teaching by tutorial work; but they have over the years become less and less significant as teaching institutions, and the modern University of Sydney, thanks to the percipience of its founder-professors, is a monolithic body, resembling the nineteenth century civic universities of England.

The second feature which differentiated the University of Sydney from its London prototype, and which revealed the influence of the ancient universities, was what Americans call 'faculty participation in government'. We have already seen how the governing body of the University of London did not include any university teachers. In Owens College, Manchester, too, the teachers at first took no part in government. The University of Sydney began in the same way; even the principal was not a member of the senate. It was not to be expected that men with the background of University College, St John's, and Marischal College, would be satisfied to be mere servants of the governing body. It was not long, therefore, before 'the professors complained, not without reason, that they had neither voice nor authority in the Institution in which they played so prominent a part ... Their complaints became unpleasantly loud, and their justice was admitted.' (So wrote Francis Merewether, the auditor-general of the colony, a founder-member of the senate and later chancellor of the university). But their justice was not admitted without prolonged resistance from the lay governors. When the professors asked for opportunities to take part in policy-making the reply they received was: 'the Senate will probably deem it conducive to the interests of the institution that you should be consulted, but they cannot compromise their freedom of action or their authority by giving a pledge that, without reference to you, no decision shall be finally pronounced.' It speaks highly of Woolley's patience that he did not resign; nine years after he was installed as principal of the university he wrote to Sheridan Moore: 'It is only quite by accident that I hear of the Senate's Proceedings, which never come before me officially.' (This was a striking contrast to the position of the president in an American college.) However in the end patience prevailed. In the revised act of 1861, provision was made for up to six seats on the senate to be occupied by professors. Thanks to the founder-professors, the faculty members had a place in university government long before their counterparts had in the civic universities of England.

The third seminal influence which the founder-professors had upon the university was over the curriculum. The senate had already shown a disposition to favour what was regarded as a liberal education for gentlemen in the unreformed ancient universities: a compulsory diet of classics and mathematics. The founder-professors consolidated this attitude. Woolley's defence of a liberal education for professional men was announced with all the vehemence and eloquence which distinguished the declarations a century later of another great advocate of liberal education in the colonies, David Balme (page 241). In a speech of singular orotundity even for those days, Woolley had declared his policy: 'The soundest lawyers come forth from schools in which law is never taught; the most accomplished physicians are nurtured where medicine is but a name. Neither of these examples will, we hope, be followed by the University of Sydney; yet she has done wisely in avoiding for the present the delusive appearance of a perfect type' (i.e. by establishing first a faculty of arts and postponing the establishment of faculties of law and medicine). The degree of social mimicry of the homeland is well illustrated from the syllabus for the first matriculation examination, held in 1852. Candidates were examined in Greek: the sixth book of the Iliad and the first book of Xenophon's *Anabasis*; in Latin: the first book of the *Aeneid* and the *Bellum Catilinarium* of Sallust; in arithmetic, algebra, and the first book of Euclid. It is a testimony to the pervasiveness of the European tradition and a tribute to the schools of the colony that twenty-four candidates passed this examination and seven were elected to scholarships on the university foundation.

When they came up to the university they encountered a severely traditional programme. In the first year all students studied classics and mathematics, together with some experimental physics and chemistry. In the second year the curriculum was leavened by the addition of lectures on the history of England. In the third year either classics or mathematics could be taken at honours level; the meaner subjects were continued only at pass level. There must have been some dissatisfaction among the public with this concept of higher education, for in 1856 the first chancellor (Charles Nicholson, a medical graduate from Edinburgh) was complaining about the 'mercenary view which deprecates as unsuitable to the Colony any outlay on objects of a not strictly utilitarian nature'. The most vivid symptom of complaint was simply that the university was not attracting enough students; and in 1859 the colonial legislature appointed a select committee to enquire into the progress of the university. When the committee asked principal Woolley: 'Is the character of the classical reading so suitable to a young country where more practical pursuits are to be followed?', his reply was: 'We have attempted to found a University here on the principles which are generally received at Home, the ruling object in the examination for the B.A. degree being first to train the mind ... for a future course of study or active exertion no previous training is so good as the training in mathematics and grammar as given through the classical languages.'

Notwithstanding these traditional opinions of education from the principal (which were disputed in the evidence given by his colleague John Smith from Aberdeen) the select committee did recommend that the university should add new faculties and widen the scope of the arts curriculum, to improve 'its capacity for adapting its teaching to the spirit of the age'. But it was not until 1865 that posts in English, German, economics, and geology were created in the university; it was not until 1886 that the arts curriculum was liberated from the constraints of the pre-1852 Oxford tradition; and it was not until a generation had passed that professional faculties were added to the university.

It is instructive to reflect on the contrast between this pattern of academic orthodoxy and the pattern which was adopted only ten years later by the land grant colleges in America. One has to admit that even by 1862, after ten years' experience of a colonial society, the University of Sydney had generated no new ideas, no fresh thinking, no reassessment of the function of a colonial university; whereas the land grant colleges from their very foundation embodied a new idea, namely that utilitarian studies could be at the core of an academic curriculum; a man's vocation could be embedded in his culture. A century later the university colleges of East and West Africa were to display a somewhat similar academic orthodoxy which remained practically unshaken until, in the 1960s, it was challenged by the implantation of a land grant college in the African bush.

During the 1850s in India, and again during the 1950s in Africa, policy over the foundation of universities was greatly influenced, if not determined, by advice from the metropolitan government in London. It seems that this did not happen over the foundation of universities in Australia. The act of incorporation of the University of Sydney had to have royal assent, which the governor of New South Wales, Sir Charles Fitzroy, secured through the colonial office in 1850. In his despatch enclosing the act for approval, Fitzroy said he would elaborate on the proposed university in a future despatch. But there is no record that he ever did. The most likely reason for this is that within a month or two gold was discovered at Summer Hill Creek, and Fitzroy's energy and interest not unnaturally turned to this more urgent and promising source of prosperity.*

The act of incorporation for the University of Sydney received the royal assent in October 1850, a few weeks after the names of the royal commissioners for Oxford and Cambridge had been announced in London. Two and a half years later, in January 1853, a similar act was passed in the legislature of the colony of Victoria, and the University of Melbourne came into being.

The universities in Sydney and Melbourne were inspired by similar sentiments and founded by men of similar convictions. But from the beginning there were important differences between them which illustrate vividly the nature of the forces which determine the patterns of universities.

* We are indebted to Mr D. S. Macmillan, archivist of the University of Sydney, for this information.

Sydney University was founded before the royal commissioners on Oxford and Cambridge published their reports, when public opinion was still suspending judgement on the function of Britain's universities; Melbourne University was founded when the reports had been out for a year and had already set British higher education on a new course. This undoubtedly had some influence on the planning of Australia's second university; proposals which would have seemed risky in 1850 seemed quite reasonable in 1853. Secondly, Melbourne was watching Sydney closely and was able to profit from Sydney's mistakes, such as the assumption that the university would be nothing more than an examining body. But the chief influence which gave shape to Melbourne University was undoubtedly the experience brought by its founder-professors.

It was the enthusiasm of a Cambridge graduate, Wentworth, which persuaded the legislative council of New South Wales to establish a university; it was the enthusiasm of another Cambridge graduate, Childers, in the legislative council of Victoria, which started a university in Melbourne. It appears that from the beginning Childers intended it to be a teaching, and not just an examining, university. There was no proposal to found colleges, though 'colleges established by private founders' could seek affiliation with the university. The pattern of government suggested for the university bore the imprint of reformed Cambridge; although control was at first to be vested in a council appointed by the governor, subsequently, when there were one hundred graduates who were masters of arts or doctors in any faculty, the graduates should (as at Cambridge) constitute a senate, having a veto upon the enactments of the governing body. The founders had in mind that ultimately there should be a 'complete' university conferring degrees in arts, philosophy, medicine, law, and music. So far, so good; their ideas were progressive for those days. But their image of the desirable graduate was still borrowed from England: at the core of the curriculum were to be classics and mathematics. The specification for the founder-professors required them to display 'such habits and manners as to stamp on their future pupils the character of loyal, well-bred English gentlemen'. These were the views of the first chancellor, Redmond Barry, a relic of Georgian courtliness, whose dinner parties were famous for their wine and who dressed when he was host for these parties 'in a blue tail coat with large gilt buttons, silk breeches and stockings, and buckled shoes'. Barry nevertheless realised how difficult it would be to create a tradition of patrician urbanity in the Australian bush. The professor of classics, he said, 'must be of a hopeful, persevering and constant mind, not to be discouraged at the outset', for 'the sciences are at first more likely to prove attractive than studies judged by those unaware of their intrinsic value . . . to be rather superficial embellishments'. The selection of the first four professors was entrusted to a committee in England almost identical with the committee which had nominated the professors for Sydney (Sir John Herschel as chairman; G. B. Airy; Henry Malden; Robert Lowe, who had just returned from Australia to England, and who was to play a prominent, if ominous, part in English education; and the chief justice of Victoria, William a'Beckett, who happened to be visiting Britain at the time). The subjects to be covered were: Greek and Latin, with ancient history; mathematics; natural science; modern history, including literature, political economy and logic.

The men selected by this committee had a decisive effect on the evolution of the university. Four professors were appointed to cover these fields of study. One of them, Rowe, a Cambridge classicist, died almost immediately on his arrival. This left three foundation professors: Hearn, a remarkable Irishman who took over for the time being Rowe's responsibilities, and in 1855 was lecturing not only in his own field (English, logic, political economy, and ancient and modern history) but also on Homer, Xenophon and Virgil; Wilson, a mathematician and astronomer; and McCoy, who covered the whole gamut of natural science.

The remarkable fact about these three men is that they had all come from the teaching staff of colleges in the Queen's University of Ireland. Hearn was a professor at Queen's College, Galway; Wilson and McCoy were professors at Queen's College, Belfast. We have already discussed how the Queen's Colleges, separated by the Irish sea from the temptation to ape Oxford and Cambridge, free from the undertow of tradition which delayed reform in Scotland, had embarked on a new and enlightened curriculum. The three founder-professors brought with them to Melbourne this freshness and initiative. They were determined to break away from the compulsory combination of Latin, Greek, and mathematics. Accordingly their first activity was to draw up for submission to the governing body a curriculum which closely resembled the pattern of study in the Queen's University of Ireland. Their first proposed concession was that candidates for matriculation should not be obliged to take both classics and mathematics. Their proposals for the B.A. course were even more radical: in the first year a choice of any of three subjects from (i) Greek and Latin, (ii) logic, (iii) geometry, (iv) algebra, trigonometry and botany; in the second year a choice of three from (i) natural philosophy, (ii) Greek and Latin, (iii) English language, (iv) mathematics, (v) comparative anatomy and physiology and zoology; and in the third year a choice of three from (i) Greek and Latin, (ii) natural philosophy, (iii) political economy, (iv) palaeontology and geology and physical geography, (v) chemistry and mineralogy, (vi) constitutional history of England. This scheme contained the shocking and revolutionary proposal that a Melbourne B.A. could be awarded to a candidate who had done no Latin and Greek at all. (There were limits to the iconoclasm of the professors, for they still maintained that classics should be a compulsory element for an M.A. degree!) Hearn and Wilson supported their proposals by appeal to the changes which were coming over the curriculum in England and by hinting that Australia should in any case not imitate English traditions. 'In the Colonies', they wrote in a memorandum addressed to the council, 'the conditions of Society which gave rise to the English system never existed . . . The more closely, therefore, the Colonial universities resemble those of the Mother Country, the greater the probability of failure'. The main burden of their argument was that 'all subjects would prosper if they were freed of the dead weight involved in any system of compulsory study'; in fact, Hearn and Wilson advocated the American system of 'electives' a decade or more before Eliot introduced the system into Harvard.

But the governing body was less enlightened than the professors and less willing to break away from the traditional idea of higher education. By a narrow majority they rejected the professor's proposals. This generated the first of what were to be many clashes between the lay governing body and the academic professorial board in Melbourne. In the end the governing body amended the proposals in such a way that no-one could get a degree without having passed two examinations in Greek and Latin and one examination in each of the subjects geometry and natural philosophy. Apart from these constraints the elective freedom to choose subjects remained. The course which the council introduced in 1855 was remarkably enlightened; more liberal than the curriculum offered in any English university at that time, and more flexible than the curriculum adopted in Sydney.

In Melbourne, as in Sydney, the response of the public to the university was disappointing. The total number of degrees awarded in the first four graduations (1858–61) was only eighteen. This apathy on the part of the colony's youth naturally strengthened the hands of those who wanted diversity in the curriculum. The professorial board continued to press for departures from tradition; in 1858 they returned to the attack, proposing to eliminate Greek, but not Latin, and (surprisingly) natural philosophy, from the obligatory diet for a B.A. This time the case was supported by the new professor of classics, M. H. Irving, the son of Carlyle's friend. Again, the worthy council members could not bring themselves to abandon so venerable a tradition of university education: Greek and natural philosophy remained compulsory and the matter was shelved until the 1870s. (A century later similar arguments, and similar resistances to change, were to be found in the university colleges of British tropical Africa.) What Melbourne University needed most, of course, were the professional faculties. It is consistent with the more progressive spirit of Melbourne that they were introduced there long before they were accepted in Sydney; but they did not begin to come until ten years after the university opened its doors: a law degree in 1865 and a faculty of law in 1874; the first medical graduates in 1867; the first graduates in engineering in 1884 (though the subject had been taught for a certificate since 1860); a faculty of agriculture (but no professor) in 1905.

Part 2

INDIA

CHAPTER THREE

THE INITIAL EXPORT POLICY

I THE CULTURAL CHALLENGE[1]

The University of Calcutta is altogether a foreign plant imported into this country, belonging to a type that flourished in foreign soil. The importation was an urgent necessity of the time, suddenly created by the abrupt introduction of new conditions of life with a new order of political situation; the founders of the new educational system had not the time to study the ideals and methods that were indigenous: the new system was introduced in entire ignorance and almost in complete defiance of the existing social order regulating the everyday life of an ancient people. (Ramendra Sunder Trivedi, principal of Ripon College and fellow of the University of Calcutta, in a memorandum submitted to the Calcutta University Commission, 1917–19.)[2]

These reflections of a sensitive Indian scholar vividly illuminate the character of the policy Britain adopted initially in exporting universities to India. But as an explanation of how and why she did so they are less instructive. To suggest that Britain acted on sudden impulse and in entire ignorance of the existing social system is to telescope time and to misjudge her purpose. Her defiance of the Indian scene was not unconscious, as Trivedi implied, but deliberate. The type of university Britain planted in India in 1857 was largely determined by a famous policy decision she had taken in Bengal some twenty years before; and this in turn had a history stretching back to the eighteenth century and the early days of British rule.

The East India Company faced a formidable challenge in the educational sphere as it embarked on its political career in India. It was confronted by two indigenous systems of education, each deeply rooted in a non-christian religion. Each had great traditions of scholarship behind it, but each by the eighteenth century was in decay. The unique flowering of the hindu system had long since passed: scattered tols, following a conventional and sterile pattern of studies, were all that remained of the vigorous forest culture of the vedic and buddhist eras. The muslim system, which had never attained its fullest height in India, was likewise in decline, the studies of its madrassas similarly bound by tradition, and remote from the needs of a modern and progressive society. But neither system had lost its ancient and characteristic ideals. Each preserved a spiritual quality and a reverence for disinterested scholarship; each was still lingeringly alive.

The immediate reaction of the company's local administrators was to fan the embers of these indigenous systems. In 1781 Warren Hastings established a new madrassa at Calcutta to provide the customary pattern of islamic studies; and in 1792 John Duncan, the resident at Benares, founded a comparable institution for 'the preservation and cultivation of the Laws, Literature and Religion' of the hindus. Both men were largely influenced by practical considerations: the need for native officials to assist in the administration as well as the need to cultivate the goodwill of the two Indian communities. But they were also inspired by a genuine admiration of the Indian cultural heritage, and a desire to promote its study. It was the decade of the oriental scholarship of Sir William Jones, and the formation of the Royal Asiatic Society.

But this early disposition to foster the native systems of education was promptly questioned. In the same year that Duncan was planning the Sanskrit College at Benares, Charles Grant, recently returned from service with the company in India, was appealing for a very different type of education for the Indians. In a treatise later submitted to the court of directors, he conceived for Britain the great mission of the regeneration of hindu society. Britain, he urged, must communicate to India her own 'superior lights': a knowledge not only of western philosophy and science but of christianity. And she must do so primarily through the medium of the English language. Grant's bold plea had no immediate effect; but it was the starting point of evangelical pressure which was to commit the company not only to formal responsibility for education in India, but to a policy containing within it the seeds of the future anglicist-orientalist controversy. Under the terms of the East India Company Act of 1813, the governor general in council was authorised to direct that out of any surplus revenue a sum of not less than one lac of rupees a year should be set apart and applied to two very diverse objectives: 'the revival and improvement of literature and the encouragement of the learned natives of India' and 'the introduction and promotion of a knowledge of the sciences among the inhabitants of the British territories in India'.

The inherent dilemma in this policy was not at first apparent. The court of directors at once set a clear priority on the former of the two objectives specified in the charter act, and in their first educational despatch to Bengal in June 1814, left it in no doubt that Indian susceptibilities were to be respected. Persuaded that 'natives of caste and of reputation' would not submit to the discipline of college life, they concluded that neither objective should be sought through the medium of public colleges 'if established under the rules, and upon a plan similar to those that have been founded at our universities'. The preferable method, they suggested, would be to encourage the traditional method of home instruction by conferring honorary marks of distinction, and providing financial assistance. They also urged the value of Sanskrit studies, pointing to the practical advantage they offered in administration and medicine, and indicating how in astronomy and mathematics they might be made the bridge to western learning. But it was not only caution in the East India House which served to obscure the dilemma. It was also inertia in India. For it was not until 1823 that the government of Bengal appointed a general committee of public instruction to administer the funds authorised by the act; and not until then, therefore, that the objectives of policy were seriously debated. Throughout the decade, however, pressures were building up, both in England and India, to uncover the dilemma. To the evangelical pressure in England was added the pressure of the utilitarians. In 1817, James Mill produced in his *History* the bible of utilitarian lore on India: a trenchant analysis of the defects of Indian society and culture, arguing the need of a thoroughgoing process of administrative reform to sweep away the accumulated errors of the past. Two years later he was appointed to an assistant examinership in the East India Company, and carried his ideas into the India House. Comparable influences were developing meanwhile in India, where missionary pressure for the westernisation of Indian society was being reinforced by secular pressures, Indian as well as European. Here, too, 1817 was a significant date: for it was in that year, as a result of the combined initiative of David Hare and the enlightened brahmin, Ram Mohan Roy, that the Vidyalaya or Hindu College, the first institution to introduce hindus to western learning, and later to provide on the higher side of its work the nucleus of Presidency College, was opened in Calcutta.

When, therefore, with the appointment of the general committee of public instruction, the company at last came to grips with the problem of education in India, the interpretation of the policy prescribed by the charter act was soon in dispute: and an early exchange between Calcutta and London marked the opening of a controversy that was gradually to deepen and draw to a climax over the next decade. Plans for the improvement of the two oriental institutions founded by Hastings and Duncan, and for the establishment of a new Sanskrit College in Calcutta, provoked a critical despatch from the court of directors in February 1824, and a stubborn rejoinder from the committee in the following August, the one generally attributed to James Mill,[3] the other clearly influenced by the distinguished oriental scholar, H.H. Wilson,[4] then the committee's secretary. With a view to the future, the court turned a critical eye on the past, and the policy originally adopted for the Calcutta Madrassa and the Hindu College at Benares. Whilst admitting the need to adopt hindu and muhammadan media, the importance of consulting hindu and muhammadan prejudices, the desirability of preserving all that was 'useful' in hindu and muhammadan literature, they sharply censured the exclusive concentration on oriental learning. 'In professing . . . to establish seminaries for the purpose of teaching mere Hindoo, or mere Mohammedan literature', they wrote in a famous passage, 'you bound yourselves to teach a great deal of what was frivolous, not a little of what was purely mischievous and a small remainder indeed in which utility was in any way concerned.' '. . . we apprehend that the plan of the institutions to the improvement of which our attention is now directed was originally and fundamentally erroneous. The great end should not have been to teach Hindoo learning, but useful learning.' They did not conceal their view that in the plans before them too little account had been taken of this great end. They acknowledged that in the older institutions the pace of reform must be gradual; but even here they directed that 'incessant endeavours' should be made to supersede what was 'useless, or worse' in the curricula. As for the new foundation, they pointed out that its curricula could be more closely influenced from the beginning by the principle of utility.

The committee chose to minimise the criticism: to construe it, indeed, as a broad endorsement of the plans they had submitted. But in a long letter to the government of Bengal in August 1824, they entered a careful defence of the policy originally adopted, and of the modified version of that policy they themselves were sponsoring. They argued that at the time of the founding of the older institutions, the prejudice of the natives, and the means available to the government, precluded the provision of any but the customary oriental type of instruction. And they insisted that these were factors still to be reckoned with. They did not dispute that useful learning was the ultimate objective, but they were strongly of the opinion that any attempt to force the pace of westernisation must defeat its purpose; and they also maintained that only those adequately grounded in the old learning would be effective in purveying the new. But it was not merely on these pragmatic grounds that the committee defended the emphasis on oriental studies. They claimed a positive value for them, respectfully submitting that the court had been insufficiently discriminating in their censure of them. Neither as regards the metaphysical sciences, mathematics, law or language was it 'worse than a waste of time' to provide tuition in them. The committee were especially insistent on the value of the study of oriental languages – 'the ground work upon which all future improvements must materially depend' – and incredulous that the court should have wished to deny a place to oriental poetry in the curriculum of Indian higher education. 'We do not know ... how any language and litera-ture can be successfully studied if its poetical compositions are not cultivated with considerable attention; as a part, therefore, and a very important part of Sanscrit and Arabic literature, as the source of national imagery, the expression of national feeling, and the depository of the most approved phraseology and style, the poetical writings of the Hindus and Mohammadans appear to be legitimately comprehended among the objects of literary seminaries, founded for Mohammadans and Hindus.' Whilst pledging themselves to take advantage of every opportunity to introduce European literature and science where it was practicable to do so, they reiterated the need for caution. 'We must for the present go with the tide of popular prejudice, and we have the less regret in doing so, as we trust we have said sufficient to show that the course is by no means unprofitable.'

In 1824, the climate of opinion in the committee was predominantly orientalist; the civil servants of whom it was composed were largely in agreement over the pace of westernisation, and able to offer a common front to the pressures seeking to accelerate it. But with the recruitment of new members, strongly imbued with the growing liberal influences at home, it gradually lost this early homogeneity. The controversy that had opened between Calcutta and London in 1824 came to be pursued within the committee itself; and by 1835, the cleavage of opinion over the competing claims of oriental and occidental learning was such that the secretary felt obliged to submit the issue to the arbitrament of the government. In doing so, he prompted the brilliantly tendentious minute of Macaulay, which not only precipitated the solution to the dilemma posed by the educational clause of the charter act twenty years before, but strongly coloured its character.

Macaulay narrowed the issue to the need for a decision on the medium of instruction to be adopted in the higher education financed by the government. In view of the inadequacy of the vernaculars, he concluded that the choice lay between English and the oriental classical languages. The criterion he applied was the simple one of which was the better worth knowing. On grounds of utility, and the intrinsic merit of the literature to which it would give access, he had no hesitation in asserting the superiority of English; and he discovered a further justification for it in the analogy of the great impulse Britain herself had received from an alien literature some three centuries before. 'Had our ancestors acted as the Committee of Public Instruction has hitherto acted, – had they neglected the language of Thucydides and Plato, and the language of Cicero and Tacitus, and had they confined their attention to the old dialects of our own island, had they printed nothing and taught nothing at the universities but chronicles in Anglo-Saxon and romances in Norman French, – would England ever have been what she now is? What the Greek and Latin were to the contemporaries of More and Ascham, our tongue is to the people of India.' But if the ultimate aim he held in view was a comparable renaissance in India, the means, paradoxically enough, was to be a narrow concentration on the invigorating alien culture. For Macaulay prescribed a virtual ban on the patronage of indigenous studies which he disparaged in terms as sweeping as Mill a decade before, and still more derisive. He called for an immediate end to the printing of Sanskrit and Arabic books, and for the abolition of both the madrassa and the newly founded Sanskrit College in Calcutta. He thought that the government would be doing 'enough and much more than enough' for the eastern languages if it were to retain the Hindu College at Benares and the madrassa in Delhi. Even if these colleges were retained, he was insistent that the system of stipends should be abandoned for future students. The savings effected in this way might then be used to assist the Hindu College in Calcutta, and to develop a system of English schools in the principal cities. In view of the limited funds at the government's disposal, he agreed with the 'orientalists' that the main effort should be concentrated on the higher levels of education. The aim should be to form a class of persons

'Indian in blood and colour, but English in tastes, in opinions, in morals and in intellect': a class who would serve as interpreters between the government and the masses, and who, by refining the vernaculars, would supply the means of a widespread dissemination of western learning. Macaulay's main contention was promptly conceded. Lord William Bentinck declined to abolish the two oriental colleges in Calcutta; but in March 1835, issued the memorable resolution which decisively asserted that 'the great object of the British Government ought to be the promotion of European literature and science among the natives of India; and that all the funds appropriated for the purpose of education would be best employed on English education alone'.

But the controversy was not yet over. Bentinck's sudden resolution – which specifically endorsed Macaulay's recommendations over stipends and the printing of oriental works – did not meet with complete or immediate approval in London. It ran up against resistance in the court, which now found the reforming zeal of the government in Bengal excessive. And by a curious twist of fate, it fell to the son of James Mill to put up the arguments against a policy which so largely embodied his father's philosophical ideas.[5] John Stuart Mill had entered the company's London offices in 1823. To begin with, he had shared his father's view of the uselessness of oriental learning. But he had since moved away from this early position, and in a draft despatch of October 1836, censured the new policy on the grounds that it was ill-calculated to foster either a 'disinterested love of knowledge or an intelligent wish for information'. To withhold patronage from India's scholarly class would be to destroy an element that was essential to her progress; whilst to concentrate so narrowly on western learning would be to stimulate the vocational goal of education, and prejudice the pursuit of learning for its own sake.[6] H. H. Wilson added his voice to this culmination of the debate he had figured in earlier. Writing now from Oxford, he reiterated his previous views in a contribution to the *Asiatic Journal*, insisting that a policy of making 'a whole people dependent upon a remote and unknown country for all their ideas and for the very words in which to clothe them' must 'degrade their character, depress their energies, and render them incapable of aspiring to any intellectual distinction.'[7]

The objections of the court, however, did not prevail. When Mill's draft came before the board of control for approval, the president yielded to the view of the governor general, Lord Auckland, that it would be unwise to invite a renewal of the recent bitter controversy by repudiating the decision that had been reached in India. He withheld his sanction, and the draft was quietly suppressed. But no alternative directions were prepared; and it was not until 1841, on the basis of a compromise supplied by Lord Auckland himself, that the issue raised by the committee six years before was finally settled. In a long minute towards the end of 1839, Auckland contended for a more generous support of the existing oriental institutions. He proposed that the sums recently withdrawn from the oriental seminaries should be restored;

that the full amount originally assigned should be devoted in the first instance to promoting a 'perfect efficiency' in oriental instruction, and only afterwards to supporting western learning; and that scholarships should be provided in place of the abandoned stipends. He welcomed the decision of the court to assist the indigenous learning by disbursing grants for the publication of oriental works through the Royal Asiatic Society and made a conciliatory reference to the value of the training provided in the native colleges. But he was frank in his opinion of the radical errors in the oriental system, and made it clear that the principal aim must be to communicate 'a complete education in European Literature, Philosophy and Science' through the medium of the English language to as many as were prepared to receive it. Endorsing the 'filtration theory', he argued that this instruction should be provided in the first place for the upper and middle classes by means of an urban system of education hinging on the higher college, and that it should be accompanied by a careful cultivation of the vernaculars so that ultimately it might be widely transmitted to the masses. In approving this modified programme, the court emphatically endorsed the priority Auckland had assigned to western learning. 'It is by no means our intention that the arrangement now authorized ... should interrupt the measures in progress for the dissemination of European knowledge', they wrote in 1841. 'On the contrary, we cordially subscribe to one of the principal declarations of the Resolution of 7th March 1835 that "it should be the great object of British Government to promote European Science and Literature among the Natives of India" [sic] and have no hesitation in sanctioning it, as a general principle, for the conduct of our Indian Government.' The formula supplied by Auckland fell a good deal short of what Macaulay had intended, but the emphasis was now firmly on an extended interpretation of the latter of the two objectives originally sanctioned by parliament, and any doubts as to the practicability of the new policy were quickly dispelled. In 1837, Persian had been superseded by English as the official language of the law courts; and by 1844, the Indian response to the new system was already sufficiently assured for Lord Hardinge to be able to announce that in the recruitment of natives to posts under the government, preference would be given to those who had received an English education. Stimulated by these two incentives, the new policy took firm root. The government went ahead with the provision of a series of secondary schools, some of which, by the addition of higher classes, were raised to college status; and official enterprise in providing western education was matched by a corresponding activity on the part of the missionaries, and indeed of the Indians themselves.

Britain's response to the cultural challenge of the Indian sub-continent had veered to a point almost diametrically opposed to the one at which it had started. From an early disposition to foster the indigenous learning, it had moved through the intermediate stage of a cautious grafting of western learning on the studies of the east to a policy which, whatever its ultimate objective, involved discouragement, amounting almost to displacement of oriental learning. The settlement, reached amid such acrimony in Bengal, gave a decisive lead to the other provincial governments: and British policy entered upon a course it was to pursue substantially unchanged for the rest of the century, with the prophetic warning of the younger Mill and other dissentients hanging uneasily about it.

II LAUNCHING THE UNIVERSITY SYSTEM

It was against this background that universities were launched by Sir Charles Wood in his famous educational despatch of 19 July 1854. The initiative came from London, but it was not spontaneous or unheralded. Two plans had already been put forward in Bengal, where English education was most advanced, and each claims a special interest. The first served as a prototype for the scheme that was ultimately adopted; the second offers a tantalising glimpse of how the unhappy consequences of that scheme might have been avoided.

Both were the work of Dr F. J. Mouat, who became secretary to the council of education shortly after it was set up in succession to the general committee of public instruction in 1842.[8] Having visited the schools and colleges under the supervision of the council, he was at once struck by the want of 'any definite aim and object' in the educational system, and quickly convinced that 'nothing short of a university' would supply it. Judging by the work of the Medical College, which had been founded in 1835, and the results of the council's senior scholarship examination, he was satisfied that Bengal was ready for such a step; and he was impressed by the advantages it seemed to offer. It would enable the natives to make their studies 'a source of emolument, as well as a social distinction', and so afford a powerful stimulus to education. It would meet the difficulty of devising a suitable examination for entry into government service and provide a superior type of public servant. It would also be of wider social benefit, for by calling into existence a new educated class it would diffuse 'a taste for the more refined and intellectual pleasures and pursuits of the West to the gradual extinction of the enervating and degrading superstitions of the East'. As a first move, therefore, he consulted his friend Henry Malden, who was professor of Greek in University College, London, where he himself had been a student. From Malden he received encouragement, and a copy of a study he had written on the development of the various university systems in Europe. He then approached the president of the council of education, C. H. Cameron; and Cameron, who was already thinking in terms of a university for Bengal, readily agreed that he should proceed with a draft scheme. After carefully considering the constitutions of the universities of Oxford and Cambridge, and of the recently established University of London, Mouat decided that London alone provided a suitable model for India. But he found it a peculiarly appropriate one. As an examining university, testing the studies of affiliated colleges, whatever their religious persuasion, it was well suited to meet the needs of the varied and scattered colleges in Bengal.

Besides which, a university of this type could be set up at very little expense and would soon be self-supporting. And thus, with the charter of the University of London as his guide, he proceeded to sketch out a plan which, after consultation with all interested parties, he completed in October 1845.[9]

This provided for a central university in Calcutta, with a senate or governing body consisting of a chancellor, vice-chancellor and fellows, empowered to award degrees in the four faculties of arts and science, law, civil engineering, and medicine and surgery. The governor general was to be chancellor *ex officio*, and vested with the 'powers and authority . . . such as pertain to those officers in Europe'. The president of the council of education was to be vice-chancellor; and he and the fellows, the latter mostly government officers, were to have 'entire management of and superintendence over the affairs . . . of the university'. Mouat envisaged an entry standard equivalent to the council's junior scholarship examination, and proposed that no candidate should be allowed to matriculate until he had completed his fifteenth year. But he did not attempt to enter into detail over courses of study or subjects of examination. These he reserved for the senate, in the event of the scheme being put into effect.

The plan was well received in Calcutta, both in official and non-official circles. It was cordially approved by the influential presbyterian missionary, Dr Duff, to whom it had been shown at an early stage, formally adopted by the council of education, and generally endorsed by the provincial and supreme governments. Early in 1846 it was forwarded to London with a supporting letter from the government of Bengal; and a few months later this official submission was reinforced by a further letter from the governor general, Lord Hardinge.[10] The government of Bengal did not feel competent to judge whether the time had arrived for a university, and preferred to leave the decision to more qualified opinion at home. But it fully concurred in the merits of the scheme, pointed to the beneficial results that had followed the establishment of universities in Europe, and offered the pertinent reflection that educational progress in Bengal was in advance of that in Britain, France and Germany when similar institutions were founded there. The support of the government of India was unqualified, and that of the governor general still more emphatic. To Hardinge, indeed, the proposal was a logical development of existing policy: 'a necessary part and consequence of the great measure of Education already in progress throughout the different Colleges in Bengal . . .' He did, however, make one significant reservation. Since the president of the council of education was to be vice-chancellor *ex officio*, he thought it would be a wise precaution that the appointment should rest with the supreme government. He did not fear any 'public inconvenience' from a chartered body consisting mainly of government officers, but he was nevertheless 'decidedly of opinion' that 'in the first years after the introduction of such an institution in India . . . the Government ought to have the power of direct control and interference in all the affairs of the University'.

The home government was unmoved by this warm commendation from

India. In September 1847, after a long delay, the court of directors declined to sanction the proposal.[11] They gave no reason for doing so at the time, and later they were to imply that the project had been judged premature.[12] But pencilled comment on the letters from India suggests that in fact it had been considered unnecessary and unsuitable, and that this was due in part at least to the unquestioned assumption that a university in India must necessarily reproduce the essential features of a university in Britain. There were two dissenting comments on the copy of the supporting letter from the government of Bengal in the board's collection on the subject.[13] When it was suggested that there were strong grounds for proposing a university because the range and extent of the subjects prescribed for the government's senior scholarships were greater than were required for an ordinary bachelor's degree in any British university, a marginal note ran: 'They do not come into the same category with Bachelors as the dead languages are not studied'. And when it was asserted that it might be difficult to find a better solution to the problem of providing suitable tests for government employment, a similar objection seems to have been raised by another critic: 'It would not answer because the primary qualification [i.e. for a bachelor's degree] is a familiar knowledge of the [?] Languages.' The same hand, commenting on a passage in an enclosure from the council of education, affirmed: 'It is quite right to postpone the question. The Queen can do as she likes when the Charter is no more.' A further clue to the fate of the proposal is perhaps to be found on the dockets of the original letter from the government of India in March, and a subsequent one of the following September.[14] Each bears the inscription 'Prof. Wilson': which suggests that the project may well have been referred to an adviser who was to express himself decidedly opposed to universities for India when the subject was reverted to some years later.

Nearly ten years after he had prepared his first plan, Dr Mouat drew the outlines of a very different type of university. This time the initial concept was not his, although the inspiration for it arose from a suggestion put forward by the council of education. This was to convert the Hindu College in Calcutta into a general metropolitan college.[15] The project was designed to fill a conspicuous gap in the educational structure of the presidency, for hitherto there had been no higher course of English education in the capital that was open to all creeds and classes. Dalhousie, in welcoming the idea, gave it an enlarged significance. With a perceptive awareness of what was already a dangerous weakness in Indian higher education, he directed that the new institution should be a college in reality as well as in name, and no mere compound of college and dame's school, such as he had already observed in India. To assist it in establishing this higher status, he proposed that it should be given the designation of 'Presidency College'; and he looked forward to the time when, in conjunction with the Medical College in Calcutta, it should 'expand itself into something approaching to the dignity and proportions of an Indian university'.[16]

The council of education was invited to transform the existing college into the nucleus of a teaching university along these lines, and Mouat devoted the opening months of 1854 to the task. He drew up a scheme which was submitted to the government of Bengal in March.[17] This provided for the same branches of study that he had proposed for the examining university before. But the curriculum was now outlined in greater detail; and both in the proposals for the general or arts branch, and in the commentary on them, there was a sharp reflection of the prevailing 'anglicist' viewpoint. No provision was made for Sanskrit, Arabic or Persian. These were deemed adequately provided for in the existing oriental colleges. Students were to read English and either Latin or an Indian vernacular; an arrangement that was supported with the familiar argument that English was to the native of India 'all and much more than all' that Latin and Greek were to the Englishman. It was also proposed that there should be greater stress on English literature in place of the former emphasis on mathematics: for 'what general improvement in the strength and tone of the mind, which the strongest supporter of a partially exclusive mathematical education claims for his system under ordinary circumstances, can be put for a moment into comparison with that improvement in the strength and tone of the mind which a native acquires by a large acquaintance with English literature?' Special provisions were made to extend the facilities of the college as widely as possible. Schools and colleges throughout the presidency were to be linked to it by means of a system of bursaries; and any person was to be admitted to its courses, though not to its examinations, on payment of a fee.[18] The scheme could not be as all embracing as the earlier one Mouat had planned, but it offered a much better prospect of establishing and maintaining a high standard of scholarship. Looking back on it thirty years later, with all the advantages of hindsight, he had no doubt that it would have been 'far more useful to Bengal than the form actually adopted'.[19] But the proposal for a teaching university had come too late. By the time it was forwarded to the court for approval, it had already been overtaken by events in London.

Here, the renewal of the East India Company's charter had prompted the first searching enquiry into the company's educational record. The government had come under pressure to pursue a more active educational policy; and strong pleas had been entered for universities. Among the main protagonists were two former Anglo-Indian officials who had been closely concerned in the shaping of educational policy in India: Sir C. E. Trevelyan, who had figured prominently in the controversy of the thirties, and C. H. Cameron, who, as legal member of the governor general's council, had been president of the council of education in the forties. Each urged the need of universities before the select committee of the house of lords on India in 1853, and each had distinctive ideas about the form they should take. Cameron revived the project he had sponsored in 1845 as president of the council of education, and in discussing the distribution and curriculum of universities of this type, he contributed a new 'anglicist' emphasis to the outline plan.[20] He recommended Calcutta, Bombay, Madras and Agra as suitable sites not only because they were the capital cities of the presidencies, but because they were well placed to promote the study of a dominant vernacular; and it was these four vernacular languages – Bengali, Mahrathi, Tamil and Hindi – together with English language and literature and science taught in English, that he prescribed for the curriculum. Neither Indian literature, nor the classical languages of the east were to form part of the subjects examined. Trevelyan's approach was more catholic and more utilitarian. He advocated a university for each presidency consisting of two departments: the first to test 'all comers' in a wide range of knowledge including Sanskrit and Arabic literature; and the second to provide 'positive instruction' at an advanced level in such professional subjects as law, civil engineering, surveying and architecture.[21]

But it was the missionaries, acting through their leading spokesmen, Dr A. Duff and J. C. Marshman, who exerted the most insistent pressure for universities. They had a special reason for doing so, for they wished to supersede the existing system of testing eligibility for government employment. In carrying out the terms of Lord Hardinge's resolution of 1844, the council of education had adopted a test on the lines of the government's senior scholarship examination. It was a test of very high standard,[22] confined to English secular literature and science, and it severely penalised the students of missionary colleges and colleges following a classical education. Latterly few had attempted it; but the regulation persisted and rankled. To Duff and Marshman, therefore, the concept of an examining university, testing a wide and liberal course of study, had strong attractions: and they pressed for it not only in the evidence they gave before the select committee of the house of lords[23] but in memoranda submitted directly to the government.[24] Marshman, however, was prepared to compromise. He was aware that in some quarters it was felt that the immediate establishment of universities would be premature; and if need be, he was ready to forego the form of a university if assured of the substance of an impartial examining body. 'What we want in India', he wrote, 'is the thing more than the name.'[25] But the opposition he anticipated remained remarkably quiescent. The only dissentient voice raised before the select committees of enquiry was that of the distinguished orientalist, Professor H. H. Wilson. As if re-enacting the part he had played in the educational controversy earlier, he did not know what was meant by a university in India. If it was to consist in 'wearing caps and gowns, and being called Bachelors of Arts and Masters of Arts' he did not see what was likely to accrue from it.[26]

Sir Charles Wood, as president of the board of control, did not respond to the pressure for universities with any enthusiasm. For him the question turned essentially on the part that Indians were to play in the administration. And here, although he was disposed to be more liberal than his predecessors, he did not envisage natives being admitted to senior posts in any substantial numbers.[27] Whilst the British continued to rule in India – and he expected them to do so for many years to come – he concluded they must continue to hold the key administrative positions themselves. To encourage the higher literary studies of a university in these circumstances seemed unnecessary and possibly dangerous. 'I care very little about teaching Hindoos to read Bacon and to be examined as we should be for honours at Oxford', he confided to Dalhousie, ' . . . I am inclined to think that these highly educated natives are likely to be a very discontented class unless they are employed, and we cannot find employment for them all.'[28] Nor did a university seem necessary for the practical training he saw as the essential want in India. In some fields, such as medicine, provision could be made independently; in others, such as civil engineering, he doubted whether the theoretical study of the degree course was what was really needed.[29] Throughout, it was training for the 'useful avocations in a lower sphere' that was his main concern.[30] Yet he was not insensible to the missionary grievance and the need for an impartial test of scholarship; and he had no objection to the provision of higher literary studies so long as government funds were not involved. He had no sympathy with those who desired to withhold higher education from India for fear of the political consequences. When, therefore, he came to work on his famous educational despatch, he was not beguiled by caution in the India House.[31] Under the influence of J. C. Marsham, a proposed 'previous communication' had suggested the halfway house of 'a body of examiners at each Presidency Town' which would afford 'a nucleus for a future University to be formed on the general plan of the University of London'.[32] Wood preferred to concede universities at once, but the concession was carefully trimmed to his overall policy of concentrating effort on the lower levels of education. 'I am for Universities to confer degrees and honours on candidates who come up from Colleges of all description', he explained to Dalhousie, as he was maturing his plans, 'but I am for leaving high education to be mainly supported by those who are anxious for it . . . '[33] He insisted on withdrawing the senior government scholarships and although prepared to subsidise higher training in such subjects as medicine and engineering declined to offer any special incentive for following the ordinary degree course.[34] 'I do not see the advantage of rearing up a number of highly educated gentlemen at the expense of the State, whom you cannot employ, and who will naturally become depositories of discontent', he reiterated in a later letter. 'If they choose to educate themselves, well and good, but I am against providing our own future detractors and opponents and grumblers.'[35]

Like Mouat, Wood was at once attracted to the University of London as a model for India.[36] He held no special brief for it on academic grounds: the arguments for separating the examining and teaching function did not weigh with him. But he thought it admirably conceived to get round the religious difficulty and provide the framework of a comprehensive university system; and it accorded perfectly with his basic strategy of building Indian education

U–B.I.A.—3*

on a system of grants-in-aid.[37] In his despatch of 1854, he endorsed the earlier view of the council of education and directed that the 'form, government and functions' of the University of London should be followed in India.

But it was to be followed with 'some variation . . . in points of detail': and in regard to the constitution, he proposed two significant adaptations. The first, plainly stated in his despatch, was to modify the exclusively examining character of the university. He thought it would be advisable to provide instruction in subjects that were not adequately covered in existing institutions and suggested that chairs should be instituted in law and possibly engineering, in the vernacular languages, and perhaps also in Sanskrit, Arabic and Persian. The second adaptation did not emerge so clearly. This concerned the powers of the senate and raised the vital question of government control. Under the charter of the University of London, the senate, although appointed by the crown, was empowered to fill vacancies by election. To begin with, Wood was content to adopt this procedure for India. In its original form, para. 26 of the despatch provided for senates 'with power of filling vacancies in their number'. But when the draft came before the court of directors, the provision was queried. 'May not this in time introduce a body apart from & independent of the Govt', ran a pencilled note in the margin. 'It seems to me at variance with all our other Indian institutions except only the "free Press". Should not a majority of the Senate be for the present at least appointed by Govt? Otherwise may you not have Religious & Political feuds?' The court concurred in the need for caution and Wood agreed. The objectionable phrase was discreetly excised and in its final version para. 26 contained no reference to the way in which the senate was to be replenished.[38]

In regard to curriculum and standards, Wood did not enter into detail. He dealt in general terms with the application of certain principles: and so far as the curriculum was concerned, the principles were not new. He reaffirmed the policy of religious neutrality; and he gave fresh and emphatic sanction to the fundamental aim of diffusing 'the improved arts, science, philosophy and literature of Europe'. No subject connected with religious belief was to be amongst the subjects examined by the university; European learning was to be the staple of the curriculum. Wood also gave prominence to a neglected aspect of established policy, emphasising the role of the universities in developing the vernaculars and so making them a more effective medium for disseminating the learning of the west. It was for this purpose that he tentatively advanced the suggestion of chairs for the classical languages of the east in addition to those for the vernaculars themselves. But he followed orthodox 'anglicist' doctrine in insisting that the professors in Sanskrit, Arabic and Persian should concentrate on the linguistic aspect of their subjects. He acknowledged the value of Indian classical literature for historical and antiquarian purposes and the study of hindu and muhammadan law; and he was not disposed to withdraw support from the special oriental institutions where it was taught. But he declined to bring it within the orbit of university studies.

In view of later events, a certain irony attaches to Wood's directions about standards. He regarded the question as one of great importance; but working under the shadow of the senior government scholarship, he was more concerned to prevent the standard of the ordinary degree from being fixed too high than to devise safeguards for its quality. He contemplated two levels of examination: one for the pass degree, and the other for honours. He was satisfied that the honours examination should be a real test of 'high ability and valuable attainments'. But as a matter of justice, as well as to avoid prejudicing the success of the universities, he thought the standard of the ordinary degree should be fixed considerably below, and certainly not as high as the senior government scholarship. The drafting of instructions to this effect presented some difficulty, and it was only after variants had been tried warning against the standard being set 'too high' or 'too high . . . at first' that the less objectionable formula 'with very great judgment' was found.[39] In explanation of this innocuous phrase it was added that 'the standard required should be such as to command respect without discouraging the efforts of deserving students . . .'

Owing to pressure of other business, there was a delay of several months before the government of India began to implement the court's instructions. In January 1855, however, it appointed a committee to prepare a detailed plan for a university at Calcutta which might serve as the basis for similar universities at Bombay and Madras. The committee was composed of members of the former council of education in Bengal, with its late president, Sir James Colvile, as chairman, together with other prospective fellows of the University of Calcutta and representatives from the legislative councils of Bombay and Madras. It confined itself to drawing up a scheme of examinations for the university and left to the government of India the task of framing the constitution and drafting the necessary legislation. The committee completed its scheme in August 1856 and this was 'unreservedly' adopted by the government of India in December.[40] Acts incorporating the three universities passed into law in the following year.[41] The resultant university pattern reproduced most of the essential features prescribed in the despatch of 1854; but in the course of the planning in India, some significant modifications had been made.

In view of the plans proposed for the new Presidency College, it was decided that professorships would not be needed at the University of Calcutta. The act of incorporation, therefore, which was followed for each of the other two universities, provided for examining functions only. In terms borrowed from the charter of the University of London, all three universities were established 'for the purpose of ascertaining, by means of examination, the persons who have acquired proficiency in different branches of Literature, Science, and Art, and of rewarding them by Academical Degrees as evidence of their respective attainments, and marks of honor proportioned thereunto'. In other respects, however, the legislation faithfully reflected the court's intentions, and this was notably the case over the question of government control.

At Calcutta, the office of chancellor was assigned to the governor general; and it was reserved to the governor general in council to nominate the vice-chancellor, and to appoint all but the *ex officio* fellows, whom it could also dismiss. Its approval was required for the making of by-laws and regulations, and it was also empowered to control the general fee fund and receive an annual statement of the accounts. A similar role was accorded to the local governors and governments in respect of the universities in Bombay and Madras.

In the range of subjects for examination, the committee appointed by the government of India acted closely in the spirit of the court's instructions. It provided for degrees in the four faculties of arts, law, medicine and civil engineering: and save in civil engineering, where the University of London offered no degree courses, it adapted the content of the corresponding London examinations to the purpose of transmitting western knowledge in the Indian environment. In medicine and law, the adaptation presented little difficulty. The committee thought the London medical examinations well suited for India; and it was a comparatively straightforward matter to provide for Indian municipal and positive law in the legal course. But to devise a suitable arts course was a more complex problem, and both in structure and content, the Indian version differed a good deal from its English model. It comprised five subject groups, of which three – mathematics and natural philosophy, physical sciences, mental and moral sciences – corresponded fairly closely to their London counterparts. But in place of the London 'classics', the committee substituted separate groups of languages and history; and each was carefully designed to further the special role of the Indian university. The committee did not have a free hand to fashion the language group solely with a view to assisting the transmission of western learning; it had to provide for Anglo-Indian students following a western classical education, and could not overweight the language content of the degree course unduly. But it contrived to give prominence to this purpose in the ordinary as well as the honours degree course. For the ordinary degree it specified English, one other language which might be an Indian or western classical language or an Indian vernacular, and a test of the candidate's spoken language. By this means it hoped to equip the Indian interpreter of western culture with a critical knowledge of an Indian vernacular without necessarily requiring the study of an Indian classical language. But the sub-committee entrusted with framing the arts regulations was persuaded that 'the chief reason why the students of our Anglo-Vernacular Schools and Colleges have failed to produce men who are able to communicate to their fellow-countrymen the knowledge they themselves have acquired, is that the students of those Institutions are for the most part ignorant of any one of the Classical languages of the country, without some knowledge of which they can neither acquire a critical knowledge of their own Vernacular nor command the respect which attaches only to men who are esteemed learned by the public'. For the honours course, therefore, the committee accepted its recommendation to prescribe a classical language in addition.[42] In assigning a special branch of the degree course to history, and providing a related honours examination, the committee looked for more than the mere transmission of learning. The aim acknowledged by the sub-committee was 'to enlarge the minds of Native Students, and lead them far beyond the contracted sphere in which the thoughts of the people of India have hitherto moved'; and in support of its enthusiastic claims on behalf of the study of history, it observed 'with pleasure that the establishment of a similar separate branch of Honors at Oxford was recommended in the Report of the recent Oxford University Commission'.[43]

Over standards, however, the spirit of the despatch was not so closely fol-lowed. Dalhousie was sceptical about the value of 'any one degree of the very low standard' which seemed to be contemplated by the court[44] and Sir James Colvile's committee was invited to consider the expediency of establishing a higher degree as well.[45] The committee was no less concerned to stimulate a high standard of scholarship but tackled the problem rather differently. It assumed a basic principle the court had never acknowledged and implicitly rejected: that the test of the 'first and principal academic distinction' in India should be 'as strict as those . . . in the Universities of the United Kingdom and other parts of the civilized world'. Instead of proposing a higher degree with a related honours examination, it preferred to establish a sufficient standard for the B.A. degree and to make the honours examination the test of the M.A. degree. In fixing the standard for the B.A., the committee did not transgress the court's injunctions. It drew a careful distinction between the prescribed maximum standard and the minimum which would qualify for the degree, and it ruled that even the prescribed maximum should be within the grasp of the ordinary student. But to assure the degree of the international currency it sought, the committee specified a longer period of study than was customary at London, fixing it at four years from the entrance examination instead of two. It insisted moreover that the maximum standard should be the highest the average student could attain in this period, and it prescribed a system of marking that was designed to encourage specialisation. It was significant of the more scholarly approach of the planners in India that in approving the recommendations of the committee, the governor general in council should have wished that the minimum qualifying standard, which it had been left to the examiners to determine, should have been more precisely specified.

The university which emerged from the planning in 1857 was a deliberate exotic of a strangely hybrid kind. Although based on the University of Lon-don, it had been assigned such different social functions that however much it resembled its model in outward form, it reproduced little of its academic character. As Wood conceived it, the Indian university had two main func-tions: to provide a test of eligibility for government employment, and to transmit an alien culture. These were not the true functions of a university and inevitably they obscured the proper aims of university scholarship. The government of India rescued the original concept from some of its narrowness, but the political purpose of the university remained dominant, and was underlined by the detailed government control written into its constitution.

And if the Indian university deviated from its model in England, it was a wholly alien implantation in India. In its deliberate disregard of Indian religion and culture, its character as an impersonal examining machine closely dependent on the state, its metropolitan setting in the great centres of British administration, it violated the most cherished Indian traditions. It had indeed been introduced 'almost in complete defiance of the existing social order regulating the everyday life of an ancient people'[46]: and it was small wonder that Sir James Colvile, addressing the first convocation of the University of Calcutta as vice-chancellor in 1858, should have entered a caution against expecting any quick return from the audacious enterprise he had helped to launch. '. . . we must be patient', he pleaded, '. . . we must recollect that we are not merely planting an exotic. We are planting a tree of slow growth.'[47]

III TROPICAL GROWTH AND DISILLUSION

The sequel to the transplantation is most strikingly exhibited in the development of the University of Calcutta. Despite the alien character of the institution and the absence of any special inducement, there was an eager response to the new examination system. The muhammadans and the aristocratic hindus held aloof; but the cultural scruples of the middle classes were effectively silenced by economic pressure and the lure of government employment. As early as 1861, Lord Canning spoke in convocation of the sensational increase in the number of candidates for admission which had grown from 280 in 1857 to 800: 'a much larger number than that of the London University, on which this University is modelled'.[48] Henry Maine, in his vice-chancellorial address a few years later, was still more exultant. ' . . . I do not think anything of the kind has been seen by any European University since the Middle Ages', he declared, 'and I doubt whether there is anything founded by, or connected with, the British Government in India which excites so much practical interest in Native households of the better class, from Calcutta to Lahore, as the Examinations of this University.'[49] Whereas in 1854, before the launching of the university, the number of students in government and non government colleges in Bengal was well under 200, by 1882, barely a generation later, the figure had risen to nearly 4,000.[50]

The growth was unquestionably luxuriant; yet, from the outset, there was an element of distortion and deficiency about it. Owing largely to the social traditions of their class – although partly also to the facilities available to them – the great majority of students chose to follow a literary or legal training. Medicine was not popular to begin with; engineering still less so. The faculties of arts and law developed out of all proportion to the other two, and the structure of the university acquired a pronounced imbalance.[51] But a more serious weakness marred the quality of the growth. From an early stage, the university was charged with fostering a shallow and superficial scholarship, and the charge was a source of deepening disquiet to the authorities.

C. J. Erskine was the first vice-chancellor to be seriously disturbed by the quality of the work sponsored by the university. He hinted at his misgivings in his convocation address in 1863, and succeeded in carrying a significant change in the curriculum later in the year. The option of studying a vernacular in the B.A. course was withdrawn and the more rigorous discipline of a classical language made compulsory.[52] Henry Maine welcomed the stiffening of the degree course in his address in the following year; but although he, too, dwelt on the danger of superficiality, he declined to recognise that the danger had become a reality. On this, and three subsequent occasions, he vehemently rebutted the criticism of the university. He could conscientiously say that he had not seen 'much more' superficiality in the answer papers at Calcutta than the older universities in England;[53] he had been assured by the examiners that the performance of the most able students was 'rapidly approaching the highest European standards'.[54] ' . . . I am sorry I have to repeat the thing so many times', he declared in 1867, 'but it is not true that the knowledge which is diffused under the influence of this University is slight or superficial except in a sense in which the proposition might be advanced of any University in any European country.'[55] Writing at the same time, however, C. H. Tawney, principal of Presidency College, took a less complacent view. He acknowledged that the 'mere "pass" subjects' demanded more of the student than at Oxford or Cambridge; but since there was nothing comparable to the honours courses of the older English universities, the tendency in Calcutta was to produce 'a dull and uniform level of mediocrity'. If the university was ever to meet both 'the want which the public feels of young natives well grounded in popular and practical subjects and the craving which the native mind itself is beginning to feel for deep and solid knowledge', he thought that some further specialisation would have to be adopted such as allowing the student to choose between literature and science at a certain stage in his university career.[56] By the end of the decade, Tawney's more critical judgment was widely accepted. Even in government circles there was little attempt to disguise the limited academic achievements of the Indian universities. In his review of the state of education for 1870–1, A. P. Howell found it sufficient that they provided 'a practical and uniform test' of the work of the schools and colleges. 'To call forth higher intellectual power', he concluded, 'must be the task of the future'.[57]

And it was a task that was seriously taken in hand at Calcutta in the following decade. In 1872, Tawney's plea for greater specialisation was met by precisely the sort of reform he had envisaged. Following the example of universities in England, it was decided to provide an alternative course for the F.A. (First Arts) and B.A. examination that was predominantly scientific.[58] Here the aim was not so much the deeper study Tawney had in view – although that was necessarily a by-product of the change – as the proper recognition of a young and progressive discipline that was specially relevant to the material needs of India. In 1881, however, the senate approved a more drastic revision of the degree structure that was specifically designed not only to encourage a higher level of scholarship, but to clarify the meaning of the B.A. degree in India. In the absence of an honours course comparable to those of the older English universities, it was felt that the Indians had come to place an inordinate value on the pass degree, and that this was partly why it had come to be regarded by many Englishmen in India as 'somewhat of a delusion and a sham'.[59] Again following British academic practice, it was decided to introduce a differentiated honours course at the post-intermediate stage, and a corresponding increase was made in the range and depth of the subjects prescribed for the M.A. degree. At the same time it was agreed to narrow the range of study for the ordinary pass degree by limiting it to two compulsory subjects and one optional one.[60] In this way it was hoped to dispel the 'mysterious halo' that had come to surround the holder of the pass degree, and to place the Indian B.A. on a 'more satisfactory footing' both as regards intrinsic value and public estimation.[61]

When, in the following year, a commission was appointed to review the execution of Wood's despatch, the working of the universities was explicitly excluded from its purview.[62] In his address to the convocation of the University of Calcutta, Lord Ripon explained the exclusion by a complimentary reference to the way in which the universities had performed their functions.[63] But since the commission was not debarred from considering collegiate education in other than technical subjects, it did in fact have some opportunity to reflect on the work of the universities; and despite a heavy official membership, it drew a more critical balance sheet than Lord Ripon had foreshadowed. It stressed, of course, the favourable side: not only the posts filled, and creditably filled, in government service and the judiciary, but the growth of cultural societies, the increasing output of vernacular literature, the development of the native press. But it was franker than the brief review of 1870–1 about the superficiality and want of distinction in the scholarship of the universities. In discussing the influence of the university entrance examination on the government zillah schools, the Bengal provincial committee made the ominous comment that 'examination standards frame themselves ultimately on the capacity of the examinees. They cannot be kept up even by an independent body like an examining University'.[64] It admitted that although hitherto the university had turned out men of 'good general education', it had 'hardly ever produced a student who would be called a scholar if judged by the highest European standard'.[65] The main commission also acknowledged that with 'a few brilliant exceptions', no eminent scholars were to be found in the long list of university graduates; and by quoting Sir Charles Turner's view, expressed to the convocation of the University of Madras in 1881, that the time could not be 'far distant' when modern India would produce 'her philsopher, her moralist, her reformer', it merely underlined the partial character of the Indian universities' attainment.[66] But both the commission and its satellite committees concluded on the conventional note of optimism. The Bengal provincial committee looked to the new degree structure of the University of Calcutta to effect the desired improvement; the commission, like A. P. Howell in 1870–1, looked to the passage of time.

The failure of the University of Calcutta to advance beyond a very modest academic level after twenty-five years of growth was due partly to the nature of the university Britain had planted in India and partly to Indian environmental factors. In Calcutta, as in London, the purely examining university exercised a dispiriting influence on its component colleges; and in India, the whole academic process was additionally undermined by the prominent government role in higher education. Not only was the examining subject to detailed official supervision but much of the teaching too: for most of the more important colleges at this time were government controlled, and thus staffed not by independent scholars, but by officers in government service working their way up the official promotion ladder.[67] Still more weakening, however, was the nature of the curriculum and the method by which it was prescribed. The syllabus for the ordinary and honours degree presented the Indian student with quite exceptional difficulties. It was not merely that he was required to study in a foreign tongue subjects that were culturally alien to him; but that initially at least, he was expected to range over an unreasonably broad field. This was particularly true of the history syllabus for the pass degree, which in covering Indian history, as well as a wider range of the branches of ancient and English history included in the London syllabus, prompted Tawney's not unmerited gibe that for those who had read the history before, the 'prescribed epitomes' must perform 'much the same service which we suppose a rosary does for a devout Roman Catholic'.[68] Here Tawney touched on another pernicious aspect of the system. For the fact that the university not only prescribed an absurdly extended syllabus but actually specified the 'epitomes' in which it was to be studied, inevitably led to what was later described as the 'apotheosis of the text book'.[69] Just what this was to mean in the class room emerges only too clearly from Walter Raleigh's horrified description of the practice he found at the Muhammadan Anglo-Oriental College in Aligarh in the 1880s. 'Calcutta sets *books* not subjects, even in mathematics', he wrote in amazement. 'And accordingly the normal method of teaching has been to pig through the books at so many pages a day.' No wonder he found the 'Calcutta Mill . . . much inferior to any English instrument' he knew of.[70]

But if in some respects the system was at fault, there were special features in the Indian environment to accentuate its defects and confirm the trend to shallow scholarship. With its broad spread and prescribed epitomes, the curriculum was inherently vulnerable to learning by rote; and as a result of centuries of learning by this method, the capacity and instinct of the Indian for memorisation was unusually strong. The traditional system of education had also endowed him with other intellectual qualities to hinder his progress in western scholarship: a reverence for authority which sapped his critical powers, and a speculative bias which weakened his ability to observe and appreciate facts, whether historical or scientific. The Indian, moreover, was abnormally precocious, and this, too, impeded the development of higher education for it produced a dangerous pressure to draw the level between student and schoolboy too low. A further drag on quality was the state of education in the schools and colleges. Under the stimulus of the university, there was a striking increase in the number of secondary schools in Bengal between 1854 and 1882; but the most significant feature of the development was the emergence of the self-supporting, private venture school. In the last decade of the period, the growth took place wholly within this sector; there was actually a decrease in the number of government and grant aided schools.[71] This meant that the potential university student was increasingly trained in poorly staffed, poorly equipped schools over which the government had no control, and the university very little; for although the university declined to accept students from schools it had not recognised, it had no inspectoral staff to give meaning to its recognition, which in practice was loosely and easily awarded. And since the standard of the entrance examination had not been set high to begin with,[72] and had been deliberately lowered in 1858,[73] it also meant that an increasing number of ill prepared students were admitted to the university to press on its standards. The majority of university students were still trained in government colleges in this period, but initially the colleges of the interior were quite inadequately provided for university work. Save at Hooghly, they had no professors, and as the Bengal provincial committee pertinently observed in its report of 1884 'with such colleges for its component parts, the Calcutta University could take no high place'.[74] But the most erosive indigenous influence was clearly the relentless economic pressure which stimulated the rush of students to the university's examinations. It was subversive of quality at high school and college alike; and in finally denying leisure to the graduate, caused the university to be credited with more responsibility for the lack of creative cultural activity than it properly deserved.

In the twenty years after 1882, the number of students at the University of Calcutta continued to grow at a rate 'unknown anywhere except within the tropics'.[75] The figure of those studying in Bengal rose from under 4,000 in 1882 to over 8,000 by 1902.[76] But neither the reform of the curriculum, nor the passage of time, produced the higher academic standard the commission of 1882 had looked for. As a result of the interaction of intensifying Indian pressures on the one hand, and government policy on the other, standards began to fall, first in teaching and later in examination; and in the last decade of the century, the deterioration became marked.

The enquiry of 1882 gave further sanction to the policy laid down by Wood in 1854 of gradually devolving responsibility for higher and secondary education upon private agency. The mushrooming of inferior native high schools that had been such a striking feature of the seventies continued unchecked, and the evil spread into the sphere of collegiate education. The private venture school of the pre-1882 period became the fee supported college of the period after; and by the end of the century, well over half the university students in Bengal were being trained in unaided colleges[77] where the average fees were about equivalent to the annual cost of a board-school boy in England.[78] The poverty of these colleges was reflected in the quality of their premises, their equipment, their range of studies and above all their teaching: for as the Sadler commission was to point out later, the outstanding fact about these new institutions was that 'while, like their predecessors, they gave English education, unlike them they gave it without the aid of Englishmen, their students rarely or never having any contact with anyone who spoke as his native tongue the language in which all their studies were conducted'.[79] And just as they had easily acquired university recognition when they were sub-standard schools, so they had no difficulty in obtaining affiliation when they became sub-standard colleges. The University of Calcutta made no attempt to impose strict conditions of affiliation, or indeed to ensure that a college once affiliated was worthy of continued affiliation. The government of India, with whom ultimate responsibility for affiliation and disaffiliation rested, merely acquiesced in the laxity of university policy.

But the feverish growth of poor quality schools and colleges was not the only danger to press on the university in this period. The emergence of the Indian nationalist movement constituted a fresh menace; and in face of this new pressure the government adopted policies that were to weaken the university in two significant respects.

The first was in the sphere of staffing. Here it fostered in its own colleges the very defect the Sadler commission was to deplore in the fee-supported native college of this period. In accordance with the recommendations of the Indian Education Commission of 1882, and the Public Services Commission of 1886, it admitted an increasing number of Indian graduates to senior teaching posts and in certain of its colleges aimed at an all Indian professoriate. By 1893, the author of the second *Quinquennial Review* was able to report that Indian graduates were being 'very extensively employed as professors in government colleges in most of the provinces' and found it 'worthy of note' that in several government colleges natives of India had been appointed professors of English.[80] But if this progressive Indianisation was viewed with satisfaction in government circles, it came to be more justly appraised by eminent Indian educationalists. On questioning the government about it in 1903, Dr Asutosh Mookerjee learnt that six of the nine government colleges in Bengal were almost exclusively manned by Indian professors and eight, including Presidency College, had no European to teach English literature and language. Quoting these statistics in debate in the following year, he openly censured the trend of government policy, and frankly admitted he was 'not patriotic enough' to appreciate the wisdom of it. What was needed, he insisted, was a fresh infusion of educationalists from the west, and he put his finger on a further weakness of the educational service when he urged that they should be 'really first class men'. Instead of the obscure Oxford graduates who had become the accepted apostles of western learning, he pressed for a return to professors 'of the type of Professor Cowell, Professor Tawney, Professor Gough, Professor Clarke and Sir J. Eliot', each of whom had been a 'tower of strength' to the university in its earlier days.[81]

But the university was more seriously weakened by the government's response to the nationalist pressure on its constitution. By sheer ineptitude, it allowed the senate to become dominated by a clique of native lawyers. The act of incorporation had set no upper limit on the membership of the senate, and this had risen from 40 in 1857 to 175 in 1880. Of this number, 126 were European and 49 Indian.[82] Over the next two decades, however, the preponderance was reversed: of a total of 187 fellows in 1900, 110 were Indian and only 77 European. Up to 1890, the power of appointing fellows rested entirely with the government which used it rather as a means of rewarding public service than furthering the special interests of the university. But in 1890, Lord Lansdowne took the first step towards introducing the elective principle. As a purely experimental measure, he conceded to the graduates of the university the privilege of electing two or three of their number to the senate each year, subject to government approval of their choice. Although this only added twenty-two members to the senate over the next decade, its effect was far reaching.[83] Since all twenty-two members were Indians, it increased the strength of the native party; and when so many European fellows were absentees, and so few customarily attended ordinary meetings, even a small access of strength was significant.[84] This might not have mattered if the elections had returned suitably qualified candidates. But in fact, as a result of careful canvassing by the vakil party, they invariably returned pleaders.[85] An already powerful element on the senate was reinforced, and by the end of the century the number of lawyers fell little short of all the professional educationalists put together.[86] Nor was this legal influence confined to the senate itself; it came to be reflected also in the syndicate, to which the senate delegated most of its effective powers. This was a small body, consisting of the vice-chancellor and ten members elected by the faculties; and by 1900 no fewer than five of its members were vakils and none held a degree from Oxford or Cambridge.[87]

The government had thus thrown away its powers of control. It had weakly capitulated to the very danger the court of directors had armed it to withstand. And the consequences were all but disastrous. It was not so much that the direction of policy passed into the hands of amateurs, although, as *The Times* noticed in 1901, this was particularly serious for a university still in the nature of an experiment and especially in need of skilled and delicate handling.[88] It was rather that in passing to amateurs it passed to those who were willing to connive at the lowering of examination standards. For apart from the professional educationalists the Indians at this time were far less concerned to uphold the quality of the university's distinctions than to put them within the reach of their compatriots. It was indicative of prevailing opinion that the native party should have insisted on abolishing a minimum age limit for the entrance examination against the advice of the director of public instruction; and that when this produced the inevitably higher failure rate, there should have been public agitation, followed by greater leniency in marking.[89] 'How far the educated natives themselves are still removed from understanding the true dignity of education', the bishop of Calcutta wrote in 1901, 'is shown . . . by the curious suggestion which was gravely put forward a short time ago that it would be a suitable memorial of the late Queen Empress to lower, at least temporarily, the standard of examination for an academical degree.'[90]

Evidence of the extent to which academic standards fell in the 1890s is bound to be elusive, and it was not until the university system was reviewed at the beginning of the twentieth century that any serious attempt was made to assess their level and trend. In the course of confidential proceedings at Simla in 1901 a conference of educational experts from all parts of India unanimously resolved that 'the standards of School and College Examinations generally exhibit a downward tendency' and that 'the percentage [pass] in University examinations should in many cases be raised'.[91] Pedler, the director of public instruction for Bengal, commented especially on the low level of the entrance examination at Calcutta[92]; and in debating the universities bill in 1903 and 1904, he was franker still.[93] Looking back on thirty years' experience of the University of Calcutta, he gave it as his considered opinion that the quality of higher education in Bengal had progressively deteriorated. Examination standards had been undermined by a steady decline in teaching standards. 'I am afraid it must be admitted that a very low standard of examination and therefore of work, is now required by the Calcutta University', he declared. 'Indeed, it is not, I think, going too far to say that in Bengal such standards have had to be set because of the numerous low grade institutions, that is, both Colleges and schools, which have been from time to time affiliated to the Calcutta University.' If the occasion gave edge to his strictures, they were not contested by responsible Indian opinion. A well qualified judge like Dr Asutosh Mookerjee readily admitted that 'the ebb tide of high education' had been reached.[94]

In the 1890s this candour was missing. Neither the university, nor the government, faced up to the abuses that were undermining higher education. Yet even in the guarded comments of successive chancellors and vice-chancellors to convocation, there was a note of persistent, if inadequate, concern. The buoyant optimism of the earlier years had no parallel in this later period. The best defence of Calcutta graduates that the first Indian vice-chancellor,

G. D. Banerjee, could offer in 1891, was that 'considering their number, and considering the powerful impetus that the University has given to education, we cannot have much reason to be dissatisfied'.[95] The boldest claim Sir Alfred Croft could advance in 1894 was that 'in some instances, here and there, a European standard of literary finish and scientific accuracy is even now being developed'.[96] And it was significant that, in 1893, Lord Lansdowne should have welcomed the opening of a centre for the external examinations of the University of London as a means of stimulating greater effort in the local university. It was likely, he thought, that the strict standards insisted on by the University of London would have a considerable effect on the examinations of the University of Calcutta.[97] A constant theme of these addresses was the need for greater specialisation and more thorough study; and it was a continuing source of comment and regret that the university had so little infected its graduates with 'the contagion of learning'.[98]

By the end of the century, the standards of the university were clearly in jeopardy. On academic grounds alone, the system stood condemned. But it was also exerting a baneful influence far beyond the academic sphere. Despite the fall in standards, there had been a significant increase in the percentage of students who failed the university examinations. Up to 1890, the failure rate in the B.A. examination had varied between forty and sixty per cent, which was much the same as at the University of London.[99] But during the next decade, it rose steeply to over seventy-five per cent;[100] and in doing so, it stimulated the very social and political dangers that Wood had foreseen. Even before the 1880s, the spectre of unemployment began to appear. It was objected that the university was turning out men for whom there were inadequate openings; and the issue was sufficiently prominent in 1882 to receive attention from the Indian Education Commission. The verdict seemed reassuring. Witnesses before the Bengal provincial committee were generally agreed that it was only the 'plucked' and 'half educated' who were really experiencing difficulty, and the committee itself concluded that a very large supply of well educated men was still required in the public service alone.[101] By the 1890s, the position was not essentially changed. 'The great majority of our graduates, and all the most distinguished among them, find their places without any difficulty', Sir Alfred Croft reported in 1894.[102] But the openings were inevitably reduced, whilst, as Sir Alfred himself acknowledged, the 'drifting body' of humbler passmen and those who failed to take their degrees had become a serious anxiety. Quoting from Bacon's *Of seditions and troubles*, he underlined the danger by warning that one of the chief causes of discontent was 'when more are bred scholars than preferment can take off'.[103] On political and social grounds as well, therefore, the university system, after forty years of uncontrolled growth, called imperatively for a reformer. And in 1899, it found one in Lord Curzon.

CHAPTER FOUR

TOWARDS A NEW POLICY

I THE OPENING MOVES UNDER LORD CURZON

Lord Curzon brought a fresh and vigorous approach to the problem of universities in India which owed something to the role he conceived for Indians in the administration, and something to the strong academic element in his make-up.[1] He looked forward to the maintenance of British rule with even more confidence than Wood,[2] and never doubted that whilst Britain remained in control, the higher administrative posts, though open to Indians, must be filled as a rule by Englishmen.[3] But outside this *corps d'élite* he was prepared to admit Indians into increasingly close partnership as they were suitably trained; and he foresaw no shortage of posts for the highly trained native.[4] This being so, he did not share Wood's misgiving about providing hindus with the sort of honours courses that were followed at Oxford. Indeed, this was precisely the sort of academic discipline he would have chosen for them. For once admitting the need of highly qualified natives, he was easily persuaded that the ideal university in India should be cast in the same mould as the ideal university in Europe.[5] And, as a graduate of Balliol and a former fellow of All Souls, he instinctively recognised this ideal in the pattern of the older universities in England.

Curzon was at once struck by the contrast the Indian universities offered to this high ideal. He had been prepared to find the characteristic defects of the purely examining university, but he was shocked by the extent to which they had been exaggerated by the peculiar circumstances of the environment, and the deplorable want of proper direction. His first impression was of colleges like so many jarring atoms, courses geared to the output of quantity rather than quality, senates swollen by fellows notoriously ill-equipped for their work: in fact, of 'a huge system of active but often misdirected effort', in which the 'rush of immature striplings . . . not to learn but to earn' threatened to become an all-consuming avalanche. He was under no illusion that the system could be transformed overnight. ' . . . we cannot, all in a moment, by a stroke of the pen, create an Indian Oxford or an Indian Cambridge.' But it was possible to prepare for the ultimate realisation of such an aim: and this was the task he saw ahead.[6]

Curzon's was the directing mind at each stage in the reform of the universities. But he was ably assisted by another keen university man, Thomas Raleigh, who was appointed legal member of the council early in 1899. Like Curzon, he had been an undergraduate at Balliol, and a fellow of All Souls; for over ten years he had been reader in English law at Oxford. When a vacancy occurred in the vice-chancellorship at the University of Calcutta in August 1900, Curzon selected him for the post, and a unique opportunity was created for tackling the university question. 'Such a situation as the present', Curzon wrote to Lord George Hamilton, 'with a Chancellor and Vice-Chancellor of the Calcutta University in the persons of myself and Raleigh who are both Fellows of an Oxford College and strongly imbued with the University feeling, is probably not likely to occur again for a long time in India. It would be a pity not to take advantage of it to carry out reforms which everyone admits to be essential, which nobody hitherto has dared to touch, but which I think that I have the strength of position to carry through.'[7] Curzon was not able to turn to university reform until February 1901; but he then examined the main issues in a minute which was the starting point of a programme of reform steadily pursued over the next three years.[8] In the following September, he took the advice of a conference of experts he had summoned to Simla to review all aspects of the educational system. In January 1902, he appointed a commission under the presidency of Thomas Raleigh to inquire into the 'condition and prospects' of the universities in India. Reporting in June, the commission advised on the curriculum and other matters within the competence of the senates; it also endorsed the need of legislation for constitutional reform. After consultation with the local governments, there followed the drafting of this legislation, and as a culmination of the reform campaign, the passage of the Indian universities bill in March 1904.

Curzon concentrated from the outset on constitutional reform. In his minute of February 1901, he offered a penetrating analysis of the defects that had come to mark the constitutions of all three of the older universities, but more especially the University of Calcutta. He exposed the anomalies in the composition of the senate, commenting on the unwieldy numbers, the inadequate representation of European and educational interests, and, above all, the insidious working of the system of elective fellowships: a system, he asserted, which was forging a weapon that would 'ultimately extrude European standards and influence from the Senate altogether, and ... hand over its government to a clique of political frondeurs who have no interest in education'. He drew attention to the irregular, and seemingly illegal way in which the senate had abdicated its functions to the syndicate, a body elected by the senate from its own members and similarly dominated by the legal element.[9] And turning to the wider structure of the university, he focussed by implication on a further major defect by considering the need of legislation to strengthen the system of affiliation.

All these constitutional deficiencies were vigorously tackled in the Indian

Universities Act.[10] The senates were reduced in size, and reconstructed. The number of *ex officio* fellows was limited to a maximum of ten; and at Calcutta, Bombay and Madras, the number of ordinary fellows, thenceforth appointed for a terminable period, was restricted to a maximum of a hundred. Twenty of these were to be elected. The remainder were to be nominated by the chancellor, and two fifths of his nominees were to be teachers. The composition of the syndicate, which received statutory recognition for the first time, was also carefully prescribed. The vice-chancellor was to be chairman. The director of public instruction was to be a member *ex officio*, and of the remaining members, all fellows elected by the senate or faculties, a number not falling short of a majority by more than one were to be heads of colleges affiliated to the university or professors teaching in them. To brace the system of affiliation, provision was made for the inspection of colleges by the syndicate, and the conditions they were required to satisfy were specified. These included such obviously desirable features as a properly constituted governing body, a suitably qualified staff, and adequate student welfare facilities. The aim throughout was to give responsibility to the expert. 'Higher education ought not to be run either by politicians or by amateurs' Curzon declared. 'It is a science – the science of human life and conduct – in which we must give a fair hearing and a reasonable chance to the Professor.'[11] The reforms did not ensure that the best teachers gained a place on the senates, or indeed that the senates obtained any real influence over the teaching in the colleges. But at least they achieved Curzon's main purpose. The educationalist was reinstated: and the amateur and politician displaced. And the advance was made in the face of bitter opposition. For although the aim was to secure the position of the expert, the means had to be a provocative reassertion of government control. Curzon had no thought of binding the university system in 'permanent swaddling clothes'. 'I hope, indeed', he wrote in the privacy of an official minute, 'that we are enveloping it in tightish bands now, only to be able to relax them later on, and to concede in practice a considerable emancipation within the limits of the law we shall pass'.[12] Defending the bill in the legislative council, he repeatedly disclaimed any intention of officialising the universities. The government wanted expert senates, he insisted, not servile ones: if the universities played their part, the powers of control the government had taken to ensure the effectiveness of the reforms would remain nominal.[13] But with the exception of a few educationalists, the argument was wholly unacceptable to Indian opinion, which in Bengal, owing to the large number of its independent colleges, was especially incensed at the provision for stricter conditions of affiliation. The bill met with fierce agitation in the press; and it was closely contested at each stage in its passage through the legislative council.

If Curzon was resolute in tackling the abuses that had developed in the constitutions of the universities, he was disappointingly hesitant in moving towards his vision of a teaching and residential university in India. He never looked beyond the improvement of the existing universities to the founding of a model college or university on new principles: such, indeed, as *The Times* suggested as a suitable commemoration of the coronation of Edward VII,[14] in nice contrast to the memorial the Indians had in mind for Queen Victoria.[15] He thought only of turning the older universities towards the new ideal. And he clearly regarded it as premature to attempt much in that direction. He considered the case for amending the original acts of incorporation to enable the Universities of Calcutta, Bombay and Madras to become teaching institutions in his minute of February 1901; but at that time, he showed little enthusiasm for it. He acknowledged the force of the objections offered hitherto: that the universities were already in effect discharging teaching functions through their affiliated colleges, and that there was neither the demand nor the funds to justify the creation of professorships and lectureships for higher courses. The only grounds on which he was disposed to support legislation were that it seemed anomalous to deny to the older universities what had been conceded to their younger sisters at Lahore and Allahabad;[16] that the concession might be the means of attracting endowments to the universities; and that even if not acted upon, it would result in no greater injury than 'the gift of a suit of grown-up clothes to a thriving school boy to be worn by him at a later date'. But he warmed to the idea as time went on. When the commission reported in favour of legislation to extend the functions of the universities in 1902, he endorsed its view on the further ground that it would be 'the first condition of any movement towards the ideal that we probably all have in view'.[17] The amendment was duly made in the Indian Universities Act; and thenceforth the universities were deemed to be incorporated 'for the purpose (among others) of making provision for the instruction of students, with power to appoint University Professors and Lecturers, to hold and manage educational endowments, to erect, equip and maintain University libraries, laboratories and museums, to make regulations relating to the residence and conduct of students, and to do all acts, consistent with the Act of Incorporation and this Act, which tend to the promotion of study and research'.[18] But the government of India offered no clear lead as to how the universities were to take advantage of these new powers. The commission had considered the question and found it 'one of considerable difficulty'.[19] It saw no way of associating the universities with undergraduate teaching and concluded they should concentrate on the provision of central schools for advanced study. To Curzon the proposal was 'shadowy'; nor did he think an attempt to turn sham universities into real ones by inviting them to become schools could be other than confusing in the Indian context.[20] But he had no alternative to suggest. In forwarding the draft of the universities bill to the India office, the government of India acknowledged that the whole subject was still in an 'indeterminate condition': that it was unable to submit any definite proposals either for the creation of a new teaching university, or for the development of teaching facilities at the existing universities.[21] Whilst the teaching functions of the universities remained in abeyance, the enabling legislation in regard to residence likewise remained an advance on paper only. But Curzon did make some progress towards the concept of a residential university at collegiate level; for although it was not possible to insist on a strict interpretation of the new rules of affiliation, at least they served to draw attention to the need for proper student accommodation.

Curzon gave priority to constitutional reform with a view to equipping the universities with suitable machinery to initiate a comprehensive programme of administrative reform. The Indian Universities Act of 1904 not only provided for the reconstruction of the senates; it also stipulated that the reformed senates should submit revised regulations for the approval of the government within a year of the act coming into force, or 'such further period' as the government might fix. In sanctioning the regulations, the government was empowered to make any additions or alterations it considered necessary after consultation with the senates: and it was indicative of the degree of control Curzon was prepared and determined to exert that it was further enacted that if the universities did not carry out the required revision within the prescribed time limit, 'within one year after the expiry of such period or of such further period', the government might itself draw up new regulations that would be binding on them.[22]

Curzon and his advisers looked for two main reforms in this way. The first was specific and clear cut, designed to remedy a long-standing abuse, and regarded as of such great importance as to justify recourse, if necessary, to the government's powers of control. This was to reimpose a minimum age limit for those admitted to the matriculation examinations of the three older universities, and to fix it at the age of sixteen. The want of the reform was strikingly demonstrated at the educational conference at Simla in 1901. The director of public instruction for Bengal disclosed how youths were being crammed for the entrance examination of the University of Calcutta at an absurdly early age, with deplorable consequences for the whole examination system[23]; and it was unanimously resolved that it would be desirable to establish a minimum age limit of sixteen for entrance candidates at all universities.[24] The commission of 1902 endorsed the need for an age test, but recommended that it should be fixed a year lower.[25] Curzon dissented. Convinced that the precocity of Indian youth was one of the greatest enemies of quality in the university system, he was determined not to lose the opportunity of 'giving the pendulum a backward swing'. 'I cannot think that a boy of fifteen is at all qualified to enter upon a University course, assuming that the latter is to be at all worthy of the name', he wrote in comment on the commission's proposal. 'If he may enter at fifteen, he may be a B.A. at nineteen, and B.A.s of nineteen are, I submit, a breed that ought not to be encouraged.'[26] Raleigh did not attempt to dispute his view, or indeed to put up much defence of the commission's recommendation. He admitted that all the commissioners except Dr G. D. Banerjee would have preferred the higher age limit and had only settled for the lower one from the conviction that it would lessen 'the practical difficulties' and conform with the recommendations of a recent committee of the Calcutta senate.[27] After consultation with the local governments, therefore, the universities were informally advised that they would be expected to provide for the higher limit of sixteen in the draft of their new regulations.[28]

The other and more fundamental reform for which the government of India looked to the reconstructed senates was the revision of the university curriculum. Here it recognised that it would be undesirable to impose a rigid uniformity on the work of the universities, and confined itself to offering advice which it commended to the careful consideration of the academic authorities. Its advice, however, was limited, for although it had suggestions to sponsor about the range and content of university studies, it failed to reach any firm conclusion about the structure of the degree courses, and the related problem of specialisation.

Influenced, perhaps, by Curzon's decided opinion, the conference at Simla returned a favourable though cautious verdict on the desirability of providing a separate honours school in the Indian universities. In carefully chosen terms, it recorded its view that 'the general result of an Honours school is to raise the standard in the higher courses of University education and that it is desirable where this can be shown to be the case and where it is possible to provide the requisite staff that Honours courses should, as time proceeds, be instituted'.[29] The commission of 1902, however, took a different line. On the grounds that the honours school at Calcutta had depreciated the pass degree, it recommended that there should be no separate honours course for the B.A., and that the M.A. should be regarded as the honours examination.[30] Curzon found the argument unconvincing. 'The more the pass degree is depreciated, the more will men go in for the Honours Course which is the very thing that we want to encourage', he wrote. ' . . . why should the B.A.s who mean to go no further all be huddled together in one pen if there is a desire among any of their number to lift themselves above the ruck?'[31] Here, however, Curzon did not carry his point. Raleigh stood firm on the recommendation, explaining that the commission did not consider an Indian student fit to embark on specialised studies until he had completed his undergraduate course.[32] Curzon retreated without capitulating. Reporting to London in the following year, the government of India put both sides of the question. It expressed a mild preference for the commission's view, and 'inclined to think' that ultimately the solution would be to provide honours courses in teaching universities or special university schools. But again it had no immediate recommendation to make.[33] In regard to the structure of the degree courses, therefore, the universities were offered no clear direction.[34]

In regard to the content of the courses, however, and the range of university studies, the government of India was less hesitant. It endorsed the findings of the commission with only minor reservations, and so invited the attention of the universities to recommendations which in two respects, more especially, were novel. In the first place the commission proposed an extended role for the universities in practical studies. It deplored the want of higher agricultural training in a country so predominantly agricultural as India, and contrasted it with the provision that had been made in Japan and Germany, and more recently in Britain itself. It thought the most appropriate training would be a two-part course: a period of mainly theoretical study in college, followed by a period of practical work on the farms. It acknowledged that it was 'as yet an open question' how far the universities could help in such a course of training but saw no reason why they should not be associated with the theoretical part of it. And so in recommending that the universities should encourage agricultural studies 'as far as possible', it suggested they should consider providing a test of the theoretical as opposed to the practical side of agricultural training, as indeed was already done at Bombay.[35] The commission also commented on the neglect of suitable training for those wishing to follow a commercial career. Again it contrasted the want of such courses in India with the provision that had been made elsewhere, notably in England and America. But here its proposals were more limited. While adopting the same formula that the universities should encourage the studies useful for commercial pursuits 'as far as possible', it did not think the time had come for degree work in commerce, and confined itself to the suggestion that the universities might help in the examinations of the London Chamber of Commerce, or any examinations the government itself might institute.[36] Curzon pronounced the proposals 'sound but . . . vague'; but in fact he was by no means opposed to the cautious approach of the commission in regard to agricultural training, thinking the less the universities were 'mixed up' with it at that stage the better.[37] And in regard to a faculty of commerce, he was fully persuaded that the universities had to justify themselves 'as purveyors of instruction in the ordinary sense' before embarking upon 'fresh experiments . . . then hardly attempted in Europe'.[38]

The other novel feature in the recommendations was a bolder emphasis on Indian studies. Hitherto, especially at the University of Calcutta, they had scarcely won a place in their own right in the curriculum. The primary function of the Indian university was still conceived to be the diffusion of western learning, and such Indian courses as were provided were intended to further this overall purpose. The policy Macaulay had helped to fix and Wood had adopted as the basis of the university system, had persisted; and from time to time it had been reasserted. Pressure from the Punjab for a university which should give greater recognition to eastern literature and thought drew a classic restatement of this policy from Henry Maine in 1867. Insisting that 'the question has not greatly shifted from the shape in which it presented itself to Lord Macaulay and the founders of modern education in India', he confessed that he did not see that 'the modes and courses of teaching followed in India can safely be further orientalized at present'. 'I fear', he declared, 'that the greater affinity and sympathy which we are called upon to exhibit for Eastern thought would be purchased by the sacrifice of that truth, moral, historical, and physical, which will one day bind together the European and Asiatic minds if ever they are to be united.' Until the danger had passed, he considered it would be necessary firmly to adhere to existing policy: and in a bid to disarm Indian susceptibilities, he went on to make his eloquent and famous plea for the pursuit of western studies.[39] Other and more imaginative minds were to conceive a different cultural purpose for the Indian universities, and a different status for Indian studies. In 1882, Lord Ripon looked forward to a fruitful intermingling of eastern and western learning. The aim, he asserted, should not be to impose an alien culture on the Indians at the expense of their own traditions, but 'to place without stint at their disposal all the riches of Western science and Western culture that they may blend them in one harmonious union with the treasures of their own Oriental learning'.[40] A few years earlier, Lord Lytton had acknowledged a more daring ambition. Looking further into the future, he had envisaged the Indian universities becoming great reservoirs of research on Indian topics. ' . . . I certainly hope that a day may come . . . when Europe will look to the Universities of India for the world's highest Sanskrit, Persian, and Arabic scholarship', he declared, 'a day when these Universities will be recognised as the great storehouses of original discovery made by science in the opulent realms already offered to scientific research by India's immense varieties of soil and climate, of human race and character, of vegetable and animal life . . .'[41] But this, as he admitted, was no more than a distant vision, and meantime, policy and practice conformed to the old ways. As late as 1885, Courtenay Ilbert, speaking as vice-chancellor of the University of Calcutta, and drawing attention to the provision of government scholarships for study in England, offered some significant reflections on the continuity of Britain's policy for higher education in India. The policy of Macaulay's minute, and Lord Bentinck's resolution, he affirmed, had lost none of its validity in the previous fifty years. The principles of 1835 still formed the 'very essence' of the constitution of the University of Calcutta. English was compulsory in all its courses; English was the medium of all its examinations; and whilst it did not neglect proficiency in eastern classical and vernacular languages, it was to instruction in English literature and European science that it devoted its main attention. 'But if Western learning in this country is to be anything more than a frail exotic', he went on, 'if it is to strike root, and bear fruit and propagate its kind, if the students of this University are to carry on and develop the work which their European teachers have begun, then as pioneers of the new learning, they must do what was done by the pioneers of the new learning at the close of the Middle Ages – go forth and seek it and study it in its native home.'[42]

The commission of 1902 did not disavow the principles of 1835, or seek to put a new definition on the functions of the universities. In considering the subjects offered for the arts courses, it gave priority to English on the grounds that the extension of European knowledge by means of the English language had been the declared object of the founding of the university system. But in the course of its detailed recommendations it revealed the dawn of a new attitude to the place of Indian studies in the curriculum. It was not breaking fresh ground in calling for greater attention to Indian vernacular languages; or in proposing a compulsory classical language for the arts degree course. But it was significant that it should have made suggestions to improve the quality and status of the courses in Indian classical languages; and still more significant that it should have justified its recommendation of a compulsory classical language not merely by reference to the familiar 'anglicist' argument of studying a classical language to improve its related vernacular, but by reference, too, to the essentially 'orientalist' argument of the value of studying a language 'containing a rich literature and embodying a record of the thought and action of one or other of the great races of mankind'.[43] Nor did the commission confine its attention to the languages of India. It proposed that the history course 'should be carefully adapted to the needs of Indian students'[44]; that the course in political economy should be centred on the economic problems of India;[45] and that for the M.A. courses in philosophy, the syllabus might include 'suitable portions of some of the great systems of Indian philosophy'.[46]

In putting this bolder stress on Indian studies, Raleigh and the commission seem to have been more concerned to provide a vigorous mental training than a curriculum that would harmonise with the student's cultural background.[47] It was as an antidote to cram, and a stimulus to intelligent learning, that the commission advocated the adaptation of the history courses. It was as 'an intellectual discipline such as cannot be obtained in any other way' that Raleigh extolled the study of Sanskrit and Arabic for the Indian student in his farewell address to the convocation of the University of Calcutta in 1904.[48] Curzon, however, appears to have welcomed the stronger Indian bias on its own merits. For him, it seems to have been an extension of his political creed: the principle of closer Anglo-Indian partnership carried into the academic sphere. He did not repudiate the views of Lord Macaulay and was happy to think that the British decision to give the Indians a European higher education was an irrevocable one. He viewed the 'daring alchemy' of subjecting the Indian mind to a curriculum borrowed almost exclusively from the west with optimism and complacency. He was struck, he declared, 'by the extent to which, within less than 50 years, the science and the learning of the Western world have entered into and penetrated the Oriental mind, teaching it independence of judgment and liberty of thought, and familiarising it with conceptions of politics, and law, and society to which it had for centuries been a complete stranger'. He had no fear that the experiment was nourishing 'a bastard civilisation', and was satisfied that the eastern and western intellectual streams were mixing 'in a fresh and homogeneous current with an identity and colour of its own'.[49] But although endorsing the system in its essentials, he was prepared to modify the preponderance of western studies in the curriculum to allow a greater weight to Indian subjects. He was 'very doubtful' whether Latin should be maintained at all. He was 'certainly' of the opinion that the modern languages of Europe should be excluded. 'When we have the utmost difficulty in piecing into our mosaic the required amount of study of English, of the vernaculars, and of the classical languages of the East', he argued, 'it seems to me . . . a mistake to introduce Latin, French or German as well. It is true that a Babu Engineer with a smattering of French greeted me at Manipur with a triumphal arch on which were inscribed the mottoes *Bon jour* and *Bon soir*; but this is the only instance known to me in this country in which a knowledge of that language by a Native has been turned to practical account.'[50] Perhaps the most instructive commentary on the motives underlying his choice of ingredients for the curriculum is to be found in the explanation he offered for wishing to substitute history for deductive logic as a compulsory subject in the intermediate or F.A. courses. 'If there is a subject which an Indian boy should be encouraged and even compelled to learn', he wrote, 'it appears to me to be History. Deductive Logic will never enable him to draw correct deductions as to British rule in India. History will, or at least may.'[51]

In addition to providing the machinery for reform, and guidance as to the lines it should follow, Curzon also provided funds. And this was an innovation. For hitherto the stringency of Wood's financial policy had been strictly adhered to. The universities had been expected to be self-supporting, and even the colleges had been afforded only limited assistance. But Curzon was under no illusion that a healthy university system could be maintained on a shoe string. He was convinced that generous government support would be necessary if his reforms were to be successful. Money would be needed to offset the loss of fees that was expected, as well as to enable the universities to inspect and aid the colleges, and to acquire buildings and staff. Besides which, as he urged in a private letter to Godley, it would be an act of the highest policy 'to gild' as far as possible 'the somewhat unpalatable pill' that was being offered to the natives.[52] He proposed an annual grant of five lakhs of rupees for a period of five years; and Whitehall sanctioned the expenditure.

In presenting his policy to London, Curzon prudently commended it as a logical development of the policy of 1854, not a departure from it.[53] This was true of his constitutional proposals in the sense that they prescribed for the Indian universities what progressive academic opinion in Britain had recently prescribed for the institution on which they had been modelled. In 1898 provision had been made for the reconstruction of the University of London as a teaching university. It was also true of the greater stress on Indian studies in the sense that the progress of western scholarship had diminished the danger that Maine had still considered a live one in the late sixties. The advance in both respects, moreover, was limited. Curzon and his colleagues had been unable to define the meaning of the teaching and residential university in

India; nor had they given the curriculum more than a very modest orientation in the direction of Indian studies. But Curzon had set a new ideal before the universities, and, however unconsciously,[54] paved the way for a modification in their cultural purpose. Whatever his protestations to London, he had made the opening moves in a reshaping of policy which was to be pursued more constructively and with greater imagination under his successors, and which was to culminate in the authoritative restatement of the Calcutta University Commission in 1919.

II HARCOURT BUTLER: A FURTHER ADVANCE

Besides making the opening moves in the reshaping of higher educational policy, Curzon also contributed to the development that took place under his successors. The violent outburst of nationalism that was unleashed by his scheme for the partition of Bengal sharply underlined the political importance of the educational problem in India; and this in turn prompted the early appointment of a member for education and local government to the viceroy's council, a fresh review of the university system, and a new and constructive phase in the evolution of policy.

The government of India sought authority for the appointment of a member for education in July 1910, and their request was readily granted. 'I need say nothing as to the political importance of education in India', Lord Morley wrote in a persuasive minute to the council of India. 'It is the universal opinion that our educational system is one of the roots of political unrest, and I do not see how the Government of India can possibly be in a position to deal comprehensively with either unrest or other elements in the existing social and political situation in India unless it is thoroughly well advised upon the whole system of education.' A majority of the council concurred, and the new post was sanctioned in the following November.[55] It was filled by Harcourt Butler, a member of the ICS, who had spent his probation at Balliol and served first in the North West Provinces, and latterly in the foreign department of the government of India. He entered on his new duties with characteristic speed and energy; and within a year of his appointment, the government of India were able to submit a comprehensive programme of educational development for the approval of the India office.[56]

The keynote claimed for this programme was continuity. Its purpose, the government of India explained, was to carry to completion the policy of Lord Curzon. But so far as higher education was concerned, the proposals represented a considerable advance on Curzon's policy. They acknowledged the same basic aim of developing the idea of the teaching university, endorsing the earlier policy of creating chairs in different branches of postgraduate study at the existing universities as a means of doing so. But they broke fresh ground in contemplating the establishment of new universities. Curzon had consistently deprecated the multiplication of universities,[57] and the commission of 1902 had taken a similar view.[58] It had agreed that the creation of new universities would be premature, and it had expressed the further opinion that a communal university, such as that proposed for the muslims at Aligarh, would be undesirable. But the government of India now took a different line. Arguing that the size of the existing universities rendered impossible 'any really sound system of examination ... and control', they pronounced in favour of gradually restricting the area of their jurisdiction by the creation of additional universities. They mentioned Dacca, Patna, Rangoon, and Nagpur as suitable centres for new local universities; they also referred to proposals under consideration for communal universities.

Again the initiative for a new departure in university policy had come from India. But whereas in Curzon's day the India office had accepted for the most part passively and uncritically the proposals submitted from Calcutta, in this later phase of development it played a more positive role and left a perceptible imprint on the shaping of policy. There were several reasons for this. It was partly that education had become a key political issue, and partly that proposals for new universities raised questions on which Whitehall could contribute more effectively. But it was largely that the council of India had recruited two members with strong academic interests and a unique experience of Indian universities. One was Sir Theodore Morison, who came to the council after sixteen years at the Muhammadan Anglo-Oriental College at Aligarh, first as professor and later as principal. The other was Curzon's colleague in university reform, who on leaving India had been honoured with the KCSI, Sir Thomas Raleigh.

British policy for the new universities took shape in relation to three specific projects. Two, inspired by the Indians, were for communal universities at Aligarh and Benares; a third, initiated by the government, was for a state university at Dacca. Only the Benares scheme came to fruition during Harcourt Butler's period of office: the Benares Hindu University Act passed into law in 1915 on the eve of his transfer to Burma. But the planning of all three projects served to clarify British ideas about essential principles in regard to the constitution, standards and curriculum. On each of these points there was change, but save over curriculum, where there was a marked difference of attitude, the new policy showed a curious mixture of caution and advance.

Constitution   British policy for the constitution of the new universities was worked out initially in relation to the projected communal universities; firstly over Aligarh, and later, when this scheme had temporarily fallen through, over Benares. In each case the Indian promoters drew up a draft constitution of their own choice, which they then submitted for the approval of the government of India; and British policy emerged in the terms which the government of India, with the sanction of the India office, made a condition of their assent. But the policy emerged only slowly; for sharp differences arose between Calcutta and London as to the conditions to be imposed. The government of India submitted the draft of the muslim constitution committee to the India office with their own views in November 1911,[59] but it was not until two years later (and then in relation to Benares) that the main principles of British policy were agreed; and a further year elapsed before details were finally settled.

The points at issue between the government of India and the council in London were three. The first, on which the government of India put up only a brief resistance, and which was therefore settled most easily, was whether the new universities, which had been approved in principle on the understanding they would be teaching and residential universities, should be permitted powers of affiliation: whether, in fact, there should be a complete break with the old type of examining university that had been introduced into India. The muslims, like the hindus later, set great store by the provision for affiliation. They intended their new university to preserve the teaching and residential character that had been such a marked feature of the existing college at Aligarh; but in order to foster the study of muslim culture as widely as possible, they were also determined that it should become an all-India institution. They therefore proposed that it should be empowered to affiliate colleges throughout India, although they were careful to stipulate that affiliation would only be accorded to colleges modelled on the same principles as Aligarh.[60] The government of India recognised that the proposal raised an 'anxious' question in view of the threat it contained to standards. But they were satisfied that the powers sought by the muslims would be used sparingly and with discretion. In forwarding the scheme of the constitution committee to the India office in November 1911, they thus recommended that the wishes of the muslims should be respected. In London, however, the proposal encountered strong hostility. Sir Theodore Morison regarded it as inconsistent with the type of teaching and residential university he believed the council had intended to promote when it had given its conditional sanction to the scheme in the previous July; and he was convinced it would mean a lowering of the degree standard at Aligarh to meet the capacity of the affiliated colleges. But despite his decided objection, he was not disposed to stand out against the proposal if his colleagues on the judicial and public committee were prepared to agree to it.[61] With one exception, however, they were more staunchly opposed to it than he was;[62] and in a despatch of February 1912,[63] the secretary of state announced with regret that he was unable to sanction affiliation outside the Aligarh district.[64] The government of India immediately pressed for a reconsideration of his decision, urging in a letter of March 1912 that the refusal to grant affiliation on strict terms would be 'a cause of disappointment so grave to both Hindus and Mohammedans alike as to raise a question of first class political importance . . . .'[65] They telegraphed a further strong appeal in June.[66] But resistance in London had already hardened. Sir Theodore Morison stood by the educational arguments against affiliation, and predicted that if the principle were conceded, the government of India would allow the university to affiliate laxly and ultimately be obliged to intervene 'to arrest a scandal as Ld Curzon & Sir T. Raleigh were obliged to do'.[67] A majority of his colleagues agreed that the earlier decision should be upheld; and in conveying this resolve to the government of India, the secretary of state took the opportunity of prescribing the general policy to be adopted for the future in the constitution of new universities. 'It is important', he observed, 'to draw a clear distinction between the federal university in the strict sense, in which several colleges of approximately equal standing, separated by no excessive distance or marked local individuality, are grouped together as a university – and on the other hand the affiliating university of the type with which India is familiar, which in its inception was merely an examining body and though limited as regards the area of its operations by the act of 1904 has not been able to insist upon an identity of standard in the various institutions which are conjoined with it.' He did not rule out the possibility that the first type, which had come to be regarded as a transitional form in England, might be found useful in a similar way in India. He admitted that the time was probably distant when India would be able to dispense altogether with the affiliating university. ' . . . but now that we are confronted in a practical shape with the conditions under which a new University is to be established', he declared, 'it seems expedient, in the highest interests of education, to lay down the principle that the power of affiliation must not receive a fresh extension.' Until experience had shown the type of university most suited to India, it was essential that new institutions should be founded 'in harmony with the best modern opinion of the right road to educational efficiency'.[68] The government of India telegraphed regret but submission,[69] and despite renewed appeals from the Indians, the ruling was duly reflected in the provision of the Benares Hindu University Act. Introducing the bill in the legislative council in March 1915, Sir Harcourt Butler enthusiastically acclaimed the birth of the teaching and residential university in India.[70] Whitehall, by building on the initiative of the government of India, had enhanced the significance of the occasion.

A second difference of opinion between the government of India and the council in London arose over the means of ensuring a proper influence to academic opinion in the constitution of the new universities, although here there was also a wide measure of agreement. When the proposal for a privately managed muslim university first came before the India office, the secretary of the judicial and public department, Sir Herbert Risley, at once fastened on the importance of securing a constitution which would provide effectively for the maintenance of academic standards. He thought the 'two-tier' pattern evolved by the modern civic universities in England well devised for the purpose, and suggested that the government of India might be invited to consider it as a possible model.[71] His advice was rejected in committee; and the muslim promoters were offered no official guidance as to the type of constitution they should adopt. But in the event they elected to follow the pattern he had envisaged, and the government of India endorsed their choice.[72] The pattern did not escape criticism in London. Sir Thomas Raleigh judged it 'unduly complicated'; understandably, perhaps, he would have preferred the simpler structure of the reformed constitution he himself had helped to provide for the other universities.[73] His colleagues, however, were not disposed to contest the principle of the 'two-tier' system; but whilst accepting the principle, they were unable to approve the interpretation it had been given.

The draft constitution provided that the supreme governing body should be a large and representative all-muslim court, with a small executive council; and that the academic body should be a senate, limited initially to forty-five members of whom a majority were to be professors, with a small executive syndicate. In lesser academic matters the senate was to have a final voice; in matters governed by regulation it was empowered to frame proposals for the approval of the council. Disputes between the senate and council were to be settled by a joint board of the two bodies, subject to the veto of the court. The government of India were satisfied that the proposals offered a reasonable safeguard against the intrusion of non-educational interests;[74] but Sir Theodore Morison considered they subjected the senate to the court or council 'in almost every important matter'.[75] The council upheld his objection and in a despatch of February 1912, the secretary of state informed the government of India that he feared the arrangement would 'not work well'. Observing that the proposed division of power was modelled on the constitutions of the newer universities in England, he pointed out that in 'the English universities ... referred to, the control of all matters relating to curriculum, discipline, and examinations is in practice left to the Senate whatever powers may be given to the Court in the written constitution. ...' He recalled the great inconvenience that had already been experienced in India from the undue influence of non-educationalists, and indicated that it would be unsafe to trust to the observance of a similar convention there. He acknowledged the difficulty arising from the need to make the senate consist of salaried employees of the governing body; but he suggested that the objection he had raised 'might be mitigated by giving some seats on the Council to representatives of the Senate'.[76]

In a desire to meet the views of the India office, the government of India, in a revised scheme submitted in the following October, proposed that the senate should be empowered to settle both curriculum and syllabuses, and that in addition it should elect five of its members to the council.[77] But even now the controversy was not over. There was to be a curious postscript, with an unexpected reversal of roles. Prompted by Sir Theodore Morison,[78] the council in London decided that five senate members on the council would be excessive. Since the quorum of the council was fixed at five, it was thought that the representatives of the senate might often be found in a majority with the result that the characteristic relationship of employer and employee between the council and senate would be destroyed. The secretary of state thus informed the government of India that he would prefer to see only the provost and one other member of the senate on the council; and at the instance of Sir Thomas Raleigh[79] he added in support of his preference that the 'experience of the newer universities in England suggests that the presence of two members of the Senate in Council secures an adequate expression of the views of the Teaching Staff'.[80] But now the government of India was to be more royalist than the king. Pursuing the same point in relation to the scheme for the hindu university at Benares, they contested the validity of Raleigh's argument. ' . . . while we recognise that in the newer universities in England two members of the Senate would suffice to represent that body on the Council', they wrote, 'political and other non-educational influences exercise in India so strong a pressure that we are constrained to adhere to our previous suggestion of the presence of five members of the Senate upon the Council.'[81] And it was for five members that provision was made in the Benares Hindu University Act.[82] As a result of the views held in London, and the new-found zeal in Calcutta, stronger safeguards for academic control were built into the constitution for Benares than had been envisaged for the similar scheme originally drafted for Aligarh. What in England was often left to convention to secure, was in India given a more explicit legislative sanction.

The third issue between the government of India and the council in London was the degree of government control to be prescribed in the constitution; and it was here that the difference was most acute and the debate most prolonged. That a 'fully satisfactory system of government control' should be insisted upon in any scheme for a university at Aligarh was not in dispute; this, indeed, was made an express condition of the sanction that was given for the planning to proceed.[83] But it took two years of hard negotiation to reach agreement on the form it should take; and yet a third to find a solution acceptable to the Indians as well.

The government of India made their position abundantly clear from the outset in the amendments they proposed to the draft constitution submitted by the muslims. The draft already conceded a large measure of control. It provided that the viceroy should be chancellor *ex officio*, and vested with wide powers. In addition to nominating five members of the senate, he was authorised 'to enquire into every matter relating to the University and give such advice to the Court as he may deem fit about the improvement, management and welfare of the University'. This latter power was somewhat illusory since the court were not bound to give effect to his advice. They were either to act on it, or record their reasons for not doing so. In other respects, however, the powers assigned to him were substantial and real. He was authorised to make enquiries to satisfy himself that the staff of the university was sufficient and competent: and here he was able to require the removal of any member of staff if, after report from the court, he considered it desirable. He was empowered at any time to call for and examine the accounts of the university, and he was to receive the annual budget. Changes in the statutes, whether by repeal, amendment or addition, were made subject to his veto; changes in the regulations subject to his approval. His approval was also required in the appointment of examiners. But wide though these powers were, the government of India found them insufficient. They wished the appointment of the provost and professors to be subject to the approval of the chancellor. They wished the chancellor to have power to insist on his advice being taken. And they wished him to be able 'to institute any enquiry with a view to ascertaining whether the provisions of the laws of the University for the time being in force are duly complied with, and, if not, to compel the members to comply with them'.[84] These proposals were in fact hardly more drastic than those already imposed on the existing universities. They represented no new departure in policy. But they met resistance in London on two grounds. Sir Theodore Morison thought that the provision of such detailed powers made government control altogether 'too palpable'.[85] And other members of the council objected to the viceroy being made the agent of control:[86] they considered it inconsistent with the policy of transferring the seat of central government to Delhi that he should be so closely involved in local work, and they feared it might create an awkward precedent when it came to establishing other universities. In his reply to the government of India, therefore, the secretary of state declined to sanction this latter aspect of the scheme. He suggested instead that the chancellor should be elected by the court; and he proposed an alternative and simplified form of control for which he drew on the current practice in Britain. Under this scheme, control was to be vested in the government of India rather than the viceroy personally, and it was to be exercised in three ways. Changes in the statutes were to be subject to the approval of the governor general in council; grants-in-aid, which were to be given for a period of years, were to be made conditional upon government inspection; and annual accounts were to be submitted to the department of education. Since these three provisions were in force in the younger universities in the United Kingdom, and had been found salutary, the secretary of state considered there could be 'no reasonable objection' to their being adopted in India. But he was averse to anything more. So that the council and senate should realise to the full the responsibilities they were to be entrusted with, he directed that all unnecessary interference should be avoided; and he specifically withheld his sanction from the proposal that professorial appointments should be subject to government approval.[87]

The despatch from the India office brought a strong riposte from the government of India. Disclaiming any desire to interfere in the details of university management, they stressed the vital importance of establishing real and effective control on both political and educational grounds. The communal university, they emphasised, was in the nature of an experiment and might well develop activities on non-educational lines. If the viceroy were not chancellor, and the government were shorn of so many of the powers claimed for it, this would not only remove the safeguards against such activities, but additionally undermine the position of the senate in relation to the council. Turning to the alternative scheme suggested, they observed that the first and third control had already been included in their own proposals (ignoring, however, that changes in the statutes had previously been made subject to veto by the viceroy, not the governor general in council); and that the third, providing for inspection at an interval of a number of years, did not admit of a crisis being forestalled. They strongly urged that theoretical considerations should not be allowed to stand in the way of clear political necessities, and contested the wisdom of seeking guidance in analogies 'adduced from English models with their widely different environment'. 'If analogies are to be regarded', they wrote, 'we desire to observe that in Colonial Universities very definite powers have been assigned to the civil authorities. In the University of Sydney, the power of interference is vested in the Governor in case the rules laid down be unduly relaxed in practice. In the Cape of Good Hope University half the Council (which is the executive body) is perpetually nominated by the Governor who can also assign additional members. In both these Universities, there are also other checks.' Arguing finally that the relaxation of control proposed would be received by the more responsible muslims with deep concern, they concluded by pressing 'with all the force at our command . . . the absolute necessity of securing adequate Government control'.[88] But the India office was adamant, and seemingly somewhat disingenuous. The secretary of state was 'surprised' that the government of India should consider his decision as practically freeing the university from government control altogether. The main decision, he pointed out, had been to place the power of control in the hands of the governor general in council rather than the governor general acting as chancellor; and this would tend to enhance the effectiveness of the control, for it ensured that each proposal submitted to him would be accompanied by 'a full statement of any objections to it that might be entertained by experienced officers of the Government'. The only substantial difference between them, he affirmed, related to the appointment of professors, and here he foresaw little danger in the absence of control, as a considerable proportion of the professors would be recruited in England, and there would be the further safeguard of the inspection provided for in connection with the renewal of the grant-in-aid. 'Apart from the appointment of professors', he concluded, 'all the powers which you propose to give to the Chancellor are conceded to the Governor General in Council.'[89]

The India office had conveniently ignored the extensive powers of intervention the government of India had originally claimed; and if this was deliberate strategy, it was cleverly countered in Calcutta. For when the muslims rejected the conditions imposed in London, and the government of India was able to come forward with compromise proposals, whilst deferring to the India office over the appointment of the chancellor and the agency of control, they promptly transferred to the governor general in council all the powers they had previously assigned to the viceroy.[90] The India office was now obliged to admit that the area of disagreement extended beyond the appointment of professors. In objecting that the powers reserved to the governor general in council appeared 'unnecessarily detailed', the secretary of state explained that he did not wish to insist on a 'minute compliance' with what he referred to as the 'suggestion' of his previous despatch that the powers originally proposed for the chancellor could be vested in the governor general in council. He repeated his preference for a simpler form of control on the lines of his earlier scheme, although this time he allowed that the governor general in council might also be empowered to 'watch over the administration of the University generally, requiring the authorities to take such action and to appoint and retain such staff as may be necessary to carry out efficiently the objects for which the University is constituted'.[91]

This still fell far short of what the government of India had been pressing for; but again they were saved from submission. The muslims declined to pursue the negotiations, and when, in July 1913, the government of India came to submit a similar draft constitution on behalf of the hindus, evidence of seditious activities at the parent colleges of the proposed universities and elsewhere gave them just the handle they needed to renew their representations. Now, indeed, they stiffened their proposals, urging that the governor general in council should have power to appoint examiners as a special measure, and even, if necessary, to suspend the constitution. And they couched their appeal in still more emphatic terms. Repeating that the universities in India were exposed to peculiar difficulties and dangers which did not exist in England, they insisted on the absolute necessity of taking explicit powers of intervention from the start. 'Under present conditions and for many years to come', they declared, 'these universities simply cannot stand alone. We do not hesitate to say that if effective powers of assistance and intervention are not secured for the Governor General in Council, we shall regard it as the lesser of two evils that the movements should collapse, notwithstanding the grave disappointment and irritation which might ensue'.[92]

The confrontation between the two governments reached its climax with an answering minute from Sir Theodore Morison. Submitting that a question of fundamental principle was involved, he made a bold plea for allowing the new universities a wide discretion. It was only by giving them latitude to make mistakes, he contended, that the experiments could have any educational value. The government should prescribe the conditions on which the universities were to be established, and then leave them to 'sink or swim by themselves'. He was not impressed by the alleged need to safeguard academic standards. If standards fell, the worst consequence would be that a section of one generation would be indifferently educated. The universities would languish and die, or they would mend their ways. The only serious danger was that they might become centres of political intrigue: and to guard against this

U–B.I.A.—4*

he considered the government should be armed with the 'ultima ratio' of the power of suppression. But to attempt any detailed control would be to cause embarrassment to the government, and to deprive the universities of vitality. 'Educationalists are a wayward race', he reflected, '& if you do not allow them to teach how they like & what they like they become spiritless & dull. That is why Government Colleges though manned by much abler men are so dead & alive when compared with Missionary or independent institutions. The Government of India should take warning from the failure of Napoleon's attempts to control education. When he had succeeded in imposing his will upon the Colleges of France, it was discovered that he had killed them & University education in France has been nursed back into life by the opposite policy of decentralization.'[93]

It was indicative of the importance attached to the issue in the India office that a solution should have been approached by way of a special committee. The suggestion was put to the secretary of state, Lord Crewe, by the clerk of the council,[94] and it was promptly accepted. 'I like the idea of a special Com^me', Crewe minuted in response, 'and it may be composed as suggested . . . These fresh proposals create a delicate situation.'[95] The committee met in October, and the upshot of its deliberations was a telegram to the government of India early in November, inviting their views on the possibility of making the lieutenant governor of the provinces concerned the chancellor of the new universities.[96] In a despatch of the same date it was explained that the appointment of the lieutenant governor would be free from the objection to the appointment of the viceroy, and that the 'difficult question of the extent of control to be exercised by the Governor General in Council might be solved by it'.[97] There was no indication as to the amount of control that would be conceded to the lieutenant governor[89]; but when in May 1914 the government of India returned an acceptance of the proposal, coupled with the suggestion that the lieutenant governor should be vested with all the powers set out in their previous letter of July 1913,[99] the India office made no further demur. Sir Theodore Morison sorrowfully acknowledged that it was 'too late to insist upon the policy of allowing the Universities liberty to make mistakes';[100] and the government of India, at length, had its way.[101]

But even now there were to be modifications in detail before the solution was finally agreed. Although the hindus were ready to accept the degree of control prescribed in the latest proposals, they were not prepared to assign the chancellorship of an all-India institution to a lieutenant governor. The government of India therefore devised an alternative distribution of offices and powers, under which the chancellor became a figurehead elected by the court, ordinary powers were vested in the lieutenant governor as visitor, and extraordinary powers were reserved to the governor general in council;[102] and since no question of principle was involved, this was readily sanctioned in London.[103] Moreover, although the government of India had been authorised to provide for all the powers detailed in their letter of July 1913, in fact they decided to dispense with a specific reference to the power to suspend the constitution. The Benares Hindu University Act, therefore, provided for precisely the type of detailed government control that Sir Theodore Morison had sought to avert.[104]

By withholding sanction to the original proposal that the viceroy should be chancellor of the new universities, and so contributing to the division of powers between the governor general in council and the lieutenant governor, the council in London had taken some of the bite from the control the government of India had originally contemplated. As Sir Harcourt Butler contended in the legislative council, it was hardly 'in human nature' that the visitor would lightly invoke the emergency powers vested in the governor general in council; whilst the whole tendency with the government of India was to avoid unnecessary interference with the details of local administration.[105] The council of India had also held out successfully against the government of India's bid to control the appointment of professorial staff. But on the essential issue their surrender had been complete. Capitulating to the argument that British academic practice was not a safe guide in the political context of India, they had conceded the principle of detailed government control. Sir Harcourt might rub his eyes at the charges of illiberality brought against the new constitution; but it was only by reference to the state universities of Europe, and indeed the existing universities in India, that he could sustain his incredulity.[106]

The negotiations for the communal universities at Aligarh and Benares had helped to clarify British policy about the principles to be followed in framing the constitution of new universities in India. But the constitution which emerged from the planning was in no sense a constitution 'provided by Government'.[107] The Benares constitution was based on a scheme prepared by the Indians and was only a partial reflection of British policy. It was otherwise, however, with the constitution planned for the new state university at Dacca. Government designed from the outset, this was a clear embodiment of British policy. And although it endorsed and developed certain essential principles adopted at Benares, in one respect, more especially, it departed from them.

The planning of the new university at Dacca developed alongside that of the communal universities, although a little later; and it, too, was protracted. The project was formally authorised by the India office in February 1912,[108] and in May a committee was appointed by the government of Bengal to frame suitable proposals.[109] This reported at the end of the year[110] and in September 1913, the government of India forwarded the broad outlines of a scheme they had agreed with the local government. But the planning then ran into difficulties.[111] The stumbling block was not opinion in London. The principles already agreed over Benares enabled the India office to give a prompt assent to the proposals submitted by the government of India.[112] But differences arose between the central and local governments on details that had not been considered in the case of Benares; and it was not until October 1915 that the government of India were able to follow up their letter of September 1913 with a detailed scheme acceptable to the government of Bengal.[113]

The main point at issue echoed the controversy over affiliation in the Aligarh negotiations, and turned on the interpretation that was to be given to the concept of the teaching university. It was agreed at the outset that the new university should be strictly local; there was never any question of its being allowed to affiliate distant colleges. The difference arose over the nature of the link that was to be established between the university and its constituent colleges. The committee had proposed that to begin with these should be government colleges; and that whilst they should retain their distinctive individuality and form the basic units of university life, they should be 'organically bound . . . into a higher and more complex unit, the teaching and residential University'.[114] The organic relationship was to be secured by entrusting much of the teaching to the university, and by giving it control of the appointment of the staff, and also of collegiate finance. It was this latter provision which led to conflict. Fearing that it would preclude the incorporation of independent colleges, the government of Bengal proposed that the constituent colleges, whether government institutions or private ones, should be allowed to retain their 'complete individual existence and separate financial arrangements'.[115] This met with strong opposition from the government of India. To deprive the university of financial control over the colleges, they insisted, would be to rob it of effective control over the teaching and defeat a major purpose of the scheme. And in support of their contention they invoked the recent emphatic opinion of the Haldane commission.[116] After prolonged discussion, the government of Bengal deferred to their view,[117] and the agreed proposals forwarded to London in 1915 provided not only for the financial arrangements originally contemplated by the committee, but for a larger share of the teaching to be conducted under the auspices of the university. In their covering letter to the secretary of state, the government of India made much of the relationship proposed for the university and its constituent colleges, and the definition they had given to the teaching university. In anticipation of criticism, perhaps, they expressly disclaimed the aim of creating 'a replica of Oxford or Cambridge'. ' . . . even if such a miracle were possible,' they wrote, 'or if it were not the fact that these time honoured institutions have recently formed the subject of criticism should we consider their type congenial to the Indian environment or the best adapted for providing a solution of the present problems of education in this country.' The aim, they emphasised, had been to create an institution which should be free of the notorious defects of the affiliating universities: a university 'where the control of teaching and much of the instruction will be in the hands of the university' and where 'the propinquity of the colleges and the fact that the highest professors will be attached to colleges and take part in their tutorial work will bring the inspiring influences of a really scholastic institution to bear upon the students of all grades'. 'We aim in fact at the type of university which we believe has proved successful in Australia.'[118]

In coming to grips with the definition of a teaching university, the government of India were developing and not departing from the policy they had pursued in relation to Benares. In their proposals for the government of the new university, however, and the place to be accorded to academic opinion, they adopted a policy that was not only distinct but different. Whereas the hindus had elected to separate the administrative and academic function, and follow the 'two-tier' pattern of government, the government of India preferred to take as their model the simpler structure of the existing universities. The Dacca University Committee recommended that the government of the university should be vested in a convocation and council on the lines of the senate and syndicate prescribed by the Indian Universities Act of 1904. But since they were persuaded that the 'detailed administration of a teaching and residential University must be entrusted mainly to its professors and executive officers' [119] they assigned a greater weight to these elements than had been considered appropriate before. Whereas in the case of the syndicate, it had been provided that a minimum of approximately one half of the members should be principals of affiliated colleges or professors, in the committee's proposals for the council, the comparable proportion was considerably increased.[120] This modest adaptation of the pattern of government originally adopted for the examining universities was readily accepted by the governments of Bengal and India; and it was sanctioned without comment by the India office.[121] Whilst over Benares, therefore, there had been acquiescence in a 'two-tier' pattern of government designed to secure a decisive voice for academic opinion in academic affairs, the proposals for Dacca revealed that the official preference was for a simpler 'one-tier' system, which gave academic opinion a predominant voice in the overall affairs of the university, financial and administrative as well as purely academic.

The Dacca proposals were also revealing on the subject of government control. And here they sharply endorsed the policy the government of India had successfully contended for in the negotiations over the communal universities. The Dacca University Committee proposed that the new university should be a state university. The government were to be vested with powers similar to those they already enjoyed in respect of the other universities; but they were also to acquire a closer and more direct control by virtue of the nature of the constituent colleges, and the provisions made for staffing, finance and inspection. The committee proposed that the constituent colleges should be government colleges, and that the staff, whether employed directly by the university or by the colleges, should be government servants. The university was to be maintained by the government. Fees were to be paid into the treasury, and the treasury was to be responsible for the payment of salaries. Other expenditure was to be met from a university fund to which the government were to make an annual grant, and over which they were to exercise a general control. And since the committee considered that 'the control of the Government over the University should be exercised directly', they recommended that 'the Director of Public Instruction should be appointed Official Visitor, with full powers to inspect all colleges and departments'.[122] The government of Bengal were satisfied with this very substantial measure of control.[123] But the government of India, in forwarding the proposed scheme to London in September 1913, reiterated the demands they had made in regard to Benares in the previous July. 'We consider that the Chancellor should be empowered to institute enquiries and to require such action to be taken and such staff to be appointed or removed as will secure the objects of the university and if necessary to suspend the constitution and see his orders carried out', they wrote. 'In our despatch no 19, dated 10th July 1913, regarding the proposed Hindu University at Benares, we have strongly represented the necessity of reserving such power to the Governor General in Council. We are not prepared in the light of the experience which we have gained in recent years to recommend to your Lordship any proposal for a new University which does not reserve such powers to competent authority.' Sir T. W. Holderness minuted that the proposed appointment of the governor of Bengal as *ex officio* chancellor with extensive powers of control was 'on all fours' with the suggestion made to the government of India with regard to the aided universities of Aligarh and Benares[124]; and the India office, already resigned, it seems, to surrender, telegraphed a general approval of the scheme.[125] In the subsequent negotiations between the local and central governments, the government of Bengal did not disguise their view that such extensive powers were unnecessary. '. . . the Dacca University will be a State institution', they wrote, 'and the principal officers of the University will be public servants subject to the discipline of the Government of Bengal who are competent in cases of emergency to exercise such powers as it is now proposed to vest in the Chancellor'.[126] But in deference to the emphatic opinion of the government of India, they did not press the point; and in the detailed scheme submitted to the India office in October 1915,[127] and approved in the following December,[128] provision was made for the emergency powers envisaged in the government of India's letter of September 1913, couched, however, in terms to harmonise with the form finally adopted in the Benares Hindu University Act.[129]

The most significant change in constitutional policy in this period was the decisive break with affiliation and the substantial approach towards the unitary teaching university. Affiliation was expressly prohibited in the case of the communal universities; it was ruled out no less decisively in the case of Dacca. And whilst at Dacca the new university was given a collegiate basis and not a strictly unitary one, great care was taken to ensure that it would have effective control over the teaching. This insistence on the purely teaching university, which was strongly criticised in many Indian quarters at the time,[130] was soon acknowledged to be impractical, and modified;[131] but it was indicative of the strength of official reaction against the examining university, and the importance attached to a wholly new departure, that the teaching university should have been born in this uncompromising form. The change in regard to university government was more modest. Official preference was still for the undifferentiated, single tier structure of the older universities, suitably modified to give the greater control to university officers that was considered appropriate for the self-contained teaching university. The grounds of the objection to the more modern two tier structure are not entirely clear. Sir Harcourt Butler in the legislative council,[132] like Sir Thomas Raleigh in his note for the council,[133] remarked simply on its undue complexity. But comment from the local governments on the constitution proposed for Benares suggests that the preference was due less to a belief in the innate superiority of the composite structure than a recognition of the difficulty, in Indian circumstances, of obtaining the suitably qualified court demanded by the differentiated one.[134] In the measure of government control prescribed for the constitution the change was greater; and it was retrogressive. Here, indeed, British policy was caught up in something of a paradox. For the fact that the teaching university should have happened to be planned in the aftermath of unprecedented nationalist agitation dictated that the increase of academic influence in the internal structure of the university should be accompanied by a decrease of autonomy in its external relations. Government control became more stringent and more explicit.

Standards   It was not only in constitutional terms that the government of India defined their meaning of the teaching university. In planning their own scheme at Dacca – the first of the official 'oases' with which it was hoped to refresh the desert of affiliation[135] – they also prescribed a number of other distinctive features, similarly designed to foster the broader education and above all the higher standard of scholarship for which they looked to this type of university.

These new features stemmed from the recommendations of the Dacca University Committee; and for the most part their proposals were bold and progressive. But in one respect, and an important one, they were notably cautious. This was over the level of entry where, as a temporary measure, it was proposed that the standard of the Calcutta matriculation should be adopted. The committee were well aware of the inadequacy of this standard. They recommended it only because they thought it would be impractical to attempt an alternative; and they suggested it should be supplemented by a policy of careful selection on the part of the colleges.[136] The proposal was clearly an uneasy one, and it was not unanimous. Several members would have liked a special scholarship examination as well, whilst one of them, Mohamed Ali, bitterly regretted the committee had not measured up to the challenge of 'an ideal scheme for an ideal university' by boldly opting for a new line of demarcation between the schools and the colleges.[137] Neither local nor central government was at first disposed to question the committee's recommendation, or indeed to embark on the sort of radical reorganisation Mohamed Ali pressed for.[138] Later they had misgivings, and seriously considered the possibility of a localised experiment in transferring the intermediate courses to the schools. But each saw insuperable difficulties in the way. The government of Bengal pointed to the inadequate staffing and equipment of the schools, and the government of India to a number of other objections: that public opinion was not ripe for the change; that it would present particular difficulties in the case of Dacca where the university would be drawing on the same schools as Calcutta; and that it would defer the creation of other new university centres. Like the committee, therefore, both governments fell back on the policy of mitigating the defects of the Calcutta standard. The government of Bengal suggested differentiating more clearly between the type of instruction given to junior and senior undergraduates: if the intermediate courses could not be put back into the schools, at least they could be segregated in the colleges, with all post-intermediate work reserved to the university. The government of India agreed; and in finally endorsing the committee's proposals, drew especial attention to the role assigned to the colleges. After all, they reflected, was it not the promiscuous and unselected admission of matriculants that did the damage to university standards?[139]

In other respects, the committee were able to offer a more stimulating lead, and a remarkable feature of their recommendations was the extent to which they took their cue from the west. For despite the predominantly Indian membership of the committee,[140] and the strong current of nationalism that was flowing in India in 1912, they deliberately set themselves to capture something of the spirit and quality of the teaching university that had grown up over the centuries in Europe and more particularly in Britain herself.

The committee had been specifically directed to provide for residence in their blueprint for the new university, and they made their recommendations under this head a pivotal point of their scheme. They prefaced their report with a significant reference to the general movement in favour of residence elsewhere: to the way Oxford and Cambridge had added to the accommodation they provided, and Scottish universities were becoming converts to the residential principle; how the provision of some sort of accommodation featured in the newly founded civic universities in Britain, and how in America and to a lesser extent Germany, there had been increasing recognition of the contribution residence could make to university life. They acknowledged that this widespread movement had already begun to have repercussions in India where, since the beginning of the century, greater attention had been paid to the provision of hostels, and there had been growing appreciation of the English collegiate system.[141] But they insisted that the movement was still embryonic; and that at Dacca the advance should be such as to constitute a change in 'kind' as well as 'degree'. At an early stage they decided in favour of the collegiate system of residence and they couched their recommendation in bold and vigorous terms. Emphasising that they attached 'the utmost importance to the principle that as large a proportion of students as possible should be in residence, since it is only on such students that the full benefits of University life can be conferred', they urged that all students not living with parents or guardians should be required to live in college, and that neither student messes, nor non-collegiate hostels should be permitted.[142]

It was largely to foster a broader and more comprehensive type of higher education that the committee championed the residential principle. They looked to the residential university for the moral and physical training that had found so little place in the university system in the past.[143] But they also looked for a more stimulating academic environment. It was a major part of their purpose to prescribe for a higher standard of scholarship; and they went on to make a series of proposals more specifically directed to this end.

In the first place they made important recommendations to ensure the quality of the teaching. Influenced, no doubt, by the example of government colleges in which the policy of Indianisation had been pressed too far, they recommended that approximately one sixth of the appointments should be set aside for members of the Indian educational service recruited in England.[144] Recognising, too, that young English scholars, however promising, often fell away in the discouraging intellectual climate of India, they took the further precaution of suggesting a number of special posts for distinguished senior scholars. It was 'almost impossible', they thought, to over-estimate the invigorating influence that even one man of great ability and enthusiasm could exert in a university; and it was indicative of their general orientation that they should have reinforced their own view with the assertion that the value of such men was 'thoroughly well recognized in Europe . . .' The committee were careful to explain that these scholars need not necessarily be drawn from England; those in India, they considered, should in fact be selected first. But they clearly envisaged attracting some men from the west, and they welcomed this way of keeping the university in touch with western centres of learning and research.[145] In regard to the method of instruction, the committee proposed a bold departure from the practice in the affiliating colleges. In place of the heavy reliance on the mass lecture, they prescribed a more varied and personal system, with lectures supplemented by classes, tutorial instruction, laboratory and seminar work and supervised private study.[146] Anticipating to some extent the recommendation of the government of Bengal, they pointed to the importance of adjusting the method of teaching to the developing capacity of the student; with more classes and fewer lecturers in the junior courses, and a more ambitious lecturing programme coupled with closer individual supervision in the senior ones. But the recommendation to which they attached most importance, and to which they gave greatest emphasis, was the introduction of the tutorial system. It was to this well tried instrument of the western teaching university that they looked for 'that steady progress on the part of the student' which they acknowledged to be 'the aim of all good teaching'.

In the pattern of degree courses they prescribed, the committee were somewhat restricted by their decision to accept the Calcutta standard of matriculation. This almost inevitably committed them to a four-year degree course in arts and science as at Calcutta, with an intermediate examination at the end of the second year. But within this general framework, they were able to suggest a number of innovations. The principle on which they based their recommendations was a clear bifurcation of studies for honours and pass students beyond the intermediate stage; and here again they were careful to range themselves with 'the general movement of thought upon the subject'.[147] The principle was not new to India; it had been followed at Calcutta for some thirty years. But it was now more sharply defined. For whilst at Calcutta the honours course was little more than an extended version of the comparable pass course, the committee urged that at Dacca it should be given a distinctive quality of its own. The committee also proposed changes in the pass degree courses. To remedy a notorious defect in the Calcutta system, they recommended that students should be prohibited from selecting an unsuitable grouping of subjects; and they suggested furthermore that the examinations should be conducted by compartment.[148] They followed up these recommendations with proposals for a structure of higher degrees, and again with a view to lifting the level of scholarship, stressed that postgraduate study should be made a special feature of the university.[149]

In their recommendations for the examining system at Dacca, the committee necessarily prescribed a fundamental change of principle. It was the very essence of their task to plan a university in which the teaching was not only closely associated with the examining but assured of a dominating influence over it. Insisting this should be so, they proposed a board of examiners for each subject, with the majority chosen from professors and assistants engaged in teaching it in the university.[150] If 'suitable persons' could be found, it was suggested that one or more external examiners should be appointed;[151] but curiously enough, the committee do not seem to have set much store by this conventional safeguard of standards in the west. At least they did not press it. They also advised on two points of detail. With the warning of the existing system before them, they proposed a more sparing and discriminating use of the text book in the prescription of syllabuses.[152] And for all examinations beyond the intermediate stage, they recommended that the numerical system of marking should be abandoned in favour of the symbol indicating overall impression. 'This system', so ran the familiar refrain, 'is in accordance with the best traditions of a teaching University.'[153]

All these recommendations met with the unqualified approval of the government of Bengal; and in forwarding the committee's report to the government of India, they too chose to commend and defend by reference to the practice of the west.[154] Although the committee acknowledged no particular model for the type of residence they proposed,[155] the government of Bengal supplied the persuasive explanation that the trend of the proposals was 'towards residence in college such as prevails at Oxford and Cambridge . . .'. And on several points which had attracted public criticism, they offered a defence which underlined the assumption that Dacca was to be created in the western image and moreover that western practice was the ultimate criterion of judgement. Commenting on a section of opinion which contended that the number of teaching posts reserved for the Indian educational service was too large, the government of Bengal endorsed the committee's recommendation with the argument that 'the European element suggested is the very least that will be required to infuse into the system the spirit of the Western Universities and to raise the general level of the teaching to the standard which is essential for success . . .'. They made a similar defence, too, of the committee's proposal that the senior pass examination for the B.A. and B.Sc. degrees should be conducted by compartment. A number of important critics, including the syndicate of the University of Calcutta, opposed the suggestion, and in support of their view, quoted the opinion of the commissioners of 1902 that such a system would be likely to lower standards. But the government of Bengal swept aside this objection with the argument that had the commissioners been prescribing for a teaching university with comparatively small numbers they might very well have come to the same conclusion as the Dacca university committee 'with the example of Oxford and Cambridge and other universities of the West before them'. 'It is not unnatural for persons who conceive a University to be a great examining body to regard an encyclopaedic public examination as the appropriate crown of a student's career', they wrote. 'But this is not the highest ideal of either examining or teaching, and the system proposed by the Committee, if carefully used, should promote more thorough study and encourage greater interest in work.' Far from lowering standards, it should permit a higher level of instruction and examination.

The government of India fully endorsed these views, and warmly commended the new policy to London.[156] They readily concurred in the committee's interpretation of the residential principle; and they were confident that the system proposed for the teaching, courses and examining would constitute 'a vast improvement' on existing practice. They especially welcomed the prospect of an effective system of tuition, recognising that this would supply 'a long felt want'. They were enthusiastic, too, about the revised examining system which they pronounced 'a new and desirable development'. They also singled out for special mention the staffing arrangements. The novelty of the provision for men of 'years and reputation' received an approving acknowledgement; but the recommendation they endorsed most emphatically was the reservation of a fixed proportion of teaching posts for Europeans. This they regarded as indispensably necessary for the introduction of 'methods of teaching and modes of collegiate life' so largely alien to Indian experience.

The India office sealed the new policy without comment.[157] And this perhaps was hardly surprising. The committee's proposals for leavening the quality of university scholarship in India constituted a major advance; but they conformed so exactly to the trend of academic thinking in Britain that the India office, already disposed to argue the relevance of British practice for India,[158] may well have felt a brief expression of general approval sufficed.

Curriculum   It was over the content of the curriculum of the new universities that British policy changed most decisively. The prejudices of Lord Macaulay were set aside; and the former disparagement of oriental studies was replaced by zeal and enthusiasm. The change was not a sudden resolve of these years. A more liberal attitude to oriental studies had been growing for a generation or more, influenced partly by the evolution of educational theory in the west and the pleas of western orientalists, and more especially by the developing cultural renaissance in India and the pressures of Indian nationalism. But it was not until the advent of Harcourt Butler that the cultivation of oriental studies was acknowledged as a major objective of policy and vigorously pursued.

One of Harcourt Butler's earliest decisions was to summon a conference of orientalists to Simla.[159] Distinguished scholars from all parts of India assembled there in July 1911 and discussion focussed on the neglect of oriental studies, and the best way of remedying it. It was generally agreed that the universities' record in oriental scholarship was poor. Dr Venis commented on the lack of 'mental context' provided for oriental subjects in the undergraduate courses,[160] and their low prestige value. Was not one of the problems simply 'how to make Orientalia respectable'? Dr Thibaut pointed to the few orientalists on the teaching staffs of the universities, and others to the want of a suitable atmosphere for research. Criticism also centred on the unproductiveness of the scholarship pursued on traditional lines, and to the absence of co-ordination between the various agencies for oriental scholarship. It was felt that the most effective stimulus would be a central research institute, located in Calcutta. This would be able to set its own pace of research, uninhibited by the universities. It would provide a suitable meeting place for scholars working on western and indigenous lines, and it would be able to draw on the unique record material of the capital. The proposal was promptly endorsed by the government of India, and in forwarding a detailed scheme to London, they enlarged on the grounds for their new approach. 'There are at the present time forces at work in India which aim at the restoration of the dreams and yearnings of an ancient civilisation', they wrote in a passage which attracted some amused comment from the purists in the India office. 'They are exemplified in many ways, not least in the demand for religious instruction in our schools and colleges and for Universities of a new type resting on a religious basis. Such a movement, if wisely guided, is likely to prove beneficial; if neglected it cannot but be reactionary. It is necessary to keep the impact of western scholarship strong and dynamic and to present the best elements of Indian civilisation through the medium of western methods of research and in relation with modern ideas and progress. To effect this we require highly trained teachers in Orientalia for our Universities and colleges and through them competent instructors for our schools. These we have not got at present nor do we seem likely to obtain them under the present system . . . We desire, therefore, to rearrange and concentrate our forces. And we think that an institution framed somewhat on the lines of the schools at Hanoi and Vladivostok would best serve our purpose . . .'[161] A few months later they indicated their standpoint still more succinctly. A draft resolution on educational policy submitted to London in October 1912 contained the simple but novel proposition that the government of India 'attached great importance to the cultivation and improvement of oriental studies'.[162]

The India office was no less keen for a new departure. The secretary of state fully acknowledged the advantage of a central institution 'to foster those Oriental studies which have fallen into comparative neglect in the curriculum of higher education in India . . .'. His only doubt was over the government of India's proposal to site it in Delhi instead of Calcutta in view of the forthcoming transfer of the capital. This in itself was a measure of the change that had come over official thinking, for it sprang in part from the fear that an institute sited away from the universities might diminish their interest in oriental studies. 'I need not labour the point that our purpose should be to supplement and not to impair the present opportunities for higher teaching in this branch of learning.' Before approving a scheme of 'such great and lasting importance', he invited the government of India to take the opinion of the local governments on the question of location.[163] Fortified by the majority view in favour of Delhi, the government of India persisted in their preference. Marshalling all the advantages of Delhi, they thought it 'not out of place' to recall that 'Lord Macaulay in his Minute of 1835 describes Delhi as the great seat of Arabic learning just as Benares was of Brahminical learning . . . [and] that he proposed to transfer to those cities the famous Calcutta Madrassa and the Sanskrit College, thereby implying that these were the most suitable locations for them and that they were unlikely to fulfil their proper aim in Calcutta'.[164] But the India office remained unconvinced. Lionel Abrahams made the significant comment: 'When the G. of I. have to rely on Lord Macaulay . . . their case must be somewhat desperate.'[165] And Sir Thomas Holderness continued to press the university argument. In a long departmental minute, he informed the secretary of state that Sir Alfred Hopkinson, who had recently been invited to advise on university development at Bombay, considered 'the money would be better laid out in helping existing Universities to found chairs of Oriental learning and grant scholarships for postgraduate study'; he also recalled that Lord Haldane's commission had advised against relegating postgraduate work to separate institutions.[166] In the end, the governing consideration was judged to be 'the disastrous frustration of the hopes entertained for the advancement of Oriental scholarship in India that might follow from a premature and unwise decision as to the site of the Institute': and in July 1914, it was decided to postpone a decision pending a clarification of the issues involved.[167] Paradoxically, the project foundered on the very importance the India office had come to attach to the policy underlying it.

It was in this new climate of official opinion that the curriculum of the new universities was planned, and the planning not only reflected but helped to shape and fix the new attitude. For the question of the cultural purpose of the new universities was first raised in the extreme form of whether official sanction was to be extended to communal universities, and the decision to allow them was not taken without much anxious debate. The Aligarh project ran up against opposition at the outset; whilst the scheme for Benares had to overcome widespread and determined hostility before it got off the ground.

The government of India had no hesitation in sponsoring a muhammadan university at Aligarh. Shortly before proclaiming their new interest in oriental studies by summoning the Conference of Orientalists, they telegraphed to London for permission to proceed with preliminary negotiations.[168] But the idea of a communal university was not so immediately acceptable in London: it provoked arguments and counter arguments which, in touching on fundamental issues, reacted on the general evolution of policy. It had always been the ambition of Sir Syed Ahmed Khan to develop the Anglo-Oriental College at Aligarh into a university and the project had been considered by the Indian Universities Commission in 1902.[169] They had opposed it; and when the scheme came before the India office in 1911, it met the preconceived hostility of Sir Thomas Raleigh who saw no reason to revise his earlier opinion.[170] The parliamentary under-secretary, E.S. Montagu, was another opponent. Disclaiming any special knowledge of the Indian factors involved, he took his stand quite simply on the evils of denominationalism, and the impolicy of following a principle that was calculated to undermine the unity Britain had brought to India.[171] But if the scheme had a long-standing opponent in Sir Thomas Raleigh, it had a very special champion, of still longer standing, in Sir Theodore Morison: and in answer to the political objections of E.S. Montagu, he produced a classic exposition of the educational advantages of a policy of cultural adaptation. He began by challenging the assumption that the muhammadan movement in India was a species of denominationalism. Muhammadanism, like hinduism, was not merely a creed: it was a social organisation, a particular type of civilisation with ideals and historical traditions of its own. He went on to welcome the signs of growing unity in India, but argued that a really catholic Indian nationalism was still a very tender plant which premature forcing in the educational field was likely to endanger,

And he then turned to the educational considerations. 'As long as you teach only reading, writing & arithmetic, you can disregard the differences in culture between the two communities; but directly you probe the deeper questions of education you are brought face to face with the necessity of inquiring into the intellectual antecedents of your pupils. When you want to mould character & impress certain ideals on your pupils you can't appeal only to the head, you must touch the heart which really governs action. There are certain rules of conduct, certain conventional standards of honour which are part of one's moral & intellectual inheritance, there are certain venerable names and chivalrous figures which every people cherishes as the most valuable part of its history; it is these, fortified sometimes by direct religious teaching, which create standards of conduct. The Muhamadans have a very distinct moral and intellectual inheritance of this kind . . . But all this legend & history, charged with sentiment for a Muhamadan, will leave a Hindu quite cold: and conversely, you can't appeal to a Muhamadan boy with stories from the Mahabharata or any Indian legend; you might as well try to influence an English schoolboy with a story of Krishna. But Hindu civilization has stories & traditions which touch the Hindu boy, & Muhamadan civilization has stories & traditions which move the Muhamadan boy, and what the Hindus & Muhamadans are now asking is that they should be allowed to use these powerful forces in the education of their sons. We are not able to do it ourselves, but we have no business to take away the key of knowledge & while not entering in ourselves hinder those who are ready to enter in.' 'I have written at very great length', he concluded, '& I hope that none of my colleagues who have Indian experience will have toiled so far, but I do think that the point is one of such paramount importance in all domains of Indian policy that those who have not lived in India will take the trouble to get at the Indian point of view.'[172] Influenced, perhaps, by this earnest plea, the other members of the judicial and public committee came out in strong support of the scheme: Sir William Lee-Warner with a significant indictment of 'our unbending system, our insular ideas, our conceits', which had resulted in 'the practical exclusion of sixty-five millions from University education';[173] and Sir James La Touche with an instructive reference to the analogy of Ireland, where the recently established National University seemed to offer a suitable precedent for a similar university in India.[174] The decision, therefore, was to concede the principle of a communal university, and the approval that was telegraphed to India in July 1911 constituted a landmark in Britain's higher educational policy there, both confirming and strengthening the disposition to 'get at the Indian point of view'.[175]

The Benares project raised more complex issues and forced a more searching examination of the place of indigenous studies in the university curriculum. The proposal for a hindu university was initially entangled with a scheme of Mrs Besant's for a University of India. In July 1910, she and a number of prominent Indians petitioned for a new university 'on National lines and under National control'. It was to start as an examining university on the pattern of the existing ones, but it was to have three special features. The first, to which greatest importance was attached, related to its powers of affiliation. These were to be strictly confined to colleges in which religion and morality formed 'an integral part' of the instruction given. The other two were concerned with the curriculum. In the first place, Indian philosophy, history and literature were to be put in the 'first rank' of subjects studied: these together with the classical languages of India were to supply the 'chief means of culture'. 'While Western thought will be amply studied, Eastern will take the lead, and Western knowledge will be used to enrich, but not to distort or cripple, the expanding national life.' Secondly, special emphasis was to be placed on those branches of learning best calculated to develop the material resources of the country. And here it was indicated that scientific education would be interpreted to include 'a knowledge of the scientific truths embodied in Oriental learning'; and medical education, in particular, 'a knowledge of such scientific truths as are to be found in the Ayur vedik and Hakimi systems'. The overall design, in fact, was 'to incorporate with the best Oriental ideals of life and thought, the best assimilable ideals of the West . . .'.[176]

The government of India's immediate reaction to the scheme was to reject it.[177] The perpetuation of the discredited system of affiliation and the absence of government control, the blatant nationalist overtones and the association with Mrs Besant and the theosophists: all these factors made it suspect and objectionable. But in view of the negotiations that had begun with the muhammadans, it was decided to consult the opinion of the local governments. They were unanimously opposed to the project. They were especially critical of the cultural objective; and their criticism on this fundamental issue of policy affords an interesting cross section of official opinion. Only the government of the Punjab were prepared to approve the elevation of Indian philosophy, history and literature to first place, and even so, they were sceptical of the response this was likely to evoke.[178] Other governments, like Madras, felt that any further emphasis on these studies would be narrowing and retrogressive. '. . . it is open to question whether culture on these lines is not of a somewhat retrograde character and likely if *generally* promoted to endanger the educational future of the country', they wrote. 'The critical appraisement of Indian philosophy and literature are subjects well worthy of the attention of educated Indians, and the study of Indian history on scholarly and scientific lines is an object deserving of nothing but commendation, but it is very doubtful whether these topics are fitted to take the *first* place in a modern university education.'[179] More serious objection was raised to the proposal to teach oriental medicine[180]; and trenchant criticism was levelled at the nebulous philosophical ideas underlying the whole scheme. The government of Eastern Bengal commented on the 'vague notion running through the petition and draft Charter of a novel admixture of Oriental and Western studies in which the two are to shed a new light upon one another and thus to evoke some vaguely conceived fresh form of culture'. They doubted whether the memorialists themselves understood precisely what they meant; and concluded it would be 'a rash and dangerous expedient to grant a Royal Charter and a dominant position in the educational world to an institution for the pursuit of a dream which its champions have been at so little pains to describe and interpret'.[181] As the Aligarh scheme took shape, Mrs Besant saw fit to modify her proposals. In April 1911, she wrote to inform the viceroy that she was preparing a revised petition for a university that would be predominantly hindu in tone, immediately residential, and subject to a measure of government control. She added that she would be consulting the secretary of state on this revised scheme during a forthcoming visit to England.[182] The concessions, however, did not disarm the opposition of the government of India; and in May 1911, they telegraphed an urgent warning to London.[183]

Mrs Besant arrived at the India office with her plans for a hindu university just six days after the decision had been taken to approve a muhammadan university at Aligarh.[184] But the scheme fared no better in London than Calcutta. 'We *cannot* be too cautious in dealing with the lady and her statements', was the instinctive reaction of one member of council.[185] Another reminded his colleagues that the scheme was 'one of the products of the same imaginative mind whose gropings in the realms of occultism and mysticism' had led to 'no useful or tangible results'.[186] It was not so much the association with Mrs Besant that was the cause of the hostility as a fundamental disquiet over the cultural aims of the scheme. The grounds of anxiety were twofold. Firstly there was the objection that had been raised by the local governments: that undue emphasis was placed on Indian studies. One of the Indian members of council, Mirza Baig, made an approving reference to the way in which the Aligarh promoters had recognised that 'culture in the widest sense of the term is not confined to any particular part of the world' and had thus followed the opposite course of placing 'the achievements of modern science and Western thought' in the forefront of the curriculum.[187] Sir William Lee-Warner quoted the view of John Stuart Mill that the function of the university was to teach 'the philosophy of knowledge' and demonstrate the relation of the parts to the whole.[188] There was also the further objection, not touched on by the local governments, that the scheme was based on a shadowy ideal which contained a possible threat to fundamental human liberties. This was a point raised by Sir William Lee-Warner, and the one on which he took his main stand. He put it first of all in a series of agitated questions: 'What is this religious spirit which the British Government is to patronise? Is it a Hindu spirit of religious intolerance such as we are meeting with in Mysore? ... Is caste to be riveted more tightly on society? are the Brahmans' claims to a monopoly of education and Government patronage to be inculcated? What does national mean? Does it reckon 53m of untouchables as beyond the care of the state? are we to revert to Sati?' 'If the aims of the projectors are really a restoration of Indian society to the post Vedantic period and the laws of

Manu', he went on, 'let us part company at once . . . We must stand by what we call principles of civilised countries, and as far as I understand Mrs Besant's aims, her principles and what I mean by principles of civilisation do not agree in the very least. Nay, they are antagonistic . . .'.[189] Later he pressed it with other objections in a carefully reasoned statement; and it was significant of his assessment of the climate of opinion at the India office that he should have sought to persuade his colleagues by reference to the policy of 1854 and the declared preference for European knowledge. He had abandoned the prejudices of Lord Macaulay, but assumed the continuing validity of the essential principle of the Wood despatch.[190] As before, however, a more liberal note was struck by Sir Theodore Morison. Provided the same conditions could be satisfied, he saw no reason why encouragement should not be given for a university at Benares as at Aligarh. 'All the educational arguments in favour of a teaching University in which a Mohammedan atmosphere prevails hold good of a teaching University in which a Hindu atmosphere prevails', he wrote. 'If the Hindus can arrive at agreement upon the social and religious ideals which they want to impart at Benares they ought to be given a chance of doing so under the conditions already mentioned. If they fail to arrive at agreement, *cadit questio*.'[191]

Hindu initiative enabled his advice to be followed. Later in 1911, a body of orthodox hindus came forward to sponsor the project at Benares, and in October, Harcourt Butler indicated the terms on which government support would be forthcoming.[192] Details were worked out in the following months, and a draft bill was submitted to the government of India exactly a year later.[193] Clause three of the bill, which set out the objects of the university, was clearly based on Mrs Besant's earlier draft charter.[194] It provided that the university should promote 'in a special degree the study of Hindu religion, literature, philosophy, history, medicine and science'; and curiously enough, despite their earlier objections, neither the government of India, nor the India office made any demur at the phraseology.[195] But under the terms of the act as finally passed, the university was deemed to have been incorporated merely for the purpose among others 'of giving instruction in hindu theology and religion, and of promoting the study of literature, art, philosophy, history, medicine and science, and of imparting physical and moral training'.[196] And it was significant that when Sir Harcourt Butler introduced the bill into the legislative council it was the combination of 'the ancient and honoured culture of India with the culture of the modern western world' that he acclaimed.[197] The earlier emphasis on Indian studies had thus been diminished; and the protracted negotiations had served to define the limits of the official encouragement that was to be extended to them.

As in the case of the constitution, however, it was in the planning of the new state university at Dacca that British policy emerged most clearly. Aligarh and Benares had raised the cultural issue in a specialised form, and in terms of general principle. Dacca, on the other hand, called for the interpretation of principle: a detailed scheme that would serve as prototype for other institutions in the development of the university system. But here, too, there were special circumstances. For a specific purpose of the scheme was to mollify the muhammadans and compensate them for the surrender to hindu clamour over partition. That was why Dacca was chosen as the site for the pilot project.[198] And although the educational precocity of the hindus in East Bengal was advanced as one reason for the need of a new centre there, a more compelling consideration was the backwardness of the muhammadans. The new university was designed to supply the want of an institution in which muhammadan needs would be specially catered for, and in the administration of which muhammadans would have a substantial voice. The government of India made this clear in their initial directions to the government of Bengal: and they underlined the point by throwing out the suggestion that special provision might be made for a faculty of islamic studies.[199]

In the course of detailed proposals for the curriculum, the Dacca University Committee gave a prominent place to Indian studies. Taking up the suggestion of the government of India, they recommended that a department of islamic studies should figure as a distinctive feature of the academic organisation.[200] This was to provide a degree course that would be a fitting culmination for the recently reformed madrassa curriculum, comprising the pass degree course in English, together with a course in Arabic and kindred subjects, developed gradually to 'a very high level of attainment'. The islamic side was to be conducted on western scientific lines, but it was to draw on the oriental scholarship of those trained in the traditional way. The aim was to provide 'ripe Arabic scholars who possess in addition a thorough knowledge of English': men of culture who would make good government officers or suitable recruits for the professions. Recognising, however, that the culture would be 'different in kind' from that acquired in the arts department, the committee proposed that the distinctive terminology of bachelor and master of islamic studies should be adopted for the degrees awarded. But they emphasised that the distinction should imply no difference in standard: and that the B.I. and B.A. should rank together for purposes of government employment or proceeding to a professional or higher arts degree.

Despite considerable pressure from the hindu community in East Bengal, the committee rejected the suggestion of a comparable anglo-sanskritic course, based on a tol in Dacca, and a separate department of brahminical studies in the university. If such a course were to be established, they took the view that it should be provided in association with the Sanskrit College in Calcutta. But they were strongly of the opinion that sanskritic studies should be given a prominent place in the new university, and they made recommendations to this effect in their proposals for the arts curriculum.[201] Here, they followed the University of Calcutta in making both English and a vernacular language compulsory for the pass degree course.[202] They attached great importance to the development and teaching of Bengali, urging the use of a wide variety of texts to enrich the vocabulary, and going beyond Calcutta in prescribing classical texts for an alternative part of the post-intermediate course.[203] So far as the other subjects were concerned, their main aim was to improve the quality of the courses in the classical languages of India, and to give the curriculum as a whole a suitable relevance to the Indian setting. To check the neglect of Arabic, as well as to improve the courses in Persian, they prescribed a Persian syllabus which required 'a very thorough knowledge of language and literature and an acquaintance with Persian history'.[204] And as a chief means of reviving interest in Arabic they looked to the stimulating influence of the department of islamic studies which was to assist in the teaching of the senior arts courses. The main stimulus they suggested for sanskritic studies was the encouragement of postgraduate work. They recommended the appointment of three professors for the M.A. classes in Sanskrit as against two for other arts subjects.[205] But they also addressed themselves to the defect Dr Venis had noticed at Simla, and warmly endorsed the proposals made by the sub-committee for bringing the study of Sanskrit at undergraduate level into closer relation with other subjects.[206] In outlining the economics syllabus, the committee showed a special concern for the needs of the Indian student. They stressed the importance of giving descriptive economics a prominent place in the B.A. course, and they urged that particular attention should be paid to local economic conditions and activities in courses at all levels.[207] In history and philosophy, they also provided for the study of Indian aspects; but here, especially in philosophy, they did not press the Indian bias so far.[208]

In forwarding the committee's report to the government of India, the government of Bengal fully endorsed the new emphasis on Indian studies. They defended it against criticism; and pressed it further. The main target of criticism was the proposed department of islamic studies. The syndicate of the University of Calcutta objected that the 'ancient and medieval' studies prescribed were unsuited to modern needs and inappropriately placed in a modern university. Other critics urged that the courses should be absorbed in the arts department and so qualify for the ordinary arts degree. But the government of Bengal would have none of the criticism; and the grounds of their counter-objections provide an ironical commentary on the change that had overtaken British policy. In reply to the syndicate, they made two points, the first as notable for its irrelevance as the second for its novelty. 'If the idea underlying the suggestion is that such studies should not be encouraged', they argued, 'then it is opposed to the policy of the Government which maintains, and has for a long time past maintained, large and expensive madrassas for their encouragement; the only change made in this respect is to improve the instruction and to raise the standard of the examination.' '. . . Arabic is one of the great classical languages of the world', they went on, 'and a profound study of its literature and of the culture of the people which developed it merits among the Muhammadans of India a place at least as important as that which Latin and Greek occupy in the older universities of England.' Passing to the other criticism, they made the further instructive comment that the alternative arrangement proposed would not be effective in encouraging 'the deep study of Moslem culture'. It was in their attitude to Sanskrit studies, however, that the government of Bengal revealed their mind most clearly. Here they went beyond the committee in thinking that the demand for a separate department should be satisfied, and again for a significant reason: that 'professors of Sanskrit and distinguished pandits could thus be brought into close contact and the opportunities for intercourse and co-operation which are afforded by a residential University could be utilised in a very admirable manner to improve Sanskrit studies in both their Western and indigenous aspects'. They suggested, therefore, that both branches of Indian studies, islamic and sanskritic, should be combined in a single oriental department: and that the degrees awarded by the department should be those of bachelor, master and doctor of oriental learning.[209] The government of India concurred in the desirability of this further emphasis on Indian studies[210] and the overall policy received the tacit assent of the India office.[211]

In their proposals for the state university at Dacca, the government of India had given convincing proof of the 'great importance'[212] they attached to oriental studies. They had taken account of the criticism of the Conference of Orientalists in their recommendations for the arts courses. They had prescribed a special degree course in oriental learning for the first time; for although there was already a course which masqueraded under this description at the University of the Punjab, it was merely the customary curriculum of the Indian arts department taught and examined in the vernacular. Still more significant, for it marked a radical change of attitude, the government had made a determined attempt to fertilise the university study of indology with the traditional learning of the maulvis and pandits. And at Dacca, as well as at Aligarh and Benares, they had made the advance with a wary eye on the status of western subjects and methods. They had insisted on the anglo-islamic, anglo-sanskritic character of the new courses in Indian studies, the western scientific method of approach, and the need of a special degree to denote the distinctive character of the culture imparted. If it was British policy to create the new Indian universities in the image of the west so far as type and method were concerned, it had equally come to be British policy to give them a carefully controlled cultural bias to the east.

The cycle of reform set in motion at the beginning of the century had been dramatically accelerated during Sir Harcourt Butler's term of office. Curzon's distant vision of an Indian teaching university had been unexpectedly realised; but it had been realised only in respect of schemes for new universities. There had been no comparable advance in the university system as a whole. The government of India had made further grants for postgraduate teaching facilities at the older universities, and Sir Asutosh Mookerjee had put Calcutta in the van of this new development. But as the viceroy, Lord Hardinge, frankly admitted in a chancellorial address to the University of Calcutta in 1915,[213] the metamorphosis of the affiliating university had barely begun. The key to it had still to be found. And meantime, although the worst of the abuses of the affiliating system had been removed by the legislation of 1904, and the affiliating universities were already turning towards some of the new policies proposed for the teaching universities, the essential defects of the system remained. At Calcutta, indeed, where the pressure of numbers continued to grow, the picture was very little changed from what it had been in Curzon's day. If the cycle of reform were to be carried to a fitting conclusion, a more fundamental approach was called for: one which would tackle the aridity of the desert on a broad front and not merely by way of a series of alleviating oases.

CHAPTER FIVE

A REDEFINITION

I THE CALCUTTA UNIVERSITY COMMISSION

The momentum behind the new phase of reform ushered in by the appointment of Harcourt Butler died away in the early years of the war. Shortage of funds, coupled with the policy of avoiding controversial legislation in wartime, inevitably put a curb on further experiment. But indirectly the war was also responsible for stimulating a fresh phase of development which, in the sphere of planning at least, was to complete the evolutionary cycle of reform initiated at the beginning of the century. By creating a new respect for political liberty and so forcing the pace of constitutional advance, as well as by placing Britain in debt to her Indian subjects for their contribution to the war effort, it provided an exactly similar impetus for educational development in India that world war II was to provide in the colonial dependencies of the empire nearly a generation later. In August 1917 the secretary of state made his momentous declaration in the house of commons that the policy of his majesty's government was that of 'the increasing association of Indians in every branch of the administration, and the gradual development of self-governing institutions, with a view to the progressive realisation of responsible Government in India as an integral part of the British Empire'.[1] Barely a month later, the government of India announced their decision to appoint a commission 'to enquire into the condition and prospects of the University of Calcutta . . .'.[2] There was no public indication of any connection between the two pronouncements. But in raising the question of an enquiry with the secretary of state, the viceroy, Lord Chelmsford, had already confided his hope of solving 'the big political problems through the solution of the educational problems'[3]; and in issuing invitations to serve on the commission, the secretary of state, Austen Chamberlain, had made it abundantly clear that the government had in view 'the desirability of raising the standard of higher education in India to meet the needs of new political ideals'.[4]

Hitherto, every committee or commission which had advised on the developconment of higher education in India had borne a distinctly official character, but there was now a significant break with tradition. Lord Chelmsford was convinced of the need for a commission which should have 'no political side to it at all but which would be entirely composed of educationalists of the highest stamp'.[5] He accordingly sought the assistance of the secretary of state in finding a chairman, and a proportion of the members, from those 'fully acquainted with recent developments of university education in the United Kingdom'.[6] To fill the post of chairman, Chamberlain turned instinctively to the man who had recently directed the massive enquiry into the English university which had served as prototype for the universities in India. But Haldane refused;[7] and Chamberlain was then able to make the happier choice of Michael Sadler whom Curzon had already tried to entice out to India as educational adviser nearly twenty years before.[8] Sadler was now vice-chancellor of the University of Leeds, and peculiarly well fitted to lead the commission in India, both on account of his personal qualities and his unique educational experience. Three other members were chosen from England to serve with him: P. J. Hartog, who as academic registrar of the University of London since 1903 had been deeply involved in precisely the sort of reconstruction that faced the University of Calcutta; Ramsay Muir, professor of modern history at the University of Manchester, who had recently gained an insight into the problems of Indian higher education as a 'cold weather' lecturer at Lahore;[9] and J. W. Gregory, professor of geology at the University of Glasgow. To these members, the government of India added three more, all chosen for their acquaintance with the special conditions in India: W. W. Hornell, director of public instruction in Bengal, and the only official on the commission; Zia-ud-din Ahmad, professor of mathematics at the Muhammadan Anglo-Oriental College in Aligarh; and the dominating figure in Indian higher education, who had already advised the commission of 1902 as well as the Dacca University Committee, and who had served four terms as vice-chancellor of the University of Calcutta, Sir Asutosh Mookerjee.

The commission were invited to focus their enquiry on the problems of Bengal.[10] They were empowered to examine the existing organisation of the University of Calcutta with special reference to its standards and examinations, its constitution, its relations with the affiliated colleges and with the government; and to recommend 'any changes of constitution, administration and educational policy which may appear desirable'. They were also empowered to consider 'at what places and in what manner provision should be made in Bengal for teaching and research for persons above the secondary school age'. But it was clear from the further suggestion that they might like to extend their enquiries to other universities in India 'for purposes of comparison' that they were expected to frame a body of recommendations that would be relevant to the university system as a whole: that if the government of India had chosen to concentrate on the problems of Bengal because it was there that the defects of the affiliating university were most acute, it was also because Bengal offered a representative cross section of the problems which called for solution in Indian higher education.

Sadler went out to India deeply impressed by the importance of the task which lay ahead of the commission: '. . . *the* most important task in India (not in Bengal only)', he wrote in May 1918, 'one of the three or four most difficult tasks in the world; vitally and crucially urgent for the Empire and (what is more) for civilisation at this juncture . . .'.[11] Like Curzon at the turn of the century, he was profoundly shocked by the education he found.[12] At the close of an exhaustive enquiry, he and his colleagues, franker than their predecessors in 1902, pronounced the university system of Bengal 'fundamentally defective in almost every aspect'.[13] To remedy the ills of the system, as well as to provide for the political and economic development in prospect, they too saw the high quality teaching university as the essential need in India.[14] They conceived it as their task, therefore, to give sharp outlines to what Curzon had left blurred: to build on to what Sir Harcourt Butler had achieved by reviewing afresh the scheme for a unitary teaching university at Dacca and prescribing in detail for the transformation of the affiliating university at Calcutta. And bearing in mind the suggestion made by the government of India, they sought to give their recommendations a general validity by framing them against the background of the university system as a whole.[15]

But as educationalists rather than politicians or administrators, they brought a new sensitivity to the cultural issue involved. Unlike Curzon, they did not seek a solution to India's problems in terms of a shadowy approximation to Oxford or Cambridge; nor did they grope empirically towards a policy which should take account of the ancient culture of the east as well as the modern aspirations of the west. They followed Sir Harcourt Butler in making this their specific aim; and they went beyond him both in attempting a closer definition of it and making it their central objective. It was not merely 'an administrative solution' they sought, but 'an intellectual synthesis' and 'a moral reconciliation'[16]; and they enlarged on their purpose, with a tactful diplomacy, by quoting with sympathy the views of the Indian principal of Ripon College, R. S. Trivedi.[17] In a remarkably perceptive memorandum,[18] Trivedi reflected on the merits and demerits of the type of university Britain had planted in India, and the need to reshape it in face of the new forces released by the spread of western learning. Under the influence of western thought and culture, he wrote, India was astir with the promptings of a new life and 'striving to bring forth a type of Indian humanity which, broadly and securely based on the foundations of its own special culture, will assert itself in the presence of the manhood of the world'. But as 'a foreign plant', paying all too little regard to the culture and traditions of an ancient people, the Indian university in its existing form was singularly ill adapted to assist in the birth of this new life. He pleaded, therefore, for a careful comparative study of the educational ideals of the east and west so that a new policy might be evolved, more closely attuned to India's special needs. He did not attempt to suggest the lines of this new policy, but he pointed briefly to the way in which the university system imported from abroad had violated the characteristic ideals of the east. Whereas the indigenous system was prescribed by the Indian scriptures and inspired by a religious purpose, the imported system was shaped to the secular needs of the state. Higher education as a result was no longer freely available to all; it was no longer marked by a close relationship between the teacher and his pupil; no longer screened from interference by the state. The ideal of learning for its own sake had become sadly obscured, and the whole process of higher education reduced to 'a series of sifting operations for the selection of useful and competent servants for the State. . . '. 'Western education has given us much', he concluded, 'we have been great gainers; but there has been a cost, a cost as regards culture, a cost as regards respect for self and reverence for others, a cost as regards the nobility and dignity of life.' The commission readily acknowledged the justice of his criticism, although they insisted that the ideals he had cited as characteristic of the east were equally to be found as persistent threads in the educational policy of the west. They warmly endorsed his plea for a new departure in higher education in India; and in expressing the belief that the drastic changes they had proposed would enable university teachers 'to combine what was best in the ancient traditions of India with what is best in the educational aspirations of the West', indicated that it was just such a synthesis as he had envisaged which had inspired the recommendations of their report.[19]

Constitution   In the constitutional sphere, the commission proposed radical changes. Addressing themselves primarily to the outstanding problem at Calcutta, they devised a detailed scheme for transforming the overgrown affiliating university into a viable teaching institution. But in doing so, they did more than prescribe a new relationship between the university and its component colleges. They prescribed a new form of university government, and a new connection between the university and the state. Thus in catering for the special needs of Calcutta, they not only supplied the key to the metamorphosis of the affiliating university: they supplied also the constitutional formula for a new and more ambitious type of teaching university. The government of India, planning for Dacca, had taken the view that both as regards internal government and external control, the existing practice of the affiliating university afforded a broadly suitable precedent for the teaching university. But the commission, striving to put a new interpretation on the teaching university, judged it fundamentally inappropriate.

   Their immediate problem in replanning the University of Calcutta was to decide between the competing claims of the unitary and federal structure. They were in no doubt as to the superiority of the centralised form where this was possible; they recommended it for Dacca, and they expressed the hope it would be adopted for any other new universities established in Bengal.[20] But they were quickly agreed 'as to the inapplicability of doctrinaire theories of the so called "Unitary University" ' to the complex conditions of Calcutta.[21] In view of the vast student members, the strong collegiate traditions, and the differing requirements of the metropolis and the mufassal they were convinced that a single centralised organisation was 'at once unattainable and undesirable'.[22] And since they were equally persuaded that the creation of new universities within the area of the existing jurisdiction of the University of Calcutta was immediately impractical,[23] they concluded that the basic framework of the new teaching university must be multicollegiate. In deciding on a federal structure, however, they drew a careful distinction between the organisation they proposed for the colleges in Calcutta, and those situated in the outlying districts.

For the colleges in Calcutta, which would form the core of the teaching university, they prescribed 'a university of colleges superficially resembling Oxford and Cambridge, and, more closely, the reconstructed University of London'; though even as they made the comparison they underlined the qualification by emphasising that 'in many respects' the analogy with Oxford and Cambridge and even with London, would not hold, and might be misleading.[24] In its main features, however, the organisation they envisaged bore a striking similarity to the reformed structure of the University of London; and in speaking of it shortly after his return from India, Hartog acknowledged that it had been shaped to a pattern which from experience in London they knew to be viable.[25] Their proposal, in essence, was for a federal university of 'constituent' colleges. In place of the affiliating system of isolated self-contained colleges submitting to the dictates of a university in whose government they had no assured representation, they prescribed a system of inter-collegiate co-operation, guided by a university in which each college would be a full member and partner.[26] It was a concept wholly unfamiliar to India; and the commission therefore explained the implications of their scheme in some detail. They dwelt in particular on the new role they envisaged for the colleges,[27] outlining the wider and more varied tuitional functions they would be called upon to perform, the new requirements they would need to fulfil to qualify for constituent status, and the privileges they would be accorded in return. They also outlined the special role they conceived for the university,[28] indicating how it would be called upon to supplement the resources of the colleges, assist in the collegiate teaching, and perform in a modified way its former functions of defining the curricula, conducting the examinations, and exercising an overall direction of policy. Whilst the university would thus acquire more effective control over the instruction given in its name, the colleges would obtain more real freedom to develop the quality of their teaching. It was this latter consideration which the commission regarded as the really vital one. They repeatedly stressed the importance they attached to increasing the strength and prestige of the colleges; and they left it in no doubt that the success of their proposals would depend on the ability of the colleges to respond to the new and higher ideal placed before them 'of being free co-operating partners in a great enterprise, each making its own

distinctive contribution to the common strength and each enriched by the
strength of its fellows'.[29]

Such a federal system was admirably adapted to the strong collegiate
tradition in Indian higher education; but the commission did not propose
that it should be extended to the colleges of the mufassal.[30] Fearing for the
standards of the university if this were done, they recommended that the
outlying colleges should be separately administered by a special board of the
university which would be responsible for conducting examinations on different curricula but a broadly equivalent standard. The mufassal colleges
were to be represented on this board; but otherwise the connection with the
university was to be of the old affiliating type. The commission prescribed
this variation of a discredited system with some reluctance; but it was to be a
reactionary agent in a liberal purpose. For the commission conceived this
subsidiary organisation as a means of fostering the nuclei of new universities –
universities which they hoped would be unitary, but whose form they were
careful not to prejudge – and their aim in doing so was not merely to reduce
the unwieldy proportions of the University of Calcutta, but to adapt the
university system more closely to its immediate environment. They wished to
see the University of Calcutta 'genuinely a city University', intimately associated with the city life going on around it, and specialising in those studies most
conveniently and usefully pursued in a city milieu.[31] And they acknowledged
a similar purpose in the mufassal although they did not state it with quite the
same clarity. Despite their reluctance to saddle the new teaching university
with an affiliating organisation even of a modified kind, they welcomed the
prospect it offered of bringing relevance and variety into the academic life of
the mufassal. They looked to the new board to frame courses more suited to
the mufassal colleges: and whilst to begin with they envisaged little more than
adaptation to limited resources, they hinted at adaptation of a more thoroughgoing kind for the future. They had made special arrangements to assist the
rise of the more active and progressive colleges to university status; and in
referring to the greater degree of autonomy provided for them, expressed the
hope that they would take advantage of it 'to devise special courses suited to
the needs of their own students or of their own districts'.[32] So that for these
colleges, too, the commission held out a new and inspiring prospect: that of
playing, ultimately as full universities, 'a great and distinctive part in the
intellectual progress of their own districts, and of Bengal as a whole'.[33]

In redrawing the structure of the university, the commission had concentrated on two main objectives: providing the larger measure of freedom
and responsibility called for in the teaching body of a teaching university, and
stimulating the growth of a university system that would be more responsive
to the needs of the community it served. And it was these same two objectives
they kept chiefly in mind in prescribing for the government of the university.
Here they were more dogmatic, prefacing their recommendations with a bold
definition of the theory of university government drawn from the practice of

the civic universities in Britain. 'A university needs, for its proper governance, bodies of three kinds', they wrote. 'In the first place, in order that it may be kept in touch with the community which it exists to serve, it needs a large body, widely representative of all the varied interests which are affected by university work ... In the second place, a great university which deals with many complex matters needs a small and efficient administrative body, including men with a wide knowledge of affairs, who will be especially responsible for finance and for the conduct of general policy ... But the most essential element in the structure of a teaching university is a strong body, or series of bodies, representing the teachers and endowed with large independent powers in all purely academic matters ...'[34] Applying these criteria to the constitution of the University of Calcutta, they found it seriously wanting in all three respects.[35] The senate, because of the duties assigned to it, had to be kept within limits which prevented it from being sufficiently representative of the life and interests of Bengal. The syndicate, whilst congested by all manner of miscellaneous business, was denied the powers and responsibility appropriate to the executive body of a great university. And most serious of all, there was no provision for 'any authoritative direction by a body of scholars'.[36] Responsibility for academic affairs rested with the senate; but because of its other responsibilities, the senate included a lay element which deprived it of 'the special character and value of an expert academic body'.[37] Nor could the faculties and boards of studies lay claim to such a character; for each were in effect standing committees of the senate and thus liable both to include non-specialists and exclude distinguished and experienced teachers. For the University of Calcutta, therefore, and for the University of Dacca, the commission prescribed a form of government which differed radically from the official prescription hitherto. In place of the senate and syndicate of the old system, they proposed three new organs of the type they had already foreshadowed. And to mark the change and avoid confusion, they chose to give them the designation, new to India, of 'court', 'executive council', and 'academic council'.[38]

The most significant feature of their recommendations was the proposal to assign responsibility for academic affairs to a hierarchy of expert academic bodies.[39] In providing for an 'academic council' or supreme academic body, they were providing for a body which, as they stressed themselves, had never before existed in any Indian university of the older type; and whilst faculties and subsidiary boards were to survive in name from the older system, they were now to be composed, like the academic council, almost exclusively of teachers. Collectively, these bodies were to have a 'predominant voice' over curricula and examinations, and a 'very great, though not decisive, influence' in other matters affecting teaching.[40] For the University of Calcutta they envisaged an academic council of some 80–100 members, so constituted as to include representatives of all the constituent colleges, representatives of all the chief subjects, and all the most distinguished teachers. And in outlining its functions both in relation to the central teaching organisation, and those sections of the university which lay outside, they emphasised the high importance and responsibility of its role. Here, indeed, was to be the 'real heart' of the university:[41] 'the main pivot of the new system of teaching which we advocate'.[42]

Their recommendations for the 'court' or supreme governing body were hardly less significant.[43] For this was to be a body so differently constituted and empowered from the senate of the Indian Universities Act, or indeed the convocation planned for Dacca, that again the change promised to bring new and important influences to bear on the shaping of the university system. The commission were insistent that the court should be representative of 'every important element in the public opinion of the areas specially served by the University, and every kind of expert judgement whose criticism on university policy would be of value'. To ensure this wide and comprehensive representation, they recommended that membership should be assigned largely by *ex officio* status and election, rather than by nomination as hitherto. And it was perhaps significant of their purpose that in indicating the sort of body they had in mind, they should have been more concerned to define the categories of opinion that called for representation than to fix their relative proportions. They did not prescribe any specific balance between the academic and non-academic elements; nor did they provide the data from which this could be deduced. But although they did not attempt to suggest a precise numerical strength for the various constituent elements, they emphasised that the total membership must be large. To enable the court at Calcutta to be representative of 'all that was best in the intellectual life of Bengal',[44] they envisaged a body of not less than four or five hundred members, with a quorum of not less than fifty.

Despite its size, it was to exercise 'a real influence and ultimate control' over university policy.[45] The commission considered that its main functions should be those of 'watchfulness and criticism, and of keeping the University in touch with the movements of public opinion on educational questions',[46] and to enable it to discharge these functions with effect, they proposed that the court receive an annual report from the executive and academic councils, together with a full statement of the accounts. They also assigned it important legislative functions, recommending that its assent should be required to the ordinances made by the executive council as well as the proposals submitted by it for changes in the statutes. But this was not all. They provided in addition that it should exercise effective supervision over university finance by means of a standing committee of reference. This was especially significant: not only because university finance, as the commission themselves acknowledged, 'in so many cases involves policy';[47] but because, as Hartog was to point out later, it was a deliberate departure from what was customary in the corresponding courts of English universities.[48] Neither he nor they offered any explanation of the deviation. But to give a governing body so fully representative of Indian opinion a real voice in the shaping of university policy was well calculated to turn 'the university system of Bengal into a living and growing system, which has to render to the community services far greater and more varied than it has hitherto been able to render'.[49] It was admirably designed to generate a continuing process of adaptation.

Passing to the nature of the relationship between the universities and the government, the commission prescribed a further change of policy which mirrored their purpose still more clearly. For here they specifically related their recommendations to the new role they conceived for the universities, emphasising that the degree of control appropriate for an affiliating university primarily concerned with administrative functions delegated by the state, was no longer necessary or desirable for a teaching university primarily devoted to the pursuit of learning.[50] Critical of the existing degree of control on the grounds that it was too rigid even for an affiliating university[51] – and still more critical of the proposal to resort to direct state control at Dacca[52] – they insisted that an entirely new form of government supervision was required if the teaching university in India were to be assured of its essential freedom to teach.

In prescribing this new form of supervision, they aimed at a type of control that would not only increase the freedom of the universities, but enable the government to play a more valuable part in the shaping of the university system.[53] The government were to discharge the same basic responsibilities.[54] As trustees for 'the highest training grounds of the nation', they would continue to be responsible for the form in which the universities were established; and thereafter for ensuring that standards were properly maintained and finances properly administered. It would continue to be a special part of their function to safeguard the rights of the various classes and communities in India and to co-ordinate the development of the university system as a whole. But these responsibilities were to be discharged in a very different way: less directly, with the help of new methods and machinery, and in accordance with a fresh allocation of powers between the local and central governments.

In the case of both Calcutta and Dacca, immediate responsibility was assigned to the local government.[55] Following the practice of the modern universities in England, the assent of the government of Bengal was to be required to all changes in regulations dealing with broad and fundamental questions. Hitherto, no distinction had been drawn between the relative importance of regulations, and all, even the most trivial, had been subject to government approval. But they were now to be graded; and only 'statutes', as opposed to 'ordinances' and 'regulations', were to require government confirmation. The government of Bengal were similarly to exercise a general but not a detailed control over university finance. They were to issue block grants on an annual basis, and these the universities were to be free to spend subject only to an annual return of expenditure. Since, however, the bulk of the cost of the universities was to be met by the state, the government of Bengal were to have a small direct representation on their governing bodies. The governor of Bengal was to be *ex officio* chancellor of each university: and it was to be his special task to hold the balance between the various classes and interests calling for representation in them. To enable him to do so, 'ordinances' were to be subject to his veto, and he was to have power to nominate members to the main governing bodies of the universities, and appoint the external experts that were to be included on the staff selection committees proposed. As a further safeguard in the face of so many potentially conflicting elements, he was additionally empowered to appoint a committee of enquiry on appeal from any aggrieved party, and to communicate its findings to the executive council.

Despite the trend to devolution in the political sphere, the commission reserved important powers and responsibilities for the central government.[56] Indeed, regarding the problem of higher education in India as increasingly an all-India one,[57] they represented an effective co-ordinating influence at the centre as more vitally necessary than before. In view of the number of new universities likely to be created in the future, they strongly recommended that the power of passing acts or charters bringing them into existence should remain with the government of India: only in this way would it be possible to ensure 'a reasonable degree of unity' in the university system, and 'a standard of training such as will be respected and recognised throughout the world'.[58] And they went on to suggest new powers and duties for the government of India, all designed to bring a more bracing and constructive influence to bear on the development of the university system. To assist the maintenance of a proper academic standard, as well as to keep the whole system under review, they recommended that the 'visitorial power . . . inherent in the Governments of all countries' should be vested in the governor general, and that a committee 'including at least one distinguished scholar from overseas, with experience of university methods and organisation in various countries' should conduct a periodic visitation of the universities throughout India.[59] The commission also proposed the creation of a central organisation to meet the new needs created by the rapid expansion and changing character of the university system. They envisaged a variety of functions for this organisation, but prominent amongst them were the co-ordination of specialist training in such subjects as agriculture and technology, and the promotion and subsidy of projects of research, as for instance 'the production of a great series of *monumenta historica Indica*', comparable to the similar publications prepared under government auspices in England.[60]

Two further proposals emphasised the new measure of autonomy the commission judged necessary for the teaching university; and each promised a decisive break with the past. Just as they had rejected the notion of direct state control for the teaching university – and called for a drastic change in the plans for Dacca – so they rejected it for the college engaged in university teaching. For a number of reasons, but more especially the one Sir Theodore

Morison had advanced in the council of India some years before,[61] they recommended that all government colleges, including the premier Presidency College, should gradually be made over to independent management.[62] They proposed too, therefore, that the service system of staffing hitherto adopted in all government controlled colleges should be abandoned; and that in future all university posts should be individually and independently filled by the governing bodies of the universities and colleges concerned.[63] The commission attached great importance to this latter aspect of their recommendation. They urged that it would facilitater ecruitment, since the claims of seniority would no longer need to be considered; supply the incentive to scholarship which had been wanting in a system where all the more senior posts lay in the sphere of administration; and above all enable the staff to command a greater loyalty from their students, and exert a wider and more effective social influence. 'A body of university teachers of this character', they wrote, 'well selected, holding their posts by a secure tenure, and therefore independent, would form an element in the shaping of public thought in India the value of which it is impossible to over-estimate. One of the greatest defects of the service system has been the fact that their very position as Government officers has robbed members of the services of the influence upon opinion which they ought to be able to exercise, and has precluded them from the expression of their judgement upon many questions on which it would have carried very great weight.'[64]

The other proposal was designed to free the university system from an indirect but more sinister influence exerted by the government: the influence stemming from the acceptance of university examinations as sufficient test for entry into the public service. Although Sir Charles Wood had approved the imposition of additional tests 'where practicable', this had been done only to a very limited extent[65]; and by the end of the century, the system of nomination in conjunction with university qualifications had produced such pressure on government posts that the secretary of state, with a reference to the possible political danger involved, had intervened to suggest the alternative of separate government examinations.[66] The proposal was discussed at the Simla conference of 1901, but Curzon and his advisers took the view that it would adversely affect the universities, and divert 'the main stream of educational effort ... into a narrow and sordid channel'.[67] The system went on unchanged, therefore, and it was within the main stream itself that pollution developed. University classes came to be flooded by inferior students who aimed no higher than a minor post in the government; and the whole character of university work was increasingly vitiated by a system which attracted students not so much to learn as simply to gain a foothold in the public services. Many witnesses before the commission offered a crushing indictment of the system, representing it as a chief cause of the deterioration in university scholarship, and a major obstacle in the way of reform. 'All the evils existing under the present system are mostly attributable to university degrees being considered as passports to places under Government service' was the emphatic opinion of one correspondent;[68] whilst another concluded that true progress and advancement of learning must be 'out of the question' so long as a university degree was to be treated as 'a bridge to a post under Government'.[69] Fully sympathising with the concern of such critics, the commission prescribed a characteristically skilful solution to the problem Curzon had dismissed so lightly at the beginning of the century.[70] They proposed that recruitment to the public services in future should be by way of special competitive tests closely related to the existing educational system. Small civil service commissions should be appointed by the central and local governments; and these should then classify the posts open to competition, define the level of educational attainment required as a preliminary qualification, and prescribe and conduct a series of supplementary competitive tests. Such a system, they claimed, would be advantageous alike to the students, the educational system and the public services: in particular it would relieve the universities of a host of ill-equipped students who would seek admission to the services at an earlier stage and so free the universities to concentrate on serious scholarship. It was a system which they also re-presented as 'a return to the sound principles enumerated in the great despatch of 1854';[71] but here they were more modest, for in fact they could claim to have given clarity and compulsion to what Wood had left vague and per-missive.

In their constitutional proposals, the commission had thus drawn heavily on the practice of the west. In reconstructing the University of Calcutta, they had been closely influenced by the recent precedent afforded by the University of London. In proposing a new form of government, they had confidently prescribed the 'two-tier' pattern of the British civic university which hitherto had been considered too complex for India.[72] Moreover they had advanced a peculiarly British interpretation of the concept of university autonomy: discreetly ignoring the political difficulties in India, they had disallowed the earlier contention of the government of India and endorsed the opposite conviction of the India office.[73] Yet they had been careful to underplay this aspect of their recommendations, to demonstrate their awareness that analo-gies between east and west could not be pressed too far, and to offer their proposals as specially adapted to the peculiar environment of India. Nor was this mere tactful presentation. In many instances, they had in fact shaped British practice to Indian requirements; and where they had not, there were often underlying affinities to warrant the conformity. They had adapted the constitutional pattern of the civic university to give enhanced power and status to the court; they had assigned special arbitral functions to the chan-cellor, and permitted the government a more immediate influence than was the practice at home. In each case the modification was an acknowledgement of special features in the Indian situation. But in conceiving the University of Calcutta as a great city university like the modern universities of the west they had done no more than recognise the logic of its urban setting;[74] whilst in conceiving the Indian teaching university as a corporate body of learning enjoying a large measure of freedom from state control, they were seeking an ideal 'not less faithful to the best Indian traditions' for being in harmony with the 'educational aspirations of the West'.[75]

Standards   In a further series of proposals more specifically directed towards improving the quality of university training, the commission recommended a bold departure from existing practice, though by no means a radical change in official policy. For with one notable exception, the policies they proposed for the university system as a whole were largely an elaboration of the policies already approved for the teaching university at Dacca. And even the exception had been clearly foreshadowed in the earlier official discussions on that scheme.

The exception was an urgent recommendation to raise the level of entry to the university. In planning for Dacca, the government of India had reluctantly concluded that such a reform would be premature;[76] but the commission now insisted that it was a matter of the highest priority, an essential pre-condition of any successful reconstruction of the university system.[77] They proposed that the intermediate examination should be made the point of entry to the university instead of the existing matriculation, and that the intermediate courses should be put back into the schools.[78] But they did not regard this as sufficient reform in itself. They urged that it should be accompanied by changes in the nature of the intermediate courses, and a fundamental reorganisation of the system of secondary education. They proposed that the intermediate courses should offer a wide variety of vocational training as well as a sound liberal education,[79] and that they should be provided in some thirty to forty specially constituted 'intermediate colleges'.[80] They recommended that a few of these should be self-contained, but the majority attached to selected high schools; and that both colleges and high schools should be administered by a new and independently controlled board of secondary and intermediate education.[81] The commission hoped in this way that many students would be diverted to practical careers more suited to their ability, and that fewer, better equipped students would go on to the university. But they were well aware that a scheme specifically designed to relieve the congestion in the university classes was peculiarly liable to misconstruction by Bengali opinion. They were careful to explain that it was not as 'a limiting or restrictive measure' that they had proposed the new line of demarcation between school and university, but as one which would 'liberate for other and more fruitful use two important, and often misdirected, years in a student's life'.[82] They also commended their proposals by a nicely balanced reference to the experience and practice of the west. They recalled that many universities of the west had dropped their elementary classes as they entered more fully upon their right province in higher education; that 'good precedent' for assigning higher secondary education to 'colleges' could be found in some of the most famous schools in the west: 'for example, Winchester and Eton among the ancient foundations; Marlborough, Haileybury and Clifton, among the new'.[83] But they were no less ready to invoke a departure from western precedent where it could be shown to be inspired by the special circumstances of the presidency. Acknowledging that the proposed board of secondary and intermediate education had 'no exact counterpart either in India or the West',[84] they represented it as specially adapted to the peculiar conditions in Bengal where there were no such safeguards against excessive government control as there were in England.

Having prescribed a new level of entry to the university, the commission went on to prescribe important changes in the structure of its degree courses. No longer hampered by the Calcutta matriculation standard, they were able to recommend that the basic degree courses in arts and science should be extended from two years to three: the honours courses at once, and the pass courses as soon as the intermediate classes had been transferred to the schools.[85] Again there was the persuasive reference to the experience of the west which seemed to show that 'a generous and well-balanced scheme of training in the arts or the sciences cannot well be fitted into a shorter period . . .'.[86] They also recommended significant changes in the character of the courses: but here they did little more than endorse the main proposals of the Dacca University Committee. They made out a more reasoned case for the reforms they recommended; they indicated in more detail how they might be carried out. But the reforms themselves were essentially the same.

The defect they most deplored in the existing system was the neglect of the abler student. Pointing to the poverty and scarcity of the honours courses, they pronounced this disregard of the needs of the élite as 'not only the most disheartening, but the most dangerous, feature of the educational life of Bengal'. 'For the fate and fortunes of every people depend upon the opportunities which it affords to its ablest sons, who must be the leaders and guides of the next generation in every field of activity', they wrote. 'And while a soundly devised educational system will not neglect the training of the ordinary mass of men, any system stands self-condemned which fails to make itself a means of selecting men of promise and of affording to them every possible opportunity of bringing their powers to full fruition. . . .'[87] Like the Dacca University Committee, therefore, they recommended the provision of clearly differentiated honours courses; and they looked to the new system of intercollegiate teaching they proposed to make them generally available.[88] But in making the recommendation, they at once entered a caution against the danger of over-specialisation. The honours course, they stressed, had no need to be highly specialised. Save in certain science subjects, a high degree of specialisation was undesirable. This type of course should be distinguished not by its range – which might even be wider than the pass course – but by a more closely articulated content, and by a method of teaching which called for more intellectual effort on the part of the student.[89] The main defect they diagnosed in the pass courses was the 'grotesquely unconnected groups of subjects' devised by the misplaced ingenuity of the student seeking an easy passage to his degree, so that again their recipe was that of the Dacca committee: a careful co-ordination of the constitutent parts of the course.[90] But both here, and in their recommendations for the honours degrees, they went beyond the committee in prescribing new administrative machinery to give effect to their proposals. They suggested that each of the main pass groups of subjects might be placed under the direction of a special 'committee on courses'; and since they envisaged no honours course so specialised as to be confined to a single subject, they proposed that each of the main honours schools should be placed under a similar body.[91]

In the postgraduate sphere, they had few changes to suggest. They followed up their recommendations for the honours courses by prescribing a variant pattern for the masters degree. They proposed that the new honours graduate should be permitted to take the degree within one year of graduating instead of two; and that instead of following a systematic course of instruction and sitting a written examination, he should be allowed to present an original piece of work.[92] But in general, it was expansion rather than reform that they looked for at this level: a vigorous development of postgraduate study and research, with generous provision for the maintenance of the advanced student.[93]

The commission also prescribed for the quality of the teaching, offering detailed recommendations both in regard to the recruitment of staff and to teaching methods. In place of the service system of recruitment on which the Dacca planners had relied, they proposed that all teaching posts should be individually filled by specially constituted selection committees.[94] In the case of senior posts, they suggested that these committees should include the vice-chancellor, representatives from the academic and executive councils, a high official appointed by the chancellor, and three experts in the subject from outside, also appointed by the chancellor. They acknowledged that such a method might seem unduly elaborate; but they insisted that 'too much care' could not be taken in the appointment of university teachers.[95] They added, besides, that a 'very similar device' had been successfully adopted in the University of London.[96] This, however, was not their only recommendation. They were strongly impressed by the need to attract more western-trained scholars to India; and so long as English figured prominently in the curriculum, especially concerned to attract more Englishmen.[97] Like the Dacca University Committee, therefore, they made special provisions to ensure a steady flow of teachers from the west. In prescribing for Calcutta, they suggested that a number of chairs and readerships should be specially set aside for this purpose in Presidency College, which had a unique tradition, through its western-trained staff of 'keeping Bengal students in touch with the constantly changing methods and outlook of western learning . . .'.[98]

They made a similar recommendation for Dacca so that the new university might be 'started on right lines'.[99] Such posts, they suggested, should be filled not in India but in England. Like many similar posts in the dominions, they should be filled by the secretary of state acting on the advice of a specialist committee which would include representatives from the university and college concerned. Western-trained Indians would be eligible for such posts, and it would be for the university and college seeking the appointment to forward details of any Indians they wished to be considered. In this way they hoped to secure 'a steady recruitment of western-trained teachers of high ability ... without indue invasion of the prerogatives of the University or the College, and without overlooking the claims of suitable candidates in India'.[100]

In regard to teaching methods, the commission again reinforced the views of the Dacca committee, pressing as they had done for fewer, better lectures, supplemented, as an essential part of the instruction, by class work, library work, and above all tutorial guidance which connoted a real and intimate contact between teacher and student.[101] The commission attached even greater importance to the development of the tutorial system than the committee, adducing fresh arguments in favour of it, and representing it, characteristically, as peculiarly well suited to take root in Indian soil. However anomalous the tutorial system might have been in the mechanically contrived training of the past, they were emphatic that it was indispensable to the higher type of education they were striving for.[102] And they ventured to add a further persuasive argument in support of it from the political context of the times. ' ... of all the present day needs of Bengal', they wrote, 'none is greater than the need of just such wise and sympathetic guidance for its ardent young men, who find themselves, when they plunge into the learning of the West, often adrift without rudder or compass; eager to serve their country, but having no one to give them counsel as to how they can best use themselves for her service. In their fresh and easily lighted enthusiasms, students are very apt to be led into wild and dangerous courses, from which they would often be saved if they could talk freely to older and wiser men. But in the places to which they now go to learn wisdom, no such chance is offered to them, only an endless routine of lectures ... ' The commission did not dispute that the tutorial system was peculiarly an English tradition. It was partly for this reason that they wished to enlist more English teachers in the service of Indian higher education. But they also recalled that it was 'closely akin with an ancient Indian tradition':[103] an old and characteristic skill to be rediscovered, not a new and possibly uncongenial one to be acquired. Already, in the smaller numbers of the scientific laboratories, they detected the symptoms of rediscovery. 'May we not therefore hope', they asked 'that, given favourable opportunities, it might very readily grow up and thrive in the colleges of Bengal?'[104]

The commission had made their essential recommendation for the examining system when they prescribed the substitution of the teaching university for the affiliating one. But, like the Dacca committee, they also suggested a number of reforms more immediately concerned with the examining process: reforms not only designed to remedy the 'sterilising tyranny' of the existing system, but also its inefficiency, and in particular its failure to uphold a proper academic standard.[105] They began, like the committee, by prescribing changes in the machinery of the examining. Here they had little to add. They proposed, as the committee had done, that for all degree examinations, 'teachers actually engaged in the teaching for the degree in question' should be included in the boards of examiners.[106] This, they hoped, would ensure that the tests would be suitably subordinated to the teaching, and easily adapted to its changing needs.[107] They also proposed, and rather more insistently than the committee, that as a safeguard of standards, the board should 'always, if practicable', include one or more external examiners.[108] But fired by the enthusiasm of P. J. Hartog, who had made a special study of the science of examining, the commission went on to pursue the quality of the examining system more closely. As an essential preliminary to reform, they urged a systematic review of all university examinations to ensure that the purpose of each was clearly defined.[109] They also recommended that a special 'examinations board' should be set up with inspecting and advisory powers to keep the working of the whole examining system under continuous review. It was to suggest improvements as well as uncover defects; and it was to assume a special responsibility for safeguarding standards.[110] It was a wholly novel device, which owed nothing to western precedent: for as the commission themselves observed, it was the 'somewhat remarkable' fact that no university had hitherto devoted itself to 'a systematic audit and survey of its own examination system in the same way that a large firm periodically audits its accounts'.[111]

The scheme planned for Dacca had been conceived in deliberate reaction from the type of university India had known before. It had been designed to provide a fuller and more comprehensive education than the affiliating university: a moral and physical training, as well as a higher intellectual training. In pursuit of this wider aim, the Dacca committee had given careful thought to the interpretation of the residential principle; they had acknowledged the importance of fostering a corporate life in the university, and they had put a novel emphasis on physical training and organised games. The commission now confirmed this broader concept of university training, not only endorsing it for Dacca, but seeking to extend it to the more complex circumstances of the university in Calcutta. ' . . . the constituent colleges of the Teaching University are not to be mere purveyors of instruction for examinations', they wrote, 'they are to be living societies, real training-places for men . . .'[112]

To enable the individual college to achieve something of the corporate life that was envisaged for the small unitary university at Dacca, they urged that it should be allowed to develop its moral and religious training in the fullest freedom; that it should be provided with additional structural amenities; and that there should be a number of staff residences in close proximity to it.[113] But the condition on which they laid most stress was the provision of suitable student accommodation. This was a condition that was notoriously unfulfilled, especially in Calcutta itself; and the commission offered a comprehensive plan to remedy it.[114] They prescribed a careful division of responsibility between the college, the university, and the government; and recommended new administrative machinery to enable the university to exercise a more effective and constructive supervision. They also advised on the scale and character of the new accommodation needed. But here they were more tentative. They pointed out that it was impossible to make any accurate assessment of the demand until the intermediate colleges had been set up. And whilst they gave it as their opinion that the best form of residence for students living away from home was the collegiate hostel, they warned against the precipitate provision of such accommodation. 'The hostel system is comparatively new to India', they wrote, 'and has not yet been well-adapted, save under exceptionally favourable circumstances, to Indian social conditions. Differences of caste and creed might well become serious if compulsory residence in hostels were hurriedly enforced. . . . It is only by gradual steps and cautious experiment that the residential system can be made a real success in India.'[115] In pressing for a systematic solution of the problem of student residence, the commission had prominently in mind the related problem of student health, and like the Dacca committee, they too put fresh emphasis on this aspect of student care. They proposed the establishment of a new board of student welfare, with special responsibility for organising a general system of physical training throughout the university,[116] and in support of the proposal made one of their rare references to trans-Atlantic practice. 'A system of this kind', they recalled, 'has been adopted with success at several American universities.'[117]

In this further series of proposals, the commission had again drawn heavily on the west. They had endorsed the earlier recommendation of the Dacca University Committee because on these topics the committee had drawn on the same source. But again the commission had been discriminating and selective in their borrowing. Whether in their proposals for the administration of a system of higher secondary education, or in their approach to the problem of student accommodation in Calcutta, they had demonstrated their acknowledgement of special features in the Indian scene. And whilst quoting western precedent rather more freely than they had done in prescribing for the constitution, they had presented their proposals in eastern dress wherever possible. They had pressed for the development of the tutorial system as a return to a method that had been the strength of Indian education in the past: and it was significant of their sensitivity to the Indian viewpoint that they should have represented the success of their proposals as dependent less on the growth of a new tradition than on 'the gradual revival of the best elements in the older Indian tradition of teaching and scholarship'.[118]

Curriculum   But it was not only a higher quality the commission sought in the training provided by the universities; it was also a new and more purposeful orientation. They completed their scheme of reform, therefore, with a series of recommendations for the content of the curriculum; and here, where they came to define their concept of the Indian university most closely, they did more than range themselves with the latest trends of official policy.

Their essential criticism of the existing curriculum was that it catered ineffectively for the contemporary needs of Bengal. It was too predominantly literary in character, too narrow in scope, too uniform and stereotyped.[119] They quoted with sympathy the view that university studies were 'out of touch with the requirements of modern life' and pursued no 'conscious definite aim';[120] and they fully endorsed the plea for a curriculum that should harmonise with the political and social aspirations of modern Bengal.[121] Having laid the foundation for this new orientation in their constitutional proposals,[122] they now indicated the two main lines they considered it should take.

In the first place they recommended a bold expansion of the facilities for professional and vocational training; and in no sphere did they regard this as more urgently needed than in that of teacher-training.[123] They were in no doubt that the root cause of the educational malaise in Bengal was to be found in the dearth of well trained teachers, and they were emphatic that no substantial improvement could be looked for until this had been remedied.[124] For Dacca as well as for Calcutta, therefore, they recommended the immediate provision of a well staffed department of education, directed by a professor, and having under its control a training college, and a practising and demonstration school. An important part of its function was to be the training of graduate teachers: a training in which special attention would be given to the methods of teaching languages and science. It was also to play a part in undergraduate teaching, for drawing on the practice of universities in the west, the commission proposed that students might be permitted to offer the principles of education as one of the subjects they chose for the B.A. pass degree course. But its main function was to be more fundamental: that of pursuing a systematic study of the art and science of education, and in particular of conducting a scientific enquiry into the special educational needs of India. Just as departments of education in the universities of Europe and America had helped to guide the development of a new movement of education in the west, so they hoped for a similar result from the establishment of vigorous and independent centres of educational research in the universities of India. 'A new school of educational thought might arise here', they wrote, 'stimulated by the thought of the West but founded upon a scientific study of India's needs and conditions.'[125] To enable the departments to carry out this dual role of training and research with maximum effect, they attached great importance to the first professors of education being well versed in the educational experiments of the west, and so recommended that the posts should be filled in England, by the same procedure they had already proposed for a number of other special appointments.[126]

But it was in the sphere of technology and commerce that they recommended the most significant development of the curriculum. Here they were responding not only to the consensus of opinion amongst their witnesses,[127] but to specific proposals already submitted to the government by the University of Calcutta.[128] Judging from the experience of universities in the west – particularly those in Britain, France and America – they were in no doubt that such studies were well placed in a modern university, and they acknowledged a special need for them in the Indian university. They would help to open up the new avenues of employment that were so much needed; they would also help to correct the too 'bookish' and literary tradition in Indian education.[129] But although giving eager sanction and support for this new departure, they did so with certain reservations.

They readily endorsed the senate's proposals for degree courses in agriculture. They recommended that they should be provided at Dacca as well as at Calcutta, and that they should follow the main lines proposed by the commission of 1902: three years of mainly theoretical training in college, followed by one or two years of practical training at a government agricultural institute. But they were careful to qualify their proposals, insisting not only that the courses should be deferred until full training facilities were available, but that admission to them should be strictly limited. For despite Bengal's supreme interest in agriculture, they foresaw few openings for the highly trained expert. In view of the prevailing system of cultivation and land-holding, they considered that the main demand must always be for men with a less specialised introduction to agricultural science, and this they endeavoured to provide for in the courses they prescribed for some of the intermediate colleges in rural areas.[130] In endorsing the senate's proposals for courses in other branches of technology, they sounded the same note of caution. They were emphatic that in 'a great city like Calcutta, one of the chief functions of a university is to meet the intellectual needs of the industrial and commercial world and to establish such contacts between the different groups of investigators and of students as will make the whole academic body an active school of thought, of citizenship and of public service'.[131] In addition to proposing a radical reorganisation of the College of Engineering, and a substantial extension of its range of studies, they recommended the establishment of departments of technology in association with the University College of Science to provide courses in such subjects as technological chemistry, dyeing and tanning. But again they warned against any sudden or precipitate development. Even in a highly industrialised society, the openings for expert technologists were comparatively few; in a country at an early stage of industrialisation they would be more limited still. University courses in technology should not be begun until the necessary teaching facilities were assured and the preliminary intermediate training properly established; and once started, the output of trained students should be carefully controlled with the aid of advisory committees fully representative of the various industries concerned.[132] Over the development of university training in commerce, the commission were still more diffident. Since British employers were generally sceptical of the value of higher commercial education, they concluded that the number of students likely to benefit from it would be small. Like the commission of 1902, they considered that the provision of degree courses would be premature. Yet they by no means discounted the university's role in commerce. Indeed, they assigned it increasingly important, although essentially limited functions. They thought that the University of Calcutta might well develop the study of commercial subjects in the existing honours courses in economics. They also proposed that it should be given power to institute an extended faculty of economics and commerce when the training in the schools and intermediate colleges was sufficiently improved, and the demand for diploma and degree courses sufficiently established. And again they relied on an advisory committee to guide the pace of development.[133]

The commission had deliberately refrained from prescribing an immediate or rapid advance in the sphere of practical studies. In many respects, their proposals recalled the cautious approach of the commission of 1902.[134] But unlike their predecessors, they had laid a firm foundation for the future. Both in their provision for preparatory vocational courses in the intermediate colleges, and in their proposals for bringing representatives of the various interests of the community into close association with the administration of the universities, they had paved the way for a steady growth of studies that were designed to give the curriculum a new and vital relevance to the developing needs of Bengal.

But however diversified its studies were to become, the commission saw no prospect of the Indian university being regarded with 'pride and satisfaction' unless it exhibited 'a special excellence in the domain of oriental learning'.[135] They sought a further relevance for the curriculum, therefore, in the field of oriental studies: and here, in pressing for the accentuation of an existing facet of policy, they came to set a new cultural purpose before the Indian university. They not only asserted that the 'systematic development and encouragement of oriental studies' was 'one of the most natural and important functions of an oriental university';[136] they ventured on the more heretical assertion that the development of western learning was no longer the primary concern of the university in India.[137]

The commission offered detailed and complex recommendations for developing the classical learning of the east. They proposed the establishment of two constituent colleges in Calcutta to serve as the principal centres of sanskritic and islamic studies in the university: a reconstituted Sanskrit

College, and a newly formed Islamia College. Each was to be provided with university chairs and special facilities for research.[138] They also confirmed the recommendations of the Dacca University Committee for strong departments of eastern classical languages in the faculty of arts at Dacca.[139] But their main concern was to remedy the stultifying dichotomy in Indian oriental scholarship: to provide for a new and fruitful co-operation between the studies pursued on western lines in the university, and those pursued according to traditional methods in the tols and madrassas. The government of India had already pointed the way to this co-operation in their plans for Dacca,[140] and the commission now built on that earlier policy.

In their proposals for Dacca, the government of India had provided for a department of islamic studies to offer courses that would be a fitting sequel to those in the reformed madrassas. The courses were to include English, and although they were to be taught in accordance with the critical methods of the west, they were also to require a knowledge of the traditional learning. A comparable arrangement had been envisaged for sanskritic studies. Since the cultural content of the courses was to be different from those of the arts departments, they were to lead to distinctive degrees in oriental learning. The commission warmly endorsed these proposals to bridge the gap between the two systems of learning;[141] and in two respects sought to carry them further. In the first place they proposed that the departments of islamic and sanskritic studies should be brought into the faculty of arts.[142] This was to encourage a more effective co-operation between the oriental departments and those of the faculties of arts and science; and it was not merely to promote a closer mingling of cultures, but to open up new possibilities in oriental research. 'In the past', they wrote, 'owing to the fact that men of science have as a rule had no adequate training in Arabic, and Arabic scholars have had no adequate training in science, great difficulty has arisen in studying the specialised contributions to mathematics, science (especially astronomy), and philosophy, which form so important a part of Arabic writings. If our proposals could be carried out, the Dacca University might play a really important part in the elucidation of a great period of history and civilisation.'[143] In the second place, they recommended the development of modified oriental courses, leading up to the ordinary arts degrees.[144] The western content of these courses was to be increased, but they were still to retain their essentially oriental character. Here the recommendation was more far reaching, for hitherto it had always been assumed that the primary purpose of the basic arts course was the transmission of western learning. The commission pursued a similar policy in regard to Calcutta. In outlining detailed proposals for bringing the Sanskrit College into contact with the adjacent tol, and moreover the Islamia College into contact with the orthodox and unreformed Calcutta Madrassa, they again indicated how students of the university might be given access to the teaching of the pandits and maulvis, and how scholars of the tol and the madrassa might be offered courses recognised by the university. The commission had deliberately refrained from proposing a fusion of the two systems of learning; but they had prescribed a working relationship between them that promised new cultural roots for the Indian university, and a new respect from India's indigenous scholars.

Whilst critical of the neglect of the Indian classics in the university system, they were still more outspoken about the neglect of the vernaculars. This they regarded as 'one of the greatest defects' of college education in Bengal:[145] and all the more surprising for the unequivocal policy laid down in the despatch of 1854.[146] To assist the earlier stages of education, as well as to develop an effective medium for instructing the masses, they were emphatic that a systematic effort should be made to promote the serious study of the vernaculars at all levels in the educational structure.[147] In pressing this view, they claimed simply to be endorsing the earlier policy of the court of directors. But in fact they were giving it an added dimension: for they looked to a study of the vernaculars not merely to develop a literature capable of transmitting the learning of the west, but a literature that should be 'representative of the genius of the people'.[148]

The commission were not in favour of remedying the neglect by compulsion. They were prepared to concede that the existing test in vernacular composition which was imposed on all arts students might be made more stringent, and indeed that it might be extended to students reading science.[149] But since not all students were 'interested, or capable of doing good work, in either literature or philosophy', they were persuaded that compulsory attendance at such courses would 'reduce the quality of the work done'. Their main prescription, therefore, was the inclusion of the literature and philology of vernacular languages among the optional subjects which students might offer for pass and honours degrees;[150] and to encourage the growth of these studies they recommended the provision of chairs or readerships in Bengali, Urdu and other vernaculars.[151]

But in urging the claims of oriental learning, they were careful to safeguard the learning of the west, and indeed to extend its range and influence. In prescribing the option of a larger eastern content in the arts courses, they were insistent that the arts degree must continue to denote an adequate training in western education.[152] And in listing the departments to be added to the University of Calcutta, as funds permitted, they included such fundamental elements in western culture as Greek and Latin which had hitherto failed to establish a position in the curriculum.[153] Their recommendations in regard to English were also significant. They prescribed an end to the compulsory study of English literature for all arts students:[154] but only to substitute more effective means of achieving what they conceived to be the two-fold purpose of the existing courses: on the one hand that of giving the students an efficient command of the language; on the other, that of conveying to them 'through a study of the riches of English literature, a comprehension of the fundamental ideas and outlook of the western world'.[155] Until the system of intermediate education was properly established, they considered that all students should receive some practical training in the English language; and until western education was more fully developed they recommended that standard English works should be prescribed in all courses so that students might gain an introduction to the ideas of the west through the study of the subjects they were most interested in.[156] In addition to these transitory provisions, they urged the development of strong departments of English, with English literature a compulsory subject in many of the courses.[157] They also concurred in the view of the great majority of their witnesses that English should be retained as the main medium of instruction: and whilst disclaiming any wish to prejudge the future, they concluded that there was unlikely to be any change in this respect. The educated classes, they thought, would wish to remain bilingual; English would continue to be their choice 'for the mutual interchange and stimulation of ideas in the sphere of scholarship and science'.[158]

In seeking a new relevance for the curriculum in the field of practical studies, the commission were doing no more than recall the university system to the purpose originally conceived for it. They were prescribing in the spirit of the Wood despatch. But in seeking a fresh emphasis on oriental studies they were adding their voice to the swelling denunciation of one of the most cherished and essential principles of that despatch. They were pressing policy into new channels, and setting before the university system a modified cultural ideal which they epitomised with greatest clarity in summarising their ambitions for Dacca. Like the government of India, the commission held out great hopes of this much planned project. ' . . . in many ways', they wrote, 'the opportunities of Dacca will be unique. We hope that it will serve as a new home for the study of that Arabic philosophy and science which gave fresh intellectual life to Europe during the middle ages; that Sanskritic studies will find a worthy and equal place alongside Islamic studies; and that in this quiet intellectual centre in the great plains and waters of Eastern Bengal, and in touch with a historic city, there may spring up a fresh synthesis of eastern and western studies. These are the possibilities. . . .'[159]

In the new definition they had given to the Indian university, the commission had gone far to justify their claim to have prescribed in the sense of Trivedi's plea.[160] They had proposed a radically new departure in higher education; and one that took much closer account of the ideals of the east. They had not attempted to give religion the place traditionally accorded to it, although they had in fact made special arrangements to strengthen the religious influences in which students pursued their studies,[161] and indeed to include some religious teaching in the curriculum. They had not discussed, as their predecessors of 1902 had done, the delicate question of developing a faculty of theology.[162] But they had expressed the view that it would be 'eminently desirable' to provide for teaching in the history of religions at Calcutta,[163] and religion, of course, lay at the root of the courses they had envisaged in islamic and sanskritic culture at both Dacca and Calcutta. But if the commission had found it impractical to give religion a prominent place in the studies of the university, they had prescribed an end of the narrow concentration on the secular needs of the state. In providing for a new freedom from state control, and a more intimate relationship between the teacher and the student, they had met the essence of Trivedi's criticism and set up a new ideal of disinterested learning in harmony with India's most cherished traditions. In their proposals for a fresh emphasis on oriental learning, they had also met his plea for a new cultural orientation which, in acclimatising the university system, would enable it to assist in the birth of the new life struggling to be born in India.

Yet the western, and more especially British element in their prescription was still strong. Despite their tactful presentation, the constitutional framework they proposed for the university system, and much of the spirit, were staunchly British. And for all their emphasis on oriental studies it was not a specifically Indian civilisation they sought as India's salvation, but a civilisation that would be a blend of the hindu, islamic and European civilisations.[164] For although planning for Indian independence, they planned in the conviction that India would wish to remain a member of the Commonwealth, and, indeed, that she would want to preserve the essentially British character of her institutions.[165] They were influenced, too, by a further political consideration. Inspired, no doubt, by the special interest of their chairman, they foresaw a great role for the universities of the Commonwealth in strengthening the unity of the Empire. Dwelling on the benefits of fostering a close fellowship between them, they were careful to stress that the sort of association they envisaged was such as would 'in no way restrict or interfere with the freedom of each to cultivate its own garden, in its own way'.[166] But in considering the practical problems involved, they admitted the desirability of establishing some correlation between them, particularly in the sphere of examination standards,[167] and they acknowledged that in re-planning the system of university training in India they had felt obliged to 'hold in mind the whole organised movement of ideas, the whole organisation of learning and study, in the great complex of varied nations of which India is a part'.[168] In touching on this great imperial theme, they were far out-ranging their terms of reference, as they themselves admitted; but they were sounding a fitting note for what was to be the culmination of Britain's policy for higher education in India.[169] They were anticipating, besides, a similar theme that was to be developed in relation to another great transplantation of universities overseas, this time to Britain's colonial dependencies, nearly a generation later.

II CASTING A BALANCE

Soon after 1947, when India became independent, another commission looked into the state of her universities. The commission was under the chairmanship of one of India's great intellectuals, S. Radhakrishnan, and it drew its membership from America and Britain as well as from India. Nearly a century had passed since the British had planted universities in India; the commission could not look back on this century of academic history with much satisfaction, nor into the future with much optimism. Enormous numbers of students had streamed through India's universities since 1857. The system had produced distinguished scholars and notable leaders, and a significant intellectual community, but compared with the impact of universities in, say, Australia, over about the same stretch of time, the impact of universities on Indian society had been deeply disappointing.[170]

The greatest disappointment was that the chronic malaise in Indian academic life, analysed so brilliantly by the Sadler commission a generation earlier, had not been cured. When a committee under Hartog's chairmanship reviewed Indian education in 1929 it still complained about the low quality of education and the poor standards of achievement expected of graduates.[171] Failure rates were still high. Command of the English language was still weakening. Students worked to pass examinations, not to understand subjects. There was, wrote the committee, no sign of any sustained resolve to grapple with the evils which resulted from the large intake of unfit students. The cloud of disillusion over quality and standards, which had darkened Indian higher education since the 1870s, had not lifted. Nor, despite the Sadler commission, had two other chronic afflictions of Indian universities been overcome. The preference for clerkly rather than technological and vocational studies was undiminished. Reflective scholars felt themselves to be frustrated, a company of intellectually displaced persons;[172] under-employment of graduates was as serious as ever: on the eve of independence it was estimated that only a third of India's graduates found employment in work commensurate with their attainments.[173] And defects in university government, which had plagued Indian academic life since the time of the vakils, persisted in a new form: even in 1960 one of India's distinguished vice-chancellors was complaining of government interference in academic policy-making.[174] Anyone who studies the story of universities in India since 1857 cannot escape the conclusion that the system of higher education inherited at independence from the British raj was dangerously weak in three ways: (i) During British rule we failed to set and maintain the quality of teaching and the standards of achievement essential to a university if its degree is to be freely acceptable in universities overseas. (ii) We failed to devise, and to persuade Indians to accept, a content of higher education suited to India's social and economic needs. (iii) We failed to establish patterns of academic government and relations between universities and the state, which would accord to universities that degree of autonomy without which they cannot serve society properly.

The foregoing chapters contain our evidence for these assertions. Over quality and standards there was the initial ambivalence of Wood's despatch;

the abdication of responsibility for teaching, implicit in the system of affiliation of colleges without control of them; the surrender to parrot-learning and the abject reliance on epitomes and examination drill-manuals; the failure of governments, despite their power over the university system, to shore up sagging standards in the 1890s; the inability of the system through its sheer size to respond to the challenge of the recommendations made by Sadler's commission in 1919. These maladies enfeebled the whole tone and style of Indian intellectual life. At independence the Indians inherited in their universities a massive invalid unable to respond to any simple treatment.

Over the content of higher education there was a similarly unfortunate legacy. Very early in the history of Indian universities it was observed that students displayed a disquieting preference for literary studies,[175] and that the universities, for their part, seemed indisposed 'to make any attempt to connect themselves with the material interests of the country'.[176] Both in its economic policy, and in its policy of using the degree as a qualification for entry into the public service, the government encouraged these tendencies; and it was not until early in the twentieth century that even in the literary courses, Macaulay's insular assumption about what Indians ought to learn yielded to more liberal ideas. In Curzon's time, the study of Indian civilisation was still neglected, but by the time the Dacca committee reported in 1912 academic evolution had brought about some desirable changes: the acceptance, for instance, of oriental studies and islamic studies as co-equal in merit with western learning. But science, technology, and vocational subjects were still inadequately provided for. The Sadler commission said 'it is difficult to resist the conclusion that an unduly large proportion of the able young men of Bengal are being trained in a manner too purely literary'.[177] And again: 'Educational reform on a bold and generous plan may save Bengal from the loss and danger which threaten a country when the training of its educated classes has got out of gear with the economic needs of the nation . . . A new kind of education is needed to fit young Bengal for the new kinds of work which it is in the interest of themselves and of their country that they should be better prepared to undertake.'[178] But during the remaining generation of British rule the bold and generous plan did not materialise; the new kind of education was not devised; at independence the university had not adapted itself fully to the Indian environment.

A university can be no better than its teachers and its students, and governments might say in exoneration of these charges that since the turn of the century the universities had been so far 'Indianised' that the governments in India and Whitehall could not be expected to take responsibility for a university's domestic affairs. But this sort of defence would be disingenuous; for the third weakness of Indian universities, which successive commissions failed to remedy, was that they were never treated by governments as adult, autonomous, institutions. As far off as 1854 little was known about the constitutions of universities and it was therefore not surprising that the court

of directors should have thought it prudent that the government should retain control over the composition of the senates (p. 60). As it turned out, the
government failed to use this power effectively, with the result that the senates
degenerated into popular assemblies, and more especially at Calcutta (p. 70)
became infested with lawyers and laymen ignorant of academic affairs and
grinding axes of their own. This degeneration of university senates was perhaps
an excuse for the paternalistic attitude adopted by Curzon and the commission
of 1902, which indeed reformed the corrupt governing bodies in Calcutta,
Bombay and Madras, but substituted a degree of government control which
would have been anathema to British civic universities, which by that date
had established robust traditions of autonomy and freedom from state intervention. For the act of 1904, which was based on the work of the 1902 commission, prescribed that up to four-fifths of the governing body should be
nominees of the chancellor, a post held at Calcutta by the governor general,
and at Bombay and Madras by the local governor; also that the government
should be empowered not only to approve, but to add to or alter, the revised
body of regulations which the universities were required to submit.[179] Ten
years later, with the rising tide of nationalism, the attitude of the government
of India became still more oppressive, and the India office (despite the liberal
influence of Theodore Morison) seemed unable to stem the growing spirit of
reaction. For the proposed university at Aligarh, the government of India
wanted to endow the viceroy, as *ex officio* chancellor, with an astonishing
array of powers, including the right to insist that his advice should be taken
on any matter relating to the welfare of the university. Even more shocking,
though it was abandoned in the end, was the intention of the government of
India that the governor general in council should have power to suspend the
university's constitution (p. 91). Half a century later the British academic
world was shocked when Dr Nkrumah, as chancellor of the University of
Ghana, assumed to himself powers more modest than these, though somewhat similar to them! Of course the government's intentions were benevolent
and in the interests of the natives: that is the excuse for all paternalism. And
the fact that power over the universities was to be exercised by men like Lord
Curzon rather than by men like Dr Nkrumah was, of course, reassuring.
British officials, indeed, had from the first tried to operate the constitutions of
the Indian universities in such a way as to foster in them something of the
tradition of academic autonomy that had grown up in England.[180] Governments, on the whole, had been forbearing in the use of the powers reserved to
them.[181] When the Sadler commission came to report in 1919, it acknowledged that although in theory the universities in India were 'among the most
completely governmental universities in the world', in practice this was not
so.[182] But as Asutosh Mookerjee protested in debate on the Indian universities bill in 1904, it was 'quite possible to stunt the growth of a beautiful tree
by ... too affectionate care'.[183] The fact that universities were subjected to
state control in almost every detail of their administration was bound to under-

mine their sense of responsibility. Despite the benevolence of her intentions, Britain failed to lay the foundations for a tradition of academic autonomy in India.[184]

From 1854 to 1919 the British rulers of India deliberately maintained powers of governmental control over universities which no British university would have tolerated. It was left to the Sadler commission in 1919 to prescribe a more enlightened pattern of government, which maintained, indirectly, the influence of the state on universities, but assured them a large measure of autonomy in academic affairs. Even so, the memorandum of evidence from Sharp to the commission (p. 407) showed how persistent was the tradition of paternalism among Indian civil servants.

Some of the universities founded since 1919 have on paper the pattern of constitution which the Sadler commission recommended; but in practice the old abuses remain. Academic policy-making is not left to academics; politicians meddle; governments interfere. Three generations of surveillance have sapped the universities' initiative. It is hard for them to become tough, self-governing societies.

So although, as Trivedi said in his perceptive memorandum to the Sadler commission (p. 115), India has been greatly enriched by western education, nevertheless 'there has been a cost, a cost as regards culture, a cost as regards respect for self and reverence for others, a cost as regards the nobility and dignity of life'. We can be justly proud of many features of British rule in India and of much of the legacy bequeathed at independence. But the export of the western university to India was not one of our successful ventures. There were substantial reasons for our failure. Neither the institution we introduced, nor the environment in which it developed, were conducive to the creation of an academic community. The model exported to India reflected the state of British universities in the mid-nineteenth century which we summarised in the first chapter of this book. Neither Oxford nor Cambridge nor the Scottish universities in the 1850s were suitable as paradigms. The University of London was the only institution with administrative experience relevant to India's needs. As an examining machine it was a good model, but it could give little guidance over quality of teaching, and even as an examining machine it offered no safeguard of standards of achievement. Such safeguards as are now provided by external examiners were not at that time taken very seriously. Degrees in Britain were not at that time anchored, as they are now, to an approximately common standard. Neither could the University of London offer much guidance on the pattern of academic government, or the delicate diplomacy of relations between the university and the state. University constitutions and university-state relations were, as we discuss in part three, chapter 10, slowly evolving through the nineteenth century. When universities were devised for India, the conventions surrounding them were very imperfectly understood.

Not only the seed: the seed-bed, too, was unsuitable. The cultural environment was an initial handicap; for students were required to study subjects that were culturally alien to them in a language that was not their own. But it was the poverty of the Indian territories, and the political status of the Indian peoples that were chiefly to undermine the migrant institution. Poverty, by giving an unnatural momentum to the university system and so diluting the quality of its staff and students, was a major cause of the disastrous fall in standards. And it was a major obstacle in the way of reform. It was poverty which so largely nullified the work of the Sadler commission. The political environment was not at first a weakening influence, although from the start it dictated an unusual degree of governmental control. But from the 1880s, the university system became drawn into the developing nationalist struggle. Popular elements contended for control of the senates, and governments resorted to an increasing degree of state control. Teachers came to be held in less respect, and student indiscipline emerged as a familiar feature of the university scene.

Out of our partial failure in India grew our partial success in Africa. For the lessons learnt in India were not forgotten. The last great British pronouncement on Indian higher education was the report of the Sadler commission. In 1923, three years after this report was published, the colonial office set up a committee (described in the next part of this book) to advise on education in tropical Africa; and almost at once the committee began to consider the possibilities of higher education there. Sadler was a member of this committee; so, later, was Mayhew, who was familiar with Indian education and had written persuasively about it; so also was George Anderson who had acted as secretary of the Sadler commission and served on the Hartog committee. The next transplantation of universities to Britain's overseas possessions did not occur until after world war II, but the policies then adopted by the British government were the result of twenty years of reflection and maturation of ideas. Throughout this period the example of India was never far from the counsels of the colonial office. It affected British policy in a variety of ways. First there was a much greater awareness of the dangers which accompany the export of higher education. The Indian experience had taught those who determine government policy to enlist the continuous co-operation of practising academics in any future export of universities. It had taught them that something must be done to ensure quality of teaching; this meant emphasis on scholarship and research and on conditions of academic autonomy incompatible with close government supervision or control. It had taught them also – although in the event the lesson was not heeded as much as it ought to have been – that higher education is unlikely to bring its full benefit to a country unless its content, emphasis, and balance between different fields of study, are adapted to the indigenous culture and the nation's economic environment.

The Indian experience served also as a warning of a different kind. In a country under foreign rule education breeds disaffection. It is common knowledge that nationalism begins among the intellectuals, though at a later stage the intellectuals are likely to be displaced by demagogues. The report of the Pakistan commission pays tribute to the part played by both staff and students in the struggle for independence, but political agitation did not stop with independence and the commissioners deplore the tradition (it persists in India too) which makes universities a perpetual thorn in the side of government. There is little doubt that some of the colonial governors of African territories, aware of this Indian experience, resisted the development of higher education in Africa. Because of this resistance the tempo of planning, and, as a result, the character of the institutions which were ultimately set up in African territories, were influenced by this experience.

So the transplantation of universities to British tropical Africa was not an act of British government *sui generis*. It was a fresh chapter in a story which began with F.J. Mouat's proposal for a university in Calcutta, despatched to London in 1846. To this fresh chapter we now turn.

Part 3

AFRICA

Note. Since this book was written there have been profound political changes in several African countries. The narrative in this part of the book refers to these countries as they were at the end of 1965.

CHAPTER SIX

ASPIRATIONS WITHOUT A POLICY

I INTRODUCTION

'Salt from the north, gold from the south, and silver from the white man's country; but the word of God and the treasures of wisdom are to be found in Timbuctoo.' So runs a Soudanese proverb. The sons of Songhoi kings, we are told, quitted the palaces of Gao, and the children of the Touaregs deserted their great tents to receive an education at the University of Sankoré. That was four centuries ago. The famous scholar of Timbuctoo, Mohammed ben Abou Bekr, 'gave lectures from early morning till ten o'clock ... he recited the mid-day prayer in public, and taught in his own house till three o'clock; he then said the prayer of *asr*, and went out to teach in a different place until dusk, and after sunset he gave a final lecture in the mosque'.[1]

There is no longer a university in the mosque of Sankoré in Timbuctoo; but two other muslim universities in Africa – the Qarawiyin madrassa in Fez and Al-Azhar in Cairo – still flourish. For over a thousand years students have gathered round teachers in the mosques there, listening to expositions of islamic science. Until recently the basic curriculum had scarcely changed for centuries. Now both these venerable institutions are undergoing reluctan metamorphosis into universities on a European pattern: a cité universitaire has been built in Fez; and Al-Azhar, though it retains its school of traditional islamic studies, has in addition a school of business and public administration and is about to have a school of engineering.[2]

So higher education is not new to the continent of Africa, but the modern universities in Africa owe nothing to this ancient tradition of scholarship. The islamic curriculum was medieval. Its technique was to learn by rote. Its truths rested on authority, not on observation or enquiry. It was not fitted to transmit western learning. Nor were the indigenous systems of education still to be found among sub-Saharan tribes fitted to do so: for these were inward looking, conducted by members of the extended family, directed to ensuring conformity with social custom and acquiescence in the hierarchy of the community. The modern universities of Africa have their roots not in any indigenous system of education, but in a system brought from the west.

It was in West Africa that Britain first introduced this system; and it was the missionaries who were largely responsible for developing it. But from the early years of the nineteenth century the government also played a part in the provision of education, and by the end of the century the foundations of a regular system of state-aided education had been laid throughout the British possessions in West Africa. In East and Central Africa the comparable development came much later. The missionaries began to pioneer in the educational field from the middle of the nineteenth century; but they were far ahead of the flag, and it was not until after the first world war that colonial governments turned seriously to co-ordinate and develop the education of their territories. There was no official policy for higher education in any of the British dependencies in tropical Africa before that time. But when planning began in the colonial office shortly afterwards, it was against the background of a significant evolution of policy towards the lower levels of education in West Africa; and also in face of two unofficial and contrasting patterns of higher education there: one actual but stagnating, provided by the missionaries; the other still hazy and unrealised, but forward looking and of the future, which the Africans themselves had set as their goal.

II THE EDUCATIONAL BACKGROUND

The educational problem which faced the British government when it assumed political control over Sierra Leone in 1808 differed in many essential respects from the contemporary one which faced the East India Company. The company was confronted with an oriental society which still preserved ancient and impressive traditions of scholarship; the government was confronted with an African society which despite its many sophistications was essentially pre-literate and relied on oral tradition. The company had to deal with a population to be reckoned in tens of millions; the government with numbers which by comparison were minute. The response inevitably reflected the difference. In India such limited funds as were available were concentrated on the higher levels of education. The 'downward filtration' theory was adopted to bring education to the masses through a small class of highly trained interpreters. In Africa the process was reversed. In the absence of a literate society, education was built from below. But on the fundamental issue, the reaction of government and company was the same. Just as in India the decision was to train 'a class of persons Indian in blood and colour, but English in tastes, in opinions, in morals and in intellect', so in Africa the decision was to give the negro an English education. The only difference was that in India the decision was taken deliberately, after a period of fierce controversy, whilst in Africa it was taken instinctively, on the assumption that no other course was open. And just as in India this initial approach was gradually abandoned from the turn of the century, so in Africa, and from about the same time, there came a move towards a new and more consciously defined policy which was fixed some decades later in a body of carefully devised principles. The story of this evolution in West Africa has a special place in the history of African universities, for the assumptions upon which higher education in all the tropical dependencies was planned arose from this evolution of opinion. In India, universities were planned in the full tide of enthusiasm for the earlier policy; in Africa, planning began in the first vigour of reaction against it.

The earlier policy in West Africa was shaped largely in relation to Sierra Leone and this in itself was to contribute to the form it assumed. For owing to the origin of the colony as a settlement for emancipated slaves, the negro community was highly artificial; the problem of education, as a result, was over-simplified and distorted. It was many years before the home government attempted to guide the educational development of the new colony. For all its vigour in freeing the negro slave, it did not care to concern itself with the details of his schooling. It preferred to observe its customary restraint in matters of education. Even when parliament voted sums of up to £30,000 per annum for the education of emancipated negroes between 1835 and 1845, the colonial office took little interest in the detailed appropriation of the funds. A professional enquiry from the committee of privy council on education in 1843 drew the disarming reply that 'it could not, with accuracy, be stated that the British Government has adopted any particular system for the education of emancipated negroes';[3] that responsibility had been delegated to various religious bodies, subject to the right of inspection. In Sierra Leone, as elsewhere, the colonial office had been content to leave the development of education largely to local initiative, and official and private endeavour had proceeded side by side.

The sort of education that had taken root in the early years of the settlement emerges clearly from the report of an inspection carried out by the local government in 1841.[4] By that date some forty-two schools had been established in the colony: fourteen by the colonial government and twenty-eight by the Church Missionary and Wesleyan Societies. Since most of the teachers in the government schools had been trained in the schools of the missionaries, the instruction in both types was broadly the same. It was a faithful reproduction of the pattern of the charity school education in England, both in method and content. The basic skills of reading and writing were taught, and the elements of arithmetic, grammar and geography. But the main emphasis was on religious instruction: to the exclusion, the inspector reported 'of, every other species of learning'.[5] There had been attempts to vary the pattern on the part of individual governors and missionaries. A Mr Weeks of the CMS had contrived to combine a system of industrial training with the current type of scriptural education. Boys at his school learnt trades and were taught to cultivate cotton and coffee; girls were instructed in housecraft and needlework. H. D. Campbell had admired the system and established a series of government schools on similar lines during his governorship in the thirties.[6] But these experiments had largely disappeared with their authors,[7] and although in 1841 the inspector noted farms attached to some of the boarding schools for liberated Africans, the overall picture he painted was of an educational system 'clerkly' in the most literal sense of that term.

The blueprint of a very different type of education came shortly afterwards from the colonial office. The initiative for this unusual intervention was Lord Grey's, prompted largely by a desire to offset the effect of the withdrawal of the parliamentary grant for the education of emancipated negroes. Seeing in the industrial schools at home a system of education that was both economical and apparently appropriate to the needs of negro communities, he sought a suitably adapted prescription from the committee of privy council on education.[8] This was provided at characteristic length by the secretary, J.P. Kay Shuttleworth.[9] He advocated the provision of day schools of industry and model farm schools: schools which would offer a practical as well as an intellectual training, and whose cost would be partially offset by the work of the pupils. The curriculum of the day schools was to include household economy and gardening; that of the model farm schools, land surveying, agricultural chemistry and veterinary medicine. In each the three Rs were to be taught in the context of the practical training. He also prescribed normal schools for the training of teachers in which the main emphasis was to be placed on the building of character. In all three institutions, the primary object was to be training in the duties of a religious life, and priority given to instruction from the holy scriptures. It was a far-sighted and imaginative conception; and even more remarkable was the prefatory reflection that it would have been 'advantageous to know more of the details of colonial culture and the peculiarities of household life in this class [i.e. the negro population] and thus to descend from the general description into a closer adaptation of the plans of the School to the wants of the Coloured Races'. But Kay Shuttleworth no more than glimpsed the possibilities of cultural adaptation and faithfully reflected the trend of current thought in proclaiming the diffusion of a grammatical knowledge of the English language 'the most important agent of civilization for the coloured population of the colonies'. The scheme had a mixed reception at the colonial office. The parliamentary under-secretary, Benjamin Hawes, was inclined to think that the privy council's letter required 'too much' and might 'deter'. He was doubtful whether it was worth circulating.[10] But Grey did not share his scepticism:[11] and the document was transmitted in its entirety, first to the West Indies for which it was primarily designed and shortly afterwards to all British colonies, including the West African dependencies.[12]

The circular was certainly too demanding for the resources of West Africa, where its influence was negligible. Nevertheless, as missionary activity spread along the coast and inland, new elements did enter into the developing pattern of West African education and one of them was a growing recognition of the value of industrial training. This was particularly apparent in the Gold Coast. Here the pioneers were the Basel missionaries. As an educational as well as a missionary organisation, they had decided views about negro education. They were convinced that the civilising process could never be achieved through the agency of literary training alone. When, therefore, they began to develop a network of schools after their return to the Coast in 1843, they made manual labour compulsory at all stages. In the elementary day schools, this took the form of agricultural work and handicrafts; in the higher, boarding schools, additional technical instruction was provided in such trades as masonry, carpentry and book binding. These subjects were also taught in the training schools for teachers and catechists. And the object of the instruction was not simply to convey practical skills, but to give lessons in the value of time and the dignity of labour.[13] Industrial training did not form an essential part of the educational policies of other missionary societies at this time;[14] but there were a number of individual experiments on these lines, most notably the industrial garden which T. B. Freeman established at Beulah as a 'moral out-work' to the wesleyan school system on the Gold Coast.[15]

Another new element in the educational approach of these middle years of the nineteenth century was an increasing tendency to teach native languages in preference to English in the lower standards. Again it was the Basel missionaries who were the most convinced exponents of the method. They confined their language teaching to the vernacular in the lower classes, partly because they recognised an intrinsic value in teaching the native tongue, and partly also because they saw danger in imparting what could only be, for the bulk of their pupils, the smattering of a foreign language.[16] Other missionary societies developed this practice as their study of the indigenous languages permitted, but less consistently; teaching in the vernacular was given at selected stations only, and then perhaps, as in the CMS Yoruba mission, in addition to English, not in place of it.[17]

Neither of these developments affected the general picture at Sierra Leone. Here, of course, with the mixture of languages, teaching in the vernacular was hardly practical or, indeed, particularly desirable. English was the obvious means of communication for the settlers and thus an essential subject and medium of instruction. There were no such disincentives for industrial training. But little was done in this direction, and particularly in the CMS educational system, the 'clerkly' bias became more pronounced. After the disastrous expedition to the Niger in 1841, with its horrifying revelation of the European's vulnerability to malaria, the society turned more urgently to the training of African mission agents. It reorganised its seminary at Fourah Bay, and, as a feeder to it, established a grammar school closely patterned on the classical model current in England.[18] The whole trend of missionary education became the despair of successive governors.[19] They deplored both the exclusiveness of the 'book education' given,[20] and the form it assumed: in particular the 'parrot-like education in Hebrew, Greek [and] Latin'[21] provided in the higher institutions of the CMS, but also the curriculum and method of presentation in the general run of missionary elementary school. The latter criticism centred chiefly on disregard of African environment: in the setting of English readers, the syllabus of the geography taught, and the omission of nature study. This deficiency in African emphasis was by no means confined to education in Sierra Leone. In the dearth of suitable textbooks, it was inevitably widespread. And it was considerably enhanced by the instinctive tendency of most missionaries at this time to dismiss African culture as something essentially evil and debased. It was typical of this approach that William Fox, writing in 1851 of wesleyan missions on the West Coast, should have ʲudged the reality of conversions in terms of the abandonment of the 'tom-tom, the song and the dance'.[22]

In 1867, this developing picture of West African education was unexpectedly reviewed by the colonial office. In July of that year the acting administrator of Sierra Leone sent home for approval an ordinance designed to lay the foundation of a regularly inspected school system in the colony.[23] Wishing to give a considered decision, the secretary of state, then the duke of Buckingham, referred to his department for information. Little was forthcoming. Practically all he could discover was the existence of some hundred schools of all kinds in the colony 'representing with sufficient minuteness the various religious denominations of the Mother Country'.[24] He was driven to the conclusion that for all past reports the colonial office was 'wholly in the dark' about the schools in 'these out of the way places'.[25] There could have been no more striking indication of the way his predecessors had conceived their role in education. He decided to despatch a qualified inspector from Britain to obtain a report on the spot, and he carried his resolve in the face of doubts raised in the office and objections urged by his parliamentary under-secretary, C. B. Adderley.[26] He was clearly influenced in his stand by the importance which witnesses before the select committee of 1865 had attached to developing the educational facilities of the West Coast.[27] He may well have been guided, too, by the quickening political interest in education at home. He drew support, moreover, from a powerful recurring stimulus in the development of education overseas: the enthusiasm of the governor for the time being, in this instance, Sir Arthur E. Kennedy.

But in one respect, Sir Arthur Kennedy did not advance the cause of West African education. It was on his advice that the inspection, which the duke had been prepared to extend to the lesser West African settlements, was confined to Sierra Leone.[28] As a result, colonial office thinking on West African education came to be unduly influenced by an untypical aspect of the problem.

This was hardly the fault of the inspector, J. S. Laurie. Indeed, he was so vividly impressed by the un-African character of the colony that he introduced his report in all seriousness by enumerating the features it shared with the Isle of Wight. He found the same size of territory and population; the same proportion of people employed on the land; the same division into parishes and no appreciable distinction in 'religious organisation, civil machinery and social economy'. He so warmed to his theme as to conclude 'that in no essential respect was there any formal difference except in race, colour, costume and the peculiar determination with which the people style themselves "English"': a passage in which the word 'race' not unreasonably attracted, in the colonial office, the pencilled marginalia of 'slight diff^ce'. With such a preamble, he was naturally led on to prescribe an English pattern of education for the Sierra Leoneans. He recommended the introduction of a system of grants-in-aid, based on the English revised code, in which the three Rs should be compulsory subjects, and grammar, geography and history optional ones. It was to be supervised by a director of public instruction who was also to be responsible for establishing and running a government model school. Two provisions catered for industrial training: the suggestion of workshops for the model school, and of special grants for instructors of optional classes in carpentry or agriculture for boys and sewing or domestic work for girls.[29] The scheme inevitably encountered some scepticism in the colonial office. Adderley doubted whether 'our advanced prescriptions' were suitable for Sierra Leone; the recommendations seemed to him 'too good for the materials to be operated on'.[30] But as before he was running against the tide. The scheme survived reference to the privy council and to Sierra Leone.[31] Only the wesleyans stood out against it: and it was launched essentially as Laurie had devised it, except that the special industrial grants for carpentry and agriculture were unaccountably lost sight of.[32]

The colonial office intervention had confirmed the direction of earlier endeavour. The English, clerkly education, developed by the missionaries, received sanction and encouragement. But just as it promised to become systematised, Britain's approach to the education of the West African negro was suddenly and bitterly assailed from an unexpected quarter. In 1871, Edward Blyden arrived in Sierra Leone.

A pure African negro, though born in the West Indies, he had for the past ten years held the chair of languages at the College of Liberia. Coming to Sierra Leone to further the interests of his race in a more practical way, he led a number of missions into the interior and interested himself particularly in the subject of education.[33] He was deeply impressed by the degeneracy of the educated negro on the Coast and convinced that existing educational methods were fundamentally wrong. They were wrong because they ignored race sentiment. In subjecting the African to 'unmodified European training', they were producing, in his opinion, a slavery 'far more subversive of the real welfare of the race than the ancient physical fetters'.[34] He voiced his criticism in the *Negro* – a paper he had helped to found in Sierra Leone shortly after his arrival – and he pressed his views on successive governors. He struck a particularly responsive note in J. Pope Hennessy, who readily agreed, in correspondence that was published, not only that education in the settlements was defective, but that the failure was 'mainly owing to the idea that the Negro should be Europeanized to be educated'.[35] He even succeeded momentarily in gaining the ear of the secretary of state: for when Hennessy made Blyden's criticism his own in an unusually candid annual report, Kimberley found 'great force in Mr H's remarks as to the want of a good *secular* education in Arabic and the vernacular. We should study what is doing in India to promote education', he concluded, '& endeavour to introduce a similar system into these African settlements. Mere missionary education will never effect much . . .'[36] Three months later, in May 1873, the post of director of public instruction fell vacant, and Blyden applied for it.[37] It seemed just possible that West African education might take a new departure.

But Blyden's application was never seriously considered. The colonial office had no mind to set the cat amongst the pigeons with the missionaries, nor, for all the interest taken in his views, any intention of courting interference with the well-tried British system so recently introduced.[38] Blyden was informed that a person with experience of elementary schools in England was considered desirable for the post[39], and after a long search, a candidate was found. The system went on unchanged until 1877, when it was allowed to lapse following a despairing report from the director about the standard of teaching and the uselessness of further inspection.[40] It was revived, however, in 1882, in essentially the same form, except that this time, owing to the vigilance of a clerk in the colonial office, special industrial grants were provided for.[41] And this time, the system was not confined to Sierra Leone. It was extended, with minor variations, to all the West African dependencies. For the next ten years, the course of West African education was largely guided by the man appointed to the marathon task of conducting the annual inspection: the Rev. Metcalfe Sunter.[42]

Sunter came to the inspectorate from Fourah Bay College where he had been principal since 1871.[43] He had acted as director of public instruction for a short time in 1876, and shown some aptitude for the work. But he owed his appointment less to his ability than to his long residence on the Coast and his physical acclimatisation.[44] He was not a man of any great mental attainments; he brought to his work vigour and common sense rather than any special intellectual qualities. He had no 'lofty views or ideas', as he acknowledged, about what was to be taught in the classroom.[45] He scarcely looked beyond a sound training in the three Rs and did not seriously envisage giving the teaching a more African bias. Occasionally he inveighed against the unsuitability of the reading books. 'Is there no native scholar who will undertake, being conversant with native manners, customs and grooves of thought to adapt an English Reading Book to his country's requirements?'[46] But he brushed aside his misgivings about the value of teaching English history with the reflection that the Africans had 'no history of their own' and that England was a country 'of which they ought to know something'.[47] He was staunchly opposed, moreover, to encouraging the study of the vernacular. He took the utilitarian standpoint: that the languages were still imperfectly reduced to written form, that the dialects were no more than locally useful, that English was the language of commerce and the ruling power.[48] Since English was being successfully introduced into nearly all the schools of the Coast, it was best to 'let "well alone", spread the knowledge of English, and by its means teach civilization and refinement'. But in one important respect he was less complacent about the education the Africans were receiving. In keeping with his practical approach, he strongly deprecated the widespread disregard of industrial training. The criticism had often been made before, but sporadically; Sunter put new drive and continuity behind it. He made industrial training the great 'hobby' of his inspectorate. Echoing Buxton's earlier plea,[49] he called for the 'pick axe, the plane and the spade' to go hand in hand with the 'white man's Bible'.[50] His object was not only to develop the resources of the country but to predispose the heathen to christianity:[51] to *civilize practically.*'[52] He urged that industrial workshops should be attached to government schools, and that greater financial inducement should be offered for industrial training in non-government schools.[53] He suggested setting up special industrial centres where skilled instruction might do more good 'than all the desultory teaching that was ever started'.[54] He wanted to make manual training compulsory.[55] Whether writing from Sierra Leone, the Gambia or the Gold Coast, the industrial theme was almost always dominant. When at last the fever claimed him, he was contemplating a comprehensive report on the subject for the whole Coast.[56] Sunter wished to give the negro a practical education, but not otherwise a specially 'African' one.

The colonial office were in broad agreement with his views, although increasingly critical of the way he did his work.[57] They supported him in his stand on the vernacular. Despite pressure from the missionaries, they declined to subsidise vernacular teaching and so effectively discouraged it. The only concession they were prepared to make was a small temporary grant for the subject at Lagos pending conformity with the new regulations.[58] They also acknowledged the importance of industrial education. In view of the frequent changes of personnel on the Coast, they did not consider it desirable for the government to take any direct action in the matter.[59] They preferred the course of offering more generous grants for the subject; and this in fact was done in the rules drawn up under educational ordinances for the Gold Coast and Lagos in 1887.[60] To that extent Sunter's exertions had borne fruit.

But his main achievement was the administrative one of having brought all British West Africa under the effective operation of the educational system inaugurated at Sierra Leone. He had thus helped to fix the missionary approach in an essentially English image of education, which took little account of the practical needs of the African and almost none of his cultural susceptibilities. The European teacher had too often assumed that the negro was 'inferior' and that it was 'needful in everything to give him a foreign model to copy'; that the peculiarities of his language, modes of thought, social habits and even physical environment could be ignored.[61] The African, for his part, had eagerly grasped at European ways, and in particular at English 'bookish' learning as the royal road to social betterment. Both pressures had contributed to the educational picture of the nineteenth century. Sunter, however, had set in train a movement towards a more practical education; and this was soon to be accompanied by a comparable trend in the cultural field. A new approach to West African education, specifically designed to unloosen the 'straight jacket of unmodified European training' slowly began to emerge.[62]

Nearly all the measures which Sunter had pressed for as a means of counteracting the literary bias of the education that had grown up on the Coast came to be adopted by the various colonial governments in the following years. In 1896, a technical institute was opened by the CMS at Freetown with substantial aid from the Sierra Leone government.[63] In 1898, a technical department was added to the government school at Accra; and a similar arrangement was made at Cape Coast a few years later.[64] In 1899, a government technical school was opened in Lagos.[65] But it was in the early twentieth century that the real breakthrough came, with a stimulating lead from the governor appointed to the Gold Coast late in 1903, J. P. Rodger. Influenced by a tour of negro schools in America,[66] he resolved on a radical reorganisation of the Gold Coast educational system, and towards the end of 1907, appointed a committee to consider the introduction of compulsory manual training.[67] Under revised education rules approved in 1909, some form of 'hand and eye' training was made obligatory in all government and government-aided primary schools; and to assist in giving effect to this new system of combined literary and technical instruction, the government established in Accra, in the same year, both a training institution for teachers and a technical school.[68] The example of the Gold Coast was quickly followed in Southern Nigeria and Sierra Leone. In 1908, the secretary of the Gold Coast committee, E. G. Rowden, was appointed director of education in Southern Nigeria; and in the following year, a new education code drawn up for the recently amalgamated territories there made similar provision for compulsory manual training in the primary schools. It was an innovation of special significance for the colony of Lagos where hitherto the education had been almost exclusively literary.[69] Rowden also played a part in establishing the new policy in the original home of the 'clerkly' system.[70] Early in 1909 he conducted an enquiry into the education of Sierra Leone; and two years later an education ordinance promulgated for the colony provided that no assistance should be given to any public elementary school unless 'some handicraft, manufacturing processes or agricultural work, and, in the case of females, domestic science' were taught in the school.[71]

But it was in the cultural sphere that official policy began to change most decisively in the years after Sunter's death. And even before he died there was a significant pointer to the change in the amended education rules prescribed for Lagos in 1891. Among the 'specific' or optional subjects qualifying for subsidy in the upper primary standards was one entitled 'African Matters'. This had already figured in the rules of 1887. But whereas in 1887 it had been given a practical bias, with special emphasis on West African economic botany, it was now defined as requiring an acquaintance with the history and geography of the African continent, and, moreover, with the 'institutions, religions, traditions and customs' of its various tribes.[72] This new interpretation would seem to have originated not with the practical Sunter, but with the African sub-inspector appointed for Lagos in the previous year, Henry Carr. If so, it adds to the speculation of the consequences for West African education had Blyden been entrusted with the post he applied for in 1873.[73] But the re-definition of 'African Matters' was not the beginning of any systematic attempt to give the curriculum a more African bias. The example of Lagos was not followed in any of the other British possessions on the Coast, and even in Lagos itself it seems that the innovation remained what it had always, perhaps, been intended: the acknowledgement of a distant goal, rather than an immediately practicable objective. However that may be, it indicated the dawn of a respect for African culture in official quarters, an attitude that was to deepen with the political pressures of the twentieth century.

As the frontiers of the British possessions were pushed back into the hinterland, colonial governments were faced with the need for an educational policy that would bolster the indigenous institutions through which they planned to administer their new territories, and some of the earliest and most notable experiments in cultural adaptation were attempts to meet this need in parts of the interior where muhammadanism presented an additional challenge. One of the first experiments of this kind was a scheme sanctioned by the colonial office in 1905 for the establishment of a school for the sons and nominees of chiefs at Bo in the protectorate of Sierra Leone.[74] Designed for pagans and muhammadans alike, it was planned to introduce the future chiefs and leaders to the learning of the west without divorcing them from their own cultural background: to train them, in the words of the official report, 'not in an alien system of thought and education' but in such a way as would equip them most usefully for the part they were destined to play. Science figured prominently in the curriculum; also practical training in farming, carpentry, bridge building, road making and land surveying. Special care was taken over the teaching of English. The school was residential, and the conditions of western civilisation so far simulated as for pupils to be assigned to 'towns' bearing the names of European capitals: London, Paris, Berlin. But otherwise the traditional features of native life were carefully preserved. The curriculum was strictly secular, and the religious beliefs of the pupils scrupulously safeguarded. Tribal customs were encouraged; pupils were known by their native names and native dress was compulsory.[75] It was a wholly novel experiment: and the philosophy underlying it was closely akin to what Blyden had been expounding for the past thirty years or more. Yet ironically enough, it was not to Blyden that the governor turned for assistance in developing the new policy – although Blyden was then occupying the position of director of mohammedan education – but to the missionaries whose educational work Blyden had repeatedly decried.[76] It was W. T. Balmer, of Richmond College, and Thomas

Rowan, of Fourah Bay College, who were invited to draw the outlines of the new scheme.[77] Still more surprisingly, it was another missionary, James Proudfoot, who was appointed as headmaster.

Almost contemporaneously with this development in the protectorate of Sierra Leone, a similar policy was being worked out, more systematically, in the muslim states of Northern Nigeria. In 1909, Hanns Vischer, a political officer seconded to education, began to lay the foundation of a system of government schools, again specifically directed to introducing the population to western learning without undermining the cultural basis of their society. Although planning on more comprehensive lines than the government of Sierra Leone, Vischer's prescription was much the same. It was for schools in which the curriculum was wholly secular. Emphasis was placed on practical training and the native way of life was carefully preserved. The time-table was so arranged that pupils were free to pursue their Koranic studies, attend their mosques, and keep the muslim holidays. They lived in their own compounds; they wore native dress. But in one respect Vischer was more cautious than those who had planned the curriculum at Bo. In Bo, English was assigned a prominent place throughout the curriculum. In Nigeria, possibly because of its more dangerous political climate, Vischer carried adaptation further than this: he arranged that teaching in the lower standards should be confined to Hausa, and even in the upper standards English was left as an optional subject. Like the earlier project in Sierra Leone, Vischer's scheme met with ready support in the colonial office, and by 1915 a senior official was confidently asserting that his system of 'native education on native lines' was 'certainly the most promising new departure in education in West Africa'.[78]

It was not merely where muhammadanism was a dominant or influential factor that this new approach was adopted. When, in 1910, the system of grants-in-aid was applied throughout the protectorate of Sierra Leone, it was provided that no school was to be eligible for aid unless 'an intelligent understanding of, and respect for, tribal law and authority' had featured as objectives of the curriculum.[79] After Vischer had laid the foundation of a network of government schools in the muslim states of Northern Nigeria, he turned to devise a similar system in the more southerly pagan districts of the protectorate. Moreover, it was not only in the context of indirect rule that the new approach was developed. It came to be adopted in other parts of the Coast where political pressures were less insistent, and where cultural adaptation was sought primarily as a matter of educational principle. The comprehensive education code drawn up for the whole of Southern Nigeria in 1909 provided that wherever possible a child should be taught to read and write in his own language before he began the study of English.[80] The goal prescribed by governor Rodger in the same year for the new system of education in the Gold Coast was still more significant. In briefing the principal of the training college that was designed to produce its main exponents, he was emphatic that the objective to be kept in mind was that African boys and girls should be trained not merely to read and write the English language, but 'to develop the best in African custom and character for the enrichment of a definite African culture'.[81]

Both these trends in official policy – towards a more practical training and a training more closely adapted to the African cultural background – had their counterpart in missionary policy as well. The changing character of the missionary approach was clearly reflected in the proceedings of the World Missionary Conference held in Edinburgh in 1910, when for the first time the whole problem of missionary education was subjected to a searching review.[82] The task was entrusted to a commission which included Michael Sadler amongst its members; and the enquiry was conducted by means of a questionnaire sent out to the various mission fields. The questionnaire, in itself, was indicative of the lines on which progressive missionary opinion was moving. Mission workers were invited to assess the results of past policy in terms of the degree of success that had been achieved in raising up men and women who were 'at once Christian in conviction and indigenous in thought, feeling and outlook upon life'.[83] They were asked to submit their views about future policy with special reference to the use of English and the need for industrial and agricultural training.[84] The consensus of the replies strongly confirmed the disquiet implied in the questions. It was generally agreed that missionary education had tended to denationalise those brought into contact with it; and, moreover, that it had exhibited the same characteristic weaknesses as education at home.[85] Too much stress had been placed on the teaching of English, and too much emphasis on the transmission of mere book learning. The replies from Africa enlarged on these shortcomings, and the report from Sierra Leone was especially frank. Here it was explained that a large number of schools had been established; but since they were mainly supported by government aid, the curriculum was framed to suit code requirements closely modelled on those originally prescribed for England. As a result, the mission school on the West Coast was largely a reproduction of the English elementary school: a type whose methods were judged 'very one sided' even for England, and 'far more unsatisfactory' when imported into Africa without adaptation to 'changed environment or to the different cast of the native mind'.[86] But guided, perhaps, by the insight and expertise of Sadler, the commission were not unduly alarmed by the reports from the African mission field. They were satisfied that the new movement of educational thought in Europe and America was already at work in Africa. The educational policy of the government and of the missionary societies was in course of rapid change, and a wholly new attitude towards native education beginning to take shape.[87] 'Regulations are being reconsidered and revised,' they wrote, 'more regard is being paid to the teaching of the vernacular ... manual and industrial training are being encouraged; the course of education is being gradually brought into more vital relation to the real needs of the different categories of native pupils. The movement is still in an early stage, but, so far as it has gone, it affords ground for hope and has already begun to remove some of the capital defects of native education.'[88] With teachers and administrators groping towards new methods, and the complexity of the educational problem recognised as never before, the commission felt unable to generalise about the present, and still less to predict the future. But they had no hesitation in putting their support behind the new movement of ideas, and pressing for the development of recent trends of policy. They fully endorsed the need for more practical training in the elementary schools and the training colleges. And backing a more radical change of policy, they urged 'a quite fresh effort' to nationalise the training of the native evangelist.[89] They were confident that in this, its primary task, 'modern missionary enterprise is wholly right in its increasing tendency to avoid attacking needlessly the ethical systems current amongst the people for whom it labours, and instead to commend and conserve all that is good in their thought and practice'.[90]

New movements of opinion in the west, coupled with new elements in the situation in Africa, were gradually shaping native education afresh. The wider social purpose assigned to education in Europe and America, and the growing interest in the study of anthropology, the practical needs created by the social and economic development of the dependencies and the new respect for African culture compelled by the political implications of indirect rule: all these were factors combining to give it a more practical bias, and a more specifically African orientation. But in one respect there was an exception to the prevailing trend. Just as the elementary education was beginning to move forward on its own lines, so the emerging secondary education was taking a contrary, retrogressive course. Secondary education, at the opening of the twentieth century, was still in its infancy in the British dependencies on the West Coast. With the exception of the Basel seminaries in the Gold Coast, and the Hope Waddell Training Institute in the protectorate of Southern Nigeria, there was no provision for secondary education in either of these territories.[91] In Lagos there were four secondary schools,[92] and in Sierra Leone, where grammar school education had begun as early as 1845, some half dozen.[93] But particularly in Lagos, the secondary schools were little more than higher grade elementary ones; and such secondary education as there was on the Coast was provided almost exclusively by the missions, and directed primarily to the training of teachers and catechists. There were no government-controlled secondary schools, and very little government aid contributed to the secondary schools of the missions. Early in the twentieth century, however, governments began to take a hand with the missions in responding to the growing demand for more highly trained personnel. In 1911, the government of Sierra Leone brought secondary education within the sphere of the grant aided system in an attempt to wean it from its narrow concentration on literary studies[94]; and in the same year, a small advance was made in the Gold Coast where the government made its first grant to a secondary school.[95] But it was in Southern Nigeria, two years earlier, that the most significant step was taken. In 1909, King's

School, the first government-controlled secondary school to be established on the Coast, was opened at Lagos.[96] It was planned to provide a higher education than was available at any of the other secondary schools; and its secondary classes were specifically designed to prepare pupils for the entrance examinations of British universities. This, in itself, was no new departure. Lagos had been recognised as a centre for the examinations of the University of London as far back as 1887, but it was not until a suitable training was provided that the arrangement came to have any real significance.[97] In 1910, in furtherance of the purpose of the school, Lagos became a centre for the Cambridge University local examinations as well,[98] and by 1914 the practice had spread to Sierra Leone.[99] A new element had entered into the educational system which was not only to curb the developing policy of adaptation at the lower levels, but to put wholly unforeseen obstacles in the way of its extension to the upper levels still unplanned.

In the stimulating aftermath of the first world war, the missionaries organised a further and more detailed survey of education overseas, this time confined to the continent of Africa, and in the first place to the South, West and Equatorial parts of it. The initiative came from America. At the instigation of the American Baptist Foreign Mission Society, the Foreign Missions Conference of North America prevailed on the Phelps-Stokes fund to finance an international enquiry led by their educational director, Dr Thomas Jesse Jones; an admirable choice, since he had been trained as a sociologist in Columbia. The commission sailed for Africa in 1920 and published a comprehensive report two years later.[100] Like the earlier commission of the World Missionary Conference, the African Education Commission found much to criticise in the British possessions on the West Coast. In common with the other colonial territories, the education was too closely modelled on the methods of the Mother Country and insufficiently adapted to the vital needs of the African people. 'The wholesale transfer', they wrote, 'of the educational conventions of Europe and America to the peoples of Africa has certainly not been an act of wisdom, however justly it may be defended as a proof of genuine interest in the native people.'[101] The elementary education, despite recent improvements, remained too narrowly literary; whilst at secondary level the educational slavery was still more pronounced.[102] The curriculum of the secondary schools managed by the missions in Freetown was too predominantly classical[103]; that of the higher schools in Lagos too exclusively devoted to 'the conventional requirements of university preparation'.[104] Repeatedly, therefore, the commission preached the doctrine of educational adaptation. But it was significant of the distance British policy had travelled since the early part of the nineteenth century that they should have preached it not as a doctrine still to win acceptance, but as a doctrine very imperfectly applied.[105] And even here their criticism was qualified. They acknowledged that partly owing to the enlightened work of the Basel missionaries, and partly owing to the inspiring lead of governor Rodger, the policy of educational adaptation had been carried further in the Gold Coast than in any of the other territories they had visited.[106]

III THE MISSIONARY APPROACH TO HIGHER EDUCATION

Although it was not until after the first world war that Britain began to formulate an official policy for higher education in the dependencies of tropical Africa, for many years before this the subject had been tackled by the missionaries, and from time to time it had stirred the imagination of the Africans. As early as 1876, the Church Missionary Society had established university courses at its theological seminary overlooking Fourah Bay in Sierra Leone. From a still earlier date, African intellectuals had begun to press for indigenous university facilities and to prescribe the form they should take.

It was African pressure, in fact, which played the decisive part in launching university studies at Fourah Bay College in 1876, although the initiative had come from the missionaries themselves several years before. At the beginning of 1871, Metcalfe Sunter arrived in Sierra Leone to take up his duties as principal of the college. He had travelled out to Freetown with Henry Cheetham, the newly appointed bishop of Sierra Leone, and a joint inspection of the college quickly convinced them that its functions should be extended.[107] Although originally established as a school for recaptives on Leicester Mountain in 1816, it had been transformed two years later into a seminary designed primarily for the training of ministers and catechists; shortly afterwards it had moved to Regent, and then in 1827 to the estate at Fourah Bay where new and larger premises had been opened in 1848. The college had had a continuously chequered career, chiefly on account of the difficulty of finding suitable staff, and in 1871 it was undergoing one of its periodic phases of eclipse.[108] The building had fallen into disrepair, the grounds were overrun with high bush grass, and only a handful of students were in training.[109] But the structure was substantial and, properly put in order, capable of accommodating some sixty students or more. Inspired by the possibilities it offered, Sunter and the bishop conceived the idea of throwing open the college to fee-paying students and giving it 'more of the University aspect'.[110] The suggestion was welcomed at a special meeting of the finance committee in Sierra Leone, and the bishop invited to recommend it to the parent committee.[111] Writing to the secretary, Henry Venn, early in May 1871, he represented it as the view of 'all the brethren here' that the time had come to establish a high school or college at Fourah Bay 'to correspond – at a most respectful distance – to Cambridge & Oxford'. This would not only make the most economical use of the buildings, but greatly reduce the number of Africans obliged to seek training overseas, benefit those reading for the ministry by giving them a wider outlook, and, above all, enable the society to set the tone of higher educational institutions in the British settlements. The bishop saw a great future for the college in this new guise, 'nicely started', as he put it, under the patronage of the CMS, the governor, and other prominent local figures; it might well develop into the University of West Africa.[112]

Sunter wrote in support of the scheme, stressing in particular the valuable part it would play in spreading the influence of the church along the whole of the West Coast.[113] But the proposal made little headway at the society's headquarters in Salisbury Square. Venn saw insuperable difficulties in the way of making Fourah Bay 'a kind of University for lay students as well as a theological Institution'.[114] He disliked the idea of mingling fee-paying students with students under training for the society, and inclined to think that the 'embryo Cambridge' would be better as a separate establishment.[115] For some months the proposal hung fire; but it was revived by the bishop when he was on leave during the following year, and in October 1872 it was submitted to a special sub-committee appointed to confer with him at Salisbury Square.[116] Acting on its recommendations, the society decided in December to authorise the principal to forward applications from students willing to pay for their courses provided they were suitably qualified scholastically and of proved christian character.[117] The concession was disappointingly small. Sunter saw it only as 'the very thin edge of a very small wedge' and the bishop as no more than 'leaving the door not actually shut'.[118] The finance committee thought that insistence on the preliminary sanction of the parent committee would virtually nullify the change.[119] And certainly the decision was unlikely to alter the picture very much, for the curriculum was left as it was, and lay students had never been rigidly excluded from the college.

But events in Sierra Leone then intervened. In a bold bid to cure the educational malaise he had diagnosed in the British settlements,[120] Edward Blyden came forward with the radical prescription of a native-controlled West African university. He had already broached the subject with a native member of the legislative council, the Hon. William Grant, in May 1872, and in the following December made a direct appeal to the administrator-in-chief, J. Pope Hennessy. His main concern was to secure the teachers and literature needed to lay the foundation of an educational system properly adapted to African requirements: and, in a passage reminiscent of the appeal by Wyse for a university in Ireland (above, p. 29), he insisted that it was for the government to provide this means of unfettering the negro mind in expiation of past wrongs to the African race. Hennessy, susceptible as ever to native pressure, readily supported the scheme. In forwarding his correspondence with Blyden to the colonial office, he expressed himself in favour of establishing a West African university – albeit 'on a very humble basis' – and even indicated the disused wesleyan training college on King Tom's Point, then in government hands, as a suitable building in which the university might be accommodated in its earlier years. But since he was only acting in a temporary capacity, he suggested that the proposal should be referred to the governor designate, Robert W. Keate.[121] The scheme met a cautious but not unfavourable reception at the colonial office. Even the most critical permanent official recommended that Keate should be invited to 'master the pros & cons';[122] and Kimberley concurred. He found 'some shrewd and just observations' in Blyden's letters – to the extent indeed of discovering in them the very defects Blyden himself attributed to 'the engrafting European ideas on a negro mind' – and whilst explicitly reserving judgement on the proposal, nevertheless commended it to Keate's 'careful attention'.[123]

Hennessy had not only undertaken to forward his correspondence with Blyden to the colonial office; he had also agreed that it should be published in Sierra Leone. When the bishop arrived back from leave early in 1873, he found the colony 'ablaze' with the educational issue and race feeling running high.[124] Deeply incensed by the disparagement of missionary methods and achievements, he and Sunter were scathing in their criticism of the projected university. In fact, they could scarcely bring themselves to regard it as a practical possibility. For how could a fully fledged university be started by negroes alone? Was it reasonable to suppose that 'the African baby' could 'at once go off at the gallop'?[125] Yet the very thought of a university in which muslim and christian would be equal was profoundly disturbing. They redoubled their efforts to get the society to capture higher studies for Fourah Bay, and Sunter offered a detailed memorandum on the new look he considered it required.[126] The christian character of the college was of course axiomatic in his scheme of things, although he was quite prepared to consider special arrangements for the admission of muslims. He was emphatic, too, that the college would need European supervision for many years to come. But he considered that it should offer a more advanced education than was available at the grammar school to all suitably qualified students who were prepared to pay for it. And for this purpose he thought the curriculum should be widened to include Arabic, history and geography, French, German and Spanish, and 'such an amount' of science 'as would be required'. With a touch of the jauntiness that was to give such offence at a later stage of his career, he added that a 'knowledge of Political Economy would not harm our friends but on the contrary . . . benefit them very much and make them a little more practical' than they were. If the college prospered on this wider basis he thought it might then be affiliated so that degrees could be obtained from a university such as London; in the meantime it should issue its own certificate. He insisted on the importance of taking a step at a time. Sunter's ideas on higher education differed in many essential respects from Blyden's.

The society had reacted swiftly to news of Hennessy's correspondence with Blyden. Unprompted by the mission in Sierra Leone, it had spontaneously reconstituted the sub-committee appointed to confer with the bishop in the previous year, and the sub-committee, faced with the prospect of a 'godless' university, had at once dropped its earlier reluctance to develop Fourah Bay. It had agreed in principle that the college should be made 'more of a University' when it first met in March 1873;[127] in November it reported in detail on how this should be done.[128] It recommended that the college should be open to any fee paying student who could pass the matriculation and provide satisfactory testimony of moral character. It considered free places should cease, but that a number of scholarships should be made available for theological students. Religious tests should be applied to these students only. As for the curriculum, it proposed that this should be extended on the lines Sunter had suggested. The society found no difficulty in approving these recommendations; it had 'quite come to the conclusion that it would be well to have a General College at Fourah Bay with a Theological Class attached to it'.[129] The scheme was referred to Sierra Leone, and unanimously endorsed by the mission conference at Freetown in June 1874.[130]

Earlier that month, the government had turned its back on Blyden's 'godless' university. But all the time the society had been maturing its plans for Fourah Bay it had seemed that the outcome might be different. When Blyden applied for the directorship of public instruction in June 1873, a clerk in the colonial office minuted that he would be more suited for a professorship in 'the coming West Africa University'.[131] After an interview with Kimberley in the following November, the Rev. James Johnson, a member of the native pastorate, was satisfied that the government intended to pursue the question of higher education in West Africa.[132] And when Blyden made a further appeal for the university in the latter part of 1873, Kimberley confirmed his interest in the subject. In a despatch to governor Berkeley, reminding him of the outstanding enquiry to Keate – Keate had died only a few weeks after taking up his appointment – he wrote that he would be glad of his opinion upon a subject which seemed to him 'one of much importance'.[133] Berkeley replied in a confidential despatch in May 1874. Less impulsive than Hennessy, and less sensitive to native blandishment, he accepted the bishop's view that the development of Fourah Bay made further action unnecessary.[134] By the time his despatch reached the colonial office, the scheme had no support there. Kimberley had gone; and permanent official opinion had crystallised in opposition. The new parliamentary under-secretary doubted whether Blyden was 'a very wise person' and was disinclined to embark on any of his 'educational crotchets' at the expense of the state.[135] Carnarvon made no attempt to save the scheme. In terms suggested by his assistant under-secretary, he informed Berkeley that 'more reliable data ... would be required' before he could sanction such an undertaking 'which must of necessity be costly' and for which the natives were 'not yet sufficiently prepared'.[136]

Although abortive itself, the projected West African University had been effective as a stimulus. But for Blyden's intervention, it is unlikely that the Church Missionary Society would have undertaken to pioneer the cause of higher education in West Africa so soon. Sunter rejoiced at the dénouement and the role assigned to 'our glorious old Socy'.[137] He came home early in 1874, and during a prolonged leave, planned details of the proposed development at Fourah Bay with Salisbury Square. He was now persuaded that immediate affiliation to an English university would greatly assist the venture, not only by attracting students, but by testing the work, and so ensuring a good standard of performance from the outset. Although he had originally envisaged an arrangement with the University of London, by the end of 1874 he appears to have advocated a link with Durham, presumably on account of the strong theological school there.[138] The society also favoured affiliating the college. It too thought instinctively of an association with London; but influenced, it seems, by Sunter's preference, and by the example of Codrington College, Barbados, which Durham took into affiliation early in 1875,[139] it resolved in July on an approach to the northern university.[140] At first it looked as though the negotiations would be successful,[141] but by February 1876 the outcome appeared less promising.[142] The Durham senate had raised further queries, and Henry Wright, who had succeeded Venn as secretary, suspected it of preparing a retreat. He began to think again of London. But Sunter was privately assured from Durham that the delay was owing to the dean's not liking the society seemingly to gain its point 'too readily'.[143] In March, the senate agreed to recommend the affiliation to convocation early in the following term,[144] and on 16 May 1876, the recommendation was carried by a unanimous vote.[145]

The vote of convocation determined the mould in which the nascent university studies at Fourah Bay were to set. By the terms of the affiliation, the students in Sierra Leone were enabled, on certain conditions, to sit the same examinations as the students at Durham; the university authorities undertook to send out the papers, and mark the returned scripts.[146] The curriculum at Fourah Bay was accordingly shaped to the requirements of Durham and modelled on its two basic courses: those leading to the B.A. pass degree and the licence in theology.[147] The latter course had been devised for candidates intending ordination in the church of England and had a strong denominational bias. The former, which also offered a suitable preparation for the ministry, stressed scriptural study and the classics, and prescribed in addition English history and mathematics with the option of certain other literary disciplines in the second and final year. Sunter saw nothing incongruous in planting these studies in West Africa. He was as untroubled as were most missionaries of his time about generating an exotic, controversial type of christianity. It seemed as natural to him as to the society to train the native pastorate in the tenets of the church of England. He had no qualms about the suitability of the L.Th. nor had he misgivings about the arts course, for it was his stout conviction that the needs of Africa would best be served by the white man first laying a firm foundation of his own civilisation, and the African subsequently adapting it to his own requirements.[148] But he did acknowledge that a curriculum followed in the north of England might at least be inadequate, if not unsuitable, when transferred to the West of Africa. The L.Th. did not prescribe the study of comparative religion; it offered no intellectual armoury against the inroads of islam. Sunter therefore arranged that the theological students should be carefully taught in Arabic and the muhammadan controversy in addition to the subjects specified by Durham.[149] But that was the extent of his deference to the theory of adaptation.

The conditions of affiliation gave Durham no control over the teaching at Fourah Bay, and this was in fact little affected by the introduction of university courses. The society had thought of trying to get a university man to take 'the kind of position of a Theol. Professor'; but in view of the difficulty of finding such a person, and the danger of unsettling Sunter, who was not university trained, it had abandoned the idea.[150] Sunter continued to shoulder the bulk of the teaching himself, assisted first by a christian Israelite, Alexander Schapira, who undertook the Hebrew and Arabic, and then by a talented linguist, C. A. L. Reichardt who rejoined the college in 1877 as professor of classics.[151] Two native tutors were also appointed, one of whom, N. S. Davis, achieved the distinction in 1878 of being the first West African to gain an arts degree on his own soil. But although the staff was small and, save on the linguistic side, not highly qualified, it proved adequate for its purpose. As Sunter had foreseen, there was no sudden influx of students. The grammar school supplied a trickle of candidates to qualify for the scholarships the society offered, but the Sierra Leoneans were not easily reconciled to the notion of fee paying, and although Lagos took advantage of the new regulations, comparatively few paying students were forthcoming to begin with. Sunter was able to enter eleven students for examination in 1876 – six for the matriculation in arts, and five for the admission examination in theology – but the numbers fell off in 1877; and in each of the next two years, N. S. Davis was sent to lecture at Cape Coast, Accra and Lagos to publicise the facilities offered at Fourah Bay. So few students precluded the appointment of a more specialised staff, but the want of it was not reflected in the examination results. All the examinees presented in 1876 were successful, as were four of the five who sat the first year B.A. examination in 1877. And after the examinations in the autumn of 1878, when N. S. Davis entered successfully for the B.A. final, and five other candidates for the L.Th., Dr Farrar, professor of divinity at Durham, wrote appreciatively to Sunter of the performance of his students.[152]

Higher education at Fourah Bay had begun in a small way, in a specialised field. The range of studies was closely attuned to the missionary purpose, but more narrowly conceived than Sunter had originally intended. His concept of a general college, so far as its degree courses were concerned, had hardly materialised.[153] In its emphasis on theology and the humanities, and its disregard of African environment, the character of the instruction was simply the current type of missionary elementary education writ large. The higher studies launched by the society were indeed an ironical by-product of Blyden's intervention.

Some fifty years later, the picture at Fourah Bay was not essentially different. The fortunes of the college had continued to fluctuate after affiliation, as before. Funds, always short, became acutely so in 1908, and the society was obliged to announce that it might not be possible to continue the 'University side' of the work after 1911. Rigid economy, however, together with certain gifts, enabled the university courses to continue, but it was not until 1918, when the society managed to secure the co-operation of the wesleyans, which it had tried for unsuccessfully in 1909, that the financial position stabilised. The number of students pursuing university courses grew only slowly: those matriculating averaged four in the first ten years after affiliation, six in the next twenty years, ten in the uncertainty between 1908 and 1911, and fourteen from 1912 until the college jubilee in 1926, when the 400th student was entered on the Durham University roll. On the staff side, too, progress was slow. After Sunter's time it became customary for the principal to be a university man; but there was no sustained advance in the teaching strength of the college until the worst of the financial stress in the early twentieth century had passed. For nearly a decade after 1905, the acting principal carried on the university work of the college with only three or four native tutors trained in one or other of its main courses. After amalgamation with the wesleyans, it became possible to maintain a more effective teaching strength, and the sort of structure that emerged was a principal, vice-principal, two or three lecturers qualified in a specialised field, and three or four tutors.

The curriculum altered very little over the years. It was adjusted from time to time to meet changes in the regulations at Durham, and, to a lesser extent, its level was lifted as more promising students presented themselves. But hardly any attempt was made to broaden the range of studies, and the work of the college remained firmly centred in theology and the classics. Under Sunter's successors it became customary for theology students to read for the honours L.Th., and when that was abolished in 1907, for a theological version of the ordinary arts degree; after 1916, some students went on to take the newly instituted diploma in theology. Other students, with very few exceptions, read for the B.A. pass degree – none yet attempted the honours examination – and in 1918, the course was extended to three years. Amalgamation with the wesleyans in the latter year confirmed this pattern of studies. It was agreed that the arts course prescribed by Durham should remain the basis of the university work of the college, although the principal was authorised to arrange other courses in consultation with the vice-principal, subject to the consent of the council and the two parent committees. And occasionally students did venture into other fields such as law, as they had done exceptionally in the past.

Higher studies at Fourah Bay had remained quite untouched by the new current of thought that was bringing African education at lower levels into closer relation with local needs. Shortage of funds was perhaps the major obstacle to experiments in adaptation, but African opinion was a further deterrent. The African student greatly prized the connection with Durham for the British degree it put within his grasp; he also placed a high value on the classical education which he regarded as a source of the white man's power. Any attempt to have given an African bias to the education or to have instituted a local qualification would almost certainly have invited opposition.[154] The pattern of studies thus remained much as it had been in Sunter's day; and when the African Education Commission surveyed the college in 1920, it strongly criticised the way in which the curriculum lagged behind the dictates of modern educational theory. It pointed not only to the absence of adequate provision for such subjects as science, including agriculture, social studies and modern languages, which were increasingly to be found in progressive colleges and universities elsewhere, but also to the similar omission of the more specifically African subjects, such as native languages, called for by the special setting of the college.[155] On the eve of official interest in the planning of higher education, Fourah Bay enjoyed a great reputation with the Africans as the only college in British West Africa at which degrees could be obtained; but it hovered uncertainly between a theological college and an incipient university.

IV AFRICAN PIONEERS FOR HIGHER EDUCATION

Meantime there had also been African pioneers in the field of higher education: independent thinkers who, from the early 1860s, had appealed for official support of schemes of their own. Three Africans had been especially prominent in this intermittent pressure; and although their projects had differed, the ideas underlying them had shown a progressive development which had helped to create a new image of African higher education, contrasting sharply with the missionary provision at Fourah Bay.

The first of the three Africans to urge the need of local facilities for higher education was a Creole of Sierra Leone: James Africanus Beale Horton. Horton was a doctor. He had been selected from Fourah Bay College in 1855 to be trained in medicine in Britain under a new scheme sponsored by the war office. After taking his M.R.C.S. and M.D., he entered the army in 1859 as a staff assistant-surgeon.[156] Two years later, he made his first proposal for higher education in British West Africa: a modest one, prompted by the difficulties he himself had experienced in England. He suggested to the war office that a small government medical school should be set up in Sierra Leone where young Africans might be prepared by an African in the preliminaries of medicine before proceeding to their studies in England. His idea was that students who had attained some proficiency in Latin, Greek and mathematics and were not above the age of twenty, should be given a grounding in 'Anatomy, Physiology, Chemistry, Botany (of Africa), Natural History, Hospital Practice and Pharmacy' for a period of up to two years. During that time they should also continue their classical studies. Since an African, in his view, would take a far greater interest in what would tend to 'elevate' his country than a European, he attached importance to the master being a native, and offered himself for the post.[157] But the proposal was still-born. The war office referred to his superiors on the Gold Coast, asking how far African M.O.s had succeeded in winning the confidence of the European and native community. On learning that the strong predilection was for European doctors, they decided to abandon the further training of natives. So far as the war office was concerned, the raison d'être for the government medical school had gone, and Horton was informed accordingly.[158] He renewed the proposal at the end of 1863 and won the warm support of governor Pine.[159] Pine felt strongly that the medical profession should be broken of its 'mischievous prejudice against colour'. But the appeal was no more successful; the war office remained unresponsive.

Already, however, Horton's ideas were growing more ambitious. As early as 1862 he had begun to advocate a full scale university for British West Africa;[160] and in 1865, encouraged by the findings of the select committee of that year, he reiterated the plea in a pamphlet which he expanded into book form in 1868.[161] Boldly proclaiming 'We want a University of West Africa', he called on the government to provide this 'focus of learning' by building on the foundations laid by the missionaries and endowing the college at Fourah Bay. He urged the appointment of a highly qualified staff and indicated in some detail the field of studies he wished to see covered. Listing the subjects in a somewhat haphazard sequence, he wrote that lectures should be given in 'the theory and practice of education, classics, mathematics, natural philosophy, mensuration, and book-keeping; English language and literature; French, German, Hebrew, history in general, mineralogy, physiology, zoology, botany, chemistry, moral and political philosophy, civil and commercial law, drawing and music, besides the various subjects which might be included under the term theology'. He laid special emphasis on the study of the physical sciences as 'closely connected with our daily wants' and well designed 'to cultivate the reasoning faculties'. Mathematics was commended on similar grounds. But the long list of studies made no mention of specifically African subjects. No place was found for Arabic or the vernacular languages; history was significantly 'general'.[162]

In 1873, Horton joined the small band of Africans campaigning with Blyden for indigenous facilities for higher education.[163] He contributed a 'brief sketch' of his opinion on 'the question of the day' to the *Negro*, in which he gave his wholehearted support for the projected university envisaged in Blyden's correspondence with Hennessy. He congratulated the promoters on pursuing the scheme in face of hostility and confessed himself at a loss to understand the grounds of the opposition. Where, he asked, 'are the schools for the study of Botany, of Mineralogy, of Physiology, of Chemistry, of Engineering, of Architecture, and of other kindred subjects which are the fundamental sciences which elevate the mind and develop the intellectual growth of any race which aims at occupying a high status in the human nationality? Is it . . . in the Grammar School, the Fourah Bay College, or the

Wesleyan Institution?' He no longer looked for a government-endowed university at Fourah Bay: he thought that a more central site than either Fourah Bay or King Tom's Point was needed so that day students might be admitted as well as residential ones. But he emphasised the importance of securing adequate official support and suggested that, following the practice in German state universities, professorial chairs should be endowed by the government. His ideas on the curriculum showed little advance on what he had written five years before. He now acknowledged the need for Arabic, but otherwise continued to ignore the provision of African studies. His chief concern was still to supply the means of scientific instruction which he declared more conspicuously wanting in British West Africa than in any other country of the British empire. 'The study of physiology and chemistry, which every literary mind should possess some knowledge of, is entirely unknown to natives on the coast', he wrote; 'these, with the more extensive studies of humanity, Belles Lettres, Arabic, Law, Medicine, Engineering &c must form parts of the curriculum of a University for the thorough elevation of a community.'[164]

Horton made a last attempt to introduce higher scientific education under the terms of his will. On retiring from the army in 1880, he settled in Freetown at Horton Hall; and this he bequeathed for the establishment of a superior school, to be known as Horton's Collegiate High School, which should specialise in 'high Scientific Classes of study'. He expressed the hope that every effort would be made to raise the standard of work at the school and to secure affiliation with an English university. But even here he was cheated of his goal. When he died in 1883, it was found that his estate was unable to support a fraction of the bequests he had made, and Horton's Collegiate High School remained a tribute on paper only to his efforts on behalf of higher education.[165]

In prescribing a pattern of higher studies for West Africa, Horton had kept in mind not so much the special needs of the West African as the requirements of 'any race'[166] at a primitive stage of development. His concept of a West African university was based on what he knew of European universities and allowed for the minimum of adaptation. Despite the 'Africanus' he added to his name, he remained insensitive to the claims of African culture. He brought the instinctively imitative approach of the early pioneer working in a field not his own; the approach, moreover, of a mind accustomed by its training to think in universal terms.

The second of the three Africans examined the problem of higher education in British West Africa more closely. Edward Blyden brought a more original mind to the task, and a decade's experience of teaching in a negro college. When he raised the question of a West African university in 1872,[167] he was already clear that it must bear a distinctive, indigenous character.[168] For he assigned it a special function. It was not merely to provide the advanced training that Horton had envisaged; it was to release the whole educational system from the grip of the despotic, Europeanising influences which had warped and crushed the negro mind. The West African University was to point the way to a new liberal system of training, properly adapted to the peculiarities of the African race. It was to be the means of counteracting the degeneracy of the negro, restoring his self-respect, and developing in him the qualities he would need for self-government.

Blyden did not disclose his formula for an indigenous university when corresponding with Hennessy in 1872. But some indication of what he had in mind may perhaps be gathered from the presidential address he gave to Liberia College in 1881.[169] Under the title of 'The aims and methods of a liberal education for Africans', he discussed the sort of training he considered suitable not only for the students of Liberia College but for 'Negro youth everywhere in Africa' who hoped to take a leading part in the work of 'the race and of the country'. There were two ways in which he considered the curriculum of an African negro college should differ from that of a college in Europe or America. It should foster the full and free development of African race instincts, partly by excluding some of the studies customarily pursued in a western society, and partly by adding new ones. It should also give increased emphasis to the 'purely disciplinary agencies' needed by a society at an early stage of development. Blyden wished to eliminate the study of modern western civilisation from the curriculum of a young African college, for it was then that 'the transatlantic slave trade arose and those theories – theological, social and political – were invented for the degradation and proscription of the Negro'. But although the African must advance along a different road from the Anglo-Saxon, he must seek his inspiration from the same source. He must draw on the experience of the earlier epochs of western civilisation and study in particular the Greek and Latin languages and literatures. The classics would give him 'nourishment . . . without . . . race poison' and teach him all he needed to know to build the moral, political and religious character of his country. With mathematics, they would provide the chief means of disciplining and strengthening the mind, and they would prepare the way for the study of the sciences. If Blyden looked primarily to western learning to stimulate the development of a healthy African society, he looked to African studies to reinforce its indigenous quality. He was keen that Arabic and some of the principal native languages should find a place in the curriculum, for in providing the means of communication with the interior, they held the key to a fund of African custom and tradition which would invigorate the African race. We must listen, he said, 'to the songs of our unsophisticated brethren as they sing of their history, as they tell of their traditions, of the wonderful and mysterious events of their tribal or national life, of the achievements of what we call their superstitions; we must lend a ready ear to the ditties of the Kroomen who pull our boats, of the Pesseh and Golah men who till our farms; we must read the compositions, rude as we may think them, of the Mandingoes and the Veys. We shall in this way get back the strength of the race, like the giant of the ancients who always gained strength, for his conflict with Hercules, whenever he touched his Mother Earth'. It was for this reason that he wished to see the African college sited away from the foreign influences of the seaboard and within reach of the stimulus of the interior. Blyden also provided for biblical instruction in his scheme of studies. He wished christianity to be the pervasive influence in the new African civilisation, but a characteristically African form of christianity. The bible was to be taught 'without note or comment'; there was to be no reference to the confusing and irrelevant dogmatic controversies of the west.

Whether or not this was the sort of curriculum Blyden envisaged for a West African university in 1872, many of its features were certainly reproduced in the scheme of studies he devised for a centre of higher learning in Lagos in 1896.[170] When he made this second attempt to introduce higher education into the British settlements in West Africa he avowed a less ambitious purpose than when he made his unsuccessful bid for a university in Sierra Leone in 1872. In raising the question in correspondence with the governor, Sir Gilbert Carter, he rested his plea on the need to check the practice of sending Africans abroad for higher training.[171] This was wasteful of time, money and life; and it was weakening, besides, to African racial integrity, for the negro receiving his education overseas did not 'breathe African air' through any of the lessons he imbibed. The 'smell of African ground' was not in them; everything was 'Europe and European'. Blyden did not assert any additional need to reorientate the educational system. He made a tactful reference to what the missionaries had done in the past and declared that the new departure was not meant to disparage or conflict with what they were doing currently, but simply to supply the more advanced training that limits of 'sphere and resources' prevented them from giving. But his reticence may well have been calculated. He had clearly reflected on the lessons of 1872 and the need for a more diplomatic approach. He set himself, indeed, to conciliate not only the missionaries but officialdom as well. He was careful to keep his project within modest bounds. It was not a university he tried to interest the government in, but initially at least, a small, unpretentious institute.

He gave some indication of the curriculum he envisaged for it both in correspondence with Sir Gilbert Carter and in a formal prospectus drawn up for circulation to the other West African dependencies.[172] The prospectus listed the subjects of study in general terms. Announcing that the proposed institute would consist of a literary and industrial department, it stated that the branches of study to be taught in the former would include 'Ancient and Modern Languages, Mathematics, History, Mental and Moral Philosophy and Natural Science' and those in the latter 'the various handicrafts, and scientific and practical agriculture'. An earlier letter to the governor revealed something of the ideas behind the curriculum for the literary department.[173] Blyden considered that the purpose of the instruction should be partly to convey 'useful knowledge', but more especially to inculcate the 'habits of attention, self-control and reflection' needed by African youth fresh from primitive conditions. In the belief that ancient languages and mathematics would be the most effective disciplinary studies, he assigned them pride of place in the curriculum.[174] He gave prominence to the study of languages for another reason too. It was a sphere specially suited to the talent of the African: one in which he could still hope to match, if not excel, the achievements of other races. It was 'not his to measure the distances of the planets and mark their courses ... to plough unknown seas and find his way across trackless waters', but 'he might from his point of vision bring forward new translations of the classics and of the Bible which would both astonish and instruct Europeans'. Scientific studies did not figure high in Blyden's list of priorities, but he acknowledged that there were some branches of science that would be useful to the African. Botany, mineralogy and geology should be taught; and it would be desirable that he should know something of 'the laws of the moral and physical world as ... unfolded by contemporaneous discoveries'. In his correspondence with the governor, though not in the prospectus, Blyden also indicated the need for religious instruction. The religious instinct in the African was strong, and any system of education which disregarded it would fail. The teaching should be based on the concepts of the christian faith but resolutely eschew dogmatic controversy.[175]

The scheme of higher studies for Lagos was thus based on many of the ideas that Blyden had developed in his presidential address to Liberia College fifteen years before. Yet one of the most characteristic features of the model curriculum of 1881 seemed to be missing. Lecturing in Liberia, Blyden had pointed to two ways in which the college in Africa should differ from its western counterpart. Prescribing for Lagos, he had apparently catered for only one. He had allowed for the greater emphasis on disciplinary studies; but he had not disclosed any special design to foster African racial qualities. When he specified ancient and modern languages in the prospectus, he may have meant to include Arabic and some of the native languages; when he specified history he may have intended to follow a syllabus specially adapted to permit the free development of African race instincts. But if the purpose was there, it was concealed, and in its place was a new emphasis on industrial training. Blyden's criterion of a suitable site for the Lagos project was not one that would give access to the springs of African culture, but one that would lend itself most conveniently to the practical aspects of the training. He thought a government site across the lagoon at Ebute Metta, hitherto used as a botanic station, but no longer adequate for the purpose, would provide an admirable setting for 'The Lagos Training College and Industrial Institute'.[176]

The absence of any explicit reference to the need for an African bias in the curriculum may well have been a further element in Blyden's strategy. He probably judged that it would be expedient to keep the academic syllabus to simple English lines and allow the industrial features of the scheme to plead for it in official quarters. If this was his reasoning, it was certainly effective.

The prospect of sound industrial training made a strong appeal both to Sir Gilbert Carter and the colonial office; and the secretary of state agreed that the colonial government might give financial and other assistance once the natives had shown by their own contributions that they were in earnest.[177] But although the colonial office welcomed Blyden's 'much more practical line', it hardly expected the scheme to succeed.[178] 'There is not much public spirit in the West African', reflected one of the permanent officials, '& Mr Blyden will be a clever man if he can extract much in the way of subscriptions from his fellow countrymen. . . .'[179] The cynicism was only too well justified. Blyden was soon obliged to admit that the support he had hoped for was not forthcoming, and that for the time being at least the scheme would have to be abandoned.[180] In bitter disgust at the 'invincible apathy' of the 'so-called Christian native', and his irresponsible preoccupation with 'England and English things', he turned back to the task which had chiefly engaged him for the past fifteen years: that of bringing western education to the muslims of the British settlements.

And it was for the muslims that he devised a final scheme of higher education for British West Africa in 1899. Prompted by Britain's developing responsibilities in the Western Soudan, he suggested that the government should establish a training centre in Sierra Leone for the muslims of West Africa on similar lines to those proposed for the Gordon Memorial College at Khartoum.[181] In view of his earlier tirades against Europeanising the Negro, the purpose of the 'Central Training Institution' reads somewhat oddly. ' . . . the object', he wrote, ' – and I should think the main object – of an Educational Institution for the Mohammedans under the British Government would be to get them imbued – saturated so to speak with English ideas and modes of expression. . . .' A very far cry, or so it seemed, from raising the Negro on his own idiosyncracies. But the inconsistency was only apparent. Blyden wished the muhammadans to be suitably trained to assist in Britain's new task in Nigeria; he welcomed the extension of British influence and had consistently advocated it. Even when his criticism of British educational methods had been most severe, he had never doubted that Britain was marked out as the regenerator of inner Africa. At the very time he was pressing the device of a West African university to correct the alien bias in the educational system, he was inviting the British government to take charge of the Western Soudan.[182] He wished the British to disseminate western ideas and western knowledge, but not to impose them. Western culture was to make an indispensable contribution to the new African civilisation, but not to dominate it. And this was the spirit in which he conceived the new Moslem Training Institution. He wished to 'saturate' the muslims with English ideas to equip them as auxiliaries in the civilising mission he assigned to the British. But he had no thought of pressing English ideas to the point of challenging their own distinctive culture. This was to be scrupulously safeguarded. He chose Sierra Leone as the setting for the new institution not only on account of its markedly English atmosphere, but because of the multiplicity of African tribes residing there. The muslim student training in Sierra Leone could learn English in a peculiarly English environment, and still hear his own vernacular spoken; he could absorb something of English ideas, and yet keep in touch with his own background.

The same twofold purposes emerged in Blyden's choice of studies for the institution. He proposed that to begin with the subjects and methods of study should be similar to those he had adopted in his elementary school for muslims in Freetown. Here he had taught English, Arabic and native languages, with general history, arithmetic and geography. The emphasis had been on languages, with daily reading from standard English authors, and translation from Arabic into English, and into the vernaculars of the pupils present. A reference to Gibbon's chapters on the rise and progress of muhammadanism suggested that he had given thought to the selection of appropriate texts. It was a careful balance of western and African elements that he had in mind for the curriculum of the Central Training Institution.

Although Blyden wished the new training centre to be in Sierra Leone, he first disclosed his plans for it in Lagos. He knew the acting governor, G.C. Denton, personally, and took advantage of a voyage along the Coast to enlist his support. In outlining his proposals, Blyden not only offered his services as principal, but suggested that the post should carry with it the title of superintendent of government mohammedan schools. He hoped in this way that the institution might serve the further purpose of fostering the development of a system of muslim elementary education throughout British West Africa. Denton was disposed to support the scheme if only to obtain the teachers that would be needed as the number of muhammadan schools grew.[183] He thought Blyden particularly well suited for the delicate task of enlisting muslim co-operation, and was only hesitant on the score of his age: Blyden was thought to be in his late sixties, and recently had not been well. The colonial office displayed considerable interest in the project. Blyden's astute reference to the part the institution might play in furthering British imperial objects in the Soudan did not miss its mark. A senior official found his communication 'a remarkable letter from a remarkable man' and thought he had fully proved that education in English was 'of vital necessity for the expansion of British influence'.[184] But before any action could be taken on Captain Denton's despatch, a less favourable view of the scheme was received from the acting governor of Sierra Leone, Major Nathan.[185] Nathan considered it premature to proceed with plans for the institution whilst the muslims showed so little interest in elementary schools; he preferred to tackle the problem of muslim education at the lower level first. The colonial office adjusted its attitude accordingly. Whilst assuring the governor of Lagos that the scheme would receive 'the careful attention' which it deserved, it regretted that owing to the many more urgent problems in West Africa, it would not be possible to take any immediate steps to give effect to it.[186] Eventually it agreed to give

Blyden a short-term appointment to develop muslim elementary education in Sierra Leone. It evidently judged, with one of its officials, that a modest scheme of that kind was 'far more likely to be carried out and be productive of good than the ambitious proposal put forward by Dr Blyden for the estab*- of a Mohammedan Training College'.[187]

Blyden's schemes of higher education were devised over a period of nearly thirty years. Inevitably they reflected something of the differing circumstances in which they were conceived, and the differing purposes they were intended to achieve. A pattern of higher education specifically designed to introduce the muslim to western learning was bound to differ in emphasis from one that was planned to counter the indiscriminate Europeanising of the African. But Blyden's basic formula for African higher education seems to have remained unchanged. Reduced to its simplest terms, this was a curriculum based on the study of early western civilisation and mathematics; supplemented by the study of African subjects with special reference to African languages; taught in a free and liberal atmosphere, if possible by native teachers. His concept of higher studies differed both in character and purpose from Horton's. Horton, as a scientist, had given precedence to vocational training with the material needs of African society chiefly in mind; Blyden, as a linguist, put the stress on academic subjects with the wider aim of building the moral character of the new African civilisation and supplying its cultural needs. Unlike Horton, Blyden made a deliberate attempt to give his pattern of higher education an indigenous character. But he still put western learning in the forefront of his courses of study. He was influenced by his cosmopolitan background as well as by the special bent of his academic interests.

Early in the twentieth century, the torch of higher education in British West Africa passed from Blyden to the Gold Coast political leader, J.E. Casely Hayford. Casely Hayford rested the case for a West African university on the need for teachers who would free the educational system from foreign influences. It was Blyden's argument over again. But whereas Blyden had wished to strengthen African race consciousness, Casely Hayford acknowledged the aim of developing African nationality. And the difference was not merely one of terminology. Blyden was not much concerned about the African's political status: in the 1870s he spoke of training the West Africans for eventual self-government, but in the 1890s he was quite content to envisage a continuing state of political subjection for the muslims of the Western Soudan. He trimmed his views to what he conceived to be the prevailing current of British colonial policy. But Casely Hayford wanted to see the African determining his own political destiny. He was an outspoken champion of African political rights. He had an additional motive for desiring a distinctively African type of higher education.

It was in 1911, when Blyden was still alive, that Casely Hayford revived the question of a university in British West Africa. He chose a curious literary form in which to do so: a series of studies, published under the title *Ethiopia unbound*, in which he cast his ideas largely, though not wholly, in the form of fiction. He described the founding of an imaginary Mfantsipim National University, and he also prescribed the characteristic features of a national university for the Gold Coast and Ashanti.[188]

The Mfantsipim National University was the product of a wave of national consciousness that had swept through Fanti-land at the time of the formation of the Aborigines Rights Protection Society. A small band of enthusiastic workers had preached the gospel of education to the people, and as the gong-gong of the Amanhin went round the villages on Jubilee Day, the appeal for the National Education Fund met with a ready and generous response. Kwamankra, a young journalist, already marked out as one of the coming leaders of his people, left his newspaper to join the staff of the new university. He took a leading part in devising schemes to prevent it becoming 'a mere foreign imitation' and 'kept constantly before the Committee from the first the fact that no people could despise its own language, customs, and institutions and hope to avoid national death'. Most of the teaching, as a result, was given in the vernacular, and special attention was directed to the translation of text books into Fanti. The students were required to assume a distinctive national dress, suitably adapted to a progressive state of society. And the Mfantsipim authorities were apparently on their guard to preserve the indigenous character of the university in the machinery they devised to establish the standard of its scholarship. The university was not only affiliated to the University of London but 'in working correspondence with some of the best teaching institutions in Japan, England, Germany and America': a somewhat complex arrangement, it would seem, but at any rate less likely to be productive of a dominating foreign influence than an exclusive agreement with a single sponsoring university.

In turning to consider a future university for the Gold Coast, Casely Hayford continued to pursue the same ideas on a more realistic plane although with Kwamankra still as his mouthpiece. The Gold Coast University, no less than the University of Mfantsipim, was to be a centre of 'national conservancy and evolution'; it was to be created in the image of Mfantsipim and reproduce its essential features. Once again he thought the special function of a national university should be to stimulate interest in the vernacular languages. He envisaged separate chairs for Fanti, Hausa and Yoruba, and he wished the vernacular to be the medium of instruction, as in Japan. In defence of this novel emphasis on native languages he pointed to the experience of Denmark and Ireland where use of the vernacular had proved effective in developing national consciousness. He also assigned an important role to the chair of history in furthering his general purpose. The sort of history he wanted to see taught was universal history, with special reference to the part played in world affairs by Ethiopia. 'I would lay stress upon the fact that while Rameses II was dedicating temples to "the God of gods and secondly to his own glory", the God of the Hebrews had not yet appeared unto Moses in the burning bush', he wrote, 'that Africa was the cradle of the world's systems and philosophies, and the nursing mother of its religions. In short, that Africa has nothing to be ashamed of of [sic] its place among the nations of the earth. . . .' In his search for ways of raising Africans in their own esteem and sharpening their national identity, Casely Hayford again stressed the value of a distinctive national dress. Students should come to the Gold Coast University 'not in top hat and broad cloth, but in the sober garb in which the Romans conquered the material world, and in which [the Africans might] conquer the spiritual world'. To safeguard the national character of the university and insulate it from the foreign influence of the Coast, he thought it would be a wise precaution to site it well inland, preferably in a suitable suburb of Kumasi.

Casely Hayford had left Blyden far behind in his definition of an indigenous university: in his extravagant allocation of professorial chairs to native languages; and his desire for instruction in the medium of the vernacular; in the special slant of his historical studies and in his repudiation of western dress for the cultured African. He had maintained a complete silence, moreover, on the place of western learning in an African university. But Casely Hayford had not attempted a comprehensive picture of the university he wished to see established. He had confined himself to indicating the unique requirements of a university dedicated to the building of African nationality. Even so, there was an element of symbolism and romance in his image. He had not entirely abandoned the realm of fantasy when he turned to contemplate a national university for the Gold Coast and Ashanti.

Casely Hayford had discussed the need for a university in British West Africa in the studies he published in 1911, but he had not represented it in a particularly urgent light. He had not called for immediate action from the government as Horton had done in 1868, and nearly a decade passed before he made any serious attempt to arouse official interest in higher education. He did so then through the First Conference of Africans of British West Africa, which it was largely his achievement to have convened, and which met in Accra in March, 1920. The question of 'Education with particular reference to a West African University' was brought before the conference at its second session, and in one of seven resolutions on the subject, it was declared that the time had come 'to found a British West African University on such lines as would preserve in the students a sense of African Nationality. . . .'[189] This was the plea of *Ethiopia unbound*, given a more immediate significance; and it was now brought before the British government. It was embodied, with other resolutions, in a memorial addressed to the king in council, and it was presented to the secretary of state for the colonies by a special delegation in London.[190]

The colonial office declined to take any immediate steps to establish a West African university, and it is perhaps doubtful whether Casely Hayford and his associates really intended it should. It seems more likely that their purpose was to stimulate official planning: to define the goal of higher education and bring it into nearer focus. Casely Hayford had recently served on a special education committee in the Gold Coast, and must have been aware of the prior claims of secondary education there.[191] He did not comment on the demand for higher education in his speech at the inaugural session of the conference and left it to the president, T. Hutton-Mills, to do so. With a special view to ending the discrimination against Africans in the higher appointments of the civil service, Hutton-Mills declared it 'highly necessary' that a British West African university should be established 'as soon as may be'. He expressed the hope that the conference might be able to suggest a scheme for it, based, he implied, on King's College in Nigeria, Fourah Bay College in Sierra Leone, and 'the vast educational scheme' contemplated by the governor of the Gold Coast.[192] But it was significant that neither Casely Hayford, nor the National Congress of British West Africa into which the conference resolved itself, put much zest behind the campaign for a university in the following years. Casely Hayford still spoke of the need to 'press upon the attention of Government the early foundation of the British West African University' when he addressed the second session of congress, as president, in 1923.[193] But at the third session, two years later, he seemed to consider the developing scheme at Achimota a justification for relaxing pressure for a West African university.[194] And when he came to give his presidential address to the fourth and last session of congress in 1929 – the year in which university classes started at Achimota – he was apparently able to persuade himself that the plea for higher education, advanced nine years before, had been satisfactorily answered. 'Looking down the passage of time to the memorable conference at Accra in the Gold Coast in March, 1920', he declared, 'it is true to say that the main resolutions of Congress have passed the stage of controversy to the domain of actualities ... The effort in the Gold Coast to establish Achimota College is a direct response to the resolution of Congress that in its opinion the time "had come to found a British West African University on such lines as would preserve in the students a sense of African nationality".[195]

This was the special pleading of a tired politician. The 'vast educational scheme' on the Gold Coast was already envisaged when the First Conference of Africans of British West Africa foregathered in Accra, and although its outlines had still to be determined, there seems little reason to suppose they were much affected by the resolution in favour of a West African university taken in 1920. African pressure for a West African university was not immediately effective as a stimulus as it had been in 1872. But like that earlier abortive appeal, it helped to fix the image of an indigenous university; and it did so at a time when the colonial office was about to abandon its stand of aloof tolerance towards projects of higher education for one of constructive planning.

V THE OFFICIAL ATTITUDE

The British government had consistently declined to sponsor the various schemes of higher education which the Africans had urged upon it; and it had taken no initiative in the matter itself. But it had not been unsympathetic towards the aspirations of the Africans, and save in the case of the early medical school proposed by Africanus Horton,[196] had disclosed no wish to limit the educational opportunities of the natives. Despite a growing tendency to disparage the African 'scholar' and to view him as a source of friction and discontent,[197] there had been no official disposition either locally or in London, deliberately to withhold the provision of more advanced training. The shadow of the British experience in India had not yet begun to fall on tropical Africa; and the reluctance to embark on schemes of higher education on the West Coast had stemmed quite simply from the conviction that limitations of finance and educational progress made it inexpedient. Political factors, however, had also contributed to the official stand. Educational policy had inevitably been attuned to the wider trends of imperial policy, and as the prospects of an early withdrawal from the Coast had receded – and with them the urgency for training the natives for self-government – so the response to appeals for higher education had weakened. Hence the paradox of the cautious interest in the proposal for a West African university in the 1870s, and the impatient rejection of it nearly half a century later.

The character and evolution of the official view were partly disclosed in the periodic decisions forced on the government by African initiative. When Blyden made his early appeal for an indigenous university in 1872, it met with an initially encouraging response not only from the administrator on the Coast, but from the colonial office as well. Hennessy forwarded the proposal to London with the persuasive argument that the practice of sending Africans abroad for higher education had 'a direct tendency to defeat the policy laid down by the Parliamentary Committee in 1865 and by Her Majesty's Government in wishing to see Africans capable of Governing their Country';[198] and although there was some scepticism amongst the senior permanent officials of the colonial office, Lord Kimberley's liberal sympathies were genuinely aroused. It was only after the Church Missionary Society were firmly committed to opening Fourah Bay to laymen that the scheme was finally dismissed, and it was then turned down by a Conservative colonial secretary, acting on the advice of a less impetuous administrator on the Coast, on grounds that were to be deemed valid for many years to come: that the educational progress of the natives did not warrant the very considerable expenditure that would be involved.[199] Despite the rising tide of imperialism towards the end of the century, Blyden's later schemes were also received with considerable official interest, for both the Lagos Training College and Industrial Institute he proposed in 1896 and the Central Training Institution he planned for muhammadans in 1899 were essentially modest projects, carefully designed to harmonise with current objectives of educational and imperial policy.[200] But when the more ambitious plea for a West African university was renewed in 1920, it met with scant support in official circles. The opposition was especially pronounced locally, where both Clifford in Nigeria and Guggisberg in the Gold Coast were uncompromising in their hostility. Neither offered any objection on political grounds. Each was identified with a liberal policy towards the 'Africanisation' of the public service and combined a progressive attitude towards the admission of Africans to higher posts with a corresponding interest in educational development. Neither questioned the ultimate desirability of a university; but each insisted that for the time being it was premature – Guggisberg, indeed, protesting that it was mischievously so. Such decided opposition was partly due to a general impatience with the claims and objectives of the National Congress. But it was largely owing to the firm assumption that political independence for the territories of British West Africa was still far in the future, and that educational development should be built systematically from below. Clifford anticipated the very similar reaction of Guggisberg when he assured the colonial office that to devote any large sums to the establishment and maintenance of a university would be to put the cart before the horse and achieve no useful purpose. The colonial office did not dispute the conclusion; but it was in keeping with the official approach of the past half century that a permanent official, reflecting on the fact that universities flourished in Europe before there was a comprehensive system of secondary education, should have questioned the assumption that this kind of cart should inevitably follow a horse! He took the view that a West African university would not be premature or useless if private generosity could be prevailed upon to provide all or most of the funds that would be needed.

To judge from the response to the sporadic pleas of the Africans, the official attitude was essentially one of benevolent neutrality; but it was more than this, for there was also a constructive side to it, stemming from the official initiative on the Coast. From the early years of the twentieth century, local governments began to plan towards the ultimate provision of higher education in their territories. And shortly before this, in the last decade of the nineteenth century, there was an interesting attempt to supply an alternative route to higher training in the Gold Coast. It was singularly unsuccessful, but it affords fresh evidence of the official readiness to admit natives to higher education, and it throws light, too, on the deepening official conviction that it would be premature to provide local facilities for the purpose.

In 1893, the governor of the Gold Coast, Sir W. Brandford Griffith, took advantage of a recent increase of revenue to propose a scheme of government scholarships that would enable natives to pursue higher studies in Britain.[201] Such a scheme, he considered, would serve as a more effective stimulus to education than expenditure on the necessary facilities for 'secondary or first grade education' in the colony itself; besides which it would greatly assist the government in recruiting suitable staff for 'superior positions'. Whilst no longer arguing the need to train natives for self-government as Hennessy had done twenty years before, he was careful to relate the proposal to 'the recommendations of the Reports of the Parliamentary Committees of 1842 and 1865 and the wishes of Her Majesty's Government in respect of employing native officers as far as possible in this climate'. He also recalled the success of the similar system of Island scholarships he had recently introduced in Barbados. The clerks in the colonial office were at once persuaded that the scheme was premature. One of them, with a reference to the disparity in the educational development of the Gold Coast and Barbados, took the conventional line that technical education was the prime need of the African colony. Moreover he thought it would be 'much safer' to keep to the existing system of selecting natives already in the service for training abroad, for a native 'coming from a country so little civilised as the Gold Coast at the age of 20 . . . might very possibly go to the dogs and save the Colonial Government the trouble of testing his official capabilities'.[202] Another took the view that it seemed to be a case of 'trying to run before you can walk';[203] and a third minuted his full agreement with their objections.[204] But in the early 1890s, there was a still stronger Liberal influence in the office than in the early 1870s. Not only was there a colonial secretary with advanced radical views in Lord Ripon, but a permanent under-secretary to share his liberal convictions in Robert Meade. Meade promptly dissented from the opinion of his junior colleagues. Provided a proper standard was set up, 'measured by the capacity to derive real solid advantage from further training in England', he saw no reason why the scheme should not be sanctioned. 'We do but little to encourage education', he observed, 'and the Governor is on the right path in seeking to obtain local material as lawyers, Doctors, Foremen of Works, etc.'[205] Ripon agreed; and in conveying his approval in principle to Brandford Griffith, adopted a significant passage which Meade had contributed to the official draft. 'I shall be much gratified', he assured the governor, 'if you should find yourself in a position to promote higher education in the colony under your government.'[206]

The sequel was also significant. It was decided to establish four government scholarships: to award one each year, and to make each tenable initially for three years. The qualifying standard was fixed at a pass in the Cambridge senior local examination with either a first or second class honours, or a third class honours with a distinction in one subject. The examination was to be held annually in Accra.[207] The scheme was introduced in 1895; but no valid application was received in that year, and of the four candidates who sat the examination in 1896, and the three in 1897, none came near even to passing.[208] The director of education considered the Cambridge senior examination far too hard for the Gold Coast, but held out no prospect of a different result if the junior examination were substituted for it. In these unpromising circumstances, the governor felt obliged to suspend the scheme; and in notifying the colonial office of his intention, expressed the view that the energies of the government should be devoted 'for some years longer' to raising the standard of elementary education, and pushing as far as possible all branches of industrial training. 'Higher education' he concluded, 'will follow as a natural result of such work.'[209] The colonial office acquiesced in his decision; and not only endorsed his view of the need for industrial training, but his view too of the right road to higher education.[210]

Shortly after the turn of the century, progress along this road began to quicken. New projects, both in the Gold Coast and in Southern Nigeria, brought higher education on to the horizon of official planning. But before they could take shape, rumours of such schemes led the governor of Sierra Leone to intervene with the first official proposal for a West African university. In a bold bid to retain Sierra Leone's lead in higher education, Probyn seized on the financial difficulties of Fourah Bay to suggest that the college should be incorporated as an independent university. After some preliminary soundings on the Coast, he outlined his proposal in simultaneous communications to the Church Missionary Society and the colonial office in January 1905.[211]

In planning the elementary school for sons of chiefs at Bo, Probyn was at pains to break away from the type of western education that had prevailed in the past.[212] In his scheme for higher studies at Fourah Bay he was content to adopt a more conventional approach, aiming quite simply at a pocket size version of the civic university at home. He envisaged a university of some fifty students, drawn from all parts of British West Africa. It was to be organised with a court consisting of the governor and the members of the executive or legislative councils, a council that would be half lay and half academic, and a senate composed of representatives of the various faculties. The governor was to be chancellor; and in the first instance the warden was to be chosen from the anglican community, and the sub-warden from the wesleyan. Probyn did not contemplate any break in the link with Durham. Students were still to be able to follow the existing courses in arts and divinity. But courses were also to be provided, at a less advanced level, in a wide variety of other subjects. The university was to be empowered by its charter to award diplomas in medicine, education, engineering, science, and agriculture; and these were to be given a specified and regionally limited validity. He gave only a vague indication of the staff that would be needed to support such a programme, and his financial estimate was still more unrealistic. He was optimistic enough to put the annual running cost between £2,000 and £2,500, and suggested that this might well be assured if local governments and the Church Missionary Society were to guarantee the fees of a stated number of students.

In view of the massive responsibilities Britain had recently incurred on the West Coast, it was hardly to be expected that such a scheme would find favour in the colonial office, and in fact it met with harsher handling than any previous proposal for higher education. The first clerk to comment on it judged that 'any scheme' for a university in West Africa was 'altogether premature'. 'We wish to encourage agricultural and industrial training rather than "arts" and divinity', he wrote, 'and for the former there is no need for a university for carpenters & farmers. It is ludicrous to expect that adequate valuable instruction of a university standard could be given in Medicine, Engineering, or Science on a seventh part of £2,500 a year.'[213] His view was readily endorsed by his superiors, and it was not thought necessary to take the opinion of the colonial secretary before putting up a draft reply. Probyn was duly informed that 'in the present circumstances and state of development of the Colony', no promise of financial support could be sanctioned.[214] Undeterred by this ruling, however, Probyn repeated the request, in slightly different form, a few weeks later. As a result of further correspondence with the Church Missionary Society, he was emboldened to ask whether, if the university were sufficiently endowed at the outset, the colonial office would be prepared to ensure the continuity of the work.[215] This time the response was still more emphatic. Declining to authorise this assurance, the colonial secretary stated the grounds of his refusal in unequivocal terms. 'I have given careful consideration to this subject', he wrote, 'but I have not been able to convince myself that the time has come to establish a University in West Africa. . . .'[216] Towards the end of 1907, Probyn raised the question of the disposal of the property at Fourah Bay in the belief that the closure of the college was imminent.[217] But even this brought no change of heart in the colonial office. It remained staunchly of the opinion that it would be premature to direct local revenue to the purposes of higher education.

Meantime, the more modest schemes that Probyn had hoped to forestall had been going ahead with colonial office approval. In April 1907, the governor of Southern Nigeria, Sir Walter Egerton, submitted details of a scheme for the establishment of a 'Government College' in Lagos.[218] The proposal was for a day school that would teach to a higher level than the existing secondary schools, and bring students to the threshold of university studies. It was designed primarily as a training ground for clerks and for those intending a professional career. Preparation for the matriculation and intermediate examinations of the University of London was to be a special feature of its work. The colonial office made no demur to the principle of a government secondary school; but it raised two issues in connection with the character it was to assume, each seeming to threaten a modification in the previous official stand on higher education.

The first concerned the nature of the courses to be provided. Inevitably there was a clerk in the colonial office to question the desirability of a predominantly literary training; and he did so not only from the point of view of the needs of the country, but of the effect likely to be produced on the native character. 'The proposed College would, it seems to me, turn out young Africans of the clerk and office class and little more', he wrote. 'But I have always understood that of this class, the kind of young man who aims at a subordinate post in a Government office, there is already a surplus and that this particular brand of educated African is not on the whole a very satisfactory product. I imagined that the real need was for technical and industrial education which would teach the native the 'dignity of labour' and would ultimately be a far more potent factor in the development of the country than a knowledge of French, Greek and elementary maths or even of letter writing or book-keeping.'[219] Referred to the Coast for comment, these views were firmly rejected. Egerton protested that owing to the very rapid development of Southern Nigeria since the beginning of the century there was in fact an acute shortage of natives suitably equipped to serve as clerks. An increased supply was the country's most urgent need. It was literary education, therefore, that was the essential want, not technical or industrial training, for which there was adequate provision already.[220] The inspector of schools, Henry Carr, was no less emphatic in refuting the alleged effect of a predominantly literary education on the native character. He attributed the unattractive traits in the 'educated' African to an insufficiency of cultural training, not a surfeit. He sensed behind the official phraseology the further suspicion that a higher literary training must invite political troubles, and went on to argue the need of an education that would serve to dispel ignorance of government activities.[221] Carr put great stress on the need for a type of secondary education that would be suitably adapted to the special circumstances of the country, and he saw in the generous options of the London matriculation a means of providing precisely the sort of general cultural education that was wanted. It would not only meet the requirements of those planning to take up a clerkship, or to follow a professional career: it would train the leaders that would surely be needed in a country where the white man could never be permanently acclimatised.[222] Such considerations were allowed weight in the colonial office. The secretary of state, Lord Crewe, felt obliged to admit that a good case had been made out for giving special prominence to commercial and literary training 'at any rate for the present';[223] and it was agreed that whilst some manual and technical instruction should be given, the main emphasis should be on sound English literary education.[224] The colonial office had thus acquiesced in a significant step towards higher education, and conformed to its practice of putting no obstacle in the way of the higher training of natives.

The second issue involved the approach to higher education more directly. This was formulated not by the colonial office itself, but by the board of education to whom it had submitted the scheme for comment. With an eye to what had happened in India and other parts of the empire, the board expressed concern lest the government in Southern Nigeria were aiming at an unduly pretentious establishment. It saw in the use of the terms 'college' and 'professor', and indeed in some of the subjects suggested for the curriculum, an attempt to give something of a university character to the new institution.[225] Asked to comment on this apparent 'confusion of aim and ideal',

Egerton at once disclaimed any desire for a university, insisting that what was wanted was 'a good Secondary School'.[226] The director of education was a little more equivocal: not concealing his hope that the new venture might form 'the nucleus and birthplace of a College system, giving instruction beyond the proposed present high-water mark of the Matriculation Examination of the University of London' but acknowledging that it should at least begin as a secondary school.[227] After prolonged discussion it was finally agreed that whilst special post-secondary classes of a vocational type might be added to the school, the normal goal of students would be the London matriculation, and that the point of entry should be temporarily lowered to provide for a model sub-secondary department. It was also agreed that both in designation and general organisation its character as a school should be clearly and unambiguously proclaimed. Final approval of the details of the scheme went out from London in June 1909 and King's School, Lagos, opened its doors to students in the following September.[228] In endorsing the views of the board of education, the colonial office had divested the school of any university character it might have assumed; it had defined its purpose in a more modest sense than some of its promoters had intended. But in identifying itself with the views of the board it had not dissociated itself from the considerations which had dictated them; and the board had made it abundantly clear that its purpose was not simply to delay the advent of higher education but rather to avoid prejudicing its healthy development. 'It may well be', its memorandum had run, 'that in time the need for education higher than secondary will make itself felt in Lagos but nothing is more likely to retard the early development of higher education than the attempt to treat as higher what in fact is only secondary. If the new institution were frankly started as a first rate Secondary School there would be nothing to prevent it giving instruction to specially bright pupils beyond the ordinary school age in the same way that many schools do in this country. In that way it would be preparing the road for the development of a true University college; but if the staff who are engaged for most of their time in doing what in fact is secondary work are called professors, and the institution given a name which seems to claim for it the rank of a University college, these things will stand in the way of further developments when the need for them arises.'[229] The long debate over the government secondary school for Lagos had not only confirmed the readiness of the colonial office to admit natives to higher education; it had supplied an additional reason to confirm it in its conviction of the educational importance of a gradual and systematic approach to that goal.

The contemporary scheme in the Gold Coast was rather different, but again a significant landmark in the local planning towards higher education. In the same month that Egerton submitted details for a government secondary school in Lagos, Sir John Rodger forwarded proposals for a government training institution for teachers in Accra.[230] Designed as part of his wider scheme for introducing a new system of elementary education in the colony, this met with immediate and unquestioning approval in the colonial office.[231] But Rodger, no less than the director of education in Southern Nigeria, was already looking beyond the immediate future. On a moonlit evening, on the battlements of Christiansborg Castle, he confided in the principal of the new institution his distant ambitions, speaking of how he envisaged a West African university with constituent colleges in Sierra Leone, the Gold Coast and Nigeria, and how the college at Accra was 'but the small beginning in his mind, of the great educational scheme which would give to Africans a full and adequate place in the scholarship of the world'.[232]

With the opening of a new phase of local planning immediately after the war, progress towards higher education became more marked, especially in the Gold Coast. In 1919, a special committee appointed by Sir Hugh Clifford reported in favour of the immediate introduction of government secondary education, recommending for this purpose the establishment of a Royal College on the lines of an English public school, in or near Accra.[233] The recommendation was enthusiastically adopted by Guggisberg when he came to the Gold Coast later in the year, and in Achimota he planned a college comparable in many ways to the secondary school devised for Lagos over a decade before. But there were interesting contrasts. Achimota was to be residential whilst King's was not. Achimota was to be given a special cultural orientation which King's did not aspire to. Achimota, above all, was specifically assigned the role of preparing the way for higher education. For although Guggisberg was adamant in rejecting the plea of the National Congress for a university in 1920, it was his intention from the outset that the new secondary school should be a 'stepping stone' towards one.[234] And this was no mere hazy ambition in his mind. It was a deliberately planned policy, publicly proclaimed in a pamphlet he published in 1924. Here, in *The keystone*, he put the case for indigenous facilities for higher education with a vigour and sense of urgency that were altogether new. Whilst insisting that higher education must be approached by way of a carefully planned system of secondary schools, he represented it as a pressing need both economically and politically; and he strongly challenged the arguments of those who wished to delay or withhold it. Asserting his confidence in the capacity of the Africans to fill higher posts with credit, he was emphatic that the Gold Coast could not afford to fill the increasing number of these posts with Europeans. As for the belief that higher education would invite political troubles, he took precisely the opposite view. The greatest danger, he contended, would be to leave the gap between the European educated Africans and the semi-educated Africans of the primary schools unbridged.

Soon after world war I, therefore, higher education was firmly on the horizon of official planning in at least one of the West African dependencies. When the scheme for Achimota came to be submitted to London, its implications for higher education were readily endorsed in the colonial office. But if higher education had become an acknowledged aspiration in official circles, it was an aspiration that was still vague and undefined. Apart from Probyn's sketchy attempt at the beginning of the century, no thought had yet been given to the type it was to assume. A couple of decades were to pass before Britain had a clearly formulated policy for higher education in tropical Africa.

CHAPTER SEVEN

EVOLUTION OF A POLICY

I THE ADVISORY COMMITTEE ON EDUCATION IN THE COLONIES

Up to the end of the first world war the colonial office had taken only a fitful interest in the development of education in the British dependencies in tropical Africa. It had assumed that education was primarily a matter for local initiative and private agency; apart from an occasional effective intervention, it had confined itself to a routine and unimaginative control over the appropriation of local revenue to educational purposes. But the growing scale and complexity of the problem of native education, the new concept of trusteeship for subject races that emerged from the peace negotiations, and the publication in 1922 of the findings of the African Education Commission, together made an unanswerable case for more effective leadership in Whitehall. And thus in 1923, in response to missionary pressure, the colonial office decided to set up a permanent advisory committee on native education in tropical Africa, later extending its terms of reference to all colonial territories. It was constituted under the chairmanship of the parliamentary under-secretary, W. Ormsby-Gore, with a distinguished membership which included Sir Frederick Lugard, who had been closely concerned in educational development in Nigeria and Hong Kong; Sir James Currie, a former director of education in the Sudan and first head of Gordon College, Khartoum; Sir Michael Sadler, master of University College, Oxford, who brought to the committee his profound understanding of higher education in India; J. H. Oldham, representing protestant missionaries; and Hanns Vischer, who, as director of education, had been a sensitive and effective pioneer of western education in Northern Nigeria. In addition to his membership of the committee, Vischer was also appointed full-time secretary.[1]

The committee met for the first time in 1924. A year later it had sufficiently clarified its ideas to set down in a memorandum the principles on which it considered British policy should be based. After submission to the secretary of state, this memorandum was circulated to all African governments as a guide for further planning. It was issued as a white paper, and it constitutes the first definitive statement of British policy for education in Africa.[2] It asserted that, while voluntary educational effort will be encouraged, government 'reserves to itself the general direction of educational policy and the supervision of all Educational Institutions'. Its most significant pronouncement was that 'education should be adapted to the mentality, aptitudes, occupations and traditions of the various peoples, conserving as far as possible all sound and healthy elements in the fabric of their social life'. To this end it proposed that 'the content and method of teaching in all subjects, especially History and Geography, should be adapted to the conditions of Africa. Textbooks prepared for use in English schools should be replaced where necessary by others better adapted . . . Provision will need to be made for this by setting aside temporarily men possessing the necessary qualifications.' These were not novel ideas. They had influenced some teachers and administrators in Africa from the early part of the century. They had inspired some particularly interesting experiments amongst the muslim communities in the hinterland of the West Coast, notably the educational system which Hanns Vischer had introduced in Northern Nigeria between 1909 and 1919, and which was itself based on the earlier work of Sir James Currie in the Sudan.[3] By the time the African Education Commission made its survey in 1920, one of its members was able to report that 'the doctrine of the adaptation of education to the needs of the community' was 'universally approved' although 'far from universally practised'.[4] The significance of the pronouncement, therefore, lay not in its originality but in the fact that it put the weight of official sanction behind a recently developed educational philosophy. Thenceforth the principle of 'educational adaptation' was the accepted starting point for educational experiments at all levels.[5]

The committee also made a cautious reference to the provision of higher education in its memorandum. Whilst asserting that 'the first task of education is to raise the standard alike of character and efficiency of the bulk of the people' it recognised that 'provision must also be made for the training of those who are required to fill posts in the administrative and technical services as well as of those who as chiefs will occupy positions of exceptional trust and responsibility'; and it concluded that 'as resources permit, the door of advancement through higher education in Africa must be increasingly opened for those who by character, ability and temperament show themselves fitted to profit by such education'. It acknowledged the need for an expansion of facilities for higher education, therefore, but on a carefully controlled basis: it was clearly determined to avoid the mistakes that had been made in India. In view of financial limitations, it did not regard any substantial development as practicable in the near future; and in fact many years passed before the committee became closely concerned in the shaping of Britain's educational policy at that level. But already it had had a foretaste of the problems of higher education in two schemes submitted from East and West Africa, and under the stimulus of discussion on these projects, its ideas had begun to emerge.

In 1924, the committee was invited to examine a proposal from the government of Uganda for transforming a technical school at Makerere into a central training college for East Africa. The scheme had been devised by E. R. J. Hussey, an educational officer seconded (at the request of the advisory committee) from the Sudan, to make a report on education in Uganda. Hussey's scheme provided for preparatory courses in medicine, agriculture and veterinary science, and surveying, with an advanced literary course for sons of chiefs, school masters, and high grade clerks. Some members of the committee questioned the wisdom of developing a costly central institution at the expense of elementary education; but none criticised the character of the scheme itself. All were agreed that the type of advanced education Africa needed at that time was a vocational one. The project was warmly commended in a memorandum drafted by Sir Michael Sadler, who saw in it a close analogy with the type of intermediate college he had recently recommended for India;[6] although he was perhaps sounding a note of warning when he expressed his confidence that the corporate life at Makerere would be strong enough to enable a vocational colour to be given to many of its courses without diminishing their value as sound and liberal training.

It has to be remembered that in 1924 there were only fifty-six elementary vernacular schools in the whole of Uganda, and nine intermediate schools which took children from 12–16 years old but did not bring them to the level of London matriculation. Hussey's idea was to use Makerere as a means of raising the educational ceiling above this modest level. He was told in the terms of reference given to him: 'Among certain classes of natives there is a growing demand for a higher standard of education than that obtainable locally.' The intention of Makerere is clear from a comment made by the governor of Uganda in 1924. He regarded it as a bold and costly experiment, aimed at producing in Uganda natives who would be capable of filling all the minor posts and the crafts and trades in their own country. This was consistent with Hussey's own views; in his report on Uganda he deprecates the idea that students should be prepared at Makerere to qualify for entrance to European universities (though a few Ugandans were already going to America or Britain for their education). He was a firm believer in adaptation. He wanted to devise a curriculum which would 'build on without destroying the finely adjusted fabric of social life which is the heritage of centuries'. But he saw clearly that life in Africa would approximate more and more 'to the ordinary social conditions of the civilised world'. So somehow the African must be led into the life of Europe; but: 'for the present the aim should be rather to provide in the country such higher education as will fit students for careers in it than to base the instruction on the subjects required for entrance examinations to foreign schools and universities'.

The advisory committee approved the proposals, and transmitted its approval to the colonial office in October 1924. Some members of the committee saw, in the arrangements to be made for training teachers in Makerere, the germ out of which in future a university college would grow. Thus the first step was taken towards a policy for higher education in East Africa.

A few months later, in February 1925, the advisory committee had before it another plan which included proposals for higher education of Africans, this time from F.G.Guggisberg, governor of the Gold Coast. For those interested in the education of Africans, Guggisberg remains the most remarkable and distinguished of all British colonial governors. On his arrival to take up the governorship in 1919 he stated that he regarded education as the first and foremost step in the progress of the races of the Gold Coast and, therefore, as the most important item in the government's work. He enlisted the help of A.G.Fraser, who had been principal of Trinity College, Kandy, in Ceylon, to establish a school and college at Achimota. Under Fraser's leadership there was to be instruction at all levels from kindergarten to university, each to be a model of its kind. It was not proposed to form university classes to begin with, but to allow these to develop naturally from the work done in the lower standards. Fraser looked forward to the college reaching the level of London matriculation in four years after it opened, of the intermediate examinations in arts and science a couple of years later, and of the final degrees at a suitable stage after that.[7] The feature of the scheme the committee fastened on was the proposed link with the University of London. Here it recognised a dilemma which was to bedevil the planning of higher education for the next twenty years. How was it possible to foster the indigenous African university prescribed by current educational theory if it was to be dominated from the outset by a foreign examination system? And yet how were the proper standards of achievement – on which Africans would rightly insist – to be secured without it? Sir James Currie raised the problem in the committee. He strongly opposed the connection with London and pressed for the substitution of local standards supported by external inspection; this was a system he had found worked well in Khartoum. Sir Frederick Lugard, however, arguing from experience in Hong Kong, maintained that an initial period of tutelage was inevitable if satisfactory standards were to be set up. He saw the solution in getting the University of London's examinations suitably modified. Sir Michael Sadler, fresh from his experience in Calcutta, reluctantly took the same view, and the university authorities were approached accordingly. But when the advisory committee learnt that this would be a departure from normal practice, the matter was dropped. The committee accepted the fact that the question of the final degree examination would not arise for some time to come; in the meantime it was agreed that Achimota College might adopt the London matriculation and intermediate examinations.

II THE CURRIE REPORT

Eight years later, the same problem arose in connection with the college at Makerere, on a report from the conference of the directors of education of the East African territories, held in Zanzibar in June 1932. Again the proposal to adopt London examinations was debated in the committee, and the same arguments were rehearsed. But this time the question was not shelved. It was referred in January 1933 to a sub-committee under the chairmanship of Sir James Currie, which proceeded to review the whole subject of higher education in British tropical Africa, and produced a bold and imaginative report.[8] The report is of such historic interest that we reproduce it in an appendix.

The report called for an immediate and publicly announced programme of university development; in doing so it was strongly influenced by political considerations. It saw serious political trouble and a very real danger of alienating enlightened African opinion unless adequate provision were promptly made for the growing demand for higher education in Africa: and it regarded it as damaging to British prestige that an increasing number of Africans should be seeking training in foreign countries; even the supply of Sudanese staff for the Gordon College at Khartoum had to be secured largely from the American University at Beirut. It reinforced its plea by reference to cultural, social and economic arguments. It acknowledged the need to regulate the supply of graduates to the absorptive capacity of the African territories, but was emphatic that the time had come for advance.

It recommended that selected colleges in Africa should be progressively raised to full university status. Whilst not attempting to forecast with any precision the number of such university institutions that would be required, it considered that Gordon College and Makerere College would provide a sufficient nucleus for higher studies in the Sudan and East Africa; and the colleges at Yaba and Achimota supplemented by Fourah Bay College, in West Africa. Despite the earlier views of its chairman, the sub-committee decided that an African university must proceed through the stages by which university colleges in England reached university status: and that for a time it must be dependent for the granting of degrees on an English university. Since Africans saw in the London degree the hall mark they required, it suggested that the University of London should be asked whether it would be willing to modify its external examination system by allowing suitable changes in the syllabuses and the participation of African examiners in the marking of papers. The sub-committee did not look exclusively to the University of London and its examinations to raise African universities of proper standard. It expressed the hope that other British universities would be prepared to help, partly by seconding staff, but more especially by contributing to the work of inspection. For if Sir James Currie had been obliged – after a long rearguard action – to concede the necessity of a foreign examination system, the sub-committee had fully endorsed his belief in the efficacy of external inspection. It stressed that this would provide a valuable means of securing that the colleges developed along the best lines and adopted from the outset a sufficient academic standard. It added the important proviso, however, that care should be taken to see that such delegations of inspection did not function narrowly;

their aim should be to encourage the free and fruitful development of all local possibilities to meet all worthy local needs. The sub-committee did not make any detailed recommendations about the curricula to be followed in these African colleges, but it was emphatic that priority should be given to vocational courses and the applied sciences until a reasonable degree of social and economic security had been achieved. It envisaged the inclusion of general degree courses and the study of education. But it did not attempt to define the essential studies of the indigenous university it aimed to create; it limited itself to the more modest objective of providing the conditions in which they could be established and develop free from the distorting influence of foreign academic practice.

The report was received with enthusiasm in the committee and its recommendations were fully endorsed by the colonial office. It was never published, although subsequently (see ref. 8) it was made available to the public on application to the committee. But it was at once circulated to all governors of East and West Africa for their views.

Here the impetus was lost. It was not until January 1935 that the proposals were considered by the East African directors of education at a conference in Nairobi; and not until the following May that they were examined by educational representatives from West Africa at a specially convened conference in Lagos. Even then, with the exception of Uganda, there was further delay on the part of the governments. It took an urgent reminder from the colonial office, despatched at the special request of the secretary of state, to extract their views; and it was the early part of 1936 before all replies were received.

The delay was indicative of local official opinion. The East African directors of education fully recognised the desirability of Africans being able to follow suitable undergraduate courses at home; but they could not agree that the existing demand for higher education was 'vehement', nor were they in favour of stimulating it. The reaction of the conference at Lagos was similar: it did not consider the time had come for taking active steps to co-ordinate the development of facilities for higher education in West Africa although it recommended that a biennial conference should keep the matter under review. The West African governors were equally unresponsive. The governor of the Gold Coast was satisfied that existing facilities at Achimota were adequate to meet the demand for higher education in his territory. He preferred to strengthen intermediate courses rather than proceed to more advanced studies; partly because it was necessary to prepare African opinion gradually for the acceptance of local degree courses and partly because a sudden increase in facilities for higher education would create a danger of training more African graduates than could be absorbed into the higher posts. The governor of Sierra Leone thought that a system of government scholarships to the colleges at Achimota and Yaba would meet the outstanding demands in his colony. The governor of Nigeria was also reluctant to force the pace of higher education. Identifying himself with the views of his director of education, E. R. J. Hussey, he did not wish to hasten the stage at which colleges such as Yaba would proceed to courses of full university standard. The rate of progress should be determined by the developing capabilities of the students. Moreover, it was important to concentrate in the first instance on providing African personnel to fill the junior posts held by Europeans.

This official policy of the colonial government in Nigeria determined the pattern of post-secondary education in the government college at Yaba, on the mainland near Lagos. From the outset Yaba was significantly referred to by its founder, E. R. J. Hussey, as a centre for higher *training*. It was to give training 'of a university type though not necessarily of university standard'. The college was formally opened on 14th January, 1934, though classes had been held in temporary buildings for the previous three years. At the formal opening the governor, Sir Donald Cameron, said:

The object of the College is to give a training of a university or professional character, although as a great deal of attention will be devoted to the practical side ... the course will not be so wide, especially on the theoretical side, as would be necessary to obtain university or professional qualifications in the United Kingdom.

Admission was through a competitive entrance examination in English, geography, history, chemistry, physics, biology, and mathematics. The number admitted was related to the number of prospective vacancies in the Nigerian government service (the highest entry in any one year was 36). The courses offered were engineering (4 years); medicine ($1\frac{1}{2}$ years at Yaba, followed by 5 years at Lagos General Hospital); veterinary science ($1\frac{1}{2}$ years at Yaba, followed by $5\frac{1}{2}$ years at Vom); agriculture, forestry, and surveying (all 2 years at Yaba followed by 2 years at vocational training centres: Ibadan for agriculture and forestry, and Oyo for surveying); teacher-training (3 years at Yaba followed by 1 year of professional training). None of these courses led to degrees; indeed students were discouraged from taking any external examinations, notwithstanding the fact that members of the advisory committee on education in the colonies were in favour of a link with the University of London and Sir Percy Nunn had assured the committee that the university would regard sympathetically any approach made by colonial colleges for help over examinations. Furthermore the government posts to which these courses led were of lower status and were less well paid than posts open to graduates. In 1947, for instance, a Yaba-trained doctor was a 'medical assistant' on a salary scale of £120 rising to £400 after fifteen years' service, whereas a doctor trained in the United Kingdom was a 'medical officer' on a salary scale of £400–£720, though both might be performing exactly similar duties. It is not surprising that the handful of educated Nigerians bitterly resented this substitute for a university. As one witness to the Elliot commission put it: 'It is essentially a government vocational school. It has no governing body outside the Education Department. Its constitution leaves much to be desired. It has no published syllabus. The number of boys entering and leaving it is restricted to the needs of the government departments which it serves . . . the diploma is recognised only by the Nigerian government . . . Yaba fails to satisfy the Nigerian youth's craving for higher education.'[9]

III THE DE LA WARR REPORT

Although Currie's vigorous and urgent proposals met with such a half-hearted response from the West African colonial governments and failed to impress the East African directors of education, in Uganda there was a more progressive outlook. Here the governor welcomed a review of the functions of Makerere College, which had risen in the fourteen years since its foundation in 1921 from being a centre for training artisans to being a school which had reached the standard of the London matriculation examination. While on leave in London in September 1935 the director of education, Jowitt, was invited to examine the question with the advisory committee's sub-committee on higher education under Sir James Currie. As a result of these discussions, it was recommended that a small influential commission should be sent to Uganda at an early date to advise on the development of the college. The recommendation was endorsed by the committee, approved by the colonial office, and warmly welcomed in Uganda itself, where the recently appointed governor, Philip Mitchell, was a particularly keen advocate of higher education. A final decision was deferred pending the next meeting of the East African directors of education fixed for May 1936, and it was perhaps appropriate that when the all-clear came from East Africa, it should have been Ormsby-Gore, pioneer chairman of the advisory committee, and latterly secretary of state, who brought the proposed commission into being. It was appointed in the latter part of 1936, under the chairmanship of Earl De La Warr, parliamentary under secretary, and *ex officio* chairman of the advisory committee. Three other members were also drawn from the advisory committee, including Hanns Vischer, and all had served on Sir James Currie's sub-committee on higher education in 1933. Vischer was prevented by ill health from accompanying the commission to Uganda, but he was present when the preliminary evidence was taken in London, and associated himself with the findings of the commission when it reported in September 1937.[10]

We have already mentioned that Sir James Currie's report on the need for university education in Africa was never published (indeed, it was forgotten: by an astonishing oversight it was not before the Asquith commission which largely reiterated Currie's findings twelve years later!).[11] Accordingly the De La Warr report, although its formal concern is with the functions and status of Makerere College in Uganda, is a seminal document; it is the first published exposition of British policy for university education in tropical Africa. In importance it stands beside the advisory committee's white paper of 1925.[12]

The report opens with a clear challenge to the educational philosophers. It quotes the secretary of state (Ormsby-Gore) as saying: 'One of the essential aims not only of every university, but of every school, should be to preserve and enhance indigenous local tradition and culture.' Then the report goes on to say:

Should we take the existing needs of African society as the foundation upon which the educational system is to be built and by which it would in effect be limited? Or should we assume that European education is the most perfect yet devised by the ingenuity of man and impose that education upon the African without considering whether in fact it is the form best suited to his capacity or his needs?... The African background today comprises not the native alone, and not the European alone, but the interaction between the African theory of traditionalism and the European theory of progress. The infiltration of European culture, whether good or bad, has irretrievably occasioned a new and additional state of mind ... Is it optimistic to believe that this enhanced awareness of the nature of our difficulties ... may enable Governments to plan an educational system which will give to Africa the opportunity to fashion an indigenous culture which would be no less African because it represented a synthesis of both African and European elements?[13]

The commission modestly hoped that its recommendations would 'form the preface, and perhaps even the first chapter, in a progressive theory of African education'.[14] Their hopes were abundantly justified, for the De La Warr report was not only the first, but (in our view) remained for two decades the most enlightened statement of policy for universities in British colonial Africa. It emphasises the need to teach English as a foreign language and not as it is taught to Englishmen. It advocates a programme of English education by broadcasts. Over the teaching of arts subjects at university level it has something to say which is very relevant to the subsequent history of faculties of arts in African universities:

The development of an arts course will afford an opportunity of giving a fitting place to subjects peculiarly African. There is danger lest the Higher College should become totally divorced from anything African, and steps should be taken at once to establish African Studies including courses in – (a) African languages with special reference to East Africa. (b) Social anthropology; the study of the changing organism of present day society. (c) African law, custom, and administration. (d) Economics as applied to Africa ... The whole system of native government in Africa deserves serious study by educated Africans.[15]

Over medicine, already being taught at sub-professional level, the commission was 'gratified to note that every attention has been paid to bringing the course into close relation with the actual conditions in East Africa. For example, the syllabus for preventive medicine stresses nutrition, the sanitation of labour camps and other factors which are of special concern to medical men in East Africa.'[16]

The commission displayed courage and foresight notably lacking among official circles in West Africa. The East African colonies were far less advanced in secondary education than the West African colonies. At the time of the commission's visit there were no schools for Africans, of full secondary standard, in Kenya, Nyasaland, Northern Rhodesia, or Zanzibar. Tanganyika had Tabora School, founded for the sons of chiefs, and Uganda had Makerere. Moreover the various government departments, when asked how many Africans with higher education they could employ, gave depressingly short-sighted replies: in Uganda the medical and veterinary services had in mind only African medical assistants, not full medical or veterinary officers; the director of public works was prepared to employ Africans in the assistant engineer grade as an experiment but doubted the possibility of training them to this level in the next ten years; in Kenya the attorney-general did not anticipate that there would be any vacancies for Africans of the type under consideration for some time; in Tanganyika the director of public works, while sympathetic towards the training of Africans, did not feel able to estimate how many college-trained African engineers his department could employ. As for the international services, there was no opportunity for employment in the customs for the time being; on the railways the maximum number of Africans who could be absorbed in the next ten years was eight or nine.[17]

Notwithstanding this dampening information the commission concluded its report: 'We are proposing the establishment of a University College in the near future, and of a University at no very distant date. We are aware of the present very flimsy foundations of primary and secondary education upon which such institutions will need to be based, and realize the possible risks of too rapid advance and of a top-heavy structure. Nevertheless we are convinced that the material needs of the country and the intellectual needs of its people require that such risks as there may be should be taken.'[18]

Yet it was no university-on-the-cheap that the commission recommended for East Africa. There was unambiguous emphasis on high entry standards, though the commission wisely (but in vain) suggested an East African school leaving certificate comparable in standard, though not in content, with British school leaving examinations. And over Latin for East Africans, the report records that strong opinions were expressed by African witnesses in favour of the teaching of Latin, and it comments: 'The conception of Latin as a magic privilege which is being withheld from the African is one which should be resisted.'[19] The commission recommended that in the first instance Makerere should award its own diplomas (with priority for medicine, agriculture, and teacher-training) and should progress by way of London external degrees to complete autonomy in the award of its own degrees. The policy should be that East Africans take their first degree in their own country, though the commission adds the interesting suggestion that students might be allowed to count toward their degree a year's study overseas. In contrast to most other reports by British educational missions until the late 1950s, the De La Warr commission was prepared to incorporate ideas from across the Atlantic; they commend the American system of Junior Year Abroad Study: 'Various American colleges allow students to spend the third year of their four-year degree course in European Universities . . .'[20] Finally the commission recommend an enlightened and (for that time) novel pattern of government for the Higher College: an assembly of not less than thirty persons, including Africans, and with some representation from the academic staff; a council not exceeding seven, also including Africans, to control finance and to exercise general supervision; an academic board, to include all heads of departments and not less than two other members of the teaching staff. It proposed external examiners and regular inspection from outside. It even went so far as to propose co-operation between Achimota, Fourah Bay, Khartoum, Makerere, and Yaba 'in approaching examining bodies and Universities in Great Britain with a view to securing special syllabuses and concessions'.[21]

The De La Warr commission emerged as a convinced and enthusiastic exponent of the policy of adaptation. It set itself to provide for the material needs of an essentially agricultural community; and to foster the development of an indigenous culture which would take note of the growing infiltration of European ideas. Like the Currie sub-committee, it assigned priority to vocational courses, again with the object of meeting the immediate demands of a developing economy. But it also showed awareness of the essential needs of East Africa in placing agriculture next in importance to teacher-training and medicine, and a similar concern in considering the content of the courses. Both in teaching and in research the commission prescribed an emphasis on East African subjects. And to ensure that the college became deeply rooted in African soil and an integral part of the society it was to serve, it stressed the need for all students to acquire a sense of citizenship and a knowledge of the political and social structure of their country.

The advisory committee recognised a liberal and progressive policy in the proposals of the De La Warr commission, and cordially supported them. The approval of the colonial office followed, and with the promise of financial assistance from the British government, the scheme for the Higher College was put in hand. But the aspirations of the report were only partially achieved. The atmosphere of Africa at the time, as a member of the advisory committee recalled later, was 'all against the creation of a place of learning and strongly in favour of a place where students could be taught to work.' Professional courses were firmly established, but academic courses were neglected; and there was no attempt to introduce the African studies on which the commission had set such store. The Higher College developed a narrowly vocational outlook and in its first few years fell far short of what the De La Warr commission had hoped to make it; indeed the principal of the college from 1939 to 1946, George Turner, did not find himself in sympathy with some of the commission's sentiments. But this does not detract from the significance of the report: it remains the first British attempt to define in any detail the meaning of an indigenous university in tropical Africa.

IV A POLICY MATURES

In West Africa, meanwhile, matters continued to drag. The fact that existing arrangements there for higher education were at a more advanced stage than in East Africa made the problem more complex; and it contributed besides to the caution and complacency of local official opinion. But in one respect there was a development that was to be important for the future. In February 1935, Sir James Currie's sub-committee on higher education entered into negotiation with the University of London. It explained that the advisory committee was considering how selected institutions in Africa could be raised to university standard, and more particularly how they could be brought within the ambit of English university education without being forced into an uncongenial mould. It referred to the desire the university had already shown to adapt examination regulations to African needs and enquired whether further assistance might be expected along these lines. On receiving an encouraging response, it proceeded cautiously. It submitted detailed proposals, but confined them to the matriculation examinations. In view of the less developed state of education in East Africa, they related only to the West African dependencies. They involved changes in the prescribed courses for English, science and geography, and exemption from the requirement to offer a second language. The university was given to understand that these proposals would not necessarily be followed by requests for changes in the degree courses. It seemed likely that the existing professional and technical courses would satisfy African needs, although changes might be desirable in the arts courses and this was being considered. The university was assured, however, that any decision it might reach in regard to the matriculation examination would not be considered to commit it in regard to degree courses. The caution was effective. The university agreed to sanction the proposed changes, with the exception of those relating to the English course, on which a decision was postponed. In July 1937, copies of the new regulations were transmitted to West Africa. This was a precursor of the 'special relationship' developed ten years later. The trend in favour of raising African universities on a suitably adapted version of the University of London's external examination system had been confirmed.

A new momentum was given to the development of higher education in West Africa by the quinquennial inspection of Achimota College in 1938. The inspection was carried out by a small committee under the chairmanship of Dr Pickard Cambridge, with Hanns Vischer amongst its members.[22] In addition to its general terms of reference, a number of specific problems were submitted to it, including those on higher education. It was invited by the governors to consider the contribution Achimota might make to a scheme of higher education for British West Africa as a whole; and it was asked by the Achimota college council to examine certain proposals for developing the university work of the college, in particular the introduction of courses for the B.A.

pass degree. On both subjects, the committee was unexpectedly timorous. It did not consider that there was a sufficient supply of suitable recruits from the secondary schools, or a sufficient demand for native graduates in government or industry to justify the institution of the B.A. pass degree courses. The classes would inevitably be small and therefore costly, and they would fall short of the standard the Africans demanded. The committee recognised that an increased demand for university classes at Achimota might follow from an organised division of university work between the three West African colleges; but it did not consider that such a demand should be anticipated. And whilst it favoured a more economic distribution of work between the existing institutions of higher education in West Africa, it was emphatic that the time had not yet come for the establishment of a West African university. Again it backed its view by reference to well-worn arguments about the state of secondary education and the prospects of employment: '. . . however much we may individually sympathise with African aspirations [for equality of opportunity in securing higher posts in government service] it would seem to be prudent to wait for some indication of a change in the practice of Government and Industry as regards appointments, before encouraging the production of any considerable number of graduates who may be doomed to disappointment so long as the alleged indifference of Governments and Employers to the graduate qualification remains.'[23] But there was also a strong liberal purpose behind this reactionary stand; with Hanns Vischer on the committee it would have been strange had it been otherwise. The committee was deeply concerned that the West African university when it came should be 'really adapted to African needs' and no 'mere reproduction of an English University in its curriculum, its examinations and its methods of work'.[24] It saw no prospect of establishing such a university until university-trained Africans were available in greater numbers to fashion and direct it; or until a more suitable type of recruit, less dominated by the English examination system, could be provided from the secondary schools to supply it. It therefore advocated delay; but in doing so, it made the pertinent suggestion that 'those who are qualified to do so – whether European or African – should be thinking about the lines upon which a genuinely African University and its work might be framed'.[25] And it looked to the proposed Institute of West African Culture to assist in this work of preliminary planning.

One encouragement to delay was the attitude of the Africans themselves. It appeared that some of the enthusiasm for an indigenous African university had evaporated since the days of Casely Hayford and the West African Congress of 1920. A small anglicised African élite, educated at British universities, was making its voice heard, and its message was on the side of caution. Here is the impression made on the committee which inspected Achimota in 1938:

We had the advantage of listening to the speeches of the African members of the Council [i.e. the college council] at the Council meeting on December 3rd. These gentlemen insisted most strongly upon their demand for opportunities for the African to obtain the very highest academic qualifications and the fullest participation in University life, in order that highly qualified Africans might be as eligible as Europeans for direct appointment to higher posts in Government. No provision of University classes at Achimota can secure anything like this. . . . The very ablest men must still for many years go to Europe; and it is only so that they can get (what these speakers also required) such an effective contact with the greater world as would assist them to acquire vision and initiative for the improvement of public and industrial life on their return. Some of the speakers also laid stress on the influence of *English* University life, as something which could not be reproduced elsewhere. Several of them expressed themselves emphatically against the idea of a West African University—giving its own degrees, certificates, etc.—for many years to come.[26]

The report of the inspection at Achimota brought the question of higher education into prominence at the West African Governors' Conference at Lagos in August 1939. The conference also had before it the report of a commission appointed to inquire into the affairs of Fourah Bay College[27]; but it was on the broad issues of policy raised in connection with Achimota that the conference chiefly dwelt. Following a full discussion, the governors of the four territories recorded their agreement that a West African university, conferring its own degrees, was the ideal at which they should aim; and they stressed two familiar objectives in connection with it. Firstly, the university should be 'West African in spirit and reality as well as in name, and not a mere colourless imitation of a British University'. They welcomed the proposed Institute of West African Culture at Achimota as a means of achieving this. Secondly, it should be of high quality, its degrees standing comparison with those of a first-class university in Britain; and for this, a period of affiliation with a British university or universities would be necessary. Like the committee which reported on Achimota, the West African governors regarded the projected university as a somewhat distant goal and they agreed that it could best be approached by planning an unhurried development of existing institutions of higher education on a carefully co-ordinated basis. They envisaged for the West African colonies a duplication of courses to intermediate level; and beyond that a distribution of studies, Achimota providing the later stages in engineering, Yaba assuming responsibility for the full medical course, and Fourah Bay concentrating on theological training. Recognising, however, the intricacy of the problems involved, they unanimously recommended that a commission should be appointed to advise on the details of the scheme. On the question of developing B.A. pass degree courses at Achimota, the governors were divided. The governor of the Gold Coast supported this extension of university work; he considered it would give added status to teachers and provide suitably equipped Africans to take over intermediate grade posts. But the other governors agreed with the committee in opposing the proposal: not because they regarded an arts degree as premature but because they had serious misgivings about the qualification it led to.

The proceedings of the West African Governors' Conference, together with the reports on the colleges at Achimota and Fourah Bay, were discussed by the advisory committee at successive meetings in April and May 1940. It was a largely reconstituted committee: Currie was dead; Sadler and Lugard were no longer on the scene; Vischer and Mayhew had just retired;[28] a system of rotation of membership with a three-year limit (followed by ineligibility for re-election for a year) had been introduced in 1939. An educational adviser to the secretary of state for the colonies, Christopher Cox, had taken up his duties and continued to have a profound effect on policy until the colonial era ended some twenty years later. Doubtless this discontinuity, together with the dislocations of war, accounts for the fact that a good deal of the thinking about policy for higher education in Africa, which had been done since 1933 by the sub-committee under Currie's leadership, was unfamiliar to the advisory committee and had to be done over again. However the new advisory committee soon proved itself responsive to the need to pursue a policy over higher education. Despite the crucial stage which the war was entering, a sub-committee was appointed under the chairmanship of B. Mouat Jones to consider the specific recommendations of the West African Governors' Conference, with the exception of the proposed Institute of West African Culture which the committee had already approved; and this sub-committee reported in the following December.[29] It brought a fresh and vigorous approach to the problem of university development in West Africa.

The sub-committee strongly favoured the extension of university work at Achimota. To provide a more balanced scheme of studies, and above all to offer as good a training as possible for the post-primary teacher of the future, it considered that the arts courses, and possibly the science courses as well, should be developed to full degree standard. It was not deterred by the argument about the state of secondary education. It considered that the number of schools, and the standard of work achieved in them, offered sufficient basis for a further development of university work. It stressed the fallacy of assuming that growth in the educational structure should be 'pyramidal'; a gradual elevation layer by layer of the stages of education from bush school to university was, in the sub-committee's view, historically ill-grounded and practically not feasible. (One wonders, for instance, when Oxford and Cambridge would have been founded if education in Britain had been 'pyramidal'.) For a pyramid the sub-committee substituted the analogy of the volcano: for the volcano 'built up its cone in all stages at once' and had 'a spontaneity about it altogether lacking in a pyramid built of blood and tears'. Higher education and secondary education were interdependent and should advance together. But although the sub-committee was keen to proceed at once with the development of university courses, it recognised that there were certain issues which would have to be carefully examined first.

One of them was the question of employment. Before increasing the number of African graduates, it was essential to ascertain how far the government was prepared to admit them to higher posts. Sir George Anderson was able to issue a warning from his experience of India, where he had seen the ideals of the universities blunted by the admission of large numbers of students whose aim was lowly paid clerical posts in government service. Another issue was the question of the qualifications the courses would lead to, and here the sub-committee examined afresh the vexed topic of the relative merits of the local diploma and the external degree of the University of London. A commission on higher education in Malaya had recently drawn attention to features of the university's external B.A. degree course which made them unsuitable for colonial students.[30] It had objected in particular to the requirement that all students should offer Latin or one of certain other classical languages at the intermediate examination, and that students taking English should be examined in Middle English in the intermediate, and Anglo-Saxon and Middle English in the final examination. The sub-committee fully acknowledged the validity of these objections; but it considered that the movement towards affiliation with the University of London had probably gone too far at Achimota for a local diploma to be acceptable to the Gold Coast African. Instead, therefore, of following the Malayan commission in its novel expedient of a local diploma backed by a statutory board of external examiners in England, it inclined to the increasingly favoured solution of a suitably adapted London degree. Echoing the Currie sub-committee, it concluded that the time was at hand when the University of London should on imperial grounds be asked authoritatively to take up the question of providing curricula suitable for external students in colonial territories.

But the sub-committee under Mouat Jones recognised that the problems raised in connection with Achimota would have to be settled against the wider background of university development in West Africa as a whole. Turning to this broader field, it again urged a progressive policy. It regarded the establishment of a university for West Africa as vitally important for the development of its territories. It endorsed the governors' view of the need for closer co-operation between the three West African colleges and approved the proposed division of function between them. But it regarded this approach to the West African university as wholly inadequate. It was not enough to talk of co-operation and to say, 'By all means let us aim at a university in some indefinite future.' Discounting, or at least ignoring, the grounds on which the Achimota committee under Pickard Cambridge had counselled delay, it insisted that positive steps should be taken at once to bring the new university into being. Higher education had reached a complex stage in West Africa. Unless a preliminary federal body were set up forthwith there was danger that the university would become little more than an examining body. The West African Governors' Conference had suggested that a predominantly local commission should be set up to plan the development of the West African colleges. The sub-committee went further. It strongly recommended that an authoritative commission should be appointed at the earliest opportunity to enquire into the whole policy of higher education in West Africa. The advisory committee, catching the note of urgency behind the sub-committee's report, fully endorsed the recommendation. Despite the sombre prospect of the war, it took the view that a commission should be set up at once: it could then make an immediate survey at home of the more pressing problems, present an interim report on those, and proceed to West Africa as soon as it was practicable to do so.

V THE CHANNON REPORT

Some of the drive behind the sub-committee's report, and many of the ideas, had come from a member of the advisory committee specially co-opted to assist in the work of preparing it: Professor H. J. Channon. He had taken a leading part in the educational commission which had gone out to Malaya in 1938; and from the time of his appointment to the advisory committee in 1940 he increasingly dominated its discussions on higher education. He stepped quickly into the role that Sir James Currie had played until his death in 1937.

Professor Channon's visit to Malaya, which had included a brief stop at Colombo, had greatly stimulated his interest in the development of higher education in the colonies; and shortly after his return, as a postscript to the official report, he had drawn up a memorandum of his personal views on the problems involved.[31] His object had been to clarify his own ideas and no use had been made of the memorandum at the time. But in February 1941, at the suggestion of the educational adviser, Christopher Cox, it was brought forward for discussion in the advisory committee, and the consequences were exceptionally fruitful.

The memorandum made a bold plea for an entirely new conception of higher education in the colonies. With the warning of India before them, colonial governments had tended to narrow the function of the higher college to that of a vocational training centre. In doing so, they had aggravated the very danger they had sought to avert, and provided an inferior education in no way adequate for training the leaders and responsible citizens so vitally needed. What was wanted in the colonial territories was not a large number of men with specialised technical training and little else; but a smaller number, carefully prepared for wider service. The answer to the fears of the governments and to the needs of the colonial peoples was the high grade university, not the mass production vocational machine. The basic problem of higher education, therefore, was the complex one of raising higher colleges to university status. And this involved two questions of special difficulty: what kind of examination system should there be in colonial universities, and how was academic staff to be found for these universities?

Professor Channon was convinced that colonial universities should dispense as soon as possible with the London external degree. From what he had seen of it in Malaya, and more especially in Ceylon, he could only liken it to an avalanche 'which from trifling beginnings ultimately carries all before it, leaving destruction in its trail'. To lessen the period of dependence on London degrees, he was strongly in favour of bringing forward the time at which universities were empowered to confer their own degrees. He considered that this should be done at the pass degree stage. He did not fear that an indigenous degree might have no value, provided a good standard of entrance examination was maintained and a proper emphasis on the educational, as opposed to the vocational, character of the curriculum. But he was by no means reconciled to the London external degree as the inevitable route to university status. He acknowledged that in some colonies the movement towards the University of London had probably gone too far to be checked, and where that was so he concurred in the importance of getting the syllabus suitably adapted. But in others it might still be practicable to adopt an alternative approach, and he strongly recommended that the possibility should be explored before it was too late. He revealed in discussion that the sort of scheme he had in mind was a local test backed by a joint examining board provided by the universities at home: a group of British universities might agree to sponsor the development of a particular colonial institution in this way. On the question of staffing the universities, which he regarded as one of peculiar complexity and importance, he again offered a radical and novel solution: and again it involved participation by the home universities. He suggested that they should co-operate in seconding staff to the colonial universities at different teaching levels: junior and senior lecturers for up to three years, visiting professors on sabbatical leave for a term at each of several colleges. Up to a quarter of the staff of a colonial university might be recruited in this way until sufficient local graduates had undertaken a period of postgraduate study in England and were available to take their place. He envisaged, indeed, a great intellectual partnership between the British universities and the colonial institutions overseas: one that would not only promote the welfare of the colonial peoples, but foster the unity of the empire and help to realise the ideals underlying it.

Professor Channon had given a new significance to the problem of university development in the colonies; and his conception of an imperial university system was warmly welcomed in the advisory committee. It strongly recommended that a suitable body should be set up to advise the secretary of state on the means whereby the universities of Great Britain could assist in the development of higher education in the colonies. It was inclined to the view that a commission was required, and that its terms of reference should be kept distinct from those of the enquiry proposed four months earlier for West Africa. But it referred the question of the form and nature the investigation should take to a sub-committee appointed in April 1941, under the chairmanship of Professor Channon.[32]

Over two years elapsed before the sub-committee reported. Shortly after its appointment it met on a number of occasions under gruesome conditions of blackout, bombing, and the anxieties of war; but before long, discussions had to be postponed owing to the complexity of the problems involved and the impossibility of carrying out the necessary consultation with the heads of the African higher colleges at that stage in the war. It was not until the principals of Makerere and Achimota were able to visit England at the end of 1942 that the work was actively resumed. By that time the sub-committee's work was greatly stimulated by the interest taken in it by the secretary of state, Oliver Stanley. Stanley had been appointed to the colonial office in October 1942; and in the following months he caught something of Channon's fervent enthusiasm for the development of higher education overseas. He became deeply impressed by the importance and urgency of the subject, and at his request in February 1943, Professor Channon agreed to undertake part-time duties at the colonial office to speed the production of the sub-committee's report and assist in following it up. Thus encouraged, the sub-committee presented an interim report in March 1943, in which it formally recommended that an authoritative commission should be charged with the proposed enquiry; and in May it presented its final report.[33]

The Channon report became the pacemaker for all subsequent development in higher education overseas. It set out in a more systematic and comprehensive way the ideas which Professor Channon had embodied in the memorandum he wrote after his visit to Malaya. It re-stated the need for high grade universities, which would also be centres of research where the potential leaders of the colonial peoples could be trained in the background of their own countries. But it represented the need in a still more urgent light. The prospects of an early termination of the war were immeasurably stronger than they had been in 1941, and government pledges of self-government for the colonies had given a new importance to university development. Also by 1943 the sub-committee could count more confidently on the support of the home universities. Unofficial discussions had been held with Sir F. Sibly, chairman of the committee of vice-chancellors and principals, and Sir J. Stopford, chairman of the universities bureau; both had agreed that the home universities had obligations to the colonies and welcomed the proposed association between them. The sub-committee, as a result, had been encouraged to examine in more detail certain aspects of the problem of raising the colonial colleges to university status.

The most important of these was the way in which degrees were to be awarded before colonial colleges received their own charters. Since it was essential that the degrees should be equivalent in standing to those of a British university, the sub-committee regarded some sort of external system as inevitable. But it regarded the existing systems, including that of the University of London, the most widely adopted, as seriously deficient 'and likely to undermine the best purposes of higher education'. It came down unambiguously in favour of adaptation. The vital need in the colonies was for men and women suitably equipped to develop their own countries; the universities in which they were educated 'must therefore be indigenous and must not be subject to some arbitrary pattern introduced from Great Britain. Apart from providing the customary facilities for professional study, these Universities must be designed to fructify native cultural possibilities, and to study problems in their local, rather than in their foreign forms. This seems to us a compelling reason why the curriculum in some subjects should differ from that in use in Great Britain.'[34] But the curriculum in many of the London external degree courses was largely inappropriate for overseas students: not only in the insistence on a classical language in the intermediate B.A. examination and the requirement of Anglo-Saxon and Middle English in the B.A. final examination in English, but also in the character of the syllabus for such subjects as the biological sciences, history and geography, the social sciences and economics. The method by which the external examination was conducted was also unsatisfactory, for the non-participation of the staff in the colonies made for an impersonal atmosphere in the college and lessened the efficiency of the teaching. The sub-committee therefore suggested three possible ways in which a new external degree system could be introduced to meet these objections. The first was to secure a substantial modification of the existing system practised by the University of London. The university might be asked to set up a visiting panel of examiners to share with the colonial colleges the work of setting and marking papers and so bring the examination for the external degree into line with internal examination practice. The panel would also be asked to assist in the examination of the local diploma. The degree examination would be conducted on a specially adapted curriculum. If the University of London were unable to accept this arrangement, the sub-committee suggested as a second possibility that the university might be prepared to delegate its responsibility for conducting the external examination to an examining body composed of representatives drawn from all the home universities, even though the degree conferred would still be that of the University of London. Its third possibility was a novel and interesting one: the creation of an academic body representative of all the universities of Great Britain and including also representatives from the colonial colleges, empowered by charter to award degrees in the colonies and bearing some such title as 'The Colonial University'. The sub-committee acknowledged that this idea of a University in Trust was unprecedented; but, 'in our opinion, we ought not slavishly to translate into the Colonies methods which have served well enough in the very different conditions of our own country without imaginative exploration of possible new methods of approach'.[35] The sub-committee did not consider it a part of its duty to advise on the relative merits of the three solutions; but it emphasised the advantage of bringing as many of the home universities as possible into contact with the colonial colleges. And the very enthusiasm of its references to 'The Colonial University', with the British universities as joint trustees, left little doubt where its ultimate preference lay.

The sub-committee had also been emboldened to outline the sort of machinery that would be necessary to give effect to the concept of a colonial university system. Since the universities had no detailed knowledge of the colonies, and the advisory committee was insufficiently informed on the intricacies of higher education, it suggested that a new body should be set up to advise the secretary of state which should be composed of representatives from the universities and those conversant with the needs of the colonies. This would have to take into account the recently constituted colonial research council and the sub-committee therefore envisaged the creation of a body entitled 'The Colonial University and Research Council' consisting of two committees: one, the existing colonial research council which would chiefly confine its activites to research institutions; and the other, the university committee, which would concern itself with all matters relating to the colonial colleges. The latter committee would assist in the recruitment of staff, and, dependent on the method finally adopted, might also play a part in the conduct of the examinations. It would be available for consultation on any questions the colonial colleges liked to refer to it and would keep itself informed about the development of standards in the colleges. If empowered to recommend grants from the development and welfare fund, and able, also, to call on a block grant from the colonial research council, its effectiveness would be greatly enhanced.

The sub-committee recognised that this machinery might be considered over-elaborate and examined the less radical alternative of affiliation between individual colonial colleges and particular universities in Britain. There was already a precedent for this, because in 1940 a decree had been passed in congregation at Oxford, at the request of Makerere College, making arrangements to advise the college on curriculum and examinations, and to nominate representatives to inspect the work at Makerere. Nothing much had come of the arrangement but this was doubtless due to the war. The sub-committee acknowledged that such connections might be valuable to supplement the wider organisation it had envisaged, but it did not consider they would be sufficient in themselves. A particular university might not have the necessary resources to advise adequately on colonial problems or to supply the right type of staff; there would be danger too that a colonial institution might model itself too closely on the parent university. The sub-committee recommended that the idea of affiliation should be carefully explored, but dismissed it as an alternative to the scheme it had outlined.

Over the recruitment of staff, the sub-committee made an eloquent plea for support from the British universities. It urged the merits of a widespread system of secondment, even though it would entail some inconvenience and sacrifice on the part of the universities, and it pointed out that even if only one or two per cent of university teachers in Britain were at any one time on secondment, this would mean (even on 1943 figures) some 40–80 scholars to staff the colonial universities. It suggested generous conditions of service for university teachers in the colonies, and it reminded the British universities that they, too, would have much to gain if some of their staff were to have first hand experience of the colonies. And it put forward a suggestion which unfortunately did not reappear in subsequent statements of British policy: that there should be a unified colonial higher education and research service, which might introduce 'a new and inspiring outlook on colonial problems'.

The sub-committee's proposals were not too radical for the advisory committee. The suggested colonial university system attracted nothing but praise; and it was its more ambitious features, in particular the projected 'Colonial University' which were specially applauded. Indeed the hope was expressed that the Channon report would become one of the historic documents in colonial education.[37] The advisory committee recorded its view that the report was well calculated to focus attention on the problems requiring investigation by the commission; it strongly reiterated its earlier resolution in favour of the appointment of a commission, and emphasised the importance and urgency of immediate action.

VI THE ASQUITH AND ELLIOT COMMISSIONS

The inspiration to create new universities in Britain's colonies had its source in the reports of Currie in 1933 and Channon in 1943, and its first practical consequences are embodied in the De La Warr report on Makerere, published in 1937. Channon's report came at a more propitious time than Currie's or De La Warr's: by 1943 the tide of war had turned, the British colonial service was becoming reconciled to the pace of development of the indigenous peoples they ruled, and there was a secretary of state for the colonies who considered university education to be 'one of the most important questions in connection with the post-war reconstruction and development of the Colonial Empire. . . .'[38] The ideas necessary for creating colonial universities had been supplied by Currie, De La Warr, and Channon; what was now needed was a strategy to turn the ideas into accomplishments. This strategy arose from conversations between Channon and Stanley in the early months of 1943. While the Allied general staff worked out a greater and more dramatic strategy in Casablanca and Washington and Quebec, Stanley and his advisers were devising ways to mobilise the British universities to carry higher education into the colonial empire.

The ground was very carefully prepared. On 20 May Channon's report was discussed by the advisory committee on education in the colonies. At the same time a copy of the report was sent to the principal of London University, who commented on it in some detail. Nine days later Stanley issued a long confidential letter to the vice-chancellors of the British universities, saying that 'His Majesty's Government is deeply committed to quickening the progress of Colonial peoples towards a higher level of social well-being and towards the ultimate goal of self-government. It is essential to the success of this policy that the supply of leaders from the indigenous people themselves should be rapidly increased. There is, therefore, an urgent and fundamental need to enlarge our facilities for higher education without which these leaders cannot be created. 'He then went on to suggest that he should appoint a commission: 'to consider the principles which should guide the promotion of higher education, learning, and research and the development of universities in the Colonies; and to explore means whereby universities and other appropriate bodies in the United Kingdom may be able to co-operate with institutions of higher education in the Colonies in order to give effect to these principles'. Stanley saw the future with what was, for British statesmen at that time, a novel clarity. 'The Universities of this country', he wrote, 'have in the past made their vast contributions to the successful growth of the overseas dependencies by themselves training and nourishing the administrators and specialists on whom their progress has depended. We are now entering on an era when this contribution may become more indirect but no less vital by taking the form of assistance in the development of Colonial Universities which will rear the local leaders of the future.'[39]

Stanley asked for an expression of sympathetic interest from the British universities. He received a ready response, notably from the University of London which had already a deep interest in colonial affairs. Invitations to serve on the commission went out early in July. On 13 July he announced to the house of commons that he was setting up a commission under the chairmanship of Sir Cyril Asquith.[40] Simultaneously he announced that a second commission, under Walter Elliot, was being appointed to make recommendations on higher education in West Africa.[41]

The Asquith commission began work in the autumn. From the outset its members were in close consultation with the University of London. In a memorandum to the principal, one of the members (Sir Fred Clarke) indicated even as early as December 1943 that the commission 'appear to be rather strongly desirous that a way may be found of adapting the London external degree to the needs of such institutions'. Clarke realised the difficulty which Currie and others had foreseen and which indeed still confronts universities in Britain's former colonies, namely how to reconcile relevance and quality: on the one hand the necessity for adaptation to indigenous needs and conditions in tropical communities, and on the other hand the necessity to maintain degree standards at a level equivalent to those in Britain. And he outlined clearly the sort of arrangements which the university might contemplate, in anticipation of a formal request from the commission.[42]

The request came in the following March. Asquith wrote to the vice-chancellor of London[43] with a summary of the trend of the discussions, sounding out the university as to how it might respond to a request to undertake what he admitted would be massive responsibilities: to adapt its syllabuses and curricula to the specific needs of different colonial colleges, to send out examiners, to allow the staffs of the overseas colleges to take part in examining, and in brief to enter into partnership with institutions thousands of miles from London. There was a swift and generous response from the University senate; before the end of May the vice-chancellor was able to tell Asquith that 'the University of London would be proud ... to accept the special responsibilities which the commission has suggested that it should undertake'.[44] The senate then proceeded to set out its own ideas of a policy for partnership with colonial colleges. It was a remarkably enlightened policy; indeed, as events have shown, it was in some respects too enlightened for the colleges to accept or for the University of London to implement. 'A University', the senate memorandum runs, 'should be an integral part of the intellectual, technical, and economic life of the community it serves. It should accordingly be the prime duty of the Academic Body established in a Colonial College to frame its courses of study with due regard to local needs and circumstances. In so far as it appeared that the subjects and syllabuses of the London External Degree examinations were not well adapted to the studies pursued in the College, the University would give sympathetic consideration to the recommendations of the Academic Body for the approval of new subjects, modified syllabuses, or special examination papers for candidates from the College.' And the memorandum went on to emphasise that success in the university's participation in any such arrangement as Asquith had suggested could not be ensured by regulations alone but would depend on the establishment of a close personal relationship between the academic staffs of the overseas colleges and those in London who would be responsible for examining and approving courses of study.

The commission was greatly encouraged by this response from the University of London. An exchange of correspondence between the two sides continued. While the commission was clarifying its ideas over the pattern of partnership which there might be between the British and overseas universities, the University of London gave thought to the conditions under which it might offer its degrees to overseas universities if asked to do so. 'It would be a welcome change', wrote the principal, 'to be able to plan one at least of our post-war activities without the usual last minute rush.'[45] Even though the University of London had behind it a century of experience of external degrees, the problem before it was a novel one. It was considering how to offer its degrees, without any suspicion of a depreciation of their currency, to remote colleges in non-European societies; moreover to encourage the teaching staff in those colleges to take part in the examining and to propose modifications in syllabus. In October 1944, eight months before the Asquith commission's report was published, the university anticipated the role it was to be asked to play: it set up a special senate committee on higher education in the colonies, with A. M. Carr-Saunders (a member of the commission) as chairman, charged with the duty (among other things) of preparing a scheme for a special relationship between the university and the colonial colleges.[46] The beneficial effect of this foresight cannot be exaggerated. It ensured that when the commission's recommendations were made public in the following July, all the tortuous and time-consuming motions of academic diplomacy which are essential before a university can be persuaded to agree to anything, had already been completed.

Although the University of London was to be asked to carry the responsibility for granting the degrees earned in the colonial colleges, it was essential to enlist the support of all British universities for the ambitious postwar programme of higher education which the colonial office by then had in mind. So as soon as he had received the commission's report, and before it was made public, Stanley wrote again to the vice-chancellors.[47] He asked them to support the commission's proposal that an inter-university council should be established, with a membership to include nominees from every British university, 'to secure the active interest and co-operation of the Home Universities in the furtherance of university development in the Colonies on which . . . the progress of Colonial peoples toward self-government must in no small measure depend'.

In July 1945 the commission's report was published.[48] Even before publication it had achieved its object: it had devised machinery for translating into action the ideas developed between 1933 and 1943 on the advisory committee on education in the colonies; it had secured the co-operation of the University of London to supervise the chief element in this machinery, and it was assured of support from all the British universities. It was a splendid piece of timing: the report appeared simultaneously with the Elliot report on higher education in West Africa and the Irvine report on higher education in the West Indies.[49] All three were well received by the press.[50] Britain was in the mood to turn from war to post-war reconstruction. The government gave a general endorsement to the Asquith report and promptly referred it to colonial governments for comment. After consultation between the colonial office and the committee of vice-chancellors and principals, an inter-university council for higher education in the colonies was set up, with representation from all home and colonial universities. It was a body independent of the colonial office; nominations for its membership came from the universities themselves. Its first meeting was held on 8 March, 1946, with Sir James Irvine as chairman and Walter Adams as secretary. A colonial university grants advisory committee was set up to administer the funds (under the colonial development and welfare acts)[51] which were to be used to finance the activities sponsored by the inter-university council. The University of London's special senate committee on higher education in the colonies began its new task. At long last Britain had published a blueprint for the export of universities to her people overseas.

For a dozen years the Asquith report remained the basis of British policy for higher education in the colonial territories. The institutions established under the arrangements proposed in the report became known as 'Asquith colleges'. The purpose of the report was to achieve a practical result, but of course the report could not avoid making assumptions which amount to a hypothesis for the philosophy of higher education in non-European societies. As a hypothesis it was very fruitful; it has made an enduring contribution to many overseas universities. But at the hands of some of its enthusiasts it was, in the 1950s, elevated from hypothesis to doctrine. To question the doctrine was not to start a discussion; it was to utter heresy. Yet in some respects, which we mention below, the doctrine did not even accord with the Asquith plan. So it is important, at this moment in the history of these emerging universities, to re-examine the Asquith report objectively: its sources of opinion, its assumptions, and the ways it has been interpreted in practice.

The Asquith report with its two daughter reports in West Africa and the West Indies constitute a coherent body of advice which was adopted almost in its entirety by the British government. Apart from the De La Warr report (p. 197) it was the first publicly declared general policy on higher education in British dependencies since the famous despatch of 1854 which gave birth to the universities of India. It is a climacteric in educational history. As to the sources of opinion expressed in it, one has to remember that these three reports are not, and were not intended to be, seminal documents. The Asquith commission was brought into being to mobilise support from the British universities for ideas which had already been worked out by members of the advisory committee on education in the colonies. The commission had to confer prestige on these ideas and to prepare them for acceptance by the public. Asquith was Aaron to Channon's Moses. It is, therefore, no criticism of the reports to say that they add very little by way of ideas to the recommendations made by Currie's sub-committee twelve years earlier, by the perceptive De La Warr report on East Africa in 1937, and by Channon's sub-committee in 1943. Indeed some passages in the Asquith report are lifted verbatim from Channon's report.[52]

The seminal ideas are to be found in Currie's brief memorandum, which is written with an urgency and passion not to be found in the Asquith report. Currie's prime emphasis was upon relevance and quality. Universities in African societies must be truly indigenous, adapted to local needs and conditions, and they must grant degrees and diplomas which 'would rank equally with those of extra-African Universities in respect of Government employment'. External European tests of academic attainment may 'exert an actually harmful influence upon the development of indigenous education of the type best adapted to . . . local needs and in order to build up a true and genuine African culture'. To ensure relevance, priority should be given to medicine, engineering, agriculture, veterinary science, commerce, law, and the education of teachers, over what Currie's report calls 'purely academic studies', on the grounds that the country's prime need is a reasonable degree of social and economic security 'without which there can be no solid or lasting basis for any real cultural life'. There was also the realistic suggestion that there should be some relation between the needs for professional manpower in a country and the numbers of students admitted to the various faculties. To ensure quality, Currie's sub-committee made suggestions almost identical with those adopted twelve years later: dependence for the time being on an English university; an approach to the University of London to find out whether it would be willing to modify its degree requirements to suit African needs; a combination of internal and external examiners; periodic inspection through overseas delegations; the secondment of teachers from British universities to African institutions; and the planning of university education as a whole.[53]

Almost exactly ten years later Channon's sub-committee reported to the advisory committee on education in the colonies. We have already summarised the gist of this report. Suffice it to say that it included, though independently, most of the ideas Currie had put out in 1933. There was a similar emphasis on quality and relevance, but by 1943 the balance of emphasis had shifted; there was less about the need for adaptation (although the De La Warr commission in 1937 had regarded adaptation as of prime importance) and more about the need to guarantee standards. To ensure quality the colonial universities must be places where 'carefully chosen young people of promise are fitted to take their place in the different professions . . . Only through the training of leaders of solid worth can the goal of self-government ever be achieved.'

This was the legacy of ideas which the Asquith commission inherited from the advisory committee. Most of Channon's ideas reappear in the commission's recommendations, though the balance of emphasis is shifted a little more away from utilitarianism, and it is a very different emphasis from that advocated by the De La Warr commission for East Africa. Pride of place is given by Asquith to the quality of the education to be provided and the standard of the degree; and, over curriculum, the pragmatic approach of the De La Warr commission gives way to 'the production of men and women with the standards of public service and capacity for leadership which self-rule requires'.[54]

It is worth pausing for a moment to speculate on the reasons for this change of emphasis. Undoubtedly one reason for it was a conviction that if these colonies were to become independent nations their leading citizens would need that kind of intellectual integrity and acuteness which comes only from high quality of education. Although it was commonly believed that independence was still half a century away, nevertheless it was not too early to prepare the colonial peoples for self-government; and of course the surest way to do this was to provide them with the pattern and quality of education which commanded the highest prestige among those who governed them. Another reason may have been that the advisory committee had become more deeply imbued with the ideas of the British academic world than it was in Currie's time. Thirdly there was evidence of a certain disenchantment with the way Makerere had developed since the De La Warr commission reported. 'No country', said George Turner when he was principal of Makerere, 'can be safely ruled by specialists.' He believed that in order to form balanced judgements on political matters Africans should pursue humane studies, not simply qualify themselves to hold down jobs; and similar views were undoubtedly shared by members of the Asquith commission.

Such original contributions as there are in the Asquith report concern ways and means to achieve the high aspirations which the commissioners propounded. A university which has as its prime function education for leadership has an easier task if it is a residential society. So, apart from practical considerations, it is natural that the Asquith report should insist that colonial universities should be completely residential. It was a wise recommendation, for it is in any case a shock for an African or an Asian to be swept suddenly into the stream of European higher education, and it would be intolerable for him to have to reconcile this with his daily life among his own people, subject to traditional constraints and obligations and family duties. In residence, too, lay the hope that tribal rivalries would evaporate, and cohesion would appear among the future leaders of the heterogeneous communities which constitute the new African states; a hope which unhappily is not being realised.

A second consequence flows from the assumption that a university is a nursery for leaders, namely the need for a balance between what the report describes as 'professional' and 'other' studies; by which is meant the old (and now outdated) antithesis between liberal and vocational education. 'Professional' studies include medicine, agriculture, veterinary training, law, and engineering; 'other' studies are assumed to be those in the faculties of arts and science. The commission did not want to see too much concentration on professional training. One very wise recommendation of the commission, which unfortunately was never incorporated into the Asquith doctrine, was the need, at university level, for a broad general education. Let the report speak for itself:

> Every student, whatever subject or subjects he is studying in his regular course, should be given an opportunity to become aware of certain great conceptions. He should know something of the place of science in modern civilization and the use of scientific method; he should have learnt something of what is meant by sociology, so that he is aware of the other elements and forms of civilization. He should be enabled to gain some apprehension of what is involved in philosophy in its widest meaning, and some sense of the past as expressed in great literature and in the record of history.[55]

These aspirations, though they would have been consistent with the pattern of curriculum in a Scottish university, did not fit the pattern of a London degree, and even the generous concessions of special relationship could not reconcile the two. So one finds, ten years later, an obsession with specialisation which excludes formal study of this range of 'great conceptions' from colonial higher education as effectively as it was at that time excluded from degree courses in the universities of England.

A third feature of the Asquith plan is that staff of the highest quality must be attracted to the colonial universities. To this end the commission was pre-pared to recommend a salary-differential for expatriate staff, generous arrangements for leave, with frequent visits to Great Britain and a liberal provision of free passages, extended study leave every fifth year; and, over secondment from British universities, it adopted the recommendations of Channon's sub-committee. Throughout the report there is repeated emphasis on the university as a seat of learning and research; there must be an obliga-tion on colonial universities to provide money, facilities and sufficient leisure for the staff to pursue research. And the research should be 'fundamental', the disinterested pursuit of knowledge 'for its own intrinsic value' . . . 'utilitarian results must not be demanded from the research activities of members of the staff of a university . . .'[56]

The commission was correct in assuming that unless the colonial univer-sities emphasised the importance of research, they would fail to recruit good academic staff. But the commission's concept of research, which was faith-fully adopted in the Asquith colleges, is one of the reasons why some of the colleges were later on criticised as 'ivory towers'. For the commissioners frowned upon the view that the universities should take a direct part in using science to improve health, agriculture, or industry in the colonies. ' . . . it is not the function of universities directly to provide this kind of help . . . to expect them to do so would indicate a fundamental misapprehension of the place of research in universities'.[57] And when the commission advocates, as it does very clearly, that research should be done on local problems in such fields as biology, anthropology, and political science, it does so not primarily as an essential step towards adaptation of the curriculum, but as an induce-ment to academics who might be deterred from taking up posts in the colonies because of the relative poverty of library resources and equipment. Although the commission was prepared to see adaptation in the topics selected for research, it was not prepared to entertain an adapted concept of what constitutes research, such as the land grant colleges of America had encouraged for half a century. The commission's idea of the place of research in the university was in the pure line of nineteenth century German tradition.

The lofty concept of a university as 'an organ of higher learning inspired throughout by devotion to search after knowledge' is inextricably bound up with the commission's assumption that colonial universities are to exist for the education of what was at that time the English (certainly not the Scottish) conception of an élite. 'If university teachers', the report says, 'for any reason such as the type of student sent to them . . . have to adopt the attitude of in-structors rather than of guides to junior . . . seekers after learning, they are subjected to a strain that they should not be required to bear.'[58] So the com-mission, doubtless warned by the mistakes made in India, set great store by a high entrance requirement for colonial universities. All students of educa-tional history are familiar with the fact that good universities preceded good systems of schooling. European universities in the middle ages (and Scottish universities up to the end of the nineteenth century) compensated for deficiencies in the school system by admitting students who were ill-prepared and giving them a rudimentary training before they embarked on higher studies. There is something to be said for regarding the colonial universities as facing a similar problem, and so for setting their entrance standards below those current in twentieth-century Britain and providing a longer course of study for the degree. For there is a world of difference between setting and controlling standards lower than those current in England (on the level, say, of those in Australia or Canada), and, as happened in India, having standards which are neither firmly set nor controlled. However, this the Asquith commission was unable to recommend, even if it had wished to do so, because the prime contribution which the commission made was to propose that the colonial colleges should be 'in special relation' with the University of London, taking London degrees, modified where necessary in content, but with no modification whatever in pattern or standard of achievement. It was necessary, therefore, for aspirants to degree courses to spend two years in a sixth form and to pass an examination appropriate to this level of attainment, before being qualified to enter a degree course at a colonial university.[59]

We have explained how, even before the commission completed its report, arrangements had been made with the University of London to sponsor university colleges in the colonies, through a scheme of 'special relationship'. We discuss in the next chapter the immense benefits which this scheme conferred on the colleges. The commission's chief contribution to educational thought was to devise, with the co-operation of the University of London, a formula which went some way toward reconciling two essential needs: relevance and the maintenance of international standards of achievement. A local degree might have ensured the first but endangered the second; an ordinary external degree from London would have assured the second need, but inevitably at the expense of achieving the first.

The Elliot report[60] was concerned with detailed arrangements for higher education in West Africa rather than with overall strategy; hence it has been overshadowed by the Asquith report. This is a pity, for the Elliot report is in its own right a very interesting document. Unlike the Asquith commission, the Elliot commission had Africans among its members. The Asquith report is written lucidly but it lacks any literary distinction; parts of the Elliot report (particularly the chapter on the West African background) are written with an eloquence which merits their inclusion in any anthology of writing about Africa. The Elliot commission was plainly aware of the massive need for African graduates and its report stressed the urgency for providing 'trained African research workers in sociology and linguistics'[61] as well as in education itself. The impact of the Elliot report was undoubtedly lessened by an irreconcilable division of opinion among members of the commission, which resulted in an uncompromising minority report. The split occurred chiefly over the number of university institutions to be established in West Africa. The chairman and eight of the commissioners recommended three colleges of university rank: one in the Gold Coast, one in Nigeria, and one in Sierra Leone, with a distribution of professional faculties between them, co-ordinated by a West African advisory council on higher education. They recommended, too, that the level of entry to the university should be at school certificate (roughly equivalent to O-level G.C.E.) not at higher certificate (roughly equivalent to A-level G.C.E.).

Five of the commissioners disagreed with these, and other, recommendations of the majority; and in their minority report[62] they argue for a single West African University College to be situated in Ibadan in Nigeria. Admission to this single college was not to be straight from school, but after two years in one or other of three territorial colleges: Achimota for the Gold Coast, a new college for Nigeria, and a reconstituted Fourah Bay College for Sierra Leone and the Gambia.[63]

The Asquith and Elliot commissions prepared working drawings, as it were, from the imaginative sketches bequeathed to them by the advisory committee on education in the colonies. But one sketch was not elaborated into a working drawing. Central to Currie's proposals (though these apparently never reached the commissions) was the idea that a colonial university should be truly indigenous and adapted to the needs of the society which supports it. De La Warr was equally emphatic that we should not without question impose European education upon Africans. And Channon, though he was less committed than were Currie and De La Warr to the importance of adaptation, subscribed to the view that the colonial universities must become indigenous and must not remain facsimiles of British models.[64] And the vice-chancellor of the University of London, during the exchange of letters and memoranda between the university and Asquith while the commission was still sitting, commented on the problems of adapting syllabuses as follows:

> In some of the [colonial] colleges interesting experiments have already been made in the devising of courses specifically adjusted to local interests and needs, and the building up of degree courses on a sound academic basis may well involve the taking into consideration of the more elementary type of course which terminates in a local diploma ... As far as the problems can be envisaged at present, some seem to be more difficult than others. The devising of courses and syllabuses in Science and Engineering does not appear likely to present major difficulties ... Greater difficulties will arise in connection with certain Arts subjects and in Economics. *Something more will be needed than the adaptation of existing syllabuses. It is, indeed, even likely that a new form of subject or grouping of subjects will be necessary.*[65]

The University of London, clearly, was prepared to take adaptation seriously. Given this lead, and bearing in mind that the major philosophical problem confronting the Asquith commission was how to reconcile local relevance with international quality, how to achieve adaptation to non-European societies, the commission might have been expected to devote a major section of its report to this problem. But this was not done; an opportunity was lost to give emphasis and prominence to the fact that although the first colonial universities established by Britain would inevitably be facsimiles of British universities, they must not remain so if they are to be viable in their new environments. It must be made clear that the Asquith and Elliot commissions did not ignore this problem. Indeed, quietly diffused through the reports of both commissions is much sensible and pertinent advice on the first steps to be taken in adapting curricula to local conditions. What is missing is a sense of the critical importance of the issue. No-one reading the reports is likely to come away with the impression that the long-term prospects of these universities depend upon their becoming indigenous, and that research, design of curriculum, pattern of government, should all contribute to this end; always, of course, with safeguards to ensure that colonial universities remain on the gold standard of learning. In view of the importance of this problem (it is indeed the central theme of this book) it is worth while to gather together the scattered comments which the Asquith and Elliot commissions made upon it.

The Asquith report asserts[66] that one purpose of universities is to refine and maintain all that is best in local traditions and cultures. It recognises that this cannot be done unless the local traditions and cultures are studied and codified into a corpus of knowledge which can be taught and examined; in brief, that the first step towards this sort of adaptation is research and the writing of text books. To this end the commission regarded 'as most important the institution at the outset of posts wholly or mainly devoted to research on these fields' (i.e. history, geography, and the social sciences).[67] The Elliot report makes a similar recommendation.[68]

Over linguistics and the study of vernacular languages, too, both the Asquith and Elliot commissions had wise advice to give. They realised that the teaching of English as a foreign language raised problems unfamiliar to conventional English scholars, and that these problems need special study. And they make another important point, namely that colonial universities should study the local languages and particularly the comparative linguistics of English and vernacular languages, in order to understand the differences in patterns of thinking between those whose native language is English and those whose native language is (say) Ibo or Hausa. This research, in close association with anthropological and sociological studies, 'might with advantage' (the Asquith report says) 'be put in hand during the earliest stages of the development of a Colonial university institution'.[69]

This advice – to study from the outset local languages and cultures so that eventually they could be incorporated into the undergraduate curriculum – in other words to take immediately the first step in a major adaptation of the traditional content of the arts faculty, was not followed. Nor, so it was said, did the new colonial colleges always take full advantage of the flexibility which the University of London offered them.[70] There are several reasons for this, some of which are discussed in later chapters. But one reason has its place here: it is the lack of conviction which both the Asquith and Elliot commissions displayed toward anything more than minor modifications in the British pattern of higher education. In the study of biology they approved, of course, the substitution of local for European animals and plants. In history they expected to see alternative papers in the examinations, so that colonial students could give emphasis to the history of their own countries.[71] In medicine the Asquith report declared that a too 'British emphasis in pathological or clinical teaching would be inappropriate. . . '.[72] In arts subjects and social sciences it had in mind the gradual incorporation of material of local relevance as research proceeded and the text books came to be written. But from the edge of any major reconsideration of the pattern of higher education suitable for non-European communities, both the Asquith and Elliot commissions circumspectly withdrew. In discussing the function of a faculty of arts under *Academic life and range of studies* the Asquith commission, notwithstanding the advice received from the vice-chancellor of London, was not prepared to go further than to say that, wherever possible, due attention should be paid to local conditions. The Elliot commission is even more cautious: 'It is a matter for discussion, when preparations have further advanced, whether the range of departments to be included in an arts faculty should be identical with that usually found in a British university.'[73] This was hardly an encouragement to the pioneer universities to give first priority to the research necessary to adapt arts faculties to African societies. Similarly over teacher-training, the Asquith report would 'deprecate any special adjustment of ordinary degree courses to meet the needs of intending teachers';[74] over veterinary education there should be modifications but only such as 'can be introduced without so altering the curriculum that it becomes too specialised for acceptance in Great Britain'.[75] The commission would like to see some changes in the medical curriculum (emphasis, for instance, on social and preventive medicine), but a special curriculum for colonial medical colleges 'is not in our minds, for we believe that what we consider desirable can be accomplished by re-arrangements in the teaching without alterations in the curriculum'.[76]

In justice to the two commissions it must be said that they were working under severe difficulties, and against time, to produce an immediate practical result, and perhaps the Asquith commissioners (like the Nigerian commissioners we discuss on p. 268) did not realise how the very nuances of their phrasing would be interpreted with the fidelity accorded the scrutiny of holy writ. Nevertheless it is the historian's business to exercise hindsight; and we must put on record our opinion that the prime intellectual challenge which confronted the architects of the Asquith plan was how to reconcile, in non-European societies, a university's dual loyalty: on one hand to the community it serves, on the other hand to the international fraternity of universities. This challenge did not receive from the Asquith commission the emphasis it deserved. It is not as though it was a problem no-one had thought about. The history of higher education in India is full of discussions of the problem. Earlier policy statements from official British sources had emphasised it. And one member of the Asquith commission, Sir Fred Clarke, had made a special study of it.

CHAPTER EIGHT

THE TRANSPLANTATION

I BRITISH UNIVERSITIES IN 1945

Underlying British enterprise in providing higher education for her people overseas was one massive assumption: that the pattern of university appropriate for Manchester, Exeter and Hull was *ipso facto* appropriate for Ibadan, Kampala and Singapore. If we were going to export universities to our overseas dependencies they would of course be British universities, just as the cars we export there are British cars. As with cars, so with universities: we willingly made minor modifications to suit the climate, but we proposed no radical change in design; and we did not regard it as our business to enquire whether French or American models might be more suitable. This assumption – it is almost an axiom – ran through a great deal of official thinking which preceded the Asquith report; it was accepted without question by the Asquith commission; and, until recently, it lay hidden in the foundations of all universities in the new Commonwealth countries.

If we now examine this assumption critically, it is not because we believe it to have been unsound or unwise in the light of what was known at that time, but because it illuminates much that has happened, and may well illuminate much that will happen, to higher education in the developing countries of the Commonwealth. It was linked to another assumption, namely that the colonies where universities were to be planted would be likely to remain under British rule for most of the rest of this century; and that even after independence the 'ties of academic fraternity' (as the Asquith report put it) would not be loosened. Even so, it was in one way a surprising assumption to make; for there is no historical justification for supposing that universities do not vary among different societies. In many ways the modern British universities bear little resemblance even to Oxford and Cambridge, still less to the German universities from which they derived the pattern of the professoriate and their preoccupation with research. American universities, though initially inspired from England and Germany, differ from them profoundly in government, in curriculum, and even in social purpose. Russian universities show little kinship with the institutions in France and Prussia from which they sprang. What grounds are there for believing that an institution with a constitution borrowed from industrial Manchester and a curriculum borrowed from cosmopolitan London is the best pattern to offer Ghanaians or Nigerians or Malayans? Indeed is there not some reason to suppose that these emergent countries, with an exiguous exchequer and a predominantly peasant population and a paucity of leaders, would have been better suited with an institution modelled on the American land grant college, which was created to serve a pioneer agricultural community; or with one modelled on the highly centralised French university system; or, as the Africans themselves suggested as long ago as 1920 (p. 475), with a model drawn from Japan where western universities have been successfully grafted on to an ancient non-European tradition?

At no stage in the evolution of British policy for higher education overseas were these questions seriously considered. Even if they had been considered, the reasonable and pragmatic answer to them would have been that the export of higher education to British colonies is a British responsibility; the British pattern of university may or may not be the most suitable for emergent nations in the tropics, but it is the best we have to offer, and it would certainly not be improved by removing components here and there and substituting components belonging to the American or French systems of higher education: like trying to fit a Chevrolet gear-box into an Austin chassis. Besides, the university had to fit the system of schooling. The British school system was already rooted in tropical Africa and Malaya and the West Indies: it was too late to pull the system up and to plant a new one. But it was not solely on grounds of expediency and suitability that the pattern adopted was British. There was a political motive too. Thirty years ago Sadler was astute enough to urge that Britain should retain an intellectual influence over universities in her dependencies; and as self-rule for the colonies drew in sight, the British government saw how universities in the British tradition would become valuable entry-points where British ideas could flow into the newly independent states. Adaptation, therefore, was not prominently in the minds of those who transplanted higher education overseas. It was left to the colonial people themselves to make the adaptations; 'it is not for us', said one of the founder-members of the inter-university council, 'to invent a specially adapted form or standard of intellectual life for their needs. Let us face the truth . . . that in the university sphere we have to offer almost everything. We must give what we ourselves value most highly and keep nothing back.'[1]

From this basic assumption many consequences flow. Just as the first Australian and Indian universities reflected English contemporary academic opinion around 1850, so the first university colleges in British tropical Africa reflected English contemporary academic opinion around 1950. Indeed, since the prime purpose of the Asquith commission was to enlist the support of British universities, the more conventional its views were, the better. It is therefore worth while to recall the British academic climate of that time and to revive for a moment some of the discussions and controversies of the post-war years.

For the men and women who had to administer universities or to teach in them it was no time for placid reflection. Their days were filled with improvisation and emergency action. Returned service men, eager to re-equip themselves for civil life, flooded into the universities. The number of full-time students rose from 37,830 in 1944 to 76,764 in 1947. And this was not simply a return to pre-war conditions; the number in 1938 was only 50,246. In 1938 there were only some 4,000 university teachers; many of them had spent the war years away from their disciplines; fresh recruits for the profession had to wait for their training until the war was over. Most university buildings were obsolescent and many of them severely damaged by bombs. It was not a fruitful moment for innovation. Those who conceived the idea of the Asquith colleges; those who brought them into being in the colonies themselves; those in Britain who approved curricula and recruited staff for the colleges – all these were people preoccupied with the need to make urgent and frequent decisions: they had scant time for philosophical speculations about the mission of the university. They had to act, and to base their actions on assumptions inherited from the uneasy 1930s.

What were these assumptions? The British university of the 1930s did not attract much public interest. The press gave it very little attention. The mass of the people did not regard the university as something affecting them or their children. From 1931 to 1938 the number of students remained virtually unchanged. The dilemma of the 1960s – too many candidates competing for too few places – would have seemed fantastic in the 1930s. The dilemma of the 1930s for some of the smaller institutions was how to attract enough students to justify their survival. Thus in 1937 the principal of University College, Leicester, was saying that the prime need for the college was to attract more students. The number of full-time students reading for degrees, sixteen years after the college was founded, was only seventy-five. Nevertheless such writing as there was about higher education at that time did not advocate any departure from the faith that a university should confine its ministrations to a select élite. Ernest Barker[2] pointed to the dangers of a democratic enthusiasm about higher education which would increase quantity at the expense of quality. Herklots,[3] writing at a time when there were fewer than 45,000 students in Britain, wanted British universities even to diminish in size. Grant Robertson, vice-chancellor of Birmingham University which at that time had little over a thousand students, nevertheless issued a jeremiad against the expansion of opportunity for university education. For him, even in 1930, more meant worse; he deplored the dangerous idea that universities might produce a 'highly competent mediocrity' (he apparently saw less danger in an incompetent mediocrity).[4] These élitist sentiments were reinforced by two essays which attracted considerable attention at the time. One was Julien Benda's *La trahison des clercs*,[5] which enjoined intellectuals to withdraw themselves from the market place and not to dirty their consciences with Europe's ephemeral problems. 'My kingdom', the intellectual must say, 'is not of this world.' The other was Flexner's comparison of American, English, and German universities, which has become a classic in the literature of *academe*.[6] Flexner poured corrosive scorn on the vocationalism of American universities; he rooted out and indicted what he considered to be signs of a similar corruption in English universities: brewing and even social study in Birmingham, domestic science in Bristol, colour chemistry in Leeds, glass technology in Sheffield, civic design in Liverpool, librarianship and journalism in London: all, in Flexner's view, slight stains on the otherwise commendable purity of the English universities, but in their modest way just as deplorable as the brash utilitarianism of American universities. Inasmuch as the empirical British could be said to acknowledge a mission of the university at all, it was a dual mission: on one hand to produce 'all-rounders', civilised by the inherited cultures of Greece and Rome and selected primarily on their promise as recruits for the professions or as servants of the public: men with the integrity, sense of duty, code of beliefs, and respect for tradition necessary for leadership in state affairs; and on the other hand to produce professional intellectuals: men with a rigorous and specialised training in the techniques of science or scholarship. The flower of the English universities was therefore of two kinds: one, the Oxford Greats man with a rowing blue who governed a province, or silently controlled the treasury, or sat on a front bench in the house of commons; the other, the man with a 'first' in natural science who became a professor and, in the German tradition, assembled disciples round him and made his laboratory in Cambridge or Manchester a world-centre for research. Commerce, business, industry, drew their recruits from the sixth forms of public schools. Except to pick up a few experts in technology, they made no demands upon the universities.

Between these assumptions in the 1930s and post-war Britain there had occurred a silent social revolution. But there was no spare time for the assumptions to be examined by those senior academics faced in 1945 with the tremendous task of rehabilitating Britain's universities. Nevertheless the assumptions did not lie unchallenged. The war had given universities a new relevance in a new society. Some of the pre-war faiths were weakened. Admiration for the German tradition, as proclaimed by Flexner, was shaken by the compliance of German universities in the Nazi mythology. Realisation that it was not the public-school type, but the boffin, who had saved Britain in 1940 was a challenge to Benda's intellectual isolationism. There were signs, in magazine articles and at conferences, of a broader concept of the scope and function of universities. It even occurred to some responsible intellectuals that British universities might have something to learn from the United States. The master of Balliol, Lord Lindsay, writing about a commission on which he had served to consider the future of German universities, said: 'To abandon the German universities to be mere research institutes seemed a counsel of despair. The Commission therefore addressed itself to the consideration of the isolation of the universities from the rest of the community. It began with a significant change in the statement of the function of the university. Its aim, they stated, is the pursuit of truth through research and teaching *in the service of man*. Truth is no longer to be regarded, is the implication, as a self-sufficient independent word. The worth of its pursuit is qualified by those significant five last words.'[7]

It must have come as a shock to German universities to have their function redefined in this way; such a definition had been a commonplace in America for eighty years, but even in Britain its blunt tendentiousness would have been repudiated by a great many academics. Lindsay ended his article with these heretical words: 'If I had to choose between the American university system with its great variety and its frequent lapses from any standard, and the German with its exclusive occupation with a high standard in research, I should choose the former.'

Lindsay's advice was not heeded at the time; even his prestige as master of Balliol was not enough to persuade the Germans or the British to take lessons from America. There was among the newer universities in Britain a 'lingering desire' as an American observer, T. R. McConnell, put it, 'to make these institutions conform as closely as possible to the conservative position of the old universities'. McConnell saw signs, however, that British universities would become more responsive to social needs: 'One feels that ultimately Britain will work out her own counterpart of the Land Grant movement if she is to give reality to her new social and economic ideals . . . Important as is the rigorous education of the most gifted students for positions of distinguished leadership and high scholarship – in which Britain has attained preeminence – it is insufficient in a modern democratic state'.[8]

Lindsay was only one of a number of gentle revolutionaries who challenged pre-war assumptions about the function of universities. Indeed the period 1945–50 was momentous in academic history; during these years there appeared a trickle of writing about universities which has since become a swollen stream. Up to the 1930s one could assemble the books about universities (other than official histories, the reports of commissions, and the like) on one small shelf: von Humboldt, Newman, Paulsen, Rashdall, Flexner, and a few others. It was in the 1940s, while the war was still on, that the literature of academic self-examination began. In 1940 Adolf Löwe proposed a new culture for post-war society and a new curriculum adapted to it.[9] Three years later a professor of Spanish at Liverpool, writing under the impenetrable anonymity of Bruce Truscot, created a new word in the language: the redbrick university. In doing so he brought into the area of controversy such obscure topics as university organisation, the rival claims of teaching and research, and halls of residence.[10] In 1946 an English translation of Ortega y Gasset's *Mission of the university* (a tract published in Spain in 1930) added to the dialectic by asserting that not only a handful of scholars, but also the mass of the population must be educated to live, as he put it, 'at the height of the times'.[11] Two years later came a pamphlet from Nuffield College, which was a forerunner of the Robbins report, for it examined the manpower needs of the professions and the claims which Britain was likely to make on her universities for graduates. But the authors of this statement adhered to the orthodoxy of Flexner: they admitted that universities must expand, but in doing so they 'must limit themselves to what is consistent with preserving the special character of the education they give; which means, in a period of expansion like the present, giving first priority, so far as they are in a position to do so, to increasing the supply of university teachers and research workers'.[12]

The book which caused the greatest stir in Britain was Walter Moberly's *The crisis in the university*, published in 1949.[13] It represented the reflections in retirement of a man who had been vice-chancellor of Manchester University and chairman of the university grants committee. The book is permeated with a nostalgia for the days when universities were concerned with moral and spiritual issues. Having asked the question: do Newman's ideas still constitute the doctrine on which British universities are based? Moberly concludes regretfully that they do not. To acquire a clear and worthy view of life based on accepted moral and religious principles is no longer the purpose of higher education; indeed higher education puts so much stress on specialisation that students are kept in ignorance even of the philosophical assumptions which underly their specialisms. Moberly criticises the crude vocationalism of many university curricula on the grounds that they are adapted only to the secondary, not to the paramount need of post-war society. The paramount need is that educated men should be men who have made up their minds about their 'ultimate loyalties', men who have, during their undergraduate course, been confronted with the necessity to choose which faith they will live by.

Moberly's book was heavily criticised as emotional, tendentious, even (because it advocated involvement in the social issues of the day) treacherous to the traditional isolationism which universities ought to preserve. But the critics were plainly embarrassed. They could be (some of them were) supercilious, captious, waspish, but they had no adequate reply to Moberly's challenge: 'If you want a bomb the chemistry department will teach you how to make it, if you want a cathedral the department of architecture will teach you how to build it . . . But when you ask whether and why you should want bombs or cathedrals the university . . . must be content to be dumb and impotent.'[14] The impression left after public discussion of the book was that the universities faced a dilemma rather than a crisis. With Hitler fresh in their memories they found it hard to agree that they should equip each student with a coherent philosophy and a repertory of convictions about political and moral issues. With Hiroshima fresh in their memories they found it hard to deny that research workers should take some responsibility for the social consequences of their discoveries.[15] Löwe and Truscot and Moberly had acted as spokesmen for scores of thoughtful university teachers and the sustained discussions which followed over the ensuing ten years gradually changed the climate of academic opinion in Britain. Early issues of the *Universities Quarterly* (founded in 1946 and itself a symptom of the new social relevance of universities) and the reports of proceedings of the annual home universities conference between 1946 and 1950 provide illuminating evidence of the ideas current in the academic world at the time the new colonial colleges were being founded. Those who had time to reflect on universities were concerned about the rival virtues of general education and specialised professional training; about the nurture of the humanities in a world where academic éclat had passed from the classicist to the physicist; about the novel problem of how to select students for admission to universities; about the problem, also novel, of a conflict of loyalties between the claims of teaching and research; about the need to introduce the social sciences more fully into British universities; about the relation between universities and the state now that the parliamentary grant to universities exceeded half their total income.

It was not only in Britain that the function of the university was being reexamined. In the United States discussion was at a deeper philosophical level than in Britain. Maynard Hutchins at the University of Chicago propounded with wit and eloquence a view of higher education medieval in its rigidity and fundamentalist in its faith in unchanging values. His views on whether or not education should respond to environment are expressed in a typically entertaining, if somewhat dubious, syllogism:

> Education implies teaching
> Teaching implies knowledge
> Knowledge is truth
> The truth is everywhere the same
> Hence education should be everywhere the same.[16]

Sidney Hook at New York University rejected this attitude, and put forward an alternative: that higher education should be experimental, empirical, pragmatic, and constantly adjusted to social needs. Both schools of thought had their practical exponents; indeed the University of Chicago became a proving ground for Hutchins' ideas. Harvard University entrusted its self-examination to a committee which issued a practical guide to modernisation of the curriculum, the famous 'Red Book'.[17] Its recommendations, although not fully put into practice, have guided the undergraduate curriculum at Harvard until very recently, when another committee reviewed general education in Harvard twenty years after the publication of the 'Red Book'.[18]

For reasons already mentioned, the wave of innovation in American universities and the exercises in academic self-criticism in Britain did not lead to immediate reforms in British universities, nor did they have any influence on the new colonial colleges. There were two bodies where academic opinion was concentrated and where innovation might have been expected to originate: the committee of vice-chancellors and principals and the university grants committee. But both these bodies had established the convention that the initiative for innovation should come from universities themselves; both repudiated *dirigisme* in the academic world. The individual universities were far too busy with physical and material crises to worry about philosophical and moral problems. Not only did they have to find places for returned service men: they had also to decide how to respond to a stream of government reports on the needs of the professions; the advancing shadow of a planned society: the Barlow report (1946) which recommended that the output of scientists and technologists should be doubled; and reports on medical schools (1944), dentistry (1945), agriculture (1945), veterinary education (1944), oriental, Slavonic, East European and African studies (1947), and social and economic research (1946).[19] From these committees and other sources the Nuffield College group estimated that the annual intake for a score of the commoner professions must rise from 14,000 to 22,000. The university grants committee foresaw an expansion of the student population from 50,000 in 1938 to 90,000: 'an expansion out of all proportion to anything which has previously been attempted in the universities of Britain'.[20] Clearly immense new responsibilities were about to be put upon the universities. Accompanying these responsibilities came financial help from parliament. In 1938 the recurrent parliamentary grant to universities was £2.1 million, representing about 30 per cent of university expenditure; in 1951, when student-numbers had reached their first post-war peak, the recurrent parliamentary grant was £16.6 million, representing about 62 per cent of university expenditure. Was this (some people asked) not only the shadow of a planned society but the shadow of state control? With such monstrous practical problems to be tackled, it is not surprising that speculation about the mission of the universities did not get on to the agenda of senates and faculty boards and that all the talk at that time about new curricula: area-studies, modern greats, social sciences, general education, humanities for scientists, and the like, did not lead to immediate reforms.[21] It could be said that the ethos of the immediate post-war university was the ethos of the 1930s, strengthened to defend traditional values. The university was to offer a high quality education to a carefully selected proportion of the age group. This posed new problems of selection and of finance, because in the post-war world no child should be denied higher education through lack of money. But standards must be maintained; research must remain a prime duty of university teachers; staff–student ratios must remain high. Over liberal education, particularly over Moberly's plea that a 'spiritual' element should be restored to higher education, the universities were in some embarrassment. Liberal studies seemed inimical to depth, and anything smacking of indoctrination, even of 'the good' was repugnant. In the end all but the new university college at Keele shelved the problem, though all universities and the university grants committee encouraged an oblique attack on the problem through a wider use of the tutorial system and the building of halls of residence where students could educate one another.

On top of all these preoccupations and responsibilities came an appeal to help the new colonial colleges. It is indicative of the interest which British universities were prepared to take in these colleges that the first session of the first Home Universities Conference held after the war was devoted to 'the relation of the Home Universities to Colonial Universities and Colleges'. Sir James Irvine, who was chairman of the newly formed inter-university council for higher education in the colonies, opened the discussion. Margery Perham, who had served on the Asquith commission, made a moving appeal to the British universities to come to the aid of the colonial peoples by sending staff to colonial colleges, by accepting colonial students in their own classrooms, by building up new links with the colonies as they grew toward independence and the influence of the colonial office diminished. Her address was an emphatic summary of the Asquith plan. She rejected the idea that colonial colleges should offer 'an esperanto of culture, divorced from any national heritage', or that they should at the beginning concentrate on cherishing and developing the indigenous culture; what the colonial peoples needed was what we could best offer them: our own culture. Miss Perham asked her audience to accept as evidence for this view the enthusiasm which Africans show for western learning: she spoke of boys on the Gold Coast acting Euripides with 'tremendous satisfaction', and an African graduate at Fort Hare whose eyes lit up when he confessed that his research problem was the poetry of Dryden and Pope! She drove home to her audience the two features which most clearly distinguish the Asquith plan and which were the burden of academic writing in the 1930s: the special function of the university as a training ground for leaders and the immense importance of insisting on the same standards of achievement as are required from students in Britain.[22]

Thus the Asquith colleges were founded before British universities had had time to adapt themselves to the new society, and were still living in the ideology of the 1930s. But the ferment for reform had begun. The 1944 Education Act democratised secondary schooling. By 1950 the proportion of any age group reaching the university was about 1 in 31, compared with about 1 in 60 before the war. By 1959 the proportion had risen to 1 in 24. By 1963 Grant Robertson's worst hopes were realised, for in the white paper approving the recommendations of the Robbins report Britain had committed herself by 1980 to the higher education of what Grant Robertson would have regarded as a mediocrity: one in six of the age group. In the 1960s this quantitative change in the dimensions of higher education has brought with it (to use a phrase coined for the University of Sussex) a re-drawing of the map of knowledge. A fresh classification of arts curricula into European studies, African studies, and the like has been adopted by some of the new universities (not so fresh, perhaps, for Oxford Greats is no more than an area-study of classical Greece and Rome; and in 1919 Sadler proposed for Indian universities honours courses distinguished by articulation of several subjects rather than concentration upon one subject – p. 127).

An Asquith commission in 1965 would doubtless have based its recommendations on an idea of the university quite different from that current in 1945, and one more appropriate for developing countries. But this is idle hindsight. In fact if the Asquith commission had not reported by 1945, or if action on it had been delayed, the opportunity would have been lost to set the colonies on the road to independence. They would have taken the road just the same; but with consequences one can only guess from observing the Belgian Congo, where (it is said) there were only thirty-one Congolese graduates at the time of independence.

II THE ASQUITH COLLEGES

No sooner were the Asquith and Elliot reports published than action was taken upon them, in a way which makes the years 1945 to 1948 stand enduringly on the credit side of the balance sheet of British colonial policy. The inter-university council for higher education in the colonies, which was set up in 1946, was an independent body, not – as the old advisory committee was – an official government body. It included representatives from British and colonial university institutions. It settled down with commendable speed to turn the Asquith and Elliot reports into working drawings. The government provided money. The universities provided men and advice. The University of London co-operated splendidly by establishing a scheme of special relationship to give the colonial colleges the maximum opportunities for initiative and adaptation within the framework of London degrees (see p. 239). Between 1946 and 1949 the university had entered into this special relationship with colleges in the Sudan (though it was not a British colony), the West Indies, Nigeria, the Gold Coast, and Uganda. Special relationship was later on extended to the university colleges in Salisbury, Nairobi, and in Dar-es-Salaam. In 1948, 104 students enrolled at University College, Ibadan, and 90 students, taken over from Achimota College, at the University College of the Gold Coast. Vigorous and imaginative Englishmen were appointed as principals of these two colleges, a nucleus of keen and able academics was recruited, and an ambitious building programme was launched. The two other colleges in Africa brought into special relationship with the University of London were Gordon College, Khartoum, and Makerere College, Uganda. Before the Asquith commission published its report some steps had already been taken to transform these colleges into institutions of higher education; had it not been for the war, they would have benefited much more from the enlightened and imaginative De La Warr report of 1937. Gordon College, Khartoum, was admitted into special relationship in 1946, with 188 students from whom the first candidates for London degrees would be selected. Makerere College, which for various good reasons had been unable to achieve its promise foretold by the De La Warr commission, was made an autonomous institution, and was admitted into special relationship, in 1949.[23]

The pioneers in these new university colleges faced a formidable task. On the new sites selected for the colleges in the Gold Coast and Nigeria, for instance, they had to do much more than establish a university: they had to build a town, for both sites were in uncleared bush some way from the city. Roads, homes for staff, halls for students, drainage, water supply, electricity, transport, schools, chapels, mosques, even a cemetery, became the responsibility of academic administrators. The first professors had to set standards of teaching which would qualify the students to enter for London degrees in subjects already in the London syllabus. Clearly the pioneers had no choice but to adopt the pattern of an English university. Equally clearly this was the pattern which Africans themselves wanted. The African intellectual, educated in London or Cambridge or Manchester, would have been indignant at any softening of standards, and substitution of easier options, any cheapened version of higher education. The African wanted a replica of the British university at its best; the expatriate staff had no other model to offer.

For ten years buildings went up, numbers increased, the machinery of administration was assembled. Gordon College, Khartoum, became an independent university in 1956, but the other colleges remained in special relationship with London. In varying degree – much more pronounced in West Africa than in East Africa – each college made an impact on the community it served.[24] Each college created its own characteristic pattern, but each bore the unmistakable image of its British origin. Some of this was superficial, a social mimicry of the fripperies of British academic life: gowns, high tables, Latin grace read by a scholar, assembly in combination rooms after dinner with port assiduously passed in the proper direction.[25] But the imported pattern was not just a veneer. It permeated the whole institution: its constitution, its standards and curriculum, its social function.

The controversial questions of university constitutions and academic freedom in African countries are dealt with in chapter 10. The social function of the Asquith colleges emerges when they are compared with some other patterns of higher education in Africa; this we do in chapter 11. For the present let us discuss the standards and curricula of the Asquith colleges, taking those in Africa as examples.

Both standards and curricula were anchored to those of the University of London, under the guidance of a senate committee to deal with special relationship. Of the many contributions which the University of London has made to higher education in the British Commonwealth, the achievements of this committee are undoubtedly the most important.

On the one hand, the link with the University of London ensured that degrees in the colleges in special relationship would be on the gold standard of learning; this has been of inestimable benefit to the African people. Indeed

Britain's greatest gift to higher education in Africa has been to demonstrate to Africans that they can compete successfully on their own soil with under-graduate education in England. In 1960, for instance (the last year before the links with the University of London were loosened) some 300 students in East and West Africa sat for degree examinations of the University of London. Eighty per cent of them passed. This percentage pass was about the same as that in the same year for internal candidates of the university. Within ten years the colonial colleges had earned their hallmarks of excellence. Their graduates carried away the modern equivalent of *ius ubique docendi*.

On the other hand, the link with the University of London was one of partnership, not merely of patronage. Teachers in the colonial colleges took part in examining. London examiners visited the colonial colleges; they be-came familiar with, and inevitably interested in, the problems of teaching and research in Africa and the West Indies. In 1960–61, for example, at about the peak of the activities of the senate committee on special relationship, 655 staff members of the five colleges in special relation were appointed as university examiners, 200 members of the University of London took part in special relation examinations, and 68 visits were made by members of the university to colleges in special relation.[26]

Moreover the University of London was prepared to admit, within the framework of its degree structure, substantial modifications in syllabus. In biology courses, African plants and animals took the place of European ones. Papers in African history and geography were introduced. The university consented even to examine students in subjects not within its ordinary reper-toire: the study of government, for instance, was incorporated into the degree structure at Ibadan and the study of East African legal systems into that in Dar-es-Salaam.[27] By the mid-1950s nearly three hundred special syllabuses had been approved by the university.

The initial African response to the Asquith colleges was, in essential matters, gratifying to the founders. Insofar as there was any expressed public opinion on higher education, it welcomed the importation of English stan-dards and English curricula. In East Africa there was until recently very little notice taken by the press in the university colleges, but in Ghana and Nigeria, ever since the colleges opened their doors, there has scarcely been a week without comment about higher education. No detail was too trivial, no issue too technical, for the West African public. Over some issues, such as academic standards, the content of the curriculum, and the relation between universi-ties and the state, there has been a running debate for fifteen years. To follow the course of this debate, and to listen to the pronouncements of political leaders, academics, and students on university affairs, is to watch African nationalism confronting the British academic heritage. Let us consider a sample of the comments on standards and curricula between 1950 and 1960

III THE DEBATE OVER STANDARDS AND CURRICULA

Over standards and quality of education the debate was overwhelmingly in favour of preserving the British academic heritage. It is true that from time to time there were murmurs of complaint in the press (often from disgruntled contributors to the correspondence columns) about the 'rigid method of selection of candidates for entrance to the University'.[28] Entrance examinations should be lowered as a way to hasten Nigerianisation.[29] It was alleged that degree standards were too high (or teaching was inefficient) because candidates rejected by University College, Ibadan, were getting places in British or American universities and doing well; it was protested that it is the colonial mentality which had led Nigerians to regard American degrees as 'cheap'.[30]

All these attacks were vigorously repulsed. In Nigeria over standards of admission at one end and quality of degrees at the other neither government nor university college made any compromise even when the flow of suitably qualified candidates diminished and there was a danger of empty beds in the college. 'We don't want another Yaba', said the minister of education in the Western Region, defending the standard of the London degree. A suggestion made by several critics – that Nigeria should look to Egypt for a pattern of higher education (with easy entrance, enormous classes, non-residential students, and teaching at night) was rejected with contempt in the editorials of the Lagos *Daily Times*.

In the Gold Coast, as it then was, public opinion about standards flowed in similar channels. There was at first no murmur of dispute against the dedication to quality, the need to set standards, so eloquently and emphatically enunciated by the first principal, David Balme.[31] A proposal made at the college convocation in 1953, that the college should grant its own degrees, was rejected by a large majority with evident approval from the press. But murmurs did begin in 1955, when there were a hundred empty places in the university college and the college nevertheless raised its entrance requirements 'in conformity with the requirements of the University of London'. For a time the press commented on the thin trickle of graduates and regretted the policy of sending down students who failed their examinations when the need for graduates was so great. The 'obsession' (as the students' magazine put it) 'of satisfying London examination requirements is too great for this College'. And concerning agricultural education, in 1958 the head of the school of agriculture at the Kumasi College of Technology is reported to have uttered the following heretical sentiments:

> I am convinced that since we in this country are not producing agriculturalists for any other country there is very little point in basing our course on an imaginary universal or even British standard. The whole question of standards is relative . . . A standard in education is high enough when it can adequately serve the needs of the community for which it is designed. As the problems become complex so the standard must grow to deal with them.[32]

All such criticism was summarily dismissed by the principal of the University College of the Gold Coast and editorial comment in the press supported him. Standards, he declared, are 'unchangeable'. A new institution making its reputation 'cannot afford any weakening of standards'. Authority, in the person of Dr Nkrumah, defended this declaration. Speaking after his installation as chancellor of the newly created University of Ghana, he said that for nearly thirteen years as a college it had been in special relationship with the University of London in order to ensure high standards. And he ended with these words: 'By the attainment of University status I trust that both the lecturers and the students of the College have accepted the challenge to maintain the high academic standards already set.'[33]

From East Africa comes a similar story. 'East Africa is fortunate', says an editorial in the *Uganda Herald*, 'in that within 50 years she has an educational institution at which her students can acquire degrees of one of the most highly considered universities in England.'[34] As the University College of East Africa approached the time when it should sever its connection with London, the Uganda minister of education defended the admissions policy of the college, which 'had never yet failed to ensure a high calibre annual intake to Makerere'.[35] A few months later an editorial, discussing the proposed federal University of East Africa, declared: 'It is particularly important that East Africa's own degrees shall have a standing at least comparable with the London University degrees which are now awarded.'[36] Even when, in 1961, there were fifty empty places at Makerere, and when one correspondent to the press complained that it was easier to get a degree in a British university than in East Africa, half a dozen other correspondents came to the defence of the high standards at Makerere; and a leading article in the *Uganda Argus* said, concerning the new autonomous University of East Africa, that it 'must certainly be able to resist pressure on the maintenance of standards . . .'.[37]

In Khartoum, Dakar, and Leopoldville, there is a similar climate of opinion about standards of achievement for degrees and diplomas. The mistakes made in India have not been repeated in tropical Africa. Wherever European countries have exported universities to tropical Africa they have set and guaranteed standards. Louvain still underwrites the licence at the university in Leopoldville. Paris and Bordeaux guaranteed the licence in Senegal, and, as we describe below, Senegal responded by asking, after independence, for Dakar University to be adopted as the eighteenth university of France. London's guarantee to Ghana, Nigeria, and the Sudan was willingly received and gratefully acknowledged.[38] Apart from a few lapses, discussed in chapter 10, African nationalism has exerted no pressure upon the universities to cheapen their degrees. Indeed, the zeal to maintain standards has not been an unmixed blessing, for the need to set standards in quality of teaching and learning, which is essential, has frequently been confused with a need which is not essential: namely to set levels of achievement in particular subjects which would be identical with those current in Britain. A common consequence of this confusion is that the pattern of degree characteristic of the English university system in the 1950s (i.e. the concentration upon one-subject honours degrees), and even the range of courses offered by faculties, have persisted in some African universities, where they are not appropriate, after severance from metropolitan control. This matter is discussed in detail on p. 249.

We turn now to consider curricula in the colonial university colleges, with particular reference to those in Africa. Our discussion falls into two parts, first, curricula in these colleges while they were still in special relation with the University of London; second, curricula devised after the colleges had become independent universities.

The University of London generously encouraged adaptation in the content of curricula in individual subjects, but it was uncompromising in resisting any departure from the pattern of the degree.[39] In all the Asquith colleges, therefore, the programme for arts had to fit into a general degree course, for which candidates studied three subjects for three years, or into an honours degree course, for which candidates studied one subject in depth and, where prescribed, an ancillary subject; either course leading to a degree of the University of London. The general course, though it meets some of the needs of a developing country more satisfactorily than an honours course, was by general agreement both unpopular and difficult; accordingly, in some of the colleges more than others, there was a drift towards specialised degrees, carried on two converging currents of opinion: the acknowledged difficulty of the general degree course and the desire to imitate the prevailing fashion of degree-pattern in England. Similarly in science there were pass courses, in which two subjects were taken at the final examination, and special courses, in which candidates concentrated upon one subject; and again the drift was toward the one-subject honours degree. By 1960, the degrees granted to the colleges since they entered into special relation were distributed as follows:[40]

UNIVERSITY COLLEGE	B.A.		B.SC.	
	GENERAL	HONOURS	GENERAL	SPECIAL
East Africa	155	19	49	0
Ghana	106	165	117	43
Ibadan	170	144	102	100
West Indies	178	99	157	5
Rhodesia and Nyasaland	17	0	6	0

It is evident from this table that the colleges differed in their policies over the balance between general and special degrees, but in all of them except the infant college in Rhodesia, the balance was moving in favour of one-subject special or honours degrees.

Within this uniformity there was, as we have already mentioned, a growing diversity in content of courses. In agriculture and the biological sciences the organisms, and to some extent the problems studied, were rapidly adapted to local conditions. In geography and history some papers were introduced which reflected the regional interests of the colleges; though there were sometimes difficulties about this: in the Gold Coast in 1954, for instance, it was said that the University of London disallowed a request for a paper on West African history before about 1500 on the grounds that the history of this region before European contact with it was not well-enough known. But if one looks at the curricula approved by the University of London at the end of the period of special relation, one is impressed with the diversity in content of courses which had been achieved under the University of London degree. In history, for instance, Ghanaians could take general papers on African history together with special subjects including British policy toward West Africa with special reference to the Gold Coast, 1820–80; European contact with West Africa, 1415–1580; states and peoples of the Niger basin, 1822–57; all alternatives to the economic and social history of Tudor England. Nigerians could take some, though rather less, African history. East Africans had a general paper on the history of tropical Africa from the mid-eighteenth century, and among the special subjects offered were: Buganda and her neighbours, 1877–1901; or the evolution of British policy in the administration of the tropical dependencies in East and West Africa since 1884. The West Indian student had opportunities to specialise on the history of the Americas, the history of the West Indies since 1604, Jamaica and the amelioration of the slave laws, 1823–31, and the growth of the British Commonwealth 1880–1932. The student in Rhodesia could take papers on central African history. In religious studies there were equally laudable adaptations: work was not confined to the study of christianity. In both Ibadan and Accra something could be learnt of islam and of the indigenous African religions; there were even lectures, felicitously classified under religious studies, on witchcraft. In sociology and social anthropology a good deal of research had to be done before the subjects could be taught with local relevance; but vigorous starts were made in Uganda, where the institute for social research under Audrey Richards built a firm foundation of distinguished scholarship for East Africa; and in Ghana as early as 1950 K. A. Busia put before the academic board proposals for an honours degree in sociology which had as its object the introduction of undergraduates to European society, African society, and contemporary problems of social change. In economics courses the colleges were able to emphasise topics such as the primary industries and African or West Indian economic history. In law the college at Dar-es-Salaam paid attention to land tenure in East Africa. Even in classics it was found possible to make a gesture of adaptation: the college at Ibadan offered a special subject in Roman rule in North Africa, 146 BC to 337 AD.

From the outset the Asquith colleges set themselves to cultivate research. Among the generous inducements offered by the University of London was one which allowed staff members in the colleges in special relation to work for the Ph.D. degree as internal students; eighty-five were so registered in 1960–61.

This was an encouragement to junior academics, and some of the more senior found golden opportunities for research in topics which could not have been pursued in Europe. Thus – to give only random examples of work with special relevance to Africa – research distinguished on world standards has been published from Makerere on tropical diseases, social anthropology, and fresh-water biology. Ibadan is a distinguished centre for African history and archaeology; its chemistry department has an impressive record of work on African natural products, and its physics department on ionospheric research. Our understanding of religious experience in Africa has been enriched by work from Makerere and Ibadan. From Legon in Ghana have come notable contributions on African music, sociology and economics.

All this scholarly work, and there is now a great deal of it, is leading to a codification of knowledge about Africa (and similar work has been done for the Caribbean and for Malaya) which is the prerequisite for teaching what are collectively called African studies at university level. The idea of African studies in African universities is a controversial one. Some people believe that there should be institutes of African studies, with some sort of physical presence, separate from other departments or faculties; others maintain that this is an artificial and contrived approach to knowledge about Africa, and that all subjects (even, so it is maintained, Latin and Greek) can and should be taught, and are being taught, with an African bias; so that African studies are diffused through the whole university. We have no useful contribution to make to this controversy. In our section on India (p. 133) we discuss the homologous problem of the place of oriental studies in Indian universities, but the circumstances of India are so different that we do not think any useful parallel can be drawn. Suffice it to say that without the centres for African studies in American, British and French universities our knowledge of African cultures would be immeasurably poorer; and where there are mature institutes of African studies in Africa, e.g. in the universities of Dakar, Ghana, and Ibadan, they are proving a great stimulus to research and are establishing valuable canons of criticism in new fields of scholarship. Where these institutes organise formal courses, as in the University of Ghana, which offers an M.A. degree and a diploma in African studies, they are proving also to be effective instruments of education. In our present context, the interesting question about African studies is whether they should be taught to undergraduates in African universities; and this brings us to a discussion of the African response to the curricula we have been describing.

As we have seen above, the African response to the demand for quality made upon them by the British system of higher education was to accept it eagerly and to prove quickly that it was a standard well within the reach of African students and scholars. It would not be an exaggeration to say that Africans themselves have been the most enthusiastic defenders of these standards; so much so that at first some of them regarded with suspicion adaptations in the curriculum (such as the substitution of African for Tudor history, or Arabic for Latin and Greek) in case they might be soft options to the traditional English curriculum. Despite the admirable detailed adaptations of the content of courses which we have described, one finds, therefore, a certain implicit conspiracy to resist major adaptations and to preserve the overall pattern of higher education as it is found in England. This pattern is what the African wants because this is what he would have got if he had graduated from London or Cambridge; this is what the expatriate wants because it is the pattern in which he himself was trained.[41] Some scholars go even further and defend the traditional English pattern of higher education on the ground that it is as relevant for Africa as it is for England. The higher learning, in their view, is always and everywhere the same. An eloquent exponent of this view was the distinguished pioneer principal of the University College of the Gold Coast, David Balme. In his inaugural address he discussed whether a university in Africa should be any different from universities anywhere else. He made the point that the diversities between (say) historians from different universities are quite trivial compared with the diversities between (say) historians and chemists within the same university. Then he went on to say:

The whole issue has been bedevilled by our careless use of the phrase 'European civilisation'. It may be justifiable that the things which are studied at universities . . . are themselves the instruments of civilisation. If so, then it follows that there is only one modern civilisation. It happens to have started in Greece . . . and it spread first through Europe. But it is high time we stopped calling it European as though there were some other from which to distinguish it. . . . I was astonished when I came here to find myself called a European. I had never thought of myself as one before, and I don't now.[42]

Balme admitted that within the one world-civilisation there are different national cultures, though he doubted whether universities were concerned with these or whether national cultures could (or should) be kept alive by teaching them. After all (he said) folk dancing is dying out in England and hand-looms have been replaced by machinery. 'I don't think we need weep when national traditions go . . . it is only a matter of pride in superficial things.'

The African people were enjoined to look across the Sahara for their intellectual nourishment. The Mediterranean, they were told, 'is the cradle of all the civilisation that has conquered the world. Happy is Africa, whose shore is on that sea.' These sentiments vividly recall Maine's convocation address in Calcutta eighty-three years earlier: 'except the blind force of nature, nothing moves in this world which is not Greek in its origin.'[43] Now it is one thing to exclude the African heritage as a matter of expediency; for a university exported from Britain to concentrate on the disciplines lying within its own tradition is a sensible pragmatic decision. It is quite a different thing to elevate this pragmatism to the dignity of a dogma. To speak as though African cultures were perhaps not even worth teaching at the university level (though despite what Balme said it is unfair to him to assume that he did have this view, for under his leadership there were from the outset plans for African studies in Ghana) is to confront the heady enthusiasms of African nationalism. It is not surprising, therefore, that African opinion over curriculum revision, unlike African opinion over standards, changed in the 1950s. By 1960, although there were still many African intellectuals prepared to swallow for Africa all the assumptions made about university education in England and to defend a degree pattern modified in detail but in all essentials based on that of the English civic university, there was a growing body of Africans, influenced by their experience of American universities (discussed in chapter 9), who were dissatisfied with the pattern of higher education and who questioned the validity of the English assumptions for the African environment. The dialectic between these two bodies of opinion is likely to continue for many years. Those who are involved in African higher education are obliged to have an opinion, if only a provisional one, about the issue. Before giving our opinion we summarise some of the arguments on both sides.

Everyone agrees that subjects such as mathematics and physics cannot be taught any differently just because the students belong to a Hamitic race living in latitude 10° and not to a Nordic race living in latitude 50°. There is a universality about natural science which requires not only its logic but also its content to be similar wherever it is practised. A scientist, wherever he works, must not only conform to certain recognised principles in his style of thinking; he must also have mastered an internationally recognised repertoire of information. There is, of course, a universality about many arts subjects too. In history the canons of criticism, the decision about what constitutes evidence, the standard of integrity expected over the accurate presentation of facts: these are shared by reputable historians everywhere. But in arts subjects there can be a much greater diversity of content. It would be inexcusable ignorance on the part of a medieval historian in Britain to be unaware of the Angevin empire; he would be forgiven if he happened to be unfamiliar with the empires of Sailendra and Cambodia. Nevertheless it can be maintained that the historian should select for his teaching episodes which are important historically, whether they have local relevance or not. The French revolution, for instance, is obviously of great importance to students of history in Africa; so is the industrial revolution; so, for that matter, is the muslim invasion of India. Furthermore, there is a persuasive argument that universities are concerned primarily to train students in a style of thinking, not in vocational skills, and as Samuel Alexander once said, a liberal education is a spirit of pursuit, not a choice of subject. Now it can be argued that an excellent spirit of pursuit is deeply rooted in traditional subjects – classics, European history, English literature – taught in the traditional way. Any classical scholar can recognise excellence in a student's knowledge of classics. It is hard for any scholar to recognise excellence in (let us say) a student's knowledge of Ibo land law or Dogon philosophy. Many university teachers in tropical Africa, both expatriates and Africans, are therefore content with the traditional content of degree courses, and see no urgent need to depart except incidentally from the patterns to be found in Britain. But there is a different side to the question. It is simply unrealistic to suppose that universities in tropical Africa are at this stage of their history concerned *primarily* with the conservation and advancement of western learning. They are concerned with training thousands of men and women who will not become scholars and whose lives will be spent working among communities deeply rooted in an indigenous ancient tradition. Obviously the African graduate must be familiar with the western heritage, for Africa has chosen to adopt this heritage. But if African universities are not to become esoteric, cut off from the mass of people, exposing themselves to the gibe of being 'ivory towers', their graduates must possess two other qualifications: (i) they must have an objective and scholarly understanding of the society from which they themselves have come, and (ii) their education must be seen, by those who are paying for it, to be relevant to Africa's needs for high-level manpower.

If only minor adaptations are made to the pattern of degree courses in African universities, their graduates, however well schooled in the western tradition, will be deficient in these two additional qualifications. In some African universities a student can graduate even in the humanities in ignorance of the roots of his own heritage, knowing practically nothing about the intricate political and social structure of the peoples of his own continent: the fascinating network of organisation among the Kede tribe along the Niger, which includes even a sliding scale of income tax according to the number of canoes a man owns; the ingenious checks and balances among the Tallensi which protect them from autocracy and which contribute to good government; the dignified and sophisticated pattern of judicial procedure among the Bemba; the philosophical ideas of the Dogon. This is not just interesting antiquarian knowledge. A teacher who does not understand or respect the village culture of his pupils cannot reach their minds. An administrator unfamiliar with the customs of the people in his charge cannot earn their confidence.[44] A lawyer, a doctor, an engineer, who is uninformed about the society he serves, cannot serve that society well. Years ago Britain recognised this by giving postgraduate training to recruits to the colonial civil service before sending them overseas. It cannot be assumed that Africans do not need similar training, and African universities have a duty to provide it. We have described (p. 62) how British policy in Indian higher education was to emphasise the vernacular languages so that Indian graduates could interpret western civilisation to the common people. For similar reasons it is important that African graduates should have a scholarly understanding of the beliefs and traditions of the common people of Africa.

As to the second qualification, that of visible and obvious relevance, it is claimed (and rightly, of course) that many Africans who have pursued traditional courses of study, concentrating, for instance, on Greats at Oxford or history at Cambridge, have given outstanding service to their own nations; and in African universities, as in Britain, the single-subject honours degree without any vocational bias has proved its success from its products; the African has not failed to notice that the most favoured background of the British colonial administrator was an arts degree from Oxford or Cambridge.[45] But this is a spurious argument. If these same persons had been equally well educated in economics or social anthropology or engineering they might have been even more effective. It is an odd train of reasoning which insists on the most austere standards of professional training before a man can be regarded as a classicist or an historian; but is satisfied that this same man will pick up in an amateur way enough knowledge of statistics and economics and political science to run the nation's overseas trade or foreign affairs, or enough social anthropology and law to become a provincial commissioner.

It is a question of priorities rather than of the intrinsic merit of different subjects of study. If there were world enough and time it would be admirable to expose first year arts students (as Lovanium University in the Congo does) to medieval French, with mimeographed sheets of *Chanson de Roland* circulated to each student; or to devote time (as the University of the West Indies did while in special relation with London) to Anglo-Saxon in the English course. These subjects have an illustrious tradition and an honourable place in the university curriculum. But, in developing countries, universities which wish to preserve such subjects as these are under an obligation to assure the public that other, more vocational, subjects are not being neglected. This assurance has not always been forthcoming. In Nigeria, for instance, ten years after the university college was founded, no courses were offered in engineering, economics, law, geology, anthropology, sociology, public administration, or Arabic and islamic studies, and it had taken eight years to establish a department of education. A new university institution in Britain might well be considered wise to defer teaching in such subjects as these until its 'basic' curriculum was well developed, for students who want to study any of the subjects could easily go elsewhere. But in Africa a good case can be made for giving priority to professional subjects including economics, education, anthropology, and public administration, if for no other reason than to establish them as scholarly disciplines; and the traditional arts and science subjects could have been clustered round these disciplines; a pattern of development common in French colonial territories and advocated over thirty years ago by Currie; it was also the pattern followed by the University of Lagos when it was founded in 1962.

In retrospect the most unfortunate decision about priorities in the Asquith colleges was to keep technology out of the universities. The source of this policy lay not in the colleges themselves but in England, for these attitudes to applied science were imposed upon Ibadan, Accra, and Makerere, by the decision, made in London, to put engineering training into the so-called colleges of arts, science, and technology, which were below university status. In African countries, as in India, the clerkly office job has for a long time enjoyed an exaggerated prestige and it has been difficult to persuade Africans to accord an equally high status to jobs in technology. The road-builder, the sanitary engineer, the telephone expert, could not command the esteem given to the functionary behind a desk in a government office in Lagos. There are many historical reasons for this attitude; but it is an attitude that everyone deplores, and it is a pity that it was reinforced by the decision to relegate all technology except agriculture, medicine, and veterinary science to colleges below university level; for in Africa, even more than in Britain, prestige in occupations goes with the right to wear a gown and coloured hood on festive occasions. Here, surely, a lesson could have been learnt from Indian experience.

Public opinion in African countries is difficult to assess, but some significance can be attached to discussions in the press and to statements made by political leaders. It can be assumed that in Africa, as elsewhere, both these sources of opinion commonly reflect what sections of the public like to hear. Adaptation of university curricula to the short term needs of African society was a common topic of discussion in West Africa (though very little in East Africa) during the 1950s. Thus, soon after a university college was founded in the Gold Coast, the local press was asking for facilities for training accountants, bankers, and business managers,[46] and for greater emphasis on vocational training.[47] An overture in 1954 from the Gold Coast ministry of defence and external affairs for a school of public administration in the college was resisted by the college authorities. Warnings of the need for adaptation came also from the highest levels. As early as 1954, Dr Nkrumah was reported as saying: 'While I fully subscribe to the vital principle of academic freedom, a University must relate its activities to the needs of the society in which it exists....'[48] And Dr Azikiwe turned his views on this matter into action, by creating at Nsukka, in Nigeria, a new university to operate on the lines of an American land grant college, with its emphasis on vocational training. 'We cannot afford', he said, 'to continue to produce ... an upper class of parasites who shall prey upon a stagnant and sterile class of workers and peasants. ... We must frankly admit that we can no longer afford to flood only the white collar jobs at the expense of the basic occupations and productive vocations ... particularly in the fields of agriculture, engineering, business administration, education and domestic science.'[49] Among some thoughtful Africans there was unease that higher, and even secondary, education was disrupting the stability of African society by alienating Africans from the core of their culture: the land, the village, the family. Must education be destructive? 'It seems ironical', wrote one observer, 'that the Nigerian community is approaching the point at which every child allowed to proceed to secondary school becomes a liability, not only in his unproductiveness, but also in his demand from society for a place he does not merit.'[50] Gradually public opinion crystallised into a demand that a university in Africa should serve the needs of the state for expertise and high-level manpower. The new African leaders were not content to see reproduced in the African bush a replica of a traditional European temple of learning, although this was the very policy which had, a dozen years earlier, given Africans confidence in themselves. Scores of times the taunt of 'ivory tower' was thrown at the university colleges in Ghana and Nigeria.

Accompanying the pressure from public opinion for relevance in the curriculum was pressure in another and quite different form, namely a desire to see incorporated into the undergraduate course material about the indigenous cultures of tropical Africa: its traditional political systems, with their subtle checks and balances; its passionate identification with the soil through religion, customary law, the cultivation of crops and the care of animals; its philosophies and codes of behaviour; its languages; its folklore and music and dance. This was indeed foreseen by the perceptive De La Warr commission as long ago as 1937; and the famous Achimota College, in 1927, set an admirable precedent at school level: African music and drumming was practised there; Diedrich Westermann joined the staff to create a common script for Twi and Fanti. Folk tales and oral traditions were collected. The colonial university colleges had, as we have indicated, laid firm foundations of research into African societies (one recalls, in particular, the work of Busia and Nketia in Ghana, Dike in Nigeria, and Audrey Richards in Uganda). But in the period we are now considering, this material was not, except incidentally, being handed on to African undergraduates; and this – accepted at first without question – is what gradually raised doubts among the more progressive African intellectuals. As long ago as 1955 the Lagos press was advocating a faculty of vernacular languages at Ibadan[51] (before independence no African language could be studied in any English-speaking university in tropical Africa) and in 1956, in an editorial, there was a plea that Arabic, the language of the book sacred for millions of Nigerians, should be studied there.[52] From Ghana came similar opinions. In 1951 a columnist in the Accra *Daily Graphic* was asking whether higher education 'should be related to local histories, traditions, and environments' – and he answered his own question by pointing to the 'cultural renaissance' already at that time evident on the Gold Coast. And Dr Nkrumah, when he opened Akuafo hall of residence at the university college in February 1956, made his policy clear: 'We must in the development of our University bear in mind that once it had been planted in African soil it must take root amidst African traditions and culture.'[53]

Of course there has been opposition to these pleas for adapting the curriculum more radically to the African environment. Some African intellectuals, especially those educated in Britain, resist changes in curriculum or in pattern of courses because they confuse such changes with a lowering of standards. They are accordingly suspicious of any divergence from the British pattern. Some of them are particularly allergic to proposals for incorporating African studies into the curriculum. Is this, they say, the first step toward disarming us intellectually; to substitute Arabic and African languages for the classics; to teach English to Africans as Chinese is taught to Englishmen, not as Englishmen learn English at Cambridge; to neglect Tudor history in favour of the history of Africa; to regard oral tradition as legitimate material for scholarship; to take seriously the political institutions of a Yoruba town; to reflect on the indigenous ethical systems of animists and muslims as well as on christian ethics? There are, of course, sound reasons for caution. To teach African studies at undergraduate level is a much harder task than to teach European or Middle Eastern or Russian studies. The subject is only now being codified. The documents are incomplete. But one suspects that these arguments are sometimes used disingenuously by those who are afraid of adaptation. It is evident from the curricula in *philologie Africaine* at Leopold-ville and in *sociologie musulmane africaine* at Dakar, and in certain subjects at Ibadan, such as religious studies and history, to say nothing of the courses at the London School of Oriental and African Studies or at Birmingham and Edinburgh, Northwestern and Boston universities, that the subject is already being taught in a scholarly way at undergraduate level and with no softening of standards.[54]

In view of the strong arguments on both sides it is not surprising that the confusing debate on curriculum reform in West African universities has not yet led to any clear-cut policies. But since independence changes have occurred; the best summary of the state of the discussion is to sample some of the patterns of university study which have appeared since then.

We begin by emphasising one point, so that it can be disengaged from the rest of our discussion: this is that in subjects where it has been practicable the *content* of curricula in individual subjects has, since independence from London, been modified to suit African conditions as far as any critic familiar with Africa could reasonably expect. Our main discussion, therefore, concentrates on the wider and more difficult problems of the pattern of degree courses and the introduction of unconventional subjects of study. But first let us illustrate the extent of adaptation in content in individual courses, choosing one example: history.

In the University of Khartoum which has been independent since 1956 students reading history take a three year curriculum for the degree of B.A. (general). In the first year students take two courses, one in the history of the Near East and Mediterranean up to 600 AD; the other an introduction to historical criticism. In the intermediate year they deal with medieval history and islam and Arab expansion. In their third year they study the history of the Sudan together with four other subjects chosen from the following: modern Europe from 1500; early Sudan; modern British history from 1485; Abbasid and Ottoman history; the history of Africa south of the Sahara to 1884.[55]

The University of East Africa has had little opportunity yet to put its new ideas into practice, but an example of an imaginative syllabus in history comes from Dar-es-Salaam. Students reading history in their first year work entirely on the history of Africa, including one paper, out of two to be taken, on pre-colonial history. In the two following years students do four compulsory papers: (i) the history of eastern Africa; (ii) comparative studies in colonialism and nationalism; (iii) historians and revolutions, a study of the English, French, and Russian revolutions; (iv) the rise of the industrial state; and in addition one specialised paper chosen from a number of options.[56] In Makerere the history curriculum, since the special relation with London ended, has considerably increased its emphasis on African material. A student who takes a B.A. in history as a single subject has in his final examination eight papers one of which is in African history; another optional one is in the history of islam; another option is the history from original documents of East or West Africa.[57]

In Ghana the state of affairs is similar to that in Makerere; or at any rate it was until the recent crumbling of autonomy in the University of Ghana (see p. 327). African history occupied something like half the available teaching time. For the rest of the time a selection was made, so that some topics could be studied in depth. The criterion for selection is the proximity of the episodes studied in space and time to the circumstances of modern Ghana. Thus British and European history and the history of islamic civilisation have a prominent place.

The history course at Ibadan University falls into two parts. In part I the curriculum in history is concerned solely with Africa. The part II curriculum offers (in 1965–6) a choice of two papers among ten alternatives. These include Nigerian history, African history, history of islam, and history of the Middle East, besides more conventional topics.[58]

The University of Nigeria offers a B.A. in history to students who pass examinations in seven main courses covering archaeology, African history, the history of Nigeria, medieval and modern European history, and a conspectus of world history since 1815. Among the special subjects which may be taken are East African history, 1890–1923, and the history of christianity and missionary thought in West Africa.[59]

From this brief catalogue of the content of history courses in five African universities, four of which were formerly in special relation with the University of London, two conclusions can be drawn. The first is that since the institutions became independent they have clearly demonstrated their conviction that the content of the history courses (and something similar could be said of many other subjects) should be relevant, and that relevance is not inimical to a scholarly attitude, even in history. The second conclusion, not evident from our summary, but very evident from a perusal of the books, papers, and documents which comprise the material for these courses and confirmed in our discussion of French scholarship in Africa (p. 374), is that the common objection which in the past has often been raised against the

adaptation of curricula to African conditions – that the prerequisite research
has not yet been done – is, for African history at any rate, a totally groundless
objection.

But there is much more to the pattern of degree courses than the curricula
in individual subjects, and to this wider question we now turn.

IV PATTERNS OF DEGREES

It must be repeated that while the colonial colleges were preparing candidates
for degrees of the University of London they had to adopt the London pattern
of degree. In arts this meant a general course in which three subjects were
studied for each of three years (3:3:3), or an honours course in which the
candidate was examined in one principal subject and, where prescribed, a
subsidiary one. The tendency in most of the colleges was toward the honours
course. As they approached independence the various colleges replanned their
degree structure. With some exceptions, their replanning can be summarised
as strongly coloured by English precedent: the common degree pattern remains one in which study in depth takes precedence over breadth of education. We offer some examples.

The University of Khartoum has been independent since 1956. It admits
students on a pass with five 'credits' in the Sudan school certificate (roughly
equivalent to O-level G.C.E.). Both general and special degrees are offered in
arts and in science; the general degree course takes four years, the special
degree course takes five. All arts students do Arabic and English in the first
year together with two other subjects. In the second year they do three subjects, in the third and fourth years, two. Those who do a special degree concentrate on one subject in the fifth year. The general pattern, therefore, is
4:3:2:2:1. The university has preserved virtually unchanged the standards it
set during its special relationship with London. It has external examiners
mainly from Britain, but (in 1964) there were examiners, too, from Beirut,
Dakar, Helsinki, Salisbury (Rhodesia), and The Hague.

The federated University of East Africa had difficulty in devising a degree
structure agreeable to its three very diverse colleges and in the end it settled
upon three alternatives. Entrance is at the level of Cambridge higher school
certificate (approximately A-level G.C.E.). The B.A. course lasts three years.
There is no alternative of pass or honours courses. The three patterns of
courses are as follows:

ALTERNATIVES	X	Y	Z
YEAR			
1	3	3	3 subjects
2	2	2	1 ⎫ selected from the 3 taken
3	2	1	1 ⎭ in first year

Opinion about the patterns of degrees in British universities has changed so much in recent years that the z alternative, at any rate, would not be regarded as suitable for general purpose arts students; and the x alternative seems very similar to that to be found in the English double honours degree. If these patterns came after a broad education at school they could be more easily defended; but they are based on the specialised sixth form work required for the Cambridge higher certificate. It might be said in defence of the decision that the East African countries are independent, and this is the sort of higher education they want. But is it? In 1963 a Uganda education commission published a report on the whole of the education system below university level.[60] Over university entrance and the pattern of degree the report has this to say:

It is doubtful whether an entrance level adopted in the United Kingdom only after the Second World War, in order to select university entrants from an almost over-whelming number of Sixth Form applicants, is necessarily appropriate to East African conditions. The standard required for the East African University Colleges is higher than that demanded in many parts of the English-speaking world, and suggests that the University Colleges are more concerned to educate an élite than to produce a large number of graduates and diplomates suitably trained for East Africa's present needs.[61]

And on the same page, commenting on the degree structure, the commissioners say: 'We suggest that consideration should be given to the design of a less specialised degree on the lines of the Scottish Ordinary degree.'

Despite this suggestion about the Scottish degree, and a similar criticism from a committee on needs and priorities appointed by the university (discussed on page 284) the university's development plan for 1964–7 did not depart from the proposed degree pattern, though the development plan does say that the university is willing to discuss the possibilities of a four-year curriculum in arts and science with a school certificate level of entry; it also looks favourably on the possibility (to put it no higher) of junior colleges, even in association with the university, to provide a better foundation for the university course.[62]

In West Africa there has been a proliferation of new degree patterns, including those adopted by two colleges previously in special relation with London. We consider these two colleges first.

Academic planning in the University of Ghana has been so bedevilled by interference from the government that it is impossible to see clearly what the university's own ideas of degree-structure might otherwise have been. When the academics started in 1959 to discuss what the new degree structure should be like there was a general agreement to maintain the standard set by London but to bring the honours degree within reach of students who, because of their inadequate school training, could not be expected to achieve this standard after only three years at the university. It was proposed, therefore, that, as in some Scottish and Australian universities, all arts students should work for three years for a pass degree, and some would be allowed to stay on for a fourth year to read for an honours degree. The university realised that Ghana's immediate need was for 'a large output of broadly qualified graduates'. At this point came a government directive that courses for first degrees in arts and science should not last longer than three years. It was further directed (but later rescinded) that all students should pursue a common first-year course: this would have left only two years for students to be brought to honours standard in arts and science. All that emerges from the present confusion is that the entrance requirement remains at A-level of G.C.E. i.e. after two years of sixth form work. The current calendar[63] gives no details of degree patterns, but it seems as though the pattern is similar to that which existed under special relation with London, i.e. for the B.A., a general degree in three subjects and an honours degree in one subject; with a somewhat similar arrangement for degrees in science. It would seem that a courageous effort is being maintained to keep the degrees on internationally respectable standards and within these standards the balance will tilt in favour of a higher proportion of pass or general degrees.

The University of Ibadan has chosen a degree pattern different from that proposed by the academic board in Ghana. We describe it as it was in 1965–6.[64]

Entry to degree courses is at A-level G.C.E. and several faculties specify subjects which must have been passed at G.C.E. Thus candidates reading any language but Greek must have passed the G.C.E. at A-level, or its equivalent, in that language and candidates for degree courses in chemistry, physics, or mathematics must have studied these subjects before up to A-level.[65] Specialisation at school at sixth form level is therefore preserved and the practice in England, which many regard as pernicious, to channel pupils into science or non-science streams in the upper classes of schools, has been confirmed for Nigeria. For candidates who have not satisfied these requirements there is still a concessional entry, on a special entrance examination, for a propaedeutic year which provides tuition up to about A-level in the subjects the candidate requires for entry to a degree course.

There is no separation of pass or general, and honours or special, courses for the degree. In the faculty of arts the degree course takes three years. Three subjects, selected from a prescribed list which strays very little outside the faculty's own field of study, are studied in the first year. For the remaining two years the student has to select a *single-subject school* (in 1965–6 the single subjects were: Arabic and islamic studies, classics, English, French, geography, history, Latin, pure mathematics, applied mathematics, statistics, and religious studies, either christian or islam); or he may select one of the following combinations of *combined subjects*: biblical and English literature, English and drama, English and French, English and Latin, French and drama, French and Latin, Greek and religious studies, Latin and religious studies, religious studies and drama, history and political science, two combinations of mathematics and geography, and three combinations of mathematics. So far the student-response has been overwhelmingly in favour of the single-subject schools. Each single-subject school prescribes a subsidiary subject: so the common pattern of degree could be summarised as three subjects in the first year, and one-plus-a-subsidiary in the two subsequent years.[66] There are no compulsory subjects: the student's curriculum is settled according to the special school he selects.

In science the pattern is somewhat similar: three subjects in the first year chosen entirely from among scientific subjects (and in chemistry, physics, and mathematics, requiring these subjects to have been done at school if they are to be taken as degree courses), followed normally by two subjects for the subsequent two years, though under certain conditions one subject alone can be pursued in the third year: a pattern of 3:2:2 or 3:2:1.[67]

In other faculties there are interesting innovations and concessions to local conditions. The faculty of education requires no specific subjects at G.C.E. other than those prescribed for entry to the university. It offers a three-year course leading to a B.Ed. degree in which education as a subject and practical teaching are built into the course. It is open to the criticism made of a similar course in Makerere: that only two subjects, apart from education, are studied in the first year; the same two are continued in the second year; and one of these is pursued in the third year (together with education). So the pattern is: 2 + education: 2: 1 + education.[68] The international committee on needs and priorities in East Africa (p. 282) censured a similar arrangement there on the grounds that it provides too narrow a repertoire for the intending school teacher; and it would seem that the same criticism could be applied to the B.Ed. course in Ibadan; but it is nevertheless a valuable innovation in a country as desperately short of teachers as Nigeria is, to recognise the status of the teaching profession by offering a professional degree in the field.

The faculty of the social sciences offers degrees in economics, political science, and sociology, and the structure and emphasis of the courses show a realistic adaptation to African needs. Thus there is breadth: two subsidiary subjects are required in addition to the major subjects, so the pattern of degree is 3: 1 + 2: 1 + 2. In the first-year courses emphasis is on African studies; thus in sociology the papers include social structure in contemporary Africa, and the history papers are on African history.[69]

The faculty of medicine has made impressive changes in curriculum since it was released from the very rigorous requirements for London medical degrees; but the faculty's most important and enlightened innovations are five B.Sc. (med) degrees: in basic medical sciences, nursing, laboratory technology, physiotherapy, and radiography.[70]

Finally the University of Ibadan has instituted a number of certificates and diplomas, some of which are at sub-degree level and which are likely to fulfil an important function in a country where opportunities for higher education are so recent and so unevenly distributed. Thus there are certificates in Arabic, religious studies, and educational drama; and for graduates (it would have been even more timely if it had been at sub-degree level) there is provision for a diploma in agricultural extension.[71]

The degree pattern in the University of Nigeria is based on that of an American land grant college, and we consider it in the section which deals with the American influence on African higher education (p. 276).

There remain three other Nigerian universities to be considered. The University of Lagos is constructed fundamentally on an English pattern, but under the enlightened leadership of one of the most eminent of Nigerians, Eni Njoku, it modified this pattern in a way which – until it was wrecked by political jobbery in 1965 – made it a model of how there could be a continuity of evolution from the anglophile Asquith college towards an indigenous African university.

The first noteworthy point is that the university gave priority, in the order in which it set up its faculties, to fields of study for which there was a national need. Instead of the assumption, regarded as an axiom by those who designed the Asquith colleges, that all professional studies must be built on a foundation of faculties of arts and science, the university began in 1962 with business and social studies, law, and a medical school.[72] In its third year of operation the university added education, engineering, arts, and science; and it was made clear that the teaching of arts and science subjects would be closely associated with the faculty of education and with other professional schools.[73] It is by a similar process that the Massachusetts Institute of Technology built up its very distinguished departments of humanities. At Lagos all students learn something of African history and culture in their first year; also for their final examinations all science students take an 'introduction to modern thought' and all arts students take an 'introduction to science and technology'. Thus the pattern of arts degree is:

First year: Three subjects + African history and culture, with a choice which includes two African languages, some social science subjects, and education.
Second and third years: Two subjects + introduction to science and technology. The choice of subjects in 1965 is English, geography, history, and mathematics.

For a degree in the faculty of science there is a similar 3:2:2 pattern with the addition of African history and culture in the first year and introduction to modern thought for the final examination. The pattern of degree in law, designed under the deanship of the distinguished English jurist L.C.B. Gower, has a refreshingly realistic approach:

The subjects included in the curriculum are not exclusively legal ones. Every effort is being made to produce a well-educated and well-rounded graduate who understands the economic and social environment in which the law operates. . . . Among the subjects in the curriculum are African History and Culture, the French language . . . and an introduction to Economics with particular emphasis on the problems and institutions of West Africa.[74]

The University of Ife has suffered from various financial setbacks and a serious weakness in its mode of government, so that no clear policy for its degree pattern has emerged. Its degree structure in the faculty of arts seems very similar to that adopted by Ibadan: A-level entry, a part I of three subjects, and a part II which is either a one-subject 'special honours' degree or a two-subject 'combined honours' degree. One notes at the University of Ife the regrettable preoccupation with specialised honours degrees. The general purpose arts candidate is not catered for; and the pass degree is devalued by the statement: 'Students failing to reach the necessary standard for an Honours degree may be awarded a pass degree. . . .'[75] The contrast between the capital 'H' and the small 'p' is probably a printer's slip, but it reflects the difference in esteem which Africans accord to what should be two equally valuable patterns of higher education.

One useful feature of the University of Ife is its institute of administration, which aims to 'professionalise' members of the Western Nigeria government service through in-service training, including what are felicitously called 'bootstrap tutorials'.[76] Projects in adult education which are severely vocational, as the institute of administration is (there is a similar one in Zaria in Northern Nigeria), are an immensely important activity for universities in Africa.

The Ahmadu Bello University in Northern Nigeria is still in process of organising its courses, but mention should be made of the degree pattern proposed for it by a delegation from the inter-university council which visited Zaria in 1961 to produce, on the lines laid down by the Nigerian commission (see p. 268), a working plan for the new university.[77] The delegation recommended a pattern of degree in non-professional subjects which – since it was published as early as 1961 – might have been expected to have more influence on curriculum reform at the older Asquith colleges than has in fact been the case. If its advice had been taken more widely, the status of the general degree might have been restored in African universities. The proposal[78] was as follows:

First year: Five subjects, including two main subjects and three subsidiaries (A, B and C); five subjects in all.
Second year: Two courses in the first main subject, one in the second and two courses chosen from A, B and C in such a way that three or four subjects in all can be studied.
Third year: Three courses in the first main subject and two courses in the second.

The current degree pattern for a B.A. or B.Sc. differs somewhat from this proposal but does recognise the need to broaden the scope of higher education in an African university. The entry standard is after sixth form work at A-level (although concessional entry to preliminary courses equivalent to A-level is permitted), followed by a degree course as follows:

Year 1: Three subjects; and in addition one supplementary subject which in 1965 was 'intensive' English, French, or mathematics.

Years 2 *and* 3: Two subjects continued from the first year with a subsidiary subject chosen from among the subjects taken in the first year.

There is no separation of the curriculum into special or general courses. Education, if taken as one of the B.A. subjects throughout the course, qualifies the candidate for a teaching diploma as well as a degree.[79]

This pattern of 3 + 1: 2 + 1: 2 + 1, is less of a general degree than that which the IUC delegation recommended; it is, nevertheless, a good deal less narrow in scope than the patterns offered at the universities of East Africa or Ibadan.

It is worth putting on record, by way of conclusion to this section of our discussion, that since 1961, at any rate, such influence as Britain could exert through the inter-university council has encouraged universities in developing Commonwealth countries to broaden their degree-structure. The University of Nigeria needed no such encouragement, but there was, when its first year survey course was being planned, consultation with Keele University, which has a 'foundation year' of similar character. The IUC delegation to Northern Nigeria, as we have illustrated above, suggested a broad-based general degree in arts. The University of East Africa came under some criticism for the narrowness of its degrees, especially for those students who include education in the curriculum. And, as we show in chapter 9, it is largely due to the influence of an ex-vice-chancellor of the University of London, John Lockwood, that the new universities of Central Africa will have a less specialised and narrow degree structure than was developed, and seems to be persisting, in the institutions which began as Asquith colleges.

CHAPTER NINE

HIGHER EDUCATION TAKES ROOT

I INTERPRETATION OF THE ASQUITH PLAN

Until late in the 1950s the Asquith report remained Britain's blueprint for the export of universities to her people overseas. Considering the purposes for which it was prepared it has proved a remarkably effective and successful plan. This is due largely to the quality of its practitioners – the staff of the Asquith colleges – who succeeded in implanting into non-European societies the rigorous discipline of learning, the high standards of teaching, and the commitment to research characteristic of English academic life.

But, in common with so many other plans for the colonial territories, the Asquith plan was soon overtaken by events. In the eloquent and vivid introduction to the Elliot commission's report (said to have been written by Walter Elliot himself) are the words:

Somewhere, in West Africa within a century, within half a century . . . a new African state will be born. It will be strong. Its voice will be listened to, wherever there are Africans or African-descended communities, and that is to say both in the Old World and in the New. It will have a vital need for counsellors, its own counsellors. Now is the time, and the time is already late, to train them for their work.[1]

Within a quarter of a century this prophecy is being fulfilled. One consequence of its fulfilment is that some institutions which the British exported to Africa, notably parliamentary government and the universities, have been under pressure to change. On the whole, universities have yielded very little to these pressures. But in the decade between the founding of the Asquith colleges and the coming of independence there were considerable changes in British attitudes to the patterns of higher education overseas. Let us now examine these changes.

The first major comment on the Asquith plan was the report, published in 1953, of a commission of higher education in Central Africa.[2] The commission was appointed by the Central African Council to draw up a plan for a university college to serve Southern Rhodesia, Northern Rhodesia, and

Nyasaland. It had a difficult task, for Central Africa has a substantial population of Europeans and the commissioners were confronted with a problem which is negligible in East and West Africa, namely whether a Central African university should segregate black and white students. The report comes down courageously and firmly in favour of an inter-racial college (although one member, Alexander Kerr from Fort Hare in South Africa, entered a reservation on this point). The main interest of the report for our present theme is that it emphatically reaffirms the Asquith plan as the basis for the proposed university college. One whole chapter reiterates the plan, and the commissioners then go on to recommend the familiar bi-cameral constitution of predominantly lay council and exclusively professional academic board; a scheme of study which the report describes as 'of a normal kind'; and (since the new college was to be in special relationship with the University of London) an entrance standard consistent with the requirements for degree courses in special relation. In this report, as in the Asquith report, the suggestion is put forward that students who have not reached the standard for admission for a degree course might be enrolled for a preliminary course leading to an examination which would qualify them for admission to a degree course. But this scheme of concessional entry was not adopted by the college, with unfortunate consequences which are discussed below.

One comment of the commissioners deserves special mention, for it records the first encounter, in an official report on African higher education, with patterns of education from outside Britain. Some of the witnesses, the report says:

laid emphasis on the importance of general education; they believe that students are poorly informed about matters of general interest and of relevance to the life of a member of a modern community. They were interested in certain experiments which are being made in Europe and the United States of America. These experiments take various forms; in some places so-called 'orientation' courses are given; in others a full year is devoted to a survey of the various fields of learning. We believe that these experiments are concerned with a real problem . . . But unsatisfactory as things may be in this respect in universities, wherever they are situated, we are not convinced that an innovation in university practice is the best way to make them better.[3]

The encounter ends with a rebuff to the 'experiments' in Europe and America (by which are presumably meant such practices as the Keele foundation year, the *Studium generale* in some German universities, and the general education course at Harvard). Not deterred by the distinction of some of the universities undertaking these experiments, the commissioners went on to say: 'To distinguish between real knowledge and half or superficial knowledge is one of the greatest lessons that a university can teach; the danger of 'orientation' or survey courses is not merely that this lesson may never be learnt, but even that the student may be encouraged to be satisfied with superficial knowledge.'[4] This is the first sign of a resistance to the incorporation of ideas from outside the English system which, unfortunately and unnecessarily, put the Asquith plan on the defensive against adaptation. General education, according to the commissioners, must be picked up by the student in other ways: for example, students must be encouraged to explore for themselves the historical and philosophical questions which arise out of their scientific studies: a tall order even for Oxford or London; totally unrealistic for Southern Rhodesia. So the studies were to be, as the report says, 'of a normal kind'. And 'normal' meant the kind to be found in English civic universities in 1952.

The University College of Rhodesia and Nyasaland was the last institution to be founded on the Asquith model. Like its predecessors, it acquired a vigorous and imaginative principal, an excellent academic staff, and attractive buildings; and it demonstrated that a multi-racial university could exist in a society not by any means free from racial segregation. But its insistence on excluding all candidates who had not acquired two A-level passes or their equivalent effectively closed its doors to large numbers of Africans; ten years later, although the Europeans in Rhodesia and Nyasaland constituted only about three per cent of the population, they constituted about seventy-six per cent of the student body at the university college.

In 1955 the secretary of state for the colonies presented to parliament a report on the activities of the inter-university council over its first eight years.[5] It records the state of the nine institutions which came under its influence: the Royal University of Malta; the universities of Hong Kong, Khartoum, and Malaya; the university colleges of the West Indies, the Gold Coast, Ibadan, and East Africa; and the college recently founded in Salisbury for Rhodesia and Nyasaland. It is a gratifying success story. Under the Colonial Development and Welfare Acts of 1945 and 1950 Britain had spent £7,750,000 on the nine institutions, nearly all of it on capital expenditure. The total contributions of the various local governments came to an even larger sum. There were in all about 800 staff and over 4,000 students, though student numbers in the new Asquith colleges were not increasing fast: Ibadan in its seventh year had only 527 students, Makerere in its ninth year only 448, and the College of the Gold Coast in its seventh year only 349. However if quantity was disappointing, quality was not. In the University of London B.A. examinations in 1954, for example, 94 candidates sat and 77 passed; in the Gold Coast there was only one failure out of 32 entries. The chairman of the inter-university council could justifiably say in his letter of transmission that the report was presented 'with some pride'.

But even justified pride is a close neighbour to complacency. Already by 1955 there were signs that the Asquith plan needed reconsideration, especially in the light of the rapidly changing political conditions of West Africa. Yet the report includes a euphoric reassertion of the principles of the Asquith plan. It is at this point of time that one can discern among some people concerned with higher education in the colonies a consolidation of orthodoxy. An admirable plan which ought to have remained a flexible working policy was becoming hardened into a doctrine. Working policies can always be discussed, argued over, and amended: doctrine can only be defended. The report ends with a statement that the apparent ease with which the programme has been carried through 'masks the risks and dangers that may yet defeat or imperil the whole enterprise'.[6] It is interesting to note the kind of dangers foreseen in the report. The chief danger is that 'there are growing signs of a demand for the establishment of more universities in the immediate future'! This demand, the report says, might be better diverted into the provision of technical colleges. If universities are allowed to proliferate there 'would soon be the deliberate acceptance of standards lower than those acceptable among British universities . . . There might be started a chain reaction that led rapidly to the lowering of standards in the public services and professions in yet further appeasement of the political demands of the under-qualified.'[7] Earlier in the report there is an eloquent manifesto on standards: 'There can be no compromise on this issue of standards. In all spheres in which we have advised or could have influence, whether in staff recruitment, student selection, the protection of examination standards, the appointment of external examiners, facilities for research or library resources, we have urged that the maintenance of high academic standards is paramount.'[8]

The supreme merit of the Asquith plan was that it established in the colonial countries a quality of higher education which brought the Asquith colleges into the international family of universities. But the loose employment of the word 'standards' and its confusion with the word 'quality' have bedevilled discussion of higher education in developing countries ever since. Quality in higher education is (as Alan Pifer has put it) 'a virtue that is immutable and timeless. It has to do with the integrity of an educational enterprise, with the teacher's pride in his craft, with excellence of performance for its own sake, with intolerance of shoddiness in any form.'[9] Anyone who suggests that universities should compromise on quality is guilty of academic treason. But (Pifer went on to say) 'standards have meaning only as they relate to a particular situation at a particular time'. The concept of standards is quite different from the concept of quality. It would be difficult to maintain that the quality of higher education in (say) the University of London is higher than that in Harvard or Göttingen or Melbourne. It would be nonsense to assert that the standards of achievement for admission or for the award of a degree are the same in these universities. While the Asquith colleges were in special relation with London, clearly not only quality but standards had to be similar to those in London. But it was recognised from the outset that the Asquith colleges would ultimately become autonomous degree-granting institutions; and much acrimonious and fruitless discussion would have been saved if the Asquith plan, as reasserted in the report of 1955, had distinguished between quality, which is limited only by human frailty, and standards, which must assuredly be *set* (this is essential) and adhered to, but set at levels which vary with time and place. It is, for example, only a few years since the University of London awarded an honours degree on three years' work after the equivalent of five passes at O-level. Standards were set lower than they are today; but the quality of higher education was certainly not lower.

From confusion between standards and quality it is but a step to confusion between standards and curriculum. 'It is an odd paradox', wrote John Lockwood, one of the wisest and most sensitive architects of new universities in the Commonwealth, 'that standards are at their highest when a subject is studied in depth', and he criticised the transmission to colonial universities 'of a quasi-mystical concept of high standards, which often possess a narrowness directly proportionate to their so-called height'.[10] The second danger foreseen by the inter-university council in 1954 was that the colleges might not grow fast enough to maintain their momentum and to hold their staff. But, the report says, growth must not mean undertaking tasks for which they are not ready; though, as an example of the tasks they should be ready to undertake, the report mentions the development of honours as well as general degree courses. The advice was followed: there was a notable increase in the proportion of single-subject honours or special degrees between 1954 and 1960.

The report from the inter-university council, with its vigorous enunciation of what was beginning to be regarded by some people as the Asquith 'doctrine' was issued in June 1955. In the very same month the principals of six Asquith university institutions (East Africa, the Gold Coast, Malaya, Nigeria, the Sudan, and the West Indies) met informally in Jamaica. They agreed that it was urgently necessary to re-examine the principles of the Asquith plan; indeed some of the principals plunged into heresy by asking whether post-secondary education in a developing country might not have something to learn from a 'mass' university, on the American land grant model, like that in Puerto Rico; and whether it might not be desirable to include in institutions of higher education a far higher proportion of the school product and a far broader range of studies and standards than are to be found in British universities. Some principals even questioned whether the present pattern of higher education, according to what were described as 'Asquith principles', in the absence of other post-secondary facilities, was in the best interests of the societies the colleges were attempting to serve; and one of them suggested that the Asquith colleges might accept students to read for an ordinary B.A. degree or a diploma that would be of much lower standard than the honours B.A. degree. The fact that the pioneer principals of six colonial university institutions should be deeply concerned on these lines is an indication that they were sensitive to the needs of the emerging nations and willing to contemplate modifications in the Asquith plan.

The prime cause of this concern did not lie in the Asquith colleges themselves but in the unpopularity of such alternative provision as was made for post-secondary education. In Britain in the 1950s only about half those who received post-secondary education attended universities: there were well organised alternatives in the technical colleges and the colleges of art and commerce. To provide a binary system of higher education in the colonies, colleges of arts, science, and technology had been established in East Africa, the Gold Coast, and Nigeria, to cover work of 'professional or near-professional standard', but, emphatically, not leading to the award of degrees. (It was an overtone of the somewhat hypocritical attitude of the British universities at that time, which opposed the award of degrees by colleges of advanced technology, but advocated the award of the Dip.Tech. which was to be 'approximately equivalent to an honours degree'.) But these COCAST colleges, as they were called,[11] finding themselves solely responsible for higher education in engineering and pharmacy and architecture, subjects which did lead to degrees in Britain, pressed for degree-status for some of their work. In 1954 the COCAST college at Kumasi, in the Gold Coast, applied to the University of London for recognition for the award of external degrees in engineering, and its application was granted. Shortly afterwards the engineering department of the COCAST college in Nigeria, at Zaria, became the faculty of engineering of University College, Ibadan (the college is now a separate university); and the COCAST college in East Africa was incorporated in the federated University of East Africa. In short, the binary system of post-secondary education never took root in the colonial territories, and by 1955 the principals of the Asquith colleges were asking themselves whether their colleges might have to assume responsibility for a wider spectrum of studies and for a larger proportion of the student population.

The views of the principals were made known to the inter-university council in July 1955. For about three years the council toyed with the question of reviewing the Asquith policy; but no decisive steps were taken, no review was issued, and in the end events overtook the agenda paper. During these three years the most significant element in the discussions was a growing awareness that the Asquith colleges might profitably look outside Britain for lessons in adaptation to colonial conditions. For example the vice-chancellor of the University of Malaya, Sir Sydney Caine, in his convocation address in 1955, said how he had been struck by the great variety and vigour of experimentation in new subjects and methods in universities in the United States. Their standards, he said, are not all the same, and it is easy to find things to criticise; out of their experimentation much good and occasional harm emerges. But Malaya could learn from the United States, particularly over the provision of courses which in more developed countries might be thought to be outside the university field. A couple of years later a British vice-chancellor, recognising the difference between quality and standards, was suggesting that insistence on British degree standards was a little doctrinaire, and suggested that – although standards must never be allowed to collapse – they might be set in a colonial university, awarding its own degrees, at a level similar (for example) to the levels set in Australia or New Zealand. Over the development of the

University of Malaya the view was expressed that the English pattern of higher education and English attitudes to it may have been taken too much for granted; and this view is confirmed in a recent study of universities in South East Asia by T.H.Silcock.[12]

In September 1957 the principals of the Asquith colleges met again, this time at Salisbury in Rhodesia. In some colleges anxieties about the lack of suitable candidates for higher education had been dispelled; their problem was now how to deal with the pressure from qualified applicants. In Ibadan, for instance, there were 1,100 applications for 300 places. Again the principals found themselves wondering what type of university was required in these rapidly developing countries, and asking themselves the dangerous question: should the universities be comprehensive on the American style or selective in accordance with the British tradition? Obviously it was important to preserve what was best in the British tradition. It was not a question of rejecting the imported model, but of adapting it to meet a wider range of needs. All that was needed was flexibility in the Asquith plan; but this is just what some of its proponents would not concede. A year later, in August 1958, when the principals met again, their views were unchanged. They were no longer anxious about the supply of candidates; they therefore felt themselves able to advocate a response to local needs on their own terms, undeterred by the dangers of lowering standards.

The year 1958 marks the end of a chapter in British policy for her overseas universities, for it turned out that the working party which reported in that year on the future of higher education in East Africa was the last major visitation with an exclusively British membership. It was invited by the secretary of state for the colonies on behalf of the four East African colonial governments.[13] Lockwood's liberal chairmanship of the party ensured that the recommendations would not be bound by convention, and the report (which was adopted as official policy) testifies to several significant changes in policy.

The main recommendation was that there should be a federated University of East Africa, granting its own degrees, with constituent colleges in Uganda, Kenya, and what was then Tanganyika. Makerere, then with 800 students, was to be one college; the Royal Technical College at Nairobi (formerly a college for sub-degree work) was to be the second; and a new college near Dar-es-Salaam was to be the third. For Nairobi the report recommended a departure from the conventional form of overseas university college: an 'adventurous experiment' to combine academic and some professional studies not commonly found in British universities. Special relationship with the University of London had of course to be abandoned. In its place the working party recommended a system of sponsorship by the University of London, whereby London would guarantee the standard of degrees from the University of East Africa. The University of London indicated that it would be willing to offer sponsorship on condition that the University of East Africa would appoint external examiners for its degree examinations, would consult the inter-university council before appointing academic staff, and would arrange some machinery of consultation with the University of London over regulations and syllabuses. This proposal had the great merit that it would give the new university much more freedom to vary the pattern of degree than was possible under special relationship: for although the University of London had been generous in allowing variations in the control of courses, it had not allowed any variation in the pattern of general or special degrees; and the patterns of both these degrees were manifestly unsuitable for the needs of some Commonwealth countries. In the event the proposal for sponsorship was not adopted, though both the university, which was set up under East African legislation in 1962, and its constituent colleges, keep in touch with British academic thought in other ways: through council members from Britain, external examiners, and the assessors whose advice is sought over senior appointments to the university.

II AMERICAN INFLUENCE ON AFRICAN UNIVERSITIES

We have already noticed the first ripples of American influence on British policy for colonial universities. We now proceed to describe how this influence has become a major factor in the English-speaking countries of tropical Africa, and to discuss its consequences for the future of higher education there.

The story starts some way back. For a generation or more there has been a tenuous connection between tropical Africa – especially West Africa – and American higher education. Both Azikiwe and Nkrumah had part of their higher education in America. Aggrey, one of the founders of Achimota School, had an American education. The Phelps-Stokes commission brought an American viewpoint to its discussion of education in Africa. And even before the first world war a few West Africans had done postgraduate work in American universities.

It is instructive to compare the Ph.D. theses of Africans who have done research on education in England with those done in America. A period of study in Britain frequently consolidates in an African a respect for the British educational system, and indeed may make him resistant to innovations in curricula in African schools and colleges. A period of study in America frequently nurtures a dissatisfaction with the British system, though not always for very profound reasons. U. Okeke, for instance, writes in his Ph.D. thesis[14] that he saw a peculiar relevance in the pattern of American education, for this pattern was worked out while America was a colony fighting to gain its independence. Therefore the history of American education is a valuable tool 'in the hands of colonials struggling to obtain their freedom from alien rule'. Okeke was impatient with British gradualism: 'The British were in Nigeria for many years before the ascendancy of the USSR, the modernisation of Japan, the revival of Turkey'; yet, apart from the endeavours of christian missionaries, nothing until recently was achieved in Nigerian education. In particular Okeke is troubled about the difficulties (some caused by Africans themselves) in the way of adapting the patterns of western education to African needs: 'The present Nigerian education is outside-orientated. Its program does not spring from the life of the people. It is imposed upon the people by outsiders, most of whom know little of the social life of the people ... who find little worthy in the life of the people and therefore attempt to make them over in their own image. This has created superficiality among the people ... The educated Nigerian is living on somebody else's ideas and philosophy of life.' Another African Ph.D. student, as long ago as 1946, was similarly impressed by what he considered to be the relevance of American education to the needs of American society, and he wrote: 'The ideal of adapting education to local environment is contradicted by the octopus of British-sponsored external examinations.... One of the strongest charges that could be made against education in Nigeria and one around which all other charges revolve, is that it lacks adaptation.'[15]

It is not difficult to imagine how the American educational system strikes an African whose only experience of western education has been in the English pattern.

First, he notices that in America there is an absence of control by extraneous examining bodies. He has been brought up to believe that the only valid passport to higher education is a certificate granted by a panel of examiners centred in England on a syllabus decided in England. Now he begins to question the need for control of standards from abroad; and if he is looking for popular arguments against the English system, he can even see in the external examination system – deciding in England whether *he* shall get a place in a university – a sign of neo-imperialism.

Second, he has been told in Africa that anyone who could not pass in at least two subjects at A-level general certificate of education was not qualified for higher education leading to a degree. He discovers that five passes at O-level are sufficient to give him a place in a reputable, even in a famous, American university.

Third, the English pattern of university education sets great store by specialisation. There is an austere emphasis on rigidity in the curriculum. It is true that the University of London awards a general degree, but the African knows that it is the honours or special degree which carries prestige; that some eighty per cent of undergraduates in Britain are reading for honours degrees and that by a process of social mimicry, African universities are following this fashion.[16] He finds in an American university a bewildering variety of courses, all deemed worthy of study. In Cornell, one of the more distinguished universities of America, there is a choice of 12,500 different courses including journalism and hotel management: both subjects in which expertise is sorely needed in Africa. The University of California at Berkeley, which attracts scholars from all over the world, includes in its degree offerings such subjects as home furnishing, advertising, and household sanitation. In England these subjects, if they are taught at all, are relegated to non-degree courses in non-university institutions. Yet (thinks the African) these are subjects which need prestige in Africa, and they are regarded as prestigious enough to be included in one of the famous universities in the most prosperous and powerful nation in the world. Prosperity and power do not of course impress academics, but academics cannot fail to be impressed by the dedication to learning, the striving after excellence, and the impressive scholarly achievements even in the humanities, which are to be found in the best American state universities.

Fourth, the African is likely to be impressed by the democratization of education in America. Stratification in the system of secondary schooling, although it exists in America, is less evident than it is in England. At the American university he finds that there is no assumption of élitism: there are facilities for the brilliant undergraduate who will become a scholar or a leader; there are on the same campus facilities for the mediocre undergraduate whose pinnacle of ambition is to be a poultry extension officer or a salesman or a sanitary inspector. He has heard in Africa how subjects like this must not be admitted to universities, for they would depress standards. He wonders why.

To suggest that Africa should have to choose between an American and a British pattern of education is to distort the problem and to generate futile and mischievous rivalries between advocates of the two patterns. But this is not to say that Africans have not much to learn from each pattern. The British commitment to high quality (if only it is not confused with the spurious assumption that standards must everywhere be the same) is essential in a country where quality might easily be eroded on grounds of political expediency. The American emphasis on relevance is essential in a country where, for a time, the need for skilled manpower at middle levels as well as at the highest levels must take precedence over the traditional English pattern of liberal education in depth through one-subject honours courses. Many African intellectuals are now beginning to realise this, and there is, therefore, a predisposition among them to examine other systems of higher education and to welcome discussion on reasonable adaptations to the original Asquith plan. Eclectic choice among educational systems is never easy; but it is a choice which Africans will have to exercise.

In the 1960s the United States was discovering a new frontier in Africa: the frontier between western education and African ignorance of western techniques. Enthusiasts, from the Atlantic states to California, determined to man this new frontier. The pioneer tradition was renewed with what one American described as 'a bland instinct for virtuous deeds'.[17] It began in 1959 with the American scholarship invasion in Kenya.

This was organised by Tom Mboya, the vigorous and colourful Kenya politician and trade union leader. He saw that the output of graduates from the University College of East Africa (there were forty graduates in 1957 and thirty-six in 1958) would be totally inadequate after independence; and he doubtless saw, too, considerable prestige for any politician who could bring the loaves and fishes of higher education to the degree-hungry students of Kenya. He paid a visit to America at the time of Kennedy's presidential campaign, and returned with a promise of 250 scholarships tenable in American colleges, and a grant from the Kennedy Foundation to finance an airlift from Nairobi to New York. In 1959 the first batch of eighty-one East Africans left Kenya. In September 1960 four chartered planes left with another 288 students. Pressure from aspirants for the airlift far exceeded resources. Queues of applicants besieged the office in Nairobi to be interviewed by Mboya and his assistants. A Kenya education trust was started to raise funds for more passages; cash was collected from auctions of bulls, goats, sheep, and chickens; the Asian community, anxious to be in the good books of the Africans, gave some £10,000; there were tribal levies, subscription dances, and so on. But the whole scheme, on both sides of the Atlantic, was hopelessly ill-conceived. Many of the Africans transported to America were unprepared for higher education; most of them were not qualified to enter the University College of East Africa. Some of the host-colleges in the United States were pretty poor places. Financial provision was sometimes inadequate. Many students were frustrated and disillusioned by hardship, shoddy standards, and failure. Only four per cent of the students were getting A grades; fifty-eight per cent were getting C grades or failing. And the scheme was not free from jobbery: there were strong charges that the selection of students was biassed by tribal and political discrimination.

This abortive piece of philanthropy irritated the British colonial government and alarmed the inter-university council for higher education; but it helped to precipitate one very important decision: it brought leaders of higher education from Britain and the United States together to discuss co-operation in Africa. Much benefit has come from this co-operation, as we shall presently observe. But first we must describe how the United States, after this initial mistake, revised its policy of scholarship invasion.

There are still many unsponsored African students in the United States, and many who are sponsored and financed by their own governments; but nearly half the African students now studying in American colleges are supported either by the colleges themselves or by the United States government. The main organ of sponsorship is the African Scholarship Program of American Universities (ASPAU), based on Harvard, in association with the African-American Institute in New York. The scheme started on a pilot scale in 1960; nineteen institutions, including Harvard, awarded scholarships to twenty-four Nigerian undergraduates, carefully selected in Nigeria by a Nigerian-American board. The scheme grew rapidly. By 1965, 750 Africans from twenty-nine countries were enrolled under ASPAU, in universities which included Harvard, Yale, Princeton, Columbia, California, Cornell, Chicago, and Michigan. The home government pays for their travel to and from America. The United States government, through AID, covers their expenses in America over and above any scholarships they receive from universities. They have no financial worries. They are insured against sickness. They are well looked after by advisers and counsellors. Their academic performance is substantially above the American average (twenty-three per cent had A grades, forty per cent Bs, twenty-nine per cent Cs, six per cent Ds and two per cent failed).[18] And it has to be remembered that the qualification required for an award under ASPAU is a good pass at O-level G.C.E. Very many of the Africans brought to America under the auspices of ASPAU or the African-American Institute would not have been admitted to degree courses in the Asquith colleges in Africa.

The ASPAU scheme has not passed uncriticised by the British-type university colleges in Africa. Objections to the scheme take two diametrically opposed forms. On one hand it is asserted that ASPAU has siphoned off the best student talent available for university training. On the other hand it is asserted that ASPAU offers African students 'a short cut to a cheap university degree'.[19] Both these criticisms have been taken seriously by those who organise the scheme. Endeavours are now made to give ASPAU awards only to students who cannot receive the training they need in their own countries; awards to Nigeria, for instance, are being drastically reduced.[20] As for the charge that American degrees are 'cheap', they do, as everyone knows, denote a more diverse and less specialised higher education than is denoted by an English (though not necessarily a Scottish) degree. But the pernicious innuendo that diversity means cheapness, and that the American degree therefore has a lower market value in Africa than an English or African degree, causes the ASPAU managers much concern; for it is so widely believed that many African students cannot be persuaded to return to their own countries after taking the bachelor's degree: they importune to stay on for a master's degree, believing that this is necessary if they are not to start at a handicap compared with their brothers at Ibadan or Makerere. To help dispel this embarrassment the governments of some African countries (Malawi, Sudan, and Zambia, for instance) have given public assurances that American bachelor's degrees will receive the same recognition in government employment as bachelor's degrees or the licence from European and African universities: they have declared against what Hastings Banda once called an 'academic protective tariff'.

The American scholarship invasion was not the only confrontation between American and British systems of higher education in Africa; for in 1955 the Eastern Regional legislature in Nigeria passed the University of Nigeria Law, 1955. It was another five years before the university opened its doors, and discussion of it belongs to a later section of this book. But long before it opened, its founder, Dr Azikiwe, made it clear that he had in mind an institution similar to an American land grant college; this announcement was viewed with concern not only by members of the inter-university council in Britain and by some of the staff of the university college at Ibadan; even in the Lagos *Daily Times* there was a protest with a headline: 'Zik wants a Yank-style university at cut rates.'

It became evident that if the Americans and British did not co-operate over education in Africa – particularly if they became rivals peddling competing patterns of education – great damage might be done. As so often happens, it was not governments but private foundations which had the prescience to see this first. In May 1958, the Carnegie Corporation of New York sponsored a small off-the-record meeting at the Greenbrier in White Sulphur Springs, West Virginia. It was attended by Americans and British from universities, foundations, business, and government agencies. Its purpose was to discuss Anglo-American co-operation over aid to Africa in several fields: agriculture, the stimulation of private industry, economic development, scientific research, education. Its discussions were not published but they became the starting point for much useful Anglo-American partnership in Africa.[21]

For our present theme, the most important consequences of the Greenbrier meeting were, first, a meeting which was held eight months later (on 17–18 January 1959) in New York to set up machinery for Anglo-American co-operation over higher education in Africa;[22] and second, a decision made at the Greenbrier meeting to promote a comprehensive study of higher education in one African country (Nigeria), in which Africans, Americans, and British would take part. At the New York meeting it was decided to ask the American council of education to set up a committee to assist higher education in Africa, and it was agreed that there should be frequent consultation between this committee and the inter-university council in Britain. The committee was set up with the aid of a grant from the Carnegie Corporation; and about the same time, in March 1959, the Nigerian federal government invited a commission to prepare a blueprint for post-secondary education for the first twenty years of independence, 1960–80.

III THE NIGERIAN COMMISSION

The Commission on Post-school Certificate and Higher Education in Nigeria (hereinafter called the Nigerian commission) was an entirely new kind of instrument for policy-making in a British colonial possession; it comprised three Africans, three Americans, and three Englishmen; it reported to the Nigerian federal government, not to the colonial office or the inter-university council; and it was financed by an American private foundation, the Carnegie Corporation of New York. We say 'entirely new', but in fact the precedent had been set ten years earlier. The Radhakrishnan commission which surveyed university education in India in 1948–9 had on it seven Indians, one Englishman (Sir James Duff, who was on the Asquith commission), and two

Americans; and the report is strongly coloured by American experience.[23] It is worth a passing comment that this precedent set by a commission in India was not followed in Africa until ten years later.

The report of the Nigerian commission was signed on 2 September 1960[24]. Copies of it were before the Nigerian federal legislature at its first meeting after independence in October 1960. Early in 1961, as Sessional Paper No. 3, the Nigerian government published a white paper accepting the report.[25]

Although it is little over five years since the Nigerian commission's report was published, and although one of us was chairman of the commission and drafted much of the report himself, we find it is already possible (and desirable) to inspect the report under the ungracious illumination of hindsight in the same way as we did the Asquith report in chapter 7. It is already possible to separate out some of the virtues and some of the defects of the report.

The commissioners had to bear in mind all the time that they were writing a political document, not an academic study. Their recommendations therefore had on the one hand to be sufficiently deeply rooted in the existing pattern of Nigerian education to be acceptable and practicable (universities are like organisms in that they evolve and adapt themselves by successive small mutations, and large mutations are very commonly lethal); on the other hand the recommendations had to promote adaptation, to stimulate innovation, and to prevent Nigerian higher education from congealing into a neo-British mould.[26]

The detailed recommendations are of no interest to the general reader: it will suffice for our present discussion to mention such innovations in educational theory as are to be found in the report.

(i) In the short term it is prudent for a country to design an educational system it can afford to pay for. But it was just this policy of prudence which had starved West African education throughout the colonial period, at any rate until after the second world war; and it was clear that there was no future for Nigeria unless she received aid from more prosperous countries. So the commission deliberately recommended an educational system which could not be sustained without massive outside aid in the confident belief, which has turned out to be justified, that the more prosperous countries would come to Nigeria's assistance during the early years of independence.

(ii) Since finance was not to be the limiting factor for the system of education proposed by the Nigerian commission, there had to be some other firm and realistic limit to the size of the proposed system. The commissioners adopted the earthy and utilitarian criterion that the provision for higher education should be linked firmly to manpower needs. To this end Frederic Harbison, from Princeton University, made a survey of Nigeria's needs for graduates and other professionally trained people. His essay *High level manpower and Nigeria's future*, which is included in the report, is the foundation upon which all the recommendations rest. It has brought a new dimension into educational planning in several developing countries. Harbison estimated the resources in high level manpower which would be necessary to permit a rate of economic growth in Nigeria during the first ten years after independence equivalent to the rate of growth over the ten years preceding independence. He emphasised (and his critics are apt to forget this) that his estimates would be worthless unless they were reviewed each year by an expert manpower board, and that sustained planning for manpower needs, and the adaptation of educational systems to supply these needs, were essential accompaniments to his recommendations. The blueprint for Nigerian post-secondary education was, therefore, severely pragmatic, though the commissioners did not fear that the reflective and civilising functions of education would suffer thereby; the myth that there is an inevitable antithesis between liberal and vocational education has long ago been dispelled. If manpower predictions are constantly reviewed, and if the size and shape of higher education is adjusted to manpower needs, then Nigeria could on one hand ensure that her development is not inhibited by lack of skilled men, and on the other hand she could minimise the danger, so oppressively present in India, of under-employment among graduates.

(iii) By 1959, when the commission was at work, there had been schools on an English pattern in Nigeria for over a century; for fully half a century the criterion of achievement had been success in examinations set in England by English examining boards; for twenty-five years there had been some form of post-secondary education, also on an English pattern, and for twelve years there had been a university institution teaching for degrees of the University of London. There were many and obvious defects in the colonial system of education, but to have suggested that there should be root-and-branch changes would have been to jettison much that was admirable and to throw the whole system into confusion. This would have been a great disservice to Nigeria. Accordingly – to the surprise of some observers – the commission did not advocate novel institutions (such as junior colleges) which would have been inconsistent with the educational inheritance; instead it confirmed the pattern of secondary schooling with sixth forms, simply for the pragmatic reasons that sixth forms were relatively well established in Nigeria, the Nigerians wanted them, it is cheaper to do intermediate work in schools than in universities, and (the paramount reason) the less the shock administered to the Nigerian educational system after independence, the greater chance the system would have of growing to meet the nation's needs: you don't transplant a tree just as it is expected to bear fruit. For a similar paramount reason the commission advocated that the binary system of post-secondary education should continue; universities should limit their responsibilities to work of degree standard and leave to other institutions responsibility for awarding sub-degree qualifications. The commission did not advocate an 'umbrella' system of higher education, whereby the university would play some part in all post-secondary education in its region, though it deliberately left the door open for Nigerians to work toward such a system by suggesting that universities should act as 'foster-mothers' to teacher-training colleges and that universities should take – as they do in the land grant colleges – a much more prominent part in agricultural extension work. In brief, the commissioners advocated an evolutionary, not a revolutionary programme for post-secondary education; it was impressive to discover how the aspirations of the Nigerian members, the wealth of new experience brought by the American members, and the somewhat critical approach toward traditional practices shared by the English members, were disciplined into unanimity of purpose by the conviction that the future educational system must be built upon the past and must not be discontinuous with it.

(iv) In university education, however, drastic changes had to be made. University College, Ibadan, was meeting one of Nigeria's needs admirably: the provision of a highly trained specialised élite; but (as one sympathetic and friendly American critic, writing about the Asquith colleges, put it) 'the fault lay rather in their restricted view of the range of society's needs it was their responsibility to meet. They concentrated on the upper level academic and professional pursuits and left the middle level of academic, technical, and professional pursuits to others.' The problem the commissioners faced was how to correct this fault without imperilling the prestige of Nigerian higher education in the eyes of British academics. Their attitude was unambiguous:

Our views amount to this: that there must be more diversity and more flexibility in university education if it is to be relevant to the needs of the Nigerian people. The British system of university education suits Britain because there are so many alternative routes to professional training. . . . In a country where these alternative routes are missing or carry less prestige, the British university system is too inflexible and too academic to meet national needs. We think it is very unlikely that in Nigeria these alternative routes will, in the foreseeable future, acquire the prestige which universities already have. Accordingly a much greater diversity of demand is likely to be made on Nigerian universities than on their British counterparts. We believe that Nigerian universities should meet this demand on one condition: that what is required of them is indeed greater diversity and not lower standards. University standards are an indispensable anchor for the whole intellectual and professional life of Nigeria; if this anchor drags, Nigeria will fail to take her rightful place among the nations.

However a country can stay on the intellectual gold standard without, as it were, having to adopt the imprint of another coinage. Fortunately there are models for diversification of university studies without lowering of standards. The land-grant universities of the United States have had to fulfil functions similar to those which Nigerian universities are now called upon to fulfil, and the best of them have done so without in any way surrendering their integrity. Let us add that Nigeria should not imitate American land-grant universities any more than she should imitate British universities. Neither kind of university should be imported unchanged to Nigeria; but both kinds have something to teach this country, and the lessons to be learnt from America include diversity and flexibility.[27]

The commissioners made it clear elsewhere[28] (though perhaps not clear enough) that by 'standards' they did not mean some unalterable and universal level of achievement, always and everywhere the same; they meant acceptance by 'the international company of universities all over the world', which is something quite different. A degree from (say) Cornell University certainly is 'legal tender' in Cambridge, though no-one supposes that a Cornell B.A. who has majored in history has reached the same standard as a Cambridge B.A. in history; nor (to regard the question from the American standpoint) does it mean that the history graduate from Cambridge has reached such a high standard as the Cornell graduate in the natural and social sciences. But both degrees are on the gold standard of learning.

All the same, standards have to be 'set': in a country like Nigeria standards would not – as they would in America – adjust themselves by open competition among universities. There were two ways in which standards might be set. One was to have a federated university system, with all institutions of higher education in Nigeria taking a common degree which was safeguarded by teams of external examiners; the other, still relying on external examiners, was to propose a number of independent universities, each offering its own degrees, but each new university sponsored by some overseas university. The sponsoring university might expect to have a place on the new university's governing body, to appoint some examiners, to be consulted about courses, and to be assured about the new university's constitution and finances.

The commissioners were unanimously opposed to a federated university: it would merely have replaced the constraints of special relation with London by the constraints of competing colleges, hindering one another's development.[29] In this the commissioners were undoubtedly correct, as the difficulties encountered by the federated University of East Africa have shown. They therefore recommended that there should be four independent and autonomous universities: Ibadan (about to achieve its independence in any event) and three new universities: one in the Eastern Region (already created as an independent university, though not at that time operating), one in the Northern Region, and one in Lagos. And they recommended that the new universities should seek sponsorship from universities overseas.[30]

With this safeguard about setting standards (it would have been better if they had emphasised quality rather than just standards) the commissioners went on to make specific proposals about diversity. Their proposals included a much greater emphasis on African studies (which has been enthusiastically adopted by all universities); and – an essential point – the injection of these studies into undergraduate courses. They included degree courses for accountants, bankers, company secretaries, insurance men, and transport executives, including 'office-based' sandwich courses for men already in posts. Other proposed innovations were a three-year course leading to a bachelor of education degree, with the pedagogical training incorporated in the undergraduate course; a 'down-to-earth' engineering course, biased toward the practical side, and equivalent in standard to membership of the professional engineering institutions (it would be at a lower, or at any rate, different, standard of achievement from the degree course in many British universities); a release of medical and veterinary education from the rigidities imposed from London; and a development of the applied social sciences, by which was meant:

the applications of academic social studies to community needs: applied economics itself, social welfare, and the legal and administrative problems which have to be solved as the social structure of tribal life becomes transformed into the social structure of urban and national life.[31]

Another innovation – judged by British conventions – was a recommendation that one university (Lagos) should conduct correspondence courses leading to degrees. For there was (there still is) a danger that thousands of young Nigerians in banks, offices, schools, and in junior ranks of the government service would be saying to themselves: 'if only I had been born five, ten years later, I could have benefited by this new provision for higher education' – and being deprived of it, would harbour a resentment against the wave of graduates coming up behind them. The chance to get degrees by evening study or correspondence would at any rate lessen this danger.

The commissioners described their recommendations as 'massive, expensive, and unconventional'. As a blueprint to be turned into a new edifice of higher education, this description was correct (though the Nigerian government, once it had recovered from the initial shock of the scope of the recommendations, decided they were in some respects too modest, and revised them so that they became even more massive and expensive); but as a venture in educational thinking the recommendations were in fact deliberately cautious and rooted in the existing system; their purpose was to stimulate and guide adaptation without breaking continuity.

The Nigerian report was received in Nigeria with embarrassing enthusiasm and quoted with alarming fidelity; embarrassing and alarming, because the commissioners intended it to be no more than a working policy, and the last thing they wanted was that the report should become (as to some people the Asquith report had become) as inviolable as holy writ. The inter-university council welcomed it on the ground that it endorsed the lines of development pursued since the Asquith commission made its recommendation. In fact it did nothing of the sort: its aim was to free Nigerian higher education as painlessly as possible from some of the imperfections of the Asquith plan, while preserving the virtues of the plan. Its real importance for the theme of this book is that it was the first piece of educational planning which was a joint operation on the part of Africans, Americans, and British, and which represented a fusion of ideas from the American and British educational systems. It marked the beginning of formal participation by Americans in the educational affairs of tropical Africa.

The Nigerian governments, federal and regional, acted on the report with commendable speed. The British and American governments and a number

of foundations adopted it as a basis for aid to Nigerian post-secondary education. Universities, teacher-training colleges, special sixth forms, a manpower unit, a permanent national universities commission: all these were
brought into being by the report. So fast is the pace of development in Africa
that the first fruits of the Nigerian commission's report are already ripening
on the tree; so it is possible to make a few tentative and preliminary judgements on the commissioners' wisdom.

One basic assumption in the report is open to challenge, namely that investment in education in an under-developed country will pay off. No-one is
likely to challenge the assumption that there can be no economic growth in
the western sense without skilled manpower; but the assumption that heavy
investment in the production of skilled manpower will ensure economic
growth, or is even the best way to get the economy of a country 'off the
ground', has been challenged. To support the challenge there is in some
developing countries the depressing spectacle of graduate unemployment and
massive educational systems co-existing with penury. Even in Nigeria there
is already unemployment among school-leavers. It is no exaggeration to say
that in some parts of Nigeria the overriding effect of primary education is to
draw the child away from the land where the nation's wealth lies, from the extended family where the nation's moral stability and self-discipline are to be
found, into the glitter of cheap western 'civilisation' in the cities, where he
finds himself unqualified for a job: it is, as one perceptive American has put it,
'education for frustration'.[32] The slick remedy is more education, using more
scarce resources in teachers and money. Thus the Western Region of Nigeria
responded to unemployment among primary school-leavers by setting up
secondary modern schools. Already secondary modern school-leavers are a
problem on the employment market. About this problem, Hanson writes:

This, then, is the first great dilemma of African education: the dream of a population that is entirely schooled, the tapping of Africa's 'greatest resource' (its people),
and the stark reality of a growing mass of disillusioned, unproductive, uprooted,
schooled children, flocking to the cities where they join the ranks of the unemployed
... disgruntled and convinced their 'education' entitled them to better things.[33]

The answer to this doubt is not to go slow on education but ruthlessly to
ensure that education is relevant, even if it means radical departure from the
forms and patterns associated with education in modern industrial societies.
With the aid of hindsight it can be said that the Nigerian commission did not
emphasise this point forcefully enough; American influence on the commission might with profit have been more powerful. For whether one uses the
controversial word 'élite' or not for the products of the Asquith colleges, the
assumptions behind the high status of the one-subject honours degree were
that a privileged class was being produced. Now the number of posts which
can be filled by such products is very limited, and these posts are already within sight of being filled. Therefore not only the numbers going into higher

education, but the content of curricula in higher education, need to be austerely adjusted to manpower needs. If, for example, arts graduates are produced in too narrow a range of subjects, or in subjects which are not taught at school, and if (as is already happening in Nigeria) there is no longer much immediate need for arts graduates in the foreign service and the home civil services, then one is confronted with the first symptoms of graduate unemployment. The assertion that Nigeria would need some 30,000 graduates by 1970 is doubtless as good a prediction as anyone could have made from the data available. What the report might have said more emphatically is that if too much of the national product is spent producing these graduates there will not be enough left over for capital investment to create employment for them; and that if Nigerian commerce, transport, and communications (for example) need economists and statisticians, it will not do in an impoverished developing country to provide these services with honours graduates in history and English.

Related to this is a second point of perspective which was present in the commissioners' minds but is muted in their report. For reasons already mentioned the commissioners decided to retain sixth forms and to regard a standard equivalent to A-level G.C.E. as the normal starting-point for an undergraduate course. It may turn out that this was an unwise decision: under American influence this policy has been abandoned in Malawi and Zambia and there may even be a retreat from it in Nigeria. What was certainly an unwise decision of the commissioners was to leave uncriticised the whole pattern of the post-school certificate curriculum. Consequently one of the most objectionable features of the British system – the obligation to concentrate either upon arts subjects or upon science subjects immediately after O-level G.C.E. – was allowed to persist in Nigeria. The commissioners (we believe) under-estimated the reluctance of many Africans and of many expatriates in African universities after independence to contemplate a break from the British pattern of curriculum. The consequences are already unfortunate: a valuable opportunity to provide flexibility in the educational system has been lost, and one university has found it advisable to circumvent the rigidities of the British pattern of schooling by admitting students at O-level for a four-year degree course and giving them a general education in the humanities and the natural and social sciences in their first year. As Hanson, speaking of school systems (but his remarks are equally valid for systems of higher education) says:

Most African educators are deeply concerned lest modified programs be viewed as being of lower stature or less value than their original European counterparts. . . . The surest way to avoid any such implications . . . is to pay lip service to adaptation, or make token modifications, but to adhere essentially to patterns, syllabi, and examinations which vary little, if at all, from inherited European models.[34]

This is the first point on which the report was, as it were, too muted. A second provisional criticism is that the recommendations have up to the present failed to lead to an acceptable plan for sub-professional education. It is true that great emphasis was put on the need to produce many more people with middle-level qualifications than people with degrees – at any rate with degrees in the British tradition – and the commissioners proposed that there should be at least six institutes for technical and commercial education. But (again in order to build upon foundations already in the country) the report retains a binary system of higher education and proposes no links between the universities and the technical institutes. One wonders already whether this was a mistake. In a country where the university degree is a passport to status and prosperity and where success is measured by the possession of certificates rather than by ability, there are certain values in an 'umbrella' system whereby the university accepts responsibility for some sub-degree work (not necessarily on its own campus), provided always that it keeps uncontaminated the thin stream of excellence on which the nation's development depends. To orthodox British academics the umbrella system is anathema and the binary system or some variant of it is regarded as essential for the preservation of standards. Americans, and British academics familiar with American universities, would not share this view. It is possible (though it must be emphasised that this suggestion needs much more careful reflection than the Nigerian commission gave it) that the best ultimate pattern for African higher education might be one in which universities take a much greater share of responsibility for all education after secondary school, with the exception of the simpler forms of vocational training, thus conferring prestige and setting standards in certain key sub-professional fields.

To sum up: it now seems as though it might have been better if the Nigerian commission had administered a greater shock to the orthodoxy of the educational pattern in Nigeria, making proposals which would have aroused hostility from the traditionalists, in the hope that educational planning might be freed from the grip of orthodoxy – a grip which is turning out to be tighter than the commissioners foresaw. And yet there are arguments to the contrary; for if the recommendations had been too unorthodox they might not have been accepted and they might not have secured the backing in money and men which overseas countries have given them; perhaps, too, enough of a chain reaction was started by the report to lead Africans themselves to remedy its deficiencies. There are indeed signs that this is happening and that British policy has been considerably modified through recent Anglo-American co-operation. We now consider four examples of this: the development of the University of Nigeria, the establishment of the University of East Africa, the plans for higher education in Zambia, and the plans for higher education in Malawi.

IV THE LAND GRANT COLLEGE IN AFRICA

The University of Nigeria was conceived five years before it was born, by a bill passed in the Eastern Region legislature in 1955. Its founder, and until 1966 its executive chancellor, is Dr Azikiwe, who was in 1955 premier of the Eastern Region and later president of the republic. From a reading of Azikiwe's speeches one is left in no doubt whatever about the purpose of the university he founded. The university's activities were to be related:

to the social and economic needs and the day-to-day life of the people of Nigeria. . . . This calls for a realistic approach to the problems of higher learning in our system of education. We must frankly admit that we can no longer afford to flood only the white collar jobs at the expense of the basic occupations and productive vocations, which can be so intelligently directed to create wealth, health, and happiness among the greatest number of our people, particularly in the fields of agriculture, engineering, business administration, education, and domestic science.[35]

In other speeches Azikiwe made it clear that as a model for his university he had in mind the American land grant college rather than the British civic university, and that he proposed to look to the United States for help.

This proposal aroused apprehension in British government and academic circles, and the inter-university council was asked by the colonial office, and agreed, to offer advice from Britain. The decision to do this was not solely political. At least one member of the council, John Lockwood, was beginning to think that a compromise between the British and American patterns of higher education might – alongside the British traditional institution at Ibadan – be suitable in the Nigerian context.[36] Meanwhile Michigan State University was considering undertaking a contract, with federal finance from AID,[37] to provide help. The outcome was that a representative of British academic life, J. W. Cook, vice-chancellor of Exeter University, and Glen Taggart, dean of international programmes at Michigan State University, visited Nigeria and produced a joint report.[38] This document is interesting as further evidence of a willingness to combine American and British ideas. It emphasises that 'a great contribution can be made to Nigeria by the proposed university if the Government established a university of unquestioned academic standards interested in Nigerian problems'.[39] It proposes ways to display this interest: through agriculture, including a feature not to be found in Britain – an agricultural extension service based on the university; engineering, with special reference to Nigeria's needs; home economics, especially with a view to improving the level of nutrition; marketing procedures; and, included in the humanities, an interest in indigenous religion and culture. From this report there developed a very satisfactory co-operation between the Americans and the British. Credit for this on the British side is due largely to the flexible and liberal attitude of the University of London, influenced by the enlightened diplomacy of John Lockwood. The university decided to co-operate with Michigan State University in a largely informal joint sponsorship. The University of London senate committee on colleges overseas in special relation has this significant passage in its annual report for 1959–60:

We have great faith in schemes of Special Relation as a well tried and flexible method of guiding new academic institutions rapidly forward. . . . But the wind of change can be felt in education as elsewhere, as Africa advances to self-government at a speed unforeseen even 15 years ago. We have not before tried to launch a new institution in an independent territory, and we have not before encountered the welcome new American interest in African education. When, therefore, we were asked to advise upon the development of a new institution in Eastern Nigeria . . . and to do so in co-operation with Michigan State University, it was apparent that an entirely new approach would be called for.[40]

The main responsibility for external aid to the University of Nigeria has come from Michigan State University, but the University of London has retained a useful influence in the new university's academic affairs. The joint operation has not only strengthened the University of Nigeria more than either partner alone could have done: it has also dispelled misunderstandings which initially existed between those who shared the partnership and it has promoted an understanding of each other's educational systems.

The university opened its doors on 12 October 1960, with 256 students. There was no water on the campus until 1 October, and no electricity until 6 October. The residence halls were not ready; students had to unpack their own linen. In more serious ways, too, the university made a shaky start: its buildings were put up without adequate foresight; some of its academic staff were recruited without adequate enquiry as to their quality, appointed, it was commented, 'by mail order'. These very evident defects encouraged its hostile critics (of whom there were many) to spread abroad the view that it was bound to be an inferior institution with lower standards. Not for the first time critics failed to disentangle comment on a new pattern of education from comment on the quality with which the pattern was being woven. Some traditionally educated Africans could be heard speaking of it with contempt. Some British academics in Africa and in Britain made no secret of their prejudice against it. So far as the quality of teaching in some subjects was inferior to that in Ibadan or London, the criticisms were justified, though the grounds for legitimate criticism are rapidly vanishing. So far as the University of Nigeria was criticised because it was introducing a new pattern into the country, the criticisms were bigoted and parochial. The fact is that in its first five years the university has made massive contributions to the whole concept of higher education in an African country, contributions different from those made by Ibadan, but in their way no less important.

The university draws heavily upon what Americans call the 'land grant philosophy'. Although a good deal has been written about this philosophy and its relevance for African higher education, it is still frequently misunderstood in Britain.[41] Very briefly it is an attitude to higher education which in no sense rejects the virtues of the European tradition, such as high quality, study in depth (though at the graduate, not the undergraduate, stage), and a commitment to 'pure' scholarship. Its novelty lies in its belief that these virtues can co-exist, and even benefit from, a lively interest in the teaching of vocational skills and education in the arts of community living. The university, according to the land grant philosophy, should concern itself with the making of citizens, not just leaders; it should become involved in 'persistent and significant problems of society', it should be prepared even to act as 'an instrument in the reconstruction of society'. In subjects which are studied for their utility, curricula should be experimental and amenable to change; the criterion for including a subject in the curriculum should be primarily – as in Europe – its intellectual content, but if a choice has to be made among subjects of appropriate intellectual content, then utility and relevance to the community should be admitted as valid criteria. Finally universities with the land grant philosophy do not, as British universities do, limit their interest to the enrolled student, with a comparatively minor ancillary commitment to conduct adult education classes in 'cultural' subjects.[42] Highly vocational extension work is regarded as an essential function of the land grant university. Its campus is the whole state. 'Making the products of university research available in terms of "know-how" at the practical level, with the "feed-back" of new problems worthy of research has been deemed an integral part of any university genuinely committed to service.'[43]

It is these principles, translated into the Nigerian context, which constitute the most dramatic impact which American thought has had on African higher education. Here are some examples of the impact. First, the question of entry. In the University of Nigeria, as in most of the Asquith colleges, there are two levels of entry: with O-level entry a student may graduate in four years; with appropriate A-level entry he may graduate in three years. But in the Asquith colleges, O-level entry is called 'concessional'; it does not admit to a degree course: it simply provides A-level work in (usually) two subjects. Consequently there is no continuity or cohesion between the preliminary course and the three-year degree course. In the University of Nigeria the freshman course after O-level is an integral part of the degree course; moreover it obliges every student to learn something of the humanities, social science, and natural science. This, in Africa, has two merits: it postpones until the second year at the university the need for a student to decide whether to specialise in arts or science; and it compensates for the very great differences in quality and curriculum among the schools from which the students come.

Programmes of this kind are not easy to devise, and some of those at the University of Nigeria have in the past lacked quality. But this is no reason to dismiss the whole idea of general courses (as the Central African Commission did in 1953) as superficial and unworthy of higher education. The social science ingredient of the general course at the University of Nigeria (to take one example) is entitled 'Conflict and unity in the contemporary world'. It includes readings, seminars, and lectures on the phenomenon of war; race, caste, and class, as factors dividing societies; the end of the colonial era; international organisations. This approach to history and political science can, like any other approach, be didactic and superficial; but if rigorously taught and examined, it is surely a valuable discipline for African students; and if it is an obligatory ingredient of the curriculum it may begin to create a common core of culture which has been missing in British education for generations.[44]

As for the rest of the curriculum in the University of Nigeria, it follows a pattern familiar enough to those who have worked in a mid-West American state university.[45] Courses have so many credit points attached to them; an undergraduate must accumulate at least 192 credit-hours to qualify for a degree. Performance in each course is graded from A (excellent) to F (failure); undergraduates whose grades are deemed too low are put on probation and may eventually be required to withdraw. In addition to this normal American practice two important British practices are incorporated into the undergraduate education: there are final written examinations of five three-hour papers the results of which carry half the weight (the other half is the accumulated grade-point average) in determining the final degree; and there are external examiners who (an unusual feature anywhere) are required to submit a report of the examination to the vice-chancellor.

There is every reason to believe that the University of Nigeria is determined to set standards as firmly as they were set by the Asquith colleges, though the standards will represent a different pattern of achievement, for the courses offered cover a much broader spectrum than is permitted on the English tradition. Courses as conventional as the French revolution, 1789–99, ethics, and algebraic analysis rub shoulders with courses on home management (an option in the agriculture course), newspaper editing (in the department of journalism), and book-keeping (in a sub-department of secretarial studies). On one hand it is possible to specialise: there is a two-subject degree in arts or science and there are 'professional' degrees in agriculture, education, engineering, law, and social studies. On the other hand subjects of modest intellectual content can be studied in an objective way in the liberal environment of a university. It is reasonable to suppose that the dignity and professional standards of such occupations as journalism, higher grade clerical work, social work in rural areas, and commercial art will be enhanced by their inclusion in the campus community; and it is difficult to see how their inclusion need diminish the quality of work done in the humanities and the sciences. Moreover, there would seem to be two secondary advantages in this pattern peculiarly relevant to African needs. Everyone who has experience of higher education in Africa is disturbed by the inflated status accorded to those who hold degrees and as a consequence the snob-prestige accorded to the subjects for which degrees are traditionally awarded. Any organisation of post-secondary education which spreads this status among more occupations is likely to improve the standards in these occupations and to promote social cohesion in the community. The danger, of course, is that an institution which tries to do too much will do nothing well. The University of Nigeria will be judged by the success with which it avoids this danger. It had a difficult start:

its founders were in too much of a hurry; it had to suffer the forebodings of traditionally minded critics;[46] its American sponsors were unfamiliar with the African environment. But it represents a fundamentally new transplantation in African higher education; and time will show whether it takes root in African soil and adapts itself to African conditions.

By the beginning of 1962 it was possible to discern the new shape of higher education in the British-speaking parts of West Africa. Nigeria had resolutely set itself upon the course charted by the Nigerian commission. The University of Ibadan had grown over fourteen years to a student population a little over a thousand and was in transition between special relationship with London and new courses for its own degrees. The University of Nigeria, with 900 students enrolled one year after opening its doors, had temporarily over-stretched its capacities, but was soon to embark on a policy of consolidation. The Ahmadu Bello University, the University of Ife, and the University of Lagos, were just beginning. In Sierra Leone little Fourah Bay College, which had played such a vital role in the intellectual life of West Africa, was still attached to the University of Durham; but it had acquired a charter as an independent university college and under the leadership of one of the great intellectuals of Africa, Davidson Nicol, it was embarking on a ten-year development plan. The university college in Ghana, an Asquith college which had acquired a reputation for the high quality of its work and for its remark-able mode of government (see chapter 10) was launched into independence after a somewhat unhelpful report of an international commission – unhelpful partly because it is distinguished by the profusion of dissenting footnotes by individual members dissociating themselves from its views, and partly be-cause the Ghanaian government gave only a qualified approval to its recom-mendations.[47] But more serious than this was the damage done during 1961 by a shocking interference in the autonomy of the new university which we describe elsewhere (p. 328); though in 1962 a new vice-chancellor, Conor Cruise O'Brien, was making a courageous effort to revive the university's fortunes. One very successful venture in Ghana is worth recording in the context of this chapter: it is the establishment of courses about African society for all undergraduates, conducted by a vigorous and enlightened department of African studies.

V INTERNATIONAL COMMITTEES IN EAST AND CENTRAL AFRICA

To study further signs of a blending of American and British experience in African higher education we have to turn to East and Central Africa. First we give an example from East Africa.

When a working party went out from Britain in 1955 to advise on the future of higher education in East Africa it presented a report which was the pure milk of English orthodoxy. This is exemplified by the inclusion of a summary of policy over entry qualifications. 'It is necessary', says the report:

to insist upon one matter connected with fitness for acceptance by a university. In some countries those who pass an examination, which is of a high level, are entitled to enter a university. In Great Britain it is different. British universities set a minimum entrance qualification which candidates for entrance must possess. There is an impression, widespread in East Africa, that the possession of this minimum qualification entitles the holder to enter a British university. It does not do so; it merely makes the holder eligible to be considered for admission. The policy of British universities is to set this minimum at a level which produces more candidates for admission than there are places; the universities then choose for admission such candidates as seem fully able to profit from university education, and those who are not selected have no legitimate grievance.[48]

Since the working party felt moved to make this statement at a time when Makerere was graduating only about forty students a year for the whole of East Africa, and since no alternative policy for admissions to higher education in East Africa was proposed, one can only suppose that East Africans were being told to accept the British policy (a consequence of post-war improvements in secondary education) as appropriate for themselves.

The second working party which went out three years later under John Lockwood, and to which we have already referred (p. 262) proposed some substantial departures from the conventional pattern, but it was left to another visitation of mixed nationality to introduce some elements of a transatlantic philosophy of education into East Africa. The Lockwood visitation recommended a federated university for the three territories. This recommendation was accepted and a provisional council for the university was set up. This council had the very delicate and difficult task of co-ordinating the aspirations of three otherwise independent territorial colleges at very different stages of development: Makerere in Uganda, a mature institution which had been in special relation with the University of London for thirteen years; the Royal College, Nairobi, which had only just been transformed from being a technical college into being a university college; and a college at Dar-es-Salaam which had just come into existence. The provincial council accordingly invited in 1962 a committee to advise the university on its needs and priorities. The chairman was the distinguished African principal of Fourah Bay College, Davidson Nicol, and the committee included an American, a Canadian, and two Englishmen. Their report[49] is an important and illuminating document.

A good deal of the report deals with the apportionment of finance between the three colleges, the necessity for all three of them to be interterritorial, the need to avoid duplication in professional faculties, and other ephemeral matters not related to our present theme. But the committee made some observations about the educational needs of East Africa which display a cautious but determined departure from the trends of higher education in East and West Africa over the 1950s; and these are worth putting on record.

Over admission to the university the committee was evidently in some embarrassment. The East African governments had decided on a policy of sixth forms in schools; they therefore did not want the colleges to admit students without passes in the Cambridge higher school certificate (which is the equivalent of A-level G.C.E.). This policy was accompanied by two dangers, albeit only temporary ones: one, that students could get admission to reputable universities overseas on passes in the school certificate, without waiting another two years or so to qualify for the higher certificate; and two, that the output from sixth forms would for a time be inadequate to fill places available at the university. The principal of the college at Dar-es-Salaam put before the committee nine arguments for and against the higher certificate entry level. In favour of it was a financial saving, the closer tuition afforded by sixth form work, the damage to schools if sixth forms were withdrawn, the possibility that sixth forms were not after all a bottleneck, and the belief that most university staff would be reluctant to teach at pre-intermediate level. Against the present entry level there was 'the incongruity of East African colleges requiring higher entrance qualifications than most overseas universities', the likelihood of empty places over the next few years unless entry requirements were lowered, the probability that a more broadly based university year would be better educationally than the highly specialised sixth form work, and the possibility of bottlenecks in the schools.[50] The committee decided in favour of the higher certificate level of entry for degree courses, though they nevertheless encouraged colleges to accept students for pre-entry courses at lower levels, and they spoke with approval even of junior colleges as 'an alternative device toward the same end'. It appears that their decision – like a similar decision about entry level made by the Nigerian commission – was probably based on expediency rather than educational theory.

Over curricula in the East African colleges the committee had some sensible things to say. Mindful, perhaps, of the way faculties of arts had developed in West Africa, they prescribed five 'basic' needs for a faculty of arts and social science: English, history including African history, economics, government including political science and public administration, and what they describe as 'facilities for learning the French language'. 'We are unanimously agreed' they wrote, that none of the colleges would be justified in 'offering courses of a traditional character in French literature and civilisation ... The courses offered should be utilitarian in nature, designed to afford students a reading – and a speaking – knowledge of French.'[51] Among other vocational subjects which the committee was prepared to envisage sooner or later in the degree courses were some which would qualify graduates to enter banking and journalism; and they gave approval to proposals to have courses leading to degrees in land economics, quantity surveying, and business administration.[52] The committee laid powerful emphasis on the university's duty to train graduate teachers, to conduct educational research (the colleges are criticised for having paid too little attention to this), and to become involved in the whole educational system through institutes of education.

Involvement, in fact, is the keynote of this committee's report; throughout

U–B.I.A.—10*

it one discerns the sense of responsibility which a university has toward its community in America and Canada. Extra-mural work (which was always good in Makerere, but was stretched hopelessly beyond its capacity, in a territory the size of Europe) must be emphasised; and the committee cautiously proposed that the university should (as the land grant colleges do in America) become committed to some extension work in agriculture and public health, a view which was rejected by the Asquith commission.

The report encourages involvement in African studies too. 'We think', the report says in one place, 'that suitable combinations of African subjects could be arranged within the courses of the B.A. degree ... We think that a Board of African Studies would help to focus attention on an important aspect of the teaching programme of the College which has not hitherto been emphasised'; and they infer that hitherto the university has not been sufficiently concerned with African topics.[53] That statements of this sort could be made of a college which had for a decade housed the East African institute of economic and social research demonstrates how reluctant the colonial university colleges were to incorporate African material into the undergraduate curriculum except as modifications in the content of individual subjects.

The most revealing sign of a change of outlook, undoubtedly influenced by American opinion, was the committee's views about the pattern of the degree. It will be recollected that the London B.A. could be taken either as a general degree, in which three subjects were studied for each of three years (3:3:3); or as an honours degree, in which a principal subject is studied for three years sometimes accompanied by a subsidiary subject. The trend in African universities, as in British universities, was toward the one-subject honours degree, although bodies as authoritative as the British university grants committee were by the 1960s deploring this trend. We have already described (p. 249) how the University of East Africa settled upon three degree patterns. In all three the candidate reads three subjects in the first year; he can then read two for two more years (3:2:2); or two for one year and one for the next (3:2:1); or specialise on one subject for the remaining two years (3:1:1). The report roundly criticises this decision; it even records 'our dismay at the abandonment of the 3:3:3 structure, which we consider to have continued validity in East African conditions'.[54] Here is a sign of transatlantic influence, for it is common knowledge that British opinion was not in favour of a 3:3:3 pattern of degree.

Finally the report declares itself unambiguously in favour of the idea of adaptation in an African university. After the protestations of some expatriate enthusiasts for European learning, giving the impression that universities, if they are to remain universities, are always and everywhere the same, it is refreshing to read in Davidson Nicol's report about 'one other urgent responsibility ... We refer to the desirability of these institutions [the university and its colleges] attaining, as soon as possible, a genuinely African character. This will involve an openness of mind on the part of university and college authorities, and a receptiveness to new ideas in what is, after all, an exhilarating period in the history of East Africa. We do not suggest a wholesale jettisoning of the principles and practices of the past era; far from it ... yet those responsible for shaping policy in the colleges and in the University should not be unnecessarily conservative in the discharge of their duties.'[55]

Of course it was not only the influence of American opinion which was working to change British policies over higher education in Africa. The experience of perceptive British expatriates, and the maturing concepts of Africans engaged in university work, all tended toward a more receptive attitude toward change. In March 1962 the heads of the university institutions in East and West Africa, Rhodesia, and Sierra Leone, met again for informal discussions. It was evident from their discussions how far views in the former colonial colleges were changing. The consensus of opinion was that some broadening of the curriculum was necessary and that the single subject honours course was not well suited to African conditions. Concern was expressed as to whether the overseas institutions were too preoccupied with the problem of standards. Now that standards had been set there might be room in the institutions for broad middle-grade courses. It was noted that many universities of international repute awarded degrees on examinations held four years after O-level G.C.E.; to pursue the implications of this would lead to a reconsideration of the very delicate problem of the future of sixth forms in Africa. It was confessed that in Central Africa the adoption of British standards of admission to the university college in Salisbury had left a serious gap in university provision in that part of Africa. There was a demonstrable need for opportunities for Africans to read for a pass degree with lower entrance requirements, providing a broad rather than an academically deep training. Such a degree would equip them admirably for many posts in the Central African territories: a degree which, as the principal of one Asquith college put it, 'is a normal feature of university education in Australia, Canada, and the United States'. This constituted a major concession of opinion to the pressures for a more widely available university education in Africa. There was still the *caveat*, of course; that provision of this kind should not weaken institutions in the Asquith tradition, which would continue to provide for an academic élite; and the difference in quality between the two sorts of degrees should be recognised by a salary differential in public service appointments.

The working party on East African higher education and the committee on needs and priorities which followed it (see p. 282) had set a course for the university there. The remaining problem in educational planning was in Central Africa, a region already at that time running into severe political storms. By 1962 American influence in African higher education had become powerful, and British policy, largely due to the influence of John Lockwood (who was willing to allow himself to be regarded as a patient heretic over the Asquith doctrine) had become much more flexible. In Central Africa there grew up something which might be regarded as a synthesis of American and British influence over models of new university institutions. It is worth while to trace this last phase of the story in some detail.

The story begins with a joint meeting under Lockwood's chairmanship, of British and Americans early in 1962, to discuss higher education in Central Africa. It was agreed without difficulty that an urgent need in Central Africa was for graduates at pass level, not honours, in arts, education, and social studies, and for persons qualified for such occupations as accountancy, commerce, and pharmacy. The view of the Americans was that in Central Africa it was essential to have a more comprehensive system of higher education, one that did not restrict itself to a thin trickle of entrants with A-level qualifications, largely in clerkly subjects; they pressed for a four-year degree course, widely based, for which the entry qualification should be the equivalent of O-level G.C.E.

These and similar discussions, and much exchange of views between the inter-university council and the American liaison committee, led to two reports which (since they have been accepted in Britain as a basis for aid) may be taken as indicators of British opinion on universities in developing Commonwealth countries.

The first of these reports, written in 1963, is a blueprint for a university in what was still Northern Rhodesia and is now Zambia.[56] The committee which visited the country and wrote the report was a mature product of the new co-operation between Britain and America. It was appointed on the initiative of the governor of Northern Rhodesia, financed jointly by the department of technical co-operation in Britain and Carnegie Corporation of New York, and its membership was determined by the American council on education and the inter-university council for higher education overseas in London. It was fortunate in having as its chairman John Lockwood, who served on the pioneer Nigerian commission four years earlier. Lockwood paid a preliminary visit to Northern Rhodesia early in 1963. His comments made on the occasion of this visit summarise brilliantly the evolution of ideas which had occurred in Britain. Since Lockwood himself was responsible for some of this evolution of ideas, and since his views are leading to a policy which preserves the virtues of the Asquith plan while rejecting the uncompromising dogmatism of some of its more zealous disciples, his opinions should be put on record. In a private communication to one of us after his first visit to Lusaka in 1963, he wrote:

The special relationship schemes with London and Durham have been extremely successful within the limits of their possibilities. Their weakness is that they have carried over into Africa the highly selective processes and types of degree courses which have grown up in the United Kingdom since the 1939–45 war. In a sense, African university development has been the victim of our own educational history in the last 20 years. Expatriate staff have naturally taken with them habits and ideas current in the United Kingdom but not necessarily relevant to the urgent needs of an African country. What they have done, they have done remarkably well and deserve the highest praise. But a nagging question has become more and more insistent during the last few years whether we and they were right to concentrate as we did on converting the university colleges into academic counterparts of English university institutions with high entrance standards and highly specialised honours courses.[57]

The report faces this 'nagging question' with courage and initiative. In it there is a better integration of American and British concepts of higher education than was achieved in the Nigerian report. It offers Northern Rhodesia very different advice from the advice offered to Rhodesia and Nyasaland by the commission from Britain ten years earlier. Northern Rhodesia must have an independent university, not one under the tutelage of another university; and the reason given for this is significant:

If it were the objective of the foundation of a university institution to produce a relatively small *élite* of graduates to fill senior posts in government, schools, university, the professions and business, a special relationship arrangement would have something to commend it. But when well-trained men and women will be wanted in a broad spectrum of types of employment, a university free from the unavoidably constricting authority which the degree structures of another university would require is better fitted to encompass this wider range and need.[58]

An independent university could contemplate 'degree courses of a more vocational type'. 'Subjects or areas of study which are described in the United Kingdom as "further" education could be considered as suitable for degree courses. The United States and some countries of the Commonwealth, not to mention other parts of the world, find no apparent difficulty in including them within the framework of university studies.'[59]

It is in fact made clear in the report that the committee was attracted to the 'umbrella' concept of higher education which would combine higher and further education in a single university complex. They abandoned it 'only with great reluctance', and then mainly because of the administrative problems it would involve. In any case they recommend a 'multi-purpose and multi-level' university awarding not only degrees after four-year courses but diplomas or associate degrees after two-year courses; and they prescribe O-level G.C.E. as the normal entrance requirement for admission to a degree course.[60] It is indicative of the long distance that British opinion had travelled since the Carr-Saunders commission to Central Africa in 1953 that the Lockwood committee – whose chairman was a classicist and an ex-vice-chancellor of the University of London – could support its recommendation with the following quotation from one of Lockwood's former colleagues:

A university will not serve its social purpose if it sets its standards of admission so high that it is concerned only with a tiny minority of extremely able students and does nothing for the larger numbers of less spectacular ability who will not realise their full potential in service unless they have the advantage of a university education.[61]

One problem which must be solved in a multi-level university is to preserve one of the traditional functions of the university, to be a centre for disinterested scholarship, in the midst of its more narrowly vocational functions. The committee proposes the normal American solution (in fact, the solution to be found already in the University of Nigeria) that different degrees should be differently labelled, e.g. B.Agric., B.Tech., B.Econ., B.Admin., and so on. Another problem, since a multi-level university destroys the sharp division between what in Britain are distinguished as higher and further education, is to create links with institutions dedicated to technical education. To solve this problem the Lockwood committee make an ingenious proposal: that the university should recognise work done in the technical college as qualifying for the award of an associate degree, and that some who reach this level in the technical college (the committee estimate about twenty per cent) could transfer to the university for degree work.

While the Lockwood committee was working in Northern Rhodesia, another team, entirely American-inspired, was preparing an educational plan for newly independent Malawi. It was organised by the American council on education on contract to the United States agency for international development (AID). Its terms of reference were much wider: it had to propose an educational plan for the next fifteen years for all age groups. Its membership – this time on American initiative – was drawn from four countries and was clearly intended to incorporate experience from West Africa.[62] Its report was published in 1964.[63]

Our concern here is principally with its findings on higher education, but it begins with an outspoken criticism of the secondary school curriculum:

The classical type of academic education found in the traditional grammar secondary school is inappropriate in Malawi. It misses the largest manpower targets and its misses relevance for African schoolboys ... The orthodox approach is simply not enough. A revitalized curriculum should make the traditional vie with the practical and technical. It should be comprehensive, as life is comprehensive.[64]

The survey team found that sixth forms had barely secured a toe-hold in Malawi; they recommend that such sixth form work as has started should cease and that entry to the university should be at O-level G.C.E. or its equivalent.[65]

Having regard to the composition of the survey team, in which the one American representative was outnumbered by two Africans (both of whom graduated from the University of Cambridge) and an Englishman, the proposals for a University of Malawi are of great interest. The team are careful to recommend a small institution which for the time being will not provide expensive fields of study such as architecture, medicine, and engineering: students in these fields should continue to study overseas. Its constituent parts should be a college of arts and sciences, a college of education, and a college of natural resources. The degree course should last four years, and the report adds: 'An essential part of the "package" is a common compulsory first year course, emphasising general studies.' (Elsewhere the report adds that this course 'must not be a disguised substitute for the sixth form'.) 'This will put degree holders at an academic level comparable to that adhered to in universities in many parts of Africa and overseas, and will qualify for admission to excellent postgraduate programs abroad. This is a test of adequacy.'[66] The degree course should be grouped around two major subjects, so that students in their fourth year have experience of some study in depth, a pattern which the report advocates 'not only because it is intellectually stimulating and liberalising, but also because it is a fitting response to the current high-level manpower needs of a nation in which flexibility and adaptability are at an extraordinarily high premium'.[67]

Finally, the team was attracted, as the Lockwood committee was, by the 'umbrella' concept for higher education in an African country; and notwithstanding the administrative problems involved, the Malawi team decided in favour of a university-complex, with links with a variety of other institutions: 'the University should be given responsibility for all existing post-secondary education and its future development, with the exception of a special relationship to Government-operated education for the agricultural services and to the training of primary schoolteachers'.[68]

This brings us to the end of our analysis of the evolution of British ideas on African higher education since the Asquith commission reported in 1945. Within twenty years universities have been transplanted and have taken root in nations which were formerly British colonies. Through the foresight of the Asquith commission, the transplantation brought with it criteria of academic quality accepted by the University of London; this attracted to the colonial colleges expatriate teachers of high standing, and this in turn set standards of achievement in teaching and research.

Over the last twenty years three sets of influences have acted upon the ideas inherent in the Asquith plan. There have been local influences arising from national needs and aspirations of the newly independent nations; there has been the influence of academics from the United States of America who believed (and in the event have convinced the British that their belief was right) that American concepts of higher education have relevance to Africa; there has been the influence of a few British academics, such as John Lockwood, who have encouraged flexibility and adaptation in African higher education. Under these influences the Asquith plan has been greatly modified. In its original form it is no longer acceptable as a pattern for higher education in a developing country. But it takes a proud and honourable place in history: where it was weak it has been replaced by better plans; its virtues remain, and they secure for the universities which practise them a firm place in the international fraternity of scholarship.

CHAPTER TEN

AUTONOMY AND ACADEMIC FREEDOM

I CONCEPTS OF ACADEMIC FREEDOM AND AUTONOMY

Academic freedom and university autonomy are emotive expressions. They include concepts which are essential to a university if it is to fulfil its function in society. They are visceral in the structure of academic man everywhere. Yet there is constant confusion about what the expressions really mean and how they are related to each other. They are sometimes regarded as synonyms, though it is a commonplace of history that an autonomous university can deny academic freedom to some of its members (as Oxford did in the early nineteenth century), and a university which is not autonomous can safeguard academic freedom (as Prussian universities did in Humboldt's time). Both expressions are frequently equated to the constitutional structure of universities although it is evident from experience that academic freedom and university autonomy are more effectively protected by unwritten conventions than by charters and statutes. The purpose of this chapter is to disentangle these ideas and to discuss them with particular reference to higher education in English-speaking countries in tropical Africa.

We begin with some general observations about academic freedom and the autonomy of universities. We then proceed to a discussion of university constitutions, for these constitute the framework round which autonomy and freedom in academic communities are built. And we provide some case histories to illustrate our views on the export of British formulae for preserving autonomy and freedom in African universities.

Academic freedom has not, so far as we know, been defined in an English court of law; nor, so far as we know, do the statutes of any British university specifically guarantee academic freedom to its members.[1] It has developed in civilized countries as a specially protected corner of intellectual freedom. It is not so much a personal privilege claimed by members of the academic community: it is a condition of work, granted because it is believed to be essential for teaching and learning the truth as scholars see it; and (as Michael Polanyi pointed out many years ago[2]) because a climate of academic freedom is the most efficient medium for research. It has been well defined as:

that freedom of members of the academic community, assembled in colleges and universities, which underlies the effective performance of their functions of teaching, learning, practice of the arts, and research. The right to academic freedom is recognized in order to enable faculty members and students to carry on their roles.[3]

The idea that scholars in universities ought to be free to teach and learn what and how they wish goes back to the middle ages, but the custom of guaranteeing this privilege by popular consent dates only from the nineteenth century. It was formulated in Germany, in universities which were directly under the supervision of the state, as *Lehrfreiheit* (a privilege of the teacher) and *Lernfreiheit* (a privilege of the research worker and the student). As defined in Germany, it had certain limitations: according to Paulsen a professor of theology, for instance, 'must be in sympathy with the great religious event of humanity which we call Christianity'; a professor of political and social science who is hostile towards the state and who aims at its dismemberment or destruction 'cannot as an honest man accept an office and a commission from the hands of the people or the state'.[4] The concept of *Lehrfreiheit* has been adopted in English-speaking countries and greatly broadened. In Britain and the United States it would be considered an infringement of academic freedom for a university to impose any censorship on the utterances of any member of its staff on any subject, whether it lies within his field of expertise or not, whether or not it deals with religion or politics, and whether or not it was uttered in the classroom. In Britain, and in most university institutions in the United States today, a biochemist (for instance) may deny God, advocate communism, or speak approvingly of free love, without endangering his security of tenure. In passing, let it be added that *Lernfreiheit*, as freedom to choose one's field of research within the limits of the facilities available, has also been adopted in the English-speaking academic world; but *Lernfreiheit* for the undergraduate has not fared so well. The tradition, strong in Britain, that the university is *in loco parentis* toward its undergraduates, gives rise to the belief (which would be indignantly repudiated on the Continent) that a student, having chosen his field of study, should pursue a programme in it in ways which his teacher thinks are best for him. The British undergraduate cannot easily migrate from one university to another. He must complete his course of study in a strictly limited period. He must select combinations of subjects approved by faculty boards. There are, of course, very important and valuable developments of student-*Lernfreiheit* in both the British Commonwealth and the United States, such as the declaration, which appears in the constitutions of many universities, that students may not be excluded, or suffer any disability, on account of religious or political opinions, or colour, race, or tribe. Also students are free (provided their entrance qualifications permit it) to choose their major field of study. But the uninhibited student-*Lernfreiheit* of nineteenth-century Germany has not been imported into Britain.

Accordingly, when we think of academic freedom in English-speaking countries, we are thinking of *Lehrfreiheit*; and *Lehrfreiheit*, although it has not been defined in law or codified in statutes, has a precise and narrow meaning. It would be infringed if any authority, either inside or outside the university, were to forbid a university officer to take a certain line in his teaching or in his published work;[5] and it would be a scandalous infringement if he were to be dismissed from his office for refusing to comply.[6]

Lord Chorley, who has had a unique opportunity to observe the operation of *Lehrfreiheit* in Britain, wrote recently (in a discussion of academic freedom in the United Kingdom): 'There does not appear to have been any case where even a colorable argument has been advanced that a dismissal took place which involved a breach of academic freedom.'[7] And he concludes that academic freedom is enjoyed as fully in English universities as anywhere else in the world. Lest this picture seems too optimistic, it must be added that anyone seeking for examples of crypto-infringement of *Lehrfreiheit* in Britain can find them. At the domestic level an autocratic professor of botany may instruct one of his junior staff to lecture on the fungi and not on the ferns; and in some universities the assignment of teaching duties is in the hands of a faculty board which might see to it that both A and B do not deliver a lecture course on the French revolution, though both might wish to do so. At the research level, a research council or an industry may offer a professor of physics a grant to do research in a specific field, and to the extent that he yields to the temptation against his better judgement (or persuades some of his staff to take up the research against their better judgement), academic freedom has been constrained. But such minor irritations as these beset all academic communities and cannot seriously be regarded as erosions of academic freedom. In its strict connotation, which is the freedom of the individual university teacher to teach according to his conscience and convictions, and to publish his views on his own subject (or for that matter on any subject permitted by the law of the land), academic freedom is now secure in British universities and – with a handful of exceptions some of which we discuss later – it seems not to have been seriously challenged in the new universities of the Commonwealth. In the cases where teaching officers have been dismissed from Commonwealth universities the grounds given were not criticism of the officers' teaching or research, though there have been cases (e.g. in the Universities of Ghana and Ife) which come under a broad interpretation of infringements of academic freedom, where contracts were terminated because teaching officers were alleged to have political opinions distasteful to the government. And some teaching officers at the University of Lagos recently had their contracts terminated because they supported the senate against the council over the failure to renew the appointment of the vice-chancellor (see p. 327). There are, however, no grounds for complacency or for a relaxation of vigilance. The melancholy example of South Africa shows how easily, in a nation which claims to have a democratic constitution, academics can be victimised by the state for their opinions on political and racial questions; and the poisonous influence of Senator McCarthy, in a great nation where civil liberties are guaranteed by the constitution, is barely a decade behind us. The bulwark which protects *Lehrfreiheit* is a simple one: it is security of tenure, either established as a legal right (as is frequently the case in the United States) or (as in Britain) established as a principle held uncompromisingly by the governing bodies of universities. Academic freedom cannot of course exceed the liberties allowed by the law of the land. So a country which does not permit freedom of speech and publication to its ordinary citizens cannot grant academic freedom to its universities. In such countries academic freedom is in eclipse and accordingly universities cannot flourish. Spain and South Africa and (recently) Ghana are examples.

It should be clear from the foregoing that academic freedom and university autonomy are two quite distinct concepts. They impinge on each other at many points. They both depend in the last resort on a public opinion which understands what universities are for and is prepared to respect them. But whereas academic freedom (or rather that part of it called *Lehrfreiheit*) is an internationally recognised and unambiguous privilege of university teachers,[8] the question as to what constitutes autonomy in universities is anything but unambiguous, and the patterns of autonomy which satisfy academics in different countries are very diverse. One example, generally acknowledged to be a feature of autonomy, will suffice to illustrate this: the procedure for appointing professors. In Glasgow and elsewhere in Britain regius chairs are filled by the crown, after taking such advice as may be thought appropriate. In Cambridge sole responsibility rests with a board of electors, appointed by decision of the university as a whole. In Belfast the predominantly lay governing body makes the appointment on the recommendation of a board of curators comprising some laymen and some academics, and there was a time when the governing body insisted on having more than one recommendation from which to make its choice. In Germany the minister of the *Land* (state) makes the appointment on a recommendation from the university faculty. In France the appointment has to be made from among the names on a list of the *cadre* of candidates held by the central ministry of education. In many American universities the initiative for making recommendations comes from a staff meeting of all permanent members of the department concerned (a practice which gives the non-professorial members of a department a degree of participation unknown in Britain). Over the emoluments attached to chairs there is a similar diversity of practice. American universities have virtually complete autonomy in deciding the salary to be offered to a professor; British universities are obliged by the state to adhere to a very narrow range of permitted salaries. German professors receive the salary appropriate to civil servants of that grade. Freedom to make professorial appointments is one of the essential features of university autonomy; the amount and nature of the freedom allowed by these different practices are very diverse: yet none of the practices is regarded as inimical to autonomy in the countries where they occur.

The truth, though it is often blurred by rhetoric, is that nowadays no university can expect to be *completely* self-governing in the sense that an independent state or a municipality is self-governing. Consider a few examples.

Most universities on the continent of Europe are branches of the civil service, though their autonomy may be protected, as it is in the German *Länder*, by provisions written into the constitutions of the states. When a German commission (with one British member, Lord Lindsay, then master of Balliol) considered the reform of German universities in 1948, it recommended that German universities should continue to come under the state. Its reasons are significant for our discussion. It asserted that 'a complete separation of universities from the State would not protect the universities in the event of a serious conflict';[9] and it made this suggestion:

If the right of the State to supervise the universities is laid down in the State constitutions, this naturally means that the State may not exceed this right. It may not interfere with the universities' affairs. It is generally recognised today that State supervision must be limited to safeguarding the law. It does not imply any supervision of academic standards. The State has only to ensure that its laws are not infringed by the proceedings of the universities. These powers of the State should be exactly defined. There should be an arbitration court for dispute between the State and the universities.[10]

The degree of protection given to universities by the state in Germany is, on paper at any rate, impressive; though there is some ambiguity about the interpretation of the clauses which guarantee autonomy. It is worth while to quote examples of these clauses. The constitutional law of the German Federal Republic [*Grundgesetz*, article 5 (iii)] provides the basic guarantee: '*Kunst und Wissenschaft, Forschung und Lehre sind frei.*' This is interpreted to mean that *academic* self-government is assured in universities, though this limited degree of autonomy has to be distinguished from self-government as found in, for example, municipal authorities. The universities are organs of the *Länder* (states), and the constitutions of some of the *Länder* spell out in more detail the degree of autonomy guaranteed to the universities. Thus article 39 of the constitution of Rheinland-Pfalz of 18 May 1947 contains this passage:

Die Hochschulen haben das Recht der Selbstverwaltung. Die Freiheit von Forschung und Lehre wird ihnen verbürgt.

And the constitution of Baden-Württemberg of 11 November 1953 contains these passages (articles 20 and 85):

Die Hochschule ist frei in Forschung und Lehre. . . . Die Hochschule hat unbeschadet der staatlichen Aufsicht das Recht auf eine ihrem besonderen Charakter entsprechende Selbstverwaltung im Rahmen der Gesetze und ihrer staatlich anerkannten Satzungen (art. 20)

Die Universitäten und Hochschulen mit Promotionsrecht bleiben in ihrem Bestand erhalten. (art. 85).

We refer again to these devices for safeguarding the autonomy of universities when we come to consider the African universities.

In the United States there is a great diversity of patterns of control, from those to be found in private institutions managed by religious bodies, to the state universities which have to submit annual budgets to the legislature. The more distinguished private institutions are as self-governing as are the British universities and have a greater degree of autonomy, for they are not subject to supervision by any authority above their own self-perpetuating boards of trustees. Their internal government is nevertheless liable to be strongly influenced by the alumni, on whose annual subscriptions many of these universities rely even to pay the salary bill. At first sight the American state universities might seem to have comparatively little autonomy, since they work on an itemised budget approved by the state legislature. But very commonly (e.g. in Michigan) the government of a state university is delegated by the state constitution to a board of trustees or regents who are elected by general suffrage in the state and who have absolute sovereignty – and cannot be overruled even by the legislature – in the government of the state university. In such cases the remaining sanction (but it is a powerful one) which rests with the legislature is control of financial appropriations.

In Britain all universities have *de jure* self-government though changes in constitution have to be approved by the privy council; and the statutes of a new university have to be approved by the privy council after consultation with the university grants committee, which scrutinises the draft statutes carefully and often suggests amendments to them. Remarkable care is taken by the university grants committee (which advises the minister of education and science) not to interfere in the running of universities; but recently the universities themselves have come to expect a more *dirigiste* attitude from the state[11] and the university grants committee, as the agent of the state, has had to consent to the imposition of certain financial controls: over salary scales, for example, the overall cost per student of halls of residence put up with public money, and the dimensions of rooms in some university buildings. The committee is obliged also to invade the sovereignty of universities by deciding (for example) that it could not provide a grant for the foundation of a medical school in one university or an engineering school in another. The committee uses these powers with great discretion and a scrupulous respect for the universities. Nevertheless there are Jeremiahs who see in these tendencies the twilight of autonomy in British universities; though it is safe to assert that these forebodings are not shared by most of those who have to take the main responsibility for preserving self-government. Anyone who has served on the university grants committee or the committee of vice-chancellors and principals has experience of the strength of the conviction that the British universities should in all essential matters maintain their autonomy.

The safeguard for autonomy in British universities, therefore, is not to be sought in overall declarations about the virtues of academic self-government; these may be taken for granted. It is rather to be sought by deciding and defining the essential ingredients for autonomy and ensuring that these are widely understood among the public, politicians, and civil servants. What are these essential ingredients?

There is a wide measure of agreement about the ingredients which matter most. To be autonomous a university must be free to select its students and its staff and to determine the conditions under which they remain in the university (it is here that autonomy impinges on, and may even conflict with, academic freedom). An autonomous university must be free to set its own standards and to decide to whom to award its degrees, even if, as in Britain, universities voluntarily set limits to their own freedom by the appointment of external examiners. An autonomous university must be free to design its own curriculum although it may in practice have to do so within certain constraints, such as the requirements of professional bodies which recognise the degree as a right to practise, and the financial sanctions which may be imposed from outside to prevent a university creating (for example) a medical school. Finally – and this lies at the root of the tenaciously-held belief in Britain that parliament should not inspect the accounts of universities – an autonomous university, having received its income from state or private sources, must be free to decide how to allocate it among the different categories of expenditure. It is this last prerequisite for autonomy which is most in danger of erosion.[12]

Finally, there is a further condition of autonomy without which these ingredients are ineffective. In a university where non-academics participate in its self-government, and where they are in fact in a majority on the body where sovereignty resides, it is essential that non-academics should identify themselves with the university, and not consider themselves representatives of interests outside the university. It is essential, too, that all academic decisions should be delegated to the academics themselves, who must always be regarded as members of a society, not employees. Without this internal coherence and internal balance of power, a university may be free of intervention from outside, and yet have its autonomy betrayed from inside. Several cases of this sort have occurred in African universities.

II EVOLUTION OF UNIVERSITY CONSTITUTIONS IN BRITAIN

We have drawn a distinction between the concepts of academic freedom on one hand and the autonomy of universities on the other. We shall return to both these topics in the context of African universities. We now turn to consider university constitutions, which are commonly regarded as the outward and visible evidence of these concepts.

The British civic universities have provided tropical countries in the Commonwealth not only with patterns of syllabus and curriculum; they have provided them also with the patterns of academic government. We have already discussed (chapter 4) how the government of India, in order to retain control over universities, adopted constitutions which would nowadays be considered quite inconsistent with university autonomy. This history was not repeated in Africa. With one exception (which is described separately below) the constitution of colleges founded on the Asquith plan were modelled on a pattern which has proved suitable to universities in English industrial cities. Before discussing how these constitutions work in the tropics it is necessary to understand how they arose in Britain and how they are being adapted to meet changing conditions in Britain.

The urge early in the nineteenth century to found new universities in Britain came from dissatisfaction with the existing universities. The shortcomings of Cambridge and Oxford in those days are too well known to need repetition here. But even the Scottish universities, which the poorest student could afford to attend, and where sectarian tests were not applied, were under heavy criticism, especially over their manner of government. Glasgow University was controlled by an oligarchy of college professors who querulously defended their power even against their colleagues who held regius chairs. Edinburgh University was ruled by the city magistrates with the lord provost as rector. Accordingly neither the English nor the Scottish universities offered acceptable models of university government for the founders of new universities to copy. The founders did not devise, at one leap of imagination, the pattern of constitution which is now common to all the English civic universities and which (with modifications) is to be found also in other parts of Britain and all over the Commonwealth; this pattern has emerged gradually during the evolution of universities over the last 125 years.

The original pattern was very simple. Higher education in the industrial cities of Victorian England began as private enterprise, financed by a joint stock company, as was University College, London; or by individual benefactors, as were Owens College, Manchester, and Mason College, Birmingham; or by groups of citizens, as were the colleges in Leeds and Liverpool. The trustees for the endowments and subscriptions acted as governing bodies; they began by regarding the professors as employees, and they considered it as part of their duty as trustees to decide policy in the colleges they governed.

Thus in Manchester, up to 1870, there was no organised internal administration. The trustees 'as one of their first acts laid down, could dismiss a professor at their absolute discretion. ... Even the most trivial matters required [the trustees'] sanction.' The teachers 'could only represent their views to the Trustees through the Principal'. There was no curriculum, no senate, no boards of study or faculties, no calendar.[13] In Mason College Birmingham, there was a similar employer-employee relationship between the teaching staff and the governing body. Indeed, a vigorous attempt was made to perpetuate this relationship when the draft charter for a university of Birmingham was being drawn up in 1898. The city's idea (we are told) was 'a small local institution . . . whose control should be strictly confined to the hands of an autocratic and provincial governing body'. And the draft charter prepared by the management sub-committee of the executive committee of the court of governors proposed a 'Senate of Professors entirely at the mercy of a Council [the lay governing body] . . . no proposal for fuller faculty organisation, no hint of academic self-government, no suggestion that the professoriate were to exercise independent authority over their own departments'.[14] Nottingham University College was for many years run by a committee of management under the city corporation, composed predominantly of town councillors. Even when a board of professors was formally constituted in 1887, the board was given scarcely any powers and a 'very slender list of duties'. The principal (who was one of the professors) was not even a member of the committee of management of the college.[15] A similar start was made by the University of Sydney, whose foundation is described in chapter 2. Some of the citizens who were instrumental in founding the university were appointed to the first governing body (called in Sydney, as in India, the senate). This body in its pioneer enthusiasm began to run the embryo university without proper consultation with the three distinguished foundation professors who had been brought out from Britain. It is on record that, within three years of the university's foundation 'the professors complained, not without reason, that they had neither voice nor authority in the Institution in which they played so prominent a part. They were, in fact, mere servants of the Senate. Their complaints became unpleasantly loud, and their justice was admitted.'[16]

The three foundation professors in the University of Sydney were fighting a battle for the delegation of academic government to academics, which has had to be fought by many other professors in many other universities from Birmingham and Reading to New Zealand and Nigeria. The forces at play were very similar in different places. On the one hand there were the laymen-founders, determined to shape the new university to their own image of what a university should be; on the other hand there were the foundation-professors, graduates of older universities, determined to establish in the new university the traditions of autonomy so jealously preserved in the institutions from which they had come. Each side was right in its own way. The laymen-founders in the nineteenth century were determined to break with the prejudices which had insulated the ancient universities from the consequences – social and economic – of the industrial revolution. They wanted their new universities to be relevant to the time and place of their foundation. The foundation professors – many of them just as anxious as the laymen to free themselves from these prejudices – nevertheless believed passionately that no university could remain viable in which the teaching staff abdicated its right to control academic affairs; a university must remain (as one of them said) 'a hearth and home of autonomy on every range, a training ground consecrate to self-government'.[17]

The resultant of these opposing forces was the emergence of the familiar 'two-tier' system of university government. In supreme control is a predominantly lay governing body (commonly called the council) where *de jure* sovereignty lies. This body retains control of finance and property, and acts as an upper house, receiving from the academic bodies below it recommendations to be approved; but despite its sovereignty the custom is firmly established that it does not issue to the bodies below it directives to be obeyed, although some university constitutions e.g. those for Birmingham and Sussex, expressly empower it to do this.[18] Under the council there is an exclusively academic body (commonly called the senate) which is obliged to submit practically all its decisions to the council for ratification but to which the council entrusts, originally by convention and latterly by statute, responsibility for the whole academic business of the university. It is on the senate's initiative that new subjects are taught, new chairs established, new faculties created. The senate, either itself or through the faculty boards which report to it, prescribes curricula and controls examinations; it is responsible for policy over admission of students; in many universities it recommends the names of persons to fill academic posts. The convention has grown up, and is now so firmly established that it is regarded as an inalienable right, that on all academic matters initiative lies with the academic staff; so that today, if a university lay council, wishing to achieve some educational change in the university, were to issue an instruction to the senate, there would be massive obstruction, a dragging of feet, and even murmurs about infringement of academic freedom, notwithstanding charters and statutes which unambiguously confer sovereignty on the lay council. For reasons which are explained below, in the civic universities this tradition of academic self-government deteriorated for a time into government by professorial oligarchy; but this weakness within the universities is being eradicated.

The 'two-tier' pattern of university government, with its allocation of power and responsibility between the lay council and the academic senate, did not appear suddenly; it has emerged gradually during a century of evolution in English civic universities, and it owes much to the work of men familiar with the democratic traditions of government in Cambridge and Oxford. Henry Malden, a fellow of Trinity College, Cambridge and subsequently professor of Greek at University College, London, was the first to describe its virtues. In 1834, when University College, London, was petitioning the privy council for a charter as a university, Malden was asked to write an explanatory essay on the constitutions of universities. He ends his essay with this passage:

But if we were to imagine a university, in which the ordinary discipline, and the details inseparable from the business of education, should be entrusted to the body of professors; in which they should be entitled to tender their advice upon the election to vacant chairs, the institution of new professorships, and other graver matters, but without a final voice, in which all financial business, and the supreme government of the university, and the administration of its patronage, should be committed to a body of gentlemen . . . chosen expressly and solely for that purpose, responsible for the due discharge of their functions, and bound to make an annual report on their management; we should form the idea of a well-balanced constitution . . . This constitution is realised in the University of London.[19]

In Owens College, Manchester, the transition from 'one-tier' to 'two-tier' government came slowly. The original college had no differentiated pattern of government at all. In 1870, a draft of a new constitution was prepared by Bryce[20] which divided power between lay governors, professors, and alumni (known as associates). The bill was passed and the new governing body at its first meeting (on 23 September 1870) 'constituted a Senate of professors'. There still remained some sign of an employer-employee relation between the governing body and the academic staff. For example, in the bye-laws adopted on 23 April 1873 (para. 80, p. 21) there is a passage: 'Professors may communicate with the Council only in exceptional cases and then only directly in writing addressed to the Chairman or through the Principal.' But there were signs, too, in this proto-constitution, of delegation to the academics. The functions of the teaching staff were, for instance, subject to direction by the council, but para. 79, p. 21, reads: 'no act of such direction or revision shall be resolved upon except after a report on the matter from the Senate'. Soon there began to appear evidences of the working of the new pattern of government. On 6 October 1871, the council 'requested the Senate to draw up a statement as to whether any additional teaching power or other appliances were required'. Even over financial matters it was not long before the convention was established that academic policy should flow upwards as recommendations from faculty and senate to council and not downwards as instructions from council to the academic bodies beneath it; in 1886 (for example) the council 'felt it their painful duty to state that in their opinion it was expedient that the estimated expenditure for the session 1886-7 should be reduced by at least £200 and resolved that the Senate be requested to report to the Council concerning the best manner in which this reduction might be effected'.[21]

In Manchester a division of responsibility and a balance of power between the lay governing body and the academic senate was firmly established before the turn of the century; but new foundations did not all accept the precedent set by Manchester. In 1898, when Chamberlain's energy transformed Mason College into the University of Birmingham, there was an exciting dispute between the sub-committee charged with the drafting of a charter and a group of professors on the management committee led by Sonnenschein, who had the chair of classics. The draft charter reached members of the management committee of the court of governors on 6 December 1898, with notice that they would be asked to vote upon it on 7 December. In Sonnenschein's view the draft was deliberately reactionary and completely excluded participation in government by the academic staff. He and his colleagues hurriedly drafted 'Suggestions towards the constitution of the proposed University of Birmingham' and had it printed in a few hours on 7 December, the day the management committee met.[22] Fortunately a decision on the draft was postponed, and this gave Sonnenschein time to 'riddle the draft charter with criticism' and to prepare an alternative draft, which based its claim for genuine faculty-participation in government on Ordinance 31 of the Scottish University Commission;[23] and a week later the management committee approved the more important of Sonnenschein's amendments, including the essential limitation of the powers of the lay council over the academic senate. 'It is clear that we were only just in time', wrote Sonnenschein, 'had it not been for the preparation of the previous month . . . the "enemy" would have perpetuated the College method of government by the Council unchanged. There would have been no academic autonomy.'[24] At subsequent meetings Sonnenschein secured further concessions from the 'enemy': the right, for example, for faculties to elect their own deans (though the dean of the faculty of medicine is still appointed by the council). And so another civic university reached an equilibrium between the two levels of its 'two-tier' government. The scars of battle are still visible in the constitution. One can hear Sonnenschein's voice (and the echo of a still more eloquent voice: J. M. Mackay of Liverpool, who was a friend of Sonnenschein and gave him much help and encouragement) in the unusual influence given to faculty boards in Birmingham – they are responsible even for recommending candidates for chairs – and one can sense the resistance of the opposition of 1898 in some of the phrasing of the first charter (e.g. 'The supreme governing body shall be the Court of Governors [which shall have] absolute power within the University'; 'At no time shall the members of Council who are members of Senate be more in number than the number of members of Council divided by four').

Birmingham's first charter and statutes (1900) and the revised charters and statutes for unitary universities in Leeds, Liverpool and Manchester which replaced the federal Victoria University in 1903, established the conventions for the 'two-tier' pattern of university government. But even in the twentieth century each university college, as it came of age as a full university, had to establish in its own region a proper equilibrium between the two tiers of government. At one time it seemed that Reading would try a new pattern: a single governing body composed of equal numbers of lay and academic members (the proposal was to have sixteen of each). This proposal was made by W. M. Childs, who was principal of the university college and became the first vice-chancellor, on the grounds that it would simplify business and promote co-operation between laymen and academics and that it was an appropriate mode of government for a university which did not aspire to be as large or as wealthy as the big civic universities. But the proposal was successfully challenged by a minority group of professors, and Reading emerged with the normal 'two-tier' government; indeed one in which academic representation on the council was high compared with that found in some other universities at the time.[25]

In Scottish universities the 'two-tier' pattern (there called court and senatus) dates also from the nineteenth century. It is true that in eighteenth century Edinburgh there was a senatus of professors under the sovereignty of the town council, but its working bore little resemblance to that of the senate in a modern university. The royal commmission of 1831 recommended for Edinburgh a court under the chairmanship of the rector together with a senatus of professors, but it was many years before this pattern was adopted.[26]

In 1939, when the preoccupations of war pushed aside plans for the development of British universities, the pattern of government among British civic universities was set. Apart from Cambridge, London and Oxford, there were eight universities in England, one federal university in Wales, four universities in Scotland and one in Northern Ireland. The charters and statutes of the modern English universities show considerable diversity in detail and a confusing variety of nomenclature, but in principle, and (what is far more important) in the conventions which surround their interpretation, they are remarkably similar. Their general pattern has been admirably summarised by the vice-chancellor of Liverpool University, Sir James Mountford, as follows:

The three major bodies are the court, the council and the senate. The court is the supreme governing authority; it is a large body, often between 300 and 400 in number, containing not only the professors and representatives of the graduates of the university and heads of schools, but persons nominated by other universities, by local authorities and educational organizations within the university area, by religious denominations, and by learned societies. It meets annually to receive the financial accounts and other reports on the work of the university and to appoint certain university officers; it may also meet specially for other purposes; and in most cases it is the body which elects the chancellor. The council, generally containing between 30 and 40 persons, is the body which administers the finances of the university; it confirms the recommendations of senate for academic appointments; usually but not invariably its formal approval is necessary for academic regulations proposed by senate; and in most universities, generally in consultation with the senate, it appoints the vice-chancellor. The largest single element in its composition consists of members appointed by the court; a restricted number is nominated by senate or faculties from amongst the professoriate and other teaching staff, and some are nominated by local authorities; the chancellor and vice-chancellor are *ex-officio* members. The council is thus not a predominantly academic body, though some or many of its lay members may in fact be graduates of a university. Though it has wide powers which could be used to thwart the considered advice and recommendations of the senate, it refrains in practice from interfering in matters of purely academic policy, and in academic appointments: and it is generally agreed that the worldly wisdom and experience of affairs collectively possessed by the council has in many ways brought very considerable advantages to the new universities. The senate, of which the vice-chancellor is *ex-officio* chairman, is, subject to the powers of council, the chief academic body; it approves and co-ordinates the work of the faculties, makes recommendations for the filling of professorships and other academic posts, and is responsible for the teaching and discipline of the undergraduates. Its membership consists of the professors of the university with the addition in most cases of a limited number of representatives of the other teaching staff, who apart from their wide representation on faculties and boards of studies do not have a share in the university government comparable to that afforded by the congregation at Oxford or regent house at Cambridge.[27]

Between 1948 and 1957, five more university colleges were raised by royal charter to the status of universities: Nottingham (1948), Southampton (1952), Hull (1954), Exeter (1955) and Leicester (1957). Their constitutions followed very closely the pattern set by Manchester and Birmingham. In some universities more than others faculty boards play a greater or lesser part in shaping senate opinion; in some more than others departments exercise a powerful anarchy over faculties; in some universities deans are important administrative officers, in others they are simply chairmen of faculties. But in all of them similar conventions are established for the movement of academic business. It flows from below upwards. It originates in departments or faculty boards; it ascends as recommendations to the senate. The senate may hold it up or refer it back; only rarely would the senate change it. If it is approved by senate, it ascends to the council, where its financial implications may have to be examined by a finance committee (presided over by a lay honorary treasurer). Finally (there may be several other steps), it comes to the governing body, the council, as a recommendation to be approved. The council, like the senate, may hold it up or refer it back; it would be a grave breach of convention for the council to change it.

The mechanism of this inverted hierarchy has been discussed elsewhere.[28] Suffice it to say here that it has worked remarkably well. It may be clumsy, but by involving so many of the staff it consolidates among them loyalty to the decisions finally taken. It may be slow, but by exposing issues to so much discussion it often ends in wisdom. It condones inertia, administrators complain against it, it encourages the timid compromise, it is an exasperation to reformers; but it is the natural product of a century and a half of evolution and it has adopted some of the essentials of an academic tradition seven centuries old. To abandon it thoughtlessly would be to put the whole stability of the academic profession in jeopardy.

But evolution cannot be halted. The constitutions of universities must continue to adapt themselves to the changing condition of universities, and it is fair criticism to say that the constitutions of the British universities are not yet fully adapted to the present scale and function of the university system. Even the latest wave of university-founding in Britain does not seem to have thrown up a constitution which meets contemporary needs, though there have been promising minor innovations, some of which we mention below.

There are three shortcomings in the traditional constitutions of British civic universities which are worth noting, for all three of them have been exported to new universities in other parts of the Commonwealth. They are as follows.

The whole trend of evolution in constitution-making in the civic universities has been toward the consolidation of the idea that a university is a society, not a hierarchy. To this extent, modern universities restored a medieval tradition: one purpose of their constitutions was (and still is) to ensure that decision-making on academic matters rested with academics. In the prototype constitution – that of the Victoria University of Manchester – this was assured by giving power to the senate, for although the senate consisted mainly of professors, professors constituted all but a small minority of the permanent academic staff. The intention – that practically all the academic staff should partake in academic government – was therefore achieved.

Today the structure of the academic profession has entirely changed. In the civic universities in 1963 professors constituted less than one eighth of the full-time academic staff.[29] The career grade is the lectureship; there were, in 1963, 6,443 lecturers, together with 2,799 readers and senior lecturers. But constitutions of the civic universities have not been fully adapted to this change in structure, and although these universities now include on senates representatives elected by the non-professorial staff, it can no longer be said (except for Oxford and Cambridge) that the educational business of universities is managed by the whole educational staff: decision-making still rests primarily with the professors. A few years ago it would have been true to say that power was in the hands of a professorial oligarchy. This is no longer generally true, and the constitutions of some of the new universities provide satisfactory opportunities for representatives of the non-professorial staff to share in policy-making.[30] But these welcome adjustments in the 'Manchester' pattern of university government should not be allowed to obscure the fact that in most British universities the responsibilities of government are still concentrated in the hands of a minority of the academic staff; the important point is that this has not come about by deliberate intent as has, for instance, the hierarchical system in American universities. It has happened by default: adaptations of charters and statutes did not keep pace with changes in the structure of the academic profession, with the result that something like two-thirds of university teachers found themselves working under a system of university government which did not anticipate their existence. Over the diffusion of academic control there has been a tendency – even among universities founded since the last war – to preserve the form of the nineteenth century prototypes while departing from the intention inherent in those prototypes.[31]

This is the first shortcoming. It is one which was incorporated into all but one of the colonial university colleges, where (since expatriates predominated on the professoriate) it sometimes led to novel and unfortunate consequences.

A second shortcoming of university constitutions inherited from the nineteenth century is that they fail to legislate adequately for the department. In the constitutions of some of the older civic universities the word 'department' does not occur at all; and even recent constitutions do not define departments in the preamble to their statutes, though all the other units of government – courts, council, senate, academic advisory committee, boards of studies, are defined. Yet it is common knowledge that the department is the real locus of power in a civic university. Among all the cogs and springs which make up the mechanism of the university, the department is the most obvious and substantial, for frequently it is not only a body of people but a building. At its best it is an intensely concentrated society within the wider society of the university, dedicated to research and teaching in its speciality, jealous of its prestige, measuring itself against other similar departments in other universities, involving all its members in decision-making about curricula, examinations, and equipment. At its worst it is a cell of anarchy and autocracy, reluctant to co-operate with the rest of the society, controlled by a despot who, however vigorously he defends academic autonomy at the level of senate and council, is unwilling to concede it at the level of his own more junior staff; he does not consult his lecturers and assistant lecturers about departmental decisions; he rarely holds staff meetings; he rules his department in a way he would never allow a council to rule the senate, or the senate to rule his faculty board. Yet it is at the level of departmental decisions that the young academic can take his first steps in university government; if at this stage he does not learn the art of decision by discussion and consent (which is basic to the stability of universities) he is likely to be clumsy if he is obliged to practise it later on. When the constitutions of civic universities were conceived, subjects were represented by professors, not departments. Therefore no provision was made for what has become the most important administrative unit in a civic university. This is a second shortcoming of the pattern of constitution exported to the colonial university colleges and still widespread in Britain. There is a simple remedy to this shortcoming, namely to prescribe in statutes or regulations that there shall be departmental meetings and that the results of these meetings should be reported to faculty boards. A provision approaching this already appears in the draft constitution of at least one new British university (the Heriot-Watt University in Edinburgh, see ref. 30), but, so far as we can discover, credit for priority should go to an African university; for in the University of Cairo it is laid down that each department must have a council consisting of the professors, assistant professors, and two lecturers; the departmental council must meet at least once a month; it submits minutes of its meetings to the dean and sends its proposals to the appropriate faculty board.[32]

A third shortcoming in the constitutions of civic universities concerns their administrative structure at the apex. The chief executive officer of a civic university is the vice-chancellor. In the larger universities he administers an institution which is spending some £3 millions a year. Any chief executive officer in industry or the civil service with comparable responsibilities would be able to delegate some of them to two or three senior and well-paid full-time administrators. Not so the vice-chancellor of even the biggest civic university. His registrar, bursar, buildings officer and deans all have their statutory duties; they may relieve the vice-chancellor of a great many chores, but he still remains on a solitary pinnacle of responsibility which has no parallel outside universities. Not ten or a dozen, but scores of people, have direct access to him and will not tolerate any intermediary. On academic matters the professors resent anything resembling lay or bureaucratic or 'office' interference; so he must either do the work himself or ask some professor (whose time is already committed to keeping himself up to date in his subject) to help him as a favour. When constitutions were conceived, the principal of a university could run it as a master 'runs' a Cambridge college, depending on the chance encounter in the cloisters, the chat after lunch in hall, to preserve cohesion in the society. And the constitutions of civic universities still embalm that assumption. There can be part-time pro-vice-chancellors, who add a stint of administration to their professorial duties. But any arrangements similar to those made in American universities (i.e. the appointment of full-time vice-presidents who have *ex officio* seats on the main statutory committees of the university) would require changes in statutes, sometimes even changes in charters. So British universities have been very slow to adapt themselves to these circumstances; we believe that only one British university, Birmingham, has a full-time deputy principal. This shortcoming did not affect the colonial university colleges in their early days, when the personal, colourful influence of the principal could reach the whole staff. But this has already become difficult to sustain, and universities in the new Commonwealth countries, like universities at home, will have to adapt their constitutions to the new scale of university finance and organisation.

III CONSTITUTIONS OF SIX AFRICAN UNIVERSITIES

With this introduction we now turn to consider first the constitutions of six African universities (those in Ibadan, Accra, Nsukka, Khartoum, Zaria, and East Africa) which we select by reason of their diversity; then we discuss the conventions for academic freedom and university autonomy which are growing up around these constitutions; and at the end of this discussion we have some observations to make on the measures necessary to preserve the integrity of universities in non-European societies.

As recommended by the Asquith commission, the ordinance for the university college in Ibadan provided for the conventional 'two-tier' constitution of an English civic university: a council with some academic representation but composed predominantly of laymen, and an academic board (equivalent to the senate in an English university) composed of all the professors and a few teachers below professorial rank, to which the various faculty boards reported. But, not surprisingly, the equilibrium between council and academic board came to rest at a point different from that to be found in England.

Although by 1959 thirteen of the twenty-one council members were Africans they naturally had not the experience which council-members in English universities have to interpret the college to the public, and especially to politicians, nor to interpret the needs of the nation to the college. The council's deliberations were inevitably strongly influenced by the views of the expatriate members, including those of the two nominees who came out from Britain for one meeting each year. Furthermore the council's views before the college became independent were influenced by the quinquennial visitations from Britain which inquired into the college's progress and advised on its development over the coming quinquennium.[33]

If Africans had too little influence at the council table, they had still less at the table of the academic board. Even as late as 1961, a year after Nigeria's independence and thirteen years after the opening of the college, the board in Ibadan (by then called senate) had only six Africans out of its thirty members. (This was remedied a year or two later.) In the English civic university this is the body to which all academic policy is delegated. It is not surprising that some leading Nigerians were apprehensive about delegating such responsibility – involving the very pattern of higher education for their future leaders – to a body on which expatriates outnumbered Africans by four to one. The zeal of expatriate professors, anxious to establish in Africa British conventions of university autonomy, was interpreted by some critics as neo-colonialism; their insistence on high standards as intolerance; their engagement with British patterns of education as pedantry. And so the distribution of interests and the mutual confidence between professorial senates and lay councils, which has made the 'two-tier' constitution so successful in English universities, was not reproduced in Nigeria. The most powerful influences at both levels of university governments were academic and expatriate. Since independence the balance has substantially changed, and what might be called the public interest is now more prominent on the university council. But in the early days criticism from the African public most frequently came from outside the council; it was therefore often misinformed and unconstructive. The lay governing body was not sufficiently trusted by the public or by the African government to guide the college into measures to increase its relevance to Nigerian needs.

When the time came for University College, Ibadan, to be transformed into the University of Ibadan, a new act had to be passed in the federal legislature. The mode of preparation of the act was a model of academic rectitude. Drafts for the constitution originated at academic level. They were considered by the council and eventually an agreed draft was sent to the federal government. An attempt was made from outside the college to interfere with the council's recommended draft (this incident is discussed below, p. 322) but the attempt failed; the new constitution embodied in the University of Ibadan Act, 1962, represents the pattern which council and senate wanted.

The new constitution calls for little comment. It retains the basic features of the ordinance under which the college had worked since 1954. It adheres very closely to the traditional constitution of an English civic university, with a clear separation of the functions of council and senate, orthodox provision for tenure of office of the staff, an enlightened degree of representation of academic staff on council and of non-professorial staff on senate. The idea of a congregation, comprising the whole academic staff, introduced as an amendment to the 1954 ordinace[34] is retained, and the congregation elects representatives on council and senate. There are faculty boards which give some administrative experience to most staff members, and these boards elect their own deans. The council is heavily weighted with 'official' appointments: each region, through the regional governors, appoints two persons, and four are appointed by the federal minister of education; but the academic staff appoints six (four from the senate and two from congregation); there is a con-vocation nominee, and four co-opted members. The council makes an annual report to the prime minister which is laid before each house of parliament. The council has already (1966) established confidence in itself as an enlight-ened and statesmanlike body.

The University College of the Gold Coast (later to become the University of Ghana) started off with an ordinance somewhat similar to the one which regulated University College, Ibadan, providing for a predominantly lay council to control financial affairs and to take ultimate responsibility for the college, and an academic board to which educational policy was to be dele-gated. But its first principal, David Balme, superposed on this ordinance a machinery of government which was a Lilliputian version of the machinery to be found in the University of Cambridge. It was a bold and fascinating experiment and it is very relevant to our theme.

To initiate the reader into the mysteries of government of the University of Cambridge is beyond the purpose of this book. Suffice it to enunciate certain basic principles as they are to be found in Cambridge. The first principle is that no-one who is not on the roll of graduates has any voice in the univer-sity's affairs. The second is that sovereignty resides in all the masters of arts resident in Cambridge who take part in the work of the university or its colleges and who by reason of this work are members of the regent house. This is no formal sovereignty. No measure, however trivial, can be enacted unless approved by a majority of masters of arts voting – usually in person and not by ballot – in the Senate House on King's Parade on a Saturday afternoon. This mammoth assembly (if all its members turned up it would number about 1,350) votes on important matters such as salary scales and the founding of a medical school; it votes on unimportant matters, such as whether there should be a urinal outside the Botanic Garden and the procedure to be followed at matriculation ceremonies. Each piece of business brought before the regent house is subject to public discussion beforehand, and the discussions, which are often used as opportunities for displays of the corrosive and futile wit dear to academics, are printed and distributed.

The business of the regent house is prepared by numerous overworked committees. Academic affairs, which elsewhere would be in the hands of a professorial senate, are in Cambridge in the hands of a body called the general board, which (like other central committees in the university) is elected by the rank and file of university teachers. There is no question of an academic hierarchy on the general board. Professors and heads of departments take their chance of election along with any other M.A.s on the roll of the regent house. This is the third principle: that the bodies which prepare policy for the regent house shall not be composed of the most senior officers of the university nor of those who by virtue of their appointments have to carry the most responsibility, but of democratically elected representatives of the faculties.

It was these three principles which were incorporated into the government of the University College of the Gold Coast. The college council – the lay governing body established by law – could not be dissolved without changing the ordinance; but it could be eroded. The process of erosion began in 1951 when the lay council agreed to meet normally only twice a year: once to receive estimates and once to receive a report. By 1954 the government of the college, still *de jure* conducted according to the ordinance, was *de facto* being conducted according to a set of byelaws which followed with touching fidelity the procedures of the University of Cambridge. The Gold Coast government never approved these byelaws; nor was the original ordinance (giving sovereignty to a lay council) amended to conform to them. This working arrangement continued until 1961, when the whole constitution was swept away and replaced by a constitution dictated by the government.

Along with this singular experiment were introduced many other anachronisms and historical survivals of English academic life. The four halls of residence were made self-governing, each with its own byelaws (no two alike) and its officers: master, senior tutor, chaplain, steward to high table. As in Cambridge, the halls and not the university accountant collected the students' fees. The terms (in a country with a considerable animist and muslim population) were labelled Michaelmas, Lent, and Trinity. Grace at table was read in Latin. The purchasing officer was called a manciple.

Within the college the experiment was successful. It had one surpassing merit: it involved every member of the academic staff, once he had reached a modest level of seniority, in the affairs of the college. For a pioneer university institution in Africa this was enormously important, for it gave responsibility (at any rate responsibility to talk and criticise and vote) to African lecturers who, under the conditions of other colonial university colleges, would have had virtually no say in policy-making. Both among Africans and among expatriate staff (most of whom had no administrative experience in British universities) this pattern of government evoked loyalty to the idea of university autonomy and responsibility for maintaining it.

But the experiment overlooked some of the differences between the political environments of Accra and Cambridge. The chief oversight was a neglect of public relations. It would not be unjust to say that the University of Cambridge has no public relations. But Cambridge has the immense distinction of its scholars and the irresistible beauty of its buildings to overcome the image created by its complacent public announcements, the smug effusions of its dons in the correspondence columns of *The Times*, and the myths sedulously cultivated by Cambridge novelists and playwrights. An African university cannot afford the luxury of this cavalier attitude towards its public; it is not sufficient for it to dedicate itself in a detached way to the advancement and dissemination of knowledge; it must persuade the public that this detached dedication is a national necessity. It must educate the public into what a university stands for. Now the channel for this essential activity of the new institution was the college council, which brought together three senior members of the academic staff, two members from British universities, and seven distinguished Africans: judges, members of the legislative assembly, native rulers. This was the body which ought to have interpreted the university to the people and the people to the university, protecting the university against the hot winds of politics and providing for the public a persuasive voice in one of its precious national institutions.[35]

These functions – essential for a pioneer university – were inadequately performed. The college, established now in palatial premises on Legon Hill outside the city, drew its skirts around its affairs and became (as an architect boasted of its quadrangles) 'inward-looking'. The council, having been denuded of its responsibilities, could not be expected to dedicate itself to the public relations of the college. For four years no report from the council was published. By 1953 the chairman of the council felt constrained to say at a meeting that the college was suffering through lack of authoritative public information and that something should be done to dispel the many misconceptions which appeared to exist. The one activity which compensated for these deficiencies was the work of the department of extra-mural studies. This department did succeed in bringing the university alive to hundreds of African citizens, and its services were frequently acknowledged with gratitude in the Ghana press.

In 1959, David Balme's successor tried to abandon this experimental and informal constitution and to substitute one based on the conventional pattern of an English civic university, with authority divided between a predominantly lay council and a predominantly professorial senate. His proposals were thrown to the academic staff for discussion and there followed two long and stormy sessions of debate. The current of opinion in the debate was clear enough: there was among the academics a powerful preference for Balme's experiment and a determination not to retreat to a more conventional constitution. In the eyes of the teaching staff, both African and European, the experiment had justified itself. It continued in a modified form until 1961, when the University of Ghana Act, 1961 was passed, which imposed a new constitution upon the institution and specified that the president of the republic should be chancellor. This constitution represents the first 'indigenous' pattern of university government in Ghana, and therefore its origin and content deserve some analysis.

In preparation for its full and independent university status, the University College of Ghana had for a long time been preparing a constitution. Indeed the astonishingly archaic – but in some ways astonishingly successful – draft constitution which David Balme had devised as long ago as 1953 had anticipated full university status by underlining every word and phrase which would have to be changed if the college were elevated into a university. This constitution was never adopted by the government, although in the form of byelaws the college used it as a working machinery from 1954 until 1961, so effectively that the original ordinance of 1948 was smothered under it. In 1957, Balme's successor as principal was asked to consider the constitution of the college. He proposed a pattern of government which was as much a facsimile of an English civic university as Balme's pattern was a facsimile of Cambridge. It restored sovereignty to a predominantly lay council; over academic affairs it restored power to the professors; it diminished the influence of non-professorial members of staff. It substituted a hierarchy for a democracy. The draft was amended, after the discussions referred to above, to produce a document which incorporated some of the better features of the byelaws under which the college had operated for five years. It was this draft which was sent to the Ghanaian government for approval. It was summarily rejected by Dr Nkrumah who, it is said, himself scribbled 'totally unacceptable' on his copy of the draft.

Meanwhile Dr Nkrumah had received advice on the relations between universities and the state from another source: the international commission (already referred to on p. 281) appointed in 1960 by the Ghanaian government to advise on the development of university education. The commission's proposals about relations between the state and the university rested on two main principles: that Ghanaian universities 'should be able to respond to the immediate and future needs of the community' and 'they should have the greatest possible autonomy in their organization, teaching and research'.[36] To this end the commission proposed that the governing body should be a council consisting of approximately one third of government nominees, one third of persons selected by the senate from among the academic staff, and one third of persons nominated by various educational bodies in Ghana. Academic affairs should be delegated to a senate comprising all heads of departments and in addition two non-professorial representatives from each department, with a further proviso that it would be desirable for each department to have at least one Ghanaian representative on the senate.

These proposals amount to a modified version of the 'two-tier' structure of government in a British civic university. Nevertheless they do involve considerable adaptations to African conditions, although it may well be that these were adaptations conceived by a group of expatriates, for only one member of the commission was a Ghanaian.

The commission's report received a qualified approval from the Ghanaian government;[37] and on 1 July 1961 a University of Ghana bill received its first and second readings in the parliament in Accra.[38] The constitution in this bill can be regarded as an unrestrained African response to the problem of the status of the university in a new African nation. It includes among the aims of the university a frankly political aspiration:

In determining the subjects to be taught emphasis should be placed upon those which are of special relevance to the needs and aspirations of Ghanaians, including the furtherance of African unity.

But the pattern of academic government set out in the constitution gave the university – on paper – a reasonable prospect of autonomy. Traces of the academically democratic structure which distinguished Balme's constitution survived. There was, for example, a good academic representation on council; and a good non-professorial representation on the academic board, intended to enable Ghanaians to become involved in policy-making. Of the fifteen members of council only five (including the council's chairman) were to be directly appointed by the chancellor; though in a one-party state where even civil servants cannot escape the obligation of political alignment, some other of the council members could doubtless be relied upon to toe the party line.

The composition of the governing body is made up as follows:

The principal officers of the University shall be the Chancellor, the Chairman of the University Council, and the Vice-Chancellor ... The President [of the republic] shall hold the office of Chancellor and as such shall be the Head of the University ... The Chairman of the University Council shall be appointed by the Chancellor ... A person shall not be appointed as Vice-Chancellor unless his appointment has been approved by the Chancellor ... The governing body of the University shall consist of the following fifteen members:
(a) the principal officers of the University [the three specified above]
(b) four persons appointed by the Chancellor.
(c) the secretary for the time being of the National Council for Higher Education and Research [by definition a Ghanaian civil servant]
(d) a person selected by a body appearing to the Chancellor to be representative of heads of secondary schools.

As for the rest of the council, its composition is interesting and enlightened; namely, a member elected from an African university outside Ghana, a member elected from a university outside Africa, and four academic members (more than a quarter of the whole council – a generous proportion compared with that in some British universities) of whom two have to be below professorial rank. Altogether there is – on paper – far less government control than Curzon or Raleigh or Harcourt Butler would have tolerated for the Indian universities.

The academic board (the body which elsewhere is called the senate) is clearly only an advisory body to the council (according to the act it advises the council even on the admission of students) but it does seem, according to the statutes which have since been made under the act, to have had delegated to it responsibility for the academic affairs of the university. Its membership includes one sub-professorial representative from each department, and six representatives appointed by convocation. It is a very large body with a quorum of twenty-four, and most of its business will of necessity be done by its executive and finance committees.

We describe below how miserably this constitution failed to preserve autonomy in the University of Ghana; but, contrary to the assertions of some superficial critics, the failure is not due to weakness in the wording of the constitution: it is due to the state's disrespect for the constitution.

The University of Nigeria is the institution founded by Dr Azikiwe. The brief history of its constitution is an instructive lesson in the evolution of African ideas about the government of universities. It begins in 1955 with the enactment of the University of Nigeria Law, 1955, in the Eastern Region, which established on paper what was the first institution of full university status in Nigeria;[39] but only on paper, for it was another five years before the university opened its doors. So far as is known, those who framed the act were innocent of any formal advice from the inter-university council in London, the body whose views were normally sought before the creation of university colleges in British colonial territories. Moreover it was well known that one of the aspirations of the founder of the new university was to break away from the British tradition and to adopt some features of the American land grant college. One might therefore have expected in the act a pattern of government reminiscent of those in (say) Middle West state universities. In fact, however, the provisions for council, senate, and faculties follow almost word for word the 1954 ordinance of University College, Ibadan. The only noteworthy divergences from this very English constitution were (a) appointment of three visitors (all from the Eastern Region: the governor, the premier, and the minister of education) in place of one; (b) greater representation on the council from the Eastern Region than from other regions, at the expense of representation from the senate; (c) provision for twenty 'institutes', vague in function and miscellaneous in coverage, including architecture, domestic science, dramatics, journalism, music, physical education, public health, and secretarial studies; and (d) the appointment of deans of faculties by the council instead of by the faculty boards. The first two divergences indicated that despite its embracing title, the new university was to be a regional rather than a federal institution. The third divergence – the twenty 'institutes' – represented a step toward diversifying higher education and departing from the conventional diet offered by Ibadan. The fourth divergence – appointment of deans by the council – was a straw which showed that the wind of African academic politics was veering toward a more hierarchical and a less democratic quarter. But these divergences were comparatively trivial: the significant fact is that in the 1955 law the constitutional structure of the new university was virtually identical with that of University College, Ibadan; the free and uninhibited drafters of the constitution of Nigeria's first independent university copied the very words devised by the colonial power in London.

But the constitution did not stay this way. In April 1959 the provisional council described in the 1955 act was appointed, though even before then the plans of the Eastern Region government for the new university were well advanced. At that stage it became the provisional council's responsibility, not the Eastern Region government's, to take charge of the planning. This circumstance doubtless precipitated the amendment to the University of Nigeria Law, 1955, which appeared forthwith. Two months after the appointment of the provisional council, on 4 June 1959, a Law to amend the University of Nigeria Law was enacted. It is a very brief document about a few technical points such as auditing, power to co-opt, and investments; and tucked away in it is this sentence, referring to the university's provisional council which, in the act of 1955, was to be 'the supreme governing body' of the university: 'The Minister [of education] may give directions of a general or specific character as to the exercise and performance of [the council's] functions, and the Council shall give effect to such directions.'[40] In brief, sovereignty was transferred from an autonomous provisional council to the minister of education. But this was not the end of the story. On 14 December 1961, the final approval was given to 'a Law to Consolidate the Laws Relating to the University of Nigeria'.[41] The title of the law is singularly inappropriate; far from consolidating the pattern of constitution set out in 1955, it substitutes a totally different one: a constitution modified (according to the preamble) in the light of 'experience gained in operating the university since its inception'. This document is important; to compare its structure with that of the act of 1955 is to observe the very process of university government adapting itself to African conditions; and the process is all the more significant because it is known that the adaptation was performed under the personal supervision of one of Africa's great leaders and intellectuals, Dr Azikiwe.

What, then, is disclosed by the so-called consolidating act of 1961? The objects and powers of the university remain unchanged, and are indeed identical with those drawn up for University College, Ibadan. It is the points of concentration of power which are changed. The university council regains sovereignty over the university: it is no longer subject to directives from the minister of education. In view of the composition of the council this is not surprising; for the council is presided over not by a mere chairman but by an executive chancellor appointed for life, who is none other than Dr Azikiwe, its distinguished founder. The membership of the council has shrunk from nineteen to nine; two of the nine are the chancellor and the vice-chancellor; of the seven members who are not *ex officio*, five are appointed by the Eastern

Region government and the other two represent the academic senate. Even assuming that the vice-chancellor has freedom of action, there is always an overwhelming government majority. Much of the day-to-day business is delegated to a finance and general purposes committee. In the 1955 act not less than two members of this committee were to be academics; in the 1961 act academics are excluded altogether; all the appointed members must be from among the government nominees on council. In the 1955 act provision was made for the customary distribution of power between lay council and academic senate: the function of the senate was to 'manage the educational affairs of the University and to act for the University in all academic matters'. In the 1961 act these functions are withdrawn: the senate is now simply 'responsible to the council' for the supervision of academic matters, and one of its vitally important powers under the 1955 act – to recommend the names of persons to fill vacancies on the academic staff – is withdrawn. Its membership is less democratic too: the 1955 act provided for two non-professorial members elected by all the staff (congregation) and for other co-opted members; the 1962 act withdraws these provisions, and the senate is now reduced virtually to a committee of professors. The faculty boards have their wings clipped: their functions are all subject 'to the directions of the Vice-Chancellor'; so is their composition; and (as the straw blew in the wind in the 1955 act) they are not even permitted to elect their deans: the council does that for them.

The reasons for these changes are set out clearly in a memorandum attached to the draft bill prepared for the 1961 act. It says: 'Whilst the principles of academic freedom are highly cherished and shall be scrupulously maintained and respected in the University, it is essential that the powers of its policy-making sector should be clearly defined.' The powers are indeed clearly defined; not only clearly defined but concentrated in the lay council, and deliberately so, for the memorandum goes on to explain how the excessive concentration of power in the senates of British universities is not appropriate for Nigeria. Academics should not be burdened with executive and administrative responsibilities; they should devote their full time to teaching and research. Power should reside with a body 'the majority of whose members are appointed by the State', for the state represents the electorate and the electorate pays for the university.

Our next example of a university constitution is taken from the University of Khartoum. The conversion of the Gordon Memorial College into a centre of higher education was recommended by the De La Warr commission (which visited the Sudan as well as East Africa in 1937). The war postponed developments and the college ultimately came under the Asquith plan, and in 1946 it entered into special relation with the University of London. The college owed a great deal in its first stages as a university institution to the advice and support of Dame Lillian Penson who subsequently served as vice-chancellor of the University of London. In 1951 the Gordon College combined with the

Kitchener School of Medicine to form the University College of Khartoum; and in 1956 the college was raised to full university status, awarding its own degrees, under the University of Khartoum Act, 1956.[42]

The constitution approved under this act is a statesmanlike document, obviously very carefully drawn up to fulfil two requirements: one, to ensure that the predominantly lay council would be a body mobilising the chief interests and influences in the country, and two, to ensure that the academic staff has a high degree of autonomy over academic affairs. The overall pattern is orthodox: a 'two-tier' government by council and senate; but there are several details worth noting. These are:

(a) The chancellor is appointed by the head of the state *on the nomination of* the university council. This, according to the convention current in Britain, is a formula which prevents the head of state from appointing anyone *not* nominated by the council. (He might – though it would be a very serious step – refuse to appoint someone who *has* been nominated, but he could not substitute any other name.) It puts much more power into the hands of the council than do the formulae 'after consulting' or 'after receiving a report from'.

(b) The council appoints the vice-chancellor, though the chancellor has to consent to the appointment.

(c) The council consists of thirty people only four of whom are nominated by the government (by ministers) and two by parliament. Other bodies which nominate to the council are the Gezira Board (representing agricultural interests), the public service commission, the chamber of commerce, the graduates, and the academic staff. Academic representation is high (eleven out of thirty) and includes two nominations from those teachers not on the senate.

(d) The council cannot create or affiliate colleges or establish or discontinue faculties except after consultation with the senate.

(e) The senate has the usual *ex officio* members (including vice-chancellor, deans, and heads of departments) but it has also seven elected members, one from each faculty. It is unambiguously charged with responsibility for the academic affairs of the university.

(f) All appointments to the academic staff are made by the vice-chancellor on behalf of the council after consultation with a selection committee constituted by him for that purpose. This would be an unusual procedure in Britain; it is very similar to a procedure common in American universities. The selection committees have to include between two and four senate members and they are obliged whenever practicable to consult external assessors.

(g) A member of the academic staff may be dismissed only on account of 'grave misconduct or dereliction of duty in breach of his contract', and only by the finance and general purposes committee of council.

This is as enlightened a constitution as any to be found in English civic universities. Its efficiency as a guarantee of university autonomy is discussed below.

Ahmadu Bello University, in the Northern Region of Nigeria, was established by an act of the regional parliament in June 1962.[43] It is one of the universities recommended by the American-Anglo-Nigerian commission (p. 272). Expatriate influence is still very strong in Northern Nigeria and the new university constitution reflects this; indeed the constitution follows closely a draft proposed by a delegation of the inter-university council from London which was invited to give advice on details of organisation, curriculum, and legislation.[44] It is a very conventional constitution but, in the light of what we have to say later on, it has two interesting provisions for preserving a proper balance of power within the university. One is a provision that statutes can be made, amended, and revoked only by and with the consent of the chancellor, the council, and the senate.[45] Since the chancellor is the head of state within the Northern Region one cannot but see in this provision opportunities for embarrassment; nevertheless, it does spell out the fact that academic opinion must concur in any changes in the university's constitution. The second provision is, as our subsequent discussion will show, a really important safeguard. It concerns the mode of appointment of members of the academic staff.[46] The university council (a predominantly lay body with a good many government nominees) appoints members of staff, but only *on the recommendation of* boards of selection. These boards of selection are constituted by the council but their composition is rigidly determined by statute. Thus for a professorship the board of selection is composed of the vice-chancellor (or his deputy); the chairman of council; two members of council not on the senate; two senate members who are also on council, but nominated by the senate; the appropriate faculty dean; two external experts nominated by the senate who shall not be officers or teachers of the university. This machinery, which is similar to that operating in the university college in Rhodesia, is as good an assurance as could be devised for the proper observance of one of the essential ingredients of a university's autonomy.

The idea that there should be a federated University of East Africa (see p. 262) seems destined to frustration due to the aspirations for political and cultural autonomy of the constituent nations: Kenya, Tanzania, and Uganda. Nevertheless the evolution of the idea of an African federated university, and its proposed constitution, deserve a note.

As long ago as 1954 although the flow of students to the one Asquith college in East Africa, Makerere in Uganda, was not in excess of the places available, there was some pressure to establish institutions of higher education in Kenya and Tanganyika. Kenya already had at Nairobi an inter-territorial college of arts, science, and technology, and the Indian community had collected £200,000 to finance in Nairobi an institution to teach to degree standard arts, science, and commerce. Two delegations from Britain, looking into the future of higher education in East Africa, proposed at that stage cautious development, with Makerere for the time being remaining the prime centre for education at university level, but envisaging sooner or later new institutions in Kenya and Tanganyika.[47] The East African territories at that time still had a strongly colonial character. National movements for independence had not proceeded very far. There was practically nothing which could be described as African public opinion in the territories about university education.

These two delegations made no precise long range proposals for the development of higher education in East Africa; but in 1958, at the invitation of the combined governments of all the East African territories, a working party was appointed under John Lockwood, a man who was to play such a prominent part in encouraging the adaptation of the English university system to African conditions. The working party recommended a University of East Africa, granting its own degrees, to be founded before 1966, with three constituent colleges, all inter-territorial in the sense that they would draw their students from the whole region, and each one of which would be the sole centre for certain kinds of professional education for the whole region. The constituent colleges in Dar-es-Salaam, Nairobi, and Kampala would each be largely autonomous, under a principal; but the policies of the three colleges would be subject to decisions made by a university council and a university senate, composed largely of persons elected by the councils and academic boards of the colleges. Finance would come from contributions made by the separate territories paid into a common services fund and distributed among the three colleges by a grants committee representing all three territories.

The working party's main proposal was accepted. The Royal Technical College in Nairobi was transformed into a constituent college of the University of East Africa; a new university college sprang up with astonishing promptitude in Dar-es-Salaam; and representatives from the three constituent colleges set out to draft proposals for their own constitutions and for the constitutions of the federal university. In 1962 an act was passed by the East African Common Services Organisation creating the university, and in January 1963 it received the assent of the three territories.[48]

The constitution for the university is in principle a facsimile of the constitutions of the constituent colleges. There is the familiar predominantly lay council, including representation from the constituent colleges, the participating governments, the academic staff, and three persons from outside East Africa. The council governs the university but not its colleges: its *de facto* administrative control is therefore merely over a co-ordinating and examining office. The intention was that the principals of the colleges serve in turn as vice-chancellors, though in the event the first vice-chancellor resigned his principalship. There is a senate composed entirely of delegates from the colleges under the vice-chancellor's chairmanship. This has more substantial powers, for it has an oversight of academic standards in all the colleges and it has the power 'to make regulations for adoption by the Council' on admission to degree courses and for standards to be reached for degrees and diplomas. Presumably on this formula the council might decline to adopt the senate's recommendations, but it could not substitute alternatives. For our present discussion the most interesting feature of the constitution of the University of East Africa is the statement, written into the act, that one of the university's objects and functions is:

to preserve academic freedom and, in particular, the right of a university, or a university college, to determine who may teach, what may be taught, how it shall be taught and who may be admitted to study therein.

The constitution provides also that the university should assume responsibility for university education within East Africa. The concept of one degree-granting institution for the whole area is admirable, but federation in universities has always been accompanied by difficulties, and the University of East Africa, even if the political climate gives it a fair trial, is clearly not going to be free from these difficulties. The chief difficulty is a clash of autonomies between the colleges and the university. This has already led to differences in view over the pattern of degree (see chapter 8), over the month in which the academic year should begin, and over other matters which would more easily be solved in a unitary university. One wonders whether central control limited to finance (as happens in Nigeria and Australia) might not be a preferable pattern. Nevertheless there are potential benefits in a federated system; it has worked in Wales, and one hopes that circumstances may allow it to be given a trial in East Africa.

As to the constitutions of the constituent colleges of the University of East Africa, these call for little comment. The senior college, Makerere (to give one example), is governed by an act, similar to those governing the other Asquith colleges, passed in 1949 and amended to bring it into line with the constitution of the university of which it now forms a part.[49] The council has a strong representation, ten in all, of members nominated by the heads of the East African states. The visitor, who is by virtue of the act the president of Uganda, seems to have considerable reserve powers. He can on the council's recommendations revoke or amend the sub-sections which deal with membership of the council, or alter its quorum; and on the recommendation of the council and academic board he can vary the membership of the academic board. The principal of the college is appointed by council but only after consultation with the visitor.

This survey of six university constitutions is, we think, a sufficient introduction to patterns of government in the English-speaking universities of tropical Africa. Patterns of government in the other Nigerian universities, Ife and Lagos, are orthodox and broadly similar to that in Ibadan, though, as we discuss below, the conventions established around the draft constitutions of these two universities have so far been disastrously unorthodox. The

University College at Salisbury, in Rhodesia, has a royal charter, granted in 1955, with statutes which give the academic board power to make recommendations, not merely to submit opinions, to the council on some academic matters; and, as in Northern Nigeria, academic appointments are made on the recommendation of boards of selection.[50] Elsewhere (p. 344) we have something to say about patterns of government in four other African university systems. At this point we turn to discuss academic freedom and university autonomy in the English-speaking countries of tropical Africa.

IV ACADEMIC FREEDOM AND AUTONOMY IN AFRICAN UNIVERSITIES

There is very little evidence indeed that academic freedom (*Lehrfreiheit*) in the precise sense in which the expression is defined on page 291 of this chapter, has been curtailed at any time in any university in the African Commonwealth countries. There have occasionally been complaints and tensions about the teaching of some academics, but we doubt whether there are any well-authenticated cases of teachers being victimised for opinions they have expressed in the classroom. If the definition of academic freedom is broadened to cover the right of academics to hold political opinions distasteful to the government, then cases have occurred; but not always due to Africans. It was, for instance, not Africans but the British colonial government in Tanganyika which in 1958 tried to dictate to Makerere who should speak (and, more significantly, who should not) and on what topics, at a seminar the university college was asked to arrange for a group of American foreign service officials.[51] And it was the white Rhodesian federal government which in 1963 prevented a lecturer in history at the University College of Rhodesia and Nyasaland from carrying out his duties, solely on account of his views on racial segregation and local politics. The university college defended the lecturer with firmness and dignity, but he had to leave the country.[52] Shortly after Rhodesia declared itself to be independent it displayed a disgraceful contempt for the autonomy of the college at Salisbury, witness the indictments published in a letter to the London *Times* on 30 December 1965. It is ironic that the most shocking examples of scorn for the integrity of universities on the African continent should have come from white governments in Rhodesia and South Africa, not black governments. But Africans are not blameless. In the University of Ife, in Nigeria, the dean of the school of agriculture, Dr Oyenuga, was dismissed by the provisional council, apparently for insubordination to the vice-chancellor; but the dismissal undoubtedly had political overtones, and eight other members of the academic staff, including expatriates, resigned in protest against Oyenuga's dismissal. The dismissed dean and four of the lecturers who resigned were subsequently awarded damages and costs against the provisional council by an Ibadan high court. There is little doubt that the unrest at Ife was an attack on the civil rights of politically minded academics, not on their academic freedom.[53]

The very serious disturbances in the universities of Ghana and Lagos, which we discuss below, are interferences with university autonomy rather than with academic freedom. All in all, if one considers academic freedom in the sense in which it is defined in this chapter, the African countries may be said to have accepted it as part of the 'package deal' included in a western university; but they have not yet related it to the needs of African society and they are suspending judgement on its necessity. A distinguished Nigerian academic, Dr Eni Njoku, puts it this way:

The modern university scholar is an entirely new type of person in Nigeria, not identified with any traditional role. The condition for such a type to flourish, such as academic freedom, is therefore an entirely new conception. Nevertheless, the principle of academic freedom has been accepted in Nigeria, not by itself, but as part of a university organization. Nigerians demanded a university as good as those existing anywhere else in the world. If academic freedom is a necessary element in such universities, then it must exist in the Nigerian institution too. . . . Although the principle of academic freedom is accepted, it is important to realize that it has still to justify itself in the Nigerian context. It is not easy to argue that academic freedom is necessary in order to train the professional manpower required by the Nigerian society. On the contrary . . . this is the very reason why an insufficiently perceptive university should be given directions by the Government. . . . The really cogent arguments for academic freedom . . . although applicable to Nigeria, are derived from other situations. The scholar has not yet fully arrived in Nigeria, and the advantages to be gained by giving him freedom are not yet obvious. . . . At present it is merely one of the embellishments attached in its country of origin to an imported product.[54]

Academic freedom is a simple privilege accorded to university teachers to enable them to do their job. There is a very strong case for asserting that it cannot vary with latitude, race, politics, or creed. A country where political doctrine or commitment to a religious creed interferes with academic freedom cannot have free scholarship or good universities. By contrast university autonomy does not always and everywhere assume the same pattern. Every nation needs to have some concordat between the state and the university to safeguard the autonomy of universities, and in each nation the concordat is likely to be different. The concordat adopted for the colonial university colleges about which we are writing was, of course, the British pattern unchanged; it was assumed that the conventions would be exported with the formularies. This assumption was by and large correct while colonial governments were in the hands of British officials (though even then there were occasions when the officials wanted the colleges to be run on civil service procedures). Since African countries have become independent, the assumption is no longer correct. University autonomy now needs to be redefined for these countries and new arrangements are needed to safeguard autonomy.

To illustrate the discussion we offer a few examples of the ways in which university autonomy has been under attack in some African countries. From these examples we make a tentative diagnosis and we suggest possible remedies.

The University of Ibadan has been free from serious inroads on its autonomy, but this has been due to skilful handling of delicate situations rather than to a general acquiescence in its independence. The pioneer principal, Kenneth Mellanby, writes vividly about the ill-informed and sometimes malicious criticism which fell upon the college in its early days and under which the college had patiently to preserve its integrity.[55] More indicative of hidden dangers, though it was the voice of a dissident and irresponsible minority, were the opinions put out in an Action Group policy-statement for higher education, in 1958. Under the sub-title 'The myth of academic autonomy', it asserts:

Every time suggestions are offered by outside bodies for certain actions to be taken by the University College for the good of Nigeria the reply invariably comes that the University College is an 'autonomous institution' which would not submit to 'dictation' by any outside body. This sort of reply is, of course, sheer nonsense because no estate within a State can be absolutely autonomous. . . . This most frequently used word: *autonomy* is purely mythical. It is well known that institutions of higher education all over the world are meant to reflect, and generally do reflect, the national aspirations and needs of the countries in which they are situated. . . . Now who determines, in the first instance, what interests each University should reflect? Certainly it is not the University itself. It is the wishes of the community in which it is situated. The community makes known its demands and the university merely supplies the demands.[56]

Since the author of this manifesto illustrates his argument by asserting that the University of Manchester responds to community demands by teaching textile chemistry and Oxford and Cambridge respond by teaching classics, the depth of his misunderstanding can be guessed. But this is the significant point: that the purpose and operation of university autonomy in Britain should be so misunderstood, ten years after it had been introduced in Nigeria. This misunderstanding, by an author known to be a graduate of a British university, is a sign that university autonomy needs interpreting in the context of African politics.

Another sign that African opinion, even though it might be minority opinion swayed by politics, is questioning imported assumptions about university autonomy, is given by an episode which followed the submission to the federal government by Ibadan of a draft for its constitution as an independent university. The draft (a sound, if orthodox, document) has been described above. It was a document agreed by the college council. But the chairman of council at that time (he has since retired), an African whose interests involved him in politics, disliked the draft. He expressed his misgivings on the grounds that the new university would be a state university and that its constitution and policies should reflect the aspirations of the federal government; and he warned the council that the government would make any alterations in the draft constitution it wished or deemed necessary, notwithstanding the recommendations of the council. He then prepared a memorandum for the federal minister of education and the attorney general, which set out clearly what in his opinion (after he had consulted the visitor, who was the governor general of Nigeria) the federal government's policy touching university constitutions ought to be.

The memorandum discloses clearly the trend of thought about university autonomy in the minds of some Nigerians: doubtless only a minority but an influential minority. After explaining how in British civic universities the powers vested in the senate are almost totalitarian, the memorandum goes on to point out how in the Nigerian context the senior members of the academic staff who constitute the senate should devote their full time to scholarship and research. Academic freedom, says the memorandum, can be safeguarded without burdening the senate with executive and administrative responsibilities; these responsibilities should not be the concern of academics in a modern university. Consequently the control of policy should be vested in a council, the majority of whose members are appointed by the state. The memorandum declares that universities in Nigeria can no longer follow the pattern of the former suzerain of the colonial Nigeria, nor can the university senate any longer be used as an instrument for controlling the higher education of colonial peoples. In conformity with the above principles the memorandum went on to ask for a dozen major changes to be made in the draft constitution, notwithstanding the fact that the draft had already been agreed by the college council and submitted to the federal government for legislation. The changes, if adopted, would have established the governor general as chancellor, with power to appoint the vice-chancellor; cut down senate representation on council from four to two; rejected the proposal that congregation (the whole academic staff) should have two representatives on council and that convocation (the body of graduates) should have one; and withdrawn the power of council to co-opt members. Furthermore the memorandum proposed changes which would have removed from the council the power to appoint the chancellor and vice-chancellor and its own vice-chairman.

For some months the fate of the draft constitution remained in suspense. But in the end the federal government rejected the changes proposed in the memorandum from the chairman of the council and adopted the draft prepared by the university college.[57] Two lessons are to be learnt from this incident: the first, that the federal government, although in some embarrassment, behaved with complete propriety toward the college and respected its autonomy; the second lesson is that the memorandum, though shocking, was within the letter of the law, for according to the ordinance under which the college was still working, the visitor can take what steps he likes to ensure the fulfilment of the objects of the college and to this end the chairman of the council would be obliged to take instructions from him. What had been flagrantly transgressed by the chairman of the council was not a law but a convention. The British pattern of constitution simply cannot be worked if this convention is disregarded.

A second example comes from the University of Lagos. This university was set up by the federal government in 1962 under legislation provided by the University of Lagos Act, 1962. It was one of the new universities recommended by the American-Anglo-Nigerian commission. On the personal invitation of the prime minister of Nigeria, one of the nation's most remarkable scholars, Eni Njoku, gave up his professorship at Ibadan to accept the office of first vice-chancellor. Under Njoku the university made an excellent start: able and enthusiastic scholars were recruited to the staff; enterprising courses of study were devised; admirable buildings were put up; within a couple of years the university was the object of gratifying international confidence.

The act of 1962 was intended only to be temporary. It provided for the usual 'two-tier' pattern of government: a provisional council of eleven members nine of whom were the appointees of federal ministers and one was *ex officio* the permanent secretary of the ministry of education, and an academic senate which had power 'to give such directions as it thinks fit for the administration of the University'. The act required the provisional council to make within two years a report to the prime minister recommending a constitution for the university. It stated that the first vice-chancellor would hold office for three years, but would be eligible for reappointment. The procedure for appointing all but the first vice-chancellor was one common in Britain: according to clause 6(4) of the act the appointment was to be made by the council 'after consideration of a report of the senate'.[58]

The provisional council, in accordance with the act, and having been given an extension of time by the prime minister, produced on 30 November 1964 a unanimous report which had the complete agreement of the senate. This was sent to the prime minister. The report is a model of clarity and precision.[59] It sets out in its preamble two principles underlying the draft constitution: (i) the university 'ought to reflect the unity of the country and ought to serve, first and foremost, the needs of the State'; and (ii) in order to enjoy international recognition the university 'must have ample freedom to run its own affairs. ... Therefore the relation between the Council and the Senate has been adjusted to ensure autonomy in academic matters.'[60]

There is nothing particularly noteworthy about the draft constitution. It follows closely the English civic university pattern. The significant sentence for the incident we have to describe is one which states 'the first vice-chancellor shall be Eni Njoku . . .'[61] Anyone familiar with the draft charters and statutes of the new British universities knows exactly what this form of words means: it is a statement of intention that the person named will be confirmed as vice-chancellor under the new constitution.

The draft constitution was sent to the federal government for enactment, but by December 1964 the legislature was preparing for a general election, and business was held up. The constitution therefore did not reach the legislature until after the elections. It was laid on the table on 17 February 1965. Meanwhile the elections had brought a change in the alignment of political parties. In the new government the NPC, predominant in the Northern Region, was now allied with the NNDP, which is the ruling party in the Western Region, dominated by Yorubas; and the NCNC, which controls the Eastern Region and which is dominated by Ibos, was now in opposition.

The chairman of the provisional council of the university was a Westerner; so was a majority of his council. The vice-chancellor was an Easterner. The Westerners involved in the crisis which was about to fall upon the university indignantly deny that the crisis was due to tribal politics, but impartial and trustworthy observers are in no doubt whatever that part of the price being paid for a Western-Northern political alliance was to put Yorubas into some of the key posts in the country. Apparently the vice-chancellorship of Lagos was one of these posts; indeed it was mentioned by an NNDP spokesman during the election campaign as a post which ought to go to a Yoruba. The post was to fall conveniently vacant because under the terms of the 1962 act Eni Njoku's three-year term of office was due to expire on 31 May 1965, although he was specifically eligible for reappointment.

On 28 January 1965, the senate was asked by the registrar on the instructions of the chairman of council to submit a report on the vice-chancellorship in accordance with section 6(4) of the act.[62] The council asked for the senate's report to 'embody a list of three or more suitable candidates for the consideration of the provisional council'.[63] Since both council and senate had agreed to include Eni Njoku's name in the draft act for the new constitution completed three months earlier, this request, though it was not inconsistent with the letter of the law, and might have been just a formality to satisfy section 6(4) of the act, nevertheless aroused the suspicions of the senate. Why were three names asked for? If three names were put up by senate, even if one was given absolute priority, would this not be an opportunity for the council to appoint any one of three people and to say they had senate support for doing so?

In this atmosphere of misgiving (which proved to be completely justified) the senate met on 18 February and reported as follows:

(i) In accordance with the request of the chairman of the Provisional Council, the Senate has given careful consideration to the submission of names for appointment as vice-chancellor.

(ii) The Senate is convinced that failure to reappoint the present Vice-Chancellor would be a grave, and possibly fatal, blow to the continued successful building of the University.

(iii) Accordingly, the Senate recommends to the Provisional Council that Dr Eni Njoku, the present Vice-Chancellor, be re-appointed until normal retirement age.[64]

The council was due to meet to consider this report eight days later, on 26 February; but, without informing the vice-chancellor (who was a member of

council) and, it is said, taking advantage of the fact that the senate's representative on council would be out of the country, the registrar summoned a
council meeting for the following day, 19 February. At this meeting, the names
of three 'candidates' for the vice-chancellorship were put forward: '(i) E.
Njoku (nominated by the Senate); (ii) S. D. Biobaku (nominated by a member
of the Council); (iii) F. O. Dosekun (nominated by a member of the Council).'[65] The standing orders of council require seven days' notice for a
meeting; so after some discussion the meeting was adjourned. The council
met again on 26 February. By this time Dosekun had withdrawn. Biobaku,
a Yoruba, was elected vice-chancellor by seven votes to three. The votes in
favour of Biobaku followed tribal expectations.[66]

In the crisis that followed the bulk of the students revolted in favour of
Njoku, and disregarded his attempts to persuade them to be loyal to the new
vice-chancellor. The university had to be closed. The senate and the association of university teachers in Lagos protested vehemently, and in the end
fifty out of seventy-five members of the staff resigned. Strong representations
were made to the prime minister who deplored the situation but felt unable to
intervene in what he regarded as the domestic affairs of the university. With
these consequences, and with the grave damage to a very promising university,
we are not here concerned. But two points need to be added. The first is that
at no stage was any dissatisfaction expressed about Njoku's work as vice-
chancellor: indeed one heard nothing but golden opinions about him from
Nigerians irrespective of tribal origin; and he has as high a reputation overseas as any Nigerian living. The second point is that only a few days before
these events it was announced that Biobaku had accepted an invitation to
become vice-chancellor of the University of Zambia.

We describe this incident in some detail again in order to draw two lessons
from it. One is similar to the lesson drawn from the challenge to the draft
constitution at Ibadan, namely that on a literal and legalistic interpretation of
the provisional constitution it could be asserted that the university's autonomy
had not been infringed. The only document binding the council was the 1962
act. The vice-chancellor's term of office ended on 31 May 1965. The council
did 'consider a report of the senate'; the act does not oblige the council to
follow the senate's recommendation. As for the new draft constitution, which
cited Njoku as first vice-chancellor, it had not become law, and – according
to the sophistry of some of the council members – even if it had become law,
the citation could be said to refer to Njoku's first term of office, which was
due to expire on 31 May 1965! As over the threatened interference with the
constitution for Ibadan, so in Lagos: what had been flagrantly disregarded
were conventions which in Britain are inseparable from constitutions. The
vice-chancellor's term of office had been abruptly ended without any cause
shown, and in defiance of the senate's recommendation. A new vice-chancellor
had been appointed without consultation with the senate and on whom the
senate had made no report. The normal procedure in Britain on the very

rare occasions when council and senate disagree – namely long and patient consultation between the two bodies – had been rejected.

The second lesson is that at Lagos the autonomy of the university was wrecked from within, by its own provisional council, not by government interference. Indeed, it was an occasion when it might have been better if the government had interfered. But the minister of education, Mr Akinjide (secretary of the NNDP), in reply to parliamentary demands for a commission of enquiry, disingenuously took refuge behind the statement: 'Our universities are established primarily and in many respects, on the lines of British institutions. It is not the policy of the government to intervene unduly in the affairs of the universities.'[67] The federal government undoubtedly could have persuaded the provisional council to rise above political and tribal considerations when appointing a vice-chancellor. It was not willing to do so; and the council members were too weak, or too committed to tribal politics themselves, to respect the wishes of the senate or to put the university above their outside loyalties.

It should be on record that the academic staff made prolonged and courageous efforts to defend the university against this betrayal from inside, but they received no response from council or government. On 14 June the provisional council dismissed five of the deans; on the following day forty-five members of the academic staff (about three quarters of the whole) resigned or asked their sponsoring authorities to recall them; 150 out of 338 students, by July 1965, indicated that they would not return to the university. In an open letter to the Nigerian people, fifty-one members of the staff who were dismissed, or resigned, or had asked for recall said:

A promising young university lies mortally stricken ... We cannot see any significant distinction between discriminating against a man in Nigeria merely because he belongs to a particular ethnic group, and discriminating against a man elsewhere because he happens to be a Jew, or a Negro, or a Catholic ... in the interests of Nigeria, we cannot tolerate political or tribal interference in academic life.[68]

The third example of the state of opinion over university autonomy is taken from Ghana. We have already (p. 312) described the present constitution of the University of Ghana. The impact of the Ghanaian government on its universities has been described by eye-witnesses who have experienced its operation. With great sympathy and understanding, Adam Curle has traced the melancholy story which first became notorious in 1959, a couple of years after independence.[69] At that time Dr Nkrumah's office issued directives to the university college requiring changes in the system of leave-passages to Britain, and in other matters internal to the college. The college staff, 'constantly on the alert for infringements of academic freedom', resisted these directives. The attacks from the government were not pressed home; they were (Adam Curle says) 'more like the skirmishes of a reconnaissance party testing defensive strength, than actual assaults'. As the college mobilised (sometimes none too tactfully) its defences, the government came to regard it – especially its students – as a focus of dissent and a threat to the solidarity of the new nation. The expatriate academic staff were said by politicians who criticised them 'to do no work which was of the slightest use to Ghana, and worst of all to pervert the flower of her youth, filling their minds with pernicious non-African rubbish'.[70] The ideals of high quality and disengagement from political affairs for which the first principal, David Balme, had worked so effectively, were dismissed as machinations of neo-colonialism. The first real assault on the autonomy of the college occurred in May 1961, shortly before the college achieved the status of an independent university. The circumstances are best described in the words of an eye-witness.[71]

Then late in May an undated letter (actually despatched on the 22nd of the month) was received by the Principal from the President's Office. The main burden of this communication was that in the circumstances of transmuting the University College into a University 'all appointments of members of the academic staff will automatically be terminated'. Those who wished to apply for re-appointment must do so by 10th June. A further letter dated 27th May indicated that persons would be re-appointed without re-applying, but that it might 'be necessary to terminate certain appointments and to revise the conditions of service of others.'

These letters and the exchanges, both official and unofficial, to which they led, indicated that the President had at last decided to intervene in the affairs of the College, to get rid of persons who were for one reason or another undesirable, and to arrange for closer Government (or party) control of the institution.

This clumsy intervention provoked a storm of protest not only within the college but from other parts of the world. The Ghanaian leaders realised they had blundered and over the next few weeks they tried to smooth the matter over and to offer reasonable contracts to the great majority of the academic and administrative staff. But in the event six appointments were terminated, including that of the Ghanaian registrar and master of Commonwealth Hall, M. Dowuona. 'What mattered', as Adam Curle wrote, 'was not the number: it was the fact that the Government had established a precedent for ending academic employment on non-academic grounds.'

Two months later, in July 1961, the University of Ghana bill was introduced in the Ghanaian parliament. At that time in Ghana freedom of speech had not been stifled, and during the debate Mr Appiah is reported to have said:

Now it is said in clause 11 of the bill that internal organisation of the University shall be left in the hands of the University Council. I sincerely trust and hope that the Government mean what they have here (sic) in this Bill because we did have a University Council for the University College of Ghana at Legon and yet we know for a fact that directives came over their heads, sometimes reaching the goal of their object before even the University Council itself had occasion to hear about them. This kind of thing will not do and if they want to set up a truly independent University they must make sure that every clause set out in this Bill is respected. . . .[72]

Speaking in the debate the minister of agriculture, Kojo Botsio, who had been chairman of the commission on the university, reassured his listeners by reminding them that the government's intention, endorsed in the white paper, was that universities in Ghana, while serving the country's needs:

must be free, within the limits of the funds available to them, to plan their own programmes of teaching and research, pursue their own methods of instruction, appoint their own teachers, maintain their own standards.[73]

He went on to give an assurance that the university council would not 'exercise direct Government control over the University' though at the same time it 'will not be open to the charge of being a society for the preservation of Ivory Towers'.

The morale of the university was restored in the autumn of 1962 by the appointment of Conor Cruise O'Brien as vice-chancellor. For three years, with masterly skill and extraordinary patience, O'Brien worked to preserve autonomy in the university and to ensure that it served Ghana's needs. From the beginning he affirmed his belief that there was nothing in the university's constitution inimical to autonomy; and at his last address to congregation, when he had finally decided that he could do no more to help the university and would have to resign at the end of his contract, he reiterated this belief. Here is a passage from the address:

Now the autonomy of this University is on paper well established. The report of the 1961 Commission on University Education rests on two main principles: 'that Universities should be able to respond to the immediate and future needs of the community and that they should have the greatest possible autonomy in their organisation, teaching, and research.' The principles of the Commission's report were accepted by the Government and are embodied in the University of Ghana Act.[74]

In preparing the statutes under the new constitution a proper procedure was followed: the draft was considered and amended by the academic board and was before the council in February 1963 with the recommendation by an overwhelming majority that the draft should be approved.

But it was not long before things went wrong. Notwithstanding their assurances the government were constantly meddling with matters which clearly lay within the province of the university. Three examples must suffice to illustrate this. First, they meddled with standards. In April 1962 the university was informed that the Ghanaian cabinet, after consulting the national council for higher education and research, decided that in view of the fact that there were at that time more places at the universities than could be filled by the students available, there was no justification for the holding of separate entrance examinations. The possession of a school certificate should be accepted as a qualification for entry to the university. The cabinet therefore decided that the holding of university entrance examinations should be discontinued. Later in the same year Dr Nkrumah announced that English language should be abolished as a compulsory subject for the purpose of obtaining a West African school certificate for Ghanaian candidates and that the 230 Ghanaian candidates who were failed in the 1962 school certificate examination because they did not pass in the English language paper should be granted passes, provided they qualify for a pass in all the other subjects.

A second example of interference was over the appointment of professors. The government white paper on the report of the university commission stated that it intended to provide for a special category of professorship to bring distinguished scholars to Ghana from all parts of the world.[75] This sounds as innocent and as acceptable as (say) the research professorships sponsored by the Royal Society of London. At the first meeting of the interim council of the university in June 1961, Dr Nkrumah announced the establishment of these special professorships. On 2 December 1961 it became clear how this provision was to be used: it was announced to the council that the head of state had appointed a junior member of the department of law, Mr A.C. Kuma, to be a special government professor of law. It was emphasised that he would not be a member of the academic staff nor would he be responsible to anyone except the head of state nor have direct access to anyone else in the university save through the vice-chancellor. A month later, Dr Nunn May, already on the staff of the physics department, was appointed a government professor of physics, and came under the direct jurisdiction of the head of state. Both these appointments completely disregarded the university's right to decide on the status to be accorded to its academic staff.

The third example of interference was over the very organisation of studies in the university. In February 1962 a presidential command suddenly lifted the faculty of agriculture from the university in order to attach it to the Kwame Nkrumah University of Science and Technology at Kumasi.

The university was understandably indignant about these incidents. Over one incident – the rape of the faculty of agriculture – the academic board presented a firm and dignified memorandum to the university council, expressing concern, saying the command could have been carried out more effectively if the academic board had been consulted beforehand, and urging that machinery should be set up for harmonising views and policies between the university and the government, to be used by the government on matters affecting the university's responsibilities. The council at this point might have supported its academic staff in an approach to the government. It did not do so. It considered the suggestions were not in good taste, received them, and decided it was inexpedient to act on them. The next step was that Dr Nkrumah, as chancellor, wanted to approve all appointments to headships of departments. Criticism against the university, obviously officially inspired, mounted. On 8 January 1964 six members of the academic staff were expelled: four Americans, a West Indian and an Englishman. The reason given was that they had been 'indulging in subversive activities prejudicial to the security of the state', and the press charged one of the victims, W.B. Harvey, an American who was dean of the faculty of law, with having discussed apartheid in his lectures; so there was an element of infringement of academic freedom, too, in the expulsion. Immediately following this, Dr Nkrumah instructed the vice-chancellor to appoint three named Ghanaians to the headships of the departments of philosophy, law, and political science. This the vice-chancellor refused to do, on the grounds that none of the persons named was fit to be made head of a department, and that in any case the procedure for making appointments was laid down by the council and had to be followed. In his address to congregation in March 1964 the vice-chancellor referred to these infringements of autonomy with great firmness and delicacy, supporting his argument with quotations from one of Nkrumah's speeches.[76] O'Brien's speech drew nineteen columns of pseudo-philosophical censure in the Accra socialist weekly, *The Spark*.[77]

In O'Brien's last year as vice-chancellor (1964–5) he had to defend the university against further invasions of its autonomy. One assault, indirect but no less exasperating, was the appointment of a committee, under the chairmanship of the professor of philosophy (a notoriously zealous disciple of Nkrumah) with powers to inspect publications in bookshops and the libraries of schools, colleges, and universities, to ensure the removal from the country of publications which do not reflect the Party's ideology. The other, direct, assault on autonomy was a 'Presidential Command'[78] to the vice-chancellor removing the institute of education forthwith from the University of Ghana to the University College of Cape Coast, some hundred miles away. Although the institute was a statutory part of the University of Ghana, the university authorities were not consulted about the move. The academic board of the university asked the council to protest; but this the council was not prepared to do, because the decision had already been taken by the government. As O'Brien put it in his 1965 congregation address: 'the internal structure of the University was changed by a Government decision, its organisational autonomy disregarded and its constitutional processes overridden.'[79] But notwithstanding these events O'Brien repeated in 1965 what he had said in 1964, that:

The Constitution of the University, the Act and our University Statutes which, although of recent enactment by our Council, enshrine principles of academic freedom which are very old, will be respected and our academy will flourish.[80]

The Ghanaian Times pelted O'Brien's address, and O'Brien personally, with the clumsy invective to which some African newspapers descend when those who control them are angry or are instructed to be offensive: 'Can Legon be a State within a State?' 'Academic Freedom or Academic Blackmail?' 'O'Brien . . . no longer the faithful he was'. [81] But embedded in this rubbish there is a point of view very significant for our discussion. The editorial of *The Ghanaian Times* for 3 April 1965 quotes the passage from the University of Ghana Act which sets out that Dr Nkrumah as president of the republic 'shall hold the office of Chancellor and as such shall be the Head of the

University'; it then quotes the passage which says that 'a person shall not be appointed as Vice-Chancellor unless his appointment has been approved by the Chancellor'. It then proceeds to draw two conclusions which (after long experience of discussing such matters with Africans) we do not feel inclined to dismiss as mere prevarication. The first conclusion the editorial draws is that Dr Nkrumah, 'as head of the University', has under the act the right to participate in its direction ('the Chancellor cannot be deemed to interfere with an institution of which he is the head'). The second and somewhat less evident conclusion is that since the chancellor has to approve the appointment of the vice-chancellor, the vice-chancellor is his employee, obliged to carry out his requests.

The speeches Conor Cruise O'Brien made during his tenure of the vice-chancellorship contain the most constructive and scholarly statements which have hitherto been made about academic freedom and university autonomy in a developing African state. They will doubtless be remembered in Ghana. They have certainly educated some Ghanaians to understand why universities must have some measure of self-government. They may one day help to restore the integrity of the university – now deeply in eclipse. But the melancholy history of the university since 1961 has its lessons for us. First, although O'Brien was quite correct in saying that the autonomy of the university is on paper well established, this is no guarantee of autonomy. The charters of most British universities state that the chancellor is head of the university[82] and in some universities it is the chancellor who appoints his vice-chancellor. The lesson is that in Africa constitutions stripped of their conventions, far from being safeguards, can be positively dangerous. Another lesson is that the lay-members of council, who in an English university regard themselves as inside, and part of, a self-governing society, in Africa cannot be assumed to have this attitude; that is why the council in Ghana did not support its own academic board over the removal of the institute of education. As in Lagos, the autonomy of the university was not only attacked from outside, it was betrayed from inside.

The next example we discuss has a happier ending. We have already described the enlightened constitution of the University of Khartoum, given to it in 1956. In November 1958 a military regime seized power in the Sudan. At first this did not have any adverse effect on the University of Khartoum. The military junta displayed that indulgent tolerance which soldiers sometimes show toward intellectuals; they let the university alone and financed it generously. But, as symptoms of dictatorship appeared and democratic rights were withdrawn, the voice of criticism against the government grew louder and, not surprisingly, a good deal of this criticism came from students and staff in the university. The council of the armed forces brought pressure to bear on the vice-chancellor to crush this criticism and to persuade students and staff to keep out of politics. The vice-chancellor firmly but diplomatically defended the right of free speech in his university. Relations between the university and the military regime deteriorated. It was suspected that the university administration and some of the staff were conniving at the demonstrations, pamphlets, and posters against the government which the students were continually producing. If the university could not discipline its members, the government would have to intervene.

This was the background to the University of Khartoum (Amendment) Act passed in 1960.[83] The purpose of the act was to put the government into a position to exert direct control over the university's administration. Its main amendments to the 1956 act were these:

(1) 'The Head of State shall be the Chancellor of the University' (formerly the head of state appointed the chancellor on the nominations of the university council).

(2) The vice-chancellor 'shall be appointed by the Chancellor after consultation with the council' (formerly he was appointed by the council, with the chancellor's consent).

(3) The composition of the council was changed, strengthening the hand of the government and reducing the influence of the graduates and the academic staff.

This, of course, only increased resentment in the university, though it did not in fact make any difference at the time to the administration. The vice-chancellor remained in office and remained unswervingly loyal to the academic society.

In September 1963 trouble broke out again. During a meeting of the heads of African universities in Khartoum the students staged a demonstration against the military regime. The regime, always easily nettled by intellectuals, lost its temper and threatened to 'take over' the university. The university played for time by asking for clarification of the expression 'take over'. The reply was that the minister of education would have to become one of the 'authorities of the university' and it would be one of his responsibilities to recommend to the chancellor (the head of state) the name of the vice-chancellor. The minister of education was to have the right to 'enquire' about administration and discipline in the university. These threatened amendments were in fact never made. For nine months there was seething discontent but no open rebellion until on 30 September 1964 the government communicated to the university an order banning all public lectures or discussions over the problems of the Southern Sudan, the Achilles heel of the military regime. The students promptly announced a seminar on 'The scientific assessment of the problem of the South', to be held on 10 October. The police entered the university, broke up the meeting and arrested the student president and secretary. This was a clear, but rare, case of an infringement of *Lernfreiheit*, for the students were being forcibly prevented from discussing a topic of intense interest to them.

The rest of the story is well known:[84] more meetings about the South; more police intervention and a student killed; mass resignation of the Sudanese staff as a protest against interference with free speech in the university; resignation of the vice-chancellor: all of which precipitated the collapse of the military regime. The military government resigned. By the end of October 1964 a caretaker government was formed, to prepare for a general election. One of the first decisions of the caretaker government was to abolish all amendments to the University of Khartoum Act, 1956, and to return to the university's original constitution. The university council appointed as a result of the 1960 amendments was dissolved, and a new council set up under the original act.

This story, too, has its lessons: that the most enlightened university constitution (for such it was) is quite useless as a defence of autonomy when it can be altered by the stroke of a pen; but where, as in Khartoum, students and staff are prepared to be uncompromising over what they consider to be the essential freedoms of a university, they can, provided they are not betrayed by their own lay governing body, get their own way. Certainly without the high degree of internal cohesion which the University of Khartoum enjoyed, its autonomy would not have been so promptly restored.

The last example is the University of Nigeria, whose constitution differs from those of the other universities we have selected for discussion. The council is small and is presided over by an executive chancellor. The vice-chancellor has much more statutory power than is accorded in the English pattern of constitution; indeed the act invests him with most of the powers which in England are delegated to the senate. He is obliged to consult the senate over the admission of students, the organisation of courses, and the holding of examinations, but he is not obliged to accept the senate's advice.

This formal allocation of power between lay council, the administration (personified by the vice-chancellor), and academic staff is a familiar enough pattern in American universities. Properly worked, it is a pattern in no way inimical to university autonomy. The essential conditions for autonomy in a university with this constitution are (a) a powerful and liberal-minded vice-chancellor who does not ever disregard the advice of his senate and who restrains his council from usurping academic business; and (b) a council whose members identify themselves with the university, protect it from outside pressures, and are content not to use their sovereign powers to overrule academic opinion. The University of Nigeria was fortunate in its first vice-chancellor, who took great trouble to interpret the constitution in such a way as to establish good conventions. He found (for instance) that deans were not to be elected by academics; they were to be appointed by council. Nevertheless he arranged that the academics should nominate their deans, and that the council should accept their nominations. The university was less fortunate in some of its council members, who could not be persuaded to leave other items of academic business to the senate; but this is hardly surprising since the chancellor was not only an executive one; he was also a renowned national leader, deeply committed to integrating the university into the nation's life and not averse to participating in the university's day-to-day business. So the vice-chancellor was frequently presented with what were tantamount to directives from the chancellor: a procedure perfectly consistent with the letter of the act of parliament under which the university operates, but nevertheless an infringement of autonomy because it represented pressures which were generated entirely outside the university.

Events at Nsukka, therefore, teach a lesson similar to one we have learnt elsewhere: that constitutions without accompanying conventions can be invoked to justify infringements of autonomy. However it has to be admitted that the pattern of constitution at Nsukka, which openly confers more powers on the council and the administration and which bluntly restricts the powers of the senate, is proving capable of interpretation to produce a good measure of academic self-government. The University of Nigeria has had its troubles; but it has so far escaped the destruction of autonomy from outside which has fallen upon the University of Ghana, or the destruction from inside which has fallen upon the University of Lagos.

V SOME CONCLUSIONS

Before we draw conclusions from this summary of the way Africans are interpreting university constitutions in Africa, it is well that we should recall how, only two or three generations ago, the British interpreted university constitutions in India. The notion that the head of state should be *ex officio* chancellor and should nominate a majority of the university's governing body was held not only by Nkrumah, but also by Curzon and Raleigh.[85] Proposals that the head of state as chancellor should approve the appointment of professors and that the governor general in council should have power to appoint examiners and to suspend the university's constitution were made by the British raj in India forty years before similar proposals from Accra shocked the British academic world.[86] When Azikiwe declared in 1961 that British traditions for academic autonomy within universities are not appropriate for Africa he was only echoing views endorsed by Harcourt Butler in 1915 for the universities of India.[87] It was left to Sadler in 1919 to define for India an equilibrium between universities and the state which was consistent with contemporary practice in Britain.

If it had been left to colonial governments in Africa to draw up the constitutions of the colonial university colleges, there would probably have been a similar well-meaning paternalism, a similar 'enveloping . . . in tightish bands now, only to be able to relax them later on' (these are Curzon's words), as we have described for India.[88] But the African university colleges were designed by academics, and the inter-university council in London saw to it that from the beginning these colonial colleges should be endowed with opportunities for freedom and autonomy in every way commensurate with those to be found at home. We have seen how these opportunities have been used, and occasionally misused. Let us now draw some conclusions.

Two conclusions emerge from our summary. The first is that academic freedom as defined on page 291 is not in danger in the universities we have been considering except where civil rights for all citizens are in danger, as in Ghana or as in Rhodesia after the unilateral assumption of independence. The second is that university autonomy, as we have described it, is from time to time in danger. The danger comes from two quarters: interference from outside the university by acts of the government, and betrayal from inside by authorities of the university which usurp functions delegated by legislation or by convention to the academic body.

The university constitutions which have failed to safeguard the autonomy of these African universities are closely modelled on the constitutions of English civic universities. All of them, as in England, provide for a council which is the 'supreme governing body of the university'.[89] The councils, as in England, include a majority of laymen, some nominated by official agencies (in England usually local authorities; in Africa federal or regional governments). All of them have senates, to which are delegated certain powers and responsibilities for academic affairs, including some of those deemed essential if a university is to be considered autonomous.[90]

Constitutional patterns borrowed from English civic universities fail to guarantee autonomy in Africa for three evident reasons. First, they are, in African countries, embodied in acts of parliament, which can be changed by governments at the stroke of a pen and without consultation with the university. This happened in Khartoum and Nsukka, and it was narrowly averted over the draft constitution at Ibadan. Second, their wording is in places positively misleading as a guide to procedure. Consider the power given to the council of the University of Sussex to 'give directions' to the senate. It is a phrase not uncommon in English university statutes. No-one fears that the council at Sussex or elsewhere in England ever would give directions and therefore no-one presses for the wording to be changed. But in Africa such a phrase would be interpreted as a duty laid upon the council, whose members would feel obliged to 'give directions' when they thought fit. Because the conventions are so powerful in Britain, the constitutions have not cried out for revision. The patterns we have exported are not in fact the patterns we practise; this has caused difficulty in Lagos and Ghana. Third, there is an inherent ambiguity in the idea of an autonomous university whose governing body contains a majority of non-academics appointed from outside. What precisely is meant by 'self-government' under these conditions? The council members are designated in charter or statutes or act of parliament as belonging to the society as fully as the academic staff belong. In England this ambiguity is decently covered by the sophistication of English society. When the university council meets, the laymen serving on it really do identify themselves with the university; they are not there as agents of outside pressure groups: they are there to personify the interests of the community at large. They are the strongest defence the university has against interference from government or damage from misconceived public opinion.

In other parts of the Commonwealth one cannot always rely on this degree of sophistication among the lay members of university councils. The university governing bodies in India (the senates) deteriorated when the vakils infiltrated into them.[91] Even in Australia and Canada there have been occasions when laymen on university governing bodies have been unduly influenced by specific interests outside the university. One can hardly expect African universities to be immune from such embarrassments. Laymen serving on university councils there are likely to be so deeply committed to other causes that they cannot insulate their loyalty to the university from outside pressures; they cannot always act wholeheartedly as members of the university to the exclusion of other interests; they therefore cannot shelter themselves or the university from political pressures. The autonomy of a university cannot but be weakened when some of its own members, on its own governing body, are restrained from acting as free and independent counsellors. The failure of the council of the University of Ghana to support its academic board over the transfer of the institute of education is one example of difficulty arising from this cause; the split between the provisional council at Lagos and its senate is another.

There are several ways in which the autonomy of the new Commonwealth universities might be made more secure. One way is to retain the present patterns of constitutions basically unchanged and to concentrate upon propagating the unwritten conventions; in other words to educate public opinion. Another way is to codify the conventions, to spell them out. A third way is to devise entirely different kinds of constitutions. We offer some reflections on these alternatives.

Experience in Europe and America supports the view that if the state is willing to guarantee a measure of autonomy to its universities it can fulfil the guarantee; if it is not willing to do so, no contract between the state and its universities is safe against repudiation. To codify the conditions for freedom and to legislate for it certainly do not guarantee freedom. It is significant that some American universities have had a good deal of trouble to preserve their autonomy and to protect their staff from molestation by witch-hunters, notwithstanding the fact that civil rights are written into the American constitution and the Association of American University Professors issued, fifty years ago, a declaration on academic freedom; while British universities with demonstrably ambiguous constitutions, and in a country with no written constitution, enjoy a degree of autonomy as secure as universities have anywhere else in the world. Argument which follows this course leads to the conclusion that the only safeguards are first, a coherent body of opinion about these matters inside universities, so that the universities of a country put up a unanimous and united front in defence of their autonomy; and second, a sufficient degree of enlightenment among the public to respect this opinion and to force governments to accept it.

What are the prospects for these two safeguards in Africa? We have described recent events in the Sudan which demonstrate that autonomy can be restored by a determined university backed by public opinion. It is not easy to persuade academics to put up a united front, for there is such diversity of opinion among them, even on basic issues, that much compromise is needed before they can speak with one voice. It is a wise German saying, that a professor is a man who 'thinks otherwise'. As for public opinion, if one examines the public utterances of African leaders one finds plenty of evidence that these leaders give lip-service, at any rate, to the need for their universities to manage their own affairs: Azikiwe, Nkrumah, Akintola, Margai, Nyerere (to mention only a sample) have all, during the last five years, made quite astonishingly uncompromising declarations in favour of academic freedom or university autonomy. It is true that the deeds of some of these leaders have not been consistent with their words; but at least their words may be taken as evidence that they know what is expected of the state with regard to the freedom of its universities to run their affairs. The task of educating public opinion in an African country is simplified in that a little of it might go a long way. It would be sufficient to convince politicians, senior civil servants, and newspaper editors of the importance of these issues to secure a good deal of support for universities.

That conventions of the kind familiar in Britain can be successfully established in Africa is demonstrated by the great prestige already acquired by the national universities commission in Nigeria (the NUC), which is the Nigerian equivalent of the British university grants committee. The commission was appointed in 1962 by the federal prime minister, to whom it reports. Its main functions are to estimate the financial needs of the five Nigerian universities, to distribute federal funds to them, and to take part in planning the balanced and co-ordinated development of universities to ensure that national needs are met. The commission's task is all the more difficult because the regions of Nigeria have a high degree of self-government; only two of the universities (Ibadan and Lagos) are established by federal legislation; the other three universities were established by legislation in the regions. The commission consists of a chairman and ten members drawn from the regions and the federal territory and chosen solely for their personal qualities.[92]

Here are all the ingredients for tribal and political rivalries, exercise of vested interests, log-rolling. The universities began by being suspicious and dubious; there were murmurs that none of the members had any experience of university finance; it was feared that the commission would have no regard for the universities' autonomy.

In the event none of these forebodings was correct. The commissioners visited all the universities and impressed the academics with their sincerity and evident commitment to their difficult task. They produced a report which even its critics admit is a masterly document, commenting perceptively on the state of the universities as they found them and setting up a procedure for financing universities which has won approval and respect from each of the five vice-chancellors. The whole tone of the report assumes an attitude of non-interference with academic affairs which could be taken as a model in any country.[93]

A further reassurance comes from the University of Ibadan where the newly constituted council is showing a degree of involvement in the university and an understanding of the way it runs which promises well for a healthy equilibrium between council and senate. The presence of a good many Nigerians on the senate has created a new confidence between senate and council. If that is consolidated, the internal autonomy of the university, at any rate, will be assured.

There is a case, therefore, for believing that the constitutions under which African universities operate might become clothed with the conventions which in Britain enable them to work successfully. Undoubtedly the surest way to educate politicians and government officials to understand the nuances of academic autonomy is to involve them in university government; not – it must be emphasised – in such a way that politics are brought into the university but in such a way that the university influences politics. It is noteworthy that the need for some such involvement as this has been observed by several leaders in the academic world. The distinguished principal of the University College of Sierra Leone suggested that cabinet ministers should serve on university councils.[94] At a conference of heads of African universities held in Italy in 1962 a similar view was expressed. Sir Ivor Jennings, when vice-chancellor of the University of Ceylon, ascribed the successful maintenance of the university's autonomy to the fact that the government of Ceylon,

had maintained the conventions which it was hoped would be established when the constitution was laid down. One reason is that the Legislature is given adequate representation on the Court of the University . . . The presence of elected members of the House of Representatives and the Senate of Ceylon enables these bodies to have adequate information about University activities . . . Therefore, strangely enough, the existence of those representatives in the Court of the University has contributed to University autonomy rather than the reverse.[95]

The patient propagation of unwritten conventions is, however, not enough. African universities cannot risk the periodic repetition of events such as those we have described in this chapter. We must consider other safeguards as well.

Clearly obvious ambiguities imported from England need to be eliminated from the constitutions of African universities. If the chancellor, although he is described as head of the university, is not to have executive powers, the statutes should say so. If the vice-chancellor and professors, although formally appointed by the council, are really to be selected by bodies which include a strong representation of academics, the procedure should be spelt out in detail. If the admission of students is to remain in the hands of university teachers, it is not sufficient to hope this will become an unwritten tradition.

Apart from having glaring ambiguities removed from their constitutions, African universities could codify the conventions in other ways. Constitutional conventions such as government by cabinet have been enacted and similar enactments could be made for academic conventions. Or – since no enactment is safe against encroachment in a one-party state – it might be equally effective for the council and senate of the university to draw up and subscribe to a code of procedure, similar to the manual of procedure used by colonial governments.

To codify the conventions, provided there was flexibility for the conventions to grow with the growth of the university, would go some way toward securing a proper balance of power between council and senate and toward ensuring that those who teach take part in the making of policy. It was indeed the great virtue of David Balme's constitution for the University College of the Gold Coast[96] that it did this. But attempts to modify the English pattern of university constitution in such a way that an African government is persuaded to leave the essential autonomies in the hands of the university are not likely to succeed without other safeguards. Under what conditions could an African state be expected to delegate self-government to an institution which (as Nkrumah once put it) 'is the heart of the nation, essential to its life and progress' and which is likely to remain for a few more years powerfully influenced by expatriates? Certainly not on the basis of a literal interpretation of the constitution of an English civic university; for, on paper, such a constitution gives the impression that the government renounces all control over the university and vests it in the council. This impression is of course incorrect. Let a British university double its professorial salaries, or use public money to build halls of residence costing £2,000 a bed, or set up a medical school without the consent of the university grants committee, and the impression of complete autonomy will soon be dispelled. But none of these limitations to autonomy appear in the university's charter and statutes and, as we have seen, Africans interpret constitutions literally; for them the English pattern of constitution spells a renunciation of all state powers over the university. Hence the devices, such as the appointment of a political leader as executive chancellor, or a take-over on the council by a majority of government nominees, to circumvent the blanket autonomy which the constitution appears to give. The *de facto* situation in Britain is that there is, of course, an unwritten concordat between university and state, through the medium of the university grants committee: one side acknowledges and accepts some measure of state influence and control; the other side agrees to a rigorous code of non-intervention in the university's academic affairs.

This leads us to consider whether in African universities the conventional English constitution might not be replaced by a covenant between the state and the university which would be acceptable to the university because it assured autonomy on all essential points, and acceptable to the state because it spelt out the powers which the state reserves to itself, and which it undoubtedly possesses anyway. The covenant would specify on the one hand the powers to be delegated to the university and renounced by the state, which could not be withdrawn legally except by an amendment of the state constitution after a commission of enquiry (e.g. power over curricula, examinations, appointment of staff, admission of students); on the other hand – and equally important – it would specify the spheres of interest within the university where the state wishes to retain an influence (e.g. overall finance but not its allocation among categories of expenditure, planning higher education on a scale which will meet manpower needs). Such an arrangement as this would recognise that in Africa governments and universities cannot remain insulated from each other. It would require machinery for continuous consultation between the state and the university, and even directives from the head of state would have to pass through this machinery. If intervention then occurs it will be seen for what it is, and not disguised as action consistent with a literal interpretation of the constitution.

The novelty in this suggestion is that the covenant between state and university should be entrenched in the state constitution, preferably as brief clauses which would be elaborated in the university's own statutes. The appropriate place for the covenant would be among the 'fundamental rights'.[97] We have already quoted precedents for this from Germany[98] and we draw attention again to the passage from the German commission on university reform which we quote on page 294, especially to the suggestion that there should be arbitration machinery to deal with disputes over the interpretation of the covenant.

There is another approach to the problem of university autonomy in Africa which should be brought into the discussion although we would consider it to be less desirable than the other suggestions we have made. This approach is simply to make the universities part of the state civil service, on the grounds:

that the public is accustomed to government officials having special immunities connected with their work, and academic freedom may be more easily defended in the eyes of the public in these terms than on more abstract philosophical grounds.[99]

This is the opinion of T. H. Silcock, who has experience of universities on the French and British models in South-East Asia, and has written perceptively about them. He states his conclusion this way:

We must, however, face the question whether – if international support could be given – academic values in Southeast Asia might be better protected under a French system of relations between university and state than under a British or American system. The answer is far from clear, for given a strong regional academic life and informed intellectual and moral support from the international academic world, universities might be more secure as functional organs with a defined influence within the state structure than as separate institutions needing constitutional defences.[100]

What is clear in Africa is that the French pattern of university constitution, operated within decrees issued from Paris, has (surprisingly) transplanted more successfully, and suffered less erosion from African politics, than has the British pattern; and this is not solely due to the fact that the French-speaking universities in Africa are still managed by expatriates. It would have interrupted the narrative of this chapter to include material about academic autonomy in the French-speaking countries; some discussion of this is to be found in chapter 11. It is relevant to mention here that in the brief history of universities in French West Africa academic freedom has been respected and a degree of autonomy acceptable to French scholars has been maintained.

Any change in the constitutions of universities in British Commonwealth countries would need more reflection and detailed thought than we have given it in this chapter. This further reflection is urgently needed, for some African universities have already suffered severely from the inadequacy of their present constitutions. No form of words, no concordat between state and university, is proof against the sort of messianic leadership to be found until recently in Ghana. But dictators succumb and universities, whatever their vicissitudes, survive. So it is worth while to consolidate the present insecure bulwarks which protect autonomy and academic freedom and to discuss the building of new ones. We end with some tentative suggestions.

1. African universities, like the English models from which they are taken, do not expend much thought or money over their public relations. The only evidence we have of a university deliberately setting out to interpret to the public its need for autonomy comes from Ghana, where Conor Cruise O'Brien put into some of his speeches eloquent and persuasive arguments intended to educate public opinion. There are scattered essays in university publications in Africa some of which display an arrogance and lack of understanding calculated to cause offence among governments rather than to promote understanding.[101] There are occasional moving manifestos by groups of academics, such as one submitted to the military government of the Sudan by the academic staff at Khartoum, and one prepared, but not published, by a group of professors in Ghana, which we reproduce in full.[102] What is lacking is a pamphlet, such as might be issued jointly by all the institutions of higher education in an African state, setting out the reasons why the academic profession, like the legal and medical professions, must have some degree of autonomy guaranteed by the state in order to fulfil its purpose in the state. Universities would be unwise to ask for a blank cheque of freedom any more than the state legal or medical services do. The fewer principles they insist upon, the more united they are likely to be in defending them, and the more uncompromising they can afford to be about them. We have already indicated what these principles are. No occasion should be lost in explaining them to the public, not querulously – as tends to happen in a crisis – but coolly and patiently.

2. This measure still leaves the formal constitutions unchanged. It would be a

serious matter to throw existing constitutions into the melting pot and to start again. But something practical might be done to remove the evident ambiguities in them and, in universities where the balance of responsibilities between council and senate has not yet reached a satisfactory equilibrium, to define in more detail, either in regulations or in a code of procedure, those decisions which are the prerogative of council, those which are delegated to bodies under the council, and those which should not be made by council except (a) on the recommendation of the senate, and (b) after consultation with the senate. Codes of procedure should specify, too, an approved machinery for the conduct of business between the various bodies responsible for decision-making in the university. The principle underlying these codes of procedure should be that a high degree of internal academic autonomy is essential in universities if they are to protect themselves effectively against molestation from outside.

3. Even if it turns out to be impracticable or imprudent to replace existing constitutions with covenants between state and university of the sort we have suggested, it would nevertheless be valuable if African academics could reflect on the idea and bring it into the arena of discussion, preferably at a time when it can be disengaged from specific cases of infringements of autonomy. It would seem a wise course to assume that political leaders mean what they say about the need to guarantee autonomy to universities, even if circumstances prevent them from honouring the guarantee. It can be assumed, therefore, that they would be willing to discuss with universities the way to reconcile autonomy with compliance to the legitimate demands which a state may make upon a university. Out of these discussions an improvement in mutual understanding would certainly arise. The discussions might end in agreement about a code of procedure which would embody the conventions for autonomy and freedom in universities, with an agreed arbitration machinery to deal with disputes. There might even arise a formal concordat between state and university entrenched in the state constitution, and which would be more enduring than an act of parliament.

CHAPTER ELEVEN

OTHER PATTERNS OF HIGHER
EDUCATION IN AFRICA

I INTRODUCTION

This book is concerned primarily with the evolution of British policy for universities in the Commonwealth. We demonstrate in chapter 9 how this policy has recently been influenced by American ideas on higher education. Other European countries have implanted universities into non-European societies, and several African universities look not to England but to France or Belgium for their inspiration. Yet ideas about higher education from the continent of Europe and from other parts of Africa have scarcely affected British policy at all. There have been interesting exchanges of views, notably in 1961 at an international seminar held in Freetown[1] and in 1962 at a conference at Tananarive;[2] but there is as yet little evidence that the various patterns of higher education in Africa are influencing one another: the affinities are still with the metropolitan models from which African universities are derived.

Nevertheless there is a place in this book for a brief assessment of other patterns of higher education in Africa, if only to demonstrate the comparative virtues and the drawbacks of the pattern bequeathed by Britain. This chapter, though by no means exhaustive (it omits, for example, the universities of the United Arab Republic), attempts such an assessment. The most striking contrast to British policy is the one displayed by the Nationalist government in South Africa; this has particular relevance to some of the issues we have raised, and it must be considered in some detail.

II THE 'BANTU' COLLEGES IN SOUTH AFRICA

Concern with the further education of Europeans in South Africa began in 1858 when a board of public examiners was established in Cape Colony, to award certificates in literature, science, law, surveying, engineering, and navigation. The board was superseded in 1873 when the legislature created the University of the Cape of Good Hope. Like the University of London at that time, this university was simply an examining body with power to grant degrees; it received a royal charter from Queen Victoria in 1877.

Various colleges sprang up where students were prepared for degrees granted by the University of the Cape of Good Hope, and in course of time these colleges were raised to the status of independent degree-granting institutions. The first two promotions occurred in 1916 when the colleges in Stellenbosch and Cape Town became universities. The original university then changed its name to become the University of South Africa. Six colleges were incorporated with it: in Bloemfontein, Wellington, Pietermaritzburg, Grahamstown, Pretoria, Johannesburg, and, in 1921, a seventh: in Potchefstroom. The college at Wellington expired in 1950. By 1951 the others had all become independent universities; but the University of South Africa remained as a degree-granting institution, no longer with any incorporated colleges but conducting its teaching by correspondence. It continues to have a large enrolment: in 1964 over 16,000 students were on its books. It does more than simply act as an examining body. Its students are obliged to enrol for tuition by correspondence and are not permitted to sit for the examinations unless their written work during the course has been satisfactory.[3] Students may visit the tutors, who occupy an office block in Pretoria, for advice, and they may use a library which is housed in the same block. Both the council and senate of the University of South Africa include representatives of the eight other South African universities. For the degree examinations there are external as well as internal examiners. Notwithstanding the difficulties of preparing for university degrees by correspondence, there is every reason to believe that the standard of achievement required for a degree in the University of South Africa is about the same as that required for degrees in the other universities in the republic.

The melancholy story of the establishment of the 'Bantu' university colleges is so familiar that only a summary is needed here.[4] Before 1960 non-white students were admitted to the universities of Cape Town and the Witwatersrand and to segregated classes in the University of Natal. There was also a university college for non-whites at Fort Hare, a missionary enterprise founded under the aegis of the united free church of Scotland in 1916, and which was affiliated to Rhodes University in 1951. The compulsory introduction of apartheid into higher education dates from the publication in 1951 of the report of a Commission on Native Education, under the chairmanship of W. W. M. Eiselen.[5] Among the terms of reference were two significant clauses:

The formulation of the principles and aims of education for Natives as an independent race, in which their past and present, their inherent racial qualities, their distinctive characteristics and aptitudes, and their needs under ever-changing social conditions are taken into consideration.

The extent to which the existing primary, secondary, and vocational education system for Natives and the training of Native teachers should be modified in respect of the content and form of syllabuses, in order to conform to the proposed principles and aims, and to prepare Natives more effectively for their future occupations.

The first of these clauses considered out of its context could be regarded as a directive to study the adaptation of western curricula to the African environment: a proposal as imaginative as those made by Britain in the 1925 white paper and the De La Warr report.[6] But in the context of the Nationalist government its meaning was totally different; this was made clear by some of the declarations of Dr Verwoerd:[7]

Native education should be controlled in such a way that it should be in accord with the policy of the State . . . Good racial relations cannot exist when the education is given under the control of people who create wrong expectations on the part of the Native himself.

And again, a statement which might have been lifted from the parliamentary debates in early Victorian England:

Education must train and teach people in accordance with their opportunities in life, according to the sphere in which they live.

The minister of Bantu education, some years later, was even more explicit:

The Bantu must be so educated that they do not want to become imitators [of the Whites, but] that they will want to remain essentially Bantu.[8]

It is no surprise, therefore, that the Eiselen commission recommended that all post-matriculation training for Africans should be conducted in institutions which did not even come under the minister of education, arts, and science, but under the minister of Bantu education, to be co-ordinated with policy for the employment of Africans. Two years later, in 1953, another commission was appointed 'to investigate and report on the practicability and financial implications of providing separate training facilities for non-Europeans at universities'. There is no mention, it will be noted, of *desirability*. The commission did not go far enough in its report to satisfy the government, and in 1955 an inter-departmental committee was appointed to work out a scheme for providing separate facilities for the higher education of non-whites.

There followed three years of dignified dissent and desperate protest from liberal-minded South Africans. But the government disregarded all the pleas and petitions put before them, and in March 1957 they introduced a bill into the assembly to give effect to their intentions.[9] In other circumstances no-one would have objected to the enlargement of opportunities for the higher education of the Coloured, Indian, and Bantu people of South Africa, or to modifications in the content of education to incorporate studies of the indigenous cultures of Bantu and Indians. But the bill introduced in 1957 had in it clauses which struck at the very roots of the academic tradition. It excluded non-whites from the existing teaching universities and it made it a punishable offence (a fine of £100 or six months imprisonment) for a non-white to register at a 'white' university without permission from the minister of Bantu education. Another clause in the bill made it an offence, rewarded with the same punishment, for a white to register at a 'non-white' university college.[10] Even the positive provisions of the bill were anathema to anyone who valued the freedoms accorded elsewhere to universities; for the three 'Bantu' colleges which the minister proposed to establish were to be controlled in a manner more fitting for a reformatory than for an academic community. The minister was to have power not only to establish but to dis-establish any 'Bantu' college; the council members were to be appointed by the governor general and the senate members by the minister of Bantu education; the principal (called a rector), too, was to be appointed by the minister. The minister was to have power to refuse admission to a qualified student 'if he considers it to be in the interests of the university college to do so'; he can require a student to reside 'at a place of residence approved for the purpose by him'; and he may determine 'at which place a student shall attend for the purpose of receiving instruction'.[11] 'Power to appoint, promote, transfer or discharge' the staff was to be vested in the minister; members of the staff at any of the 'Bantu' colleges could be discharged by the minister on any one of seventeen counts, which include:

if he:
publicly comments adversely upon the administration of any department of the Government or of any province or of the territory of South West Africa . . . propagates any idea or takes part in or identifies himself with any propaganda or activity or acts in a manner calculated—(i) to cause or promote antagonism amongst any section of the population of the Union against any other section of the population of the Union; or (ii) to impede, obstruct or undermine the activities of any Government department.[12]

As a final precaution against any risk that the 'Bantu' colleges might wish to exercise some measure of academic autonomy, the minister reserved to himself the power to make regulations as to the maintenance, management, and control of the colleges; the functions, powers, duties, and the procedure at the college council meetings; conditions for admission of students; and the constitution and function of faculty boards.[13] The bill provided also for a compulsory take-over of Fort Hare College, dissolving its affiliation with Rhodes University and making it a tribal college under the minister's control. All efforts to oppose the bill failed; with minor amendments it became law under the ironical title of the Extension of University Education Act, No 45 of 1959.

Three 'Bantu' colleges are now in existence, together with a college near Cape Town, confined to Coloured people, a college for Indians in Durban, and a non-European medical school in Durban, all of whose students are Indian or African. Our concern here is only with the three 'Bantu' colleges. Each of them restricts entry not only to Bantus, but, with a few exceptions, even to certain tribal groups. Fort Hare is now mainly for the Xhosa-speaking peoples; the new College of the North at Turfloop is for the Sotho, Venda, and Tsonga peoples; the College of Zululand is for Zulu and Swazi people. The colleges are still small: their student and staff populations in 1964 were as follows:

	STUDENTS ENROLLED	ACADEMIC STAFF WHITE	NON-WHITE
Fort Hare	274	61	12
College of the North	307	47	6
Zululand College	180	37	6

Not all these students are reading for degrees, for some of them have no qualified for matriculation. Those who have matriculated are prepared for degrees of the University of South Africa. The relationship of the 'Bantu' colleges to the University of South Africa therefore resembles the relationship which the present unitary universities (e.g. Rhodes, Pretoria) had before they acquired their independence.

This is an important point to note. For it is commonly asserted that the Bantu are being offered a higher education which is entirely different from that offered to the white South African, tribally orientated, and leading to an inferior degree. In one sense, which we consider in a moment, this is true. But in another sense, which we consider now, it is not true. The curriculum followed, the examination papers set, the examiners who mark the scripts, the pass mark for award of a degree: all these are common for the Bantu students in the three colleges and for the thousands of white South Africans who are enrolled as correspondence-students of the University of South Africa.[14] Moreover the three colleges offer, in the liberal arts and social sciences at any rate, a wide choice of subjects. The College of the North, for instance, gives a list of thirty-two subjects in which students can be prepared for the B.A. degree. The list includes all the familiar arts subjects, including Latin, Greek, philosophy, history, English; and, of course, Afrikaans and three Bantu languages. It includes also subjects in the social sciences, e.g. economics, sociology, psychology, anthropology, criminology, native administration and political science. Physics, chemistry, botany, zoology, and mathematics may also be taken as ingredients of the arts degree. Where the university college cannot provide tuition, tuition by correspondence is arranged with the University of South Africa. The pattern of degree follows the common practice in South Africa: it is based on the familiar old Scottish model, and it is very similar to the pattern advocated by the inter-university council delegation for the new university in Northern Nigeria in 1961.[15] To graduate with a pass degree in arts, a student has to qualify in eleven courses; for a degree in science he qualifies in nine courses. Two of these he studies in depth for three years; the others he selects – if he is wise – to give his education an element of diversity combined with relevance. Thus a selection for an aspiring schoolteacher, suggested in the university's prospectus for 1965 is:

First year Afrikaans 1; English 1; psychology 1; history 1
Second year Afrikaans 2; English 2; sociology 1; history 2
Third year Afrikaans 3; English 3; anthropology 1; biblical studies 1

This is a broader, and doubtless a more superficial, pattern of degree than the one common in England and in the universities which began as Asquith colleges. But it has not been watered down to suit Bantu Africans; it is characteristic of all South African university education. And the 'Bantu colleges, again in common with other South African universities, offer one-subject honours degrees to those who have qualified for a pass degree and who successfully pursue a further year of advanced study. One or other of them offers, too, master's degrees and degrees in education, divinity, law, pharmacy, commerce and administration; and there are diplomas in social work, commerce, administration, nursing, and teaching. The chief deficiencies in curricula of the colleges are in technological and some professional studies. Thus engineering, mining, and (except at diploma level) agricultural science are out of reach of Bantu Africans (but, owing to job reservation, professional posts in these subjects are out of reach, too).

It is evident, therefore, that the *content* of higher education for Bantu Africans within the range of subjects available at their colleges, and the pattern and standard of achievement of the degrees they take from the colleges, do not differ significantly from those offered to white South Africans enrolled in the University of South Africa, and are broadly similar to those offered at the eight unitary universities. On these criteria the common assumption – that the Bantu are being given a special kind of higher education biased toward their tribal life – is incorrect. But on other criteria the assumption is only too correct. What the South African government has done, with cynical ingenuity, is to create in the 'Bantu' university colleges an environment utterly inimical to freedom of thought, an environment which puts young minds into intellectual quarantine for three years, a veritable academic concentration camp.

We have already quoted passages from the bill which led to the creation of the colleges. It is clear from these quotations that both academic freedom and autonomy are ruthlessly excluded. The minister of Bantu education even decides on the membership, duties, and procedure of academic committees, such as the senate, within the colleges. It is specifically stated that a university teacher may be dismissed even for commenting adversely in class upon the administration of the country (he is presumably permitted to comment favourably), or for propagating any idea which might be regarded as critical of the affairs of the country. In fact the actual pattern of government in the colleges is more deplorable than is evident from the act. For each college has *two* councils and *two* senates. The executive council is all white, and there is a non-white advisory council. All members of both bodies are appointed by the state president. Similarly the executive senate is all white, and there is a non-white advisory senate. These senates consist of professors and lecturers selected by the minister after consultation with the council. The administration of a penitentiary could not pay much less attention than this to principles of democratic government. Set beside the constitution of the 'Bantu' colleges, Nkrumah's constitution for universities in Ghana, and Azikiwe's constitution for Nsukka, are models of academic liberty.

As for the students, we have already explained how they are forbidden, under pain of fine or imprisonment, to enrol in one of the open universities (Cape Town or Witwatersrand) which are still willing to accept them; and how the minister of Bantu education may decide which of the 'Bantu' colleges they may attend, and may refuse admission to any student who might be an embarrassment to a college. To satisfy the minister is an annual hurdle to be jumped, for students must renew their registrations annually. But again the actual situation is more deplorable than is evident from the act. Each college has, of course, a set of regulations governing the discipline of students. The regulations are not made by the college council: they are made by the minister. They include the customary reasonable measures: evidence of matriculation must be produced, fees must be paid, there must be regular attendance at lectures, damage to college property must be paid for. In addition to these there are regulations quite staggering in their severity. Here is a sample of them from the University College of Zululand:[16]

A student may not admit a visitor [of either sex] to a hostel without permission from the Hostel Superintendent.

Any student organisation or organisation work in which students are concerned is subject to the prior approval of the Rector.

No meeting may be held on the grounds of the College without permission from the Rector.

No magazine, publication, or pamphlet for which students are wholly or partly responsible may be circulated without the permission of the Rector in consultation with the Advisory Senate and the Senate.

No statement may be given to the press by or on behalf of the students without the Rector's permission.

The one 'Bantu' college which had once known freedom was Fort Hare.[17] Its tranfer from its own comparatively liberal college government to the protective custody of the minister of Bantu education was accompanied by serious student unrest; indeed the unrest continued, for it was reported in the press that all students there except graduates boycotted the graduation ceremony in 1964. The standard regulations were deemed insufficient and some new ones were added,[18] viz:

No student or group of students may visit any other institution without the permission of the Rector and of the Institution concerned, and then only on such conditions as may be determined.

No student or group of students and no person or persons not under the jurisdiction of the University College, may be upon the College grounds as visitors . . . without the permission of the Rector or his duly authorized representative, and then only on such conditions as may be determined.

It is upon evidence such as we have quoted from the bill and the college regulations that we base our indictment of the 'Bantu' colleges as places unworthy to be included in the community of universities. It is not the curriculum, nor the pattern or standard of degree: it is the whole stifling intellectual environment, the obligatory segregation of tribes, the enforced isolation from currents of thought in other universities, which condemn the Africans to an inferior and contemptible system of higher education. Within this tyrannical régime there are dedicated white teachers, sincerely doing their best for their students and trying to make the system work for the benefit of the Bantu Africans. One can believe that under such teachers the apparently penal regulations are interpreted humanely, and the intellectual environment is not as sultry as one might assume from the published evidence. The colleges have pleasant buildings, growing libraries, and decent amenities for student life. So far as a tyranny can be made agreeable, some of the staff are trying to make it so. The examination results are satisfactory.[19] But morale among the students is low. They are cut off from student life in other universities; for instance, they are not allowed to affiliate with the national union of South African students (NUSAS). They live in an environment calculated to foster a resentful tribalism rather than a sense of belonging to a nation. And they face a bleak future, for even with degrees, they may have difficulty in getting employment except in native reservations. 'In terms of the Government's plan, there was no place for the Bantu in the European community above the level of certain forms of labour. Within their own areas, however, all doors were open. Education should, thus, stand with both feet in the Reserves and have its roots in the spirit and being of a Bantu society.'[20]

Some of those who support segregated higher education for the Bantu people bolster up their claim by quoting British writers who advocate – as we do in this book – the gradual adaptation of imported patterns of higher education to meet the needs of African communities.[21] It is evident from our analysis that the content of university education has not been adapted except inasmuch as it has for all South Africans. The adaptation which has occurred is one we would uncompromisingly reject, namely to seal off the environment of university education, to exclude the fresh air of dissent, to create an atmosphere which will not promote intellectual freedom among the Bantu, but will stifle it.

III HIGHER EDUCATION IN ETHIOPIA

Up to 1906 the only formal education in Ethiopia was that given by the coptic church, to enable children to read the scriptures, and by a few Roman catholic and protestant missionaries. In content and style it was analogous to the instruction given by mallams in the koranic schools of Nigeria. In 1906 the Emperor Menelik II set up a primary school in Addis Ababa. Primary education expanded slowly up to the Italian occupation in 1935, and a few Ethiopians were sent abroad for their education. The Italian occupation from 1935 to 1941 was distinguished by a cynical suppression of educational opportunity. In 1935 there were 180 missionaries in Ethiopia, most of them engaged in some form of teaching; by 1942 only eight remained. 'At the close of the occupation the governmental system of education had to be completely rebuilt. There was almost a total educational vacuum.'[22]

Since the restoration of his country's freedom, the Emperor Haile Sellassie I has taken a deep personal interest in the education of his people. The first national budget, in 1942, allotted twelve per cent of the revenue to education, and the proportion is now more than doubled. The first priority was to establish secondary schools and to send Ethiopians abroad for higher education. It is difficult to imagine the plight of an independent country of some twenty million people which had – only twenty years ago – no more than fifteen citizens who had completed secondary education and a mere two or three university graduates.

During the 1950s, as soon as a trickle of candidates issued from the secondary schools, the emperor founded a number of post-secondary institutions: a university college in Addis Ababa in 1950, a college of agriculture in Alemaya in 1951, a college of engineering in Addis Ababa in 1953, and a college of public health in Gondar in 1954. In addition to these an Ethio-Swedish institute for building technology was started in 1954 and a theological college in 1960. In 1961 an imperial charter brought all six of these institutions together as component parts of the Haile Sellassie I University, with the emperor himself as chancellor.

The university now has an annual budget equivalent to about £1·9 million, much of which comes as foreign aid. The biggest overseas contribution is from the United States; in 1964–5 the US government alone contributed over three million US dollars. Since the university is at the time we write not yet five years old, it is too soon to assess its achievements. But it is already possible to discern a distinctive pattern of higher education in Ethiopia; and some elements in this pattern are relevant to the theme of this book.[23]

The mode of government in the university follows an American pattern modified to incorporate the personal participation of the emperor. All authority issues from him. He is himself the chancellor; he appoints the governing body and the president, who is the chief executive officer. As one observer put it: 'there are no limitations upon his powers except those of self restraint'. Under the present emperor's benevolent régime the university enjoys a secure autonomy; but autonomy and academic freedom depend entirely upon conventions recognised by the emperor: they are in no way guaranteed through the wording of the charter.

The university is controlled by a board of governors consisting of the president and eight members nominated by the emperor. When there are 200 graduates of the university, they will be entitled to elect one member to the board. Consistent with American practice, representation on the board from the academic staff is expressly excluded: article 5 of the charter reads: 'No permanent member of the staff other than the President shall be eligible for appointment, nomination, or election as a member of the Board.' The board has complete sovereignty but the charter does delegate to the faculty council, which is an academic body corresponding to the senate of an English civic university, power to grant degrees (except honorary degrees), admission requirements for students, and 'the general methods and conditions for ex- aminations and the general standard for granting degrees, diplomas, and certificates'. The faculty council can also 'discuss and determine the internal policy of the University in general'.[24] The faculty council includes not only heads of departments but also three members of each of the faculties elected by the full-time members of the teaching staff; so at the academic level there is a reasonably democratic machinery of government and a good deal of dele- gated responsibility. As in American universities, the president has consider- able powers. The charter (article 20) lays it down that 'all members of the staff shall be subordinate to him and shall carry out his directions and instruc- tions . . .': and, 'after consultation with the Council and with the approval of the Board' the president employs, and fixes the terms and conditions of employment of all members of the staff.

In our discussion of academic freedom and autonomy we suggested that one possible precaution to prevent the abuse of university constitutions is for the university to draw up and subscribe to a code of procedure, similar to the manual of procedure used by colonial governments.[25] The Haile Sellassie I University has recently prepared a document of over sixty pages which has precisely this intention.[26] The document has several interesting features. It spells out the procedure to be followed when the faculty council and its com- mittees transact business. It specifies in detail the machinery for admitting students to the university and the academic achievement required of students before graduation. It prescribes the way in which decisions are to be made for dismissing students or putting them on probation when they have failed to pass examinations. Its most interesting sections deal with student life in the university. There is – and again this is traditional American practice – a dean of students, who is responsible for discipline and for overseeing all student activities. All student societies have to be registered with the dean of students. The faculty legislation goes out of its way to encourage a student-council which shall act as a channel of communication between the student body and the officers of the university; although the document wisely insists that the university will recognise only one official organisation representing student- opinion, and that this official organisation must be able to demonstrate by its constitution that it does represent the persons it purports to represent: it must, for example, be able to demonstrate that all its members have a voice in policy-making and can, if necessary, replace its officers or even dissolve the council. The faculty legislation provides detailed machinery even for the publication of a weekly students' newspaper, with a minimum of control or powers of censorship.

The most interesting feature of the faculty council's manual of procedure is a code of conduct for students. This is a remarkable document; an astonishing contrast to the minatory and suspicious measures adopted to suppress initiative in the 'Bantu' colleges. Consider the following examples:

The University regards itself as a community of scholars, a community of men of integrity. Students are entitled to the full respect due to members of such a community. They, in turn, are expected to accept the responsibilities which this membership entails.

The University will rely, as far as possible, on a system of self-discipline founded upon trust and respect reciprocally rendered, to govern student-university relationships . . .

Students enjoy the same right as faculty to criticise the University and any of its programs . . .

The University will protect students in the exercise of rights of academic freedom which, for these purposes, include:

(i) the right to discuss and express openly, controversial matters in class or in connection with academic work so long as the expression of views expressed is generally relevant to the subject under study;

(ii) the right to enjoy freedom of thought, speech, writing and association and other civil rights to the full extent these rights are protected by law.[27]

The charter of the university empowers it to take responsibility for 'all units and agencies of higher education assigned to it'. These wide terms of reference already stretch the university's resources in men and money; but there is little doubt that for the conditions of Ethiopia, where firm central planning of post-secondary education is essential, the concentration of policy-making under one governing body is at this stage a wise move. Indeed the diversity of institutions now assembled into one university under the charter leaves no alternative: already the studies under the university's umbrella comprise not only conventional subjects in the faculties of arts, science, education, engineering, agriculture, medicine, law, and theology: they include also subjects which in England (but not in America) have conventionally been regarded as 'sub-university' work: e.g. diplomas or certificates in building technology and commercial subjects, and qualifications for agricultural extension officers, health officers, community nurses, and sanitarians.

Although the university curriculum is planned on American lines, admission to degree courses is through a pass in the Ethiopian school leaving certificate, an examination reminiscent, in the level of achievement required, of the Cambridge overseas school certificate and O-level G.C.E. The minimum requirement is a 'c' average in five subjects of which English, Amharic, and mathematics are compulsory. At present the output from secondary schools is so small that the university admits every qualified student it can get. In 1964 forty three per cent of all pupils who completed the twelfth grade of secondary school were enrolled in the university. The university's policy is to give a high priority to the production of teachers: the faculty of education has the biggest enrolment in the university[28]; many of the students are recruited from the best of the untrained teachers who attend an annual summer school at the university.

To illustrate the pattern of studies at the university we give some details of the curriculum leading to degrees in the faculty of arts. Achievement is assessed course by course, as in American universities. Candidates must accumulate 130 credit-hours and must maintain a 'c grade average'. ('A' is excellent; 'B', good; 'C', satisfactory; 'D', a bare pass.) In the first year all arts students follow a common curriculum: Ethiopian studies (an introduction to the culture and political institutions of Ethiopia); Amharic language and literature; English; history of world civilisation; introduction to geography and economics; human biology; and a choice of logic, or philosophy, or sociology. A purpose of the course is to introduce the student to more mature ways of thinking than he has learnt at school, and, of course, to compensate for the general weakness in secondary schooling.

After the first year the student selects a major and a minor area of study, which he pursues for three years. During these three years he may specialise (major) in economics, English, Ethiopian languages and literature, French, geography, history, and political science. There have been difficulties in incorporating Ethiopian material into the curriculum because two-thirds of the staff are expatriates on short-term contracts: they do not stay long enough in the country to codify the special knowledge they acquire. Nevertheless much good work on Ethiopian material is being done and the university deliberately encourages research which can ultimately be incorporated in its teaching programme. The history department, for example, offers five courses in the history of Ethiopia and its other offerings include ancient and medieval history of the Mediterranean world; Ottoman history; history of islamic institutions; history of the Middle East, 1900–56; history of East Africa, 1500–1918; history of West Africa until 1900; history of Egypt and Sudan, 1820–1954; and nationalism and liberation movements in modern Africa.

As to the ethos of the university, it is very obviously coloured by American ideas. There is a healthy pragmatism about its ambitions, as is evident from the impression which it made on an observer from English academic life:

In every society and in every age there is no doubt a place for the contemplative and for the speculative researcher, for the scholar who regards learning as an absolute end; but in the world in which the Haile Sellassie I University has come into being, its general tasks are clear and undisputed, and they relate overwhelmingly to the transmission and increase of knowledge and skills for use in practical areas. . . . That is not to say, of course, that there is no room in the University for research. But in a situation, for example, in which it became necessary to choose between allocating sums of money to the pure research of individuals or to an applied research project, we assume that at the present time the latter must ordinarily receive the higher priority. And similarly, that in its policies of academic development, the University will have continually in mind not only the general education but also the training needed by young men and women if they are to play a creative role in society; in other words, that it will devote its energies in the first place to enriching the country through education, and regard as a secondary duty the satisfaction of casual intellectual curiosity on the part of those who might choose to come to it in that spirit. The creativity and eagerness of students must indeed be aroused and maintained throughout their work; but in a purposeful context. We are happy to find that this is also the approach of the University authorities, of the teaching staff, and in general of the students themselves.[29]

It is commonly the case in Africa that students are less altruistic about the purposes of higher education than those who administer and teach in universities. The Ethiopian student is no exception. For some students admission to the university is simply a windfall: he is paid a stipend for studying, with no inducement to excel in his work; he knows there is an assured post at the end; he looks forward to status in a country where status is immensely important, and to liberation from the constraints of rural life. And since the prime motivation of such students as these is self-interest and not a passion for learning, they find the intellectual discipline of academic work irksome. This is one reason for the heavy failure rate in the Haile Sellassie I University. It is estimated that some forty per cent of the students drop out of the course between their first and fourth years. There are, of course, other reasons for the failures. Instruction is in English, which many of the students read very slowly. They are not practised in using books. The techniques of learning familiar to any sixth form pupil in England are mysterious to them. Furthermore the whole atmosphere in Addis Ababa (it is not true of the outlying colleges) is inimical to learning: there are a few hostels but most students have to seek beds for themselves in the city; they live under conditions where private study is quite impossible; there is no adequate student-centre at the university where they may enjoy quiet for working or leisure for educating one another informally. The introductory first-year course, though admirably planned as a curriculum for freshmen, is dispersed among half a dozen departments and is not accompanied by any tutorial or counselling system; it is only when the student embarks on his major study that he comes closely into contact with members of the teaching staff. But these are only temporary deficiencies; the university is aware of them, and they are likely soon to be eliminated.

In the context of African universities the most remarkable feature of the Haile Sellassie I University is the Ethiopian University Service known as EUS. It was introduced in the academic year 1964–5. It requires every full-time Ethiopian student in the university to spend an academic year between the third (junior) and fourth (senior) year of his course in some form of civilian national service. The unique character of this enterprise is that it is university-based. The faculty council of the university retains jurisdiction over the programme and it is administered by an officer of the university, who is responsible for allocating students to jobs and making arrangements for their maintenance while on service. The students are paid a stipend. Unless specially exempted, they are not eligible to receive degrees or diplomas until they have discharged the service. The intention is threefold: to have something resembling an indigenous Peace Corps for helping in work such as mass education and rural hygiene, for which there is urgent need; to familiarise students with some of the social problems among their countrymen and to dispel the attitude, only too common in African countries, that students are a privileged élite who have not time to be concerned with their less fortunate fellows; and, finally, to propagate throughout Ethiopia a good image of the university and the intellectual. It is too early to decide whether EUS will succeed. 'At this stage', as one American observer remarked, 'its establishment would seem to be an inspiration of genius.'

IV PORTRAIT OF A UNIVERSITY IN THE CONGOLESE REPUBLIC[30]

Stretched along the length of Mont Amba, in unmistakable gallic symmetry six hundred feet above Leopoldville, is the cité universitaire which contains Lovanium University. It is by any standards an astonishing institution to find in tropical Africa. If one has regard to Belgian colonial policy over education in the Congo, and the melancholy history of that country since its independence, the achievement at Lovanium is an educational epic. We summarise its story here because it illustrates a pattern of European higher education transplanted to Africa which differs profoundly from the English and American patterns we have already described.

In the Congo, to a greater extent even than in the British colonies, education in colonial times was left in the hands of missionaries. By a concordat arranged in 1906 between Leopold II and Rome, state subsidies were paid for schools run by catholic missionaries, especially if they were Belgian catholics. Even government schools, financed entirely by the state, were staffed by members of catholic teaching orders. There were also schools run by protestant missionaries but until recently they had to survive without financial help from the state.

In other parts of Africa the tradition in missionary education was generally literary and clerkly; and in the Congo, too, boys selected for the catholic priesthood were given a classical education indistinguishable from that offered by the seminaries of Belgium. But for the rest, Belgian policy in the Congo was severely utilitarian. The prime purpose of education was to build the base of a pyramid which might in the unforeseeable future have an apex: to raise the economic level of a country where all responsible positions were held, and would continue to be held, by Europeans. Therefore primary and technical education were important; secondary and higher education were unimportant. The flow of pupils into secondary schools was adjusted to the opportunities for employment after schooling. Even secondary schools did not until recently provide a curriculum which would lead to university study; pupils pursued a common course for three years and thereafter specialised in vocational subjects. Furthermore the Belgians – unlike the French – were not concerned to transform even a small élite of Africans into Europeans. Therefore there was no need – as there was in French colonial Africa – to suppress the vernacular and to use a European language of instruction from the very start of schooling. In the Belgian Congo all primary education was in the vernacular: this had the virtue that it helped to insulate the Congolese from disturbing influences from outside: their main communication with the western world was through the morally and politically aseptic intermediary of the catholic church.

Within these modest and limited educational aims, the achievement in the Congo was impressive. In the 1950s it was estimated that about half the children of school age were receiving some schooling. Although the average level of education (in the western sense) was low, bare literacy, craft skills, and vocational training, reached levels higher than in any other African colony. Even as late as 1954, the Belgian minister for the colonies, André Dequae, is reported to have said:

Civilization cannot be limited to a few individuals or even to a thousand, for its purpose is to raise the whole people to a higher level. I do not think that the method which some countries have applied has had very favourable results. We have seen that those natives who have been shown Europe and given a very advanced education did not always return to their homelands in a spirit favourable to civilization and to the mother country in particular. They have gone back as blasés, estranged from their own people . . .[31]

The shock of independence laid bare the appalling weakness of Belgian educational policy in the Congo. Leaders were suddenly needed in a nation whose schools had deliberately excluded from the curriculum education for civic and political responsibility. According to the official Belgian figures, there were, at the time of independence, only thirty-one Congolese graduates. Overnight, typists became senior civil servants and sergeants became staff officers. A university, instead of being superfluous to the educational system, became the most urgent and desperate need.

Thanks to the foresight of the catholic hierarchy, some preparation had been made to meet this crisis. Secondary schooling on a more academic curriculum lasting six years had begun in 1948. By 1954, when the first qualified pupils began to leave these secondary schools, a centre universitaire opened on Mont Amba, under the sponsorship of Louvain University. In January 1954 thirty Africans were given a preparatory course to enable them to qualify for enrolment as university students. Eleven of them passed the examination and, together with twenty-two other students, embarked in the autumn of 1954 on courses for the licence. In 1964, ten years later, Lovanium had over a thousand students, drawn from twenty-eight nationalities. The output of Congolese graduates, especially in professional and technological subjects, is still pathetically small, but the limiting factor is the supply of candidates from schools, not the capacity of the university.

In September 1954 a stone from the wall of the most ancient part of Louvain University was laid in the foundation of the science building on Mont Amba. This, together with the new university's name, are vivid symbols of the ethos of Lovanium. In constitution, in standards, in content of curricula, Lovanium was to be a replica of Louvain. And even since independence, although the constitution of the university has been revised to bring it within the influence of the Congolese government, it remains a satellite of Louvain. Louvain is still represented on its governing body. The rector of Lovanium, a Napoleonic figure whose ruthless energy and administrative genius have inspired the university since its foundation, has direct teletype link with Belgium in his room on Mont Amba. He is in touch with Louvain almost every day. The recruitment of staff, which is a persistent problem for most African universities, is greatly simplified at Lovanium by the way in which scholars can be seconded from Louvain. This link firmly secures Lovanium to the standards and quality of academic work in Louvain University; it also puts some constraint upon the content of higher education in the Congo. And the whole enterprise is deeply influenced by the supra-national character of the catholic hierarchy.

The constitutional arrangements, though they are not a reliable guide to the way the university actually runs, are interesting.[32] The university is governed by a conseil d'administration which corresponds to the council of an English civic university. One hesitates to use the word 'lay' because the chairman of council is an archbishop and eight of the sixteen members are catholic clerics. Three of the members are from Louvain, one of them being the recteur magnifique of Louvain himself. The other members include cabinet ministers, senior civil servants, and the governor of the national bank. The governing body is advised by a conseil académique supérieur, which comprises three professors from Louvain, two from Lovanium, and four academics who belong neither to Louvain nor Lovanium. These two councils co-operate to determine academic policy for the university. But neither of them meets often. The governing body has an executive comprising its local members with one or two additions. Academic business is discussed by an advisory conseil rectoral, which includes the deans and heads of institutes. The real locus of decision-making is the comité de direction which consists of the rector, two vice-rectors, and the secretary general (who has the functions of a registrar). This compact body meets at least once a week and is charged with responsibility for carrying out the general policy determined by the *de jure* governing body. It has wide powers. Its members can attend any faculty boards. Subject to consultation with deans or heads of departments, it can make decisions within the general policy touching all the university's activities. It even has some control over what members of the university may or may not publish.

The constitution provides for consultation with the academic staff over all academic policy-making. There are faculty boards (at which attendance is compulsory) which meet once a month. The faculty boards do not elect their deans, but they do submit two nominations to the executive of the governing body and the executive selects one or other of these names for a two-year term of appointment. The duties of the deans are spelt out in great detail. They are the channel of communication between the academic staff and the administration (namely the comité de direction); they are charged with keeping the administration informed about activities in the faculty, and also with keeping the faculty informed about the views of the administration.

The hierarchy of posts in the university is determined by detailed and explicit regulations. A full professor must have the agrégation or a special doctorate, and at least four years' experience as a chargé de cours (lecturer). A chargé de cours must have the agrégation or a doctorate and have had experience in a junior post. Permanent full-time members of the teaching staff teach for a minimum of 180 and a maximum of 270 hours per year. They are appointed by the governing body on the recommendation of the comité de direction after consultation with the academic council and the dean in whose faculty the appointment is made. The basic establishment in each department is one professor, one chargé de corps, and one assistant. If student numbers justify addition to this establishment they are authorised by the comité de direction on the recommendation of the dean. As we noticed for the Haile Sellassie I University, the administrative procedure for Lovanium University is spelt out in such detail that when the university comes to be run by the Congolese themselves, it will at least be evident if improper procedures are followed. But this is still a long way off. In 1964 there were only five Africans on the academic staff of the university; it is evident that Louvain's responsibility will last for many years yet. Indeed, with the present constitution, which gives professors from Louvain a preponderance over Lovanium professors on the conseil académique supérieur, and which interposes this body between the staff and the administration on major matters of academic policy, there is a risk that Louvain might 'breathe down the neck' of Lovanium. While the present rector is in command, and maintains his brilliantly successful despotism, this risk may be ignored. But just as special relations between the Asquith colleges and the University of London not only conferred great benefits but involved also some unwelcome constraints, the relation between Louvain and Lovanium may do the same.

We have already mentioned that Belgian policy for educating the Congolese gave little emphasis to conventional secondary education and none to university education. The school system was equipped to produce technicians, clerks, agricultural and veterinary assistants, and craftsmen. Almost the only boys who received a literary education were those destined to be priests. Even the teaching profession was staffed predominantly by Europeans. The realisation that a country cannot run its own affairs without graduates in the

arts and social sciences came too late to save the Congo from the chaos of the
1960s. But Lovanium, while offering an impressive array of professional and
technological studies, has certainly not laid itself open to the charge of being
narrowly vocational. Rather the reverse.[33] To be admitted to a degree course
a student has to possess a diplôme homologue d'humanités grecolatines,
latines-mathématiques, latines-sciences, or modernes-scientifiques; or equivalent qualifications. The equivalent qualification for English-speaking
students is a pass in G.C.E., division I, with five O-level subjects and two A-
level subjects. These entry qualifications are prescribed by state law. Since
many Congolese schools are not yet teaching to this level, the university runs
a section propédeutique which prepares students in one year for admission to
degree courses. The curriculum for this course gives a vivid idea of the uncompromising requirements set by Lovanium. For admission to a degree
course in the faculty of arts and letters the student has to qualify in philosophy, French language and literature, Latin, English, history, African
culture and linguistics, and mathematics. For admission to degree courses in
sciences, medicine, engineering, or agriculture, the cours propédeutique comprises philosophy, French language and literature, Latin, English, mathematics, physics, and chemistry. These courses are a striking contrast to the
narrow range of subjects offered in the concessional-entry courses in English-
speaking universities in Africa.

Once admitted to the course for a degree (licence) the student faces a
pedagogic marathon. He is exposed to more than twice as many lectures as he
would have in Ibadan or Makerere, and, in science subjects, to about the
same amount of laboratory work. To illustrate the pattern of curriculum we
give some details of the courses in the faculty of philosophy and letters, which
corresponds to the faculty of arts in English-speaking universities.

The course leading to a licence takes four years from the equivalent of A-
level entry; the first two years are occupied by courses for the candidature,
and the subsequent two years culminate, if the candidate is successful, in the
licence. In level of achievement a licence from Lovanium is probably somewhat higher than an honours degree in an English university. During the first
year all students in the faculty take a common course. It includes philosophy
and logic; history, including African history; African literature; a little about
African art and archaeology; and a course on society and institutions from
classical antiquity to modern Africa. In the second year of candidature,
students can choose to specialise in philologie Africaine, philologie romane,
philologie classique, or philologie germanique.

Students who survive to the candidature (there is a heavy failure-rate)
embark on another two years of study for the licence. Whatever their specialisms they come together for a common course in philosophy with options of
aesthetics, history of music, or historical techniques. They can continue to
specialise in African studies (which include anthropology, African religions
and philosophies, African sociology, study of oral tradition, African history,

and an African language); or romance philology (which is an intensive study of French civilisation and literature including medieval French), with options in Latin, anthropology, and African religions and philosophies; or germanic philology (which is an intensive study of English, including Anglo-Saxon, with some French), with options in German, Swedish, Dutch, and African religions and philosophies. In his final year every student has to write a thesis on a special subject, which he 'defends' at a public examination.[34]

Beside the faculty of philosophy and letters there are the following:

Theology A two-year course for a licence, open to students who have a baccalauréat in theology or who have graduated from a four-year seminary.

Medicine A seven-year course, comprising (a) a three-year candidature (which covers pre-clinical subjects and some general education in philosophy and mathematics); followed by (b) a four-year clinical course, including an intern year, leading to a doctorate. There is also a school for nurses, a course for pharmacists, and a graduate diploma in tropical medicine. The hospital is on the university campus.

Law A three-year course for a licence, open to students who have completed a two-year candidature in the faculty of philosophy and letters.

Science As for arts students: a two-year candidature-course followed by a two-year course for the licence. Apart from obligatory courses on philosophy, there are no opportunities for combinations of subjects across faculties. Students can specialise in biology, chemistry, mathematics, or physics.

Politics, sociology, and economics As for art students. Students can specialise in politics and administration; sociology; economics; commerce and finance; and African social anthropology.

A faculté polytechnique which offers a five-year course for the qualification of diplôme d'ingénieur agronome des régions tropicales (it is approximately equivalent to an honours degree in agricultural science elsewhere); and a diplôme d'ingénieur civil in civil engineering.

In quality of teaching, in standard of achievement demanded for graduation, in content and range of curriculum, in the amount and sophistication of its research work, Lovanium stands very high indeed among African universities. It combines the prime virtue of the Asquith colleges – insistence on a high standard of achievement – with the prime virtue of the American university – a broad based education which incorporates indigenous material into the undergraduate curriculum. The university nevertheless has shortcomings, though some of these may disappear if the Congo consolidates its social and economic life. The most disappointing feature at present is outside the university's control, namely the distribution of enrolments among faculties. Although there is a large enrolment for medicine, very few students elect to read engineering, agriculture, or science. The heaviest enrolment is in the faculty of politics, sociology, and economics; this is a pity, for although graduates qualified in these fields are undoubtedly needed, it is not a faculty which qualifies its graduates to teach in secondary schools. The university will not be able to continue to insist on such high standards of achievement for admission and for the licence unless the secondary schools are staffed with teachers who have themselves survived this strenuous discipline.

The chief criticism which can be brought against Lovanium is one inherent in any continental model exported to Africa. American and British universities, although profoundly influenced by universities on the continent of Europe, have not adopted the laissez-faire attitude toward students which is characteristic of universities in France and Germany. English-speaking universities throughout the world, probably influenced by tradition from Oxford and Cambridge, still regard themselves as *in loco parentis* toward students. This attitude is being challenged, particularly in the United States, but there is no disposition on the part of British or American universities to abandon it; and it is a valuable feature of English-speaking universities in Africa. Not so in Lovanium. It is true that the object of the university, as set out in its constitution, is not only academic but is also to contribute 'dans le respect de leurs convictions, à leur promotion spirituelle, morale, culturelle, sociale et civique'. Lovanium has all the facilities to achieve these ends: all students reside on or near the campus, in simple but well designed hostels or married quarters; the ratio of staff to students over the first ten years was about one to five; the whole of Mont Amba is united under the discipline of the catholic church. Yet the informal personal relationship between teacher and pupil, which alone can ensure the sort of education which the constitution claims to offer, is lacking. Although the university is heavily clerical, with priests in many of the key positions, there is little evidence of tutorial and pastoral care. The authorities know a good deal about the students statistically (even when there were only 1,000 students their records were entered on IBM cards), but practically nothing about them individually. One has the impression that the attitude of most members of the teaching staff is deliberately remote and authoritarian. A prodigious amount of attention is devoted to the university as an institution: its buildings, its prestige as a centre for research, its public relations, especially overseas. But in all this the welfare and fortunes of individual students seem to have little place.

We mention this attitude not to condemn it, but to make the point that a policy of non-intervention in the lives of students, characteristic of European continental universities, could be expected to appear, and does appear, when this pattern of university is established in Africa. This is not to say that provision for student-welfare is neglected. Lovanium provides admirable amenities for its students, rather in the way a paternalistic industry provides for its employees. There are restaurants to which students can bring their friends. There are recreation rooms, reading rooms, a bar where students can hold 'longer and more boisterous gatherings', a splendid swimming pool, regular film shows, sports, a good medical service, and an advisory service organised by the institute of psychology. There is a diversity of student-clubs and societies, though all of them have to be authorised by the university authorities.

The disciplinary rules are aimed at maintaining agreeable conditions in the community rather than inculcating good habits in individual students. Thus article 8 of the hostel rules for men runs:

Students shall refrain from returning late at night to the hostels. If the hour is very late they shall remain in town rather than disturb the sleep of their fellow-students and the tranquillity of the homes.[35]

It may well be that in the context of Congolese life, which is predominantly catholic, the pastoral and tutorial functions which are such an important ingredient of university life in Britain can simply be left to the catholic church. But the catholic church in the Congo is authoritarian and didactic; and one cannot help but feel that the dialectic between teacher and pupil, the imperfect but nonetheless valuable bridge which in a residential university is thrown between two generations, is missing at Lovanium; and that this omission is detracting from the great contribution which, in other ways, Lovanium is making to Congolese society.

V   FRENCH EDUCATIONAL STRATEGY IN AFRICA[36]

Strategy in colonial education can be described as deliberate policy based on the political and economic objectives of the metropolitan power. France had such a strategy for her former African colonies; it has often been defined in Governor Carde's words: 'instruire la masse et dégager l'élite', and the élite were to be assimilated into the citizenry of France. But this definition over-simplifies the subtle and changing interplay of forces which began over a century ago and which has shaped the present system of education in some eighteen African states.

European settlement in Senegal began as early as 1639, but it was not until the nineteenth century that plans were made to establish formal education there. In 1818 the minister for the navy, who was responsible for the French colonies, decided, on the advice of the governor, that elementary education should be in the hands of laymen rather than missionaries, out of respect for the muslim faith. The notorious monitorial system of Lancaster and Bell was in vogue at that time and was recommended for Senegal.[37] A. M. Dard was sent out to lay the foundation for a system of schooling. Dard must have been a remarkable man. He learnt the local tongue, Wolof, and compiled a Wolof dictionary and grammar. He is said also to have incurred hostility from the administration because he employed Wolof as a medium of instruction in his school. He began in a modest way a system of secular schooling but after he left Senegal his policies were not consolidated.

It was decreed in 1829 that French should be the sole medium of instruction in Senegal, but in fact there was no financial provision for instruction at all. Spasmodic classes were run by soldiers or administrators in their spare time, but nothing much more. In 1837 the minister for the navy negotiated with a teaching order, the Brothers of Ploermel, to run schools in Senegal. The schools were intended to be narrowly vocational, teaching such subjects as river navigation and workshop crafts. This project, too, ran into trouble. It was not long before critics hinted that the Brothers of Ploermel were (not unnaturally) more interested in serving the interests of the catholic church than those of France. They were devoting teaching time to Latin at the expense of French, and they were arousing hostility among the muhammadans.

The year 1848 was as important for Senegal as it was for France. Ripples from the revolution reached the west coast of Africa, freed the slaves in Senegal, and gave the colony the right to send a representative to the parliament in Paris. Once more the colonial administrators were faced with the need for education; for the freed slaves had to be trained, and work had to be found for them to do. Under the vigorous governorship of Faidherbe, who went to Senegal in 1854, a foundation for a public system of schooling was laid. The native élite was to be educated in an école des otages at St Louis. The masses were to receive a simple vocational training together with a grounding in the French language. Although missionary education was not suppressed (it could even qualify for state subsidy), government schools were set up strictly under non-clerical control. 'There is no relationship', Faidherbe is reported to have said, 'between the religion of the French and the metric system'.

After Faidherbe's departure the foundations he had laid crumbled. There was no firm consistent educational policy from Paris; nor was there any financial support. Whether schools were encouraged or not depended on the interests of colonial governors. One by one, schools in the interior closed their doors; the lay schools in the coastal towns were abandoned or taken over by missionaries. By 1883, according to one government report, all the schools of Senegal were in the hands of the church.[38] In 1900 there were only ten primary schools in Senegal, with a thousand pupils; and the other French colonies in West Africa had even fewer children at school.

The next wave of interest in French colonial education was generated from a new source: the combined energies of the Alliance française and the Mission laïque française. It was secular, not to say anti-clerical, and it formulated for the first time a national purpose for overseas education. Its mouthpiece was Pierre Foncin, who was also at the time inspector general of French education and vice-chairman of the national consultative committee for colonial education. In a statement made in 1900, Foncin defined a strategy for French education overseas, reminiscent of Macaulay's strategy for Indian education:

If the administrative, economic and financial autonomy of the colonies appears to me to be very desirable, it is perhaps all the more necessary to attach them to the *Métropole* by a very solid psychological bond, against the day when their progressive emancipation ends in a form of federation, as is probable . . . that they be, and they remain, French in language, thought, and spirit.[39]

Foncin's views, backed by the influential organisations determined to propagate French civilisation in Africa, mark the beginning of an official campaign of cultural evangelism which has continued ever since. By 1903 the
first administrative arrangements for conducting this campaign were promulgated.[40] A school system run by the state and controlled as to its strategy
from Paris, was established. There were still to be two avenues of schooling:
one for Africans, with local relevance, giving emphasis to the French language
and to such useful arts as agriculture, and, in muslim areas, including Arabic;
the other for Frenchmen living in Senegal, together with a few selected 'assimilated' Africans, giving an education exactly corresponding to that in the
métropole. In brief, the masses were to learn French and to have vocational
training; the élite were to have an education identical with that provided for
Frenchmen. And so another step was taken in the westernisation of Africa.
But the efforts of the Alliance française and the Mission laïque did not go
unchallenged. There were still in French Africa – as in British Africa – colonial
administrators who believed that education would only spoil the natives for
honest toil and equip them with weapons they could turn against their
masters. 'Restrict yourself', said the secretary general of Guinea to one advocate of education, 'to oral lessons given in the shade of a tree'; and he ordered
his district officers to spend no money on schools.

As in Britain, so in France, the humanitarian aspirations which are the
aftermath of war prompted administrators to display more interest in the
welfare of colonial peoples. Up to 1914 the proposal that a few assimilated
Africans might have the benefit of a French pattern of education had been
made cautiously and had elicited little response. But in 1919 Henri Simon,
minister for the colonies, gave it great emphasis. 'We should dedicate ourselves', he said, 'to the establishment, wherever possible and as rapidly as
possible, of secondary centres of French civilisation. . . .'[41] In 1920 Simon
was followed as minister by Albert Sarraut, one of the great figures in the
history of education in the French colonies. He tightened the control of
colonial education from Paris. Colonial governors had to submit reports to
him on the state of education in their regions. He started a vigorous campaign
to recruit teachers. By 1924 Sarraut had established in West Africa a secondary
school leaving certificate corresponding to, and under certain conditions
accepted as equivalent to, the baccalauréat in France. This, like the overseas
school certificates run by English examining bodies, became a mixed blessing.
Throughout the 1920s and 1930s there was, as there was also in Britain, a good
deal of talk about adapting education to the needs and aptitudes of the African
people; Sarraut himself frequently emphasised it. But, as in the British colonies, the examination-fetish stood menacingly in the way of adaptation,
partly because most teachers could only teach effectively what they themselves
had learnt as students in France, but mainly because the Africans themselves
saw beyond the secondary school leaving certificate the faint but fantastic
allurement of becoming an évolué, sharing in equality with their masters the

management of the country. The inspector for primary education for French West Africa, M. Davesne, reported in 1932 that despite all the talk about the need for adaptation, the curriculum was evolving 'with increased acceleration toward an imitation of metropolitan education . . .'.[42] The fact was that education for the élite in the French colonies was working well, and the less it was adapted to African needs the more successful and acceptable it was.

After world war I there was vague talk, but nothing more, about eventual higher education in the French African colonies. It was not until after world war II that any action was taken. The new jolt to the conscience of French colonial administrators dates from the Brazzaville conference in 1944. The war was still being fought in Europe. But the French provisional government called a meeting, opened by de Gaulle, to consider what status French Africa should have when peace came. The conference emphatically asserted the unity of the French nation in Europe and overseas, in a memorable passage which is the key to an understanding of higher education in French Africa today:

Les fins de l'oeuvre de civilisation accomplie par la France dans les colonies écartent toute idée d'autonomie, toute possibilité d'évolution hors du bloc français de l'Empire; la constitution éventuelle, même lointaine, de *self-government* dans les colonies est à écarter.[43]

Political history since 1944 has not precisely followed these instructions; but educational history has, by and large, not disappointed those who conferred at Brazzaville. Most of the universities in the French-speaking parts of Africa (excluding the Congolese Republic) are still closely linked to France. Some still come formally under the jurisdiction of France; others – though all formal links have been dissolved – remain voluntarily close to some university in the métropole. Only Guinea has opted out altogether from the French educational system.

Already in August 1945 steps were taken to bring French higher education within easier reach of Africans. The ministry of colonies sent telegrams to the governors general of Equatorial Africa, Madagascar, West Africa, and to the governor of Cameroun requiring to know among other things how many students had qualified for higher education in France, so that an appropriate number of scholarships could be awarded; and the colonies were told that the universities of Bordeaux, Montpelier, Paris, and Toulouse had made arrangements to receive Africans who desired higher education. A year later a fund for economic and social development (called Fonds d'investissement pour le développement économique et social de la France d'outre mer: FIDES) was set up; it was similar in purpose to the British colonial development and welfare fund (CD & W), to finance development programmes in the French colonies. In the same year the French Union was created; the policy of assimilation became intensified; Senegal, Ivory Coast, and other French possessions were no longer colonies attached to the French republic: they *were* the French republic.

For education in the French territories of Africa all this meant an undertow toward conformity with patterns of education in France. By 1948 it was officially announced that secondary education in West Africa was now aligned with that of the métropole, not only in regard to curriculum and duration of studies but in regard to diplomas as well. Six years of primary schooling led to a certificat d'études: another seven years of secondary schooling led to a baccalauréat, with some choice of subjects. Those who succeeded in getting a baccalauréat were entitled to enter any university in France, at home or overseas.

Clearly the next logical step was to found universities in French Africa. But there was no strong local pressure in favour of this. Indeed African *évolués* resented the suggestion that there should be a university in Dakar, for this would deprive Africans of the privilege of going to France for their higher education and it might open the door to adaptation of the curriculum to African conditions. Thompson and Adloff quote from a speech made by a Guinean representative in the French Union Assembly in 1950:

> The day you make a distinction between higher studies in the Métropole and those you want to set up in Africa, you will not find a single African in the University of Dakar. . . . We want to have higher education at home, but we want it to be exactly equal to that of the Métropole. We want a Metropolitan curriculum . . . and the same diplomas as in France, for we are as French as are the French of the Métropole.[44]

The representative from Guinea had no need to fear. Since the West African territories were now part of France, their institutions were, with minor differences, governed by French law. French law includes meticulous and detailed decrees covering all aspects of higher education: these decrees apply to universities in Africa as strictly as to universities in France. Indeed, in order to understand the export of higher education to the French territories we have to remember that 'the university' in France is not a society of scholars: it is an administrative concept. The society of scholars is the faculty. The university administers a federation of virtually autonomous faculties, within the framework of decrees laid down by the ministry of education. Thus (to illustrate this point) the students' handbook for the University of Dakar for 1961–2 sets out the conditions for matriculation under a decree from Paris of 21 July 1897! Cheating at examinations in Dakar is punishable under disciplinary rules laid down under a law passed in France on 23 December 1901.

Between 1945 and 1950, under the scholarship system we have mentioned, hundreds of French-speaking Africans migrated to French universities. It was not long before their presence embarrassed the government. Africans in Paris organised a federation of students of black Africa (FEANF) which aligned itself with the communists. The federation became a nursery for aggressive nationalism; it agitated for better living conditions in Paris for its members; it denounced the activities of the overseas ministry; it emitted (for example in a book: 'Les étudiants noirs parlent') irritating and gushing political sentiments. Some Africans after graduation found themselves so attached to Paris that they would not return to their own continent. They sat in cafés in the university quarter indulging in endless nostalgic talk and propaganda about pan-Africanism and négritude. Moreover the ungrateful students were costing France a lot of money: according to French officials, forty or fifty students could be taught in Africa for the cost of teaching (or even failing to teach) one in France. So, despite the misgivings of some African intellectuals, the French authorities decided that higher education must be established in Africa. Although there are superficial similarities between the terms of apprenticeship prescribed for African universities by France and Britain, the prodigious centralisation of the French university system made the implantation of universities in Africa easier for the French than it was for the British. In some African countries the first step was for an individual faculty in France to sponsor professional training, sending professors and lecturers (maîtres de conférence) on secondment. Thus in 1947 the faculty of law in Aix-Marseille organised courses in Tananarive. The next step was to create an institute for higher studies, usually incorporating the pioneer operations of individual faculties in any professional colleges already existing in the country. By decree in 1950 an institute for higher studies was created in Dakar. Its activities were supervised by faculties in the universities of Paris and Bordeaux. Academic staff from these two universities was seconded to Dakar; examinations were controlled by professors from these two universities. The relationship was analogous to that established between the Asquith colleges and the University of London. In 1955 a similar institute was created at Tananarive. There followed institutes in Abidjan in 1958, sponsored by faculties in Paris, and in Brazzaville in 1959, sponsored by faculties in Bordeaux. More recently the Cameroun has acquired an institute at Yaounde.

After a few years of noviciate the institutes qualify to become universities. The first to be promoted in sub-Saharan Africa was at Dakar. By a decree from the French ministry of education of 24 February 1957, Dakar was established as the eighteenth university of France. The decree declares that the university shall be governed by the statutes which govern the universities of metropolitan France; that the academic staff at Dakar shall be part of the cadres of the French universities, eligible for all their privileges; that the regulations in force for universities in France, particularly those concerning admission, examinations, and standards of achievement, shall apply equally to Dakar University; and that, as in the métropole, each faculty should have its own administration and financial autonomy.

Shortly after this the Federation of Mali set itself up as a republic, soon afterwards to split into the republics of Senegal and Mali. One of the first acts of the Mali Federation after independence was to entrust its university to the French ministry of education: it was an astonishing tribute to the success of French educational strategy. The concordat between France and Mali (subsequently adopted as a concordat between France and Senegal) included the following:

(i) The University of Dakar is transferred to the Mali Federation.

(ii) The Mali Federation entrusts to the French Republic, which accepts this responsibility, the control and administration of the University of Dakar.

(iii) The French Republic will administer the university in such a way as to maintain and develop higher education of a quality equal to that in the universities of France.

(iv) The University of Dakar will develop its research and its curricula in a way consistent with its responsibilities to Mali, the Community, and Africa.

(v) The rector shall be nominated by agreement between the two governments (Mali and France) and the university staff shall continue under the rules and conditions for corresponding members of staff of French universities.

(vi) Grades and diplomas conferred by the University of Dakar shall, both in Mali and France, have the same value as French grades and diplomas.[45]

By 1966 there will be three national universities in Africa – at Abidjan, Dakar, and Tananarive – linked to the French university system by concordats resting on decrees from the government of France, and a centre d'enseignement supérieur at Brazzaville; all continuing to receive massive help in men and money from France. In addition there is the university at Yaounde in Cameroun, heavily subsidised from France but, because of the bilingual community it serves, with a curriculum somewhat different from that of the French universities, leading to diplomas which are not equivalent to French diplomas. The one colony which opted out altogether from the Union was Guinea, which is therefore deprived of official help from France. Guinea has no university of its own, but sends large numbers of students to European countries. In 1965 France and the USSR were receiving the largest numbers.

In addition to African universities legally attached to the French university system, there are in Tunis and Morocco independent universities which began under the French system and (as the Sudan does with Britain) still maintain voluntary links with French universities. The University of Tunis began under French direction as an institute of higher studies in 1945. It became a university in 1960. Although it is outside the French system, it still draws the chairmen of its examination boards from Paris, and recruits its academic staff according to the rigid principles laid down in France. Similarly in Morocco, there is no formal link between its institutions of higher education (in Rabat, Casablanca, and Fez) and the French system. But there is a cultural convention between France and Morocco, and Moroccan universities receive co-operation from Bordeaux. It was hardly to be expected that the curricula of higher education in Morocco would indefinitely remain replicas of the curricula in France. Already there is some diversification. Thus to speed up the production of administrators and functionaries the course for the licence in law can be taken in three years instead of the usual four years, and it can be taken in French or Arabic: 'ce qui a posé', as a French academic put it, 'un délicat problème d'équivalence'.[46] But the Moroccan universities hold to their lifeline of equivalence, for in the faculty of letters it is possible to graduate with any of three kinds of licence: a licence marocaine in Arabic, a licence marocaine in French, and (for safety) a licence marocaine de type français which corresponds to the licence granted by Bordeaux.

It is evident from what we have written that to look more closely at a university in one of the French territories in Africa is simply to look at the French university. It will be enough, therefore, to sketch very briefly the present state of one of these universities; we select the University of Dakar.

Those who designed the university dreamt that it might become a great intellectual centre for French-speaking Africans from all over the continent. The balkanisation of the French territories has made this dream unlikely of fulfilment. But the grand concept is there: a splendid approach from the city; a gallic geometry (as in Leopoldville) about the setting of the buildings; a spaciousness about the buildings themselves – the French government, through FIDES, had spent some 25 million NF on them by 1963. Admission to the university is through the French baccalauréat or its equivalent. Students are admitted to one or other of four faculties: law (which includes the social sciences), medicine, science, and letters. The first year of the course is a preparation for admission to the degree course. At the end of this first year students must pass a qualifying examination known in the faculty of letters as C.E.L.G. (certificat d'études littéraires générales). There is a 'classical' C.E.L.G. and a 'modern' C.E.L.G.: the one comprising French, Latin, and a choice of Greek, a modern language, history or geography; the other comprising French, a modern language, and choice of another modern language, or history, or geography.* There are similar qualifying certificates at the end of the first year in other faculties, except in the faculty of law and economics, where the first examination is already part of the course for the licence.

Successful candidates may then enter on the course for the licence. In the faculty of letters candidates must acquire four certificats d'études supérieures in order to obtain a licence. In 1964 the certificates had to be chosen from classics, French, English, Spanish, philosophy (including psychology), sociology, history and geography; as the faculty develops other subjects will be added. Students who are awarded a licence (which is the equivalent of a first degree) may go on to work for advanced diplomas in single subjects, necessary for the next step up the academic ladder, called aggrégation; or they may work for doctorates. In pattern, and indeed very largely in content, this is simply the prescription for undergraduate study in any French university. There are, in addition, opportunities to pursue studies not normally part of

* The C.E.L.G. system will come to an end in France from the beginning of the academic year 1966-7.

the licence: there is, for example, an institute of islamic studies which offers courses for a certificate, again a French one, awarded by the institute of islamic studies of the University of Paris. The academic staff at Dakar is still predominantly French. Most professors are in fact recruited from among those on the French cadre, to serve a term of five years (which can be renewed) under conditions of secondment, guaranteed by decree, which are very reassuring. At the end of their secondment the minister of education is obliged to reintegrate them into the academic staff in a French university. They lose no seniority while they are abroad and on their return they partake in any privileges meanwhile accorded to their colleagues in the métropole.

The mode of government of the University of Dakar, like the pattern of studies, corresponds closely with that of the sister universities in France. Shortly after the institute for higher studies was created in Dakar a decree was passed (27 November 1950) establishing the double office of rector of the institute and head of all public-education within the West African Federation. This is the metropolitan pattern, though since independence the rector has had no responsibility for primary and secondary education. The rector is appointed by the government. He is the government's agent. But by French tradition he is a university man, an ally of the academics and not their opponent. The rector presides over a council of fifteen, consisting of the four deans of faculties, two professors from each faculty, elected by the whole faculty (called the assembly), and three persons co-opted from outside the university (in 1963 the co-opted members were the president of the Senegal national assembly, the minister of justice, and the president of the chamber of commerce).

This constitution firmly puts domestic decision-making into the hands of the local university staff, and within the framework of the laws and decrees governing all French universities, day-to-day control is by academics. The genuine academic society, however, is not so much the university as the faculty. The faculty controls the disbursement of the finances allotted to it. It nominates and recommends persons to be invited to fill vacant professorships. It elects a dean-designate who is then formally appointed by the minister of education. Arrangements for student government and discipline are also characteristically French and are set out in a succession of governmental decrees valid for metropolitan France and all French territories. Each year in the first fortnight of December the students in each faculty elect five representatives by secret ballot. The votes are counted in public under the surveillance of the dean. If fewer than ten per cent of the students vote there is no election. The combined twenty student representatives (five from each of the four faculties) decide who among themselves shall negotiate with the university council or sit on committees which have student representation. If the university council has to deal with a matter touching student-discipline, the council co-opts representatives of the students: a contrast to the more paternalistic attitudes toward students common in the older universities of England and inherited by universities in the English-speaking parts of Africa.

The British are reluctant to believe that such a system of university government, in which academics are civil servants and in which policy is crystallised as decrees from Paris, could possibly be consistent with the autonomy and freedom necessary for good scholarship and good teaching. In fact it is consistent. The French are as convinced of the virtues of liberty as we are, and they have clothed university constitutions with serviceable and hard-wearing conventions, just as we have in Britain. In Africa the French may have done better in this respect than we have, for their conventions seem to be serviceable and hard-wearing in the tropics too; which has not always been true of British conventions. A senior official of the French ministry of co-operation, writing recently of the constitutional structure of French universities in Africa, had this to say:

C'est ainsi, en particulier, que les franchises universitaires traditionelles ... sont garanties par les différents accords ou par les textes législatifs ou réglementaires nationaux visés par ses accords. Ces franchises et libertés traditionelles sont évidemment la condition première de tout recrutement valable et de tout enseignement supérieur digne de ce nom.[47]

Cultural imperialism has not always been the strategy of French educational policy overseas. The Brothers of Ploermel, although under contract from the minister of the navy, concentrated their teaching upon proselytisation, moral education, and training in the useful arts. It was not until the 1920s that cultural evangelism became a declared strategy of France. Even since then there has been an ambivalence about French educational policy, as the convictions of policy makers swing between two poles of attraction: on one hand the virtues of a centralised bureaucracy, which are a powerful safeguard in preserving the integrity of the world-wide French community; on the other hand the libertarian sentiments inherited from 1789 and reaffirmed in 1848. The African attitude is ambivalent too. Many of the younger intellectuals regard the rigidity of the French curriculum as a device of crypto-imperialism:

> This beleaguered heart
> Alien to my language and my dress
> On which bite like a brace
> The borrowed sentiments and customs of Europe[48]

The attitude among the older evolués is different; even if they demand political independence they admire and accept the monolithic structure of French education and are content to remain part of it. Fulbert Youlou, a former president of the French Congo, paid a touching tribute to French educational strategy when he declared, in 1960:

In expressing myself spontaneously in French, I do not have the feeling of betraying the African culture. I simply provide an incomparable means of rendering it intelligible to the entire world.[49]

But the ambivalence persists, particularly over the pattern of higher education. The French strategy of cultural assimilation, and the common African acquiescence in this strategy, naturally preserves conformity with curricula in France and impedes movements toward adaptation. Equivalence of diplomas as between Africa and the métropole is not desirable solely (as it is to the British) on pedagogical grounds: it is important to the French on political grounds too. Furthermore equivalence has a much more precise and vivid meaning to a citizen of the French Community than it has to a citizen of the British Commonwealth. For us it means an approximate parity of esteem in the academic world; for them it means eligibility for admission to the French civil hierarchy.

The French are, however, still convinced that there must be adaptation of the content of higher education in Africa and they are thinking constructively about the problem. Claude Tardits, secretary general of the institute of ethnology, has recently commented upon this thinking. Education orientated solely to French humanities and social sciences can lead, he thinks, to a double impasse: it gives the African who receives it a privileged culture which not only cuts him off from his own culture, but which also will itself deteriorate because in Africa he will be cut off from its sources of renewal. Tardits therefore urges strongly the introduction of African studies into university curricula in Africa, and he concludes his argument with the words:

En quelques mots, seule l'étude des civilisations africaines peut permettre aux universités de ce continent de jouer un rôle stimulateur durable dans la vie intellectuelle.[50]

The common objection to incorporating African civilisation into undergraduate courses is that there is not yet sufficient material to make this practicable. Tardits dismisses this objection. The institute of ethnology in the University of Paris, to mention only one source of material in French, has published thirty-three volumes on Africa. British and American workers have made equally substantial contributions. In subjects such as land tenure, market economy, the political structure of African communities, African art and music and religions, the techniques of oral tradition: in all these, according to Tardits, there is already a sufficient accumulation of research to justify adaptation of the curriculum without danger to quality in teaching or loss of equivalence in the value of diplomas. African universities should have institutes of human sciences where these topics are codified by western techniques and integrated with western thought, and where, above all, they are taught to the young. The need is to distinguish the *structure* and *methodology* of western thinking, which are of world-wide application and which must, in the French Community, remain French; and the *content* of thinking, which must be specific to place and time. The French, in other words, believe in adaptation in the content of African school and university courses, but on their own terms, which are that there must be no weakening of links with French civilisation. After a conference of French African ministers of education, held in Paris in 1961, the French set up a 'comité d'études pour l'adaptation des programmes scolaires en Afrique'. The reflections of this committee may have significance for education all over Africa; for the problem of how to reconcile the supra-national and national ingredients of education is one confronting all African states and their metropolitan sponsors. Education, at least beyond the primary level, must have international currency: it must also incorporate regional cultures. For half a century lip-service has been paid to this principle, but no nation has yet successfully achieved a reconciliation.

REFERENCES AND NOTES

The references and notes are arranged as follows:

The sources used for part I are assembled in a bibliographical summary (pp. 380–2). There are no references in the text except to certain quotations; the sources of these are in footnotes.

For parts II and III the references and notes are numbered, and are assembled chapter by chapter.

A summary of the primary and secondary sources consulted, together with some additional background material, is given in the bibliography (pp. 527–40).

Introduction

[1] Basic documents are:

(i) For the West Indies: *Report of the West Indies committee of the commission on higher education in the colonies;* 1944–45, Cmd. 6654, V [Irvine report].

(ii) For Malaya: *Higher education in Malaya: report of the commission appointed by the secretary of state for the colonies, June 1939,* Colonial No. 173 (HMSO, 1939); *Report of the commission on university education in Malaya,* Colonial No. 229 (HMSO, 1948); *Report of the commission of enquiry on the University of Malaya, 1957,* Singapore sessional paper No. Cmd. 54 of 1957. There is a good general account and some interesting discussion of some other Far Eastern universities in T. H. Silcock, *Southeast Asian university* (Durham, N.C., 1964).

(iii) For Ceylon: *Report of the Ceylon university commission,* Ceylon sessional paper XXIII of 1959; *Report of the universities commission, 1962,* Ceylon sessional paper XVI of 1963.

(iv) For Pakistan: *Report of the commission on national education. Government of Pakistan, ministry of education, January to August 1959* (Karachi, 1960).

[2] A good brief account of the history of technical education in India is to be found in R. I. Crane's 'Technical education and economic development in India before world war I', in *Education and economic development,* ed. C. A. Anderson and M. G. Bowman (Durham, N.C., 1965) 167–201.

[3] It is, for example, less serious in the Sudan, where the salary differentials between graduates and technical college diplomates are narrower than in, say, Nigeria.

[4] Anyone wishing to pursue this aspect of Indian higher education will find valuable material in the writings of Edward Shils, e.g. 'The intellectual between tradition and modernity: the Indian situation', *Comparative studies in society and history,* supplement I (The Hague, 1961).

[5] (a) Institute of research on overseas programs, Michigan State University, *The international programs of American universities* (East Lansing, 1958).

(b) E. W. Weidner, *The world role of universities* (New York, 1962).

(c) J. W. Gardner, *AID and the universities* (New York, 1964).

[6] Eric Ashby, *African universities and western tradition* (Cambridge, Mass., 1964) 49.

[7] Ref. 4.

[8] Margery Perham, *The colonial reckoning* (London, 1961) 34.

[9] There are, nevertheless, some illuminating comments on this theme by people who have become familiar with African societies, e.g. K. A. Busia, *The challenge of Africa* (London, 1962); M. J. Herskovits, *The human factor in changing Africa* (New York, 1962); J. V. Taylor, *The primal vision* (London, 1963); also in some articles in a collection edited by W. R. Bascom and M. J. Herskovits: *Continuity and change in African cultures* (Chicago, 1959), and in the proceedings of a seminar held in 1959, edited by Aidan Southall: *Social change in modern Africa* (London, 1961).

PART I: THE SETTING

Chapters 1 and 2

In writing this introduction to our study we have relied on published material. Rather than pepper the text with references we bring together in this summary a list of sources we have consulted, together with some comments on them.

No-one who wants to learn about medieval universities need go far beyond Hastings Rashdall's brilliant essay, as expanded and corrected by F. M. Powicke and A. B. Emden: *The universities of Europe in the middle ages*, 3 vols. (London, 1936). The reader who would like to read translations of some primary sources should turn to Lynn Thorndike's *University records and life in the middle ages* (New York, 1944) which includes thirteenth century university statutes and regulations, announcements and synopses of courses, a medieval calendar of the University of Paris, and other curiosities. An entertaining brief account of medieval universities is to be found in C. H. Haskins' Colver Lectures at Brown University: *The rise of universities* (Ithaca, 1957).

The most useful history of German universities up to the turn of the century is still Friedrich Paulsen's *The German universities and university study*, trans. by Frank Thilly, (London, 1908). The philosophy of education which led to the ascendancy of German universities in the nineteenth century and their collapse under Hitler is well described by F. Lilge in *The abuse of learning* (New York, 1948); see also the chapter on universities in R. H. Samuel and R. H. Thomas: *Education and society in modern Germany* (London, 1949). There are many histories of individual German universities which describe their constitution and government; one which may be specially recommended is Ernst Gundelach's *Die Verfassung der Göttinger Universität in drei Jahrhunderten* (Göttingen, 1955). A good deal has been written on the influence of German universities on British higher education. References to this can be found in Eric Ashby, *Technology and the academics* (London, 1958). One basic document which is always worth re-reading is Matthew Arnold's *Higher schools and universities in Germany* (London, 1892).

There are separate historical accounts of each of the Scottish universities; e.g. for Aberdeen: J. M. Bulloch: *A history of the University of Aberdeen, 1495–1895* (London, 1895); for Edinburgh: Alexander Grant: *The story of the University of Edinburgh during its first 300 years* (London, 1884); for Glasgow: J. D. Mackie: *The University of Glasgow*, 1451–1951 (Glasgow, 1954); for St Andrews: R. G. Cant: *The University of St Andrews: a short history* (Edinburgh, 1946). Also there are two interesting discussions of the educational ideas and assumptions underlying Scottish higher education: one in L. J. Saunders: *Scottish democracy, 1815–1840* (Edinburgh, 1950), and the other in G. E. Davie: *The democratic intellect: Scotland and her universities in the nineteenth century* (Edinburgh, 1961). There is a charming account of student-life in Edinburgh 150 years ago in J. A. Froude's *Thomas Carlyle*, vol. 1 (London, 1882). Anyone wishing to trace the languid and tortuous history of reform in Scottish universities has to consult the reports, none of them very well written, of three royal commissions, one appointed in 1826 (H.C. 1831 (310) XII), one in 1858 (H.C. 1863 [3174] XVI), and one in 1876 (H.C. 1878, C.1935, XXXII).

The sources, in English at any rate, for the history and present state of Latin American universities are meagre, though sufficient for our purpose in the introduction. Our discussion of Latin American universities is drawn from two volumes by J.T.Lanning, which gather together an impressive amount of original material; they are: *The university in the kingdom of Guatemala* (Ithaca, 1955); and *The eighteenth century enlightenment in the University of San Carlos de Guatemala* (Ithaca, 1956). A vigorous, if somewhat coloured, account of modern Latin American universities by one who has worked in them, is given by L.P.Atcon: 'The Latin American university', *Die Deutsche Universitätszeitung* (Feb. 1962) 9–49, and there is a sober account of a Peruvian university by F.M.Rogers: *The University of San Marcos in Lima, Peru* (Lima, 1961). The part which students play in Latin American universities is discussed in great detail by Martin Lipset in an article in *Minerva*: III, No 1 (1964) 15–56.

If the published sources for the history of South American universities are disappointingly few, the sources for the history of North American universities are embarrassingly rich. There are scores of histories of individual colleges and universities and some admirable critical and historical essays on higher education in the United States. We are particularly indebted to Richard Hofstadter for a series of masterly studies in American higher education, viz. R.Hofstadter and C.D.Hardy: *The development and scope of higher education in the United States* (New York, 1952); R.Hofstadter and W.P.Metzger: *The development of academic freedom in the United States* (New York, 1955), which has a much wider scope than its title denotes and is excellently documented; R.Hofstadter and W.Smith: *American higher education: a documentary history*, 2 vols. (Chicago, 1961), which is a collection of primary documents: statutes, memoranda, speeches, and articles, illustrating the history of the American college; and – although it is concerned with much else beside universities – Hofstadter's *Anti-intellectualism in American life* (London, 1964). Another useful and copiously documented history is that of J.S.Brubacher and W.Rudy: *Higher education in transition* (New York, 1958). We drew from a few special histories (but these are only a small sample of the resources available to the student of American higher education): S.E.Morison's *Three centuries of Harvard, 1636–1936* (Cambridge, Mass., 1946); G.W.Pierson's *Yale College; an educational history, 1871–1921* (New Haven, 1952); M.Bishop's *A history of Cornell* (Ithaca, 1962); J.Gray's *The University of Minnesota, 1851–1951* (Minneapolis, 1951). For the general history of the land grant colleges we relied on E.D.Eddy's *Colleges for our land and time* (New York, 1956); and A.Nevin's *The state universities and democracy* (Urbana, 1962). In drawing conclusions about American higher education we have relied upon our own judgement, but we have of course been influenced by three major American critics in this field: A.Flexner's classical *Universities: American, English, German* (London, 1930); R.M.Hutchins' *The University of Utopia* (Chicago, 1953); and Clark Kerr's *The uses of the university* (Cambridge, Mass., 1963).

For the discussion of the state of English universities in the 1850s, our basic sources are the royal commissions on Oxford and Cambridge (H.C. 1852 [1482] XXII and H.C. 1852–53 [1559] XLIV) and the well known books on the histories of these two universities: C.Mallet's three-volume book on Oxford and the unique tudies of Victorian Cambridge by D. A. Winstanley. For those who find royal commission reports unpalatable, there is a good summary by A. I. Tillyard: *A history of university reform* (Cambridge, 1913). Two memoirs greatly illuminate Oxford academic history at the time universities were being founded in India: G. Faber's *Jowett* (London, 1957); and V. H. H. Green's *Oxford common room* (London, 1957), which describes the exertions of Mark Pattison, another great Oxford reformer. For the labyrinthine history of the University of London, the serious reader has to go to the reports of royal commissions (Selborne, 1889; Gresham, 1893–4; and Haldane, 1910–13). But there are short cuts, notably a series of articles by W. H. Allchin, collected together as *An account of the reconstruction of the University of London* (London, 1905); and D. Logan's admirable brief essay: *The University of London* (London, 1962). A little known essay of great interest, because it contains a description of university government in the early nineteenth century, is Henry Malden's *On the origin of universities and academical degrees* (London, 1835). Malden was consulted about universities in India and Australia. H. H. Bellot's *University College, London, 1826–1926* (London, 1929), has much useful information; and W. H. G. Armytage's *Civic universities: some aspects of a British tradition* (London, 1953), covers in fascinating detail the whole canvas of English higher education from Celtic monasteries to the College of Horology.

For the discussion of the Queen's University of Ireland we have drawn materials from the two-volume history by T. W. Moody and J. C. Beckett: *Queen's, Belfast, 1845–1949* (London, 1959). For the discussion of the universities of Sydney and Melbourne we have drawn materials from H. E. Barff: *A short historical account of the University of Sydney* (Sydney, 1902); E. Scott: *A history of the University of Melbourne* (Melbourne, 1936), and G. Blainey: *A centenary history of the University of Melbourne* (Melbourne, 1957). Other useful sources have been a brilliant forgotten pamphlet by the vice-president of Queen's College, Belfast, Thomas Andrews, entitled *Studium generale, a chapter of contemporary history* (London, 1867), and two recent papers on early Australian academic history, one by I. Westbury: 'The Sydney and Melbourne arts courses, 1852–1861', in E. L. French, *Melbourne studies in education, 1961–62* (Melbourne, 1964) 256; and the other by D. S. Macmillan: 'The University of Sydney – the pattern and the public reaction, 1850–70', *The Australian university*, I, No 1 (1963) 27–59.

We have not discussed the impact of Europe and the United States upon the Canadian universities. Any reader who would like to inform himself on this matter will find interesting material in three papers by R. Falconer in the *Transactions of the Royal Society of Canada*. Scottish influence is described in vol. XXI, sect. II (1927) 7–20; English influence in vol. XXII, sect. II (1928) 33–48; and American influence in vol. XXIV, Sect. II (1930) 23–38. The influence of France on the foundations of Canadian education is described in an essay by R. M. Saunders in *Essays in Canadian history*, edited by R. Flenley (Toronto, 1939); and W. Kirkconnell has written two articles on the French tradition in Canadian universities, to be found in *The humanities in Canada*, edited by W. Kirkconnell and A. S. P. Woodhouse (Ottawa, 1947).

PART II: INDIA

Full particulars of the sources given below will be found in a classified bibliography on p. 527.

Chapter 3 *The initial export policy*

[1] In briefly recalling the well known controversy in Bengal, we have drawn mainly on the documentary material published in H. Sharp and J. A. Richey (eds) *Selections from educational records, I. 1781–1839, II. 1840–1859* (Calcutta, 1920, 22); the detailed analysis by Percival Spear: 'Bentinck and education', *Camb. Hist. J.*, VI, No 1 (1938) 78–101, supplemented by K. A. Ballhatchet's 'The home government and Bentinck's educational policy', *ibid.*, X, No 2 (1951) 224–9; and two more general studies: Eric Stokes, *The English utilitarians and India* (London, 1959) and G. D. Bearce, *British attitudes towards India, 1784–1858* (London, 1961).

[2] Calcutta University Commission, 1917–19, *Report*, VII (Calcutta, 1919) 303.

[3] *Cf.* Spear (ref. 1).

[4] *Cf.* the very similar arguments used by Wilson in 1835 (ref. 7).

[5] For the divergence in view between Macaulay and James Mill, see Ballhatchet, and Stokes (ref. 1).

[6] Quoted Bearce (ref. 1) p. 284.

[7] Letter to the editor, 5 Dec. 1835, *Asiatic Journal*, N.S. XIX, No 73 (Jan.–April 1836) 1–16. Quoted Bearce (ref. 1) pp. 171–2.

[8] For Mouat's own account of these schemes, see the paper he read before the Society of Arts in 1888: F. J. Mouat, 'The origin, progress and influence of universities in India', *J. Soc. Arts*, XXXVI (1888) 483–507.

[9] The plan was published in the council of education's *General report on public instruction in the Lower Provinces of the Bengal Presidency for 1845–46*; it was also published separately: *Proposed plan of the University of Calcutta* (Calcutta, 1845). It was reprinted as an appendix to the second report of the select committee of the house of lords on India in 1852 (*Indian territories, sel. cttee. H.L. 2nd rept.*, pp. 618–20; 1852–3 (627–I) XXXII) and Mouat gives it in full in his article (ref. 8).

[10] Home letter from India, No 7, 7 Mar. 1846, with enclosure from govt. of Bengal, No 138, 11 Feb. 1846, Letters from India and Bengal, vol. 49; home letter from Hardinge, No 2, 25 May 1846, *ibid.*, vol. 50.

[11] Public despatch to India, No 22, 22 Sept. 1847, Despatches to India and Bengal, vol. 54.

[12] See para. 24 of Wood's despatch of 19 July 1854. J. A. Richey (ed.) *Selections from educational records*, II (Calcutta, 1922) 371.

[13] Board's collection, No 108193/a, vol. 2204.

[14] Home letters from India: No 7, 7 Mar. 1846, Letters from India and Bengal, vol. 49; No 20, 7 Sept. 1846, *ibid.*, vol. 51.

[15] Mouat to Beadon, secy, govt. of Bengal, 4 Aug. 1853. *Papers relating to the establishment of the Presidency College of Bengal* (Selections from the records of the Bengal government, XIV) Calcutta 1854, pp. 1–30.

[16] Beadon to Mouat, 21 Oct. 1853, *ibid.*, pp. 31–8.

[17] Mouat to Beadon, 10 Mar. 1854, *ibid.*, pp. 39–68.

[18] Dalhousie readily approved the scheme as a whole, but was critical on two points of detail. He doubted the expediency of providing for Latin in the curriculum.

'The Council will not be disposed to suspect His Lordship of undervaluing or contemning the Classical Education which is received in the Colleges of England. If, therefore, he offers an objection to it here, it is solely because he does not think that, for the present at least, the Government system of education in India should include a course of ancient classics. The system, His Lordship conceives, should be calculated to bestow a thoroughly good and complete education in the practical and classical knowledge of England and India; but he is of opinion that those who seek a complete instruction in ancient classics should still look for it in the seminaries and universities of England.' He also made a plea for adaptation in terminology. 'His Lordship ventures further to deprecate the use in the Presidency College of these terms which in long lapse of time have become familiar to English Universities such as "bursaries", "matriculation", and the like. These terms are not descriptive and it may be feared that the use of them here might tend to create misapprehension. . . .' Beadon to Mouat, 10 April 1854, *ibid.*, pp. 69–71.

[19] Ref. 8.

[20] Paras 7316 ff., 7 July 1853. *Indian territories, sel. cttee H.L. 2nd rept.*; 1852–53 (627–I) XXXII. Cameron handed in a copy of the plan that had been drawn up in 1845, and this was printed as appendix O to the report. *Cf.* ref. 9.

[21] Paras 6627 ff., 21 June 1853. *Ibid.*

[22] Mouat considered the senior scholarship examinations 'fully equal in extent to the Bachelor's examination of Oxford, Cambridge, and Dublin, and much more so than that of the Bachelier-es-Lettres of the Sorbonne in Paris'. Mouat (ref. 8) pp. 483–507. Marshman thought the 'new rule of examination was as preposterous as the limitation of degrees at Cambridge to Senior wranglers only, would be'. 'Notes on Education in India', 12 Nov. 1853. MSS. Eur.F. 78/25.

[23] Duff, para. 6247, 6 June 1853, and Marshman, paras 6466 and 6471, 15 June 1853 (ref. 20). See also Marshman, para. 8163, 21 July 1853, before the select committee of the house of commons. *Indian territories, sel. cttee H.C. 6th rept.*; 1852–53 (897) XXIX.

[24] Marshman submitted a written statement to the board of control in November 1853, and Duff in the following January. Duff had been active in canvassing influential members of the court and of parliament since returning home on furlough in 1850, and he and Marshman were among those consulted by Wood during the preparation of his great educational despatch. Marshman (ref. 22); A. Duff, 'Brief memorandum on the subject of Government Education [in] India', 25 Jan. 1854. MSS. Eur. F. 78/25. G. Smith, *The life of Alexander Duff* (London, 1879) II, 190–91, 231 ff.; Wood in the house of commons, 8 Aug. 1853. *Parl. Deb.*, 3 ser., 135, cols 1462–3.

[25] Ref. 22.

[26] Para. 7278, 5 July 1853 (ref. 20).

[27] *Cf.* Wood to Dalhousie, 24 Nov. 1853: '. . . I am not sure whether we shall send you a public dispatch on the subject which I am going to mention but I wish to call your attention to it more particularly. Not that you have not already done much in the way of what I wish to see carried further, but I am prepared and wishful to go a good deal beyond what has hitherto been ever contemplated. I refer to the employment of natives in high situations. The point which has been most urged is their admission to the Covenanted Service. This seems to be a point of honour and we have arranged our matters so that they *may* come here and be admitted. But I

cannot say that I either expect or wish to see them do this to any extent. I am for keeping the covenanted service as the means of maintaining the European Indian servants on a high footing of acquirement and character. I hope that we shall govern India for many years, but it is clear to my mind that we shall always govern it as *aliens* not settling in the country or having much in common with the mass of the people whom we govern. This being so, I confess I do not see that any reduction of consequence can be made in the number of Europeans employed in governing India. I am now speaking of the Civil Service . . . I do not see how we can to any extent *substitute* native agency for these men if we could get men as good. That natives may occasionally be placed in situations hitherto held by Covenanted servants is another matter. I should like to see such cases from time to time but they will always be rare. It follows . . . that the employment of natives in high places must be attained by *adding* such places to those already existing, and I believe this to be advisable . . . If you educate and elevate the natives you must open a career for the intelligent and higher class whom you thus create . . . I should be very glad to hear of half a dozen natives appointed to high places. The more openings of this sort can be made the less they will feel the practical exclusion from the covenanted service. I do not suppose that the operation will go on very fast, nor do I desire it. . . .' MSS. Eur. F.78/L.B.IV.

[28] Wood to Dalhousie, 8 June 1854. MSS. Eur. F.78/L.B.V.

[29] *Cf.* para. 31 (ref. 12).

[30] Ref. 28.

[31] For the drafting of the 'Wood' despatch, see the reconstruction by R.J.Moore: 'The composition of "Wood's Education Despatch" ', *E.H.R.*, LXXX (1965) 70–85, which at last resolves the problem of its authorship.

[32] The draft of E.D.Bourdillon, a clerk in the correspondence department, and the genesis of the despatch of 19 July 1854. MSS. Eur. F.78/12. *Cf.* Moore (ref. 31).

[33] Ref. 28.

[34] *Cf.* paras 64–6 of the despatch of 19 July 1854.

[35] Wood to F.J.Halliday, lieutenant-governor of Bengal, 24 July 1854. MSS. Eur. F.78/L.B.V.

[36] Wood to Lord Elphinstone, governor of Bombay, 24 Jan. 1854. MSS. Eur. F.78/L.B.IV.

[37] 'We have taken for the model of our Indian University the London University, because its framework is quite independent of any form of religious belief which is indispensable in India', he explained to F.J.Halliday. 'We have been doing something towards removing from our Oxford system the difficulties arising from religious tests as regards the *University*, though they must remain in force as regards the *College* system. So in India your Colleges may be Christian, Mahometan, or Hindoo, or admitting all if you can manage it (which we clearly cannot do here); but leaving all religious instruction (if any) to the Colleges, the University is to be open alike to all comers from any of the affiliated Institutions.' Wood to Halliday, 24 July 1854 (ref. 35).

[38] A similar query was raised, in the same hand, about the mode of establishing the universities. The draft had envisaged incorporation 'either by Royal Charter or by Acts of the Legislative Council of India'. This prompted the comment: 'Q^y d[esira]ble. We appear sensible that the subject of Indian education embraces questions of difficulty which at this moment obstruct all progress in England, Scotland &

Ireland. Any increase of separate superintending authorities had I think better be avoided.' Again the objection was upheld, and the reference to the alternative of proceeding by royal charter deleted. From the initials appended to the first query it would seem that R. D. Mangles was the instigator of these adaptations. Draft of public despatch to India, No 49, 19 July 1854. Despatches to India and Bengal, vol. 87.

[39] The successive amendments can be traced in a bundle of Wood's papers, bearing his inscription: 'These papers contain the various stages thro' wh the Education dft of 1854 passed.' MSS. Eur. F.78/12.

[40] Colvile to Beadon, 7 Aug. 1856; govt. of India home (education) resolution, 12 Dec. 1856. *Papers connected with the establishment of universities in India* (Calcutta, 1857).

[41] All three acts are reproduced in Richey (ref. 12) pp. 408–26.

[42] The arts sub-committee produced two reports, the second after the local governments had been consulted on the first. The passage we quote appears in the first report and it is omitted from the second. But the recommendation of the second report is the same, and it is prefaced by the same explanation of the seeming deviation from established policy. 'The Sub-Committee fully participate in the Hon'ble Court's desire that so far as the direct efforts of the Government are concerned the higher branches of European knowledge should be communicated to the Natives of this country through the medium of English but they desire to combine with that principle one no less important in itself and essential to the full development of the other, namely that those who are instructed in European knowledge, through the medium of English should also be instructed in one or other of the learned languages of their country as the only means whereby they can communicate their European knowledge in an acceptable form whether by translations or by original compositions, to the mass of the people. First report of the sub-committee of arts, 24 June 1855; Second report, 2 June 1856 (ref. 40).

[43] The recommendation that history should figure as a separate branch of the honours examination was made by the sub-committee in its second report. Since making its first report it had been joined by Dr Duff; and it is tempting to attribute to him, and his recent stay in England, this new sensitivity to the contemporary trend of academic thinking at home.

[44] Minute, 30 Dec. 1854, Richey (ref. 12) p. 404.

[45] Letter of appointment from the government of India, 26 Jan. 1855 (ref. 40). Dalhousie reiterated his doubt about adopting British nomenclature for the degrees. But the committee disagreed, arguing more especially with reference to the arts faculty, and fully endorsing the view of its arts sub-committee. This considered the title 'B.A.', though 'non-descriptive', so well known and understood as to be more acceptable than any other. It saw no reason for withholding it if the standard of examination were set as high as elsewhere. 'It seems also undesirable', it reported, 'and in some degree inconsistent with the object of founding Universities in India, to adopt for the first and principal academic distinction a title which may be held to imply intellectual disparity between those who attain that distinction in India and those upon whom it is conferred in other parts of the Empire.' *Ibid.*

[46] See above p. 47.

[47] University of Calcutta, *Convocation addresses* (Calcutta, 1914) 20.

[48] *Ibid.*, p. 47.

[49] 17 Mar. 1866, *ibid.*, pp. 138–9.

[50] Calcutta University Commission, 1917–19, *Report*, I (Calcutta, 1919) 45. (The earlier figure does not include those studying in Assam, which was then a part of Bengal.)

[51] The numbers of those graduating in Bengal in 1882 were: civil engineering 6, medicine 20, law 67 and arts 95 B.A., 26 M.A. *Review of education in India in 1886*, comp. A. Croft (Calcutta, 1888) 36, 43.

[52] Apart from minor details, the first regulations for the B.A. degree, framed in 1858, were the same as those recommended by the University Committee in 1856 (p. 62 above). Students were required to study five compulsory subjects: languages, history, mathematics and natural philosophy, physical sciences, and mental and moral sciences. University of Calcutta, *Hundred years of the University of Calcutta* (Calcutta, 1957) 64.

[53] 11 Mar. 1864. *Convocation addresses* (ref. 47) p. 100.

[54] 9 Mar. 1867, *ibid.*, p. 160.

[55] *Ibid.*

[56] [C. H. Tawney] 'The studies of the Calcutta University', *Calcutta Review*, LXXXII (1865) 297–317.

[57] 'Education in British India, 1870–71', comp. A. P. Howell (Calcutta, 1872). *Educational reports, 1859–71* (Selections from educational records of the government of India, I) Delhi, 1960, p. 515.

[58] Provision had been made for a 'first arts' or intermediate examination in March 1860. 'Note on the state of education in India', comp. A. M. Monteath (Calcutta, 1862), *ibid.*, p. 6.

[59] Sir Alexander Arbuthnot, in vice-chancellorial address to convocation, 13 Mar. 1880. *Convocation addresses* (ref. 47) pp. 409–10.

[60] The subjects for the B.A. pass degree under the new regulations (formally sanctioned by the government in 1882) were:

'A' COURSE	'B' COURSE
1 English	1 English
2 philosophy	2 mathematics
3 One of the following:	3 One of the following:
a A classical language	a physics
b history	b chemistry
c mathematics	c physiology
	d geology

Honours courses were provided in each of these subjects. The subject groups for the M.A. remained unchanged: languages, history, mental and moral philosophy, mathematics, and natural and physical science. Education Commission, *Report by the Bengal provincial committee* (Calcutta, 1884) 105; *Review of education in India in 1886*, comp. A. Croft (Calcutta, 1888) 28.

[61] Ref. 59.

[62] Para. 7, Govt. of India, home dept (education) resolution, No $\frac{1}{60}$, 3 Feb. 1882. *Report of the Indian Education Commission* (Calcutta, 1883) 625.

[63] 11 Mar. 1882, *Convocation addresses* (ref. 47) pp. 440–1.

[64] Ref. 60, p. 16.

[65] *Ibid.*, p. 105.

[66] *Report of the Indian Education Commission* (Calcutta, 1883) 302–4.

[67] For the effects of the service system of staffing, see below the views of Sir

Theodore Morison, and the Sadler commission (pp. 92, 123).

[68] 'In history', he wrote, 'the most casual observer must be struck by the large field embraced. The student who presents himself for a B.A. degree has travelled over Grecian, Roman, Jewish, Indian and English history. He is equally familiar with the battle of Marathon, and the field of Flodden; the Cabal, the Gerusia, and the Sanhedrin ... the students in history have every year to wade through the appointed cram-books to get up the functions of Roman tribunes and Jewish judges, the oppressions of iniquitous harmosts and equally iniquitous major-generals, from pages illumined by no ray of wit, genius, or imagination.' Tawney was also critical of the honours syllabus, finding it too rarely changed, and too exclusively English. 'There are other great European politics besides that of England, though it is apparently not the object of the Calcutta university to let its students into the secret of the French, Germans, and Italians having had a history of their own, any more than a language or a literature. The period chosen for the honour course is that of the great English revolution. There is something quite crushing in the regularity with which it has hitherto recurred. There is no alternative, no choice. ...' [C.H.Tawney] ref. 56.

[69] 'Indian education', *The Times*, 26 June 1901.

[70] W.Raleigh, *The letters of Sir Walter Raleigh 1879–1922* ed. Lady Raleigh (London, 1926) 42–3.

[71] CUC (ref. 50) I, 42.

[72] See the assessment of the Bengal provincial committee of the Education commission of 1882. Ref. 60, p. 14.

[73] In July 1858, the senate approved a recommendation of the faculty of arts to drop natural history from the examination, omit mechanics from the subject group 'mathematics and natural philosophy', and dispense with the oral examination in languages. *Ibid.*; *Hundred years of the University of Calcutta* (ref. 52) p. 87.

[74] Ref. 72.

[75] Gooroo Dass Banerjee, in vice-chancellorial address to convocation, 18 Jan. 1900. *Convocation addresses* (ref. 47) p. 608.

[76] CUC (ref. 50) I, 62.

[77] *Ibid.*

[78] A comparison made in an article from a *Times* correspondent in Calcutta discussing the report of the Indian Universities Commission of 1902. *The Times*, 23 Sept. 1902.

[79] CUC (ref. 50) I, 61.

[80] *Progress of education in India, 1887–88 to 1891–92: second quinquennial review*, comp. A.M.Nash (Calcutta, 1893) 78–9.

[81] 21 Mar. 1904, *Govt. of India Leg. Proc.*, XLIII (1904) 279–81.

[82] Notes by Curzon for his address to the Simla educational conference of 1901. MSS. Eur. F.111/248. See also the figures given by the director of public instruction, Alexander Pedler, in a speech to the governor general's council on 18 Mar. 1904. *Govt. of India Leg. Proc.*, XLIII (1904) 167–8.

[83] 'Minute by H.E. the Viceroy on University Reform', 23 Feb. 1901. MSS. Eur. F.111/280.

[84] Commenting on the way in which fellowships had come to be conferred 'as a sort of titular reward', Curzon noted that English officials honoured in this way usually recognised 'no answering obligation'. 'A good many drift away from Cal-

cutta into other provinces and posts although their names continue to block the list. Of those who continue in Bengal, a large number never attend.' A further reason for the poor attendance was that a byelaw had been carried fixing the annual ordinary meeting for the third Saturday in April 'when the majority of the Europeans are absent from Calcutta and when the star of the Natives is in the ascendant'. *Ibid.*

[85] Of the twenty-two members elected, two had died, four had been elected in accordance with a stipulation that certain vacancies should be filled on specific grounds, and the remaining sixteen were practising lawyers. '... election is only secured by systematic and elaborate canvassing', Curzon wrote. 'Lists are kept up by the Vakils of the electors who, having taken their degrees, have dispersed throughout India. Agents are employed to hunt them out and canvass them; and very considerable expense is incurred. No candidate has a chance of being returned who does not resort to these methods and who is not supported by the Vakil party.' *Ibid.*

[86] According to a *Times* correspondent in 1901, of the total of nearly two hundred fellows, only fifty-three 'appeared' to be connected with education, while forty-six were pleaders, barristers or judges, and the remainder 'civilians, doctors, engineers and more or less distinguished nondescripts'. *The Times*, 26 June 1901.

[87] Pedler, at the Simla educational conference, 3 Sept. 1901, MSS. Eur. F.111/248; also, 'Indian education', *The Times*, 26 June 1901.

[88] *Ibid.*

[89] Pedler, at the Simla educational conference, 5 Sept. 1901, MSS. Eur. F.111/248.

[90] Letter to *The Times*, 28 June 1901. *The Times*, 2 July 1901.

[91] Proceedings of the educational conference at Simla, 6 Sept. 1901, MSS. Eur. F.111/248.

[92] Proceedings, 5 Sept. 1901, *ibid. Cf.* p. 77 below.

[93] 18 Dec. 1903, *Govt. of India Leg. Proc.*, XLII (1903) 299–301; 21 Mar. 1904, XLIII (1904) 307–9.

[94] *Ibid.* The Indian Universities Commission of 1902 had returned a similarly critical verdict, though in more guarded terms: 'Having visited a considerable number of these institutions [i.e. affiliated colleges], we are not disposed to confirm the sweeping condemnation which has sometimes been passed upon our University system.' Taking into account the early age at which many Indian students began their college career, the comparatively recent foundation of Indian universities, and the very small resources at the disposal of the universities and colleges in India, the commissioners saw 'no reason to regret the determination at which the Government arrived in 1854. At the same time we must admit that the acquirements of Indian graduates are in many cases inadequate and superficial. We make every allowance for the difficulties of a student who has to receive instruction in a foreign language. We do not forget that when western students received all their instruction in a classical tongue, the Latin of the Schools was more fluent than correct. But after all allowance is made, it is most unsatisfactory to be told that the Indian B.A. not infrequently lacks the general training which he requires to fit him for the business of life, or for a further course of study.' *Report of the Indian Universities Commission, 1902* (Simla, 1902) 5.

[95] *Convocation addresses* (ref. 47) p. 645.

[96] *Ibid.*, p. 748.

[97] *Ibid.*, p. 707.

[98] *Ibid.*, p. 754.

[99] University of London, *Calendars for 1871, 81, 91* (London, 1871–91); *cf.* G.D.Banerjee in vice-chancellorial address to convocation, 18 Jan. 1890. *Convocation addresses* (ref. 47) pp. 609–10.

[100] A figure quoted in the senate by Dr Asutosh Mookerjee when moving, on 17 August 1901, for the appointment of a committee to enquire into the conduct of the B.A. examination. University of Calcutta, *Minutes for the year 1901–02* (Calcutta, 1902).

[101] See the evidence of Kristodas Pal (editor of the *Hindu Patriot*) and Rai Rajendralala Mitra (a fellow of the University of Calcutta). Ref. 60, pp. 302, 344–5. The committee reported that only 526 arts graduates (of the total of 1,589) were employed in the public service, although there were *c.* 4,500 government and municipal posts in Bengal of Rs 50 a month upwards. 'A very large supply . . . of these educated men is still required to meet the felt wants of the public service; not to speak of the necessity of so far increasing their number as to force them by the struggle for existence into new paths of trade and industry.' *Ibid.*, p. 103.

[102] *Convocation addresses* (ref. 47) p. 735.

[103] *Ibid.*, p. 736.

Chapter 4 *Towards a new policy*

[1] '. . . I will not conceal from you that I am a University man to the core of my being; and that deep down in me, behind the mask of the official immersed in public affairs, and beneath the uniform of State, there lurks an academic element, ineradicable and strong, connecting me with my old University days, and affecting me with a natural sympathy towards those, who, although in different circumstances and under a different clime, can also claim connection with a University.' First address to the convocation of the University of Calcutta, 11 Feb. 1899. *Speeches by Lord Curzon of Kedleston*, 1 (Calcutta, 1900) 49.

[2] 'I cannot myself conceive of a time as remotely possible in which it would be either practicable or desirable that we should take our hand from the Indian plough.' Speech to the United Club, 1 Aug. 1904. *Ibid.*, IV (1906) 44.

[3] Debate on the budget, 30 Mar. 1904. *Ibid.*, III (1904) 410.

[4] Addresses to convocation, 15 Feb. 1902 and 11 Feb. 1905. *Ibid.*, II (1902) 428; IV (1906) 82.

[5] 'What ought the ideal University to be in India, as elsewhere?' Address to convocation, 13 Feb. 1904. *Ibid.*, III (1904) 275 ff. *Cf.* his speech to the educational conference at Simla, 2 Sept. 1901. *Ibid.*, II (1902) 316 ff.

[6] Speeches to the educational conferences at Simla, 2 Sept. 1901 and 20 Sept. 1905; also his summing up on the Indian Universities bill on 21 Mar. 1904. *Ibid.*, II (1902) 316, IV (1906) 142 ff.; *Govt. of India Leg. Proc.*, XLIII (1904) 334.

[7] Curzon to Hamilton, 28 Aug. 1901. MSS Eur. F.111/160.

[8] 'Minute by H.E. the Viceroy on University Reform', 23 Feb. 1901. MSS. Eur. F.111/280.

[9] *Cf.* above, p. 70.

[10] Indian Universities Act, 1904 (VIII of 1904).

[11] Speech to the educational conference at Simla, 20 Sept. 1905. *Speeches*, IV (1906) 147.

[12] Minute by Curzon, 14 July 1903. MSS. Eur. F.111/251 (Govt. of India home

dept., education A., proceedings, Dec. 1903. *Simla records, I* (1903)).

[13] 18 Dec. 1903, *Govt. of India Leg. Proc.*, XLII (1903) 321–2, 21 Mar. 1904, XLIII (1904) 334–6.

[14] *The Times*, 23 Sept. 1902.

[15] See above, p. 71.

[16] The University of the Punjab had been founded in 1882, and the University of Allahabad in 1887. Each had been empowered to assume teaching functions; but apart from the University of the Punjab taking over management of the Oriental College at Lahore, neither had chosen to do so. Each had conformed to the old examining pattern.

[17] Minute by Curzon, 20 July 1902. MSS. Eur. F.111/251 (Govt. of India home dept., education A., proceedings, Dec. 1902. *Calcutta records, I* (1902)).

[18] Sect. 3, Indian Universities Act, 1904 (VIII of 1904).

[19] *Report of the Indian Universities Commission, 1902* (Simla, 1902) 6.

[20] Ref. 17.

[21] Home letter from India, No 10, 3 Sept. 1903 (ref. 12).

[22] Sect. 26, Indian Universities Act, 1904 (VIII of 1904).

[23] 'The Entrance Exam was some years ago limited to boys of 16 years and upwards. The native members of the Senate opposed this and the age test was abolished against the advice of Sir Alfred Croft, the Director of the Education Department. Since that time the tendency has been to push forward the boys by cramming in order to shorten their School Courses so that it is not uncommon to find boys of 12, 13 and 14 coming up to the Entrance Exams at which age they are supposed to commence their University career. This reduction of age has worked badly. Great pressure is brought to bear on masters of Schools by parents or guardians to allow improperly prepared boys to go up for exams with the result that the percentage of passes in the Entrance and other exams has become low. This has caused agitation and indignation. More than one committee has been appointed to inquire into the wholesale failure of students. The natural result of the agitation has been to lower the standards and to cause certain alterations in the direction of leniency in the Regulations . . . It is almost true to say that every attempt is made to pass every possible candidate at the Entrance Exam . . .' Pedler, Simla educational conference, 5 Sept. 1901. MSS. Eur. F.111/248. *Cf.* above p. 71.

[24] Resolution 27, *ibid.*

[25] IUC (ref. 19) p. 46.

[26] Ref. 17.

[27] Minute by T. Raleigh and J. P. Hewett, 28 July 1902 (ref. 17).

[28] *Cf.* Curzon to Sir Arthur Fraser, rector of Calcutta University. 26 Jan. 1905. MSS. Eur. F.111/280.

[29] Resolution 34; proceedings of the educational conference at Simla, Sept. 1901. MSS. Eur. F.111/248.

[30] IUC (ref. 19) p. 49.

[31] It was the aim of all education, according to Curzon, to promote 'the distinction between the ambitious and the duffer'! Minute, 20 July 1902 (ref. 17).

[32] Minute, 28 July 1902 (ref. 27).

[33] Home letter from India, No 10, 3 Sept. 1903 (ref. 21).

[34] Writing to Allahabad, Curzon did suggest that in view of the ultimate solution the government had in mind, the university might like to abandon its practice of

conferring honours on those who had passed the ordinary B.A. course in the first division. But he was careful to explain that the suggestion was in no sense a requirement; and he made no attempt to influence the other universities in the structure of their degrees. Curzon to the rector of Calcutta University, and to the chancellors of the universities of Madras, Bombay, Allahabad and the Punjab, conf., 26 Jan. 1905. MSS. Eur. F.111/280.

[35] IUC (ref. 19) pp. 40–1, 68.

[36] *Ibid.*, pp. 10–11, 41–2, 68.

[37] Minute, 20 July 1902 (ref. 17).

[38] *Ibid.*

[39] '... I am aware that many cultivated Native gentlemen, scholars renowned not only among their own countrymen but in Europe, are openly or secretly revolted by the pretension of a branch of the Indo-European family, which is one of the youngest in civilization, to come and bid one of the oldest to sit at its feet and learn. And no doubt the pretension is sometimes put forward with intolerable arrogance. But the truth is, that the mind of India is undergoing a process without which all civilizations, young or old, are ultimately worthless. . . . with one single exception, no race or nationality, left entirely to itself, has developed any intellectual result which is valuable or durable, except perhaps poetry. . . . To one small people, covering in its original seat, no more than a hand's breadth of territory, it was given to create the principle of progress, of movement onwards and not backwards or downwards, of destruction tending to construction. That people was the Greek. Except the blind force of Nature, nothing moves in this world which is not Greek in its origin. A ferment spreading from that source has vitalized all the great progressive races of mankind, penetrating from one to another, and producing, in each, results accordant with its hidden and latent genius, and results of course often far greater than any exhibited in Greece itself. It is this principle of progress we English are communicating to India. We did not create it. We deserve no special credit for it. It came to us filtered through many different media. But we have received it, and, as we have received it, so we pass it on. There is no reason why, if it has time to work, it should not develope in India effects as wonderful as in any other of the societies of mankind.' Vice-chancellorial address to convocation, University of Calcutta, 9 Mar. 1867. University of Calcutta, *Convocation addresses* (Calcutta, 1914) 163–6.

[40] Address to convocation, University of Calcutta, 11 Mar. 1882, *ibid.*, pp. 448–9.

[41] 10 Mar. 1877, *ibid.*, pp. 364–5.

[42] 19 Dec. 1885, *ibid.*, pp. 514–8.

[43] IUC (ref. 19) p. 26.

[44] *Ibid.*, p. 31.

[45] *Ibid.*

[46] *Ibid.*, p. 30.

[47] *Cf.* Raleigh's response to Curzon's plea for compulsory history in preference to deductive logic: 'As H.E. is aware, the place of History in University courses has been much discussed. The Commission adhere to the opinion that the chief object of a course of University study should be, not the acquisition of useful knowledge, but a thorough mental training. High authorities at Oxford have maintained that if you wish to make a man a student of History you should direct him to the School of Literae Humaniores so that he may be thoroughly trained in scholarship and Logic. He will then be able to read History for himself. The School of Modern History can

teach the student a certain number of facts; but the Political Economy subject represents all the dialectic training received by candidates in that school. The majority of the Commissioners are in sympathy with this view of the matter; they have therefore proposed the retention of Maths and of Logic supplemented by the elements of Psychology in the programme of the Indian Universities. History they relegate to the position of an optional subject and they combine it with Political Economy . . .' Minute by T.Raleigh and J.P.Hewett, 28 July 1902 (ref. 27).

[48] '. . . if the time should come', he added, 'when Sanskrit literature is neglected because it is not of immediate use at Calcutta in the 20th century, the University will be descending to a lower plane and abandoning the high place which its founders intended to claim for it'. 13 Feb. 1904. University of Calcutta, *Minutes for the year 1903–04* (Calcutta, 1904).

[49] Address to convocation, University of Calcutta, 7 Feb. 1900. *Speeches*, I (1900) 241–5.

[50] Minute, 20 July 1902 (ref. 17).

[51] *Ibid.* A more discreet argument was found for the official letter in which the government of India's proposals were outlined: '. . . it has been suggested that owing to the metaphysical and introspective bent of the Indian mind, the intellectual discipline which is the object of all University training, can perhaps be better imparted by substituting History for Deductive Logic and Elementary Psychology in the Intermediate course . . .' Home letter from India, No 10, 3 Sept. 1903 (ref. 21).

[52] Curzon to Sir A. Godley, 23 Sept. 1903, MSS. Eur. F.111/162.

[53] Home letter from India, No 10, 3 Sept. 1903 (ref. 21).

[54] The government of India seems to have attached little importance to the proposals for Indian studies: at least it made no reference to them in the official letter of 3 Sept. 1903. *Ibid.*

[55] The government of India gave official notice of their desire for an additional member in a telegram of 14 July 1910; but Lord Morley was already forewarned of the proposal and had written in support of it for a meeting of the council on 12 July when it had been approved. The provisional sanction of the India office was given by telegraph on 7 November, in reply to a letter from the government of India on 6 October. This was followed by a further telegram on 7 December, and a despatch on 27 January 1911. J. & P. 1032.

[56] Finance letter from India, No 234, 28 Sept. 1911, J. & P. 1111A.

[57] *Cf.* his minute of 20 July 1902, commenting on the recommendation of the Indian Universities Commission that the creation of new universities should be postponed. 'I gave much the same advice when I said in opening the Simla Conference that "as time goes on the list may perhaps be extended, though consolidation rather than multiplication of academic institutions is the object that I should prefer for the present to hold in view".' MSS. Eur. F.111/251 (Govt. of India home dept, education A., proceedings, Dec. 1902. *Calcutta records, I* (1902)).

[58] *Report of the Indian Universities Commission, 1902* (Simla, 1902) 7–8.

[59] Finance letter from India, No 258, 2 Nov. 1911, enclosing 'Draft of the constitution of the Muslim University as approved by the Constitution Committee held on August 18th, 19th, and 20th 1911', J. & P. 1146.

[60] Sect. 9(6) of the draft constitution; and ch. XXIII of the draft statutes (ref. 59).

[61] 'One of the hopes entertained about a teaching University', he wrote, 'was that

it would become a genuine seat of learning at which examinations would be sub-ordinate to teaching and in which the teachers, freed from the tyranny of the text book, would carry their pupils along with them in their own branches of study. If affiiation of other institutions is allowed, this hope must go by the board.' Note, 1 Jan. 1912, *ibid.*

[62] See especially a strongly worded note from the parliamentary under-secretary, E. S. Montagu, who urged how wrong he thought it would be to inaugurate a system of university education 'wholly out of keeping with modern university ideas, wholly inconsistent with the desires of those who want better educational opportunities for Mahomedans and far removed from the principles upon which Sir Syed Ahmad Khan worked all his life'. 'The residential university is to be given up and hetero-geneous colleges are to be affiliated', he wrote. 'The worst faults in the machinery of government of Oxford and Cambridge are to be applied to the new university, and this despite the unavailing efforts which those universities are now making to throw off the shackles arresting their development through their government by a casual body composed of persons ignorant of educational problems . . . Let us then boldly refuse to permit affiliation. . . .' 9 Jan. 1912, *ibid.*

[63] Public despatch to India, No 33, 23 Feb. 1912, *ibid.*

[64] 'In using the terms "outside the Aligarh district" ', he explained in a later des-patch, 'I recognise the possibility that generous founders might one day endow other residential colleges in the immediate neighbourhood of the present college, to be clustered as at Oxford or Cambridge round the centre of University life . . .' Public despatch to India, No 114, 12 July 1912, *ibid.*

[65] Education letter from India, No 8, 28 Mar. 1912, *ibid.*

[66] Tel., 24 June 1912, *ibid.*

[67] Note, 16 April 1912, *ibid.*

[68] Public despatch to India, No 114, 12 July 1912, *ibid.*

[69] Tel., 6 Aug. 1912, *ibid.*

[70] 22 Mar. 1915, *Govt. of India Leg. Proc.*, LIII (1914–15) 522.

[71] 'Assuming, then, that the general idea is accepted', he wrote, 'the next question is what sort of model the constitution of the University should follow. Here I would submit that careful consideration should be given to the modern type of University of which we have examples at Manchester, Liverpool, Leeds, Bristol and, I think, also at Sydney & Melbourne. The constitution of the older Universities assumes the existence on the spot of the large academic body furnished by the various Colleges. But this cannot be counted on where the University itself is practically a single College and it is difficult to foresee the time when Aligarh will become a great aca-demic centre equipped with the varied culture that the requirements of a University demand. The question in fact as regards Aligarh is in many respects similar to that of the Tata Institute at Bangalore. That was organised on the model of the Bristol University with a very large "Court" which in practice could never be got together, but which would form a very effective agency for obtaining subscriptions & dona-tions. There is also a small administrative Council and an academic Syndicate which deals with courses, examinations etc. The whole organization is held together by the very large powers vested in the Viceroy as Patron, powers which he would exercise after consulting his regular educational advisers. It is submitted that the G. of I. might be invited to consider the constitution of the Tata Institute when framing their proposals.

'The great difficulty will be to secure the maintenance of adequate standards. The University will of course confer the usual degrees – nothing short of this will content the Mahomedans – and these must be accepted for the purpose of Govt appointments, the bar, medicine etc., as equivalent to the corresponding degrees of the existing Universities. With a small local body managing the University, the temptation to turn out as many B.As. as possible will be considerable & the constitution must provide effective safeguards against this . . .' Minute, 29 June 1911, on tel. of 10 June 1911 from India, J. & P. 1146.

[72] Ref. 59.

[73] He suggested the promoters might be asked to consider a constitution like that of the other universities in India. 'A governing Senate, mainly but not wholly composed of teachers, and a small Syndicate appointed by the Senate – this is all that is really needed.' Note, 11 Jan. 1912, J. & P. 1146.

[74] They acknowledged that the machinery for settling disputes between the senate and council was elaborate, but believed that in actual practice it would work smoothly. 'The Vice Chancellor, who will be President of the Court and the Council and will always be a Muhammedan of position and influence, will be President of the Joint Board; and his influence and that of the Pro Vice Chancellor will, we have little doubt, be used to produce harmony. There will be a natural disposition to settle matters in the University without invoking the final authority of the Chancellor.' Finance letter from India, 2 Nov. 1911 (ref. 59).

[75] 'The Senate, which is representative of the Educational experts in the University, is in almost every important matter subject to the Court or the Council; the functions allotted to it are mostly to frame proposals to be submitted to the Court or Council.

'Though I do not approve of this solution, I recognise that the framers of the Bill were here confronted with a very difficult problem. It was necessary to put the staff i.e. the Provost, professors, wardens etc, on the Senate for theirs is the only educational opinion worth having in the University; but the staff are the salaried employés of the Governing Body and they could not be made the judges of their own terms of service. It was necessary, therefore, to devise a solution which would enable the Governing Body to retain the power of the purse while getting the benefit of the staff's expert knowledge. That was the problem and the solution adopted is to give the Governing Body the power of overruling the Senate on almost all vital questions. I fear this will not work well. In other Universities we have found that the presence on the Senates of persons ignorant of educational problems was a great inconvenience & one of the great reforms achieved by the Act of 1904 was to disencumber the Senates of these unprofessional Fellows.' Note, 1 Jan. 1912, J. & P. 1146.

[76] Public despatch to India, No 33, 23 Feb. 1912, *ibid.*

[77] Tel. 7 Oct. 1912, *ibid.*

[78] 'As originally constituted', he observed, 'the Council was the Executive Committee of the Court; it bore the same relation to the Court as the Syndicate holds to the Senate in the Indian Universities. The proposal of the G. of I. introduces a new element if, as I conjecture, the Senate is to be at liberty to elect 5 of its own members to the Council. I am not sure that this is wise. The Senate, roughly speaking, are the employés, & the Council is the Executive Committee of the Employers. As (in the original draft) 5 constitutes a quorum, it might not infrequently happen that the 5 representatives of the Senate constituted a majority of the Council present.

'My own view is that the Provost should be ex officio a member of the Council, to be able to represent the views of his staff, but that otherwise the employers should settle among themselves the terms they are prepared to offer to their employés.' Note, 17 Oct. 1912, *ibid.*

[79] Raleigh explained the amendments he suggested in the proposed draft reply thus: 'It is often useful to refer to University experience here 1) because many Indian problems have been solved, or at least dealt with here and 2) because we get rid of the notion that we are imposing our official requirements on an academic body.' Note, 7 Nov. 1912, *ibid.*

[80] Public despatch to India, No 246, 29 Nov. 1912, *ibid.*

[81] Education letter from India, No 19, 10 July 1913, J. & P. 1087.

[82] Sect. 10(1), Benares Hindu University Act.

[83] Tel. from India, 10 June 1911; tel. to India, 18 July 1911, J. & P. 1146.

[84] Finance letter from India, No 258, 2 Nov. 1911, enclosing draft constitution with amendments proposed by the govt. of India, *ibid.*

[85] Note, 1 Jan. 1912, *ibid.*

[86] *Cf.* note by Sir T. Raleigh, 11 Jan. 1912, *ibid.*

[87] Public despatch to India, No 33, 23 Feb. 1912, *ibid.*

[88] Education letter from India, No 8, 28 Mar. 1912, *ibid.*

[89] Public despatch to India, No 114, 12 July 1912, *ibid.*

[90] Tel. from India, 7 Oct. 1912, *ibid.*

[91] Public despatch to India, No 246, 29 Nov. 1912, *ibid.*

[92] Education letter from India, No 19, 10 July 1913, J. & P. 1087.

[93] Note, 2 Sept. 1913, *ibid.*

[94] Minute by Lionel Abrahams, 9 Sept. 1913. Abrahams suggested the committee should consist of Sir T. Holderness (under-secretary), E. S. Montagu (parl. under-secretary) and four members of council: Sir D. Barr, Sir J. La Touche, Sir K. Gupta and M. A. A. Baig (the two latter, Indians). *Ibid.*

[95] Crewe added, however, that if Sir T. Morison's duties on the Public Services Commission enabled him to be on the committee, he would 'add weight'; and this was arranged. Minute, 16 Sept. 1913, *ibid.*

[96] Tel., 11 Nov. 1913, *ibid.*

[97] Public despatch to India, 11 Nov. 1913, *ibid.*

[98] See, however, Sir T. W. Holderness's minute of 10 Nov. 1913 on the Dacca proposals (p. 96 below) from which it would seem that the India office had already decided to concede the full powers sought by the government of India when it telegraphed its enquiry about the chancellor.

[99] Tel., 16 May 1914, J. & P. 1087.

[100] Note, 9 June 1914, *ibid.*

[101] Tel. to India, 24 June 1914, *ibid.*

[102] Tel. from India, 30 Nov. 1914, *ibid.*

[103] Tel. to India, 15 Dec. 1914, *ibid.*

[104] The provisions for government control, as finally enacted, were as follows: Powers of control reserved to the government under the Benares Hindu University Act, 1915.

1. Powers of inspection vested in the lieutenant governor of the United Provinces as visitor *ex officio:*

　　Section 6(2) 'The Visitor shall have the right of inspecting the University and its Colleges generally, and for the purpose of seeing that the proceedings of the

University are in conformity with this Act and the Statutes and Regulations. The Visitor may, by order in writing, annul any such proceeding which is not in conformity with this Act and the Statutes and Regulations:

'Provided that, before making any such order, he shall call upon the University to show cause why such an order should not be made, and if any cause is shown within a reasonable time, shall consider the same.'

2. Powers of financial supervision vested in the visitor:

Section 13(2) 'The accounts, when audited, [they were to be audited 'once at least in every year'] shall be published in the Gazette of India and a copy of the accounts, together with the auditor's report, shall be submitted to the Visitor.'

3. Control over statutes and regulations:

i. STATUTES

Section 17(5) 'All new Statutes or additions to the Statutes or amendments or repeals to Statutes, other than Statutes providing for the instruction of Hindu students in Hindu religion, shall require the previous approval of the Visitor, who may sanction, disallow, or remit for further consideration:

'Provided that no Statute making a change in the constitution of the Court, the Council, the Senate or the Syndicate, as provided for in the first Statutes, shall be made without the previous sanction of the Governor General in Council.'

ii. REGULATIONS

Section 18(2) 'The first Regulations shall be framed as directed by the Governor General in Council, and shall receive his previous approval.'

Section 18(5) 'All new Regulations or additions to the Regulations, or amendments or repeals to Regulations, shall require the previous approval of the Visitor, who may sanction, disallow or remit for further consideration:

'Provided that no Regulation making a change in the first Regulations as to the admission of students to the University, shall be made without the previous sanction of the Governor General in Council.'

4. Emergency powers reserved to the governor general in council:

Section 19(1) 'If, at any time, the Governor General in Council is of opinion that special reasons exist which make the removal of any member of the teaching staff desirable in the interest of the University, or that, as a special measure, the appointment of a certain examiner or examiners to report to him is desirable to maintain the standard of University examinations, or that the scale of staff of the University is inadequate, or that in any other respect the affairs of the University are not managed in the furtherance of the objects and purposes of the University or in accordance with this Act and the Statutes and Regulations, he may indicate to the Council any matter in regard to which he desires explanation, and call upon that body to offer such explanation as it may desire to offer, with any proposals which it may desire to make, within such time as he may prescribe.'

Section 19(2) 'If the Council fails to offer any explanation within the time prescribed, or offers an explanation or makes proposals which, in the opinion of the Governor General in Council, is or are unsatisfactory, the Governor

General in Council may issue such instructions, as appear to him to be necessary and desirable in the circumstances of the case, and the Court shall give effect to such instructions.'

[105] 22 Mar. 1915, *Govt. of India Leg. Proc.*, LIII (1915) 525.

[106] 'My Lord', he declared, 'I have seen this constitution described as illiberal and I have rubbed my eyes in amazement. It is far more liberal than the constitution of existing universities. No Government can allow universities to grow up without control. In most European countries the universities or at least the majority of them are entirely State universities. In the course of these discussions two policies emerged. One was a policy of trust. The other a policy of distrust. The Government might have said to the Society – You are starting a new kind of University without any experience of it in India. We must leaven the lump with officials who have the requisite experience . . . But we preferred to trust the Society, to leave them large autonomy and to reserve to Government only the necessary powers of intervention if things go wrong . . . I hope intervention will not be required. We desire . . . you should manage your own affairs; we are anxious to maintain the dignity and independence of the University. But we must in the public interest, in the interests of the rising generation, in your own interest, have powers to interfere if things go wrong . . . But with this one reservation, we wish to see you realise your own way of life, your own way of corporate life. I ask Hon'ble Members to compare the constitution of this University with that of the oldest University of India. And yet who will deny that the University of Calcutta has had in practice a measure of independence that is not accorded to universities in most countries?' *Ibid.*, p. 524.

[107] Sir Harcourt Butler, in moving that the Benares Hindu University bill be referred to select committee, 8 Sept. 1915. *Ibid.*, LIV (1916) 15. In a further speech on 1 Oct., he did not disguise the fact that the government were critical of the complexity of the constitution; this was a matter, he stressed, on which they had deferred to the wishes of the promoters 'only insisting that the real academic work of the University should be in the hands of an academic body, namely, the Senate'. *Ibid.*, p. 80.

[108] Tel., 13 Feb. 1912, J. & P. 1135. Lord Crewe had already authorised Lord Hardinge to inform the muslims of Dacca that the government of India were recommending the establishment of a university there. He gave the permission during his visit to India for the coronation durbar, and the announcement was made on 2 Feb. 1912. Note by Crewe, 12 Feb. 1912, *ibid.*

[109] Govt. of Bengal, general dept (education) resolution No 567 T.–G., 27 May 1912 enclosed in finance letter from India, No 267, 18 Sept. 1913, J. & P. 1261. The president of the committee was R. Nathan, chief secretary of the Bengal education department, and its members were as follows: G. W. Küchler; Rash Behary Ghose; Saiyid Nawab Ali Chaudhuri; Siraj-ul-Islam; Anandra Chandra Roy; Mohamed Ali; H. R. James; W. A. J. Archbold; Satis Chandra Acharji; Lalit Mohan Chattarji; C. W. Peake; Abu Nasr Muhammad Waheed.

[110] *Report of the Dacca University Committee, 1912* (Calcutta, 1912).

[111] Finance letter from India, No 267, 18 Sept. 1913, J. & P. 1261.

[112] Tel. 9 Dec. 1913, *ibid. Cf.* the minute by Sir T. W. Holderness, 10 Nov. 1913, p. 96 below.

[113] Education letter from India, No 14, 15 Oct. 1915, J. & P. 1261.

[114] *Dacca report*, p. 20.

[115] Bengal education letter, 28 Sept. 1914; enclosure in finance letter from India, 15 Oct. 1915, J. & P. 1261.

[116] Education letter to Bengal, 28 Dec. 1914, *ibid.* 'The Government of India are confirmed in their opinion on the point by the report of the Royal Commission on University Education in London', the letter ran. 'That Commission considered that the University of London (on the model of which existing Universities in India were founded) was prevented from carrying out its duties by the variety of teaching institutions connected with it and their complete financial independence of each other and of the University itself. The independence of these institutions it was found was not confined to the appointment and control of their teachers but extended to their whole financial and educational policy.' *Ibid.*

[117] Bengal education letter, 25 June 1915, *ibid.*

[118] Education letter from India, No 14, 15 Oct. 1915, *ibid.*

[119] *Dacca report*, p. 130.

[120] It was proposed that the council should consist of the vice-chancellor, the commissioner of the Dacca division, principals of incorporated colleges, six professors appointed by the chancellor and six members elected by convocation from amongst its own members. *Ibid.*, p. 133.

[121] Bengal education letter, 6 June 1913; finance letter from India, No 267, 18 Sept. 1913; tel. to India, 9 Dec. 1913, J. & P. 1261.

[122] *Dacca report*, pp. 130–44.

[123] Bengal education letter, 6 June 1913. J. & P. 1261. (At one point in their debate with the government of India, however, the government of Bengal had actually hinted that the new university might be set up as a state department by simple executive order. This was too much even for the government of India. 'Although the proposal has not been made to them officially', the joint secretary wrote in December 1914, 'I am to take this opportunity of stating that the Government of India would not be in favour of a State department created by executive order. They would consider such an arrangement open to criticism, derogatory to the dignity and the independence which the University should enjoy; and from its very novelty, calculated to excite public distrust.' Education letter to Bengal, 28 Dec. 1914, *ibid.*)

[124] Minute, 10 Nov. 1913, on finance letter from India, No 267, 18 Sept. 1913, *ibid.*

[125] Tel., 9 Dec. 1913, *ibid.*

[126] Bengal education letter, 25 June 1915, enclosed in education letter from India, No 14, 15 Oct. 1915, *ibid.*

[127] Education letter from India, No 14, 15 Oct. 1915, *ibid.*

[128] Tel., 20 Dec. 1915, *ibid.*

[129] The section relating to the chancellor reads as follows: 'The Chancellor shall be the Governor of Bengal for the time being. He will confirm all proposals for honorary degrees and all elections to Council and Convocation, and if, in his opinion, the affairs of the University demand enquiry, he shall cause enquiries to be made and shall issue such instructions as appear necessary and desirable in the circumstances, which instructions shall be incumbent on the University. He will have other powers under the Act and Regulations.' 'Outline of the Scheme of the Dacca University', Simla, 28 Aug. 1915. Enclosure No 8 in letter of 15 Oct. 1915. *Ibid.*

[130] The issue was less prominent over Dacca. But even in the report of the Dacca University Committee, which was specifically precluded from providing for affiliation by its terms of reference, the government's policy did not go unchallenged. One

of the Indian members, Mohamed Ali, protested that it was premature to dispense with the federal system altogether. 'In confining itself, as the Government desired, to framing a scheme for a purely teaching University', he wrote in a dissenting minute, 'the Committee has . . . concerned itself with the ideal more than with the needs of the situation in Eastern Bengal.' *Dacca report*, p. 163.

[131] Thus whilst the new university at Patna, established in 1917, was designed to be primarily teaching and residential, it was also permitted limited powers of affiliation. According to the *Quinquennial Review* this was in deference to the strength of local feeling. But the powers were regarded as transitory. It was intended that Patna should become a centralised institution like Dacca as soon as the local colleges were strong enough to stand alone. *Progress of education in India, 1912–17: seventh quinquennial review*, comp. H. Sharp (Calcutta, 1918) 68–9.

[132] Ref. 107.

[133] Ref. 73.

[134] *Cf.* especially the view of A. I. Mayhew, director of public instruction, Central Provinces, on the 'two-tier' structure proposed for Benares: 'The division of the government of the University into two sections, administrative and academic', he wrote, 'and the assignment of the first section to the Court and the second section to the Senate, is a notable feature of the proposed University which differentiates it from any other University already established or proposed in India. It is strongly advocated by the London University Commission, but I have grave doubts as to its practicability in India where there is not at present sufficient material for two such governing bodies. It would be far better to have one efficient governing body controlling all the business of the University whether administrative or academic than to have an efficient Senate dominated by an inefficient Court.'

He pointed to the contrast between the type of court prescribed by the commission and that provided for under the bill. Whereas the commission 'recommended that the Court . . . should be composed of men representing varied interests and sections of the community nominated for the most part by bodies of good standing and proved reputation and possessed of administrative ability', the majority of the hindu court were to be donors and their representatives or nominees. It seemed, therefore, that 'if any particular wealthy section of the Hindu community wished to control the Hindu University it would be able to . . .'

The government of the Central Provinces endorsed his concern that the supreme governing body would in fact be a plutocracy; and concluded that the constitution seemed to have been framed on a model 'which however suitable it may be to the conditions of Western civilization in Europe, is not, at least without considerable modification, adapted to the circumstances of India'. Legislative letter from India, 13 Aug. 1915, forwarding letter from the government of the Central Provinces, 31 July 1915 with enclosure from A. I. Mayhew, 15 June 1915. J. & P. 1087.

[135] Education letter from India, No 14, 15 Oct. 1915, J. & P. 1261.

[136] *Dacca report*, pp. 21–2.

[137] Dissenting minute by Siraj-ul-Islam, Saiyid Nawab, Ali Chaudhuri, and Abu Nasr Muhammad Waheed; and by Mohamed Ali. *Ibid.*, pp. 160, 166–7.

[138] Finance letter from India, No 267, 18 Sept. 1913, enclosing Bengal education letter, 6 June 1913, J. &. P. 1261.

[139] Education letter from India, No 14, 15 Oct. 1915, enclosing Bengal education letter, 25 June 1915, *ibid.*

[140] Ref. 109.

[141] *Dacca report*, p. 11.

[142] *Ibid.*, pp. 70–5.

[143] *Ibid.*, pp. 70–5, 79.

[144] *Ibid.*, p. 54.

[145] *Ibid.*, pp. 56–7.

[146] *Ibid.*, pp. 36–42.

[147] *Ibid.*, pp. 24–5.

[148] *Ibid.*, pp. 25, 29.

[149] *Ibid.*, p. 67.

[150] *Ibid.*, p. 45.

[151] *Ibid.*

[152] *Ibid.*, p. 43.

[153] *Ibid.*

[154] Bengal education letter, 6 June 1913 (ref. 138).

[155] They did mention a model, however, for one of the colleges they proposed to found. This was a college for the 'well-to-do classes': a rather curious project prompted by a peculiar defect of the existing system. 'It is notorious', they wrote, 'that in Bengal the landholders, and others of high position and comparatively ample means, have failed to take due advantage of the State system of higher education; they prefer to keep their sons at home and to give them such private tuition as they may be able to secure, or, in a few cases, to send them to Oxford or Cambridge. There can be no question that Bengal has suffered from the failure on the part of the upper classes to take their proper part in the educational system of the country, and that as education becomes more widespread and as the people take a more prominent share in the Government, this evil becomes more severely felt.' Concluding that the failure was perhaps caused by the absence of suitable residential facilities, they proposed the experiment of a special college to attract the patronage of these classes. 'The conception in the minds of the promoters of the scheme', it was explained, 'is to provide a thoroughly well-equipped and well-managed residential college on the model of one of the colleges at Oxford or Cambridge, in which the students will be cared for and will live in a style suitable to their upbringing.' Again there was the supporting reference to practice in the west where 'even in democratic countries, young men of land-owning and wealthy classes take a prominent, sometimes the foremost, part in University life . . .' But the scheme met with strong public criticism; and the government of India agreed with the government of Bengal that it should be dropped. *Dacca report*, pp. 92–6; finance letter from India, No 267, 18 Sept. 1913, J. & P. 1261.

[156] *Ibid.*

[157] Tel., 9 Dec. 1913, *ibid.*

[158] See above, pp. 86, 88, 89.

[159] *The conference of orientalists including museums and archaeology conference held at Simla, July 1911* (Simla, 1911).

[160] 'As "courses of study" are at present prescribed', he wrote in a note for the conference, '[the Indian undergraduate's] daily round of lectures may present him with a play out of Shakespeare, and a dish-up of Aristotle or Kant or some period of modern European history and, finally the Sākuntala and the Kirāta. His Sanskrit thus links on to nothing in the prescribed "course" and can find no mental context for itself. But would not the whole process become more organized, more alive, if

the study of an Oriental language were combined with the study of historical and philosophical works in that language?' Note by Dr Venis, *ibid.*, p. 54.

[161] Finance letter from India, No 85, 11 April 1912, J. & P. 1149.

[162] Enclosure in education letter from India, No 25, 10 Oct. 1912, J. & P. 1111[A].

[163] Public despatch to India, No 51, 21 Feb. 1913, J. & P. 1149.

[164] Education letter from India, No 30, 18 Dec. 1913, *ibid.*

[165] Minute, 14 April 1914, *ibid.*

[166] 19 May 1914, *ibid.*

[167] Public despatch to India, No 111, 10 July 1914, *ibid.*

[168] Tel., 10 June 1911, J. & P. 1146.

[169] IUC (ref. 58) p. 8.

[170] In a printed note for the council, he stated he would 'greatly prefer' a scheme accepting the existing division of spheres of influence as fixed by the act of 1904, and making provision for muhammadan students wherever they were found. He considered it would be 'vastly better' to bring muhammadans into the life of a mixed university than to 'pen them into a privileged enclosure of their own'. 17 July 1911, J. & P. 1146.

[171] Note [7 July 1911], *ibid.*

[172] Note [7 July 1911], *ibid.*

[173] Note, 13 July 1911, *ibid.*

[174] 'The case of Ireland seems to me analogous. Trinity College, Dublin, was originally a denominational University but has ceased to be such for 100 years. The Royal University was founded similar to our Indian Universities. Yet when a large section of the community refused to make use of the Royal University all parties in the State joined together to welcome the establishment of a National University acceptable to that large section of the Irish people. The counterpart in India is the National University for Mohammedans in Aligarh.' Note, 13 July 1911, *ibid.*

[175] Tel., 18 July, *ibid.*

[176] Mrs Annie Besant to private secy to viceroy, 27 July 1910, enclosing petition and draft charter for a University of India. Enclosure in demi-official education letter from India, No 297, conf., 11 May 1911, J. & P. 1087.

[177] *Ibid.*

[178] Punjab home letter, 7 Feb. 1911, *ibid.*

[179] Madras education letter, conf., 2 June 1911, enclosed in demi-official education letter from India, 15 June 1911, *ibid. Cf.* the replies from the United Provinces (conf., 28 Mar. 1911) and Bengal (24 May 1911) enclosed in demi-official education letters from India of 11 May and 1 June 1911, respectively. *Ibid.*

[180] *Cf.* the replies from Bombay (22 Feb. 1911), the United Provinces (conf., 28 Mar. 1911) and the Central Provinces (29 Mar. 1911) enclosed in demi-official education letter from India, conf., 11 May 1911. *Ibid.* Also the reply from Madras, ref. 179.

[181] E. Bengal education letter, 24 Feb. 1911, enclosed in demi-official education letter from India, conf., 11 May 1911, *ibid.*

[182] Mrs Annie Besant to private secy to viceroy, 13 April 1911, *ibid.*

[183] Tel., 3 May 1911, *ibid.*

[184] Minute by the secretary of state, Lord Crewe, 25 July 1911, reporting the visit from Mrs Besant on the previous day. *Ibid. Cf.* ref. 175.

[185] Note by Sir S. W. Edgerley, 1 Aug. 1911, *ibid.*

[186] Note by Mirza Ali Abbas Baig, 11 Aug. 1911, *ibid.*

[187] *Ibid.*

[188] Note, 25 Aug. 1911, *ibid.*

[189] Note, 1 Aug. 1911, *ibid.*

[190] Ref. 188.

[191] Note [Aug. 1911], *ibid.*

[192] Harcourt Butler to the Maharaja Sir Rameshwara Singh Bahadur of Darbhanga, 12 Oct. 1911. Enclosure in demi-official education letter from India, conf., 12 Oct. 1911, *ibid.*

[193] Maharaja of Darbhanga to Sir Harcourt Butler, 30 Oct. 1912, enclosing draft bill and explanatory memorandum. Enclosure in demi-official education letter from India, 7 Nov. 1912, *ibid.*, and in education letter, 10 July 1913 (ref. 195).

[194] Ref. 176.

[195] Education letter from India, No 19, 10 July 1913; whilst at the India office, attention was monopolised by the constitutional issue: tels to India, 11 Nov. 1913, 24 June 1914, *ibid.*

[196] Sect. 3(3) Benares Hindu University Act, 1915. (Act XVI of 1915). As forwarded to London in draft, the full text of this clause had read:

'3. The University shall be and shall be deemed to have been incorporated for the purposes (among others) of making provision for imparting education literary artistic and scientific as well as technical, commercial and professional, of furthering the prosecution of original research, of giving training, moral as well as religious, and aiding in the formation of character and of promoting in a special degree the study of Hindu religion, literature, philosophy, history, medicine and science.'

As finally enacted, it became:

'3. (3). The University shall be deemed to have been incorporated for the purposes, among others, of making provision for imparting education, literary, artistic and scientific, as well as agricultural, technical, commercial and professional, of furthering the prosecution of original research, and of giving instruction in Hindu theology and religion, and of promoting the study of literature, art, philosophy, history, medicine and science, and of imparting physical and moral training.'

[197] 22 Mar. 1915, *Govt. of India Leg. Proc.*, LIII (1915) 527.

[198] Note by Crewe, 12 Feb. 1912, J. & P. 1135.

[199] Education letter to Bengal, 4 April 1912, Govt. of India, educ. dept, proceedings, vol. 8942, pp. 865-7.

[200] *Dacca report*, pp. 15, 97–103.

[201] *Ibid.*, p. 32.

[202] *Ibid.*, p. 25.

[203] *Ibid.*, p. 31.

[204] *Ibid.*, p. 33.

[205] *Ibid.*, p. 32.

[206] *Cf.* ref. 160. 'The sub-committee state that the study of Sanskrit has suffered in Indian Universities by the failure to bring it into relationship with other subjects', the Dacca University Committee reported. 'By their suggestions that a candidate studying the early history of India for the B.A. degree should be permitted to offer the original text of some of the Gupta inscriptions as part of his examination in Sanskrit, and that a candidate taking philosophy should be allowed to include in his Sanskrit course a philosophical text in the original, they indicate how this defect may be removed.' *Ibid.*, p. 32.

[207] *Ibid.*, p. 34.

[208] The pass degree course in history was hardly less wide ranging than the comparable Calcutta course which had earned the strictures of C. H. Tawney (above, p. 67). It was to cover the history of England from the earliest times as well as the history of India; the outlines of European history in the nineteenth century, and an intermediate course in the history of Rome. Thus would the student be able to enjoy 'such a knowledge of history as a well-educated man should possess'. In philosophy, the emphasis of the pass degree course was firmly on western philosophy. An optional paper in the outlines of Indian philosophy was suggested for the honours course; but as in the pass course, the greatest stress was laid 'on the first-hand study of works of genius, the writings of the great succession of European philosophers from Descartes to Kant, whose works, regarded as an organically connected series, form the natural introduction to any serious consideration of the problems of modern philosophy'. The committee took Curzon's view that western classics were unnecessary (above, p. 82); but they proposed sufficient French and German to enable students to read books in those languages relating to their other studies. *Ibid.*, pp. 33, 35, 24.

[209] Bengal education letter, 6 June 1913, enclosed in finance letter from India, No 267, 18 Sept. 1913, J. & P. 1261.

[210] Finance letter from India, 18 Sept. 1913, *ibid.*

[211] Tel., 9 Dec. 1913, *ibid.*

[212] P. 103 above.

[213] 'We still stand on the threshhold and amid the preliminary difficulties of what I believe to be a new era in the history of Indian Universities, their transition from a purely examining to a partly teaching University type.' Convocation address, 6 Mar. 1915. *Speeches of H.E. the Rt. Honble Baron Hardinge of Penshurst*, II (Madras, 1917) 366.

Chapter 5 *A redefinition*

[1] E. S. Montagu, 20 Aug. 1917, *H.C. Deb.*, 5 ser., XCVII, col. 1695.

[2] Calcutta University Commission, 1917–19, *Report*, I (Calcutta, 1919) 1.

[3] M. Sadleir [i.e. M. T. H. Sadler], *Michael Ernest Sadler (Sir Michael Ernest Sadler K.C.S.I.) 1861–1943* (London, 1949) 282.

[4] P. Hartog, *Some aspects of Indian education past and present* (London, 1939) 60.

[5] H. Sharp, 'The development of Indian universities', *J. Roy. Soc. Arts*, LXXIII (1925) 513–25.

[6] CUC, *Report*, I, 1.

[7] J. R. B. Muir, *Ramsay Muir: an autobiography and some essays*, ed. Stuart Hodgson (London, 1943) 111.

[8] Writing privately to Lord George Hamilton in September 1901, Curzon referred to an official request being sent home asking for the appointment of a director general of Indian education, and for assistance in finding a suitable man. 'I think I can give you a hint in the latter direction', he added. 'Twenty years ago, when I was leaving Oxford, there was a very able young fellow named M. E. Sadler, a scholar of Trinity College who was President of the Union, took a First Class and made quite a mark on University life. After leaving Oxford he devoted himself to Education and has for many years been in the service of the Education Dept. in Whitehall . . . Some of his reports upon Secondary and Technical Education are quite excellent and he is moreover one of the great pillars of the University extension movement. I have no

idea whether he would be willing to come to India; but . . . the prospect of doubling his income might persuade him . . . I should add that I myself have neither seen him nor had any communication with him for twenty years; so that my evidence is quite disinterested in the matter. Raper, however, could probably give a very good opinion about him and would tell you how far he is qualified for the task. From my recollection of him I should say that in respect of character, ability, and above all enthusiasm he would be singularly well suited for it . . .' Curzon to Lord George Hamilton, 25 Sept. 1901, MSS. Eur. F.111/160.

[9] Muir went out to Lahore in September 1913; and before leaving India early in the following year, he was invited to Delhi by the viceroy to join a discussion on education with Sir Harcourt Butler, Sir Michael O'Dwyer, and Sir Valentine Chirol. He recalls in his *Autobiography* how after the discussion the viceroy asked him to set out his views in a memorandum, how he did so, and how this contained 'in form all the main proposals embodied in the Report of the Calcutta University Commission of which a few years later I was to be a member'. Muir attributed his invitation to serve on the commission to Austen Chamberlain having seen the memorandum. Muir, (ref. 7), pp. 99, 110.

[10] CUC, *Report*, I, 2.

[11] To his wife, 30 May 1918. Sadleir (ref. 3), pp. 299–300.

[12] *Cf.* an early letter to his father: '. . . The education is bad – and they [the Indians] seem to like it so. It is overrun by gigantic examinations. Education is chiefly parrot work. Under every part of it there are intrigues, suspicions, dirty work. The Europeans get rather cynical about it all . . .' January, 1918. *Ibid.*, p. 290.

[13] CUC, *Report*, V, 302. [*Cf.* the very similar judgement of the Haldane commission on the University of London: 'After the most careful inquiry we have been able to make into the whole organisation of the University, we have come to the conclusion that it is fundamentally defective, and as at present constituted is not calculated to promote the higher interests of University education in London . . .' *University education in London, roy. comm. final rept.*, p. 2; 1913, Cd. 6717, XL.]

[14] CUC, *Report*, V, 302.

[15] *Ibid.*, I, 15.

[16] Ref. 11.

[17] CUC, *Report*, IV, 19 ff.

[18] *Ibid.*, VII, 303–9.

[19] *Ibid.*, IV, 20.

[20] *Ibid.*, IV, 252–3.

[21] Minute by M.E.Sadler, quoted in L.Grier, *Achievement in education: the work of Michael Ernest Sadler, 1885–1935* (London, 1952) 213–5.

[22] CUC, *Report*, IV, 253.

[23] *Ibid.*, IV, 336–42.

[24] *Ibid.*, IV, 254.

[25] P.J.Hartog, 'The work of the Calcutta University Commission', *Asiatic Review*, XVI (1920) 597–608.

[26] CUC, *Report*, IV, 254–5.

[27] *Ibid.*, IV, 299–309.

[28] *Ibid.*, IV, 283–9.

[29] *Ibid.*, IV, 255.

[30] *Ibid.*, IV, 331–63.

[31] *Ibid.*, IV, 427–9.

[32] *Ibid.*, IV, 357.

[33] *Ibid.*, IV, 358.

[34] *Ibid.*, IV, 281.

[35] *Ibid.*, III, 187–221.

[36] *Ibid.*, III, 211.

[37] *Ibid.*, III, 199.

[38] *Ibid.*, IV, 376–7.

[39] *Ibid.*, IV, 394–400.

[40] *Ibid.*, IV, 282.

[41] *Ibid.*, III, 220.

[42] *Ibid.*, IV, 400.

[43] *Ibid.*, IV, 384–90.

[44] *Ibid.*, IV, 387.

[45] *Ibid.*, IV, 390.

[46] *Ibid.*, IV, 387.

[47] *Ibid.*, IV, 215.

[48] P. J. Hartog, 'Some problems of Indian education', *Educational Review*, XXVI (1920) 211–27.

[49] CUC, *Report*, IV, 375.

[50] *Ibid.*, III, 258–9.

[51] *Ibid.*, III, 259–60. Writing in ignorance of the solution that was to be found for the African universities, the commission did not dispute that 'minute and detailed' control had been necessary at the outset – 'when the western methods of university work were entirely unfamiliar, an exotic importation of whose working only those trained in western universities could have any understanding and which might have gone disastrously astray if not firmly guided from above'. *Ibid.*, III, 259.

[52] *Ibid.*, III, 260–2; also IV, 134, 150–64.

[53] *Ibid.*, III, 265.

[54] *Ibid.*, III, 263–4.

[55] *Ibid.*, V, 219–27.

[56] *Ibid.*, V, 238–45.

[57] 'Memorandum submitted by the Commission to the Subjects Committee (appointed in connexion with the Reforms)' 21 Nov. 1918. *Ibid.*, VI, appx 1, 3.

[58] *Ibid.*, V, 239.

[59] *Ibid.*, V, 239–40.

[60] *Ibid.*, V, 243.

[61] See above, p. 92.

[62] CUC, *Report*, V, 224.

[63] *Ibid.*, V, 227–33.

[64] *Ibid.*, V, 230–1. For the commission's detailed criticism of the service system see *ibid.*, III, 265–75.

[65] Public despatch to India, No 49, 19 July 1854, J. A. Richey (ed.) *Selections from educational records*, II (Calcutta, 1922) 386.

[66] Public despatch to India, No 42, 5 April 1900, J. & P. 525.

[67] Education letter to the local governments, 27 Nov. 1901, MSS. Eur. F.111/280.

[68] Syed Nawabaly Chaudhury, CUC, *Report*, III, 281.

[69] Tej Bahadur Sapru, *ibid.*

[70] *Ibid.*, V, 233–8.

[71] *Ibid.*, V, 235.

[72] See above, p. 97.

[73] Above, pp. 88–93. For the current, somewhat modified local official view, see the evidence submitted by H. Sharp, educational commissioner with the government of India. He prefaced detailed suggestions by the following general reflections:

... Next, as to the nature of the relations which should exist between the University and the Government ... one is faced with a great variety of different models, from the purely State university, such as is found on the Continent of Europe and in some of the United States of America, to those over which the control is very slight, as in the United Kingdom. The nature of the control should be fixed with regard to the local conditions. The conditions in Bengal which affect the issue are:

a. The widespread desire for a university education resulting from the lack of variety in employment.

b. The weakness of public opinion in regard to discipline and standards.

c. The insistence, urged by a certain class, upon popular control in university matters.

d. The introduction of non-educational motives into educational questions.

e. The existence in the country of local variations and conflicting interests.

These conditions are inimical to university development on proper lines and point to the desirability of establishing State universities. They have resulted in undesirable situations regarding applications for affiliation, appointments, and failure on the part of the University to observe its regulations, which indicate that the power over the framing of regulations and the other means of check at present possessed by Government are insufficient.

On the other hand, there are certain considerations which bear in the opposite direction. These are:

i. The traditional British policy regarding universities.

ii. The desirability of affording to India every opportunity of training in self-governing institutions.

iii. The existence in the country of an external power, necessitating, within all reasonable limits, discussion and advice in matters which affect the public at large.

Hence, it appears advisable to steer a middle course. This has been the aim in my general memorandum. ...

CUC, *Report*, XI, 93–5; VII, 442–9.

[74] *Ibid.*, IV, 428.

[75] *Ibid.*, IV, 23.

[76] See above, p. 98.

[77] CUC, *Report*, IV, 119; V, 297.

[78] *Ibid.*, IV, 26.

[79] *Ibid.*, IV, 99–115.

[80] *Ibid.*, IV, 54.

[81] *Ibid.*, IV, 30–52.

[82] *Ibid.*, IV, 26.

[83] *Ibid.*, IV, 54.

[84] *Ibid.*, IV, 51.

[85] *Ibid.*, IV, 167, 257.

[86] *Ibid.*, IV, 257.

[87] *Ibid.*, I, 395.

[88] *Ibid.*, IV, 167, 260.

[89] *Ibid.*, IV, 260–2

90 *Ibid.*, IV, 262.

91 *Ibid.*, IV, 221, 403–4.

92 *Ibid.*, IV, 167, 258–9.

93 *Ibid.*, IV, 170, 276–80.

94 *Ibid.*, IV, 156–7, 294–9.

95 *Ibid.*, IV, 298.

96 *Ibid.*, IV, 296.

97 *Ibid.*, I, 368; IV, 295, 323.

98 *Ibid.*, IV, 323.

99 *Ibid.*, IV, 157.

100 *Ibid.*, IV, 323–4.

101 *Ibid.*, IV, 148–50, 265–76.

102 *Ibid.*, IV, 268–9.

103 *Ibid.*, IV, 270.

104 *Ibid.*

105 The commission summarised their reactions to the current system in a poignant passage from Hartog's pen: 'It is impossible to peruse the evidence on the examination system as it exists today in Bengal without a feeling of profound sadness. The immensity of the effort, disproportionate to the results; the painful anxiety of the candidates; the mechanical award of marks encouraging the least fruitful efforts of the mind; a leniency sometimes neglecting the grave responsibility of the University to the public and tending to class the less with the more deserving students; the number of failures in spite of that leniency; the sterilising influence of the whole system on both teachers and taught, and the consequent crying waste of the intelligence of the youth of Bengal: these are evils which have been brought home to us by the most convincing evidence from witnesses of every section of the community, as well as by what we ourselves have seen.' *Ibid.*, II, 224–5. (*cf.* M. Hartog, *P. J. Hartog: a memoir* (London, 1949) 80).

106 *Ibid.*, V, 9.

107 *Ibid.*, V, 25.

108 *Ibid.*, V, 9.

109 *Ibid.*, V, 1–2.

110 *Ibid.*, V, 2–6.

111 *Ibid.*, V, 4.

112 *Ibid.*, IV, 304.

113 *Ibid.*, IV, 306, 456–8.

114 *Ibid.*, IV, 435–47.

115 *Ibid.*, IV, 239.

116 *Ibid.*, IV, 449–55.

117 *Ibid.*, IV, 452.

118 *Ibid.*, IV, 327.

119 *Ibid.*, I, 380, 397 ff; IV, 13–5; V, 302.

120 The opinion of Abdur Rahim, *ibid.*, IV, 14–5.

121 *Ibid.*

122 See above, p. 118.

123 CUC, *Report*, V, 71–97.

124 *Ibid.*, IV, 8.

125 *Ibid.*, V, 74.

[126] See above, p. 128.

[127] CUC, *Report*, III, 163, 180; IV, 193.

[128] The senate had appointed a committee on 13 October 1917 'to consider the feasibility of the University taking steps to develop the teaching of the higher branches of agricultural, technological and commercial studies'. This had reported in favour of the proposal, and draft regulations had been submitted for the sanction of the government in the following March. The government had delayed a decision pending reference to the commission. *Ibid.*, III, 174.

[129] *Ibid.*, IV, 192–3.

[130] *Ibid.*, V, 176–91, 339–40; IV, 109–10.

[131] *Ibid.*, V, 195–6.

[132] *Ibid.*, V, 192–209, 340–2.

[133] *Ibid.*, V, 209–12, 342–4.

[134] See above, p. 79.

[135] CUC, *Report*, II, 81.

[136] *Ibid.*, V, 330.

[137] This they did implicitly: by reference to the fact that 'the primary function of university work has always hitherto been held to be the development of western learning . . .' *Ibid.*

[138] *Ibid.*, IV, 326–7; V, 49–70.

[139] *Ibid.*, IV, 168.

[140] See above, p. 109.

[141] CUC, *Report*, IV, 178–9.

[142] *Ibid.*, IV, 182–3.

[143] *Ibid.*, IV, 180.

[144] *Ibid.*, IV, 180–1, 183.

[145] *Ibid.*, I, 402.

[146] *Ibid.*, V, 59.

[147] *Ibid.*, V, 58–60.

[148] *Ibid.*, V, 58.

[149] *Ibid.*, I, 402.

[150] *Ibid.*, I, 402–3.

[151] *Ibid.*, V, 333–4.

[152] See above, p. 134.

[153] CUC, *Report*, V, 286, n.1.

[154] *Ibid.*, IV, 265.

[155] *Ibid.*, IV, 262–3.

[156] *Ibid.*, IV, 263–5.

[157] *Ibid.*, IV, 167–8, 265.

[158] *Ibid.*, V, 27.

[159] *Ibid.*, IV, 240.

[160] See above, pp. 116.

[161] They had kept the needs of the muslims especially in mind, urging the provision of a muslim hall at Dacca, a muslim college in Calcutta, and special facilities for religious observance in all hostels where muslim students were accommodated. But they also emphasised the obligation of all college authorities in the matter of moral and religious training (CUC, *Report*, IV, 306, 456) and the desirability of affording opportunities for religious observance in all hostels where the need arose (*ibid.*, IV, 447).

[162] A majority of the witnesses in 1902 had objected to 'the introduction of the theology of any one religion into the curriculum of the University' and the commission had thus concluded that it was 'neither practical nor expedient to make provision for a Faculty of Theology'. *Report of the Indian Universities Commission, 1902* (Simla, 1902) 11.

[163] CUC, *Report*, IV, 285.

[164] They hoped that at Dacca 'the close association of Hindu, Muslim and European teachers will in a specially high degree afford opportunities for collaboration in thought and scholarship among the representatives of the three cultures from the blending of which a new intellectual movement may arise in India' (*Ibid.*, IV, 18). 'We have suggested elsewhere', they added in another section of their report, 'that the future of India depends upon finding a civilisation which will be a happy union of the Hindu, Islamic and European civilisations. The institution of such departments as have been recommended in this chapter [i.e. those that were to provide the special courses in islamic and sanskritic culture] would be a practical step to this end.' (*Ibid.*, V, 70). There was to be a significant change of emphasis when the Radhakrishnan commission came to report thirty years later in the full flush of Indian independence. '. . . our present fundamental cultural problem is to adapt our ancient tradition and culture to the exigencies of the new era of Western thought and culture', they wrote. 'We have to modernize our national and historical individuality by mobilising our spiritual forces and building up a new civilization from our own history, which will be neither European, nor American, but essentially Indian and human.' (*The report of the University Education Commission* (Delhi, 1950) I, 153).

[165] Hartog was disarmingly frank about this in a lecture he gave to the Royal Society of Arts. Replying to Indian suggestions that India would soon be able to follow the example of Japan in dispensing with the services of Europeans in her educational system, he insisted that there was an essential difference in the two situations. 'Japan is our very good ally. India is a country of the British Commonwealth and except for a handful of extremists desires to remain so. India desires not Japanese institutions but institutions modelled on those of Great Britain and developed to meet India's needs; and though it is not vocal there is among the bhadralog, the middle classes, a strong feeling that they have something direct to learn from Englishmen and other Europeans which is not testified to by University examinations and distinctions . . . I believe profoundly that in the new education of India the need for the help of Englishmen strong of heart and mind will be great. I hope that Englishmen will give that help. I hope that India will welcome it.' *J. Roy. Soc. Arts*, LXVIII (1920) 114–27.

[166] CUC, *Report*, V, 245–6.

[167] They considered it an essential condition of any system whereby commonwealth students went to England for courses in postgraduate research that 'there should be some general understanding as to the purpose, significance and standards of the undergraduate courses in all the universities'. It was at the postgraduate stage that they thought that Indians would most benefit from study in England; but they did not wish to rule out migration at an earlier stage and suggested that the standard they had proposed for the intermediate examination might well be accepted by British universities as a condition of entry to their undergraduate courses. But whether the Indians went to England for undergraduate or postgraduate courses, for academic studies or professional or technical ones, the commission stressed the

need of 'a clearer adjustment' between their Indian training and the courses they would follow overseas; and here they looked for the assistance of an effective inter-university body of the type which the existing Universities Bureau of the British Empire aspired to be. *Ibid.*, V, 246–50.

[168] *Ibid.*, V, 251.

[169] Under the system of dyarchy established by the Government of India Act of 1919, education became a 'transferred' subject and passed into the control of Indian ministers responsible to the provincial legislatures. The change was gravely to sabotage the work of the commission, at least so far as the University of Calcutta was concerned. In January 1920, the government of India issued a resolution commending the findings of the report to the local governments, and much of the subsequent university legislation was influenced by its ideas. The government of India also drafted a bill to give effect to the commission's proposals for the reconstruction of the University of Calcutta. But before this could be introduced, other legislation was carried, giving effect to the transfer of responsibility for the University of Calcutta from the government of India to the government of Bengal. In March 1921, the government of Bengal informed the university that, owing to financial stringency, it was unable to undertake the reforms contemplated by the commission; and thenceforth neither government did anything to implement the recommendations of the report. *Progress of education in India, 1917–22: eighth quinquennial review*, comp. J. A. Richey (Calcutta, 1923) I, 52; University of Calcutta, *Hundred years of the University of Calcutta* (Calcutta, 1957) 195–7, 268–76.

[170] *The report of the University Education Commission (December 1948–August 1949)* (Delhi, 1950). Membership of the commission was as follows: S. Radhakrishnan (chairman); Tara Chand; James F. Duff (from Britain); Zakir Hussain; Arthur E. Morgan (from USA); A. L. Mudaliar; Meghnad Saha; Karm Narayan Bahl; John J. Tigert (from USA); Nirmal Kumar Sidhanta (secretary). The commission's concern runs through the whole report. 'The marked deterioration of standards in teaching and examinations', it says (p. 5), '. . . are matters of great concern.' The universities had failed to produce in adequate numbers either 'teachers commanding fame and respect' or investigators who had won international recognition (p. 71). The amount of research did not approach what it should be, and its quality was steadily declining (p. 147). '. . . intellectual leadership', say the Radhakrishnan commissioners, 'seems to have deserted us . . . We must make a sustained effort to raise ourselves up' (p. 141). The fault lay partly in the secondary schools; by neglecting the recommendations of the Sadler commission on high schools and intermediate colleges India had lost thirty years of educational progress. It lay as well in two familiar causes: 'The purely affiliating university is today doing more harm to the good name of Indian Universities as a whole than any other single factor . . .' (p. 415). And examinations, the commissioners thought, were corrupting the moral standard of university life. Without reform 'there is danger that Indian higher education will fall into chaos' (p. 329). The Radhakrishnan commission found also a deplorable lack of social relevance in Indian higher education. Universities 'touch only the fringe of what is required in the way of higher education in the world's newest and most populous democracy' (p. 555).

Pakistan's indictment of its own universities is even more outspoken. A commission composed entirely of Pakistanis under the chairmanship of S. M. Sharif reported on the whole educational system in 1960. (*Report of the Commission on National Educa-*

U–B.I.A.—14*

tion. Government of Pakistan, ministry of education, January–August 1959 (Karachi, 1960).) It exposed similar evils in the system: unplanned expansion and a disastrous deterioration in quality (p. 16); the fetish of examinations (p. 23); neglect of national needs (p. 52). But it was on the poor quality of teachers and teaching that the commissioners mainly focussed. They say bluntly that most teachers think their duty is discharged when they have given lectures; research, personal study, and contact with students are neglected. They criticise a general slackness in the teaching programme: 'there is a growing tendency among teachers in colleges and universities to be casual about punctuality and frequently to absent themselves from classes altogether' (p. 29). And they say:

We are convinced that except for a few dedicated teachers the vast majority are spending little if any time in improving their own knowledge or keeping abreast of their subjects. . . . We may now state the crucial problem. It is to ensure that the work of a teacher ceases to be an impersonal and perfunctory routine, making little demand on his time and abilities, and becomes instead a joyous and gainful pursuit (p. 31).

[171] *Interim report of the Indian Statutory Commission (review of growth of education in British India by the Auxiliary Committee appointed by the Commission) September, 1929*; 1929–30, Cmd. 3407, X.

[172] Their dilemma has been vividly described by E. Shils, 'The intellectual between tradition and modernity: the Indian situation', *Comparative studies in society and history*, supplement I (The Hague, 1961).

[173] *Post-war educational development in India: report by the Central Advisory Board of Education, January 1944* (Delhi, 1944) 29 [Sargent report].

[174] A. L. Mudaliar, *Education in India* (London, 1960). Mudaliar wrote (p. 64 ff.): '. . . I do feel that the general trend at present is to assume that the Universities are more or less incompetent to perform their task and so to try to direct them in many insidious ways to such activities as seem desirable to particular persons, to Departments of the Government, or to particular Ministries. . . . This attitude of interference has been very prominent and felt by Universities since the attainment of independence in our country. . . . It is unfortunate that sometimes those in official circles, acting under different Ministries, should consider that the Universities should prune the syllabi and courses of studies just to fit the finished product to enter on the duties which a Government Department may require him to do. . . . Is it possible for a Secretary in an Agricultural Department to determine what the regulations should be for the candidates preparing for an academic degree in agriculture? Or for a Secretary in an Education Department to attend a meeting of an expert body on Engineering Education and to discuss the course of instruction that should be given to persons preparing for a degree in this Faculty?'

[175] *Cf.* [C. H. Tawney] 'The studies of the Calcutta University', *Calcutta Review*, LXXXII (1865) 297–317.

[176] 'Education in British India, 1870–71', comp. A. P. Howell (Calcutta, 1872), *Educational reports, 1859–71* (Selections from educational records of the government of India, I) Delhi, 1960, p. 512.

[177] Calcutta University Commission, 1917–19, *Report*, I (Calcutta, 1919) 22.

[178] *Ibid.*, IV, 24.

[179] There was, of course, strong Indian opposition to these provisions (p. 75). Speaking on the bill in the supreme council, G. K. Gokhale prophesied that if this

measure of control was to be imposed on the Indian universities, not much 'dignity or independence' would be left to the senate in such circumstances. 18 Dec. 1903, *Govt. of India Leg. Proc.*, XLII (1903) 309.

[180] S.R.Dongerkery has quoted illuminating evidence of the care taken to foster a sense of independence in the University of Bombay during its formative years. In a farewell address to the retiring chancellor, Sir Bartle Frere, in 1867, the vice-chancellor, Sir Alexander Grant, wrote:

A university like ours occupies necessarily a delicate position. Its members are all appointed by the Government; it derives all its current resources from the Imperial Treasury; and its acts are all subject to veto from the local administration. Under such circumstances . . . there cannot but be a tendency for a university to lose caste, as it were, and to come to be regarded as a mere office or department of the State.

What is to be apprehended from this tendency is not only a loss of dignity to the University itself, but a loss of the highest kind of efficiency in its working.

For, the mission of a university in a country like this is nothing else than to create an intellectual and vital soul among the people; and there can be no question whether this mission is likely best to be fulfilled by persons feeling themselves nominated merely to carry out the views of a government, or by the free and enthusiastic action of men feeling responsible to themselves for the good or bad success of the university. You have encouraged us to settle in our own assemblies all questions falling within our province.

The chancellor's reply was as follows:

I have endeavoured ever since I came to this Government to promote, as far as lay in my power, the efficiency and independence of this University, because I believe that it contains the germ of some of the most valuable gifts which England could bestow upon India . . . the political government of this country could hardly commit a greater mistake than by attempting to convert the University into a 'mere office or department of State'. I have ever felt most strongly the importance of these truths that you have so well expressed in your address . . .

S.R.Dongerkery, *A history of the University of Bombay, 1857–1957* (Bombay, 1957) 131.

[181] This was acknowledged by Dr Bhandarkar during the debate on the Indian Universities bill in 1904, when he recalled that neither government nor government officers had tried to influence 'in any way' the deliberations of the senate of the University of Bombay (*Govt. of India Leg. Proc.*, XLIII (1904) 295). It was also acknowledged by the Hon'ble Mr Dadabhoy in the debate on the Benares Hindu University bill in 1915: 'It is a point worthy of note that, under the existing Allahabad University Act and the Punjab University Act, Government have large powers of interference with the University authorities which have been rarely used' (*Ibid.*, LIV (1916) 91). But particularly after the turn of the century there were cases of government interference on political grounds, as for instance when the government of India vetoed the appointment of university lecturers at the University of Calcutta in 1913. (University of Calcutta, *Hundred years of the University of Calcutta* (Calcutta, 1957) 243–4.)

[182] CUC, *Report*, I, 69.

[183] *Govt. of India Leg. Proc.*, XLIII (1904) 277.

[184] This is evident in the recommendations of the Pakistan commission of 1960 (ref. 170) for the pattern of government for universities. The commission prescribes that the provincial governor (or, in federal areas, the head of state) should be

chancellor, and it gives him many of the powers Curzon wanted chancellors to have in his day. The chancellor is to appoint the vice-chancellor, without any obligatory consultation with the academic staff; make nominations to the syndicate, which is the university's governing body; nominate selection committees for chairs and set up committees for the evaluation of the work of professors and readers (ref. 170, pp. 48–9).

PART III: AFRICA

The main authorities given in the references to chapters 6 to 10 below have been assembled in a classified bibliography on p. 531. Full details of this material will be found there, with the exception of the annual reports from the colonies used in Chapter 6, which are too numerous to list individually. Reports for 1845 and succeeding years were presented to parliament. In the references given below, they are cited briefly by date, and after reports on individual colonies came to be published separately, by territory as well. For full bibliographical details, reference should be made to the official indexes to parliamentary papers.

Chapter 6 *Aspirations without a policy*

[1] F. Dubois, *Timbuctoo the mysterious* (London, 1897); see also Cheikh Anta Diop, *L'Afrique noire pré-coloniale* (Paris, 1960).

[2] Abdelhazi Tazi, *Onze siècles à l'université Qarawiyin: 850–1960* (Fez, 1960); Taha Husain, *The stream of days* (London, 1948); J. M. Ahmed, *The intellectual origins of Egyptian nationalism* (Oxford, 1960).

[3] C.O. to committee of privy council on education, 10 Aug. 1843, C.O. 168/29.

[4] J. Miller, 'Report on the liberated African schools and the other government schools of Sierra Leone', 1 Feb. 1841, *West Coast of Africa, sel. cttee rept.*, pp. 383–90; 1842 (551) XII.

[5] *Ibid.*, p. 386.

[6] *Ibid.*, pp. 552–6; 1842 (551) XI.

[7] *Ibid.*

[8] Minutes by Grey, 10 and 21 Nov. 1846, C.O. 318/170.

[9] To C.O., 6 Jan. 1847, *ibid.*

[10] Minute, 19 Jan. 1847, *ibid.*

[11] Minute, 21 Jan. 1847, *ibid.*

[12] 16 Jan. and 8 Feb. 1847, C.O. 854/3.

[13] W. J. Rottmann, 'The educational work of the Basel mission on the Gold Coast', 5 July 1902, *Board of education: special reports*, 13, pp. 297–307; 1905, Cd. 2378, XXVI; H. A. Dewald, 'Educational work of the Basel mission on the Gold Coast, 1828–1912', *Imperial Education Conference papers, III: Gold Coast Colony, Ashanti and the Northern Territories* (HMSO, 1914) 81–91. See also the evidence of the Basel missionary, E. Schrenk, before the select committee on Africa (western coast), 1865. *Report*, pp. 135–48; 1865 (412) V.

[14] For the policy of the CMS, see R. Maconachie, 'On the education of native

races', 28 July 1902, in *Board of education: special reports*, 14, pp. 209–49; 1905, Cd. 2379, XXVI; for that of the Wesleyan Society, the evidence of J. W. Berrie before the select committee of 1865, *Report*, pp. 281–2; 1865 (412) V.

[15] See the accounts by Freeman, enclosed in the annual reports from the Gold Coast, transmitted with the blue books for 1851 and 1853. *Reports, 1851, 53*, pp. 188–91, 184–5. See also the evidence of C. A. Gollmer, CMS, before the select committee of 1865. *Report*, p. 240; 1865 (412) V.

[16] See W. J. Rottmann (ref. 13).

[17] Evidence of C. A. Gollmer before the select committee of 1865. *Report*, p. 240; 1865 (412) V.

[18] C. P. Groves, *The planting of christianity in Africa*, II (London, 1954) 16–7.

[19] See especially the annual reports from governor N. A. Macdonald, and acting-governor Pine. *Reports, 1846–51*.

[20] Macdonald to Grey, 13 May 1847, *Reports, 1846*, p. 140.

[21] Macdonald to Pakington, 26 June 1852, *Reports, 1851*, p. 183.

[22] W. Fox, *A brief history of the wesleyan missions on the western coast of Africa* (London, 1851) 609.

[23] Yonge to Buckingham, No 80, 15 July 1867, C.O. 267/290.

[24] Memo. for draft to treasury, 6 Feb. 1868, C.O. 267/291.

[25] *Ibid.*; minute, 14 Sept. 1867, C.O. 267/90.

[26] Adderley had been an influential member of the select committee of 1865 which had recommended that Britain should ultimately withdraw from all her dependencies on the West Coast 'except, probably, Sierra Leone'; and that meantime her policy should be directed towards training the natives for self-government. (*Report*, p. iii; 1865 (412) V.) He was anxious to avoid any measures which would tend to conflict with the policy of withdrawal, even in the interests of native education: and it was only when it was established that the cost of the inspection could be borne wholly on the local estimates that he withdrew his opposition. Minutes, 18 and 23 Oct. 1867, C.O. 267/290; 9 Nov. 1867, 4 Jan. and 15 Feb. 1868, C.O. 267/291.

[27] Ref. 24; *cf.* also ref. 26.

[28] Minutes by Buckingham, 14 Sept. and 20 Oct. 1867, C.O. 267/290; memo by Kennedy, 3 Jan. 1868, C.O. 267/291.

[29] 'Report on the elementary schools of Sierra Leone by J. Stuart Laurie, formerly H.M.'s Inspector of Schools', 6 June 1868, C.O. 267/297.

[30] Minute, 12 June 1868, *ibid.*

[31] Kennedy wrote that Laurie's 'practical and well considered Report' left him little to suggest. '. . . if his recommendations be carried out it will go far to redeem the shortcomings of years and signalize Your Grace's tenure of office'. Kennedy to Buckingham, No 105, 12 Aug. 1868, C.O. 267/294.

[32] For details of the grants-in-aid system approved by the legislative council, see enclosure in Kennedy to Kimberley, No 163, 1 Oct. 1870, C.O. 267/307.

[33] The circumstances in which he entered upon his work in Sierra Leone were unfortunate; and they contributed not a little to the bitterness of the educational controversy he aroused in the colony some eighteen months later (see below p. 164). On leaving Liberia, Blyden had sailed to England and offered his services to the Church Missionary Society. He disclosed that owing to various misunderstandings he had been subjected to violent personal assaults in the African republic. Although warned by the bishop of Sierra Leone of Blyden's 'said delinquency in regard to

President Roye's wife', the society were so overjoyed at the prospect of recruiting an Arabic scholar in their crusade against the Crescent that on being assured by the Presbyterian Missionary Society in America that Blyden had in fact been unfairly treated by the Liberians, they decided to engage him as linguist and translator 'with a special view to the Arabic language & the Mahometan controversy'. In a delighted letter to Blyden of 1 August 1871, they dwelt on the 'remarkable chain of concurring providences' that had enabled them to respond to his request. They directed that he should make a start 'at once' in instructing the students at Fourah Bay in Arabic, so as to 'enlarge their minds to the contemplation of the interior of their fatherland and stamp a Missionary character on Fourah Bay'. They also expressed the hope that in other ways, too, he would be able to give help in the 'higher branches' of education in Sierra Leone. But their satisfaction was short lived. Only three days later, mail from the West Coast brought Liberian papers which contained virulent attacks on Blyden's moral character; and before the end of the month further unpalatable enlightenment came from the bishop. 'We are shocked to hear of Mr Blyden's appointment', he wrote in astonishment and consternation. 'I assume of course that you have done it in ignorance of the charge of immorality that is laid agst him . . . I did not for a moment suppose the Soc^y would have come to a favourable consider^n of his request so rapidly, therefore only mentioned in my last eno' to put you on inquiry if you were really entertaining his request. Of course now I must tell you that it is commonly reported that he was conducted out of Monrovia to the boat with a rope round his neck under a charge of adultery with the wife of President Roye. His enemies in Liberia thus executed lynch law upon him & no doubt have made his case no better by telling: but Mr Crummell, who wished to befriend him, had no doubt whatever of his moral adultery: & said that Roye was seeking a divorce. I dare say the man has talent: I think he has . . . but, he did not at all strike me as a spiritually-minded man on the only occasion when I have seen him: & alas, alas, it is spiritually minded men we want . . . Well, now', he concluded, 'what are we to do . . . I feel sure you will agree with me that bad morals is far too high a price to pay for good Arabic. . . .' The society were at first reluctant to abandon the arrangement. Having received counter evidence in Blyden's favour, they allowed him to proceed to Freetown and clung to the hope that he would be able to establish his innocence. By mid-November, however, they felt obliged to terminate their agreement with him; and since he had concealed the cause of the Liberian attacks on him, and the fact, too, that at the time of his appointment he was under suspension by the presbytery of his church, they had the less compunction in doing so. To save his exceptional gifts for Africa, they wrote to the governor of Sierra Leone to suggest that he might be employed by the government in a civil capacity; and for the next thirty-five years, Blyden served sporadically, in a variety of temporary official posts, in one or other of the British settlements in West Africa. (Henry Cheetham, bishop of Sierra Leone, to Henry Venn, secretary, CMS, 24 June 1871, C.A1/0.25e; Venn to Cheetham, 24 July 1871, C.A1/L.8; CMS to Blyden, 1 Aug. 1871, ibid.; Venn to Sunter, 5 Aug. 1871, ibid.; Cheetham to Venn, 10 Aug. 1871, C.A1/0.25e; Venn to Sunter, 5 Aug. 1871, C.A1/L.8; Venn to the Rev. Pinney, and to Sir A. E. Kennedy, 16 Nov. 1871, ibid.).

[34] Blyden to Hennessy, 11 and 14 Dec. 1872. E. W. Blyden, *The West African University* (Freetown, 1872).

[35] Hennessy to Blyden, 10 Dec. 1872, *ibid.*

[36] Minute by Kimberley, 27 Feb. 1873, on Hennessy to Kimberley, 31 Dec. 1872, C.O. 267/317.

[37] Blyden to Bravo, 13 May 1873, enclosed in Harley to Kimberley, No 42, 9 June 1873, C.O. 267/321.

[38] Minute by Wodehouse, 18 July 1873, initialled by Kimberley, 21 July 1873, on Harley to Kimberley, No 42, 9 June 1873, *ibid.*

[39] Kimberley to Harley, No 478, 23 July 1873, *ibid.*

[40] W. B. Eddy, director of public instruction, to Carnarvon, 11 Nov. 1876, C.O. 267/330; Kortright to Carnarvon, conf., 31 Mar. 1877, C.O. 267/331.

[41] Minute by Anderson on Havelock to Kimberley, No 157, 27 Aug. 1881, C.O. 267/345; Ordinance No 3 of 1882 (An ordinance for the promotion and assistance of education in the settlement of Sierra Leone) enclosed in Havelock to Kimberley, No 87, 26 April 1882, C.O. 267/348.

[42] The offer of appointment was made by the C.O. in August 1882, and Sunter entered formally upon his duties in the following December, having already conducted one inspection of the schools in Sierra Leone, acting in a temporary capacity, between June and September. Kimberley to Havelock, No 423, 23 Aug. 1882; Havelock to Kimberley, No 172, 12 Sept. 1882, and No 234, 30 Dec. 1882, C.O. 267/349.

[43] See p. 162 below.

[44] Havelock took the view that 'a gentleman possessing higher attainments' might be found, but that Sunter was 'fully competent' for the post and his record of ten years on the Coast without serious loss of health constituted a special qualification. Anderson, in the C.O., considered that since 'very superior intellectual attainments' were not required, Sunter would be a better choice than an abler man who was not acclimatised. Kimberley was disposed to agree: 'His health is a great point in his favour.' Havelock to Kimberley, No 153, 26 Aug. 1881, with minutes by Anderson, 1 Oct. and Kimberley, 2 Nov. 1881, C.O. 267/345.

[45] *General report on elementary schools in the colony of Sierra Leone, 1885,* enclosed in Sunter to Rowe, 16 May 1885, C.O. Library, vol. 7860.

[46] *General report, Sierra Leone, 1884, ibid.*

[47] *General report, Gold Coast and Lagos, 1884,* enclosed in Brandford Griffith to Granville, No 327, 25 Aug. 1886, C.O. 96/175.

[48] *General report, Central district Gold Coast, 1883,* enclosed in Rowe to Derby, No 237, 17 July 1883, C.O. 96/151.

[49] 'It is the Bible and the plough that must regenerate Africa': memo of April 1839, quoted in C. P. Groves, *The planting of christianity in Africa,* II (London, 1954) 6. Buxton had noted a similar motto used by James Read when helping to found a mission in South Africa some twenty years earlier. *Ibid.,* I (1948) 244 n. 3.

[50] *General report, Gold Coast and Lagos, 1884,* C.O. 96/175.

[51] *General report, Gambia, 1885,* C.O. Library, vol. 8234.

[52] *General report, Sierra Leone, 1886,* C.O. Library, vol. 7860.

[53] *General report, Gold Coast, 1886,* C.O. Library, vol. 8997.

[54] *General report, Sierra Leone, 1892,* C.O. Library, vol. 7860.

[55] *General reports, Gold Coast, 1886, 1887,* C.O. Library, vol. 8997.

[56] *General report, Gold Coast, 1890, ibid.*

[57] He was tactless and indiscreet, and consistently failed to measure up to the

difficulty of inspecting the widely dispersed schools of the Gold Coast. His manner set the colony against him and the inaccuracies of his report for 1888 enabled the governor to appeal successfully for the withdrawal of his services. Sunter's reaction to the charge of inaccuracy was a 'wild' communication to the colonial office, where it attracted the comment: 'Is this man a lunatic? It looks like it.' A few months earlier the colonial office had given a more considered opinion of Sunter's work. When, in September 1889, he had sought their good offices to secure a transfer to the English inspectorate, they decided to forward his letter to the privy council without comment. It was felt that he did not make the grade of an English inspector, but that his removal from the West Coast was desirable in the public interest. Sunter was not successful in getting the transfer; but on succumbing to a sudden fever in Lagos in December 1892, he received a more charitable recognition of his capacity, and of his long years of service on the Coast, from his sub-inspector, Henry Carr. 'By his death', Carr wrote, in terms of evident affection, 'West African education has lost a very able servant, and the negro a true friend.' (Brandford Griffith to Knutsford, 10 Aug. 1889, with minute by Webb, 28 Aug. 1889, C.O. 96/207; Knutsford to Brandford Griffith, conf., 18 June 1890, C.O. 96/210; Sunter to C.O., 3 Dec. 1889, with minutes by Hemming, 2 Jan., and Webb, 6 Jan. 1890, C.O. 96/207: Sunter to Knutsford, 16 Sept. 1889, with minutes by Hemming, 17 Sept., and Webb, 18 Sept. 1889, *ibid.*: *Reports, Lagos, 1892*, p. 19).

[58] Derby to Rowe, No 154, 27 April 1883, C.O. 96/149; Anderson to Sunter, 1 Oct. 1883, C.O. 96/151.

[59] Minute by Anderson, 22 Jan. 1886, on Rowe to Stanley, No 120, 28 Aug. 1885, C.O. 87/125; Granville to Rowe, No 18, 9 April 1886, *ibid.*

[60] Rules for assisted schools under the Education Ordinance for 1887 in the Gold Coast Colony, 4 Nov. 1887, enclosed in Brandford Griffith to Holland, No 458, 13 Dec. 1887, C.O. 96/185; Colony of Lagos: Rules under Education Ordinance, No 3 of 1887, 31 Dec. 1887, enclosed in Moloney to Holland, No 12, 9 Jan. 1888, C.O. 147/63.

[61] Rev. James Johnson, native pastor of Sierra Leone, to Hennessy, 24 Dec. 1872. E. W. Blyden, *The Lagos Training College and Industrial Institute* (Lagos, 1896).

[62] Blyden to Hennessy, 14 Dec. 1872. E. W. Blyden, *The West African University* (Freetown, 1872).

[63] *Reports, Sierra Leone, 1895*, 96.

[64] *Reports, Gold Coast, 1898, 1903.*

[65] *Reports, Lagos, 1899.*

[66] Phelps-Stokes Fund, *Education in Africa: a study of West, South and Equatorial Africa* (New York, 1922) 142.

[67] *Reports, Gold Coast, 1907.*

[68] *Reports, Gold Coast, 1909.*

[69] *Reports, Southern Nigeria, 1909, 10*; see also *Imperial Education Conference papers, III: Southern Nigeria* (HMSO, 1913) 18.

[70] *Reports, Sierra Leone, 1908–11.*

[71] Sect. 16 (6), Education Ordinance 1911.

[72] Schedule B, The amended and consolidated Education Rules, 1891.

[73] See above p. 154.

[74] Lyttelton to Probyn, No 60, 17 Mar. 1905, C.O. 267/473.

[75] *Reports, Sierra Leone, 1905–8*; see also Bo school prospectus, 29 Sept. 1905,

published in C. Fyfe, *Sierra Leone inheritance* (London, 1964) 303–7; and D. L. Sumner, *Education in Sierra Leone* (Freetown, 1963) 140–1. For details of the scheme submitted for the approval of the C.O., see Probyn to Lyttelton, No 320, 30 Dec. 1904, C.O. 267/473, and No 364, 1 Aug. 1905, C.O. 267/479; and for an account of the early months of the school, the report drawn up for the government of Southern Nigeria in June 1906, and enclosed in Probyn to Elgin, No 219, 11 July 1906, C.O. 267/485.

[76] Far from inspiring, or helping to plan the new project, Blyden took on the role of critic. His attitude brought him into conflict with the governor, and so contributed to bring to an end his long but fitful connection with the British government. Blyden was on leave in Europe when the details of the scheme were worked out. On his return to Sierra Leone, early in 1906, he was at first disposed to support the new venture. Although uneasy at the appointment of a christian missionary as headmaster, he welcomed the project as a healthy departure from the type of education provided hitherto in the coastal settlements, and well designed to foster the invigorating native atmosphere – 'wholesome, racy of the soil' – he had so long contended for. On learning of the prospectus that the headmaster, James Proudfoot, had put out in the previous September, his attitude changed. He lent a ready ear to the disquiet this had aroused amongst the muhammadans, and he helped them to frame a protest to the governor. Whilst giving an assurance that there would be no interference with the religious beliefs of the pupils, Proudfoot had announced that 'sound ethical teaching' would be provided. With a curious disregard for native susceptibilities, he had also announced that in order to increase the pupils' respect for women, attention would be called to 'the principal incidents in the lives of such women as Florence Nightingale, Elizabeth Fry, and the late Queen Victoria' by means of lantern lectures. Assisted by Blyden, the muhammadans entered a strong plea against both these proposals, particularly the latter. They reminded the governor that the introduction of pictures would be an affront to their beliefs; and they respectfully added that they had notable women of their own to serve as exemplars. 'According to a traditional saying of Muhammed', they wrote, 'Khadijah, Fatimah, the Virgin Mary and Asiyah – an African woman – the wife of Pharaoh were the four perfect women. These and others in Soudanic history, not generally known, are the models which the Muslim has always before him. The names mentioned by Mr Proudfoot, noble and excellent as they are, will not appeal to the Muslim but rather divert him from imitable models to unattainable ideals.' In addition to assisting the muhammadans in their protest, Blyden pressed his objection to the appointment of Proudfoot and his 'vicious and illiterate' programme in representations to the governor, and a series of private letters to Reginald Antrobus at the colonial office. With characteristic exaggeration, he excused these personal appeals to London by reference to the 'present crisis' in West African education. Whilst it was acknowledged in the colonial office that Proudfoot was probably not the most suitable choice, it was felt that the decision must stand. Blyden's letters went unanswered. The governor, meanwhile, succeeded in placating the muhammadans by appointing five of their number to act as a board of advice in connection with the school. He had the further satisfaction of allowing Blyden's own appointment to lapse when it expired on 1 July 1906. (Blyden to Antrobus, private, 2 Feb. 1906, enclosing memo to governor Probyn, 1 Feb. 1906, C.O. 267/491; Bo school prospectus, published in C. Fyfe, *Sierra Leone inheritance* (London, 1964) 304–7; Blyden to Antrobus,

private, 19 Feb. 1906, enclosing muhammadan petition to Probyn, 15 Feb. 1906 C.O. 267/491; Blyden to Antrobus, private, 3 Mar. 1906, enclosing minute from Probyn, 1 Mar. 1906, *ibid*; minutes on Blyden to Antrobus, private, 2 Feb. 1906, *ibid*.; Probyn to Elgin, No 78, 1 April 1906, C.O. 267/484).

⁷⁷ See their 'Suggestions towards a scheme for a projected school at Bo for the sons of chiefs in the Sierra Leone Protectorate', enclosed in Probyn to Lyttelton, No 320, 30 Dec. 1904, C.O. 267/473.

⁷⁸ Sonia F. Graham, *A history of education in relation to the development of the protectorate of Northern Nigeria, 1900–19, with special reference to the work of Hanns Vischer* (Unpubd Ph.D. thesis, University of London, 1955). Vischer's system of 'adapted' education is vividly summarised in the following extract from a letter written by his wife from Kano in 1912:

. . . Pour que l'arbre puisse croître, il fallait que ses racines se trouvent dans le sol africain même. C'est là la condition primordiale d'un succès utile et durable. On créa donc un système d'éducation nationale. Le noir sait que, loin de vouloir l'européaniser, on tient, au contraire, à lui laisser son caractère africain. Il est vrai que l'administrateur européen a besoin de clercs et d'employés pour l'administration, mais ce but est considéré comme secondaire dans l'organisation des écoles de Nigérie. Avant tout, on recherche le bien du noir, le developpement de ses industries, le progrès de son littérature et de ses idées propres. Toutes les branches sont enseignées en haussa. Certains élèves, doués de dispositions particulières pour recevoir une éducation plus rapprochée de la nôtre, sont admis à apprendre la langue anglaise et à suivre l'instruction secondaire. . . .

Les années d'écoles terminées, l'élève doit pouvoir rentrer dans son milieu et reprendre la vie parmi les siens, sans peine, et sans aucun sentiment d'y être dépaysé.

La surveillance et la direction du blanc sont encore indispensables à l'heure qu'il est. C'est à lui qu'incombe le travail de discernement et d'adaptation . . . Le jour viendra où les écoles n'auront plus besoin d'être dirigées par le Blanc. Avec la bénédiction d'Allah, la génération future verra l'oeuvre continuée par le corps enseignant purement indigène, qu'aura formé une universitée nigérienne. [Quoted, *ibid.*, p. 232.]

⁷⁹ *Reports, Sierra Leone, 1910.*

⁸⁰ *Reports, Southern Nigeria, 1909.*

⁸¹ W. H. Barker, 'The early days of the Accra Training Institution', *The Teachers' Journal*, I (1929) 136–40.

⁸² 'Education in relation to the christianisation of national life': report of Commission III. *World Missionary Conference, 1910*, III (Edinburgh, 1910).

⁸³ *Ibid.*, p. 2.

⁸⁴ *Ibid.*

⁸⁵ *Ibid.*, p. 6.

⁸⁶ *Ibid.*, pp. 190–2; 201. The correspondent in Sierra Leone was W. T. Balmer, who had recently helped to plan the new system of education at Bo. In his candid assessment of the education on the West Coast, he fastened on the same weakness that critics had long deplored in the education Britain had planted in India. 'The greatest disappointment', he wrote, 'is in the failure of the so-called educated native community in West Africa to evolve any original thinker or to show any signs of pre-eminent constructive ability. Everything seems to go by rote; knowledge is regarded as so much verbal matter; memory is the chief faculty relied on, and that in an artificial way.' *Ibid.*, p. 192.

⁸⁷ *Ibid.*, pp. 167–9.

[88] *Ibid.*, p. 169. Here the commission were writing with special reference to the evolution of policy in South Africa; but an exactly comparable movement was taking place in the tropical dependencies of the West.

[89] *Ibid.*, pp. 373–4.

[90] *Ibid.*, p. 264.

[91] *Reports, Gold Coast, 1902; Reports, Southern Nigeria, 1902.*

[92] Board of education, *Special reports*, 13, pp. 42, 51; 1905, Cd. 2378, XXVI.

[93] *Reports, Sierra Leone, 1902.*

[94] Education Ordinance 1911.

[95] The Church of England Grammar School at Cape Coast (later Adisadel). *Imperial Education Conference papers, III: Gold Coast Colony, Ashanti and the Northern Territories* (HMSO, 1914) 25.

[96] *Reports, Southern Nigeria, 1909.*

[97] *Reports, Lagos, 1887.*

[98] *Reports, Southern Nigeria, 1910.*

[99] *Reports, Sierra Leone, 1915.*

[100] Phelps-Stokes Fund, *Education in Africa: a study of West, South and Equatorial Africa* (New York, 1922).

[101] *Ibid.*, p. 16.

[102] *Ibid.*, p. 26.

[103] *Ibid.*, p. 119.

[104] *Ibid.*, p. 177.

[105] A. W. Wilkie, one of the British members of the commission, was explicit on the point. In an article explaining how the commission had come to preach the doctrine of 'the adaptation of education to the needs of the community', he stressed that 'more than a formal recognition' of the doctrine was called for. 'Adaptation is universally approved', he wrote, 'far from universally practised'. Quoted, *ibid.*, p. xix.

[106] *Ibid.*, pp. 121, 141.

[107] Second charge of the Rt Rev. Henry Cheetham, bishop of Sierra Leone, 21 Mar. 1877, enclosed in Cheetham to Carnarvon, 19 June 1877, C.O. 267/333.

[108] [J. Denton] 'History of Fourah Bay College', *Sierra Leone Messenger*, Nos 91, 92 (1915) 397–409, 429–41. See also T. J. Thompson, *The jubilee and centenary volume of Fourah Bay College* (Freetown, 1930).

[109] Sunter to Venn, 30 Mar. and 16 June 1871, C.A1/0.202.

[110] Cheetham to Berkeley, 17 April 1874, C.O. 879/8.

[111] Ref. 107.

[112] Cheetham to Venn, 6 May 1871, C.A1/0.25e.

[113] Sunter to Venn, 13 July 1871, C.A1/O.202.

[114] Venn to Cheetham, 5 April 1871, C.A1/L.8.

[115] Venn to Cheetham, 5 June 1871, *ibid.*

[116] Committee minutes, 14 Oct. 1872, vol. 40, f. 235.

[117] 9 Dec. 1872, *ibid.*, f. 324; minutes of finance committee, Sierra Leone, 24 Jan. 1873, C.A1/O.2.

[118] Sunter to Wright, 8 Mar. 1873, enclosing copy of Cheetham to Sunter, 6 Mar. 1873, C.A1/O.202.

[119] Minutes of finance committee, 24 Jan. 1873, C.A1/O.2.

[120] E. W. Blyden, *The West African University* (Freetown, 1872).

[121] Hennessy to Kimberley, No 159, 28 Dec. 1872, C.O. 267/317.

[122] Minute by Holland, 29 Jan. 1873, *ibid.*

[123] Minute, 1 Feb. 1873, *ibid.*

[124] Cheetham to Wright, 13 Mar. 1873, C.A1/O.25e.

[125] Sunter to E. Hutchinson, 27 Mar. 1873, C.A1/O.202.

[126] 'Education on the West Coast' [1873], enclosed in Sunter to Hutchinson, 20/21 June 1873, C.A1/O.202. See also Sunter to Hutchinson, 7 June, and to Wright, 24 June 1873, *ibid.*

[127] Wright to Cheetham, 10 Mar. 1873, C.A1/L.8.

[128] Committee minutes, 10 Nov. 1873, vol. 40, f. 703; enclosure in Hutchinson to Nicholson, 1 Jan. 1874, C.A1/L.9.

[129] C.C. Fenn to Sunter, 13 Nov. 1873, C.A1/I.1.

[130] Minutes of finance committee, recd June 1874, C.A1/O.2.

[131] Minute by Hales, 17 June 1873, on Harley to Kimberley, No 42, 9 June 1873, C.O. 267/321.

[132] ... 'I am most thankful to know that the matter of superior educational establishments for the young men of the Colony and other parts of the west African coast, is under Your Lordship's consideration; that Your Lordship contemplates teaching eventually in the Colony some of the learned professions and is anxious that the interior countries share with the British Settlements the privilege of a liberal education . . .' Johnson to Kimberley, 21 Jan. 1874, C.O. 879/8.

[133] Kimberley to Berkeley, No 590, 16 Dec. 1873, C.O. 267/324.

[134] Berkeley to Carnarvon, conf. 8 May 1874, C.O. 879/8.

[135] Minute by Lowther, 6 June 1873, C.O. 267/326.

[136] Carnarvon to Berkeley, conf., 12 June 1874, C.O. 879/8.

[137] Sunter to Fenn, 23 Dec. 1873, C.A1/O.202.

[138] Wright to Sunter, 26 Feb. 1875, G.AC2/1/558.

[139] Wright to Sunter, 18 June 1875, G.AC2/1/824.

[140] Committee minutes, 20 July 1875, vol. 40, f. 99.

[141] Wright to the dean of Durham, W.C. Lake, 29 Dec. 1875, G.AC2/2/319.

[142] Lake to Wright, 22 Feb. 1876, *ibid.*; Wright to Sunter, 25 Feb. 1876, C.A1/L.9; Sunter to Wright, 13 Mar. 1876, C.A1/O.202.

[143] Sunter to Wright, 4 April 1876, C.A1/O.202.

[144] Wright to Sunter, 31 Mar. 1876, C.A1/L.9.

[145] *Church Missionary Intelligencer and Record*, I (1876) 439.

[146] *Durham University Calendar, 1877* (1877) app., xlvi–xlvii.

[147] *Ibid.*, pp. 13–6; 21–3.

[148] Annual letter, part II, 28 Nov. 1872, C.A1/O.202.

[149] CMS annual report for 1876, pp. 13–4 in *Proceedings, 1876, 77,* XXXIV [1878].

[150] Wright to Cheetham, 12 Feb. 1874, C.A1/L.9.

[151] For these, and the following details of the early development of the 'university' side of the college, see *Durham University Calendar* (1877–); J. Denton, 'Fourah Bay College, Sierra Leone', *Durham University Journal,* XVII, iv (May 18, 1906) 40–2, 53–4; T.J. Thompson, *The jubilee and centenary volume of Fourah Bay College* (Freetown, 1930); and C.E. Whiting, *The University of Durham, 1832–1932* (London, 1932) 300–6.

[152] Wright to Sunter, 18 Oct. 1878, C.A1/L.9.

[153] Annual letter, part II, 9 Dec. 1873, C.A1/O.202.

[154] F.B.Heiser, 'Fourah Bay College', *Church Missionary Review*, LXXVII (1926) 60–72.

[155] Phelps-Stokes Fund, *Education in Africa: a study of West, South and Equatorial Africa* (New York, 1922) 75–7, 119.

[156] *Church Missionary Record*, N.S. I (1856) 25; C.Fyfe, *A history of Sierra Leone* (London, 1962) 294–5.

[157] Horton to W.O., 13 July 1861. J.A.B.Horton, *West African countries and peoples* (London, 1868) 46. See also enclosures in Horton to CMS, 13 Nov. 1863, C.A1/O.117.

[158] W.O. to Horton, 19 June 1862, enclosed in Horton to CMS, 13 Nov. 1863, *ibid.*

[159] Horton to W.O., 13 Nov. 1863, enclosed in letter of the same date to CMS., *ibid.*; Pine to Horton, 7 Dec. 1863, enclosed in Horton to CMS, 10 Dec. 1863, *ibid.*

[160] Horton to Grant, [1873]. T.J.Thompson, *The jubilee and centenary volume of Fourah Bay College* (Freetown, 1930) 54.

[161] J.A.B.Horton, *Political economy of British Western Africa* (London, 1865); *West African countries and peoples* (London, 1868).

[162] *Ibid.*, pp. 201–5.

[163] See above p. 163.

[164] Horton to Grant, [1873]. T.J.Thompson, *The jubilee and centenary volume of Fourah Bay College* (Freetown, 1930) 54–6.

[165] *Ibid.*, pp. 149–51.

[166] See above, p. 170.

[167] See above, p. 163.

[168] E.W.Blyden, *The West African University* (Freetown, 1872).

[169] E.W.Blyden, *The aims and methods of a liberal education* (Cambridge, Mass., 1882).

[170] E.W.Blyden, *The Lagos Training College and Industrial Institute* (Lagos, 1896).

[171] Blyden to Carter, 14 and 21 May, 3 June 1896, *ibid.*

[172] Enclosure in Blyden to Carter, 15 June 1896, C.O. 147/110.

[173] Blyden to Carter, 21 May 1896. E.W.Blyden, *The Lagos Training College and Industrial Institute* (Lagos, 1896).

[174] In support of his emphasis on classical studies, Blyden quoted from a recent article in the *Nineteenth Century* the famous passage in which Henry Maine had upheld the western orientation of the Indian university curriculum a generation earlier (see above, p. 392).

[175] *Ibid.*

[176] *Ibid.*

[177] Carter to C.O., 3 Aug. 1896; C.O. to Carter, 28 Sept. 1896, C.O. 147/110.

[178] Minute by Bramston, 24 Sept. 1896, *ibid.*

[179] Minute by Read, 13 Aug. 1896, *ibid.*

[180] Blyden to Carter, 10 Nov. 1896, *ibid.*

[181] Blyden to Denton, copy, 10 April 1899, enclosed in Denton to Chamberlain, No 128, 14 April 1899, C.O. 147/142.

[182] Blyden to Kimberley, 22 Oct. 1873, C.O. 267/324.

[183] Denton to Chamberlain, No 128, 14 April 1899, C.O. 147/142.

[184] Minute by Mercer, 12 May 1899, *ibid.*

[185] Nathan to Chamberlain, No 173, 23 May 1899, C.O. 267/446.

[186] Chamberlain to Macgregor, No 222, 14 July 1899, *ibid.*

[187] Minute by Antrobus on Nathan to Chamberlain, No 82, conf., 2 Oct. 1899, C.O. 267/448. Blyden did not give up hopes of the Central Institution, and as director of mohammedan education in Sierra Leone between 1901 and 1906 (above p. 176) made a number of informal attempts to enlist official support for it. In 1903 he tried to get Sir Frederick Lugard to take it up with the imperial government; and he made frequent references to it in private letters to Reginald Antrobus at the colonial office. When in 1903 he appealed for an increase of salary to enable him to settle permanently in Sierra Leone, he wrote that it was then his 'strongest desire' to see a Central Institution for the muslims of British West Africa in Freetown on similar lines to the Central College established by the French in Senegal. And when in 1906, as a result of his differences with the governor of Sierra Leone over the school at Bo (above, p. 157), he offered to transfer his services on a part-time basis to the Gambia, he suggested that Bathurst might perhaps provide a healthier site for the Central Institution than Freetown. But his overtures were quietly ignored. (Blyden to Antrobus, private, 2 Feb. 1906, C.O. 267/491; 4 July 1903, C.O. 267/471; 10 Mar. 1906, C.O. 267/491).

[188] J.E. Casely Hayford, *Ethiopia unbound* (London, 1911) 15–7, 194–7.

[189] National Congress of British West Africa, *Resolutions of the Conference of Africans of British West Africa, held at Accra, Gold Coast, from 11ᵗʰ to 29ᵗʰ March, 1920; Memorandum of the case of the National Congress of British West Africa for a memorial based upon the resolutions to be presented to his majesty the king emperor in council through the right honourable the secretary of state for the colonies* [1920]. The text of the resolutions on education is reproduced on p. 474.

[190] *Petition of the National Congress of British West Africa*, 19 Oct. 1920. G.E. Metcalfe, *Great Britain and Ghana: documents of Ghana history, 1807–1957* (London, 1964) 583–5.

[191] *Report of the special committee appointed by his excellency Sir Hugh Clifford to report upon and to make such recommendations as seem desirable in the educational system of the Gold Coast*, Sessional paper XVII of 1918–19.

[192] National Congress of British West Africa, *Memorandum of the case of the National Congress of British West Africa* [1920] exhibit D, p. 5.

[193] J.E. Casely Hayford, *West African leadership: public speeches*, ed. M.J. Sampson (Ilfracombe, 1949) 73.

[194] *Ibid.*, pp. 81–2.

[195] *Ibid.*, p. 86.

[196] See above, p. 169.

[197] For an interesting discussion of the colonial office attitude towards the educated Africans of the West Coast in the latter half of the nineteenth century, see D. Kimble, *A political history of Ghana, 1850–1928* (Oxford, 1963) 87–93.

[198] Hennessy to Kimberley, No 159, 28 Dec. 1872, C.O. 267/317.

[199] See above, p. 165.

[200] See above, pp. 173–6.

[201] Brandford Griffith to Ripon, conf., 24 Jan. 1893, C.O. 96/230.

[202] Minute by Read, 6 Mar. 1893, *ibid.*

[203] Minute by Hemming, 6 Mar. 1893, *ibid.*

[204] Minute by Bramston, *ibid.*

[205] Minute by Meade, 12 Mar. 1893, *ibid.*

[206] Ripon to Brandford Griffith, conf., 27 Mar. 1893, *ibid.*

[207] Brandford Griffith to Ripon, conf., 16 and 22 June 1894, C.O. 96/246.

[208] Hodgson to Chamberlain, conf., 18 June 1898, C.O. 96/317.

[209] *Ibid.*

[210] Chamberlain to Hodgson, conf., 3 Aug. 1898, *ibid.*

[211] Probyn to Lyttelton, No 45, 31 Jan. 1905, enclosing a letter of the same date to the secretary of the CMS, C.O. 267/475. In his letter to the CMS, Probyn explained his reason for judging the time opportune for such a proposal: '. . . In the Gold Coast, and I believe also in Lagos', he wrote, 'projects are, I understand, under discussion for the establishment of highly equipped Colleges. Should even one of these projects be carried into effect, the result will be that the number of students who would seek admission into the proposed Fourah Bay University would be proportionately diminished. The present, therefore, seems . . . to be the time for deciding whether the scope of the Fourah Bay College should be enlarged as would necessarily be the case if the proposed University was incorporated. If it is now decided that the College is to be incorporated as a University, the effect will be to arrest further action with respect to the establishment in other Colonies on the Coast of high grade schools or Colleges which, as above stated, would necessarily compete to a great extent with the proposed University.'

[212] See above, p. 157.

[213] Minute by Darnley, 7 Mar. 1905, C.O. 267/475.

[214] Lyttelton to Probyn, No 55, 14 Mar. 1905, *ibid.*

[215] Probyn to Lyttelton, No 182, 19 April 1905, C.O. 267/477.

[216] Lyttelton to Probyn, No 123, 16 May 1905, *ibid.*

[217] Probyn to Lyttelton, No 515, 29 Nov. 1907, C.O. 267/497.

[218] Egerton to Elgin, No 160, 8 April 1907, C.O. 520/44.

[219] Minute by Butler, 17 May 1907, *ibid.*

[220] Egerton to Elgin, No 105, 10 Feb. 1908, C.O. 520/58; No 609, 14 Sept. 1908, C.O. 520/65.

[221] Memorandum of 29 Jan. 1908, enclosed in Egerton to Elgin, No 105, 10 Feb. 1908, C.O. 520/58.

[222] *Ibid.*; also report of 28 Aug. 1908, enclosed in Egerton to Elgin, No 609, 14 Sept. 1908, C.O. 520/65.

[223] Minute by Crewe, 1 Nov. 1908, C.O. 520/65.

[224] Crewe to Egerton, No 912, 6 Nov. 1908, *ibid.*

[225] 'Memorandum on the proposed establishment of a University College at Lagos'; enclosure in board of education to C.O., 7 Nov. 1907, C.O.520/54.

[226] Minute by Egerton, 2 Jan. 1908, enclosed in Egerton to Elgin, No 105, 10 Feb. 1908, C.O. 520/58.

[227] Minute by J. A. Douglas, 1 Feb. 1908, *ibid.*

[228] Crewe to Thorburn, No 472, 9 June 1909, C.O. 520/77. The decision over the designation was soon abandoned. Towards the end of 1910, the principal, H. J. Hyde Johnson, recommended that the name of the school should be altered to 'King's College', as originally proposed, in order to distinguish it from the other secondary

schools of the colony and encourage it in a higher standard of attainment. Egerton agreed; and the colonial office did not hold out against a change which it accepted as being dictated by actual experience of working the new institution. Egerton to Harcourt, No 803, 13 Dec. 1910, with enclosure of 3 Dec. 1910 from H. J. Hyde Johnson; Harcourt to Egerton, No 19, 10 Jan. 1911, C.O. 520/96.

[229] 'Memorandum on the proposed establishment of a University College at Lagos'; enclosure in board of education to C.O., 7 Nov. 1907, C.O. 520/54.

[230] Rodger to Elgin, No 129, 11 April 1907, C.O. 96/456.

[231] Elgin to Rodger, No 187, 15 May 1907, *ibid.*

[232] W. H. Barker, 'The early days of the Accra Training Institution', *The Teachers' Journal*, I (1929) 136–40.

[233] *Report of the special committee appointed by His Excellency Sir Hugh Clifford to report upon and to make such recommendations as seem desirable in the educational system of the Gold Coast*, Sessional paper XVII of 1918–19.

[234] F. G. Guggisberg, *The keystone* (London, 1924) 31.

Chapter 7 *Evolution of a policy*

[1] The origin of this committee was as follows. On 6 June 1923, a conference was held at the colonial office to consider a memorandum submitted to the secretary of state on behalf of the education committee of the Conference of Missionary Societies in Great Britain and Ireland. The memorandum stressed the need for an educational advisory committee at the colonial office. Among those attending the conference were Ormsby Gore, who presided, the governors of Nigeria, the Gold Coast, Sierra Leone, Kenya, Nyasaland, a representative from Tanganyika, and Dr Jesse Jones, author of the Phelps-Stokes report. The conference recommended that the committee should be set up. It was given the following terms of reference: 'To advise the Secretary of State on any matters of native education in the British Colonies and Protectorates in Tropical Africa, which he may from time to time refer to it, and to assist him in advancing the progress of education in those Colonies and Protectorates'.

[2] *Education policy in British tropical Africa;* 1924–25, Cmd. 2374, XXI.

[3] See above p. 158.

[4] See above, p. 161.

[5] Unfortunately it often remained no more than a starting point. It was an illuminating commentary on the way in which practice continued to lag behind policy, that when the Jeffery mission came to review the education in British West Africa a generation later, it should still have found the primary schools attempting to model their organisation and curriculum on the English elementary school of forty years before. Nuffield foundation and colonial office, *African education: a study of educational policy and practice in British tropical Africa* (Oxford, 1953) 18. If 'universally approved' by British and Americans, the sentiments of the 1925 white paper were certainly not approved by some Africans, to whom the ideas of adaptation, of local standards, of indigenous curricula, were anathema. They wanted nothing less than the standards of education and content current in Britain. Emphasis on agricultural training would, in their view, merely perpetuate their status as hewers of wood and drawers of water; and they were particularly antagonistic to the paternalistic views in the report about character-training and moral education.

Cf. J. Coleman, *Nigeria, background to nationalism* (Berkeley, Cal., 1958) 119–20, 445.

[6] See above p. 125.

[7] For details of the origin of Achimota, see C. Kingsley Williams, *Achimota, the early years, 1924–1948* (Accra, 1962), and W. E. F. Ward, *Fraser of Trinity and Achimota* (Accra, 1965). See also two official reports of committees appointed to inspect the college: *Report of the committee appointed in 1932 by the governor of the Gold Coast Colony to inspect the Prince of Wales' College and School, Achimota* (Accra, 1932); and *Report of the committee appointed in 1938 by the governor of the Gold Coast Colony to inspect the Prince of Wales' College, Achimota* (Accra, 1939).

[8] *Report of the sub-committee appointed to consider the educational policy underlying paragraph 19 of the report of the conference of directors of education of Kenya, Tanganyika, Uganda, and Zanzibar, held at Zanzibar in June, 1932*, December 1933, A.C.E.C. 44/33 [Currie report]. The membership under Currie's chairmanship was: F. O. Mann, W. W. Vaughan, Miss Philippa Esdaile, W. H. McLean, A. G. Church, Hanns Vischer and A. I. Mayhew. The report was subsequently made available to the public. In *Oversea Education*, VI No 4 (July 1935) 208–9 there occurs this announcement: 'The following documents relating to education in the British dependencies are obtainable on application to the Official Secretary, Advisory committee on Education in the Colonies . . . *Higher education in Africa* (A.C.E.C. 44/33).' The report is reproduced in full on p. 476.

[9] Paper read to the Ibo Union Education Committee, Lagos, by E. Njoku, for presentation to the Elliot commission, 13 Nov. 1943.

[10] The commission comprised: The Rt. Hon. the Earl De La Warr, Robert Bernays, Miss Philippa Esdaile, B. Mouat Jones, Alexander Kerr, W. H. McLean, Z. K. Matthews, John Murray, the Hon. Harold Nicholson, Hanns Vischer.

[11] See below, ref. 53.

[12] *Higher education in East Africa: report of the commission appointed by the secretary of state for the colonies, September 1937*, Colonial No. 142 (HMSO, 1937). [De La Warr report.]

[13] *Ibid.*, pp. 9–10.

[14] *Ibid.*, p. 12.

[15] *Ibid.*, pp. 91–2.

[16] *Ibid.*, p. 98.

[17] *Ibid.*, pp. 16–23.

[18] *Ibid.*, pp. 118–9.

[19] *Ibid.*, p. 61.

[20] *Ibid.*, p. 113.

[21] *Ibid.*, p. 83.

[22] *Report of the committee appointed in 1938 by the governor of the Gold Coast Colony to inspect the Prince of Wales' College, Achimota* (Accra, 1939).

[23] *Ibid.*, p. 140.

[24] *Ibid.*, p. 144.

[25] *Ibid.*, p. 145.

[26] *Ibid.*, p. 143. This is confirmed by many similar impressions. Hussey, for instance, once told the advisory committee that Makerere and Yaba had at first met with considerable opposition from Africans who thought they were being given something inferior to that given to Europeans.

[27] *Fourah Bay College: report of the commission appointed in 1938 by the secretary of state for the colonies to report on Fourah Bay College, Freetown*, Colonial No. 169 (HMSO, 1939).

[28] Arthur Mayhew had been appointed member and joint secretary of the committee when its terms of reference were extended to include all colonial territories in 1929.

[29] Its membership was: B. Mouat Jones (chairman), Sir G. Anderson, E. Burney, H. J. Channon (co-opted), C. W. M. Cox, H. M. Grace, E. R. J. Hussey, W. M. Macmillan.

[30] *Higher education in Malaya: report of the commission appointed by the secretary of state for the colonies, June 1939*, Colonial No 173 (HMSO, 1939) 30–2.

[31] Extracts from this memorandum are reproduced on p. 481.

[32] The other members were: Sir Fred Clarke, Julian Huxley, B. Mouat Jones, W. M. Macmillan, Miss M. Perham, and R. A. McL. Davidson (a colonial office official who took C. W. M. Cox's place).

[33] *Report of the sub-committee on higher education*, 15 May 1943, A.C.E.C. 7/43, conf. print, Misc. No 507 [Channon report]. The report is reproduced in full on p. 492.

[34] *Ibid.*, p. 20.

[35] *Ibid.*, p. 22.

[36] *Ibid.*, p. 27.

[37] This was the view of A. Creech Jones, who described to us his impressions of the meeting, and who later on, as secretary of state for the colonies, was involved in translating some of the ideas into action.

[38] Stanley to Channon, 23 Feb. 1943.

[39] e.g. Stanley to F. Horton, University of London, 29 May 1943.

[40] *H.C. Deb.*, 5 ser., 391, col. 54. Stanley's announcement was well received, though a couple of Conservative back-benchers suggested that elementary education was more important for the colonies than higher education. The new look which had come over British colonial policy was evident from several passages in Stanley's speech. Political responsibility, he said, rested on the twin pillars of 'educational advance and economic development'. He displayed none of the patronising superiority which some representatives of British universities a generation earlier displayed even toward Canadian and Australian universities. Instead he saw the colonial colleges as 'partners in the circle of home universities . . . an intellectual lend-lease'.

The members of the commission were chosen, after informal discussions between Channon and Stanley, with an eye to their standing and influence among British academics. Those whose names are marked * were also on the Elliot commission on West Africa; and those marked † were on the committee under Sir James Irvine which reported on the West Indies. The commission comprised:

The Hon. Mr Justice Asquith (chairman)	Sir Richard Livingstone
Sir Donald Cameron	R. Marrs
A. M. Carr-Saunders	Miss Lillian Penson
*H. J. Channon	†*Miss Margery Perham*
Sir Fred Clarke	†*R. E. Priestley*
*J. F. Duff	J. A. Ryle
The Lord Hailey	R. V. Southwell
†Sir James Irvine	J. A. Venn

Those in italics were members of the advisory committee on education in the colonies.

[41] *Ibid.*, col. 55. The Elliot commission comprised:

The Rt. Hon. Walter Elliot (chairman)	B. Mouat Jones
H. J. Channon	K. A. Korsah
J. R. Dickinson	I. O. Ransome Kuti
J. F. Duff	Miss Eveline Martin
Sir Geoffrey Evans	Miss Margaret Read
Julian Huxley	E. H. Taylor-Cummings
A. Creech Jones	A. E. Trueman

[42] Clarke to Claughton, 6 Dec. 1943.

[43] Asquith to Horton, 10 Mar. 1944.

[44] Horton to Asquith, 24 May 1944, and enclosure.

[45] Claughton to Lillian M. Penson, 8 June 1944.

[46] Senate minutes, 25 Oct. 1944.

[47] e.g. Stanley to Horton, 14 June 1945.

[48] *Report of the commission on higher education in the colonies*, 1944–45, Cmd. 6647, IV [Asquith report].

[49] *Report of the commission on higher education in West Africa*, 1944–45, Cmd. 6655, V [Elliot report]; *Report of the West Indies committee of the commission on higher education in the colonies*, 1944–45, Cmd. 6654, V [Irvine report].

[50] See, for instance, *The Times*, 20 July 1945.

[51] In 1945, the sums voted by parliament under the Colonial Development and Welfare Act of 1940 were substantially increased; out of a total allocation of £120 m. for schemes other than research in the ten year period ending 31 March 1956, £4½ m. was set aside for higher education. (Colonial Development and Welfare Acts, 1940 and 1945: 3 & 4 Geo. VI, c. 40; 8 & 9 Geo. VI, c. 20.) The act of 1940 constituted a landmark in British colonial policy. Hitherto it had been a firmly established principle that each colonial territory should be self-supporting, and that imperial aid should be forthcoming only in exceptional circumstances. In 1929 a centrally financed colonial development fund was set up to stimulate economic development in the colonies. But this was only a partial break with tradition. It was a step taken primarily in the interests of the Mother Country: 'to promote commerce with or industry in the United Kingdom' and so bring relief to the unemployed at home. The sums then voted by parliament – up to £1 m. a year for a ten year period – were to be used only for economic development and mainly for schemes of capital expenditure. The policy and provision in 1940 were very different. The sums made available in that year were 'for any purpose likely to promote the development of the resources of any colony or the welfare of its peoples'. Up to £½ m. was authorised for research in any financial year; and up to £5 m. a year, over a ten year period, for other schemes. And it was specifically emphasised in an explanatory statement of policy that these latter funds might be used for recurrent expenditure as well as for capital schemes. Britain had thus acknowledged a new and enlarged responsibility for her dependencies overseas; for the first time colonial education became eligible for regular subsidy from the imperial exchequer. (*Ibid.*: *Statement of policy on colonial development and welfare;* 1939–40, Cmd. 6175, X).

[52] *Cf. Channon*, p. 17 and *Asquith*, p. 25. The commission, in its introduction, acknowledged the 'utmost assistance' it had received from the deliberations of the advisory committee. *Asquith*, p. 5.

[53] A. M. Carr-Saunders, in *New universities overseas* (London, 1961) states that the report of Currie's sub-committee was not before the Asquith commission and that the commission 'arrived independently at very similar views' (p. 33, ref. 16). But certainly two members of the commission must have been aware of the report; for Lord Hailey had already summarised it in his *African survey* (1st edn, 1938, pp. 1231–2), and Sir Donald Cameron would have received it when he was governor of Nigeria.

[54] *Asquith*, p. 10.

[55] *Ibid.*, p. 15.

[56] *Ibid.*, p. 27.

[57] *Ibid.*, p. 29.

[58] *Ibid.*, p. 28.

[59] This assertion requires one qualification. One or two members of the commission, realising that it might be unreasonable to expect African students, whose mother-tongue is not English, to reach a standard of entrance to universities similar to that required from British students, wanted the commission to recommend entrance qualifications which took account of this. But a majority of the commissioners preferred to set a high standard of entry and then to suggest either that there might be concessional entry to pre-university courses for students who were unqualified, or that such students might read for local diplomas and not London degrees. *Ibid.*, pp. 43–5. Some colleges adopted concessional entry: see chapter 9.

[60] See ref. 49 (Elliot report).

[61] *Elliot*, p. 52.

[62] *Ibid.*, pp. 140–76. The minority report was signed by Channon, Evans, Huxley, Creech Jones, and Margaret Read.

[63] The British government at first preferred the minority report; but this aroused such an outcry in the Gold Coast that policy was modified to allow the Gold Coast to have its own university college provided it found the funds for this itself.

[64] *Cf. Channon* (ref. 33) p. 20.

[65] Undated memo of vice-chancellor [Aug.–Sept., 1944]. Italics are ours. The italicised sentences appear, in a slightly different form, in a letter from the vice-chancellor to Asquith, dated 4 October 1944.

[66] *Asquith*, p. 10.

[67] *Ibid.*, p. 17.

[68] *Elliot*, p. 55 and p. 53, where the report specifically commends research on African history, systems of customary law, and land tenure, and goes on to say: 'Research into the past will not only stimulate local interest in the ancient traditions of the peoples, but will help to maintain their sense of continuity in the rapid changes now coming upon them.'

[69] *Asquith*, p. 93, and *Elliot*, p. 85. The Elliot report recommends that this sort of research should be temporarily located in a West African institute of education.

[70] See p. 433.

[71] The Irvine report specifically recommended a lectureship in West Indian history (ref. 49, p. 25).

[72] *Asquith*, p. 60.

[73] *Elliot*, p. 55.

[74] *Asquith*, p. 87.

[75] *Ibid.*, p. 74.

[76] *Ibid.*, p. 59.

Chapter 8 *The transplantation*

[1] Margery Perham, at a discussion. 'The relation of the home universities to colonial universities and colleges'. *Conference of the Home Universities, 1946* (Univ. Bureau of the British Empire; London, 1946) 17.

[2] Ernest Barker, 'Universities in Great Britain' in *Universities in a changing world*, ed. W. M. Kotschnig and E. Prys (London, 1932) 119.

[3] H. G. G. Herklots, *The new universities, an external examination* (London, 1928) 87–8.

[4] C. Grant Robertson, *The British universities* (London, 1930) especially pp. 72–5.

[5] Julien Benda, *La trahison des clercs* (Cahiers verts, 2, vi) Paris, 1927.

[6] Abraham Flexner, *Universities: American, English, German* (London, 1930) 255.

[7] Lord Lindsay of Birker, 'The commission on German universities'. *Universities Quarterly*, IV, No 1 (1949) 82–8.

[8] T. R. McConnell: 'Impressions of British university education'. *Universities Quarterly*, III, No 3 (1949) 656–64.

[9] Adolf Löwe, *The universities in transformation* (London, 1940).

[10] Bruce Truscot, *Redbrick university* (London, 1943); *Redbrick and these vital days* (London, 1945). Using a borrowed voice, Truscot gave two broadcasts about universities on the African service of the BBC. In one of these (on 18 November 1943) he defined the aims of higher education as ripples spreading across a pool when a stone has been thrown in. The 'very heart and centre' of university teaching is (he said) research; *teaching* he regarded as the first of the widening rings of the surface of the pool; then generally broadening the minds of students through *residence*; and finally the influence of the university on its environment through *extension work*.

[11] Ortega y Gasset, *Mission of the university* (London, 1946); a translation of a tract published in Spain in 1930.

[12] Nuffield College, Oxford, *The problem facing universities* (Oxford, 1948) 89. The signatories to the statement were: J. H. Brookes, D. N. Chester, Henry Clay, Douglas E. Cooke, Lindsay of Birker, Richard Livingstone, F. W. Ogilvie, Janet Vaughan, Douglas Veale.

[13] Walter Moberly, *The crisis in the university* (London, 1949).

[14] *Ibid.*, p. 52.

[15] See 'The mission of a university' in *Universities Quarterly*, IV, No 1 (1949) 15–81; and the discussion on 'The crisis in the University' in *Report of the proceedings of the 1949 Conference of the Universities of Great Britain and Northern Ireland* (Assoc. of Univs. of the British Commonwealth; London, 1949).

[16] R. M. Hutchins, *The higher learning in America* (New Haven, 1936) 66.

[17] Harvard University, *General education in a free society: report of the Harvard committee* (Cambridge, Mass., 1945).

[18] There is a brief discussion of this controversy in *Universities Quarterly*, II, No 2 (1947) 131–5: 'American controversy on the philosophy of education', by I. L. Kandel and R. A. C. Oliver. The reassessment of the Harvard 'red book' is in: Harvard University, *Report of the special committee to review the present status and problems of the general education program* (1964). [Mimeo.]

[19] The principal official reports at this time were:

(a) *Scientific man-power: report of a committee appointed by the lord president of the council;* 1945–46, Cmd. 6824, XIV. [Chairman, Sir Alan Barlow.]

(b) Ministry of health and department of health for Scotland, *Report of the inter-departmental committee on medical schools*, (HMSO, 1944). [Chairman, Sir William Goodenough.]

(c) *Final report of the inter-departmental committee on dentistry;* 1945–46, Cmd. 6727, XI. [Chairman, Lord Teviot.]

(d) *Report of the committee on higher agricultural education in England and Wales;* 1945–46, Cmd. 6728, X. [Chairman, Dr T. Loveday.]

(e) *Second report of the committee on veterinary education in Great Britain;* 1943–44, Cmd. 6517, IV. [Chairman, Dr T. Loveday.]

(f) Foreign office, *Report of the inter-departmental commission of enquiry on oriental, Slavonic, East European and African studies* (HMSO, 1947). [Chairman, the earl of Scarbrough.]

(g) *Report of the committee on the provision for social and economic research;* 1945–46, Cmd. 6868, XIV. [Chairman, Sir John Clapham.]

[20] *University development from 1935 to 1947, being the report of the university grants committee* (HMSO, 1948) 28.

[21] Thus when in 1948 the University College of Nottingham became autonomous and was able to divest itself of the strait-jacket of the London external degree, it made no dramatic change in the pattern of its curriculum. The only striking departure from the conventional pattern was made at the University College of Keele, which put into practice some of Lord Lindsay's ideas about general education. It was the first institution in Britain (and still is the only one) which requires all its undergraduates to take a course comprising the humanities, natural science, and social science.

[22] Ref. 1.

[23] A factual account of these colleges and the inter-university council's relationship to them is to be found in the official report of the first eight years of the council's work: *Inter-University Council for Higher Education Overseas, 1946–54; 1955–56,* Cmd. 9515, XIV. See also A. M. Carr-Saunders' *New universities overseas* (London, 1961).

[24] An example of the difference in impact is to be found in the amount of attention given in the press to the affairs of the university colleges. In West Africa over the period 1950–60 scarcely a day passed without some mention of higher education; until recently the East African newspapers were silent on the subject for months on end.

[25] Since independence some African universities have abandoned these harmless and trivial customs. Students at the new university in Kumasi, Ghana, for instance, do not wear gowns on formal occasions, but national dress.

[26] University of London, *Annual report of the senate committee on colleges overseas in special relation, 1960–61.*

[27] For details of the curricula under special relationship see University of London, *Schemes of special relation: regulations 1962.*

[28] *Daily Times* (Lagos), 3 May 1955.

[29] *Ibid.,* 28 Mar. 1956.

[30] *Ibid.,* 24 Aug. 1954.

[31] D. M. Balme, 'Reflecting on work done', *Universitas*, III, i (1957) 4–6.

[32] *Daily Graphic* (Accra), 7 Mar. 1958.

[33] *Ghana Today*, 6 Dec. 1961, p. 2.

[34] *Uganda Herald*, 11 Mar. 1950.

[35] *Uganda Argus*, 1 Oct. 1960.

[36] *Ibid.*, 24 June 1961.

[37] *Ibid.*, 9 May 1962.

[38] For example, the speech by Mr Justice McCarthy in moving the second reading of 'An ordinance to provide for the establishment of a University College in the Gold Coast . . .' on 21 July 1948 (*Leg. Co. Deb.*, 1948, No 2, 79).

[39] In 1955 Kenneth Mellanby, the principal of University College, Ibadan, had to defend the college against criticism from members of boards of studies in the University of London, that the colonial colleges had not availed themselves fully of the opportunity for adaptation and made more fundamental changes in curricula. This was reported in the Nigerian press (*Daily Times* (Lagos), 4 July 1955). Mellanby defended the need for caution over early adaptations in curriculum also in *Minerva*, I, No 2 (1963) 153. Attempts by colleges to persuade the University of London to permit changes in pattern of degree failed. Thus in 1951 the academic board of the University College of the Gold Coast was in favour of a general B.Sc. degree with two main subjects, not three, in the third year; but the board was told that such a change in structure as this would not be allowed. It was in fact later introduced throughout the University of London.

[40] University of London, *Graduates under schemes of special relation, 1961.* [Mimeo.]

[41] See the perceptive comment made by John Lockwood, quoted on p. 286.

[42] D. M. Balme, 'Inaugural address to first ordinary convocation, 2 December, 1950', *University College of the Gold Coast, Notices* (1950–1) No 5.

[43] Above, p. 80.

[44] The sort of blunders committed by Europeans who do not understand African society were well described by E. W. Smith in *The golden stool* (London, 1926). But Africans, too, can blunder in this way; indeed one recent Nigerian novel is concerned with the theme of what happens when an African government officer misjudges the attitude of his own people. See T. M. Aluko, *One man, one matchet* (London, 1964).

[45] For example, there is the touching incident related in the report of the Elliot commission, about a boy who told a member of another educational commission visiting Africa: 'We desire to learn Latin because it is your secret language, from which you derive your power.'

[46] *Daily Graphic* (Accra), 30 May 1953.

[47] *Ibid.*, 5 May 1955.

[48] *Ibid.*, 13 Dec. 1954.

[49] Inaugural address as chancellor, quoted in University of Nigeria, *Prospectus, 1962–63*, p. 7.

[50] U. Okeke, 'Educational reconstruction in an independent Nigeria'. (Unpubd Ph.D. thesis, New York University, 1955.)

[51] *Daily Times* (Lagos), 17 Nov. 1955 and 8 Feb. 1955.

[52] *Ibid.*, 19 Mar. 1956.

[53] *Daily Graphic* (Accra), 18 Feb. 1956.

[54] See also the comments of French scholars on this question, p. 374. There was another good reason why African studies should be promoted at African universities, foreseen by David Balme as long ago as 1948. In a discussion with the University of London senate committee on higher education in the colonies, Balme made a perceptive comment, to the effect that there was evidence that the people of the Gold Coast were being subjected to a dangerous racial myth and it seemed politically desirable

to provide facilities for the study of comparative anthropology, to be closely associated with the study of history and the vernacular languages. Balme anticipated a tendency which has indeed shown itself in Ghana, though there seems no danger of it at present elsewhere among African nations; namely a sort of Celtic revival of African culture, investing Africa's past in a luminous mist, with airy and undisciplined talk about the great empires of Ghana and the Sudan; an attitude which could easily lead to the injection of romance, if not downright falsification, into history.

[55] University of Khartoum, *Calendar, 1963–1964*, p. 227.

[56] A summary of the plans for the University College at Dar-es-Salaam is given in R. C. Pratt, 'East Africa's University problem', *East Africa Journal* (August, 1964) 3–11.

[57] Makerere University College, *Calendar, 1964–65*, p. 45.

[58] University of Ibadan, *Faculty of arts prospectus, 1965–66*, p. 20.

[59] The University of Nigeria, *Calendar, 1964–65*, p. 83.

[60] *Education in Uganda: the report of the Uganda education commission, 1963* (Entebbe, 1963).

[61] *Ibid.*, p. 29.

[62] University of East Africa, *Draft university development plan for the triennium 1964–67*, p. 14. [Mimeo.]

[63] University of Ghana, *Calendar 1964–65*, p. 128.

[64] University of Ibadan, *Calendar 1965–66*.

[65] *Ibid.*, p. 59.

[66] *Ibid.*, pp. 65–6. See also faculty of arts prospectus 1965–6 for the details of courses and permitted subsidiaries.

[67] *Ibid.*, p. 67.

[68] *Ibid.*, p. 98.

[69] *Ibid.*, p. 93.

[70] *Ibid.*, pp. 74–82.

[71] *Ibid.*, p. 105 ff.

[72] University of Lagos, *Calendar 1964–65*, p. 27.

[73] *Ibid.*, pp. 35–6.

[74] *Ibid.*, p. 31.

[75] University of Ife, Ibadan branch, *Calendar 1963–64*, p. 43.

[76] *Ibid.*, p. 96.

[77] *University of Northern Nigeria: report of the inter-university council delegation, April, 1961.*

[78] *Ibid.*, p. 33.

[79] Ahmadu Bello University, *Calendar 1964–65*, p. 99.

Chapter 9 *Higher education takes root*

[1] *Report of the commission on higher education in West Africa*, p. 18; 1944–45, Cmd. 6655, V.

[2] Central African Council. *Report of the commission on higher education for Africans in Central Africa* (Salisbury, S. Rhodesia, 1953). The members were: A. M. Carr-Saunders (chairman), A. V. Hill, Alexander Kerr, F. G. Young.

[3] *Ibid.*, p. 34.

[4] *Ibid.*, p. 35. This sentiment seems inconsistent with a view expressed by the Asquith commissioners: see chapter 7, ref. 55.

[5] *Inter-university council for higher education overseas, 1946–54*; 1955–56, Cmd. 9515, XIV.

[6] *Ibid.*, p. 28.

[7] *Ibid.*, p. 29.

[8] *Ibid.*, p. 4.

[9] Private communication: notes for a discussion.

[10] Private communication.

[11] i.e. colleges under the advisory committee on colonial colleges of arts, science and technology (subsequently called the council for overseas colleges); a body which performed for these colleges functions similar to those performed for the university institutions by the inter-university council.

[12] T. H. Silcock, *Southeast Asian University: a comparative account of development problems.* (Durham, N.C., 1964).

[13] *Report of the working party on higher education in East Africa, July–August 1958* [Mimeo.] The members were: J. F. Lockwood (chairman), D. L. Keir, Lillian Penson, E. Griffen, C. T. Ingold, D. H. Alexander.

[14] U. Okeke, *Educational reconstruction in an independent Nigeria* (Unpubd Ph.D. thesis, New York University, 1955).

[15] N. J. Okongwu, *History of education in Nigeria, 1842–1942* (Unpubd Ph.D. thesis, New York University, 1964).

[16] Up to 1960 the university colleges in East Africa, Ghana, and Nigeria produced 759 B.A.s of the University of London under schemes of special relation. Of these 328 were honours graduates. The figures are:

	EAST AFRICA	GHANA	IBADAN
B.A. general	155	106	170
B.A. honours	19	165	144

[17] A. G. Sims, 'Africans beat on our college doors' *Harper's Magazine*, 222 (April 1961) 53–8.

[18] African scholarship program of American universities. *Annual Report 1963–1964* (Cambridge, Mass.).

[19] D. D. Henry, *Continuity and change in ASPAU. Address given at the Fourth ASPAU Conference, October 29, 1964* (Cambridge, Mass., 1964).

[20] The difference in admission requirements between African and American university institutions sometimes makes this policy difficult to achieve. Thus in Rhodesia and Nyasaland it was agreed that awards tenable in America should not be offered to students who were assured of a place in the university college in Salisbury. This college does not admit students without passes at A-Level G.C.E. or the equivalent; whereupon some schoolboys deliberately failed their A-level examinations in the hope that they would thereby become eligible for ASPAU awards. 'In British Africa', says an American guide for sponsors of student exchange programmes with Africa, 'students who would be considered college caliber in the United States (and sometimes in the United Kingdom as well) cannot gain admission to an institution of higher education. Thus African undergraduates must look abroad if they are to achieve their aspirations, and American universities are increasingly willing to help them.' Committee on educational interchange policy, *African students in the United States* (New York, 1960) 11.

[21] A 'follow-up' meeting was held a year later, in May 1959, at Cumberland Lodge in England.

[22] Those attending this meeting were, from USA: Harvie Branscomb, chancellor, Vanderbilt University; Grayson Kirk, president, Columbia University; Clifford M. Hardin, chancellor, University of Nebraska; J. L. Morrill, president, University of Minnesota; and from the UK: Eric Ashby, vice-chancellor, the Queen's University, Belfast; Charles Morris, vice-chancellor, Leeds University; Keith Murray, chairman, university grants committee.

[23] *The report of the university education commission* (*December 1948–August 1949*) (Delhi, 1950) [Radhakrishnan report]. See p. 411.

[24] *Investment in education; the report of the commission on post-school certificate and higher education in Nigeria* (Lagos, 1960) [Ashby report]. The membership was, from Britain: Eric Ashby, J. F. Lockwood, G. W. Watts; from Nigeria: K. O. Dike, Senator Shettima Kashim, S. D. Onabamiro; from the United States: R. G. Gustavson, H. W. Hannah, F. Keppel.

[25] *Educational development 1961–70*. Federation of Nigeria, sessional paper No. 3 of 1961.

[26] A. M. Carr-Saunders, in his book *New universities overseas* (London, 1961), devotes a section to the Nigerian commission's report, which he seems to regard as an additiona' piece of proof for the immutability of the Asquith plan. '... it is therefore of the greatest interest', he says, 'to find that international commissioners of great experience, who are not motivated by any paternal sentiments for the Asquith plan, propose what is in effect a great expansion of university facilities on the lines which guided development during the first phase.' This is a misconception of the commission's recommendations: the necessity for continuity in evolution must not be assumed to mean satisfaction with the past. See the discussion, p. 259.

[27] *Investment in education*, p. 22.

[28] *Ibid.*, p. 31.

[29] *Ibid.*, p. 26.

[30] In the event, there are five universities in Nigeria, for the Western Region created the University of Ife, which was not recommended by the commissioners.

[31] *Ibid.*, p. 26.

[32] J. W. Hanson, *Imagination and hallucination in African education* (East Lansing, 1965).

[33] *Ibid.*, p. 7.

[34] *Ibid.*, p. 13.

[35] An address delivered before the inaugural convocation of the University of Nigeria, 13 October 1960; reproduced in The University of Nigeria, *Calendar*, *1964–65*.

[36] Private communication from John Lockwood. His liberal and enlightened views and his prestige as a classicist in the Oxford tradition and as an ex-vice-chancellor of the University of London, were to have a great influence in modifying the rigidities of the Asquith doctrine in African universities.

[37] AID (Agency for International Development). It was formerly called the International Co-operation Administration. It finances American universities to operate on its behalf. For an acute analysis of the educational work of AID see John W. Gardner's *AID and the universities* (New York, 1964).

[38] *Report to the government of the Eastern Region of Nigeria concerning the development of a university*. 7 July 1958. [Mimeo.]

[39] *Ibid.*, p. 5.

[40] University of London, *Senate committee on colleges overseas in special relation: report for the session 1959–60.*

[41] A good brief description is given by J.W.Hanson: 'The land grant philosophy and African higher education', in *West African Journal of Education,* VI (1962) 80–4. For an excellent scholarly discussion of it, see Allan Nevins, *The state universities and democracy* (Urbana, 1962).

[42] Extra-mural departments in British universities cannot claim grants from the ministry of education and science for classes in vocational subjects; these are by and large regarded as further education and not a university's responsibility.

[43] Hanson (ref. 32) p. 82.

[44] It is noteworthy that one of the Asquith colleges, now the University of the West Indies, has, since its independence, introduced a first year survey course. All candidates for a B.A. general honours degree in their first year take courses in the use of English, the development of civilisation, and the history of the Caribbean.

[45] The facts which follow are taken from the 1964–5 calendar of the University of Nigeria.

[46] e.g. A.M.Carr-Saunders, in a book published a few months after the university opened, gives it a discouraging start by suggesting that before the proposal to open a university on these lines is adopted 'very careful consideration should be given to other possible methods of filling the gap ...'. *New universities overseas* (London, 1961) 212.

[47] *Report of the commission on university education, December 1960–January 1961* (Accra, 1961). The members were Kojo Botsio, (chairman), D.A.Chapman; J.D. Bernal, E.E.Evans-Pritchard, D.Skilbeck, from England; H.M.Bond and Miss L.A.Bornholdt, from the United States; Davidson Nicol from Sierra Leone; and N.S.Torocheshnikov from the Soviet Union.

[48] *Report of the working party on higher education in East Africa, 1955,* p. 4. [Mimeo.] The members of the party were A.M.Carr-Saunders, D.L.Keir, F.J. Harlow, and E.Griffen.

[49] *The University of East Africa: Report of the committee on needs and priorities, 1962.* (Entebbe, Uganda, 1962). The members were: Davidson Nicol (chairman), A.M.Carr-Saunders, N.A.M.MacKenzie, H.J.Seddon, Alan Pifer.

[50] *Ibid.,* p. 76.

[51] *Ibid.,* p. 38.

[52] *Ibid.,* pp. 66–7.

[53] *Ibid.,* p. 92.

[54] *Ibid.,* p. 40.

[55] *Ibid.,* p. 98.

[56] *Report on the development of a university in Northern Rhodesia, 1963* (Lusaka, 1964). The committee consisted of J.F.Lockwood (chairman), Karl W.Bigelow, A.J.Tattersall, and Hugh A.Warren. In a foreword to the report the prime minister and minister of education of Zambia announce that they accept in principle its main recommendations.

[57] Private communication from J.F.Lockwood.

[58] Ref. 56, p. 2.

[59] *Ibid.,* p. 2.

[60] *Ibid.,* p. 3.

[61] *Ibid.,* p. 3.

[62] The membership was: Eldon L. Johnson (chairman), from the USA; J. W. Blake, from Britain; A. T. Porter, from Sierra Leone, and K. Twum-Barima, from Ghana.

[63] American Council on Education, *Education for development: report of the survey team on education in Malawi* (1964). [Mimeo.]

[64] *Ibid.*, p. 24.

[65] *Ibid.*, p. 26.

[66] *Ibid.*, p. 52.

[67] *Ibid.*, p. 54.

[68] *Ibid.*, p. 50.

Chapter 10 *Autonomy and academic freedom*

[1] See Lord Chorley, 'Academic freedom in the United Kingdom', *Law and Contemporary Problems*, XXVIII (1963) 647–71. The nearest approach to any statutory protection, according to Lord Chorley, is to be found in the articles of association of the London School of Economics and Political Science, one of which reads that no member of the staff shall be 'under any disability or disadvantage by reason only of any opinions he may hold or promulgate on any subject whatsoever'. Quoted by Lord Chorley, p. 663.

[2] M. Polanyi, *The foundations of academic freedom* (Society for Freedom in Science, Occasional pamphlet No 6) London, 1947.

[3] R. F. Fuchs, 'Academic freedom—its basic philosophy, function, and history', *Law and Contemporary Problems*, XXVIII (1963) 431.

[4] *Ibid.*, p. 435; and see F. Paulsen, *The German universities and university study* (Eng. trans., London 1908) 235, 246.

[5] As, for example, happened some years ago in Iowa. Some research at the state university was favourable to the nutritive and economic advantages of margarine. Iowa is a dairy-producing state, and members of the legislature objected to the publication of work which might favour a competitive product.

[6] In the United States such dismissals have occurred, and cases for wrongful dismissal have come to court. There is, therefore, a considerable amount of case law over infringement of *Lehrfreiheit*. For a historical account of this see R. Hofstadter, and W. P. Metzger, *The development of academic freedom in the United States* (New York, 1955); and for a recent legal symposium which includes a discussion of some of the dismissals, see essays in 'Academic freedom', *Law and Contemporary Problems*, XXVIII (1963) 429–671.

[7] Ref. 1, p. 664.

[8] We do not here enter into a discussion of whether *Lehrfreiheit* should be a privilege of *all* teachers, from primary school upwards; this is a question which has received a good deal of discussion in the United States.

[9] We quote from the English paraphrase of the report: Foreign office, *University reform in Germany: report by a German commission* (HMSO, 1949) 14.

[10] *Ibid.*, p. 16.

[11] See, for example, an important statement made twenty years ago by the committee of vice-chancellors and principals:

In the view of the Vice-Chancellors . . . the Universities may properly be expected not only individually to make proper use of the resources entrusted to them, but collectively, to devise and execute policies calculated to serve the national interest. And in that task, both individually and collectively, they will be glad to have a greater measure of guidance from Government than until quite recent days they have been accustomed to receive.

This is from *A note on university policy and finance for the decennium 1947–56* published by the committee of vice-chancellors and principals in 1956. For the background to this decision see E. Ashby, *Community of universities* (Cambridge, 1963) 61–80; and the excellent study by R. O. Berdahl, *British universities and the state* (Berkeley, Calif., 1959).

[12] Berdahl (ref. 11) gives an admirable account of the endeavours of parliamentary committees in Britain to secure for parliament some degree of supervision over university expenditure.

[13] E. Fiddes, *Chapters in the history of Owens College and of Manchester University, 1851–1914* (Manchester, 1937) 65.

[14] E. J. Somerset, *The birth of a university: a passage in the life of E. A. Sonnenschein* (Oxford, 1934) 20.

[15] A. C. Wood, *A history of the University College, Nottingham, 1881–1948* (Oxford, 1953) 32.

[16] H. E. Barff, *A short historical account of the University of Sydney* (Sydney, 1902) 70.

[17] J. M. Mackay, 'Senate and faculty...' [1897]. Reprinted in *A miscellany presented to John Macdonald Mackay, LL.D., July 1914* (Liverpool, 1914) 363–88.

[18] The powers of the university council at Birmingham include 'to review and control or disallow any act of the Senate and give directions to be obeyed by the Senate'. In the University of Sussex the council has power 'to give directions to the Senate'. The phrase does not appear in the constitutions of more recently founded universities.

[19] H. Malden, *On the origin of universities and academical degrees*, (London, 1835). Malden was a fellow-student with T. B. Macaulay at Cambridge. He was consulted about the establishment of the first universities in India. See p. 54.

[20] H. A. L. Fisher, *James Bryce* (London, 1927) I, 116.

[21] J. Thompson, *The Owens College: its foundation and growth; and its connection with the Victoria University, Manchester* (Manchester, 1886) 618.

[22] Ref. 14, p. 20.

[23] Universities (Scotland) Act, 1889. Ordinance (No 31), Glasgow, Aberdeen, and Edinburgh, No 1; 1893–94 (271) LXIX.

[24] Ref. 14, p. 21. See also articles by Sonnenschein in *Birmingham Post*, 24 April, 1 May, and 8 May 1899.

[25] W. M. Childs, *Making a university* (London, 1933). In 1960–1 there were nine academic members of council (excluding the vice-chancellor himself) out of a total of thirty-six.

[26] *State of universities in Scotland, roy. comm. rept.;* 1831 (310) XII. *Evidence taken before the commissioners: I. Edinburgh;* 1837 [92] XXXV.

[27] J. Mountford, 'The universities of the United Kingdom', in *Commonwealth Universities Yearbook* (London, 1962) 783–4.

[28] E. Ashby, *Technology and the academics* (London, 1958) 98.

[29] *University grants committee: returns from universities and university colleges in receipt of exchequer grant. Academic year 1962–1963;* 1963–64, Cmnd. 2456.

[30] Thus Statute 11 of the University of York provides for a general academic board

with considerable powers. The board consists of the vice-chancellor, the deputy vice-chancellor and:

not more than forty persons, of whom at least one fifth shall be Professors, as may be elected from among themselves by all the holders of academic posts of the grade of lecturer and above.

The statutes for the Heriot-Watt University in Edinburgh provide for departmental committees which:

shall meet not less than three times in each year and any member of the staff of the Department may make representations on any matter affecting that Department (Statute XXI).

[31] One must distinguish argument from fact in this question. It may be that modern universities, on account of their size and their cost and their contemporary structure, should no longer be regarded as societies in which all members take part in government; perhaps they should be run mainly by professors. This is a matter for argument. The fact is that the constitutions which the modern universities are copying, with minor modifications, were not designed deliberately to exclude from full participation in academic government most members of the career grade of the academic profession; yet that is the effect they frequently have.

[32] University of Cairo. *Calendar 1958–59*, p. 15.

[33] These took place in 1952, 1957, and 1961. The membership of all three of these visitations was British (on the 1961 visit there was a professor from McGill, but he was a Scotsman).

[34] Provision for the whole staff to meet as congregation, appears in the 1954 Ordinance of University College, Ibadan. It is interesting that the original draft ordinance, drawn up in 1952 in London, contained no such provision: it was added by the council of ministers in Lagos, deliberately to foster the idea that the new university college set down in the African bush was a self-governing academic society.

[35] This view of the function of laymen in university government is supported from an unexpected quarter: the president of one of the great land grant universities in the United States. The president of Cornell, discussing university autonomy, writes of the 'enormous contribution of the lay trustee' in helping to preserve academic freedom among university teachers. He says: 'We need only talk to our fellow educators in other parts of the world where the lay trustee is unknown to realize how our academic communities would otherwise be exposed to the hot pokers of special interest. The informed lay trustee who says, "Stop, it is I who represent the public's interest in this matter", is perhaps one of the greatest contributors to our free academic communities.' J.A. Perkins, 'The new conditions of autonomy', in *Emerging patterns in American higher education*, ed. Logan Wilson (Washington, 1965) 14.

[36] *Report of the commission on university education, December 1960–January 1961* (Accra, 1961) 11.

[37] *Statement by the government on the report of the commission on university education*, W.P. No 5/61.

[38] University of Ghana Act, 1961, Act 79.

[39] University of Nigeria Law, 1955, E.R. No 23 of 1955.

[40] University of Nigeria (Provisional Council) (Amendment) Law, 1959, E.R No 10 of 1959.

[41] University of Nigeria Law, 1961, E.N. Law No 21 of 1961.

[42] University of Khartoum Act, 1956, 1956 Act No 29.

[43] Ahmadu Bello University Law, 1962, N.N. No 26 of 1962.

[44] *University of Northern Nigeria: report of the inter-university council delegation, April 1961.* [Mimeo.]

[45] Ref. 43, para. 31 (1).

[46] *Ibid.,* Statute 8, p. 20.

[47] *Report of the inter-university council delegation to Makerere College, August 1954* [mimeo.] and *Report of the working party on higher education in East Africa, 1955* [mimeo.]

[48] The University of East Africa Act, 1962, E. A. Common Services Organisation Act No 16 of 1962.

[49] *The Makerere College Act, 1949,* as amended 1954, 1957, 1961, 1963, 1964; reproduced in Makerere University College, *Calendar, 1964–65,* p. 116.

[50] Charter: the University College of Rhodesia and Nyasaland, 10 February 1955, Federal notice No 103 of 1955.

[51] The US state department asked the University College of East Africa at Makerere to arrange the seminar, and the department of extra-mural studies undertook the arrangements. The Americans wanted the programme to cover contemporary political and economic problems in the East African territories, and they wanted to hear not only the official colonial office point of view but points of view of African leaders, which might not conform to colonial office policy. The strongest pressure was brought to bear on Makerere not to invite certain African leaders to speak, and the colonial government of Tanganyika made conditions which undoubtedly challenged the academic freedom of some of those who were taking part in the seminar. However, the seminar was held with the speakers the college wanted and they were allowed to speak without interference; so in the end academic freedom was not infringed.

[52] An account of this incident is given in *Minerva,* I, No 3 (1963) 395–7. The device the Rhodesian federal government used was to declare the lecturer, Dr Terence Ranger, a prohibited immigrant after he had resided in the country for six years. No reason was given. No charge was made against him which could be tested in the courts. The principal of the university college, in protesting against this action, wrote: 'The issue raised by the government's action is one of civil liberties, not of academic freedom. The action is presumably not directed against the college in its corporate capacity or against Dr Ranger's academic activities'. A somewhat similar incident occurred in Sierra Leone, when the director of extra-mural studies was deported – but this time by an African government – for views he expressed in an article published in the *New Statesman* (8 June 1962).

[53] For a brief account see *Minerva,* II, No 2 (1964) 269, II, No 3 (1964) 395–9; III, No 2 (1965) 272.

[54] E. Njoku, 'The relationship between university and society in Nigeria', in *The scholar and society* (Bulletin of the Committee on Science and Freedom, 13) Manchester, 1959, pp. 82–6.

[55] K. Mellanby, *The birth of Nigeria's university* (London, 1958).

[56] *A tract on higher education in Nigeria* [Action Group manifesto, 1958, mimeo.]

[57] University of Ibadan Act, 1962, No. 37.

[58] University of Lagos Act, 1962, No 1. Part IV Sect. 24 (1) refers to the obligation of the provisional council to present a draft constitution. Part II sect. 6 (4)

refers to the term of office of the first vice-chancellor, his eligibility for reappoint-ment, and the procedure for making an appointment.

[59] *Report on the constitution of the University of Lagos, 30th November 1964* (Unpubd, Lagos, 1964).

[60] *Ibid.*, p. 2.

[61] *Ibid.*, p. 23.

[62] A burst of pamphleteering followed the incident we are describing. One of us (E.A.) was in Lagos during part of the crisis and is familiar at first hand with some of the events. In addition we have drawn on three diverse sources of information, viz:

(a) *The crisis over the appointment of vice-chancellor of the University Lagos*, by the senior members of staff, the University, Lagos, 19 March 1965.

(b) *University of Lagos, change in vice-chancellorship*, over the signature of the chairman of council, issued on 16 June 1965, and described as an 'official publication'. It was never before council or senate and it is a grossly mis-leading and prejudiced document.

(c) *University of Lagos: the truth about the change in vice-chancellorship*, a pam-phlet published by G. K. Berrie (dean of the faculty of science), C. Fielstra (dean of the faculty of education), T. F. Nicholson (president of the Associa-tion of University Teachers), P. O. Nsugbe (head of department of African his-tory and culture), B. O. Nwabueze (senior lecturer in law), A. Nwaefuna (presi-dent of the students' union). This is a restrained and accurate account of the incident, published in July 1965.

There is an accurate account of the incident in *Minerva*, III, No 3 (1965) 412–6, III, No 4 (1965) 592–601.

[63] Ref. 62(a), p. 1; ref. 62(b), p. 5; ref. 62(c), p. 7.

[64] *Ibid.*, (a) p. 2; (b) p. 9; (c) p. 8.

[65] *Ibid.*, (a) p. 2; (b) p. 6; (c) p. 11.

[66] *Ibid.*, (a) p. 3; (b) p. 1. (the evasive remark of the chairman does not deny this); (c) p. 12. It is significant that the premier of the Western Region and leader of the NNDP, Chief S. L. Akintola, in a speech on 25 June 1965 is reported to have said, over Biobaku's appointment, that it is 'a forerunner of many good things that await the Yorubas at Federal Government level' (*Daily Times* (Lagos), 26 June 1965).

[67] 23 April 1965, *Fed. Nigeria Parl. Deb.*, 18, col. 1330.

[68] Ref. 62(c), p. 32.

[69] A. Curle, 'Nationalism and higher education in Ghana', *Universities Quar-terly*, XVI, No 3 (1962) 229–42.

[70] *Ibid.*, p. 236.

[71] *Ibid.*, p. 238.

[72] Second reading, University of Ghana bill, 31 July 1961, *Ghana Parl. Deb.*, 24, col. 880 ff.

[73] Ref. 37, p. 3.

[74] *University of Ghana Reporter*, 4, No 21 (23 April 1965) 267 .

[75] Ref. 37, para. 24, p. 7.

[76] *University of Ghana Reporter*, 3, No 20 (18 Mar. 1964) 192.

[77] 'We disagree: our critical analysis of the convocation speech by Dr Conor Cruise O'Brien . . .', *The Spark*, 17 Mar. 1964.

[78] This is the expression used by the vice-chancellor in his address to congrega-tion. See ref. 74, p. 268.

[79] Ref. 74, p. 268.

[80] *Ibid.*, p. 269.

[81] *The Ghanaian Times*, 2 April and 3 April 1965.

[82] Even very recent ones, e.g. the University of Sussex charter, para. 5(1).

[83] The University of Khartoum (Amendment) Act 1960. 1960 Act No 53.

[84] A brief and accurate account of it, well documented, is to be found in *Minerva*, III, No 2 (1965) 277–86.

[85] Above, pp. 74–5.

[86] Above, p. 89.

[87] Above, p. 93.

[88] This is not mere speculation. In the early 1950s some colonial government officials in Africa frequently expressed views about the relationship they would like to see between university colleges and colonial governments which closely resembled the Indian government's attitude over the constitutions for universities at Aligarh and Benares (above, pp. 88 ff.).

[89] This is the wording in the University of Nigeria Law, 1961, sect. 7; the University of Ibadan Act, 1962, states that the council 'shall be the governing body of the university' (sect. 4); the University of Ghana Act, 1961, states that 'the governing body of the university shall be the university council' (sect. 7); the draft act for the University of Lagos follows the wording for Ibadan; the University of Khartoum Act, 1956, states that 'the executive authority of the university shall rest in the council' (sect. 8).

[90] The following table summarises the position in some African universities:

X = Powers delegated by constitution to senate

	Ghana	Ibadan	Lagos(d)	Ife(b)	Nsukka(a)	Khartoum
Curricula and courses of study	X	X	X	X	—	X
Examinations and award of degrees	X	X	X	—	—	X
Admission of students	X(c)	X	X	—	—	X
Appointments of staff	—	X	—	—	—	—

University (column group heading over Ghana, Ibadan, Lagos(d), Ife(b), Nsukka(a), Khartoum)

Notes: (a) In Nsukka (the University of Nigeria) the senate is formally an advisory body to the council and to the vice-chancellor. It is however, 'responsible to the University Council for the development and supervision of all academic matters' and despite lapses described in this chapter a satisfactory equilibrium between council and senate is being established.

(b) according to the temporary act setting up a provisional council.

(c) power to admit is only advisory to the council.

(d) draft constitution.

[91] Above, p. 70.

[92] Unlike the membership of the British university grants committee none of the members is a practising academic. The membership (1965) is the emir of Yauri (chairman); the president and the secretary of the Nigeria Union of Teachers; the secretary to the prime minister; the chairman, board of inland revenue; the provincial secretary, Sokoto; the resident engineer, Sokoto; the minister of education, and the chief secretary to the premier, Eastern Region; a medical practitioner from Benin; and the executive director, Western Nigeria Development Corporation.

U–B.I.A.—15*

[93] *University development in Nigeria: report of the national universities commission* (Lagos, 1963).

[94] Davidson Nicol, in a memorandum to the Commission on University Education in Ghana, wrote, 'There should be at least two members of the Government of cabinet rank in each Council' [of the constituent colleges of a proposed federated University of Ghana].

[95] *Sixth congress of the universities of the British Commonwealth, 1948. Report of proceedings* (Assoc. Univs. of the British Commonwealth; London, 1951) 37.

[96] Above, p. 309.

[97] E.g., in the Nigerian constitution, Chapter iii. Nigeria (Constitution) Order in Council 1960, L.N. 159 of 1960.

[98] Above, p. 294.

[99] T.H.Silcock, *Southeast Asian university* (Durham, N.C., 1964) 87.

[100] *Ibid.*, p. 86.

[101] E.g., D.B.Heron, 'Some reflections on academic freedom', *Makerere Journal*, 9 (March, 1964) 33–43, which strikes noble attitudes about the functions of universities, but at a level which is out of reach of the Ugandans on whom he pours criticism. It is therefore ineffective. Moreover, in denying the state any rights over the university, the article is as bigoted as some African politicans are when they deny the university any immunity from control by the state.

[102] We the undersigned senior members of the University College of Ghana declare:

I That we have watched with increasing concern illiberal policies towards Universities and discrimination and differentiation within Universities in various parts of the world. In our opinion such policies and practices can never create the conditions in which a University can fulfil its true responsibilities.

II That to fulfil its true responsibilities a University must
  (1) function as a sanctuary for ideas, even if unpopular or unorthodox, promote freedom of intellectual expression and stimulate research and the extension of the frontiers of knowledge
  (2) train students in different disciplines and fields of knowledge
  (3) promote a liberal outlook which involves fostering such basic concepts as justice, freedom, equality, and human dignity and
  (4) promote a rational and scientific attitude among its members with an emphasis on truth as a supreme value.

III That if it is to fulfil these responsibilities, the body of scholars which constitutes a University must, together with the autonomous governing body
  (1) have complete authority over the appointment of academic staff
  (2) have complete control over what it teaches, including the scope, content, emphasis and other details of its course of studies
  (3) be free to admit students on the basis of merit and competence
  (4) have control over the discipline of its students and not allow outside interference in the administration of the discipline; and
  we further declare

  (1) that a University should not keep aloof from the society of which it forms a part but should on the contrary actively seek to serve the needs of that society
  (2) that problems of adjustment and adaptation should be met in a constructive and responsible spirit on the part of the University and with an appreciation on the part of higher authority of what a University stands for

(3) that academic freedom is not an end in itself but an essential condition of University life; without it a University cannot contribute fully to the development of the society which gives it birth, nor to the well being of humanity as a whole.

R. W. H. Wright
G. Walton
Adam Curle
P. L. Shinnie
G. W. Irwin

[December, 1960]

Chapter 11 *Other patterns of higher education in Africa*

[1] This was arranged by the Congress for Cultural Freedom. It was concerned with inter-university co-operation in West Africa. The seminar was attended by academics from all the West African countries from Senegal to the Congolese Republic and by individuals from Britain, France, and the United States. The papers and discussions are assembled in a book, *The West African intellectual community* (Ibadan, 1962), which has some very interesting material in it.

[2] This was arranged by UNESCO. It covered all countries on the continent except South Africa. A report was published as *The development of higher education in Africa* (Paris, 1963). There was, for the first time, co-operation between different European countries over some of the preparatory papers. Thus there was a joint study on staffing under the auspices of the British inter-university council, in which the French ministry of education co-operated.

[3] University of South Africa, *Prospectus, 1965*, p. 13. The obligation to obtain tuition (by correspondence) from the University of South Africa or from some other recognised institution which prepares students for degrees, dates only from 1962. See University of South Africa, *Calendar, 1965*, p. 48.

[4] A convenient brief account of it is to be found in M. Horrell, *A decade of Bantu education* (South African Institute of Race Relations; Johannesburg, 1964).

[5] *Report of the commission on native education, 1949–51*. U.G.53 (Pretoria, 1951). [Eiselen report.]

[6] Above, p. 190 and p. 197.

[7] S.A. Assembly, 17 September 1953, quoted in ref. 4, pp. 5–6.

[8] S.A. Assembly, 17 June 1959, *ibid.*

[9] Bill to provide for the establishment, maintenance, management and control of university colleges for non-white persons ... *Union Gazette Extraordinary*, 15 March 1957.

[10] *Ibid.*, clauses 15, 36, 37, 43.

[11] *Ibid.*, clauses 11, 13(1), 13(2).

[12] *Ibid.*, clauses 32, 33.

[13] *Ibid.*, clause 39.

[14] The *Calendar* of the University of South Africa (1965, p. 61) publishes the minimal pass marks which candidates have to obtain to qualify in courses for bachelor's degrees. The *Calendar* of the University College of Fort Hare (1965, p. 21) also publishes minimal pass marks; they are the same as those published by the university.

[15] Above, p. 254.

[16] University College of Zululand, *Calendar, 1965*, pp. 23–4.

[17] The history of the college up to its take-over by the minister of Bantu education

is charmingly told in: *A short pictorial history of the University College of Fort Hare, 1916–1959* (Lovedale, 1961).

[18] University College of Fort Hare, *Calendar 1965*, pp. 9–10.

[19] According to a statement made by the minister of Bantu education (Assembly, 2 June 1963) the percentage passes were:

	FORT HARE	COLL. OF NORTH	ZULULAND
1st year	91	66	64
2nd year	85	79	70
3rd year	88	86	90

[20] Ref. 4, p. 156.

[21] One example is a highly disingenuous pamphlet issued from the University College of the North, by C.H.Rautenbach, entitled *Open discussion on closed universities* (Turfloop, 1963).

[22] H.Kitchen (ed.) *The educated African* (London, 1962) 114.

[23] During 1965–6 a few academics from Britain and the United States, including one of us (E.A.), were asked by the university to review its progress and to make recommendations for its future. Therefore much of the material in this section was collected at first hand.

[24] Charter for Haile Sellassie I University, article 15. The charter is in the *General Catalogue* of the university, 1965, section 1, p. 38.

[25] Above, p. 340.

[26] *Legislation of the faculty council of Haile Sellassie I University* [n.d. mimeo].

[27] *Ibid.*, pp. 47–50.

[28] The total enrolments in 1964 were (approximately): agriculture, 196; arts, 290; building technology, 107; business administration, 204; education, 431; engineering (a five-year course), 200; law (a five-year course), 68; medicine, 20; public health, 76; science, 140; social work, 22; theology, 20.

[29] A.G.Lehmann, *Report on the development of higher education in Ethiopia* [unpublished, 1965].

[30] In writing this section we have used material collected by one of us who visited Leopoldville in December 1963. The history of education in the Belgian Congo is well summarised in Lord Hailey's monumental *An African survey* (London, 1957) 1206–14, and in *The educated African*, edited by Helen Kitchen (London, 1962) 191–206.

[31] Quoted in Kitchen (ref. 30) p. 192.

[32] The constitution is determined by statutes published in *Bulletin Officiel du Congo*, 4 (15 April 1949); 5 (1 March 1956); by decrees published in *Moniteur congolais*, Nos 30 and 34 (1960); and by ordinances promulgated on 27 November 1963. The statutes and regulations are reproduced in the calendar for 1963–4: *Université Lovanium*, 1954–1964 (Leopoldville, 1963) 17–41.

[33] It is, however, relevant to arguments elsewhere in this book (above p. 244) that when the centre universitaire started in 1954, opportunities for higher education were offered only in science (leading also to medicine), agriculture, engineering, and administration. Studies in arts (the faculty of philosophy and letters) followed later.

[34] One of us (E.A.) has examined several of these theses in scientific topics familiar to him. They run to about a hundred pages of typescript. The best of them

reach a standard rather lower than that expected for an M.Sc. in an English civic university.

[35] *Lovanium University, 1962–1963* (Leopoldville) 27.

[36] Our sources of material for this section are first, conversations with faculty members from the University of Dakar and information kindly supplied from the office of the inspection générale of the direction de l'enseignement supérieur, Paris. We have also drawn heavily from material in an unpublished Ph.D. thesis in the library at Stanford University: J.B.Bolibaugh, *French educational strategies for sub-Saharan Africa: their intent, derivation, and development* (Stanford, 1964).

As for published material, there are brief accounts of the systems of education in French Africa in Lord Hailey's *An African survey* (London, 1957), and in *The educated African* (London, 1962), edited by Helen Kitchen. A thoughtful discussion of Faidherbe's contribution to education in Senegal is to be found in R.Delavignette, *Freedom and authority in French West Africa* (London, 1950), and there is an excellent analysis of French educational policy in V.Thompson and R.Adloff, *French West Africa* (London, 1958). A recent issue of *Revue de l'enseignement supérieur* (No 2, 1964) is devoted to French aid to higher education overseas; it contains some illuminating essays on the French attitude toward the adaptation of curricula and the preservation of 'équivalence' in diplomas. Another useful source of French opinion is the *Compte rendu* of the first conference of the *Association des universités entièrement ou partiellement de langue française* (Montreal, 1963), held at the Sorbonne in April 1963. We have drawn also on the calendars of institutions of higher education in French-speaking Africa, especially the annual *Livret de l'étudiant* of the University of Dakar; upon the discussions at the international seminar on inter-university co-operation in West Africa, held in Freetown in 1961 and published as *The West African intellectual community* (Ibadan, 1962); and, for some statistical material, on *The development of higher education in Africa* (UNESCO, Paris, 1963).

[37] Bolibaugh (ref. 36), p. 17.

[38] *Ibid.*, p. 55.

[39] Pierre Foncin, *De l'enseignement aux colonies* (Paris, n.d.) 3, quoted in translation by Bolibaugh (ref. 36) p. 86.

[40] *Journal officiel du Sénégal et dépendences*, No 152, 48th year, 28 Nov. 1903, p. 678, quoted in translation by Bolibaugh (ref. 36) p. 90.

[41] Quoted in translation by Bolibaugh, *ibid.*, p. 111.

[42] M.Davesne, 'Rapport sur l'Afrique occidental française' in *Adaptation de l'enseignement dans les colonies*. Congrès intercolonial de l'enseignement dans les colonies et les pays d'outre mer. (Paris, 1932) p. 95. Quoted by Bolibaugh, *ibid.*, p. 126.

[43] *La conférence Africaine française, Brazzaville, 30 Jan.–8 Fév. 1944* (Paris, 1945).

[44] Quoted by Thompson and Adloff (ref. 36) p. 539.

[45] Information provided from the national ministry of education, Paris. A new decree, of 24 articles, issued on 6 January 1966, retains the firm link with France but delegates more responsibility to Senegal for policy-making in the University of Dakar. See: 'Accord de coopération entre la république française et la république du Sénégal en matière d'enseignement supérieur.' *Journal officiel de la république française*, 16 janvier, 1966, pp. 468–71.

[46] Philippe Ardant, professor at Poitiers, writing in *Revue de l'enseignement supérieur*. See ref. 36, p. 39.

[47] Jean-Pierre Dannaud, writing in *Revue de l'enseignement supérieur*. See ref. 36, p. 50.

[48] Quoted from 'Tendencies in African poetry', by Samuel Allen; *Présence Africaine* (Paris, 1958) 180.

[49] *Ministère de la coopération, France Afrique* (1960) 36, quoted in translation by Bolibaugh (ref. 36) p. 201.

[50] Claude Tardits, 'Connaissance de l'Afrique, développement de l'enseignement supérieur africain'. In *Revue de l'enseignement supérieur* (ref. 36) p. 57.

DOCUMENTS*

* An explanation of the references to the unpublished material in this appendix will be found on p. 531 of the bibliography to Part III.

I. THE UNIVERSITY QUESTION OF THE 1870s

When Blyden made his appeal for a West African university in 1872, he was not the first to urge the need of local facilities for higher education. Horton had been pioneering in the same cause for over a decade; and already the Church Missionary Society were planning to transform their theological seminary at Fourah Bay into a general college that would cater for lay students as well as those training for the ministry.[1] But it was not until Blyden pressed his demand on the government that the question took on any urgency, and although his plea failed in its immediate purpose, it was indirectly responsible for hastening the establishment of the first university courses to be provided in British West Africa. The following extracts have been chosen to indicate the novel character and purpose Blyden conceived for the new institution, the initial interest his proposal attracted in official circles, and the stimulus it afforded to the development of higher studies at Fourah Bay. The reports from the Coast disclose something of the heat engendered by what to Horton in 1873, and to native opinion generally, assumed the proportions of 'the question of the day'.[2]

A. THE PROPOSAL FOR A WEST AFRICAN UNIVERSITY, DECEMBER 1872[3]

1 *E. W. Blyden to governor Hennessy*

Freetown, December 6, 1872

In the interview I had the honor to have with your Excellency the other day, you expressed the opinion that a great effort should be made not only to spread the rudiments of technical and secular knowledge among the mass of the population on the coast and in the adjacent interior, but also to establish a sort of Educational Department of State for the purpose of securing to intelligent and studious Natives the advantage of instruction in the higher branches of learning.

The more I reflect upon the subject, the more I am convinced that we can have no thorough and permanent reform – no proper development and growth – without the means being afforded of a liberal education to the youth.

If in the Government of these Settlements, native agency is to be welcomed and encouraged and not despised and excluded; if the people are ever to become fit to be entrusted with the functions of self-government; if they are ever to become ripe for free and progressive institutions, it must be by a system of education adopted to the exigencies of the country and race: such a system as shall prepare the intelligent youth for the responsibilities which must devolve upon them; and, without inter-fering with their native instincts, and throwing them altogether out of harmony and

---

[1] See above, chapter 6.
[2] Above, p. 170; *cf.* also doc. No 5, p. 465 below.
[3] E. W. Blyden, *The West African University: correspondence between Edward W. Blyden, M.A., and his excellency J. Pope Hennessy, C.M.G., administrator-in-chief of the West Africa settlements* (Freetown, 1872).

sympathy with their own countrymen, shall qualify them to be the efficient guides and counsellors and rulers of their people.

The system unfortunately or want of system to which the natives of this country have been subjected in consequence of the conflicting dogmatic creeds introduced among them from abroad, has unduly biased their development and hampered their progress. All effort here, as in some other mission fields, seems to have been directed mainly to a solution of the question of who shall be uppermost . . . Free learning has, with very few exceptions, been substituted by the narrow and dwarfing influence of ecclesiastical dogmatism. . . .

Now to give the people the opportunity and power of a free and healthy development – to bring out that individuality and originality of character which is one of the sure results of advancing civilization and culture, the University is most important. The presence of such an Institution with able African teachers brought, if necessary, from different parts of the world – even a Negro Arabic Professor from Egypt, Timbuctoo or Futah – would have great influence in exposing and correcting the fallacies upon which our foreign teachers have proceeded in their utter misapprehension and, perhaps, contempt of African character.

And it occurs to me that so far as the organization of a suitable system of education for West Africa is concerned, your Excellency enjoys a noble opportunity, having – what very rarely falls to the lot of Colonial Governors – a sort of *tabula rasa* – an open, extensive and unencumbered field. If such a system could be organized under your Administration, or in consequence of your Administration, it would be the crown and glory of all the beneficent acts which it has been your good fortune to be instrumental in conferring upon the inhabitants of this coast and their interior neighbours.

I believe that any recommendation made by Your Excellency, looking to the establishment of an educational institution here on a broad and liberal basis, would meet with the earnest sympathy and cooperation of the Government of England, and of those races which must sympathize with the Negro, as well as of all intelligent Natives on the coast.

2 E. W. Blyden to governor Hennessy

Freetown, December 9, 1872

In taking the liberty to call your Excellency's attention again to the important subject of the Educational necessities of the West Africa Settlements, I beg to remark that for many years after the founding of these Settlements, they were regarded practically only as missionary stations and harbors of refuge for the naval and mercantile interests of Great Britain, and the improvement and training of the people with reference to a free autonomy was held in abeyance.

When important questions have arisen, therefore, having their origin purely in a race sentiment they have been entirely ignored or misunderstood by the generality of rulers who have presided over the destinies of these Colonies. . . .

The result of these things has been that there has been no marked or permanent progress of the people on the coast. The movements have been in a circle, always recurring to the point of commencement; great expense, and no doubt a great deal of effort, but no advance. Every new set of missionary or political agents have had the task of beginning the work anew.

I deem it, then, a singular privilege of the present generation to have witnessed the advent among them of a ruler of liberal and cultivated statesmanship. I believe that just at this crisis in the history of the world, when such striking revolutions are affecting the condition of the Negro race, your official residence on this coast is Providential. God sent you hither, despite the opinion of those who would practically divorce the direct Divine agency from African affairs; and I am gratified to notice in all your conversations with me your recognition of your responsibility to the Supreme Arbiter of nations. Your ardent faith and trust in Providence, and your belief in the past and future of the Negro, so apparent in all your words and actions, have been means of great instruction and encouragement to me.

There can be no doubt that your residence here, brief as it has been, has already produced a great change – a change which, if not adequately realised or understood or universally accepted, is, nevertheless, an important advance upon the past. Old maxims and policies have been rudely shaken. The owls and bats of the past are getting startled while the crude, nebulous and pernicious atmosphere in which they have delighted to shelter themselves is being penetrated by a fresh and searching light. The *de facto* is giving place to the *de jure*. Race sentiment will hereafter be allowed to have its proper place and influence on the coast. We are rising to a loftier, purer and clearer atmosphere, and arriving at the conviction that the political and commercial aggrandizement of this country is of less importance than the improvement and integrity of the people; that a Government which is more inert in developing the intellectual and moral character of these tribes than in availing itself of the material resources of the country is of very questionable utility to the race. And as a means of intensifying this conviction and rendering it operative and productive, the University which your Excellency has in view is most important.

. . . the higher and more subtle reforms after which you are aiming are understood and studied only by the few. . . .

Without help, some even of those few may succumb in the *gurgite vasto*. The help necessary is some educational institution to give shelter and nutriment to these struggling views, so as to make them the mental property of the masses; and by gradually developing and extending them, make them a permanent element of moral and even religious power on the whole coast.

Your Excellency with that keen appreciation which you possess of the power of ethnological analogies and affinities, predicted the other day that some great spirit will arise in the interior of Africa, endowed with superior intellectual power, who will diffuse an elevating influence, and kindle the dim consciousness of the people into active intelligence. This may be so. In all countries great men have risen up from time to time, far above the level of their contemporaries, and have infused into society new life, new views, and a clearer intelligence; and I see no reason why such a phenomenon may not occur in Africa. Nevertheless, we ought not to rely upon exceptional and abnormal development. We must establish the means and agencies which shall create an indigenous literature, and silently but effectually transform the moral and intellectual condition of the people; and the source and fountain of this literature must be a well-established African University, in keeping with the advancing spirit of the age and adapted to the inherent necessities of the race. . . .

3 *Governor Hennessy to E. W. Blyden*

Local. No 147   Government House, Sierra Leone,
                                                        December 10, 1872

I have read with interest the letters on the subject of Education which you have addressed to me.

2 It is impossible not to observe the defective state of Education in these settlements. The late Director of Public Instruction drew public attention to the decided want of instruction in practical morality in the schools, and to the formation of a thoughtless, idle and ignorant character. At the same time, no one can say that the Government and the various Missionary Societies have not laboured zealously to promote education. But as you point out, there has been great expense and great effort, but no advance.

3 I agree with you that the failure is mainly owing to the idea that the Negro should be Europeanized to be educated. A similar mistake was made in the early days of British rule in Hindostan, and with a similar result. Now, Indian statesmen trace the intellectual development of the East to the recognition by the Government of the fact that the spirit of race cannot be ignored.

4 On the Senate of the University of Bombay, of which the Governor is Chancellor, we see such men as Juggunath Sunkersett, Premabhai Hemabhai, and other natives, whose national habits in no degree interfere with their loyalty to the Crown or with their usefulness as promoters of Public Instruction.

5 To establish a similar University in Africa must be the work of the Africans themselves. There are so many monuments of benevolent failures in Sierra Leone, that the Government would shrink from undertaking the initiative of such an Institution, though a reasonable claim for some State support might be made, when the Promoters could show that their scheme possessed the real elements of success.

4 *E. W. Blyden to governor Hennessy*

                                                    Freetown, December 11, 1872

I beg to acknowledge the receipt of your Excellency's letter of yesterday and to thank you for bringing forward so distinctly your own sense of the importance of the recognition of the Race instincts in all efforts to educate a people; that you approve the views contained in my letters and accept the logical inferences to which they lead.

Your letter, though brief, is particularly valuable as containing the estimates and views of a disinterested and competent foreigner who has devoted time and study to these special questions: and I am glad that you have called attention to the mistaken policy formerly pursued in India and which proved to be so resultless, if not injurious to the people.

In the case of the Negro, the truth is, that the despotic and overruling method which has been pursued in his education, by good-meaning but unphilosophical philanthropists has so entirely mastered and warped his mind that, in the whole civilized world, scarce any important political or social issue can be witnessed as the result of Negro training. All educated Negroes suffer from a kind of slavery in many ways far more subversive of the real welfare of the race than the ancient physical fetters. The slavery of the mind is far more destructive than that of the body. But such is the weakness and imperfection of human nature that many even of those who bravely fought to remove the shackles from the *body* of the Negro transfer them to his *mind* with as little compunction as ever Hawkins or Da Souza prosecuted the slave-trade; and do not feel themselves called upon to give the slightest attention to questions like these.

Such, then, being the present condition of the Africans – misunderstood and compromised by many of their best friends, and often by themselves – it must be evident that to leave the work of initiating the education they need to 'the Africans themselves' would be to put it off indefinitely. Europeans owe us a great debt, not only for the unrequited physical labors we have performed in all parts of the world, but for the unnumbered miseries and untold demoralization they have brought upon Africa by the prosecution for centuries of the horrible traffic to promote their own selfish ends; and we feel that we do not simply ask it as a favor but claim it as a right when we entreat their aid as civilized and Christian Governments in the work of unfettering and enlightening the Negro mind, and placing him in a position to act well his part among the 'productive agencies' of time.

We cannot expect Missionary Societies to take up and consider questions of this nature. They look upon them rather as secular and political than religious, and therefore, as out of the sphere of their operations. Our only resource, under present circumstances, is to look to the Government – the Government, in the first instance, of SIERRA LEONE.

This Colony, from its peculiar circumstances, the multiplicity of African tribes genuinely represented in it, and the facilities which it has of communication with all parts of Negroland, must, for the present at least, be regarded as the centre of the race: here, therefore, the special educational work at which we are aiming should be begun. . . .

5 *Governor Hennessy to E. W. Blyden*

Local. No 150   Government House, Sierra Leone,
                                                                    December 11, 1872

I have the honor to acknowledge the receipt of your letter of today's date in which you indicate what you believe to be the responsibilities of the Government in the special Educational work you have at heart.

2 Without pledging the Government to any action in the matter, I shall have much pleasure in transmitting this letter and the preceding ones to the Earl of Kimberley with my Report upon them, for his Lordship's decision.

3 You have certainly thrown new light on this subject; and, whatever course respecting it the Secretary of State may instruct the Governor of this important part of Negro-land to take, I am confident he will be deeply interested in your views and suggestions.

6 *E. W. Blyden to governor Hennessy*

                                                                    Freetown, December 14, 1872

I have the honor to acknowledge with thanks the receipt of your Excellency's communication of the 11th inst.

I have submitted all the letters to the Honorable William Grant and other leading Natives, who take a deep and intelligent interest in the subject, and they have urged me to obtain your permission to publish the correspondence, that it may be scattered into all parts of the world where there are Negro communities, with a view of informing them of the steps we are taking in this important matter here in the original and natural home of the race. . . .

Your Excellency's determination to forward the letters 'to the Earl of Kimberley with your Report upon them for his Lordship's decision' makes the effort assume an importance and gather to itself an element of speedy success which I could hardly anticipate when I ventured to open the correspondence.

Pegasus will now be unbound. The tropical African blood that beats passionately in the veins of every Negro will manifest itself in a new social force, in new institutions and a new literature. The present straight jacket of unmodified European training holds back the hand of many a master. We are racked and torn on the bed of Procrustes. . . .

. . . We have lost the manliness and simplicity of our forefathers; and, before we can take our proper place as respectable factors in the work of the world's progress, we must with our own hands unravel the intricate web of the civilization by which we have been smothered, and begin anew. This looks like an ambitious and formidable work – but it is a work which must be undertaken, and for which, in some degree, the adversity of centuries has given us at least the external adaptation: and the dissemination of the views contained in the correspondence it is hoped will help to counteract the degeneracy which everywhere has marked our transit from barbarism to the complex forms of European civilization.

7 *Governor Hennessy to E.W.Blyden*

Local No 153   Government House, Sierra Leone,
                                                        December 14, 1872

I have no objection whatever to the publication of our recent correspondence.
I am sure the circulation of your letters will do good.

B. THE OFFICIAL RESPONSE

1 *Governor Hennessy to the earl of Kimberley* [C.O. 267/317]

No 159   Government House, Sierra Leone
                                                        28 December 1872

I have the honor to lay before Your Lordship copies of some correspondence that has recently passed between Professor Blyden, a Negro gentleman who was selected by Sir Arthur Kennedy last year to conduct an important mission to the Interior, The Honorable Wm Grant, a native member of the Legislative Council, and myself on the higher education of the African Race.

2 In Mr Keenan's Report to Lord Granville on the state of Education in Trinidad (House of Commons' Paper 450 of Session 1870) he refers at page 64, to the strong desire amongst the creoles to secure for their children a complete course of education without the disadvantages of sending them to Europe.

3 This feeling is seen here too, but it is much stronger in the colored people than in the creoles; and it is strongest of all in the black, or pure African.

4 Within the last fortnight I had a long conference with thirteen native clergymen of the Church of England on this subject. At Lagos and at Elmina I frequently heard the views of the leading natives as to the state of Education on the Coast. They

all appeared to concur in the opinions now expressed in Professor Blyden's letters.

5 My own observation convinces me that the system of sending the Children of the wealthier Africans to Europe has been doubly injurious: it has spoiled the characters of those who have been so treated; and it has a direct tendency to defeat the policy laid down by the Parliamentary Committee in 1865 and by Her Majesty's Government in wishing to see Africans capable of Governing their Country. It is painful to notice the contrast between such young men, who ought to be the natural leaders of public opinion in their own country, and the Chiefs and people from the Interior who have been untouched by Europeans. The latter have a manly bearing, a natural courtesy, a very keen intelligence and a frank and honest disposition. The negroes who have been educated in Europe, or who have been forced here into a sort of semi European mould, are the very reverse of all this.

6 More than two Centuries and a half ago, Sir John Hawkins reports how he visited Sierra Leone and found the negroes a courageous and manly race; just and true in all their dealings; and he adds they mostly drank nothing but water.

[C.O. marginalia:]
But not from visiting
Europe
a complimentary
valedictory address
Then why did he
believe the educated
Natives at Cape
Coast & Lagos?

7 The villages that he then visited have grown into the City of Freetown, but the negroes themselves have sadly degenerated. Sir Arthur Kennedy, in addressing them a short time before his departure for Hong Kong, said that drinking spirits, telling lies, and idleness were their chief characteristics.

8 This want of temperance, and of any regard for truth or industry, I saw along the Coast wherever the negro had come under European influence.

9 Fortunately, European influence has barely touched West Africa; and, in the interior, such negroes as Sir John Hawkins met in 1607 can still be seen in every village – men who are temperate in their habits and just and true in their dealings.

10 Seeing all this, I could not but heartily sympathise with Professor Blyden, Mr Grant, the Native Pastors and the other Africans who have spoken to me on this subject.

11 I think a West African University founded on a very humble basis ought to be established, where not only the sons of rich Africans could be educated but where, like in the early Irish Universities, and some of the Continental Universities of our own times even the poorest youths who had talents and a real taste for knowledge might by sizarships or fellowships have an opportunity of cultivating learning.

Will not
these render
it difficult to
found a
University?

12 The Wesleyan Training College on King Tom's peninsula which was purchased for £1500 in 1869 by Sir Arthur Kennedy with the idea of establishing a large Reformatory has remained unused in the hands of the Government, as the religious, and other, difficulties of getting the Reformatory to work were found to be insuperable. This commodious and conveniently situated Building would be well suited for the early days of the University.

13 Looking, however, to my very temporary tenure of office, and to the fact that Mr Keate is one of the Governors who have done most for Academic education in

the Colonies, I have left everything for his more mature and valuable judgment; and, in my reply to Professor Blyden, I have avoided entering into any details or committing the Government to any opinion in the matter. . . .

Colonial office minutes

Establishment of a West African University

Mr Holland

There is at present, I think, at S. Leone, a well supported Grammar School for the better class of Natives, superintended by a native Clergyman (of the Church of England). There is also the Fourah Bay Institution maintained by the Ch. Miss^y Soc^y for the education of Natives for the Church, but there is no establishment for carrying on secular studies commenced at school. Where one Native is sent to England to be educated, and as Mr Hennessy himself admits, to return to his Native Land spoilt, of course hundreds are unable to avail themselves of a more advanced education.

Mr Blyden hints at the employment of Native Professors, & Mr Hennessy suggests the late Wesleyan Training College on King Tom's Peninsula as the University Building.

Both he and Mr Blyden deserve credit for starting an idea which properly developed might be of incalculable advantage to W. Africa, but which could hardly come to anything without Government support, & till some further investigation as to the feasibility of the project has been made by Mr Keate.

J. H[ales][1]   28/1/73

I confess that I am not much struck with Mr Blyden's letters, or his arguments for a University. I doubt whether the plan would succeed. However there is nothing to be done except to refer the subject to Mr Keate & to desire him to report upon it when he has been long enough in the Colony to master the pros & cons.

H. T. H[olland][2] 29/1/73
R. G. W. H[erbert][3] Jan 29

Refer as proposed. An University of the kind suggested by Mr Hennessy is more easily conceived than established. There would be great difficulties – but we may await Mr Keate's report before taking any steps.

E. H. K[natchbull] H[ugessen][4] 30/1/73

Mr Hennessy's eyes seem at last to be opened to the character of the so called educated negro. The correspondence is interesting and altho' Mr Blyden's letters show strongly the defects which he himself points out as arising from the engrafting European ideas on a negro mind, they contain some shrewd and just observations. Send to Mr Keate as proposed, saying I have read with interest, and that altho' I am not prepared to express any opinion at present on the suggestion of a University, the subject deserves his careful attention.

K[imberly] feb 1

[1] First-class clerk, African and Mediterranean department.
[2] Assistant under-secretary of state.
[3] Under-secretary of state.
[4] Parliamentary under-secretary.

2 *The earl of Kimberley to governor Keate* [C.O. 267/317]

Draft

Sierra Leone, No 405 Downing Street,

5 February 1873

I have received Mr Pope Hennessy's despatch No. 159 of the 28th ult. advocating the establishment of a University at S. Leone for the Natives of West Africa and enclosing a copy of a correspondence on the subject between himself & Professor Blyden.

I have read Mr Hennessy's despatch with interest and although I am not prepared to express any opinion on the suggestion of a University, I consider the subject deserving of your careful attention.

[Keate did not live to discharge this reference; and it was not until May of the following year that a considered opinion was obtained from the coast. Kimberley, meanwhile, showed signs of warming to the project. Evidence of his growing interest is provided in the two following documents: the first (No 3), a letter written at his request by the Rev. James Johnson, a member of the native pastorate of Sierra Leone, after an interview at the colonial office in November 1873; and the second (No 4), a despatch sent to the governor of Sierra Leone as a result of a further appeal from Blyden received in the colonial office shortly after the interview with Johnson. In directing governor Berkeley's attention to the outstanding enquiry to Keate, Kimberley dropped his earlier reserve (No 2) and so phrased his reminder as to leave in no doubt where his own sympathies lay. But Berkeley, with the bishop of Sierra Leone at his elbow, took a less sanguine view of the scheme (No 5); and this was readily accepted by Kimberley's Conservative successor (No 6).]

3 *The Rev. James Johnson to the colonial office* [C.O. 879/8]

62 Gibson Square, Islington N. January 21, 1874

[Refers to the interview granted him on 25 November 1873]

I am most thankful to know that the matter of superior educational establishments for the young men of the Colony, and other parts of the west African coast, is under Your Lordship's consideration; that Your Lordship contemplates teaching eventually in the Colony some of the learned professions, and is anxious that the interior countries share with the British Settlements the privileges of a liberal education.

. . . the work of education needs now, and is capable of, an expansion on all sides for which the funds of a missionary society are not available, and which the people, unaided, are not yet able to give it. . . .

Should Your Lordship see your way to co-operate with the Church Missionary Society in this matter . . . it would very considerably lessen the expense, as that Society has a very commodious and well-situated building at Forerah [sic] Bay, and the foundation of a good library, and it contemplates throwing open its college in it to the general public.

The fact that the natives of the Colony and other parts of the West African coast have been in the habit of sending their children and other friends to this and other countries to be educated at no small expense, and with no little risk to the lives of those sent, and that there are at this time about twenty-five of them in schools here and in Germany, tell their desire for a liberal education, and afford a strong argument in favour of the efforts that may be made for enlarged schemes. . . .

4 *The earl of Kimberley to governor Berkeley* [C.O. 267/324]

Draft

Sierra Leone, No 590   Downing Street, 16 December 1873

[Refers to Blyden's letter of 22 October 1873]

Mr Blyden strongly urges the establishment at S. Leone of a West African University, and upon this subject I desire to call your attention to my despatch No 405 of the 5th February last, and the desp: from Mr Pope Hennessy (No 159 of 28 Decr. 1872) to which it was an answer.

I shall be glad to receive your opinion, when you have had time to form one, upon a subject which seems to me one of much importance.

5 *Governor Berkeley to the earl of Carnarvon* [C.O. 879/8]

Confidential.   Government House, Sierra Leone, May 8, 1874

[In reply to Sierra Leone No 590 of 16 December 1873 (No 4 above), and Sierra Leone No 26 of 26 January 1874 (forwarding Johnson's letter of 21 January), encloses an exhaustive report from the bishop of Sierra Leone.]

2 The Bishop wishes this communication to be considered as private and confidential. . . .

3 I agree generally in the suggestions made and the opinions expressed by the Bishop.

5 I consider that the Fourah Bay College, especially since it has been thrown open to laymen, possesses all the essentials requisite to promote that higher class of education in furtherance of which the establishment of a Government University is by certain parties advocated. . . .

Enclosure.

The bishop of Sierra Leone to governor Berkeley

Bishop's Court, Sierra Leone, April 17, 1874

[Prefaces his opinion of the proposal for a West African university with a reference to the published correspondence between Blyden and governor Hennessy] . . . I feel sure you will marvel with me that any gentleman representing Her Majesty the Queen should allow letters which in their language seem to me so full of the most disgusting flattery to him, of low abuse of others, and of a tendency to set class against class in this community, to be addressed to him; and you will marvel the more that they should not only be received but answered, and that the correspondence should close with a brief note from Mr Hennessey [sic] to Mr Blyden, in which he writes, 'I am sure the circulation of your letters will do good'.

[Insists that he is not opposed to 'any well thought of, well planned practical scheme' of higher education; he had not been four months in his diocese before advising the CMS to open Fourah Bay College to other than those training for the ministry, and since then the CMS had resolved to act to the full on his recommendation.]

This determination on the part of the Church Missionary Society very materially affects the question of the establishment by the Government of a West African University at the present time; and I cannot but think that it will be the wisdom of the Government to pause to count the probable cost, the possible entire failure, the extent of beneficial result the most sanguine of reasonable men could expect, for the following reasons:

1 The Church Missionary Society is willing to do very much what is now sought at the hands of the Government. The Society can do it at very much less expense than the Government can, and on a much more reliable and less fluctuating basis, being subject, I mean, to none of the risks of external pressure and an annual vote.

2 For the Government to do it, would involve a most serious outlay. First, charges in buildings, furniture &c., and then charges of maintenance, professional chairs, repairs &c. In the present condition of the Settlement, it is a more sound principle of action for the Government to encourage and stimulate, at an expense proportional to what may be otherwise raised, what the people originate, provided it be good, than for the Government to undertake the responsibility of founding. That is, spoon-meat once a necessity, is no longer needed, but hurtful. Help those who help themselves, but avoid an expenditure of 1,000*l.*, and the risk of being after all left in the lurch.

3 I usually put it down that any estimated result in connection with any object of religious benevolence on this coast needs to be divided by three to reach the probable net result of benefit, and I think it out of the power of any one to judge of the number that would avail themselves of the advantages of an university during – say, the next five years, if one were established tomorrow. Yet, some reliable data the Government should have before it plunge into so considerable an undertaking.

Mr Johnson writes of twenty-five Africans being at the present time in schools in England and Germany. I think the statement needs to be tested, before it is allowed to apply to the present case. It might appear that quite half of these would not be students in a West African University if one were in existence. For instance, one is at Oxford, one at St Augustine's, Canterbury, two at Kings College, and there happens to be just now the very large family of Mrs William Smith in England, most of whom are mere children.

India and Africa are not parallel. India has a literature far older than our own, whereas the West Coast of Africa has none. India has a population, out of which it is most certain a large percentage will avail themselves of the highest possible education, but here the percentage might be a very small one; unless, indeed, the university were to become nothing more than an upper middle-class boys' school.

The Government, though it may from prudential or other motives decline, at the present time, the direct work of establishing an university, yet may be willing to assist in developing the Fourah Bay College (of course making its own terms) if the Church Missionary Society desire its aid; and by looking upon this as a tentative experiment, may observe the right and safe path in the future.

On the subject, therefore, of a West African University, in which particularly my remarks are asked, I think your Excellency would do well to advise the Secretary of State to pause before he resolve; to become acquainted with his correspondents, to decline to act as requested without reliable data on which to estimate probable results, and to make sure that for every 1,000*l.* spent by the Government the people will contribute at least an equal sum. . . .

Colonial office minutes [C.O. 267/326]

Confidential report on affairs of the Colony

. . . As regards the Bishop's letter which is to be treated as confidential, I would express Ld C.'s sense of the ability & judgment with which he has dealt with the important subjects under his consideration.

I would add that Ld C. would gladly sanction any vote of money for the adoption of the pupil teachers scheme & improvement of elementary schools, as also for the increase of technical education of a plain character which would fit the scholars for different handicraft trades & teach them to avail themselves of the resources of the country.

That Ld C. entertains very grave doubts as to the expediency of attempting to establish a W. African University, & considers the observations of the Bishop upon such a scheme as deserving serious consideration. More reliable data would be required before he could sanction such an undertaking which must of necessity be costly & for which the natives are not yet sufficiently prepared. . .

H. T. H[olland] 5/6/74

I don't fancy the idea of carrying out the educational crotchets of these Revd gentlemen at the expense of the State. Mr Blyden does not seem to be a very wise person.

J. L[owther][1] June 6

Write as proposed by Sir H. Holland but let me see the dft. . . . the plainer & simpler the type of education given the better.

10 June C[arnarvon]

6 *The earl of Carnarvon to governor Berkeley* [C.O. 879/8]

Confidential.   Downing Street, June 12, 1874

[Acknowledges his confidential despatch of 8 May 1874]

With regard to the Bishop's letter, I have to request you to convey to His Lordship my sense of the ability and judgment with which he has dealt with the important subjects under his consideration.

I have to add that I should readily sanction any vote of money for the adoption of the pupil-teacher scheme and the improvement of elementary schools; as also for the increase of technical education of a plain character, which would fit the scholars for different handicraft trades, and teach them to avail themselves of the resources of the country.

I entertain, however, very grave doubts as to the expediency of attempting to establish a West African University; and I consider the observations of the Bishop upon such a scheme to be deserving of serious consideration.

More reliable data than have yet been furnished would be required before I could sanction such an undertaking, which must of necessity be costly, and for which the natives are not yet sufficiently prepared . . .

[1] Parliamentary under-secretary.

C. THE MISSIONARY RESPONSE

(1) *On the Coast*

(a) From Henry Cheetham, bishop of Sierra Leone

1 *Henry Cheetham to Henry Wright, hon. secretary, CMS* [C.A1/O.25e/38]

Bishopscourt, Sierra Leone. Mar 13 1873

My dear Brother,

You will recollect all that passed at Salis^y Sq^{re} on the subject of expanding very carefully & *gradually* Fourah Bay so as for it safely & quietly to meet the demand for a West Af^n University.

You will recollect the very small modicum of encouragement the Com^{ee} gave in this direction.

On my return, I find the place to be ablaze with a scheme of a West Af^n University: which is advocated in correspondence between Mr Blyden & the late Admins^r, Mr Hennessy, in words, which apart from the merits of the subject, appear to me to be highly censurable & so much in excess of the occasion, that among a more civilized community, it would be impossible for them to contribute to the success of the cause which it is sought to advocate. Protestant Missions & Missions^s are spoken of in language most derogatory: your past plans of education are smiled at, as failures: & you are complimented on having incurred great expense & great effort, with^t obtaining any advance: you are quietly excused from taking any interest in this new Univer^y as being out of your sphere: Sierra Leone established for the very purpose of providing a Xn settlement is claimed quite as much for Mohammedans: and we – your Missionaries, past & present, including myself, – are spoken of as foreign teachers; & our influence as foreign: and this after Eng^d has made the place to provide this people a home & we have settled down among them with the highest & most self sacrificing motives.

I do not know at all how the project of an University founded by the people & subsidised by the Govern^t stands; I expect it is not so far a fact as Mr Blyden represents in the Negro: & most likely in a few months it will drop out of sight, but it will not be Mr Blyden's fault, nor Mr Hennessy's: it is spoken of as a fact & King Tom already taken: & it is to be started on the *most* wide basis possible: that is, it is to be in our estimation a Godless University.

Of course the establishment of such an University, under Government & Negro control on no special Xn basis but where Mahomet will be on the same level as your & my most dear & precious Saviour, who is God over all blessed for ever, would fill me & I think you also with much regret: but my object in calling your attention to it is (1) to claim that the idea of a West Af^n Univ^y does not belong to Mr Hennessy & Mr Blyden. I have no doubt it has been discussed at Salis^y Sq^{re} years ago, in Mr Milward's day for instance: but at all events my own letter, written about April 1871 entirely negatives the claim of these two men: (2) and to suggest that that letter did not incorrectly measure a want here & perhaps had not the attention the subject merited: at all events I have not lived to change my opinion yet and (3) seeing that public opinion of an unhealthy kind has been so greatly aroused, whether the Society sh^d not give the subject a still further consideration. I am for nothing but the most cautious prudent, God dependent advances: but I would advance, looking upward continually: I would so open Fourah Bay & announce it open, as to cut to the ground the plea of necessity for another College: I would for a long time to come keep in my own hands, if I were you, the higher Education of the Coast using Governors' names & all the rest of it for ornament & patronage: but you being at the base: & spending money freely on supplying teaching power, offer an attractive syllabus: with Xnty the pervading element. To perfect the Xnty of this people & spread it along the Coast: & save us from the blight of infidelity, money, in one aspect, is no object: & you ought I think to give serious thought how to secure what you have won. I have used the words 'money freely' & you have not got it: well, are you right in risking, as you have risked, by withdrawing so much the work here & giving so much to India: & then would not Mr — (St John's Divinity Hall Patron what is his name?) or some other who feels the importance of Education on a Xn as opposed to a Godless basis, very largely help?

Mr Blyden, of course, is labouring to feather his nest & to spread his mischievous politics: I expect under a new Governor he will be mild & draw in: but he will be sowing seeds & his seeds are ruinous to our work, whether here or in the interior: & simply because he is all for the exaltation of self & not for the crowning of our King. You ought, I submit, to advance, steadily, orderly, religiously to advance, & perhaps in the mercy of God, finding his game being spoiled, he might try his fortune in another line or in another place.

> Believe me, &c.,
> (sgd) H. Sierra Leone

2 *Henry Cheetham to Henry Wright* [C.A1/O.25e/44]

> Bishopscourt, S. Leone. April 9th 1873

My dear Brother,

... One word as to the race sentiment: a week's stay here would dissipate all serious thoughts & hope about the blessing of it: national feeling & so forth is not finding expression in the Negro but the Negro is spreading it on thick before the people are ready: as Quaker aptly told Blyden that if he wants to deliver the people he must go away for 40 years as Moses was sent: patriotism & national feeling etc are plants that grow with a nation's growth & here there is not a nation yet, only a collection of persons of diff^t tribes who heartily hate & distrust one another: & in the present condition of Soc^y to write about race sentiment is understood to mean by the common folk – be good haters– hate well – everybody else but yourself . . .

> Believe me, &c.,
> (sgd) H. Sierra Leone

(b) From Metcalfe Sunter, principal of Fourah Bay College

3 *Metcalfe Sunter to Henry Wright* [C.A1/O.202/17]

> Fourah Bay, March 8th 1873

My dear Mr Wright,

I enclose a copy of a letter from the Lord Bp: Sierra Leone, addressed to me with respect to the admission of other than Missionary Students into our College at Fourah Bay.

That I am in favour of such admission is, I think, well known: and altho by the recommendation of the Sub Comm^ee appt^d to confer with the Bp: on West Af^n affairs we, as it were, have the insertion of the very thin edge of a very small wedge, I am still hoping that the Parent Comm^ee will see their way clear to its opening on a still wider scale. When I take into consideration (1) that the large building we have here is insufficiently utilized, (2) that our Wesleyan friends are striving to get hold of the Native youth on the coast, (3) that numbers are sent to England at an early age, who could well be educated at home (at least up to a much higher standard than at present) & whose health .˙. would not be endangered by too long a stay, (4) when by a bigoted Roman Catholic Governor a few are taught to expect the endowment of an African University from the Imperial Exchequer the staff of wh must be purely Negro and that, as the Bishop says, it is to be a Godless one, (5) that by too long a stay in England, African youths imbibe notions which in great measure cause them to look down on their own people, & wh I have heard publicly animadverted on by the natives, (6) that it is very important that African youth should be brought under religious influence to a much greater extent than they are at present, & (lastly) that I conceive the time has come to warrant in some measure such a step – I would earnestly urge upon our Soc^y the still further consideration of the propriety of such a step in what I consider the right direction. . . .

I am, &c.,
(sgd) Metcalfe Sunter

4 *Metcalfe Sunter to Henry Wright* [C.A1/O.202/21]

Fourah Bay, May 7th 1873

My dear Mr Wright,

. . . The introduct^n of India & its Universities into the letters in 'Negro' is neither here nor there, it is not even a case in point for they forget that the Hindoo has just as good claims to Caucasian origin as we have ourselves – and also that they have existing evidence of a civilization & literature many hundred years before the name of Anglo-Saxon even appeared in History. . . .

I am, &c.,
(sgd) M. Sunter

5 *Metcalfe Sunter to E. Hutchinson, secretary, CMS* [C.A1/O.202/22]

Fourah Bay Institution, June 7th 1873

My dear Mr Hutchinson,

. . . You say in y^r last that you would be glad to know my views on the great educational question – for great it is in the eyes of our Native brethren . . . I can really and truly say that I am the Negro's friend, and prepared, if God wills it, to devote my life to the one great desire of my soul – to evangelize and elevate the whole of the African Race. And, if I have seemed at all to feel strongly it is simply that I feel that our friends have been acting in such a way as, most materially, will damage their own interest as a Race and still more so the interests of what they love to speak of as the West African Church. Let our friends seek rather after true spirituality: let them seek after Unity – Xtian Unity I mean – let them seek after that highest developement of Race feeling . . . instead of allowing *one* or *two designing* persons to lead them at will and they will then discover that they themselves have been really – I will not say wilfully – blind . . .

A great deal of mischief here has been done by Mr John Pope Henessey [sic] –

C.M.G. – during his twelve months' tenure of office. From the very first day, almost, of his arrival, he tacked himself on to – not tacked on to himself – Mr Blyden, who, as his dealings here attest, is not only a cunning man but also a Master of the Art of Intrigue: and to the day of his leaving the Colony, he simply, I believe, was led by that gentleman at will: this is a fact well known to the Natives here: and altho' they may not say it openly, yet there are those who have admitted as much to me. Mr Henessey [sic] instead of judging for himself accepted as gospel whatever his native friend chose to stuff him with: and I regret to say too evidently has been acting merely, in one or two matters at least, as the tool of more than one designing African. It has been his aim, ever since his first arrival here, to depreciate systematically, the European, especially the Protestant Missionary: and one thing is patent, that whatever his intentions may have been, he has succeeded during his long stay of *twelve months*, in doing more to excite a hostile feeling towards Englishmen in the minds of some Natives than any previous Governor has done during his term of office, whether long or short. I sincerely hope that Mr Gladstone will not send out any more red hot Papists to this colony . . .

. . . My counsel would be to develope Education in proportion as the funds of the College derived from direct payments of parents wd allow: let our friends pay for Educ^n & they will value it the more – At the same time I fully go in with the views wh are in favour of the opening of this Instit^n & am quite prepared to devote my previous experience as a practical educationist to this much to be desired end. . . .

I am, &c.,

(sgd) Metcalfe Sunter

6 *Metcalfe Sunter to E. Hutchinson* [C.A1/O.202/23]

Fourah Bay Institution, June 20th 1873.

My dear Mr Hutchinson,

. . . I feel anxious to know what conclusion you are going to, or have arrived at, with regard to the future of Fourah Bay . . .

June 21st 3 P.M.

I have written on foolscap what I have at present to say. I have not discussed the question of the throwing open of Fourah Bay so much as I have stated the result of my matured thought on the subject . . .

I am, &c.,

(sgd) Metcalfe Sunter

[Enclosure]

In these pages I make a few remarks on:

Education on the West Coast

. . . In the next place I pass on to offer a few remarks on higher education as it affects Fourah Bay & the Society's work on the Coast. The first question would to my mind be as to what is really req^d to meet the present requirements of the Coast.

In the first place, I think it is fair to say that the time has arrived when an education of a higher kind should be provided for the youth of the Coast. Complaints have often been raised here as to the effects of a few years stay in England on the young men of this Colony: one charge is that they come back puffed up & too proud almost to speak to their old acquaintances; a second is that in some cases the health is materially affected by a prolonged stay in England; thirdly & lastly, that there is as yet, Fourah Bay being closed, no place where such a higher education is imparted as would at least considerably shorten the period of their stay, supposing they still wished to go to England. I simply express here the feelings of natives with whom I have conversed and with whom in the three above particulars I agree. . . .

I maintain then, that an education of such a character should be placed within their reach, as will, altho' not as yet intended to do away with the necessity of visiting England, at least enable them, if they wish it, to shorten the period of their children's stay; and such an education might be afforded at a cost, which would guarantee a very great saving on their part, & enable the Soc^y, in lapse of time, to make such a building as Fourah Bay, almost self-supporting.

The time has not yet arrived, as yet, [sic] for the establishment of a University, unless 'White man's money' should not only establish it but also maintain it: the time has not yet arrived for the establishment of a College in affiliation with an European University: but the time has arrived, I think, when we may fairly begin to look forward in the direction of the latter & prepare for it . . .

I will, now, as briefly as I can, state my views as to the throwing open of F. Bay & the subjects necessary to be taught as far as I can judge.

(1) I recommend that the place should be as soon as possible thrown open so that an educat^n in advance of what has hitherto been given in our Grammar Schools etc, should be within the reach of all the inhabs of the Coast.

(2) That the distinctive religious & Miss^y character of the place should be preserved, as far as possible, and that all entering should be req^d to fall in with all rules & requirements of the place. On the other hand, if we could reach the N. chiefs it would be well for us to endeavour to induce them to send their sons for Education to this Institution.

(3) A Theological department must of necessity be maintained for the training of youths for missionary work.

(4) That the education afforded should be of such a character, as would be a sufficient preparation for the majority of the professions on the Coast, excepting such of course wh will always, more or less entail upon the Student the necessity of a visit to Europe.

(5) That in addition to the present subjects, we should afford such other instruct^n as would carry out the object proposed in No 4.

The subjects at present are as follows:

Latin, Greek & Hebrew; Mathematics; English Language & Literature; Mental & Moral Science; and other subjects Theological etc I need not mention here. To the above I would add:

(1) History, Anc^t & Modern, & Geography in the first parts of the course. Both are necessary subjects & ought to be taught.

(2) I think if French & German were taught, or Spanish, according to the Nature of Commercial relations on the Coast, it would be a decided advantage. French is almost as necessary, indeed, as English, considering how large a share of the trade they possess & how many we have here on the Coast.

(3) I should recommend that a Science Class be formed in which such an amount of scientific knowledge might be gained as would be req^d, the instruction given always keeping pace with requirements.

(4) A knowledge of Political Economy would not harm our friends; but on the contrary, would benefit them very much & make them a little more practical than they are.

(5) Our friends talk of *Law & Medicine*. Well, if any of our Legal or Medical friends here or both were disposed to be patriotic, they might volunteer their services: but, I must confess, at present, I cannot see my way to at all entertain their views on this subject, seeing that they, while capital theorists in their own way, are not yet very practical.

(6) I should lay great stress on the study of the English Language & Literature, Mathematics etc: both of which are only imperfectly taught: Classics we may fairly pass over as there will be no occasion for fear in that respect. Arabic might perhaps be fairly included in the curriculum of studies.

(6) That, with the exception of Native Assistants, the place should for some time yet be superintended by Europeans: at the same time every effort must be made to train Natives for all departments of such higher educational work, preparatory to the time, when in the nat^l course of things, they must be left to themselves.

(7) That an increased staff of teachers would, if a response sufficiently encouraging was made, be needed to carry out any scheme of Education on an extended basis.

(8) That if the experiment succeeded, then in due time, the $Inst^n$ should be affiliated, so that degrees might be obtained from some such University as that of London: & pending such arrangement that a kind of Certificate should be given of having passed thro' the College.

(9) That we should, in future, rather look for Volunteers for the Mission field from among such pay students rather than maintain the Grammar School foundations on the same basis as at present.

> ... I can only say that we cannot bound at once to the top of the tree, as our friends would have: rather let us take the trouble to climb to the top by slower degrees. We want something a little in advance of the present: but let us take one step at a time & see whether that will answer before we take another. If talking & scribbling would accomplish all desire, Africa would at once be far in advance of the *front* rank of civilization: but unfortunately deeds, not words must win the day & raise the Negro till as they themselves say, 'He towers to the height of Man'. We must, in conclusion, aim at the establishment of a system of Education on a firm & solid basis: such a one alone if followed up by corresponding act^{ns} on the part of themselves, will accomplish anything like results.

(2) *At CMS headquarters, Salisbury Square, London, E.C.*

7 *Henry Wright to Henry Cheetham* [C.A1/L.8/466]

[Copy]

Church Missionary House, Salisbury Sq., London E.C.
March 10 1873

My dear Brother,

... And now I must enter upon other matters. We have been much grieved to hear from many quarters of the evil influence that the acting administrator & Mr Blyden have been exerting on the colony, in making such evil use of the race feeling. We should, I think, agree that the feeling in itself is not only natural but a hopeful sign. It is one doubtless that may readily be turned to bad account & employed by evil disposed & self interested persons to evil ends, but at the same time, I cannot resist the conviction that it is one which kindly met & properly guided & above all sanctified by the Holy Spirit may have good results in stimulating the Christian negroes to more earnest efforts on behalf of their own unenlightened fellow-country-men.

Just now, however, it is very plain that it is being turned to bad account – so that the information that you & others have given us has led us to the conviction that it is important at once to review the state of things in the Colony & try & act upon some of the suggestions that were made by you when you were with us. With this view the Sub Committee appointed to confer with yourself has been called again into activity. We have already had one meeting, & although we have not yet arrived at any definite conclusions (except on one point) I should like to shadow out what we are thinking of, that we may have the benefits of your thoughts upon it.

1 We are disposed to recommend that the Fourah Bay Institution should be made, as you suggested, more of a University, i.e. that a higher & wider education should be given in it, & its doors thrown open to any well recommended Xtian Africans who may wish to enter it & are willing to pay.

With this object our idea is that we ought to have as its Principal as good a University man as we can possibly get – & under him a Vice Principal (Mr Sunter) & native Professors – of whom H. Johnson might be a chief one – We think this arrang^t would be likely to satisfy all that is legitimate in the cry for a University – & prevent the likelihood of such an Institution being established in godless hands; though we have very little idea that Mr Blyden's university scheme is likely to be anywhere but on paper. . . .

. . . the one point we have decided upon is to request Mr J. Johnson to come over to England & see the Committee. We consulted with Mr Oldham & Mr Hamilton & they both agreed with us in the opinion that no step would be better calculated to remove the evil impressions & wrong bias that he has received from his association with Mr Blyden & the influence of Mr Pope Hennesey [sic] & we trust it will meet with your approval also, & effect, with God's blessing, the good we hope. . . .

Believe me, &c.,

(sgd) Henry Wright

8 *Henry Wright to Henry Cheetham* [C.A1/L.8/503]

[Copy]

The Heath, Hampstead, N.W. April 5 1873

My dear Brother,

. . . Yours of March 13th on the West African University is quite as if you had anticipated what was likely to occupy our thoughts – & confirms our expectation that in the main you will cordially welcome our suggestions which indeed are little more than an attempt at carrying out your own to the Committee. . .

Believe me, &c.,

(sgd) Henry Wright

9 *Committee minutes*

i General Committee, November 10 1873 [Vol. 40, f. 700]

. . .

Presented and read Report of Sierra Leone Sub Comm^{ee} respecting the subsidy to the Native Pastorate, the funds raised by the CMS Auxiliary, an alteration in the management of the School and the regulations to be proposed for the future admission of general pupils to the Fourah Bay Institution . . .

Resolved . . .

   3 That the remainder of the Report [including the proposals about Fourah Bay] be forwarded to Sierra Leone for consideration by the Mission Conference, the Native Church Council and the CMS Auxiliary there.

ii Committee of Correspondence, July 20 1875 [Vol. 42, f. 91]

West Africa Mission

The Secretaries stated that the subject of the affiliation of Fourah Bay College with some English University whereby such of the students as were qualified for it might have the advantage of a competitive examination and the opportunity of obtaining degrees had been for some time under consideration in connection with the recommendation of the Sierra Leone Sub Committee to throw open the Fourah Bay College and had been warmly advocated by friends of the Society in Africa. That the recent affiliation of Codrington College, Barbadoes [sic] with the University of Durham afforded a precedent which might be followed in the case of Fourah Bay. . . .

Resolved That it is advisable to give the students of the Fourah Bay College the opportunity of being subjected to a competitive examination and of taking degrees and that steps be taken with this object for affiliating the College with the University of Durham upon the same conditions as had been agreed upon in the case of Codrington College, Barbadoes [sic].

Referred to Minutes of the Committee of Nov. 10th 1873 and Report of Sierra Leone Sub Committee approving certain 'regulations to give effect to the Committee's determination to open the Fourah Bay College'.

The Secretaries read the said regulations with certain modifications which it was proposed to introduce.

Resolved That the modified regulations as read be adopted as the regulations for the present of the Fourah Bay College.

Regulations of the Fourah Bay College

The Sub Committee also considered Regulations to give effect to the Committee's determination to open the Fourah Bay College, and recommended the following for adoption by the Committee:

   1 That the Fourah Bay College be open to any Student who can bring satisfactory testimony of his moral character, and pass the Matriculation Examination.

   2 That the ordinary curriculum of the College shall include instruction in the Holy Scriptures and the Evidences for the Christian religion; Latin, Greek, Hebrew, Arabic and English history and Geography, Comparative Philology, Moral Philosophy, the principles of Political Economy, Logic, Mathematics, Music, and such branches of Natural Science as may be found expedient and practicable.

N.B. The subjects taken up by each Student shall depend on their previous training, their capacity for receiving instruction, and their proposed future calling. Instruction shall also be given if required, in French and German, on payment of an extra Fee.

   3 That no more Free Students be received into the College, but that two Scholarships be given every year, of the value of £40 each, to be held for three years, or, in the event of the Student being received for special training in Theology, for four

years. These Scholarships are liable to be forfeited in case of serious misconduct or of failure of health.

4 That the Scholarships be given to the most successful candidates at an Examination held yearly at the College by the College authorities on the following conditions:

(a) That all candidates bring satisfactory testimony from three persons, one of whom must be a Clergyman, and the remaining two either Clergymen, Ministers, or Church Members of some Protestant denomination, as to their moral and religious character, giving promise thereby of future usefulness in the service of Christ. In the case of candidates from the Grammar School, one of the testimonials must be from the Master.

(b) That no candidate shall be entitled to receive a Scholarship, unless the Examiners be satisfied he comes up to the required standard of attainments.

5 That Students intended for Holy Orders shall receive one year's special training in Theology.

6 That it shall be open to Catechists and Teachers who have earned for themselves a good degree in their respective callings, and are recommended by the Conference for Holy Orders, to avail themselves of this special training in Theology, in which case the Church Missionary Committee will grant for one year the sum of £50.

7 An certificate shall be given at the close of their course to all Students who shall have succeeded in passing the final Examination, stating in what class they have passed.

8 That no Student be admitted under the age of 17 years; his application for admission to be accompanied, where obtainable, by his baptismal certificate.

9 That the following be the scale of fees:

For Instruction, per Term, £5; per annum £15.

For Board and Lodging, £8; per annum £24.

10 That Students be at liberty to obtain board and lodging outside the College – provided that they conform in all other respects to the College discipline. In every case, the lodgings selected must have the sanction of the Principal.

Church Missionary House

July, 1875

iii General Committee, July 10 1876 [Vol. 42, f. 689]

Referred to Minutes of Committee of July 20, 1875 resolving that application be made to the Durham University for the affiliation of Fourah Bay with that University.

Read letter from the Rev. Thos Thornton Registrar of the Durham University dated University College Durham June 13th stating that at the meeting of the Convocation of May 16th the proposition to affiliate the Fourah Bay College, Sierra Leone, was passed unanimously.

Resolved   That the acknowledgements of the Society be given to the authorities of Durham University for this token of interest in the work of the Society.

D. THE ARRANGEMENT WITH DURHAM

1 *The terms of affiliation*

Durham University regulations: Title XI[1]

Of the affiliation of Codrington College, Barbados, and Fourah Bay College, Sierra Leone, to the University.

[1] Durham University, *The Durham University Calendar, with almanack, MDCCCLXXVII* (Durham, 1877) xlvi-xlvii.

1 Students of Codrington College, Barbados, and Fourah Bay College, Sierra Leone, may have their names placed on the Register of the University as Matriculated Students of the same, provided that the Principal of their College, or other person authorised to act in his behalf, shall have certified to the Warden that they have passed an examination similar to that required for the admission of Students, in the several faculties, in the University of Durham; and the aforesaid Colleges shall be accounted Colleges of the University of Durham.

2 Students of the affiliated Colleges, having been so Matriculated, shall be admissible to the Exercises and Public Examinations required for proceeding to Degrees, Licences, and Academical ranks in the several Faculties, provided that they shall have forwarded to the Warden certificates of having fulfilled the same conditions as to residence, attendance at lectures, and conformity to discipline, in their own College, as are required from other Students of the University so admissible, terms of residence being counted from the time of passing the Admission Examination of their own College.

3 The principals of the said Colleges shall forward to the Senior Proctor lists of Students of their respective Colleges who are Candidates for any examinations, together with the certificates required, in time for them to be received at Durham four weeks at least (and, in the case of candidates for Honours, six weeks at least) before the commencement of the examinations at Durham. The examination papers shall be sent to the Principals of the Colleges, in sealed packets, by the last mails that leave England previously to the commencement of the examination at Durham. The papers so sent shall be set to the candidates as soon as possible after their arrival, and the answers to them returned, unread, as soon as possible after the conclusion of the examination, to the Senior Proctor (who shall transmit them to the Examiners), together with a Certificate signed by the Principal of each College, or the person acting in his behalf, that the examination has been duly conducted, and the above-named conditions complied with.

4 The Examiners, after examining the papers, shall issue and publish in the usual manner supplemental lists of those who have passed the examination, and of those who have been adjudged worthy of honours; which lists shall be sent by the Registrar without delay to the respective Principals of the Colleges; and one combined list of all who have passed the examination, in England, Barbados, and Sierra Leone, shall be inserted in the next issue of the 'University Calendar'.

5 All prescribed conditions having been fulfilled, graces for Degrees, Licences or Academical ranks, shall be prayed in Convocation, in the usual manner, in behalf of Students of the affiliated Colleges; and Certificates of such graces having been granted shall be forwarded by the Registrar to the respective Principals of the Colleges, after the receipt of which the Degrees, Licences, or Academical ranks for which graces have been granted may be conferred by their Lordships the Bishops of the dioceses in which the affiliated Colleges are respectively situated, as Visitors of the same, acting under commission from the Warden.

6 The Warden and Senate shall have power to determine the fees payable by the Students of the affiliated Colleges for admission to examinations, and to Degrees, Licences, and Academical ranks; and to frame, from time to time, such further Regulations as may be deemed by them expedient.

7 The above arrangements may be terminated at any time either by the University or by the authorities of each affiliated College on notice of six months at least being given beforehand.

2 *The courses of study prescribed for the ordinary B.A. degree and the licence in theology at the time of affiliation.*

Subjects of examination, 1877[1]

For students in arts – First year

October, 1877

For students not Candidates for Honours

Herod., i, ii, iii
Virgil, i–vi
Gospels of St Mark and St John in the Greek
Greek Grammar
Latin Grammar
Ancient History:
    That contained in the first three books of Herodotus
English History:
    History of England to the Conquest
Scripture History:
    Joshua, Judges, Ruth, 1 and 2 Samuel
Arithmetic
Euclid i, ii, or Logic
Latin Composition

Final examination at the end of Easter Term, 1877,

and at the end of Michaelmas Term, 1877

For an ordinary degree

Herodotus, i, ii, iii
Virgil, Aeneid, i–vi
Gospel of St John and the Acts
Greek Grammar
Latin Grammar
Paley:
    Evidences of Christianity
    Natural Theology, omitting chapters xix–xxii
Ancient History:
    That contained in the first three books of Herodotus
Latin Composition (Optional)
Any two of the following subjects:
    1 Mechanics
    2 English History:
        History of England to the Conquest
    3 Euclid, i–iv
    4 Logic
    5 French:

[1] Durham University, *The Durham University Calendar, with almanack, MDCCCLXXVII* (Durham, 1877) 13–5, 21–2.

Guizot's 'Histoire de la Révolution d'Angleterre', Part II
Translation from English into French
Or German:
Schiller's 'Geschichte des dreiszigjahrigen Kriegs', Part I and II
Goethe's 'Tasso'

For Students in Theology
At the end of the first year
October, 1877

Cicero, De Officiis, Books i and ii
The Gospels of St Mark and St John, and the Acts of the Apostles, in Greek
The Epistles to the Hebrews and Philippians, in Greek
Paley's Evidences
Scripture History
Euclid, i, ii, or Butler's Sermons i, ii, iii, with Preface, and Analogy Part I

For a Licence in Theology
June, 1877

The Gospel of St Mark and St John, and the Acts of the Apostles, in Greek
The Epistles to the Thessalonians, Ephesians, Philippians, Colossians, Philemon,
Timothy, Titus, Hebrews, in Greek
The Ecclesiastical History of the first four Centuries
The History of the Church of England
The Liturgy and Thirty-nine Articles of the Church of England
Criticism and Interpretation of the New Testament

II. THE EDUCATION RESOLUTIONS OF THE CONFERENCE OF AFRICANS OF BRITISH WEST AFRICA, 1920

NATIONAL CONGRESS OF BRITISH WEST AFRICA

*Resolutions of the Conference of Africans of British West Africa
Held at Accra, Gold Coast, from 11th to 29th March, 1920*
. . .
Education with particular reference to a West African University

Resolutions

1 That this Conference is of the opinion that the system of Education best suited to the needs and conditions of the various British West African peoples under British influence is one which, whilst enabling the students to attain the highest possible proficiency in the many departments of learning, will least interfere with the development by the student of a proper spirit of reverence for indigenous institutions and modes of life not opposed to equity and good conscience.

2 That in the opinion of this Conference the time has come to found a British West African University on such lines as would preserve in the students a sense of African Nationality, and therefore recommends that all existing Secondary Schools throughout West Africa, or those about to be formed, should promote a course of training that shall best attain the end in view.

3 That with this object in view it recommends that the different Boards of Education of each Colony should admit on them, African and other Educationists capable of contributing practical suggestions, and that in the submission of such suggestions they be guided by the experience of such communities as Japan which have encountered similar problems to that of West African Communities.

4 That besides existing Secondary Schools the Conference recommends each section of it to promote a scheme in each Colony whereby sound Secondary Education on national lines supported by the people may be promoted, and which shall form a further nucleus for the formation of the proposed British West African University.

5 That compulsory Education throughout the British West African Colonies be introduced by law, and that the standard of both the Primary and the Secondary Schools be uniformly raised to meet the Standard of the University.

6 That the Education Schemes of the Governments of the several British West African Dependencies be considered and incorporated in the Scheme and given as far as practicable a more national tone by co-operation between the Educationists controlling the working of the Scheme and such experienced educated Africans capable of suggesting lines of African National evolution.

7 That each British West African Colony promote a National Educational Fund so as to ensure the development of a national Educational Scheme, which fund, when the Scheme is in operation, may be supplemented by Government subsidies.

III. PRECURSORS OF ASQUITH

To illuminate the evolution of policy that culminated in the Asquith report, we reproduce in full below the hitherto unpublished texts of the Currie and Channon reports (Nos 1 and 3). We also quote at length from the Channon memorandum (No 2), for this was a seminal document of unusual importance. It supplied all the essential ideas that were to give a new momentum and a new direction to British policy. And it has the further interest, derived from its informal character, of revealing the considerations which inspired them. It contains a perceptive diagnosis of the current defects in colonial higher education; and it is especially frank about the inhibiting influence of events in India.

1 THE CURRIE REPORT, DECEMBER 1933

A.C.E.C. 44/33

Report of the Sub-Committee appointed to consider the
educational policy underlying paragraph 19 of the
Report of the Conference of Directors of Education of
Kenya, Tanganyika, Uganda and Zanzibar, held at
Zanzibar in June, 1932.[1]

Paragraph 19

'Standard for Admission to Makerere College

The Directors noted with satisfaction that it is intended to start at Makerere in January 1933 a course leading to Matriculation by means of the University of London's School Examination. It was suggested that a syllabus should be drawn up covering the last five years of this matriculation course, and that the first two years of this syllabus should be undertaken in Secondary Schools, and the last three years at Makerere. As soon as a sufficient number of students have reached the stage of entering for the intermediate Arts Examination of London University, the Secondary Schools should undertake the whole matriculation course, and matriculation should become the standard for entry to Makerere.'

I   In examining the question of University Education for Africans, we have considered it necessary to keep in mind the following considerations:

(a) The educational policy approved by the Secretary of State and followed in the various African territories is based upon the principle that the education provided must be of such a character as to encourage the development of the natural aptitudes of the people concerned to the fullest possible extent, having regard to specific background and needs of the African environment.

(b) The number of African Secondary Schools is increasing, and the standard of their attainment has improved and is continuing to improve. The schools now turn out annually a continually augmenting number of pupils, not only desirous but capable of continuing their studies up to a final University standard.

(c) Africans, more especially from the West Coast territories, are increasingly leaving their own country in order to undertake undergraduate courses at Universities in Europe and America. It is not disputed that most of these Africans do in fact follow those courses with profit and success.

(d) Women's education is retarded by the understandable reluctance of women to proceed overseas. Until there is in Africa provision for University Education in some form or other, it will only be very rarely that a woman will proceed beyond the Secondary stage.

(e) With the development of more and more reliable standards in African educational institutions, there is an undoubted tendency gradually to eliminate external tests in favour of local ones. This tendency arises not only from the fact that external tests are unnecessary where local standards exist and can be relied upon, but also from the growing conviction that external European tests, devised, as they all are in

[1] For the membership of the sub-committee, see p. 427 ref. 7.

the main, to test the attainments of pupils from a European environment, exert an actually harmful influence upon the development of indigenous education of the type best adapted to, and indeed urgently called for to meet local needs and in order to build up a true and genuine African culture. Pupils in many African secondary schools are in fact now taking courses which have been designed primarily with reference not to African, but to English conditions. In this connection, the paragraph remitted to us from the Report of the Conference at Zanzibar is of course illuminating; it shows in the most striking way how local schemes of education may be abandoned at the lure of an extraneous course leading to a degree.

(f) At the moment there are in tropical Africa three Government institutions which aim at providing educational facilities up to roughly a University standard, viz. Achimota in the Gold Coast, Yaba in Nigeria, and Makerere in Uganda. Of these three institutions, Achimota is possibly the furthest advanced. The Gordon College at Khartoum must additionally be borne in mind: here the instruction in engineering and medicine approximates closely to the standard of a European University (see for example, the Report on the Khartoum Medical School made in 1932 by the visiting Commission appointed by the Governor-General).

Besides these Government institutions Fourah Bay College in Sierra Leone, a missionary institution aided by Government, has for many years prepared pupils for the Durham B.A. Degree and has also a post-graduate course for the Educational Diploma.

II The present position, as we see it, is that, while the Colleges at Achimota, Makerere, Yaba and Khartoum do not yet as a whole approach a real University standard, inevitably and of their own momentum they tend towards this final point. At the same time the African thirst for higher education remains unabated; if this is not satisfied at home it can only lead to an increasing efflux of undergraduate African students towards the Universities of Europe and America. The social and intellectual undesirability of this procedure in the African's own interest needs no labouring here. But it does perhaps require some emphasis that under present conditions University education is practically debarred to all Africans, no matter what their ability unless they are able to raise the comparatively large sums needed to meet the cost of travel and University tuition and residence abroad. Moreover, the courses standard in European Universities are naturally enough designed with no regard whatever to the special needs and social and intellectual background of African students: they are seldom, therefore, anything like as helpful to them as they might be. There is something grotesque, for example, in the fact that an African wishing for higher training in agriculture should have to seek it in an English University situated in, and very often wholly concerned with the agriculture of, a non-tropical country.

III Quite apart from these educational grounds, the present position appears to us to be open to grave objections from the broad general point of view of British prestige and administrative efficiency. There is reason to think that the absence of any African institutions for adequate higher training already cripples to some extent the recruitment of properly trained natives for higher posts where they are wanted for Government and private service and in Native Administrations and Judicial systems. It seems indefensible, for example, that the Gordon College should, at all events till very recently, have had to rely substantially upon the American University at Beyrut for the advanced training of natives needed for its own staffing. From another, and slightly different point of view it appears equally indefensible that intelligent Africans from the Gold Coast should most easily obtain further training of a University type by taking advantage of American bounty and American institutions. On the political difficulties and the economic disabilities inherent in such a position continuing, it is not necessary to enlarge.

IV   There is a grave danger, as we see it, of the Africans' zeal for education being neglected and ignored by the Government to whom they ought to be able to look for its reasonable satisfaction. There appears no prospect – nor is it in any event a prospect that can in the least be wished or desired – that the present vehement demand for higher education will slacken off. It follows then, that, if that demand is not adequately met by a natural development in Africa itself under the wise control, which only British Government and experience can afford, it will spend itself in all sorts of individual and group educational enterprises, which can hardly fail to be eccentric, often self-defeating and sterile, and attended by social and political phenomena harmful alike to the prestige of this country and the true well-being of the Africans.

V   Our conclusion upon these considerations is that the only right policy for the Government is to think out ahead a scheme of developing selected institutions in Africa up to a real University standard, and that this policy, as soon as decided upon, should be publicly announced as officially adopted. We are of opinion that such a University must almost necessarily proceed through the same stages by which the University Colleges in England (e.g. Birmingham, Leeds, Manchester, Liverpool, Reading) have gained University rank. This will involve any institution established being for a time dependent on some English University for the final examination necessary for the granting of degrees. It is suggested that, as the African students already have close relation with London University, and consider the degrees granted by London as the hall-mark they require, it might in the first instance be wise to approach London University, and find out whether it would be willing to make such modifications of its requirements as would suit the needs of Africa.

We envisage a stage when the African institutions in question would be recognised schools of the University of London, their teachers being recognised teachers, and working for the London internal degree. Careful negotiations with the University would no doubt be necessary, in order to obtain an arrangement which might fully recommend itself, but we are of the opinion that these ought to be undertaken.

VI   In making any such announcement, we regard it as of the highest importance to avoid any action that might excite African suspicion. We think it should be made clear at the outset that the adoption of such a scheme does not involve the Government putting any hindrance whatever in the way of any Africans who might still determine to proceed to Europe for University training, though no doubt (in such a case) the Government might reasonably decline to grant any financial assistance. It should be emphasised too that nothing in the scheme is meant in the slightest to discourage post-graduate students from proceeding overseas: on the contrary the proposals would envisage a steadily increased stream of such students directed upon Europe from the new African Universities, though at a riper age, and with a previous training better calculated to enable them to take advantage of European facilities than is the case at present. The immediately important point is that largely increased and improved facilities at infinitely lower cost would be made available to young Africans in their home country. Above all, it would be necessary to clear the native mind of any suspicion that the African Universities were a sham, designed merely to side-track native ambitions. This can only be effectively demonstrated in our view by a Government declaration that the degrees and diplomas granted by such Universities would rank equally with those of extra-African Universities in respect of Government employment, and by the full and continuous implementing of that declaration in administrative practice.

VII We are of the opinion that the gradual but publicly forecasted development of certain selected African institutions towards University status should be aided by assistance and advice of the British Universities and the Board of Education. The possibility of seconding teachers from British Universities, officers of the Board of Education or of Local Education Authorities, for periods of service in African University Colleges requires careful exploration; we are aware that there are many difficulties in the way, for example with regard to pensions and remuneration, but we think that the importance of the end in view makes it necessary for these to be overcome at least in some measure. Periodic inspection through overseas delegations in part composed of British University teachers and Educational officials appears to us to offer a valuable means of securing both that the Colleges develop upon the best lines, and that they adopt from the beginning a good and sufficient examination standard. It would of course be necessary to secure that the Universities and professional authorities concerned fully realised the African situation, so that such delegations did not function in any stereotyped or narrowly academic way, but so as to encourage to the full the free and fruitful development of all local possibilities to meet all worthy local needs. In the actual degree examinations, a combination of local and external examiners might well be found the best machinery, both for securing confidence in the results and consultative advice for the African University staffs.

VIII We are of the opinion that the claims of African women to University education ought to receive equal attention with those of the men. But we are aware – and some of our witnesses were particularly emphatic on this point – that the question is one of considerable though of varying local difficulty. We think, therefore, that in dealing with this particular phase of the problem, it is of the highest possible importance that no action be taken except with the closest possible co-operation and advice of the African communities concerned.

IX It is neither possible nor desirable at this stage to attempt any precise forecast of the number or range of the University institutions which Africa may require during the coming years. It appears that Achimota, Yaba, Makerere, and possibly the Gordon College, should be able to meet all the needs of their particular territories at present. These institutions might welcome the attendance of students from other parts of Africa, provided that suitable financial arrangements were made.

A general and a comprehensive view of education of university grade would have to take account of the position and contribution of Fourah Bay College.

X As regards the facilities to be provided in each University College, we are of opinion that medicine, engineering, agriculture, veterinary work, commerce and the applied sciences generally, have special claims for consideration together with law.

In making this suggestion, we do not ignore the importance of more purely academic studies. But we feel that, having regard to the situation in Africa as it exists today, the first essential is to attempt to secure for the country that reasonable degree of social and economic security, without which there can be no solid or lasting basis for any real cultural life. In the belief that the securing of such a basis is the first and essential step towards such a life, we do not hesitate to assign priority to these branches of study. But in addition the African University would supply courses leading up to a general degree and including the study of education, which would entitle the graduate to recognition by the appropriate African authorities as a trained certificated teacher. It is hardly necessary to say that it is undesirable to encourage the admission to any particular faculty in any one year of students in greater numbers than the needs and absorptive capacity of the various sources and professions in the territories served by the College seem to require.

XI In order to realise the aim of providing in Africa itself institutions at which Africans will have the opportunity of obtaining education equal in quality to that provided in European universities, co-ordination of effort between different territories is in our view indispensable. It is encouraging in this connexion that, in East Africa, Kenya and Tanganyika are looking definitely to Makerere to meet the need in higher education of the whole East African area. In West Africa similarly it is desirable that there should be every possible co-operation between the different areas in providing university education. It is doubtful whether any single territory will, within measurable time, be in a financial position to provide first-class facilities in every department of university education. Should an attempt be made to cover the whole field in each territory, it will be difficult to reach and maintain the desired standards in all departments. Only by co-ordination of effort can West Africa obtain the best university education that it is possible to provide. It is desirable therefore that from the first beginnings the problem of university education in West Africa should be envisaged as a whole, that there should be consultation between the different West African governments in regard to its development and that the Secretary of State should examine carefully all proposals for the extension of existing institutions in their relation to the largest good of West Africa as a whole.

XII In making this Report, we have abstained from any consideration of the financial issues involved. No doubt the policy advocated herein must involve considerable expenditure, in spite of the fact that in some cases (for example, those of natives who are now in a position to proceed overseas for graduate courses) tuition fees might be expected. And the question of finance must not be viewed from any narrow and exclusively educational angle; broadly envisaged, it is necessary to bring into the balance the important consideration that a system of higher education, which enables English officials to be largely replaced by natives, is a system which will effect a saving on the annual budget for Civil Service salaries and allowances. But finance apart, and in any case, we cannot too strongly emphasise our conviction that the present situation is one which cannot continue without danger, and which must be faced at all costs, if years of increasing strain and embarrassment and the growing alienation of enlightened African opinion are to be avoided. We believe that the passion of the African for higher education, properly guided, may prove a boon to the economic, social and cultural development of the country, and an advantage, support and ornament to British rule. Neglected it must create social and political confusion.

XIII We wish to record our gratitude to the gentlemen whose names follow for their kindness in meeting the Sub-Committee and giving us the benefit of their views and experience.

Sir Edgar Bonham Carter, K.C.M.G., C.I.E., former Legal Secretary to Sudan Government, later Judicial Adviser in Iraq.
The Rev. J. Horstead, Principal of Fourah Bay College, Sierra Leone.
Mr. S. J. Hogben of the Nigeria Education Department.
Mr Ladipo Solanke, Solicitor, and a number of African graduates and students at present studying in this country.

We are additionally under obligation to various Universities, other institutions and persons for supplying us with valuable information.

[Circulated to members of the ACEC, 14 December 1933.]

2 THE CHANNON MEMORANDUM, 1940

CONFIDENTIAL

Some observations on the development of Higher Education in the Colonies

1 A visit to Malaya, considerable discussion with the Vice-Chancellor of the University of Hong Kong regarding the problems of that University, a few hours spent at University College, Colombo, attendance at meetings of the Advisory Committee on Education in the Colonies and the reading of various reports represent my limited experiences of Colonial Education. These experiences leave me perplexed about many things, and in order to clear my own mind, I have thought it worth while to piece together my thoughts on the various problems to see if they would fit together to give a composite whole, or if any of them were in conflict with each other. I begin by reviewing what seem to me to be current thought and practice in Higher Education in the Colonies, and try to point out what seem to be the weaknesses; later suggestions regarding future policy are made.

2 In the first place, the attitude of mind often found in government and commercial circles regarding university development in the Colonies appears to be a somewhat reluctant recognition that universities must ultimately be created; but this is usually combined with a hope that the day of achievement may be postponed for as long as possible. There is, in fact, a genuine fear of the political and economic consequences of the production of a highly educated class among the native populations, and in this connection the example of India is usually and understandably quoted.

While the fears of the ill-effects of the possible mass production of so-called university men by colonial universities are understandable, I believe them to be largely groundless, for they are based on a misconception. They arise from a failure to realize that the difficulties in the past have arisen because the fundamental principles underlying the conception of university education have not been adequately appreciated. A university should not be, as it has so often and dangerously been, a mass production vocational machine through which are passed, regardless of their future livelihoods, students of indifferent mental calibre but of great capacity for memorising facts; it should be a place where carefully chosen young people of adequate mental attainments are fitted to take their places in the different professions, but at the same time are given the outlook necessary for them to play their part as citizens in the much wider sense. Failure to appreciate this elementary principle inevitably gives rise to political fears, and institutions of university type are then established only when it is imperative to produce men vocationally trained for some particular type of government post. Very rapidly entry to the institution comes to be regarded as entry to government service; there follows the pressure for more admissions and, later, the discontent of those who, because of lack of vacancies, fail to obtain the posts which the rapidly established tradition has led them to expect. Even if the institution was conceived at the start on a more enlightened basis, in the shortest of time it becomes a vocational training centre and little else. Once this idea of its functions has arisen, there is little or no hope of recovery; the university institution exists in no more than name, for the real justification for its existence has been forgotten. The very danger which it was sought to avoid has been brought into being.

3   The absence of a realisation of the true value of properly conceived and developed university education, is necessarily reflected in many ways, all of which contribute to impeding rather than helping its progress. Firstly, the financial policy is a stringent one in which the apparent material gains in the output of professionally trained men and women are balanced against the expenditure involved. Since any university institution is necessarily costly, the belief that university institutions are undesirable is further strengthened. Thus we frequently hear comparisons made between the cost per head of elementary, secondary and university education. The much greater cost of giving a child a secondary as compared with an elementary education is often stressed, and the stress does not always seem concerned with the financial aspect alone; it sometimes has its root in the doubt as to whether this secondary education is really desirable; the fact that the value of an article is usually reflected in its price tends to be overlooked. The anticipated dangers of university education being even greater, the financial aspects of university development are yet more brought to the front; for instance, on a number of occasions in Malaya my attention was drawn to what was considered the excessively high cost of the production in Singapore of a doctor, dentist or teacher, and the comparative cheapness of sending a relatively few selected students for training in England was often emphasised; that there could be any gain to the country other than that resulting from professional attainment was rarely contemplated.

4   Secondly, the importance of research work in university institutions is not understood. Research is regarded as a luxury, unjustifiably expensive both in time and money, unless it be directed to the solution of a problem, the results of which are of immediate practical application. This attitude towards research provides yet another factor calculated to prevent the university from achieving its purpose. Like the wider results of university education on the people as a whole, results of academic research cannot be materially assessed and therefore research is given but slight moral or financial encouragement. It is not realised that immediate public utility is not, and cannot be the standard by which universities measure the value of researches conducted within them, nor is the fact understood that teaching in any university institution becomes sterile, unless the inspiration of the teacher is maintained by some form or other of original investigation. . . .

5 Thirdly, at least in Malaya, the scope of the duties of members of the academic staffs is too narrowly defined. In reference to the staff of Raffles College I often heard such statements as 'those people have too little to do'. Further, the one section of the Malayan Report with which our secretary disagreed was that in which proposals were made to try to provide intellectual stimulation for the members of the staff by changes in the practice regarding leave and the provision of substitutes; he regarded such a proposal as impossible, because it would result in the staff of Raffles College receiving treatment different from that of government officers. This attitude of a man of considerable seniority in the Malayan Civil Service is indicative of Malayan administrative opinion as a whole.

Every one of these points, all of which have a cumulative effect in impeding the wise and fruitful development of Higher Education, has its origin in the real concern which is felt as to the wisdom of providing university education at all, and the failure to realise that a university can serve any purpose other than that of a centre for vocational training.

6 There is, in addition, a further problem which is only indirectly concerned with the matters just discussed, namely the difficulty of recruiting adequate staffs for colonial university institutions. It is unnecessary to dwell on the reasons why colonial universities do not attract the best men. Men of 45 years or more who have achieved distinction in their own subjects are by this time deeply committed to their universities, learned societies and other bodies, and they are too old. The able young men of an age from 25 onwards who have hopes of achieving academic distinction are understandably unwilling to surrender this hope by leaving the first class facilities available in this country and by losing all contact with their fellow workers in their own subjects on whom they must depend in part for help in their advancement.

As a result, the men who are appointed to posts in colonial universities often have neither the outlook nor the experience necessary for the carrying out of their work. There are, of course, exceptions to be found in occasional men who possess either the spirit of adventure or something of the missionary spirit which is most frequently found among members of the medical profession. Speaking generally, however, the men appointed are relatively young graduates of our universities; they have perhaps obtained a Ph.D. degree after pursuing two or three years of post graduate study and during this time they will have carried out a certain amount of lecturing, and in science subjects, of laboratory teaching, while some few will be men of more experience. They are, however, as a body ill-equipped for the work which will fall to them. Amid the novelty of their new environment they spend the first two or three enthusiastic years partly in making changes in their departments, but mainly in learning the subject matter which they have to teach and in building up their lecture courses. During this time the thought may or may not occur to them that research is part of their job. Here an obstacle arises however, for while they may have carried out a piece of research under the direction of the professor of their own university, they are usually insufficiently mature to initiate independent research. Combined with the further difficulty that the facilities to which they were accustomed in this country are not available this soon leads to the importance of research being forgotten and there follows the defensive attitude that it is impossible to carry on research because there are inadequate facilities. . . .

Admittedly the professor in a colonial university has many difficulties to face. He has almost certainly no post graduate students who in these days play such a big part in research in the western world. Because of the poor standard of the undergraduate student and perhaps of a limited staff, he may have to devote more time to teaching activities than is usual in this country. His desire that his students shall pass their examinations may lead to too great an emphasis being laid on teaching and almost inevitably to the adoption of too narrow a basis of instruction. Increasingly teaching dominates his life, and the other functions of the university fade into oblivion. . . .

7   Leaving aside the questions of teaching and research there is an equally important aspect of the work of the staff to consider. If we are to develop universities in the colonies, their vital objective at this stage must not be the production of large numbers of men and women with no more than a highly specialised technical knowledge; it should be the production of smaller numbers who, while they must be adequately prepared for their future professional livelihoods, must go further and be prepared for wider service.

The young native graduate has within his grasp the priceless opportunity of leading his people to a full realisation of their civic and social responsibilities and to a wise development of the material and cultural resources of their country. But technical knowledge alone will not equip him for this. He himself needs guidance in the development of his own character. His facile learning must be given depth and breadth, his personal and racial interests must be led along paths of national service and responsibility and he must be given integrity of purpose. His natural guides are the staff of his university, who should be available both within and without the classroom or laboratory. This staff can only help him if it is adequate both in numbers and in outlook, for this aspect of the work demands men of high quality and breadth of vision. It is an outlook which can only be obtained if the members of the staff have served in a university in this country long enough to have acquired an intimate knowledge of the aims and ideals of university education, and some idea as to the approaches necessary for its ordered development and administration. Such an appreciation cannot be possessed by young men leaving their universities before they have held for a sufficient period posts of some responsibility in them.

Thus from whatever point of view we regard the development of our colonial university institutions, the importance of an adequate staff appears overwhelming. Yet it has to be confessed that with the exception of the relatively few whose mental make up differs greatly from the average, it is probably true to make the harsh statement that the men who take posts in colonial universities are not good enough to obtain appointments carrying the same or even approaching the same status in this country. This question of staffing is a fundamental problem which with all its difficulties must be solved. Without its solution, there can be little hope of our colonial educational system developing in the way which is desirable, and the colonial universities will not contribute to the ordered advancement of the territories and their peoples in the way they should. If we continue on our present lines it seems to me likely that we may be laying the foundations of future unhappiness and, not improbably, of political discontent.

8   Failure to take a long enough view of educational development is another factor impeding wise development. Too often decisions have been made on the spur of the moment without adequate thought of the future, and inevitably a proportion of these decisions proves to be wrong. Later it falls to the lot of a Commission or an individual to endeavour to make the best out of the mistakes of the past, and it is usually found that many of them should not have been made and that some of them

can never be rectified. The explanation of this is not far to seek: firstly for the reasons stated earlier, education tends, in some cases, to be regarded as a wayward and difficult child in colonial government circles; secondly, only in exceptional circumstances can the administrative officers of the educational service have a broad enough view or the necessary personal experience to lay adequate foundations for the future, since they were recruited to the service at a youthful age.

9 Our policy of providing some form of elementary education for the mass of the colonial peoples is a most enlightened one and our achievement in carrying it out remarkable, even though we must all recognise that much indeed remains to be done and wish to see it done as quickly as possible. But it seems to me important that we should not forget the equally vital task of creating slowly but surely an highly educated section of the communities. This is a process which cannot be unduly accelerated, but there is a big difference between enlightened encouragement and help grudgingly given, between far sighted planning and disordered growth. It must be remembered that in contrast to this country in which education began at the top and spread downwards, in the Colonies education is beginning at the bottom and spreading upwards. The real progress of the peoples and their ability to stand on their own feet will only be ensured by early and active help and encouragement in the development of the top of the educational structure, in order that an educated section of the community may emerge as soon as possible. This demands the development of university institutions as soon as their creation can be justified. I have already stated that we must endeavour to find among the students of these universities, men, who besides becoming fully adequate for their future professional activities, go much further and develop into citizens exerting, by their powers of leadership, a real influence in the promotion of the happiness and welfare of their own people. But apart from the few who develop as leaders, all the students, irrespective of their professions, will influence the development of their people, not only by virtue of the official positions which they may hold, but also in their private lives. If they be teachers, their power to help their race is obviously great, and for this reason the importance of the provision of adequate teachers cannot be too greatly stressed. We should recognise fully that secondary education of poor quality given by teachers of the wrong outlook is not only of little value but may be as unhappy in its results as wrongly conceived university education itself.

This plea that we should do all we can to strengthen our existing university institutions does not run counter to our desire to provide elementary education for all; rather does it help to further this desire. It seems to me that we need the help of the educated native in planning the elementary education far more than we have been able to have it in the past, and we shall greatly improve the quality of the elementary education by raising the standard of teaching generally. Indirectly too, another factor will come into play. In the course of time public opinion will be developed and will be reflected in the Press. This public opinion will in the first place be that of those who have passed through the universities, and if it is an enlightened one, it will exert a powerful influence for the good and provide great stimulus for the peoples. Later too, the children who have passed through the schools will contribute to it and here their teachers have a great part to play. While we rightly lay much emphasis on the importance of education for all, it seems to me that we may not have realised fully how best to achieve this aim and that we have overestimated the importance of immediate education for all rather than realised that we shall ultimately serve our purpose better by paying greater attention for the time being to adequate higher education for the few.

10   Apart from the problems already mentioned, there are many matters of policy which ought to be determined now, for the lead can only come from us if our own minds are clear on the objectives we seek. The absence of definite objectives not only undermines the enthusiasm of the staff but also hampers the early development by the students of the nationalist pride in their own institution which is so essential for its future success.

All these matters of policy ultimately resolve themselves into the single question of how our colonial university institutions are to achieve university status, with all that this question implies. Various aspects of this problem are repeatedly discussed at length in reports of Commissions and we discuss them again on the Advisory Committee in reference to each single territory, but we rarely reach conclusions. I feel that we ought not to allow the variations which are dictated by local considera- tion to cause us to lose sight of the fact that there are problems of higher education common to all the territories. We ought to endeavour to solve these general prob- lems, for unless we do so now, far more difficult and perhaps insoluble ones will arise later. I now turn to discuss my views on some of them.

11   Before university status is conferred, the standard of achievement of a student in any degree course must be not less than that which is expected in Great Britain; there must be a rigorous avoidance of the degree of inferior standard. The accep- tance of this principle, which will doubtless be agreed upon by all, will, however, be of little value unless it carries with it full recognition by government and other employers that the colonial degree is equivalent to the English, so that adequate opportunity of employment of the graduates becomes available. This recognition can, however, only come when the universities at home accept the colonial degrees as exempting students from equivalent courses here.

I do not think we have reflected enough on the implications of the statement that the standard must be the same. Our degree courses in this country are designed adequately to occupy the mind of the average student coming to us, but they allow him a reasonable amount of time for those independent activities which do so much to mature his outlook and give him self reliance. If we expect the same examination standard from our colonial students, their courses must be longer, even though the content be the same, for these students labour under the great handicap of being educated in a foreign tongue and they have none of the advantages of the home environment and school system available to the student in England. Even without an increase in the accepted length of the course, by, say one year, the student may yet pass his examination because of the further cultivation of his peculiar ability to memorise facts. Though he thus may have reached the same *examination* standard as the English student, he will, however, be lacking in understanding and the power to apply his knowledge. In addition, even this accomplishment will only have proved possible at the cost of having sacrificed the development of all those things which are emphasised in Section 7. To me then 'the same standard' means much more than examination performance, for even apart from the wider aspects mentioned earlier, there are material factors involved, since only when the standard in the larger sense is achieved, will responsible employment in commerce and industry become avail- able. That at least is the view which I found in Malaya and it is one with which I sympathise. Some of us doubtless have experiences of our own which bear on this problem. Even though undergraduate foreign students have all the advantages of pursuing their studies within our own universities, they labour under the greatest handicap because of the deficiencies of their school education and the fact that their teaching is in English; in my experience only rarely is it that they achieve the standard in the wider sense. If this happens to these students coming to this country, it must happen even more when they study in their own university institutions.

In considering this question of standards, it is worthy of repetition that some of the peoples possess a quite remarkable facility for memorising facts, without appreciation of their significance or application; they have much information but little understanding. It may well prove necessary to try to depart from the accepted type of entrance examination, such as the matriculation or the school certificate, because facility of memory encouraged by ill-directed teaching undermines the value of this type of examination as a test of intelligence. The dangers of its use are well seen, for instance, at University College, Colombo. We ought to consider this problem and try to devise an improved method, difficult though this may be. Whatever be done in the meanwhile, it must always be remembered that the ultimate solution lies in the production by universities of teachers fully adequate for secondary school teaching. Similarly, the examinations conducted on the courses held within the university itself must be directed far more to testing understanding than to assessing knowledge of facts. My own experience of students from abroad leads me to believe that the failure to realise the importance of this matter is more responsible for the unhappy results of higher education in a number of countries than we may perhaps realise.

12 If we can solve the difficult problem of the entrance examination, if we see that an adequate standard of technical knowledge is acquired, and, equally important, that the educational as compared with the vocational value of the institution is not less great than it is in England, the well known fears from the possible production of large numbers of so-called educated people for whom no suitable employment can be found, will not arise; the institution will be distinguished not by the numbers but by the quality of its students. . . .

13 When the conditions laid down in section 11–12 can be fulfilled, I see no objection to the student who has satisfactorily passed through the institution being awarded a Pass Degree. On the contrary, it seems to me important that he should receive some outward sign of recognition, for his worth will be real and should be made obvious in order that his opinion may count among his people. In contrast to the unfortunate influence which the taking of the London External Degree examinations must unavoidably exert, the award of a Pass Degree would materially assist the most desirable object of creating nationalist pride in the institution and would lay the foundations of intellectual equality among the native populations. . . .

14 The question of the method whereby any given institution is to justify the granting to it of powers to award general degrees is a matter of policy which needs early decision. I left Malaya with the fear that the London External Degree method was fraught with danger. A few hours spent at University College, Colombo, on the way home confirmed this fear. The results there are worthy of study, for in a relatively brief space of time problems of infinite difficulty have already been created. The only analogy which seems to me appropriate is that of the avalanche which from trifling beginnings ultimately carries all before it, leaving destruction in its trail. It was for this reason that my colleague and I endeavoured to present an alternative method of approach in the report of Higher Education in Malaya.

At the present time, students from the different territories take the London External Degrees in varying numbers and even if we can find safeguards adequate to prevent such happenings, we ought to decide now whether this is the best means of achieving the aim in view or whether some better method can be found. Investigation may well show that, at least in certain of the Colonies, failure to anticipate this problem has already prevented the possibility of any alternative being adopted. We certainly ought not to adopt the London Degree method merely because it is the established avenue of approach in our own country. Even if it is found unavoidable for some Colonies or even desirable for all, I hope that it will be adopted only if the ever recurring question of modifying the curricula to suit imperial needs can be satisfactorily settled, since it is of the greatest importance that the curriculum should govern the examination, rather than that the examination should determine the curriculum. . . .

15 My own view therefore is that our main immediate object should be to develop University institutions empowered to award at this stage Pass Degrees only. By such a method a sound basis for any and every future development will be laid. We ought, I think, boldly to depart from the long established conception that a University can only come into being when the institution already possesses numerous Faculties, each consisting of a number of departments having their own Honours and Research Schools. . . .

17 I now turn to discuss the question of staffing. For the reasons stated already, I regard the question of attracting the right men to colonial university posts and the maintenance of their enthusiasm as the outstanding problem to be faced. It must be solved in spite of its many difficulties and great complexity, and I do not believe that we can achieve what we set out to do unless we change our methods. We must clearly abandon such customs as that at Raffles College of introducing schoolmasters to take the place of the members of the staff who proceed on leave. We must also realise from the start that methods which will ensure that the staffs are adequate will require further expenditure and that the justification for any extra expenditure cannot be materially assessed.

It is clear that merely increasing the existing relatively high salaries already offered for posts in colonial university institutions will have no effect in increasing the number of suitable candidates. Progress can only be made by a more radical method. In my opinion, hopes of success lie in one direction and in one direction only, and that is in our obtaining the willing help and co-operation of our own universities in building up a system by which members of their staffs may become available for service in the colonies for suitable periods and under appropriate conditions.

18 The system which I believe could be established is that members of the staffs of the universities of this country would be seconded to our colonial university institutions; they would serve there for periods of up to three years when they would return to their home universities. This system would, in effect, be the introduction of visiting lectureships of an extended type and it could be applied to various categories of the academic staff. Perhaps the most valuable category from our point of view would be that of the senior lecturer who, apart from his professional attainments and his teaching experience, would have a considerable background of university administration and would be a man of wide outlook; he would bring his experiences of university life in this country to bear on the development of our colonial institution in just those ways which are so necessary. A second category,

fulfilling another purpose, would be the junior lecturer, a young man who, after taking an M.A. or Ph.D. Degree, has served as a Grade 3 lecturer for the usual period of three years. He too might be seconded for a three-year period, and apart from the good effects of his bringing his new enthusiasm to bear on the institution, it is likely that in some cases he would find such satisfaction in his new work that he would wish to remain abroad permanently; if this were so, it would aid the problem of recruiting the permanent staff for he would be making his choice in the full knowledge of all that the step entails. This question of seconding lecturers is not the only way in which our universities might help. The practice of granting sabbatical years to senior members of the staffs is practised little in modern universities, largely because these members are financially unable to make profitable use of such a respite from their normal duties. It would clearly be a great advantage if suitably chosen professors from our own universities could, from time to time, be granted sabbatical years in order that they might visit two or three of our colonial institutions and take a serious part in their work for a period of one academic term each. Much help would be given by visits such as these and the stimulus would be great. These are only indications of some of the avenues to be explored, and it has also been pointed out to me that apart from the home Universities, the question of the Dominion universities taking part in such a scheme should not be forgotten, for the lecturer in a Dominion university may tend to be more adaptable than one in a university of Great Britain; some months spent in the University of Toronto lead me to share this view.

The scheme which I would like to see evolved is one in which perhaps three quarters of the staff of any colonial institution would be permanent members and the remaining one quarter would consist of these visiting lecturers. As time progressed we should slowly appoint to the permanent staff local graduates who have pursued post graduate study in Great Britain. By these two methods a long term policy of fruitful development would be established. The University of Liverpool has a School of Tropical Medicine with a station in Sierra Leone, and members of its staff spend varying amounts of time here and at this African station; it is not a very great extension of this principle to make it apply in some form or other to the colonial universities.

19 It is not to be denied that any scheme embracing an organized effort among the universities of Great Britain for such a purpose is full of difficulties and may meet with discouragement and perhaps opposition. But any radically new conception is very rarely favourably received at first, particularly in this country, and too often the apparent repercussions and difficulties of proposals lead us to reject them without adequate exploration. That should not, however, deter us, for while I have not discussed these proposals with any of our Vice-Chancellors, I do not see material difficulties which cannot be overcome. The universities will not, for instance, need to make any financial sacrifice, for the salaries of their absent members will be available for meeting the additional staffing costs necessitated by their absence, while at the same time the university superannuation scheme would not be affected. Further, only a very few members of a given university would be absent at one time and the work of the Departments concerned would not suffer in most cases. . .

20 While I am fully aware of the likelihood of a hesitant reaction in the first place to a departure of this kind, I believe that success can be achieved. Success will not come however unless we are prepared to work for it with persistence, skill and patience. It will only come if we feel sincerely that the problem is one of such impor-

tance that it is essential to solve it and therefore to labour for it. Unless we are convinced of the weaknesses of the present system under which we laboriously search for individuals to fill our posts instead of having individuals seeking posts – with the inevitable result that the men obtained are not good enough – it will lead us nowhere; we shall obtain no success and the attempt should not be made. On the other hand, if the problem is boldly stated to the universities and a reasoned appeal made for their help, I think that success will come, for it must be remembered that the majority of academic people in the universities of Great Britain have not heard of the existence of the problem, and therefore know nothing of its importance. I myself believe that our universities here have a responsibility to the Empire in this matter. Without denying the ideals which are their motive force they will surely find it impossible to resist an appeal which is directed to furthering their fellow universities in the Colonial Empire, and indirectly the welfare of the peoples of the Empire. Further, they will be aware of the increasing desire of the British Government to assist in the development of the Colonial peoples through the enlarged Colonial Development Fund, and this will increase their sense of moral obligation.

The recent enlightened departure regarding the Colonial Development Fund has already done much to awaken in the educated people of this country a consciousness of our responsibility to the colonial peoples, and after the war there will be an auspicious atmosphere of Empire unity. There will be great opportunities of making use of the impulses for development which will certainly occur at the end of the war, but we shall be unable to seize these opportunities unless we are fully prepared. We ought to prepare now. . . .

21 If some such scheme could be ultimately achieved, the gains would be even greater than those which are apparent at first sight. Instead of being struggling institutions of obscure mediocrity, the colonial universities would become an integral part of an imperial university system; in the course of time this system would exert a profound unifying influence on the Empire as a whole and would bring nearer the achievement of the aims of its members for the development of all its peoples. The widely varying conditions of the Colonies and Protectorates – the different stages of development of the peoples, the variations in their economic, social and religious backgrounds, the diversities of climate – provide so many vivid contrasts, that it is extremely difficult to see how each may become a member of a family working for a common end rather than the adopted child of a somewhat unenthusiastic foster parent. It seems to me that in the realm of higher education, the universities provide a common ground for all the peoples; nothing but gain can result if advantage is taken of this fact. These views are in no sense imperialistic in the old and selfish sense. If we are sincere in our belief in the value of education and in our professed wish to help the Colonial peoples to maturity, one step of the greatest value would be to endeavour to bring university institutions of the Colonies into active relationship with the university system of this country. . .

25 I have indicated the important results to be expected if we bring the colonial university institutions into close relationship with the home universities. It is useful to consider here, therefore, whether there is any desirable method of approach to the problem other than that previously discussed, and in this connection the recent association of Makerere with the University of Oxford comes to mind. It will be recalled that emphasis was laid on the informal nature of this association; its two main objects are the giving by the University of Oxford of advice regarding the

curriculum when invited to do so, and the sending of visiting lecturers to the College, if and when occasion permits. Other universities may wish to play their part in following the admirable example set by Oxford, and it is well then to reflect whether this method should replace that already suggested or whether it could usefully supplement it.

There is no doubt that this association with Oxford will mean much psychologically to the students of Makerere, while if visiting lectureships can be established, nothing but good can arise from the stimulation which they will provide. But it seems to me that this method, which must depend on the personal inspiration of the few, has too narrow a basis for our purposes. Apart from this, advice on the curriculum will only be of solid value if it is given by those who have an intimate knowledge of the background of the Colony concerned, and it is unlikely that any particular university will have on its staff continuously members with the appropriate knowledge.

Further, if the method be extended and a particular university becomes enthusiastic in its work for a given college, it will understandably feel that it has the possessive rights of a foster parent in controlling the welfare of its adopted child. Difficulties may thus arise in a conflict of views between the college and the Advisory Committee and harmonious co-operation may be impeded. Almost certainly too, the adopted college will seek advice on many other matters; it is not unlikely, for instance, that the staff of the college will tend to be recruited perhaps exclusively from the graduates of its foster parent; similarly, the college may tend to follow the practices of its foster parent instead of moulding itself to suit local conditions; I can well picture also the possibility of difficult positions arising in a conflict of interests of the parent universities at home regarding the development of their adopted colleges.

Not for one moment do I wish to underestimate the spirit which prompted the enlightened step taken by the University of Oxford. But I feel that we should consider the implications very fully in order that we may form a sound judgment as to whether the extension of this development will provide the best method of achieving our purpose. My own view is that our colonial institutions should be brought into close contact with our universities as a whole, and that they should benefit by the accumulated experience of all rather than by that of a single university, however zealously that university may be prepared to contribute to their problem.

26 This brings me to the question of research in institutions in the Colonies. Ultimately research must play as important a part in the life of our colonial universities as it does in that of our own, and even though much time must elapse before this happens, we ought to form a clear view on the more immediate objectives. The essential facts are that there lie before us many pressing needs for development in colonial education, and that research of fundamental character is often very costly, for it requires adequate staffs, it may need special buildings and equipment, while good libraries are essential. My view is that any substantial expenditure on research is only justified at this stage if it is confined to the one or two special subjects for which the local opportunities and material available are unique. In these particular subjects development ought to come now, so that the universities should, in course of time, be so outstanding as not only to be distinguished within their own countries but to attract workers from all over the world. In my opinion, we should be unsparing in our financial and moral encouragement to the development of research in these few particular subjects, and those who are appointed as directors should be

men of already established international reputation. We should recognise that we have a duty to the world in this matter, because the opportunities are in our hands and some of them are in our hands only. Thus the College of Medicine at Singapore should become as soon as possible a centre of world importance for the study of Tropical Medicine and Hygiene, and a similar development of Oriental Languages might take place at Raffles College. The recent decision regarding the formation of an Institute of West African Culture is one which gives me much pleasure, for I am confident that it will lead to results of outstanding importance.

But apart from these particular research developments which will prove costly, we ought also to encourage research in all the colonial institutions, for without it the colleges cannot hope to achieve what we expect of them. In almost all the subjects the Colonies offer problems peculiar to themselves, capable of solution in any reasonably equipped department if the members of the academic staffs are fully worthy of appointment. I am not unaware of the fact that much which passes under the name of research would be better left undone even in our own country, but it cannot be denied that good work could be done in all the colonial institutions if reasonable opportunities were provided. Research of the type which I am now discussing requires neither considerable expenditure nor special research appointments. We ought to foster it as much as possible, so that knowledge of the territories may come from their own institutions.

Finally, I wish to emphasise that I am fully conscious of the fact that some of the things which I have said might not have been written had my experience of colonial education been wider. Discussions on the Advisory Committee concerning territories other than Malaya have, however, led me to think that some at least of the problems are common to all the territories, and I hope that these problems will receive attention. My concern is that we should take a broader view of the problems of Higher Education in the Colonies and direct our policy accordingly. We should endeavour to control future events rather than wait until the pressure of events makes it necessary to take action.

H. J. CHANNON.

3 THE CHANNON REPORT, MAY 1943

Printed for the use of the Colonial Office

Miscellaneous No 507

CONFIDENTIAL   A.C.E.C. 7/43

Advisory Committee on Education in the Colonies

Report of the Sub-Committee on Higher Education

SUMMARY

(Numbers in brackets refer to the relevant paragraphs of the Report.)

Introduction (1–3)

Part 1   The present position of Higher Education in the Colonies

Names of existing institutions (4). Scope of Report (5). The political urgency for action now (6–7). Statistics concerning school populations in Malaya and East Africa (8). The social and economic advantages of the development of higher education in undeveloped territories (9). The origins of higher education in the Colonies (10). The results of present narrow policy and outlook on the Colleges: scope and functions (11–12), research (14). Factual teaching as a hindrance to progress (15–16). The lack of staffs adequate in number and quality and the difficulties of the members of staffs (17–22).

Part 2 Principles which should guide future development

The difficulties of creating universities in undeveloped countries (25). The need for far-sighted planning of the universities of East and West Africa and of Malaya (26). The necessity of training leaders (27–28). The Colleges must become active centres of research (29). The need for definition of the aims and objectives of a Colonial University (30). The method of evolution of existing Colleges to university status must be determined now (31). The basic problems of university development are the same in all the Colonies (32). A new approach on a much higher plane is essential; an appeal to the home Universities (33).

Part 3 The treatment of the problems encountered

Staffing. The need for high quality (34–36); the principal features (37–39). Proposals for secondment from home Universities and for study-leave from colonial Colleges (40–42); the result of a secondment system on the life of colonial Colleges (43), of the home Universities (44–46), in promoting knowledge of the Colonies in Great Britain and in improving colonial recruitment generally (47).

Evolution to University Status. The desire of colonial students to obtain degrees and the necessity of immediate decision as to how universities are to evolve: the example of Malaya (49–50). The standard of any colonial degree must be equal in the widest sense to that of a degree in Great Britain (51). Modifications in the present external degree system are essential (52–54). Suggestions for modifications (55–57). Proposal for an examining Panel sponsored by all the home Universities (58–59). London University in relation to the Panel proposals (60–61). Proposal for establishing "The Colonial University", sponsored by all the Universities of Great Britain (62–63). Ill effects of the use of the Matriculation Certificate (68–69).

Research. The Colonial Research Committee (70). The urgent need of accelerating research in the Colleges (71–72). Research should be concentrated in the Colleges unless overriding considerations make this impossible (74). The part of the full-time research worker in the life of the College (75). The College as the headquarters of regional research (76). Institutional, industrial and College research should be in close contact (77). The College is the acknowledged centre of learning (78). Grants for research to individuals; block grants to the Colleges (79).

Machinery. Reasons for the establishment of a new body 'The Colonial University and Research Council', with a University committee and a research committee, with their possible functions (70–84). The University committee should have powers to recommend grants, under the Development and Welfare Act (86). Relationships of any new central body to the Advisory Committee on Education, the Colonial Research Committee and the Universities Bureau (87). The functions of the University committee in creating a colonial University system (88).

Post-graduate study in Great Britain and the need for indigenous Universities. Opportunities for post-graduate study must be extended with special arrangements in the home Universities (92–93). The Pass and Honours Degree problem and its bearing on post-graduate study and the recognition in Great Britain of modified curricula appropriate to an indigenous University (94–95).

Requirements for admission to Colonial Colleges. Failure of the present methods and need for a new approach (96); the question of abolishing fees in colonial Colleges (97–98).

Problems facing the Home Universities. How can academic staffs be made Colonies-conscious (99); specific proposals for bringing the Colonies into the active life of the home Universities (100–102).

The new consciousness of our obligations which now exist in Great Britain provides opportunity for action; the expectations of the Colonies demand that the opportunity be taken (103).

INTRODUCTION

1 The Memorandum on Higher Education by Professor Channon was discussed by the Advisory Committee at its 110th and 111th meetings and at the end of the latter meeting the following Resolution was adopted:

The Committee desires to express its appreciation of Professor Channon's Memorandum and its deep sense of the importance and urgency of the issues which it raises. The Committee is in general agreement with Professor Channon's analysis of the character of the problems to be faced and strongly recommends that a suitable body should be constituted to advise the Secretary of State on the means whereby the universities of Great Britain could best assist in the development of Higher Education in the Colonies.

We were therefore appointed as a Sub-Committee consisting of Mr C. W. M. Cox, Professor H. J. Channon, Sir Fred Clarke, Mr E. R. Hussey, Dr Julian Huxley, Mr B. Mouat Jones, Professor W. M. Macmillan and Miss M. Perham to advise as to how effect could best be given to this resolution.

2 Our Interim Report in which a recommendation was made concerning the nature of the body which should undertake this enquiry with a statement of its terms of reference was adopted by the Advisory Committee at its 121st meeting.

3 The Interim Report mentioned that the Memorandum by Professor Channon is concerned with certain aspects only of the problem of Higher Education in the Colonies, and is, in effect, a supplement to the Report on Higher Education in Malaya,* in which other important aspects had already been discussed. It seems desirable to us, therefore, to present to the Committee the present Report which sets out the principal features of the problem as a whole, with a statement of some of the lines of enquiry which appear to us worthy of investigation. *Part 1* is concerned with an analysis of the present position of Higher Education in the Colonies; *Part 2* deals with the principles which should guide its post-war development; in *Part 3* consideration is given to the possible treatment of the problems set out in Part 1.

PART 1

The Present Position of Higher Education in the Colonies

4 There are two groups of institutions concerned with higher education in the Colonies. In the first group are the autonomous Universities of Ceylon, Hong

* Colonial No 173

Kong, Jerusalem and Malta; in the second group are Colleges in various stages of development which will later become the Universities of East Africa, West Africa and Malaya. In East Africa there is Makerere College, serving Kenya, Uganda, Tanganyika Territory and Zanzibar, and which will probably also draw students, in the near future, from Northern Rhodesia and Nyasaland. In West Africa, there is Achimota College serving principally the Gold Coast, but also drawing students from all the West African Colonies; Fourah Bay serving Sierra Leone and to a limited extent Nigeria; the Higher College, Yaba, and the Medical School, Yaba, serving Nigeria. In Malaya there are the King Edward VII Medical College and Raffles College, both in Singapore; it is likely that in the not far distant future a beginning will be made towards the creation of a University in the West Indies. For brevity of description these Colleges will be described in this Report as the Colleges.

5 While this Report deals with the general question of Higher Education in the Colonies, it is particularly concerned with the development to full university stage of institutions in East Africa, West Africa and Malaya, and it discusses in some detail how the existing Colleges, through wise development and fruitful progress, may achieve university status as soon as possible. Some of the suggestions made have, however, wider implications, and if carried into effect would ultimately bear on the life of many other Institutions of research and learning both at home and overseas.

6 During the present war the British Government has emphasized that the guiding principle of its colonial policy is that the Colonies shall become increasingly self-governing as the degree of their development makes the carrying out of this policy possible. These public pronouncements of policy will lead the colonial peoples rightly to expect that active help in their own development will come from Great Britain after the war. There is no doubt that there will be a spontaneous and vigorous impulse for self-development among the colonial peoples in the immediate post-war period and preparations must be made to satisfy this impulse. Long-term plans must be made now so that the course of future events may as far as possible be pre-determined. Unless such plans are so prepared, pressure of events will later compel action to be taken, and action taken under pressure lacks the ordered sequence necessary to success.

7 Clearly, the complete fruition of this declared policy cannot take place rapidly, for many years will necessarily elapse before full effect can be given to it even in the most advanced of the colonial territories. In all cases the policy must be an evolutionary one, whereby the peoples will increasingly take a more responsible part in their own administration; and gradually the more responsible and ultimately the highest posts will become available to men of proved ability. A first step, therefore, must be to provide adequate opportunities for the higher education of those few who are capable of becoming the pioneers in the evolution of their own people. Before discussing the changes which we consider necessary if these opportunities are to be made adequate, a review of the present position is desirable.

8 The development of higher education in the Colonies presents problems of peculiar difficulty, for in many of the territories a very large proportion of the children receive no education of any kind, while the numbers receiving secondary education from which the entrants to colonial colleges are drawn, are both small in themselves and form an insignificant fraction of the total child population. In the most

developed territory, Malaya, which has a population of approximately five millions, about 250,000 children, or five per cent. of the total population, receive education in Government Vernacular Schools (Chinese, Indian or Malay), or in English Schools. About 40,000 of these children attend the latter schools where English is the medium of instruction throughout, and where it is possible to pass from the kindergarten stage, through the primary sections of the schools to the secondary section proper. About one-quarter of the children attending English Schools reach the secondary school stage, and of these some 2,500 end by taking the Cambridge School Certificate examination. These 2,500 or 0·05 per cent. of the total population, provide the pool from which the entrants to the two Colleges at Singapore are drawn. Malaya with its great prosperity due to its vast resources in tin and rubber naturally presents an educational picture far more favourable than that of any other colonial territory. The position in the African Dependencies is much more complex than that in Malaya, for the variety of languages is great, there are ten different Dependencies covering a vast area, and doubts exist as to the reliability of the available statistics. Some idea of the present position may, however, be gained from the statement that the total population is some forty millions, of whom about one million, or 2·5 per cent. of the total population, are receiving some measure of education. Of these, some ten thousand attend secondary schools where the medium of instruction is English and the aim is to reach the Cambridge School Certificate examination or its equivalent. The number achieving this aim is, however, still small. In 1938, it was 1,100 but it is rapidly increasing. The ten thousand secondary school pupils are, of course, very irregularly distributed over the different Dependencies, for 6,100 of them are to be found in Nigeria, 1,340 in Uganda, while there are none in Nyasaland or Northern Rhodesia. In Great Britain, the number of children between the age of 5 and 16 in attendance at schools is 20 per cent. of the population. Accepting this percentage as representing the number of children who should be receiving education in the Colonies, the figures of 5 and 2·5 per cent. in Malaya and Africa, respectively, present a striking contrast.

9 The fact that the general problem of the education of the whole peoples awaits solution, does not make the production of a highly educated section less pressing. There is the urgent need of the social and economic services for professionally trained men – agriculturists, dentists, doctors, engineers, teachers, veterinary surgeons and others. This need will increase as the Colonies develop and as finance becomes available. It will only be possible to satisfy the demand by the provision of adequate local facilities for higher education. This development of higher education must go hand in hand with an increasing extension of primary education, for the progress of education at any level is not an independent thing; it depends in its turn on events proceeding at the different levels above and below it. Because of this interdependence the efficiency of higher education ultimately governs that of primary education, which, in its turn, determines the progress of higher education; this view of the effect of higher education in promoting primary education is how-ever, one which is not accepted in all the Colonies. In our opinion, therefore, it cannot be too strongly emphasized how important a part the colonial Colleges have to play in the educational field as a whole, and particularly in the production of teachers of quality for the secondary schools. In a developing country, the secondary-school teacher has a far greater opportunity of moulding public opinion through his pupil than he has elsewhere; the progress of the Colleges largely depends

on the quality of the pupils who have passed through his hands; his help is needed in the planning of both primary and secondary education, for up to the present there have been all too few educated local men capable of giving this vital service to their own race. Secondly, while the teaching and professional training are of great importance, it is of not less importance that the Colleges should be conceived as fulfilling the purposes of research as well as of higher education; knowledge of an area should come largely from its own centre of higher education, and the fields for research are vast and largely unexplored. Thirdly, the Colleges have a great part to play in acting as the centres from which progress in education in a variety of directions is stimulated. They should act as the centres of research into the methods and problems of education itself; by their extra mural work and extension lectures they can do much to foster adult education; they can serve as centres for the direction of any mass education movements, by refresher courses they can ensure that the stimulus of new knowledge is made available to men and women in the different professions and so help to overcome the tendency to intellectual stagnation which is inevitable in countries which are largely undeveloped. Lastly, the influence of prosperous centres of higher education is not limited to their effects on education in the narrower sense. The doctors a college produces help to improve the health of the people as a whole and improvement in child health and nutrition are essential preliminaries to education; similar arguments can be applied to the good effects resulting from the higher education of men in the other professions and to the fruitful results of research. All the activities of a college interact with one another and together affect the progress of the peoples as a whole – their health, their education and their economic development. The Colleges have therefore a large indirect part to play in the movement towards self government as well as directly by the education of leaders.

10 While the pioneer work of Christian Missions in the early introduction of the humanities must be recognised, wider facilities for higher education in undeveloped countries have usually come into being as the result of the initiative of governments, stimulated by the need for the provision of locally-trained professional men for the social services. Medicine, with its more direct impact on human welfare, has pride of place; it has been followed variously by agriculture, dentistry, engineering, and veterinary science; usually much later, and when the need for adequately-trained teachers for secondary schools comes to be appreciated, the sciences are introduced and humane studies extended.

11 In encouraging the foundation of Colonial Colleges, the Governments have been confronted with many problems and difficulties. In the first place experience in India has drawn attention to certain political and economic dangers which may result from over-production of men who have received a particular type of higher education. In some cases these dangers have been met by limiting admissions to the Colleges to the number of government posts prospectively available in a given year. As a result, entry to the College very rapidly comes to be regarded as entry to government service, and within a short time the College tends to become a centre of narrowly vocational training even if it were conceived on a wider basis at the start. There naturally follows a demand for more admissions; if this demand be granted, the inevitable result is the discontent of those who, because of lack of vacancies, fail to obtain the posts which the rapidly established tradition has led them to expect, for opportunities of employment of university graduates must depend mainly not

on the development of government activities but on the economic and social development of the country as a whole.

12 On the other hand, this economic development is inevitably restricted by the grave financial difficulties with which nearly all Colonial Governments are faced. These difficulties are in the main due to the fact that, with the exception of a few territories, the Colonies are producers of primary agricultural products and are therefore poor. In the educational field, this limitation has the inevitable result that the Colonial Government is constantly finding itself in the position of having to choose between the different stages of education which it desires to develop, and loses sight of their essential interdependence. Higher education is exceedingly costly, particularly in its early stages, and hence the funds likely to be made available for it tend to be limited to the bare amount considered sufficient to cover the very narrow conception of its needs.

13 Moreover, Colonial Governments suffer from the fact that they rarely have available to them men with personal experience of the development of higher education or with university life as a whole, for the members of the Educational Services are men who have proceeded to the Colonies in their earlier years and their experience is limited to particular territories in which universities may have yet to arise. The development of higher education is, however, a highly intricate matter needing the help of the expert, and the help of the expert is not at present available. In consequence, decisions are too often dictated by immediate needs or local pressure, and there is a lack of a long-term plan for the balanced and fruitful development of education as a whole, and perhaps especially of higher education.

14 Both this doubt of the wisdom of developing Universities and the financial stringency which is, in part, dictated by it, are reflected in the attitude to the question of research. Research in the Colonies has so far been very largely the concern of the various Government services such as those of medicine and agriculture, and has been mainly directed to the solution of problems which are of immediate practical importance. As a result, it is true to say that the Colleges are teaching institutions in the life of which research plays too little, and in some cases, no part. This divorce of research from the Colleges may be in part explained by the fact that the Government services were in existence before the Colleges became established; the conception therefore arose that research was the concern of these services; in part, it is also doubtless due to the fact that research is expensive, for it needs adequate staffs, and laboratory and library facilities, and lack of adequate finance has made provision for it difficult. Even where good facilities exist as at the King Edward VII College at Singapore, the staff are liable to be called upon to carry out many duties outside the College, and serious research under conditions such as these is not easy. Further, there is no doubt whatever that the great importance which attaches to the Colleges becoming lively centres of research is not appreciated. It is not understood, for instance, that teaching in any institution of higher education becomes sterile unless the inspiration of the teacher is maintained by some form of original investigation; that like the wider results of university education as a whole, the results of academic research cannot be assessed in immediate material terms; that many problems of applied nature cannot be solved until pure research has added to existing fundamental knowledge. The need for the investigation of urgent problems has therefore hindered recognition of the fact that immediate public utility is not and cannot be the standard by which Universities measure the value of researches conducted within

them. The failure to appreciate the importance of research is illustrated by the statement in the Annual Report of the King Edward VII Medical College, Singapore, for 1938, where it is recorded that among other changes worthy of mention in the revised College Ordinance is the fact that the 'post graduate work and research are included in the purposes of the College'. This illustration of the belated recognition of the importance of research is noteworthy, for this College was founded as long ago as 1906, and has provided the opportunity for the creation of a centre of tropical medicine which might have been of outstanding importance not only for Malaya but for the whole world.

15 The important matters discussed in paragraph 11 to paragraph 14 have a profound effect on the outlook and development of the Colonial Colleges as a whole. But the Colleges have yet two further great difficulties to face, namely, in the quality of their students and in the quality and numbers of their academic staff. At the present time, the London Matriculation or the School Certificate, defined in various ways as regards combinations, subjects, and the standards to be reached in them, are, with the exception of Yaba College, used as the entrance requirements to the Colleges. Evidence from all the Colonies shows, however, that such examinations are an uncertain guide to the intellectual capacity of the student because of the poor quality of the teaching in the secondary schools. Much of this training is given by teachers who suffer from being inadequately trained for their task, and whose belief in their own merits is largely dominated by the success of their pupils in these examinations. On their side, the pupils suffer from grave disabilities for they are being taught in a language which is not their mother tongue: very frequently they do not hear English spoken save during their school hours; they have none of the educational advantages with which the background of an English home may provide the child in Great Britain. The wrong outlook of the teacher, together with these handicaps of pupils educated in this particular way, results in much of the teaching becoming a burden to the memory rather than a development of the mind, and this factual teaching is greatly encouraged because the pupils seem often to possess a quite remarkable facility for memorising facts without an appreciation of their significance or application: they have much information, but often little understanding. The final result is that students enter the Colleges ill prepared for the work which lies before them, and not infrequently prove incapable of making further progress under present conditions.

16 This reference to the apparently outstanding facility of memory possessed by some of the peoples is not to be interpreted as meaning that real intelligence is lacking, for there is much evidence to the contrary. The fact that the teaching is given in a language which is not the mother tongue is doubtless one important factor in the present state of affairs; and the second results from the ill effects of over emphasis on the value of success in the School Certificate examination which affects both the teacher and his pupil. The former would doubtless occur in Great Britain if the teaching of our own children were suddenly given in an African or Chinese language; the latter is a phenomenon which is frequently encountered even in our own schools. These difficulties will increasingly disappear as education in the English language becomes more widespread and of improved quality, and as the examination system improves.

17 The last general matter for discussion is the all-important one of the staffing of the Colleges, and here it must be confessed the picture is not an encouraging one.

With the exception of the subjects involved in the latter years of the medical curriculum where the wealth of clinical material sometimes makes a special appeal, the
difficulties of obtaining staffs of adequate quality are great. Few young men of
promise are willing to leave the material facilities and intellectual resources of the
home Universities to take posts in the Colonial Colleges, of the very names of which
they have probably never heard, under conditions of service which make their return
to the Universities of Great Britain virtually impossible. Older men of already established reputation are even less likely to be attracted. The result of these conditions is
that, with the exception of the relatively few whose mental make-up differs greatly
from the average, men of the right calibre are not attracted.

18 New additions to the staff of a College are therefore usually young men who
bring to bear on the life of the College experience adequate neither in teaching,
administration nor research, for their own experiences of university life at home are,
in general, limited to their years spent as undergraduates and to their few later years
of post-graduate study; further, the experiences of their older colleagues of university
development in Great Britain are no greater than their own.

19 Amid the novelty of their new environment, these young men spend their first
few enthusiastic years in learning the conditions under which they have to teach and
in preparing their lecture courses. Inevitably the burden of teaching will be a heavy
one, for the staffs are limited in numbers, while the student, much less prepared for
university studies than the student of Great Britain, needs more individual tuition.
It is not unlikely also that a praiseworthy though sometimes too exclusive desire that
the students shall pass their examinations may lead to a too narrow basis of instruction. If these young men acquire a vivid interest in the people whose College they
serve – a thing greatly to be desired – teaching will, under present conditions,
increasingly dominate their lives, and other activities such as research will not find
a place. In the course of time, the teaching will lose its inspiration, for a variety of
factors, such as intellectual isolation, the difficulties of climate, the lack of the
stimulus which research provides, the strain of maintaining enthusiasm in the teaching which under these conditions requires much patience, will together not improbably lead finally to a feeling of frustration and consequent discontent. This discontent will probably occur long before the age of retirement and will increase with the
passage of time and with the growing realisation that return to a university post in
Great Britain is impossible.

20 On the research side, the position is not less difficult. Ability to conduct independent research requires maturity of knowledge and adequate previous experience
of research; it is unlikely, however, that the research experiences of these men are
more extensive than that gained in carrying out a piece of work for one or two years
under the direction of a professor in a home university, an experience which is
inadequate for their needs. They contrast their new facilities with those to which
they were accustomed at home and resign themselves to a belief that research is
impossible. On one hand, there is often a failure to realise that it is usually impossible for a college or university in the Colonies to compete at the present stage with
the highly-equipped Universities of Europe and America in the intensely developed
study of the basic problems of science, medicine and other subjects. On the other
hand, there is equally a failure to appreciate the wealth of new material available for
study in the Colonies. Many new problems of the greatest social and economic
importance as well as the study of indigenous systems of law and linguistics, provide

material which is not available to the Universities of the western world. It is not realised that study of these problems would give results of great importance for a fraction of the time, energy and money required to obtain similar rewards along the well-trodden tracks of research in Europe and America.

21 It must be freely admitted that the members of an academic staff of a college or university in the Colonies have many difficulties to face and that they deserve our sympathy. The fact that staffs are so small means that there is insufficient time available for research since teaching commitments are heavy, and climatic conditions are a handicap both from the point of view of time and energy; as mentioned in paragraph 14 research within the Colleges has received little moral or financial encouragement from Governments and in consequence facilities are often poor; in the absence of the help of post-graduate students, who in these days play such a large part in research in the western world, progress is likely to be slow. Research under all these conditions requires much initiative and resolution; initiative to find problems which can be tackled with the time and facilities available or to obtain facilities from governments who have not appreciated the importance of colleges becoming active centres of research; resolution to resist the insidious effects of the climate or the distracting pleasures which may be available. Not least of all, it requires great strength of will to resist the undermining effects of being isolated from workers in the same subject. In this country each of us knows the majority of the people working in our own subjects and comes into contact with them at the frequent meetings of learned societies held in the different Universities. We gain much from the continual stimulation of oral discussion and of written enquiry; we know what everyone else is doing and everyone else knows what we are doing; there is a healthy spirit of competition and a freedom to obtain help readily when difficulties arise.

22 It must be emphasized here that even if he overcomes all these difficulties, it is likely that a member of the staff of a College or University in the Colonies will, under present conditions, remain in his particular College or University until he retires, for his chances of appointment to a post in a home University or to another colonial College are far from bright. Save in quite exceptional circumstances, Universities here dare not take the risk of appointing to their staffs men who have been away from this country for more than a few years, particularly if they have left this country at an early age. Interviews are essential and distance forbids interviews. Apart from opinions as to the value of research publications, which can of course be readily obtained from workers in the same subject in this country, referees are required who can speak of the individual's personality and of his merits as a colleague as well as of his academic capacities. These must be sought in the country in which he is working, but it is unlikely that the country will contain many people of sufficiently established academic reputation for their opinions to count.

23 With this brief review of some of the main features of the present position, we now direct attention to what seem to us the fundamental points which must be kept in mind in the making of any decisions on policy.

PART 2

Principles Which Should Guide Future Development

24 We begin by emphasizing that there is no doubt whatever that the immediate post-war period will provide a unique opportunity for a vivid demonstration of the

seriousness of our intentions towards development of the Colonies. It is an opportunity which it would be both shortsighted and dangerous to lose, for the particular combination of circumstances will not recur. Wisely taken, it would not only bring inspiration to the Colonies themselves, but the results would be of great political value within the Empire as a whole, and might even provide a pattern to other countries.

25 The difficulties which attend the creation of universities in undeveloped countries cannot be stated too clearly: deficiencies of secondary education, poverty of staff, over-emphasis on teaching on too narrow a basis, lack of wide outlook, dearth of research, lack of adequate finance, political pressure which causes Governments to exert a rigid control of development, poverty of standards, misconceptions of objectives. In spite of all these difficulties, circumstances may compel the creation of a university at some time or other under conditions which are far from satisfactory. The new university then has to face a struggle to justify its existence and to raise its general standards to a reasonable level. For instance, even in medicine which for a variety of reasons is usually by far the most developed subject, there is a continuous fight to maintain standards of teaching and of laboratory and clinical facilities which will satisfy the requirements of the General Medical Council and allow recognition of the diploma as a registrable practising qualification. In most other subjects, in which there is no outside stimulus, the position is much less encouraging.

26 In our opinion it would show a lack of vision if we do not seize the opportunities now available to us, and profiting by past experience, plan the future universities of Africa and Malaya on sound and fruitful lines from the very beginning. This will entail expenditure but this can be made available under the Colonial Development and Welfare Act, and it is our opinion that a far greater return will be received on the relatively limited expenditure necessary to achieve these ends than would result from a similar outlay on any other single project, for this will affect all other projects in the most creative way.

27 If this view be accepted, then a radical change must be made in our methods and outlook. Firstly, if we wish to achieve the larger objective, the Colleges must concern themselves not only with the production of professional men having a highly specialised technical knowledge; they must be equally concerned with the preparation of these men for wider service, for the production of leaders from the mass of the peoples is an urgent need. These leaders may and indeed do come from all ranks of the community but indubitably the young man who has successfully passed through his university has in special degree the priceless opportunity of leading his people to a full realisation of their civic and social responsibilities and to a wise development of the material and cultural resources of their country.

28 But technical knowledge alone will not equip him for this. He himself needs guidance in the development of his own character. His facile learning must be given depth and breadth, his personal and racial interests must be led along paths of service and responsibility to his people. He must be helped to acquire a world outlook and given integrity of purpose. His natural guides are the staff of his University, who should be available both within and without the classroom or laboratory. This staff can only help him if it is adequate both in numbers and in outlook, for this aspect of the work demands men of high qualities and breadth of vision. Under present conditions it is an outlook which can be obtained only if the numbers of the staff have served in a University in this country long enough to have acquired an intimate

knowledge of the aims and ideals of University education, and some idea as to the approaches necessary for its ordered development and administration. This aspect of the work of the College is of profound importance, for only through the training of leaders of solid worth can the goal of self government ever be achieved.

29 Secondly, there is no doubt whatever that the Colleges will fail to achieve this objective if their activities are unduly concentrated on teaching, as the history of university development in India shows. It is therefore, vitally important that research should play an important part in the life of the Colleges from the very start. The argument that the Colleges can spend their earlier years in teaching only and that research can come later, is liable to prove misleading, for among developing peoples traditions become rapidly established in the early years, and a wrong atmosphere, which is difficult to change, is readily created. Apart from this reason there is the urgent intellectual and material need for the encouragement of research of all kinds in the largely unexplored colonial fields.

30 Thirdly, it is essential that steps be taken to educate the Governments, academic staffs and the peoples as a whole as to the aims and objectives of a university in the Colonies, for there is much misconception on this subject. It must be pointed out that a university is not a mass production vocational machine through which are passed, regardless of opportunities for future employment, students of indifferent mental calibre, but of great capacity for memorising facts; it should be a place where carefully chosen young people of promise are fitted to take their places in the different professions, but at the same time given the wider outlook necessary to fit them to play their part as citizens in the wider sense. The Governments must be led to appreciate this latter point of view and at the same time to be convinced that its adoption is possible without the production of a surplus 'intelligentsia'; here the question of the method of admission to the Colleges which is discussed in paragraph 92 is concerned. The academic staffs must be made to realise the importance of research, without which the institution will fail to achieve its purpose. The peoples must be educated to the wider purposes of the College and to an understanding that passage through it is not merely a means to material success, but entails responsibility and leadership. Apart from this, there is already a deep-seated desire among the more enlightened of some of the peoples that their future university shall be so distinguished as to command the admiration of the world.

31 Fourthly, it is essential that the peoples and staffs of the Colleges shall be given the inspiration of having a defined objective and a route to the attainment of university status must be presented to them. The absence of a definite objective undermines the enthusiasm of the staff; it makes their task of creating the right atmosphere and outlook much more difficult; it also hampers the early development by the students of pride in their own institution which is so vital to its future success. A developing people resemble developing children. No matter how difficult the road along which they have to travel may be, they will overcome the difficulties provided the route is definitely sketched before them. A mere vague future is demoralising in its effects and leads to false ideas and misconceptions, which rapidly end in discontent.

32 All the problems just described are involved in the single many-sided question of how the Colleges are to develop so as to merit in the course of time the conferment of university status. Various aspects of this question have been discussed at length in reports of Commissions and by the Advisory Committee in reference to individual

territories, but no final conclusions have been reached. It is, therefore, important to emphasize that the many variations consequent upon local conditions and environment do not alter the fact that the basic problems of higher education are common to all the territories wherever they may be, and that they require a common type of solution. Recent conversations with the Principals of Achimota and Makerere Colleges have, for instance, vividly shown that the fundamental issues in East and West Africa are identical with those of Malaya, even though the differences in the peoples and the economic development of these countries are so striking. A clear statement of policy regarding these general problems is needed now, for in its absence more difficult and perhaps insoluble ones will arise later. Once a general policy has been formulated, adaptation to local conditions is a relatively easy matter.

33 After considering all the evidence available to us, we consider that the desired objectives cannot be achieved under the present system, for progress will certainly be slow and uncertain and not without danger. We are convinced that a new outlook on the importance of the development of higher education in the Colonies is necessary and that the method of approach must be on a much higher plane. We do not believe that a successful approach is possible unless the home Universities with their vast intellectual resources feel able to respond generously to an appeal for their active help and guidance. We hope that in recognition of the importance of the new policy of partnership under which funds are made available for the development of the Colonies from the Imperial exchequer under the Colonial Development and Welfare Act, they will feel a desire to help on grounds of national policy. Moreover, the home Universities will doubtless recall that in spite of the widely varying conditions in the Colonies – the different stages of development of the peoples, the variations in their economic, social and religious backgrounds, the diversities of climate, the many mother tongues – all the peoples share one common property and one only, namely, that their higher education is in the English language. If advantage be taken of this fact to bring the Colonies into intimate relationship with each other through a colonial university system, which in the course of time may become an integral part of a Commonwealth university system, further unity of purpose will be given to the conception of the British Commonwealth of Nations. From every point of view, the time to act is now. On all these grounds, the home Universities will doubtless wish to do all that is in their power to further the development of the colonial Colleges and Universities, for in so doing they will be promoting the welfare of the Colonial peoples as a whole. The fruitful results of close co-operation between the home Universities of other colonial powers and their own colonies in higher education and research, such as those of Holland in the Dutch East Indies, are already well established and should be better known. There is no reason why similar success should not be achieved by ourselves even though, unlike the State Universities of Holland and other countries, our home Universities are independent bodies, for they will certainly realise their responsibilities no less than their opportunities which the present surge of world opinion lays before them. What in effect is required is that as older members of the university family, our home Universities should admit to the family circle these young Colonial members and that they should use their great experience to help to guide them to constructive development; as discussed in paragraphs 45–46, they themselves would not be without benefit from so doing. We now turn to mention particular proposals which seem to us worthy of exploration.

PART 3

The Treatment of the Problems Encountered

34 All will agree that the success of any institution, irrespective of its educational level, depends on the quality of its staff. Apart from creating the right atmosphere and providing inspiration, a staff of real quality is able to overcome considerable material and financial difficulties because its very quality ensures it obtaining help which is not otherwise available.

35 In a University in Great Britain young men are regularly absorbed into an already large academic body of established tradition and great wealth of experience; here they mature under the guidance and stimulus of their numerous colleagues until they too become part of the backbone of their University; if a few individuals fail to fulfil their early promise, no serious ill effect results, for they are absorbed in the body as a whole, or find other occupation. In contrast, in a young institution in its early years, every single failure exerts a profound effect on the whole, for the staff is necessarily limited in numbers and under present conditions in experience also. If our old established Universities need to recruit the best young men in order that their intellectual level may be maintained, it is certain that a University College – especially one in the Colonies – which has yet to establish itself, needs young men of not less ability. These men must also be imbued with an active desire to further the interests of the Colonies and their peoples.

36 A yet greater need of the colonial Colleges is the help of men of mature experience to apply their accumulated wisdom to their development. Under present conditions, the young men going out to the Colleges become in their turn the senior members of the staff; yet their experience is entirely limited to that which they have gained in the College itself and there is thus a vicious circle inimical to progress.

37 This staffing problem has two aspects; firstly, to discover the means whereby men of varying grades of seniority in teaching and research may be attracted to serve in the colonial Colleges; secondly, how to maintain the intellectual vigour of men who have already been attracted.

38 It is clear that further increasing the relatively high salaries already offered will not solve the problem; new methods must be sought. The essential fact is that men of the right calibre will not come forward unless conditions are so arranged that much greater freedom of movement is possible, and particularly that they are not virtually debarred from returning to posts in home Universities, if they so wish.

39 While exchange systems are theoretically attractive, in practice they do not work even under the best conditions in established universities, for individuals suited for undertaking each other's responsibilities are rare, and timing is always difficult. In the Colonies, there is obviously even less chance of success, for at the present stage the Colonies have relatively little to give in personnel and they need to receive much.

40 A more promising solution of the problem appears to lie in the secondment of good men of varying seniority in teaching and research under conditions which will enable them to return to posts in home Universities after varying periods of colonial service though it should be possible for them to remain indefinitely in the Colonies if they so wish. Such a scheme, the difficulties of which are discussed in paragraph 44, would need the introduction to the Colleges of a Federated Superannuation Scheme

for Universities in common with that at home; secondment might be for periods of up to five years: perhaps up to one-quarter of the staffs of the colonial Colleges might be made up of men seconded in this way, a proportion which both the Principals of Achimota and Makerere Colleges think would not undermine the team spirit of the staff as a whole.

41 Such a scheme would give great elasticity and would enable the right man to be found in one or other of the home Universities for any particular type of work, whether in teaching or research, in which a particular college or research institution needed help. It could apply to the junior lecturers who had some three years' experience after taking an M.A. or Ph.D. degree; to the dental, engineering, medical and veterinary graduates of similar standing; to the able man in his early thirties who would have much to give, not only in teaching and research, but also through his wider experience of university life as a whole; it could be applied to the professor, who, if seconded for one year, might visit one or more of the Colleges lecturing on his own special subject, or spending a year at one institution where the local conditions provided research material not available elsewhere. On the research side in general, the candidate would be selected for secondment to a particular institution, because of his general interest in a problem on which the staff could provide special guidance; alternatively, if a research worker wished to study a problem which could only be studied in a particular region, he would be seconded or attached to an institution in that region.

42 It is not less important that members of the permanent staffs of the Colonial Colleges should be given similar intellectual opportunities by their being granted sabbatical years, say every sixth year by an extension of their normal period of leave. In addition, it is desirable that they should be able to attend suitable refresher courses in the home Universities during their normal period of leave.

43 If any such scheme could be brought into being, its effect on the College would be profound. Firstly, the staff would no longer be intellectually isolated, for it would not only know that active interest was being taken in its welfare at home, but it would feel that it was a vital part of university life as a whole. Secondly, it would certainly happen that some of the young men sent out under the secondment system would be so attracted as to elect to stay. In this way, there would be gradually built up an enthusiastic and contented permanent staff of men who had chosen this life in the full knowledge of what it entailed. There is a third important thing that would be likely to happen from time to time. The young man who had served for a short period and then returned to his home University might, later still, wish to be considered for appointment to a post as a professor or principal either at the College in which he had served or elsewhere. From the point of view of the Colonial College, nothing but gain would result from the institution of such a secondment system.

44 As to the home Universities, it must be fully recognized that the institution of any such scheme would entail a radically new departure from current practice, which would be made possible only by some sacrifice and considerable endeavour. Means whereby men could be attracted in the first instance would need to be worked out, though doubtless there would be no lack of applicants once the attractions of the scheme became apparent through the return to the Universities of men who had already served a period in the Colonies. The Universities would be called upon to make sacrifices in agreeing to some of their best men being released for work in the Colonies and in making arrangements which, while not jeopardising their own

efficiency, would yet keep open the appointments of their colleague whom they had temporarily released. In this connection, the magnitude of the resources of the home Universities must, however, be remembered. In 1938–39 the academic staffs of the Universities of Great Britain contained the following full-time members; professors 889, readers, assistant professors and independent lecturers 369, lecturers 1,543, assistant lecturers and demonstrators 856, and others 337. If in the first place one to two per cent. only of this total of 3,994 were made available to the Colonies for teaching and for research, both in Universities and elsewhere, no great difficulty should result if the burden were shared in anything like equal fashion, even though it is to be hoped that the particular men concerned would be of more than average academic merit.

45 While such a scheme would entail sacrifice, the balance would certainly not be entirely on the debit side. Firstly, many will agree that anything which provides new intellectual experiences for the members of the university staffs is not only invigorating to the individual, but stimulating to the academic body as a whole; our own Universities would in effect benefit in a different degree but in just the same way as would the Colleges which they would be endeavouring to help, for their own life would be greatly enriched. It is a common experience that the lively junior members of our academic staffs are usually just those who have travelled abroad for two years on a Commonwealth, Rockefeller or some other Fellowship; the secondment system for the junior members of staff would not be dissimilar in its effects, for while stimulus to those holding these Fellowships comes largely from working on problems similar to those investigated in British Universities but under the guidance of the best brains in the United States or elsewhere, it cannot be doubted that stimulus will also be provided to the able young man working on completely new problems in a radically new environment. Lastly, it will be agreed that great benefit will accrue if the system of providing sabbatical years to professors could be extended. At present most professors are financially unable to accept the offer of a sabbatical year without salary and the secondment system would be a means of removing this disability.

46 It is obviously not for us to suggest methods whereby the Universities should ensure the carrying on of the work of their absent colleagues. Two points are, however, worthy of mention. Firstly, the dislocation of university life caused by the present war has shown that many junior men are capable of shouldering efficiently greater responsibilities than fell to them in times of peace. Secondly, one of the great weaknesses of some of our Universities is the lack of funds to enable them to retain for a year or two longer men who have already completed two or three years' research work for a Ph.D. or other high degree. Under present conditions these men leave their Universities for posts elsewhere at just the stage when they are well trained and capable of carrying out independently research work of real value. The secondment system would clearly be a very great benefit in enabling men in this category to be retained in departments from which men had been released to the Colonies.

47 Any such scheme which brought the Universities of the Colonies into intimate relationship with those of Great Britain would also have not less important results of a wider nature. Firstly, the deplorable ignorance which exists in this country regarding the Colonies would in the course of time begin to be dispelled. Knowledge of the Colonies would first permeate the Universities through the return to them of men

who had seen colonial service. Inevitably this knowledge would be reflected in the teaching in different subjects and the students' interests would be widened; later through the teachers trained in the Universities it would ultimately reach the man in the street through the schools. Secondly, interest in the Colonies within the Universities would create interest among the students, and opportunity to discuss the question of service in the Colonies with their teachers, who had had personal experience themselves, would certainly lead to dispelling many of the fears of the unknown, which often deter men from entering the colonial service. As a result, more and better candidates would be available for all the colonial services; there would be better men for medicine, dentistry, veterinary science, agriculture, administration and the educational services. The cumulative benefits of any such scheme would be great.

48 Throughout this Report we endeavour to make proposals which would bring the life of the Colonies into more intimate contact with that of Great Britain. We wonder whether it is not desirable to institute also visiting lectureships for men from other countries, for these are days when thought runs along lines of international co-operation, and visiting lectureships of this type might not only have good effects on the life of the Colleges, but would also help to dispel from the minds of other peoples, ignorance of our colonial achievements.

49 We now turn to discuss the important question of how students of colonial Colleges are to obtain degrees during the period which must necessarily elapse before the Colleges have so far advanced as to receive their own University Charters. A decision on this question is urgently needed if the growth of the Colleges to the University stage is to be constructive, and serve the best interests of the Colonies and their peoples. The present position may be summarised by saying that a few students in Malaya and rather more in West Africa sit for certain of the external degrees of the Universities of London and Durham, while a larger number take the Intermediate or other first-year examinations. The Colonies thus contain already a number of men of degree standard, and many others will prove capable of reaching it readily as soon as some improvement in the available facilities is made. The desire of colonial students to possess degrees is a natural one, just as is the desire of students elsewhere; for the colonial student, it is reinforced by the impulse to demonstrate intellectual equality with the European. If Universities are to come into being and the policy of self government is to be increasingly achieved, this impulse is one which must be encouraged under the best conditions which we can devise. If the conditions are bad, the impulse will not be thwarted; it will persist and develop along undesirable lines.

50 Attention may be focused on the general problem by brief reference to the present position in the most advanced territory, namely, Malaya. In Singapore there is an excellent well-established medical school, with clinical facilities surpassing in some respects those available in the medical schools of Great Britain, and having an adequate academic staff. As in Great Britain, the student carries out the full six-year General Medical Council course at the end of which he receives a local diploma, which is registrable as a practising qualification throughout the British Empire. A reasonable case could be presented that the standard already reached at this medical school is but little short of the degree standard of Universities in Great Britain and the students would welcome degrees rather than their local diploma. In arts and science, however, which are taught at Raffles College, the average standard is only

about one year post intermediate; here a few of the candidates sit for London Degrees. These two Colleges are the future University of Malaya. How and when is the University to be created? What are to be the criteria of standards and efficiency in teaching and research on which the decision regarding university status is to be reached? Is the curriculum to be identical in each subject with that in use in Great Britain? A decision on these questions is needed now not only for Malaya but for the other territories also.

51 Before further discussion of this problem, we wish to emphasize our conviction that it is of the utmost importance that any degree awarded to a student either of an existing College or of any future colonial University must be of a standard equivalent to that awarded by Universities in Great Britain and fully accepted as such by them. It is essential that this be made clear, for it is fundamental to the whole conception underlying this Report.

52 Clearly the award of such degrees for some time to come will be possible only if the degree examinations are conducted by a University or group of Universities in Great Britain. We now turn to discuss the external degree system as at present practised, for we consider that modifications in it are imperative. Our comments are of general application, but since the external examinations of the University of Durham are taken by the students of Fourah Bay College only, particular illustrations are taken from the London Degree Courses.

53 There is much evidence to show that the application of the present external degree methods to the Colonies is educationally unsound and likely to undermine the best purposes of higher education. In the first place, the curriculum in many subjects is largely unrelated to the background and educational needs of the peoples, and the important educational principle that the curriculum should govern the examination and that the examination should not influence the curriculum, is ignored. There are many illustrations of this, as, for example, the necessity of a classical language such as Latin in the Intermediate B.A. for students who are already being taught in a language which is not their mother tongue; the requirements of Middle English and Anglo-Saxon in the final B.A. examination in English; and the inappropriate nature of the syllabuses in the Biological Sciences, History and Geography and in Social Science and Economics. The broad question here is whether a syllabus designed as suitable for a British degree should ever be imposed in conditions differing so radically from those in Great Britain. In addition, curricula for external examinations tend to undergo alteration but rarely, and in developing subjects they may be in arrears with current thought. Secondly, the necessity of teaching in terms of a curriculum imposed from outside leads to forms of examinations which themselves have most undesirable effects, particularly upon methods of study. Under the present system it is not possible to give credit to the student for his general performance during his years of study at his College and this prevents the development of the personal atmosphere and interest which it is so necessary to encourage. The staff, too, lose greatly from the lack of stimulus provided by contact with visiting examiners. Is it wise to retain in the Colonies a system under which a College has no part in the examining and the external University has no part in the teaching? Thirdly, the retention of such a system must result in impeding in the area concerned the development of a proper sense of pride in its own future University. The students now taking these degrees form the nucleus of educated opinion and some of them doubtless will go far in the service of their own peoples. It seems of importance that a

country should begin to gather faith in its own future at an early stage and that this should come from developments from within rather than acceptance of a superimposed pattern from without. Unless there is from the start a sense of obligation to the local territory, the growth of corporate responsibility will be impeded; the present system is unlikely to encourage this growth.

54 In passing, comment on the question of equality of standards is desirable. Degrees courses in Great Britain are designed adequately to occupy the mind of the average student, but at the same time to allow him a reasonable amount of time for those independent activities which do so much to mature his outlook and give him self-reliance. If we expect from the colonial student the same educational standard in this wider sense, and if we are to avoid hasty cramming, any course of the same content must be longer, say by one year, because of the many handicaps under which the student labours; for he is being educated in a foreign medium and he lacks the advantages of the home environment and the sixth-form or post-matriculation phase of schooling available to the student in Great Britain.

55 In our opinion, the present external degree system needs substantial modification in two directions; firstly, in the curriculum, and secondly, in the method of conduct of the examinations.

56 We have indicated our views regarding the curriculum in paragraph 53. The major purpose in the creation of Universities in the Colonies must be to ensure the increasing flow of men and women fitted to promote the development of their own country and the welfare of its people. Each of these Universities must therefore be indigenous and must not be subject to some arbitrary pattern introduced from Great Britain. Apart from providing the customary facilities for professional study, these Universities must be designed to fructify native cultural possibilities, and to study problems in their local, rather than in their foreign forms. This seems to us a compelling reason why the curriculum in some subjects should differ from that in use in Great Britain.

57 Two other aspects of the curriculum question are worthy of notice. Firstly, the life and purpose of a growing colonial College is undermined by the fact of teaching two categories of students, one for external degrees on the present system and the other for internal diplomas on a reformed system. Secondly, the attainment of degrees is not only the desire of the student. The staffs realise that their Colleges cannot make material progress unless an increasing number of their students are successful in obtaining degrees. This commendable attitude has been known to lead them to make application to their Governing Bodies for permission to teach on curricula which experience shows are inappropriate. If such an application is rejected, the effects on the staff are most unfortunate, for they naturally feel that they lack an objective.

58 We now turn to discuss the second direction in which we consider changes necessary, namely, in the conduct of the external examinations. In our view the methods of examination which we have at home, whereby visiting examiners from other institutions act with the internal examiners in the setting of the papers, the marking of the scripts, and the assay of the final results, should be brought into being. This system could be introduced by the creation in Great Britain of a Panel of Examiners to serve the needs of all the colonial Colleges. The Panel, the functions of which are discussed in paragraphs 61–64 would meet under a chairman of eminence and might be composed of members drawn from a single University;

alternatively, each home University might be represented on it. The examinations in the colonial Colleges could then be conducted in a similar way to those in the Universities of Great Britain. Air communication in the post-war period will make it readily possible for the papers to be set and marked by the Internal and visiting Examiners; in addition each colonial College might be visited each year, if not by all, at least by one Examiner representing each group of subjects, such as one for arts, one for science, one for medicine and so on.

59 The advantages to be gained if such a method could be introduced are many. Firstly, since the Panel would be made up of men of academic standing, experienced in examining in Great Britain, intimate knowledge of the standards of achievement of each College, of the growth of its material facilities, of the qualities of its staff and of the nature of the research work which it was undertaking, would become available to the home Universities. Secondly, experience has already shown vividly the stimulating effect on progress in colonial Medical Colleges which results from the visits of examiners of the Conjoint Board and from those of the inspectors sent out by the General Medical Council; similar stimulus to progress in other subjects would be provided by this method. Visits by members of the Panel would obviously be of great value to the staff, for lively interest would be evoked by personal contact and discussion, by advice and by the pooling of experience, and the sense of intellectual isolation would be decreased. These visits too would be of great psychological value to the student, who would realise that this system had a much more personal approach than the present external degree system; it would aid materially in helping to overcome the narrow examination outlook discussed in paragraph 54. Thirdly, the position of the Principals and staffs of the Colleges would be greatly strengthened against political influences which are inevitable in the early stages of higher education. The introduction of this system would, in effect, result in the admission of the Colleges of the Colonies to our own university circle and would forge a further bond between the home Universities and the Colonies as a whole. It must be emphasized here that such a Panel could not provide, under present conditions, for the award of degrees. This question is, however, discussed in paragraphs 61–64.

60 In putting forward this proposal, we wish to emphasize that we are not only concerned with the few degree students who exist at the present time. We believe strongly that these visiting examiners should similarly take part in the conduct of the examinations for local diplomas, and this view is shared by the Principals of the two African Colleges.

61 How are these two desirable objectives of appropriate curricula and new methods of conducting the examinations to be achieved? The most obvious line of approach is through the University of London which alone has great experience of the award of external degrees and already examines some students in the Colonies. London University might well be asked on Imperial grounds to consider the question of the award of degrees in the Colonies as a special problem. In making this suggestion, we realise the considerable departure from its external examination practice which is entailed. We recognise, for instance, that the adoption of our proposal for a visiting Panel of Examiners would mean that the degree examination in the Colonies would be conducted in much the same way as that for the London internal degree; that special curricula would be needed for the different areas; that the examiners would have the additional task of assisting in the examination of the

candidates for the local diplomas for which London University would, of course, have no direct responsibility. On the other hand, it must be emphasized that the solution of the problems of the curriculum and examination can only be provided by a realistic approach by some University or group of Universities. There is the further point that London University has an established reputation as a Body conferring external degrees to which some students, at least in West Africa, are already beginning to turn. It might prove difficult to provide for these students an acceptable alternative to the London degree.

62 In this way London University might undertake the important task of carrying out all the examinations in the colonial Colleges until the Universities later come into being. Such a policy might, however, have wider implications which might make its adoption by London University difficult or impossible. If this proved to be so, the University might still shoulder this responsibility by a slightly modified method, assuming, as we do, that our plea for locally-adapted curricula is accepted. The examining Panel might, for instance, be composed of representatives drawn from all the home Universities as mentioned in paragraph 58. London University might then delegate to this Panel of experienced examiners the responsibility of carrying out on its behalf these particular examinations even though the degrees conferred would still be London degrees.

63 A third method of approach to this problem has been suggested to us; namely, that by an extension of the idea of the Panel of Examiners drawn from all the home Universities, there should be created an academic body representative of all the Universities of Great Britain with powers to award degrees in the Colonies; among the members of such a body representatives of the colonial Colleges themselves should be included. Such a body would need a Charter and it might bear some such title as 'The Colonial University'. In effect, the home Universities would be acting as joint trustees until the colonial Colleges had so developed as to merit receiving their own Charters. We freely recognize that this idea of a University in Trust, as it were, is novel, but we are so impressed with the importance of the problems before us that we feel fully justified in presenting it. In our opinion, we ought not slavishly to translate into the Colonies methods which have served well enough in the very different conditions of our own country without imaginative exploration of possible new methods of approach. We hope, therefore, that this idea will not be rejected without careful investigation.

64 It is an idea which has many attractions. Launched in an adequate manner with all the great authority of the combined Universities of Great Britain, such a scheme might overcome the possible difficulty of the students of West Africa regarding the new degree as an inferior substitute for the London degree; such, at least, is the opinion of the Principal of Achimota College. It would result in the Universities of this country as a whole doing well for the Colonies what is not being done well under the existing external degree system. Further, under this scheme the combined Universities might also take responsibility for the actual standards to be achieved in the diplomas, a responsibility which the University of London might not itself be prepared to undertake. In this sense, the idea is only different in emphasis from present practice in our own Universities, where, in a variety of subjects, many students obtain diplomas and not degrees. We freely admit that there is no precedent for such an imaginative conception as is presented by the idea of 'The Colonial University'. On the other hand, many of the apparent administrative

difficulties which make the proposal appear impracticable at first sight, would be overcome in the light of proposals made in paragraphs 83–88.

65 Any one of the three methods outlined in paragraphs 61–64 would achieve the objects in view. Students in the Colonies would acquire degrees based on curricula best suited to the needs of the country, yet equivalent in standard to a degree in Great Britain; the life of the Colleges would be transformed, for they would be given a real objective; in place of disordered growth there would be wise planning; Universities would come into being by a natural evolutionary process and many of the difficulties described in paragraph 25 would be avoided.

66 In discussing the important effects which would result from the conduct of the examinations in the manner we have indicated, we do not lose sight of the fact that no examination can be of real value unless the quality of the teaching is high. The importance of the teaching staff being adequate both in standing and numbers is therefore overwhelming, and for this reason we have discussed this staffing problem at length in paragraphs 34–47. Universities cannot suddenly be created in the Colonies. We believe, however, that if we call on the great wealth of accumulated experience available in Great Britain, and take the measures we have proposed for improvements in the staffs and the examinations, we can do much to accelerate their constructive development.

67 It is not for us to express opinion as to which of the three methods is most desirable. We wish, however, to emphasize one point. As we have indicated earlier, we believe that the home Universities should be brought into intimate contact with the life of the Colonies. If the Panel of Examiners were drawn from all the Universities, a further step in this direction would be taken.

68 Lessons are to be learned from the history of higher education in Ceylon which bear closely on the subject under discussion. Here the London Matriculation and the London External Degree examinations so increasingly obstructed the outlook at University College, Colombo, that the very purposes of the College were undermined, and the lure of these examinations made it impossible for development to occur along the lines which we envisage in this Report. We mention this illustration as showing the dangers which can be avoided by far-sighted planning at the present stage.

69 It is convenient here to refer to the London Matriculation examination. This examination or its School Certificate equivalent tends to be regarded by the colonial pupil as the necessary qualification for entry either to Government or other employment, just as in Great Britain the attitude of employers has encouraged similar faith in the Matriculation Certificate; it is also used for entry to some of the colonial Colleges. An illustration of the extent to which this examination may be taken is provided by Ceylon, where as many as 4,000 Ceylonese children have taken one single London Matriculation examination. Once established this outlook tends to spread at increasing speed, and it has begun to appear in the colonial territories as a whole. Recent information shows, for instance, that in West Africa, a School Cerficate carrying a matriculation exemption is preferred to one which may represent a far more worthy educational achievement. Action has already been taken in Great Britain to deal with a similar situation. In 1939 the Joint Matriculation Board of the Northern Universities recognized the ill effects of the use of the Matriculation Certificate for purposes far removed from that for which it was originally designed, and abolished it; a new standard of entrance to the Universities was then created by

requiring the passing of certain subjects in the School Certificate examination followed by the passing of others at the subsidiary standard of the Higher School Certificate one year later, but without the issue of any Matriculation certificate. While the war caused the temporary suspension of the latter new University requirements, the abolition of the Matriculation Certificate was final. This question of the Matriculation Certificate affects not only the schools but the admissions to the colonial Colleges. The Cambridge Syndicate has modified the curriculum of its School Certificate examination in a number of subjects to meet the needs of the different Colonies, and in our opinion, this examination is now much better adapted to colonial needs as a school-leaving examination. We wonder, therefore, whether London University might not take similar steps if it does not intend to follow the lead of the Northern Universities in abolishing its Matriculation examination altogether.

70 Having discussed the general problems involved in the question of how the Colleges are to evolve to university status, we now turn to elaborate in more detail the broad ideas expressed earlier concerning the part which the Colleges have to play in research. We begin by making reference to the newly-created Colonial Research Committee which is charged with the initiation and development of research within the Colonies and is empowered to recommend expenditure up to £500,000 a year. Under present conditions, research within the Colleges will come within the purview of this Committee, with the members of which we have had two valuable discussions.

71 As stated in paragraph 14, historical reasons account in part for the fact that research in the Colonies has so far been almost entirely confined to work carried out by Government Departments or other bodies, while the Colleges themselves have been little concerned with research. Under the moral and financial stimulus which the Colonial Research Committee will provide, extensive research development in the Colonies will doubtless take place in the near future. We therefore record our views as to the place which the Colleges would take in these research developments.

72 For reasons already mentioned in paragraph 29, we consider it as highly important that research should come to be regarded as being of not less importance than teaching in the life of the Colleges. Unless steps are taken greatly to broaden their life, the Colleges will certainly fail to achieve the objective of becoming the intellectual centres of their territories. The encouragement of research within the Colleges must obviously not be allowed to hinder its further development in other institutions. On the other hand, it is equally important that the present backwardness of the Colleges in research should not be regarded as a reason for a yet further concentration of research in existing institutions; it should be regarded as an incentive to taking vigorous steps towards making up the present leeway of the Colleges and to ensuring that the present divorce of research from teaching is not perpetuated.

73 Just as in Great Britain, the terms of appointment of members of academic staffs should include the duty of carrying out research as well as teaching. The inclusion of research in the terms of appointment must obviously carry with it the certainty that both facilities and staff are adequate to ensure that research is possible.

74 When any particular new programme of research is under discussion by the Colonial Research Committee the possibility of the College being made the centre at which it is carried out should always be in the forefront. Obviously in some spheres of work, geographical or climatic conditions will make it necessary to erect

new institutions or field stations far away from the sites of the Colleges. On the other hand unless there are such solid reasons to the contrary, in our opinion, any new facilities required should be provided at the Colleges either by the erection of special institutes or by additions to the accommodation of existing departments. Such Research Institutes might be either an integral part of the College, or associated with it in some way similar to those adopted in this country, where there are many precedents which might be followed.

75 When men are sent out from Great Britain for the purpose of carrying out special researches in the Colonies, their activities should not be limited to their research only. It would clearly be greatly to the gain of the Colleges if such men could give a short course of lectures or seminars each year on their own special subject, even if the lectures were only few in number. This would provide great interest and stimulation both to the students and to the staff, and in most cases, the opportunity to give these lectures would be welcomed by the research worker. If the research was being carried out in the College or in a new institute adjacent to it, activities such as these and others would present no difficulty, and would bring the research worker with all that he has to give into the active life of the College. If he were working elsewhere, it is of not less importance that he should visit the College from time to time for this same purpose. Anyone familiar with university life in this country will appreciate fully how much it owes to the occasional assistance of the distinguished visitor; in the isolated Colleges of the Colonies, the benefits of activities such as these would be very much greater.

76 Much research work which is urgently needed in the Colonies is of the regional type and includes such things as nutritional surveys and work in the social sciences. It is highly desirable that the Colleges should act as the headquarters of workers involved in these fields, for the same reasons as have just been discussed. Similarly, it is desirable that the existing complete divorce of the Colleges from research work carried out by Government departments should not continue. If research work goes forward in the Colleges, it will obviously be of great gain to the workers in these departments to be in contact with the Colleges; in their turn the Colleges will benefit much; occasional interchange of staff for short periods would obviously be of value also.

77 There is a growing opinion in Great Britain, that the present position is unsatisfactory in which researches carried out in Universities, in research institutions conducted by special Government committees and in industry are often divorced from one another. It seems desirable therefore that in planning research in the Colonies we should endeavour to bring our own experience to bear and to try to introduce a new outlook which will avoid the creation of barriers between these different types of research bodies. Admittedly there are difficulties to face but the opportunity exists to overcome them; the very backwardness of the Colonies provides this opportunity since vested interests have not had time to develop to any great extent.

78 The proposals which we have made would help greatly in creating the correct attitude towards research. They would husband the material and intellectual resources together in one centre and would ensure that the greatest use was made of them. They would make certain that in the course of time the Colleges were able to train local research workers adequately who will obviously be needed in increasing numbers as research develops. Above all, they would ensure the gradual evolution of the College as the centre of learning and intellectual life of the Colony, and this is

the primary objective. In these largely undeveloped and often vast territories what is required at the present time is an acknowledged centre of learning which will act as the focus of the intellectual development of the territory. Diffusion of resources will not accomplish this aim, for these Colleges must be developed on the broadest basis if they are to avoid political difficulties. The peoples must take just pride in them and realise that the Colleges belong to them and that the future of the Colleges and of themselves lies in their own hands. Further, the building up of real centres such as we envisage, may well prove of great importance in any regionalisation schemes which may later come into being.

79 An important matter concerning research within the Colleges calls for comment, namely, the provision of adequate facilities and of adequate staff, both of which will entail considerable expenditure. The Colonial Research Committee may well feel that its duty is confined to approving applications for grants for research into problems placed before it by individual workers who wish to carry out particular pieces of work; this method is adopted by such bodies as the Medical Research Council in Great Britain. On the other hand, there is much to be said for the view that on a longer-term policy it would prove a wise investment to give to the Colleges a block grant for a period of, say, five years in order to assist their general development in much the same way as is done by the University Grants Committee in our own country. It is true that probably little return on a grant of this type would emerge for the first few years. On the other hand, it would be a great incentive to research within the Colleges if they received grants of this type from so distinguished a Committee. Further, such grants would bring home to the local Governments and peoples the fact that research was an integral part of the life of the Colleges, and if given on a pound-for-pound basis, would introduce a new outlook. Apart from this, grants of this type might be justified on the grounds that the Colleges are responsible for the training of the local research assistants on the production of which progress in research will increasingly depend. While we recognize that grants for a variety of purposes can and doubtless will be made to the Colleges by the Colonial Development and Welfare Committee, we hope that, apart from grants in aid of specific individual researches, the possibility of a block grant from the Colonial Research Committee will be carefully considered. There is a third direction in which research grants might be made, which should present no difficulty, namely, in the grant to a particular department of funds for research in a general subject. With this mention of research, it is now possible to discuss the question of machinery to give effect to the proposals made earlier in this Report.

80 It is clear that the success of any broad scheme for promoting the welfare of the Colleges depends in very large extent on the provision of staff and examiners and on contributions in many other directions which the home Universities may feel able to make. Nevertheless, it seems unlikely that these Universities would be able to set up suitable machinery for putting a scheme into effect successfully, for its success demands detailed knowledge of the Colonies, in which the Universities are lacking. Equally, the Advisory Committee on Education itself has neither detailed knowledge of the home Universities nor is it linked sufficiently closely with them. It is a body resembling in some ways the Board of Education and concerned with general education; higher education is, however, a highly intricate form of education requiring the specialised treatment of the expert. It seems clear, therefore, that it will be necessary to create a new body responsible to the Secretary of State.

Among its members there would need to be considerable representation of the home Universities and also other members with a detailed knowledge of the Colonies and their needs.

81 Since we are obviously unable to foretell the final form which any scheme may take, it would be purposeless to discuss in detail the nature and functions of this new body. A number of points are, however, worthy of mention even at this stage.

82 Firstly, if the Colleges are to receive the full impetus to constructive development which is so desirable, it is essential that all matters connected with their welfare should be advised upon by a single body. Under present conditions, applications for grants in aid of the salaries of research workers and of research equipment and materials will come forward from the Colleges to the Colonial Research Committee; on the other hand, applications for grants for development of their teaching activities such as buildings, houses for the staff and so on will be considered by the Development and Welfare Committee, presumably after discussion by the Colonial Education Advisory Committee. This is an undesirable state of affairs, for it represents a separation of teaching and research, and in university development these two functions are too closely interlocked to be separable from one another. The co-ordinated growth of our own Universities would not, for instance, have been possible under conditions such as these. Further, unless a single body is responsible for university development as a whole, there will be much wasted effort and the Colleges will not receive the moral encouragement and help which is so necessary to them, for they require much more than channels through which applications for grants may be made.

83 For these reasons, we suggest that a new body which might be known as 'The Colonial University and Research Council' might be created; that the existing Colonial Research Committee should become a Committee of this new body; and that a second committee should be formed to deal with the development of higher education as a whole. This University Committee might concern itself with all questions of teaching and research within the Colleges; the Colonial Research Committee might, on the other hand, apply itself largely to what may be described as institutional research conducted at special institutions and research stations. Overlapping membership between the two bodies would obviously be desirable to ensure ordered progress.

84 The creation of such a 'Colonial University and Research Council' would also be a first step in making possible the formation of a unified Colonial Higher Education and Research Service, a matter which we discussed at length with the Colonial Research Committee. The institution of a new Service such as this would, in our opinion, have most important effects in helping to attract men of distinction to give to the Colonies varying periods of service either in higher education or research, for it would introduce a new and inspiring outlook on colonial problems.

85 An important point needing consideration here is whether the University Committee should receive powers to advise on grants from the Colonial Development and Welfare Fund. At the present time under the Colonial Development and Welfare Act grants can only be recommended either by the Development and Welfare Committee or by the Colonial Research Committee. The proposed University Committee would, however, receive applications for many things outside research, as mentioned in paragraph 82. It could, of course, send these forward to the Development and Welfare Committee with its comments; similarly, it could forward applications for grants in aid of research to the Research Committee. On the other hand,

the University Committee would gain greatly in importance if it were empowered to recommend grants for general university purposes from the Development and Welfare Fund, and if it were able to call upon a block grant put at its disposal by the Colonial Research Committee.

86 This is a matter of importance for two reasons. Firstly, whatever the scheme which finally emerges, it will demand much from the home Universities, in fact, no scheme will be successful unless it evokes their unstinted help. It would be unreasonable to expect this help unless the Universities through their Vice Chancellors or other representatives appointed as members of the University Committee were convinced by the importance attaching to its functions that their help was earnestly needed. Secondly, under present colonial practice, we cannot compel the Colonies to accept any scheme. We can do no more than present an offer, and the offer will inevitably be more attractive if it is backed by the opportunity of financial assistance. This appears to us a compelling reason for the University Committee being empowered to deal with applications for grants whether for teaching or research. This will rapidly focus attention on it from the Colleges and will make it more readily able to pursue its many other necessary activities.

87 Whatever new body be created, its relationship both to the Colonial Research Committee and the Advisory Committee on Education will need definition. Overlapping membership with the Advisory Committee would maintain close liaison with colonial education generally. It would also be necessary to investigate the part which the Universities Bureau might take in any scheme which was evolved, for it might prove advantageous for the Bureau to be responsible for some part of the activities.

88 If a University Committee of this type was set up, it would be an important body having many functions. (a) It would act as the Committee to which all matters concerning higher education in the Colonies were, in the first place, referred. (b) Whenever the colonial Colleges required a man for teaching or research, whether for short-term or permanent appointment it would, if invited, get into touch with the home Universities to find the best man available, both on academic grounds and on the important matter of personal qualities and outlook. The actual procedure to be adopted would depend on the wish of the institution concerned and would vary with the extent to which the institution could send or appoint its representative to the selection meeting. It must be emphasized here that, while the staffing problem has been discussed in detail in paragraphs 37 to 41 from the point of view of secondment for short periods of service, the question of finding adequate men for permanent appointment is not less vital. The men chosen would, of course, be appointed by the institutions to which they were going, and the final decision as to their appointment would need to rest with the institution. (c) The Committee would acquaint itself thoroughly with all the problems, the position and the staffing of the Colleges. It would follow the careers of members of their staffs and would gather experience as to the type of men who were most successful; it would be its duty to do its best to ensure that any man who wished for a change, either to return home or to be transferred to another Colony, might have his wish fulfilled. Above all, it would show that the conception which exists in academic circles that concern with the Colonies is a waste of time, is no longer tenable, and it would foster the idea that those who went to the Colonies would not be forgotten but had friends and advisers in academic circles at home. (d) It would make recommendations concerning grants under the Colonial

Development and Welfare Act as mentioned in paragraph 85. (*e*) It would be involved in the question of examinations, the scope of its examination activities depending on which scheme is finally adopted. (*f*) It would advise the Colonial Colleges on any matter of policy, curriculum or research on which they sought help. (*g*) It would build up a fund of information regarding the standards achieved, it would be available for advice regarding the most suitable University to which a particular man might go for post-graduate study in this country, and would advise the home University regarding his achievements. (*h*) Lastly, suitably constituted and under an imaginative policy, it would bring into being the establishment of a colonial University system which in its turn would be an integral part of an Imperial system of higher education.

89 Such a Committee would clearly need a permanent Secretariat if its functions were of the nature just described, while if the proposal concerning the creation of The Colonial University mentioned in paragraph 63 were adopted, the functions of the University Committee would need both modification and extension.

90 All the ideas so far discussed would result in the Universities of Great Britain as a whole taking a very intimate part in the development of higher education in the Colonies. It might be argued, however, that a less ambitious approach at the present stage, leading ultimately to some such wider scheme, might prove more fruitful and achieve the objectives more rapidly. In this connection, the attachment of individual colonial Colleges to particular Universities in Great Britain needs consideration, and the recent informal association of Makerere College with the University of Oxford comes to mind. The objects of this association are the giving by the University of Oxford of advice regarding the curriculum when invited to do so, and of sending visiting lecturers to the College if and when occasion permits. If this idea were developed on a more comprehensive and official basis the Colleges might be affiliated in the literal sense to particular home Universities which would thereby become largely responsible for furthering their development and catering for their needs.

91 An attraction of such a scheme would be that recruitment of members of the staff would be relatively easy, for the staff of the College would tend to regard themselves as part of the staff of the particular University to which the College was so closely connected. On the other hand, there is the danger that the staff would tend to be recruited almost exclusively from the parent University; the affiliated College might tend to mould itself too closely on the practices of its parent University in conditions in which close imitation might be unwise; and advice on the curriculum would only be of real value if the parent University had available on its staff members who had personal experience of the needs of the particular Colony. Difficulties might also arise as to which College should be affiliated to which University; there might be divided views at home as to the most fruitful lines of development; further, it might not always be possible to supply from one particular University men fully suited to the type of teaching or research needed by the colonial College. The idea of affiliation with its many implications clearly needs careful exploration before it is rejected. While our view is that the colonial Colleges should be brought into close contact with our Universities as a whole, we fully recognize that valuable results would accrue from the association of particular colonial Colleges with particular home Universities within the framework of a wider scheme. Associations of this type might arise as a result of personal interests of members of academic staffs or

of common interests in specific problems; many opportunities for liaison of this type readily come to mind.

92 Having considered the broad aspects of a possible Imperial machinery, we now turn to discuss the question of study in British Universities by students from the Colonies. All experience shows that the sending of students from the Colonies to Great Britain for undergraduate study is often unfortunate in its effects, for on their return to their home country their outlook may have been changed far too radically; inevitably they compare what they saw in Great Britain with what they find at home, and whereas before leaving their country they were satisfied, they subsequently find only discontent. The important object of producing leaders of their own countrymen is not achieved, for the conception that those who lead best are those who serve best is often undermined. Even if they are fortunate enough to avoid the social dangers, these students are far too often insufficiently mature to be able to devote themselves successfully to their studies amid their new environment.

93 On the other hand, it is of great importance to make adequate provision for post-graduate study. The student who has acquired his initial qualification is now older and more mature and less likely to fall a victim to disillusionment or worldly temptation. It may be desirable, however, that post-graduate scholarships should not be awarded until the man selected has spent a year as a junior member of the staff of his own institution, for such a year, free from the bogey of examinations and in contact with his teachers on a new footing, will enable him to emerge from his student outlook and will develop his sense of balance; experience of sending local doctors, who have already spent two or three years in Government service before coming to Great Britain to study for some diploma such as the Diploma of Tropical Hygiene, confirms this view. It is desirable also that every effort should be made to find employment for post-graduate scholars on their return; otherwise discontent and political controversy will arise. It is important to remember that it is through the development of post-graduate scholarships that it will be possible for the staffs of the colonial Colleges to be slowly but increasingly made up of local men and women.

94 This question of post-graduate study in Great Britain is a most important matter for consideration by the home Universities, since it involves the whole question of recognition by them of work done by the student in his colonial College. While post-graduate study by 'graduates' of Medical Colleges which award a registrable diploma, recognized by the General Medical Council presents no difficulty, this position holds in no other subject. Thus it cannot be of great value to award an expensive scholarship for two or three years to a student of, say, Raffles College, Singapore, who has probably reached Pass Degree standard already, if he is required to make a fresh start when he comes to England, and to begin to read for a Bachelor Degree. This is a further reason for accelerating the provision of opportunities for obtaining degrees in the Colonies, for the student naturally prefers to return home even with a Bachelor Degree rather than widen his knowledge with no visible reward for having done so. It seems reasonable, therefore, to suggest that the home Universities should be asked to make specific arrangements for the reception and training of post-graduate students, even though they may not have obtained in their colonial College degrees of the accepted type in Great Britain. In this connection it must be remembered that, if a wide scheme of the kind we have discussed comes into being, detailed information regarding the diploma standards and the

curricula at each colonial College will be available to all the Universities through the 'Colonial University and Research Council'.

95 It has been suggested earlier that degrees awarded in the Colonies should be based on curricula suited to local needs. It is important to emphasize that such a degree will only find acceptance if it is recognised by the home Universities, the Governments and employers generally as equal in standard to the English degree. From the point of view of post-graduate study, recognition by the home Universities must be complete in the sense that the student must be allowed to proceed forthwith from his initial degree to advanced study in any one of his particular subjects. It seems to us, therefore, that the creation of courses for degrees will thus involve not only the University of London or some other body conferring degrees; it will be necessary for all the Universities to be consulted at each stage in order to ensure that they are willing to accept the modified curriculum of a particular subject as exempting the student from further under-graduate study in that subject. We emphasize this point because the curricula in some subjects will doubtless differ radically from those in use in Great Britain, and academic bodies in our Universities have naturally and wisely been very conservative in their recognition, particularly for the purposes of post-graduate study, of courses given for degrees and diplomas when these curricula differ significantly from their own.

96 Reference will now be made to the question of the entrance requirements to the Colleges. There are many who share the view that the entrance requirements at present in use in the home Universities are at times inadequate to ensure that only students really capable of profiting by university education are admitted. The problem of what should be the entrance requirements for admission to Colleges in the Colonies is a far more pressing one, for results of examinations such as the London Matriculation or the School Certificate are a very uncertain guide indeed to the potentialities of the student; the reasons for this are the deficiencies of the secondary school education mentioned in paragraph 15. This matter is of great importance; firstly, because discontent follows when students who have been admitted, fail to achieve their goal; secondly, a high wastage rate has ill effects on the teaching, the general outlook and the standards of any institution, as any with experience of teaching will know; thirdly, it is important that some new method should be adopted to ensure that only the best students are admitted, if for no other reason than to remove from Governments their just anxiety about the dangers of producing a body of disillusioned unemployed. Some form of special entrance examination to serve as a test of intelligence rather than of factual knowledge seems imperative, and interviews for the same purpose seem desirable. In the absence of sixth forms in schools and their maturing influence on the mind of senior pupils, we wonder whether the difficulty of a high wastage rate might not be further met by making the first year at a College a probationary one, since it is clearly advantageous to remove, at the earliest stage possible, students who are not likely to benefit by further study. An authoritative opinion on this general question would be of great value, for it is important that the peoples be educated as soon as possible to the view that the possession of a School Certificate is not necessarily an index of general ability. Such a statement would greatly strengthen the hands of the Principals of the Colleges in introducing new methods of entrance which will inevitably tend to be unpopular at first.

97 In all the Colleges there are many scholarships or free places, and in one of

them, all the places are free under a Government bursary system. There is to-day a growing opinion in our own country that ability to pay fees should not be the factor which determines whether educational opportunity is available to any student. Is it wise to perpetuate in these newly developing territories, a system which we ourselves recognise leaves much to be desired? It cannot be too strongly emphasized that our immediate task is to find and educate the potential leaders of the peoples of the Colonies. Would it not be a gesture of great value to abolish fees in the Colleges altogether and thus give a vivid demonstration to the peoples of the seriousness of our intentions that those who showed potential powers of leadership should not lack opportunity to develop them? In making this suggestion, we realise that safeguards would need to be taken to ensure that opportunities for higher education were still available to those who might not be entirely deserving on merit in open competition but for whom it was in the interests of the country as a whole that opportunity should be available; thus it is essential to stimulate the higher education of women, the sons of chiefs and others.

98 A proposal such as this makes a wise decision on the method of entry to the Colleges even more important; it would focus attention on the Colleges as centres from which the future leaders are to emerge; it would undermine the idea of some Governments that the Colleges can serve no purpose other than as centres for vocational training, for it would establish the conception that while professional attainment was one objective, the development of wider attributes was not less important; it would, in addition, show far-sighted planning.

99 Throughout this Report, we have emphasized our opinion that it is vital both from the educational and political point of view that the home Universities should now undertake to give active help in the development of Universities in the Colonies. We wish to record here that we fully recognize the serious obligations which so radical a departure from current practice entails for them; and that many difficulties will need to be overcome if success is to be achieved. The major initial difficulty will be that of bringing home to the members of their academic bodies the intellectual opportunities in connection with the problems of the Colonies no less than our responsibilities towards them. Clearly the intimate nature of the help which we consider desirable will not be possible merely through the goodwill of a very few members of each university staff: by some means interest in colonial life must be actively brought to the notice of the academic bodies as a whole. Perhaps informal discussions in which chosen groups at each University were addressed by speakers with an intimate knowledge of the Colonies would, in the first instance, assist the Vice Chancellors in making their colleagues Colonies-conscious. But whatever form of propaganda be used, it will fail unless it is followed by action which brings the Colonies into the active daily life of the Universities.

100 In this connection, the possibility of linking Lord Hailey's proposed African Bureau with some University merits earnest consideration; similarly, the question of the creation in particular Universities of the Colonial Institutes or perhaps Regional Institutes after the model of the Indian Institute at Oxford or the Colonial Institute at Amsterdam should be explored. We should like to see lectureships established in some Universities in such subjects as colonial history or in the social and other sciences with particular reference to the Colonies. These lectureships would at first be mainly concerned with research. Their holders would contribute greatly by producing much-needed authoritative literature on colonial problems and this litera-

ture would serve as a source of information for the preparation of text-books and lectures; in providing the home students with attractive optional subjects in under-graduate courses; in relating to its colonial background the wider post-graduate studies of students who will increasingly come to Great Britain from the Colonies; in assisting the Colonial Office to carry out long-range research problems, the invest-igation of which is urgently required. All these activities would greatly stimulate the spread of knowledge and interest in colonial problems in the home Universities, both among the staff and among the students. Lastly, these lectures would in the course of time, take an active part in giving teaching to the members of the Colonial Service who are likely to come to our Universities for training of all kinds. On the research side also, it seems likely that the Colonial Products Research Council will increasingly make considerable use of the Universities for the investigation of its problems.

101 It seems to us necessary also that the opportunity of bringing the Colonies into the life of senior research students should not be overlooked. Ought it not to be possible for holders of 1851 Scholarships or Department of Scientific and Industrial Research Grants to be permitted in selected instances to proceed to the Colonies to carry out specific pieces of research work at such institutions as can afford adequate facilities and direction of their studies? Would it be possible too, for a Senior Research Fellowship to be established in each University from some source or another to enable one student a year to pursue his studies in the Colonies? The home Universities, in general, accept as part of the requirements of their higher degrees such as the Ph.D., M.D., etc., work carried out at institutions other than their own, and the question of extending this type of recognition under approved conditions to work done at institutions in the Colonies merits thought.

102 There is another important matter worthy of mention here, namely, our attitude towards students who come to this country from abroad. Many will agree that too often in the past we have failed to appreciate our responsibilities towards them, and have not recognized that their visits to us must leave a permanent mark on their lives which will largely govern their future outlook towards ourselves and the world at large. It seems to us that we have peculiar opportunities in the case of students from the Colonies and that we should seize them. We should realize that if these students return to their own peoples with a feeling of content that everything possible has been done to promote their progress in our home Universities, they will unconsciously act as unofficial ambassadors. If they return discontented, evil results will certainly occur. In this connection, ought not there to be appointed in the home Universities, specially chosen tutors who would look after the welfare of the students from the Colonies? Men of the right capacity would ensure that students returned to their own territory not only with their academic objective achieved, but with a wide appreciation of English life and culture; much could be done by this means to undermine the attitude of suspicion as to our motives, which exists at the present time.

103 Such then are our views of the problems to be faced and some of the lines of enquiry which seem to us likely to be fruitful. As we have already said, we believe that the problems must be investigated now, and that plans must be made ready, for these are days when events move rapidly and new conceptions rapidly spring into being. The very success of our own propaganda leaves us with no option but to go forward; we must, however, go forward constructively and without hurry, giving the lead rather than being pressed into action. The psychological value of the present

attitude of mind both at home and abroad is great; at home, there is a new consciousness of our obligations, and in the Colonies, pronouncements such as that of
the Atlantic Charter, have led to expectations. Advantage must be taken of the new
outlook at home, and the expectations of the Colonies must be moulded to fruitful
and constructive purpose. We ourselves are incapable of doing more than to provide
a sketch of the problem as a whole; its solution must lie in more expert hands, and
its political and educational importance with their wide implications are such that
we consider an authoritative enquiry to be essential.

> (Sgd)   H. J. CHANNON (*Chairman*)
>   F. CLARKE
>   J. HUXLEY
>   B. MOUAT JONES
>   W. M. MACMILLAN
>   M. PERHAM
>   R. A. McL. DAVIDSON (Colonial Office)

Mr C. W. M. Cox had to proceed overseas before the Report was completed and
was represented by Mr R. A. McL. Davidson. Mr E. R. Hussey had also proceeded
overseas before the Report was completed.

C. A. GROSSMITH (*Secretary*)

Colonial Office
    15th May, 1943

BIBLIOGRAPHY

INDIA

The following bibliography lists the main sources cited in the references to chapters 3–5, together with some additional background material.

PRIMARY SOURCES

I *Unpublished material*

At the India office library and record department, Commonwealth relations office.

A. Records of the East India Company and board of control.

Letters from India and Bengal.

Despatches to India and Bengal (original drafts).

Board's collections.

B. India office records.

Judicial and public department papers (classified J. & P.).

C. European manuscripts series.

MSS. Eur. F. 78: papers of Sir Charles Wood, 1st viscount Halifax (Wood collection).

MSS. Eur. F. 111: papers of George Nathaniel, marquess Curzon of Kedleston (Curzon collection).

II *Published material*

A. Official records.

1 Great Britain.

Report from the select committee of the house of lords appointed to inquire into the operation of the Act 3 & 4 Will. 4, c. 85, for the better government of her majesty's Indian territories; together with the minutes of evidence, appendix and index; 1852–53 (41) XXX, 1.

Second report; 1852–53 (627–1) XXXII, 1.

Index to reports; 1852–53 (627–111) XXXIII, 319.

Reports from the select committee on Indian territories, together with the minutes of evidence and appendices:

First report; 1852–53 (426) XXVII, 1.

Sixth report; 1852–53 (897) XXIX, 1.

Index to reports; 1852–53 (897–11) XXIX, 269.

Interim report of the Indian Statutory Commission. (Review of growth of education in British India by the Auxiliary Committee appointed by the Commission.) September, 1929; 1929–30, Cmd. 3407, X, 535.

Parliamentary debates.

2 India and Pakistan.

(a) contemporary publication.

Proposed plan of the University of Calcutta. Calcutta, 1845.

Papers relating to the establishment of the Presidency College of Bengal (Selections from the records of the Bengal government, XIV). Calcutta, 1854.

Papers connected with the establishment of universities in India. Calcutta, 1857.

Report of the Indian Education Commission. Appointed by the resolution of the government of India dated 3rd February 1882. Calcutta, 1883.

Education Commission. Report by the Bengal provincial committee; with evidence taken before the committee, etc. Calcutta, 1884.

Review of education in India in 1886 [first quinquennial review], and succeeding reviews for 1887–88 to 1891–92 etc. to 1917–22. Calcutta, 1888–1923.

Report of the Indian Universities Commission, 1902. Simla, 1902.

Indian Universities Act, 1904 (VIII of 1904).

The conference of orientalists, including museums and archaeology conference, held at Simla, July 1911. Simla, 1911.

Report of the Dacca University Committeee, 1912. Calcutta, 1912.

Benares Hindu University Act, 1915 (Act XVI of 1915).

Calcutta University Commission, 1917–19. Report. 13 vols. Calcutta, 1919–20. [Sadler report.]

Post-war educational development in India: report by the central advisory board of education, January 1944. Delhi, 1944. [Sargent report.]

The report of the University Education Commission (December 1948–August 1949). 2 vols. Delhi, 1950. [Radhakrishnan report.]

Report of the Commission on National Education. Government of Pakistan, ministry of education, January–August 1959. Karachi, 1960.

Legislative proceedings of the council of the governor general of India.

(b) later publication.

Bureau of education, India. Selections from educational records. I. 1781–1839, *ed.* H. Sharp; II. 1840–1859, *ed.* J. A. Richey. 2 vols. Calcutta, 1920–22.

National archives of India. Selections from educational records of the government of India.

I. Educational reports, 1859–71: being two notes on the State of education in India compiled by A. M. Monteath in 1862 and 1867 and part two of Education in British India prior to 1854 and in 1870–71 by A. P. Howell. Delhi, 1960.

II. Development of university education, 1860–87. *Ed.* J. P. Naik. Delhi, 1963.

B. Writing and discussion on current problems of Indian education.

Wilson, H. H. 'Education of the natives of India', *Asiatic Journal*, NS XIX, No 73 (Jan.–April 1836) 1–16 [letter to the editor, 5 Dec. 1835].

Trevelyan, C. E. On the education of the people of India. Calcutta, 1838.

Cameron, Charles Hay. An address to parliament on the duties of Great Britain to India, in respect of the education of the natives and their official employment. London, 1853.

[Tawney, C. H.] 'The studies of the Calcutta University', *Calcutta Review*, LXXXII (1865) 297–317.

Chirol, Valentine. Indian unrest: a reprint, revised and enlarged, from *The Times*, with an introduction by Sir Alfred Lyall. London, 1910.

James, H. R. Education and statemanship in India, 1797–1910. London, 1911. [Reprinted from the Calcutta *Statesman*, Jan.–Mar. 1911.]

James, H. R. Problems of higher education in India. Bombay, 1916. [Reprinted from 'Indian education' 1905–09.]

Hartog, P. J. 'Some problems of Indian education', *Educational Review*, XXVI (1920) 211–27.

— 'The work of the Calcutta University Commission', *Asiatic Review*, XVI (1920) 597–608.

Sharp, Sir H. 'The development of Indian universities', *J. Roy. Soc. Arts*, LXXIII (1925) 513–35.

Hartog, Sir P. Some aspects of Indian education past and present. London, 1939.

C. Newspapers.

The Times (London).

D. University records.

Benares Hindu University. Benares Hindu University, 1905 to 1935, *ed*. V. A. Sundaram. [Benares], 1936.

University of Calcutta. Minutes for the year 1857–. Calcutta, 1860–.

— Convocation addresses. I. 1858–1879; II. 1880–1898. 2 vols. Calcutta, 1914.

E. Autobiography, memoirs, letters and speeches.

Curzon, George Nathaniel, baron Curzon of Kedleston. Speeches by Lord Curzon of Kedleston, viceroy and governor general of India . . . 1898–1900 (—1904–1905). 4 vols. Office of the superintendent of government printing: Calcutta, 1900–06.

— Lord Curzon in India: being a selection from his speeches as viceroy & governor-general of India, 1898–1905.   With . . . an introduction by Sir Thomas Raleigh. London, 1906.

Hardinge, Charles, baron Hardinge of Penshurst. Speeches of his excellency the right hon'ble baron Hardinge of Penshurst. 2 vols. Madras [1914, 19].

— My Indian years, 1910–1916: the reminiscences of Lord Hardinge of Penshurst. London, 1948.

Maine, Sir Henry J. S. Sir Henry Maine: a brief memoir of his life by . . . Sir M. E. Grant Duff, . . ., with some of his Indian speeches and minutes selected and edited by Whitley Stokes . . . London, 1892.

Mouat, Frederic J. 'The origin, progress, and influence of universities in India', *J. Soc. Arts*, XXXVI (1888) 483–507.

Muir, J. R. B. Ramsay Muir: an autobiography and some essays, *ed*. Stuart Hodgson. London, 1943.

Raleigh, Sir W. The letters of Sir Walter Raleigh (1879–1922) *ed*. Lady Raleigh. 2 vols. London, 1926.

Ramsay, James A. B., marquess of Dalhousie. Private letters of the marquess of Dalhousie, *ed*. J. G. A. Baird. Edinburgh, 1910.

SECONDARY SOURCES

I *General*

Bearce, George D. British attitudes towards India, 1784–1858. London, 1961.

Fraser, Lovat G. India under Lord Curzon & after. London, 1911.

Misra, B. B. The Indian middle classes: their growth in modern times. London, 1961.

O'Malley, L. S. S., *ed*. Modern India and the west: a study of the interaction of their civilizations. London, 1941.

Panikkar, K. M. The foundations of new India. London, 1963.

Philips, C. H. The East India Company, 1784–1834. 2nd edn. Manchester, 1961.

Roy, Naresh Chandra. The civil service in India. 2nd edn. Calcutta, 1960.

Smith, Vincent A. The Oxford history of India. 3rd edn, *ed.* Percival Spear. Oxford, 1961.

Stokes, Eric. The English utilitarians and India. London, 1959.

II *Education*

Ballhatchet, K. A. 'The home government and Bentinck's educational policy', *Camb. Hist. J.*, X, No 2 (1951) 224–9.

— 'John Stuart Mill and Indian education', *Camb. Hist. J.*, XI, No 2 (1954) 228.

Bruce, J. F. A history of the University of the Panjab. Lahore, 1933.

Dongerkery, S. R. A history of the University of Bombay, 1857–1957. Bombay, 1957.

Grier, Lynda. Achievement in education: the work of Michael Ernest Sadler, 1885–1935. London, 1952.

Keay, F. E. Indian education in ancient and later times: an inquiry into its origin, development and ideals. Revd edn. London, 1938.

McCully, Bruce Tiebout. English education and the origins of Indian nationalism. New York, 1940.

Mayhew, A. I. The education of India: a study of British educational policy in India, 1835–1920, and of its bearing on national life and problems in India to-day. London, 1926.

Moore, R. J. 'The composition of "Wood's Education Despatch"', *Eng. Hist. R.*, LXXX (1965) 70–85.

Nurullah, Syed and Naik, J. P. A history of education in India (during the British period). Revd edn. Bombay, 1951.

Silveira, A. A. A critique of the Sadler report (1919) with special reference to later developments of university education in India. Unpubd M.A. thesis, Univ. of London, 1957.

Spear, Percival. 'Bentinck and education', *Camb. Hist. J.*, VI, No 1 (1938) 78–101.

Thomas, Frederick W. The history and prospects of British education in India: being the Le Bas prize essay for 1890. Cambridge, 1891.

University of Calcutta. Hundred years of the University of Calcutta: a history of the university issued in commemoration of the centenary celebrations. Supplement. 2 vols. Calcutta, 1957.

University of Madras. History of higher education in South India: University of Madras, 1857–1957. 2 vols. Madras, 1957.

III *Biography*

Dundas, L. J. L., earl of Ronaldshay. The life of Lord Curzon, being the authorized biography of George Nathaniel, marquess Curzon of Kedleston, K.G. 3 vols. London, 1928.

Hampton, H. V. Biographical studies in modern Indian education. Madras, 1947.

Hartog, Mabel. P. J. Hartog: a memoir by his wife. London, 1949.

Lee-Warner, Sir William. The life of the marquis of Dalhousie. 2 vols. London, 1904.

Sadleir, Michael [i.e. M. T. H. Sadler]. Michael Ernest Sadler (Sir Michael Ernest Sadler K.C.S.I.) 1861–1943. London, 1949.

Smith, George. The life of Alexander Duff, D.D., LL.D. 2 vols. London, 1879.
— Twelve Indian statesmen. London, 1897.
Trevelyan, G. Otto. The life and letters of Lord Macaulay. 2 vols. London, 1876.

AFRICA

The following bibliography lists the main sources cited in the references to chapters 6–10, together with some additional background material.

PRIMARY SOURCES

I *Unpublished material*

A. Colonial office records.

  1 At the public record office.

      C.O. 87 : original correspondence, Gambia.
      C.O. 96 :   ,,   ,,   Gold Coast.
      C.O. 147:   ,,   ,,   Lagos.
      C.O. 267:   ,,   ,,   Sierra Leone.
      C.O. 520:   ,,   ,,   S. Nigeria.
      C.O. 879/8: confidential print, Africa No 82, pt I. Sierra Leone.

  2 Records of the advisory committee on native education in tropical Africa (later, the advisory committee on education in the colonies).
      Reports mentioned in the text, and reproduced in an appendix:
      A.C.E.C. 44/33: Report of the sub-committee appointed to consider the educational policy underlying paragraph 19 of the report of the conference of directors of education of Kenya, Tanganyika, Uganda and Zanzibar, held at Zanzibar in June 1932, December 1933. [Currie report.]
      A.C.E.C. 7/43: Report of the sub-committee on higher education, 15 May 1943. Confidential print, Misc. No 507. [Channon report.]

B. Records of the Church Missionary Society at CMS headquarters, 6 Salisbury Square, London.
    Committee minutes.
    G.AC: General secretary's papers, home correspondence.
      2. letter books (outgoing).
      4. original letters (incoming).
    C.A1: West African Mission.
      I. individual letter book (outgoing).
      L. letter books (outgoing).
      O. original letters, journals and papers (incoming).

C. Records of the inter-university council for higher education in the colonies (later, inter-university council for higher education overseas).
    Minutes of the council and executive committee, 1946–62.
    Reports mentioned in the text:
      Report of inter-university council delegation to Makerere College, the University College of East Africa. August, 1954.
      Report of the working party on higher education in East Africa, July–August 1955 [sponsored jointly with the ACEC].

Report of the working party on higher education in East Africa, July–August 1958.

University of Northern Nigeria; report of the inter-university council delegation, April 1961.

D. Records of the University of London.

Minutes of the senate.

Minutes and reports of the special committee of the senate on higher education in the colonies (later, senate committee on colleges overseas in special relation) 1944–62.

Correspondence with the Asquith commission.

E. Miscellaneous.

Report to the government of the Eastern Region of Nigeria concerning the development of a university. 7 July 1958.

American council on education. Education for development: report of the survey team on education in Malawi. 1964.

Harvard University. Report of the special committee to review the present status and problems of the general education programme. 1964.

University of East Africa. Draft university development plan for the triennium 1964–67.

University of Lagos. Report on the constitution of the University of Lagos. 30 November 1964.

II *Published material*

A. Official records.

1 Great Britain.

(a) Parliamentary papers.

Report from the select committee on the west coast of Africa; together with the minutes of evidence, appendix and index. Part I, report and evidence; 1842 (551) XI, 1. Part II, appendix and index; 1842 (551) XII, 1.

Annual reports from the dependencies of the west coast of Africa: for 1845– . [See note, p. 414 above.]

Report from the select committee on Africa (western coast); together with the proceedings of the committee, minutes of evidence and appendix; 1865 (412) V, 1.

Board of education: special reports on educational subjects.

Vol. 13. Educational systems of the chief crown colonies and possessions of the British empire, including reports on the training of native races. Part II. West Africa, Basutoland, Southern Rhodesia, East African protectorate, Uganda, Mauritius, Seychelles; 1905, Cd. 2378, XXVI, 1.

Vol. 14. Educational systems, etc. Part III. Federated Malay States, Hong Kong, Straits Settlements, Fiji, Falkland Islands; 1905, Cd. 2379, XXVI, 385.

Education policy in British tropical Africa: memorandum submitted to the secretary of state for the colonies by the advisory committee on native education in the British tropical African dependencies; 1924–25, Cmd. 2374, XXI, 27.

Report of the commission on higher education in the colonies; 1944–45, Cmd. 6647, IV, 673. [Asquith report.]

Report of the West Indies committee of the commission on higher education in the colonies; 1944–45, Cmd. 6654, V, 791. [Irvine report.]

Report of the commission on higher education in West Africa; 1944–45, Cmd. 6655, V, 593. [Elliot report.]

Inter-university council for higher education overseas, 1946–54; 1955–56, Cmd. 9515, XIV, 843.

Parliamentary debates.

(b) Other official papers.

Imperial Education Conference papers. III. Educational systems of the chief colonies not possessing responsible government: Gold Coast Colony, Ashanti and the Northern territories, HMSO, 1914; Northern Nigeria, HMSO, 1913; Southern Nigeria, HMSO, 1913.

Higher education in East Africa: report of the commission appointed by the secretary of state for the colonies. September, 1937. Colonial No 142. HMSO, 1937.

Fourah Bay College: report of the commission appointed in 1938 by the secretary of state for the colonies to report on Fourah Bay College, Freetown. Colonial No 169. HMSO, 1939.

Higher education in Malaya: report of the commission appointed by the secretary of state for the colonies. June, 1939. Colonial No 173. HMSO, 1939.

2 Africa.

(a) Central Africa.

Central African Council. Report of the commission on higher education for Africans in Central Africa. Salisbury, S. Rhodesia, 1953.

Charter: the University College of Rhodesia and Nyasaland, 10 February 1955, Federal notice, No 103 of 1955.

Report on the development of a university in Northern Rhodesia, 1963. Lusaka, 1964.

(b) East Africa.

The Makerere College Act 1949 [amended 1954, 61, 63, 64.]

The University of East Africa: report of the committee on needs and priorities, 1962. Entebbe, Uganda, 1962.

The University of East Africa Act, 1962, E. A. Common Services Organisation Act No 16 of 1962.

Education in Uganda: the report of the Uganda education commission, 1963. Entebbe, 1963.

(c) Gold Coast, later Ghana.

Report of the special committee appointed by his excellency Sir Hugh Clifford to report upon and to make such recommendations as seem desirable in the educational system of the Gold Coast. Sessional paper XVII of 1918–19.

Report of the educationists' committee appointed by his excellency the governor on 5th March, 1920 to advise the government on educational matters, together with minutes of the meetings of the committee. Accra, 1920.

Achimota College: report of the committee appointed in 1932 by the governor of the Gold Coast Colony to inspect the Prince of Wales' College and School, Achimota. Accra, 1932.

Achimota College: report of the committee appointed in 1938 by the governor of the Gold Coast Colony to inspect the Prince of Wales' College, Achimota. Accra, 1939.

Report of the education committee, 1937–41. Gold Coast, 1942.

Report of the committee on higher education, August–November, 1946. No VII of 1946. [Bradley report.]

The University College of the Gold Coast Ordinance, 1948, G.C. No 6 of 1948.

Report of the commission on university education, December 1960–January 1961. Ministry of information, Accra, 1961.

Statement by the government on the report of the commission on university education, December, 1960. January, 1961. W.P. No 5/61.

University of Ghana Act, 1961, Act 79.

Gold Coast legislative council debates.
Gold Coast legislative assembly debates.
Ghana parliamentary debates.

(d) Nigeria.

University College, Ibadan, Ordinance, 1954, No 10 of 1954.

University of Nigeria Law, 1955, E.R. No 23 of 1955.

University of Nigeria (Provincial Council) (Amendment) Law, 1959, E.R. No 10 of 1959.

Investment in education: the report of the commission on post-school certificate and higher education in Nigeria. Federal ministry of education, Lagos, 1960. [Ashby report.]

Educational development 1961–70. Federation of Nigeria, sessional paper No 3 of 1961.

University of Nigeria Law, 1961, E.N. Law No 21 of 1961.

University of Ife (Provisional Council) Law, 1961, W.N. No 6 of 1961.

Ahmadu Bello University Law, 1962, N.N. No 26 of 1962.

University of Ibadan Act, 1962, No 37.

University of Lagos Act, 1962, No 1.

University development in Nigeria: report of the national universities commission. Federal ministry of information, Lagos, 1963.

Federal house of representatives debates.
Federal republic of Nigeria parliamentary debates.

(e) Sudan.

University of Khartoum Act, 1956, 1956 Act No 29.
The University of Khartoum (Amendment) Act 1960, 1960 Act No 53.

3 United nations.

United nations economic commission for Africa, and united nations educational, scientific and cultural organization. Conference of African states on the development of education in Africa, Addis Ababa, 15–25 May 1961. Outline of a plan for African educational development [Paris] 1961; Final report [Paris] 1961.

UNESCO. The development of higher education in Africa: conclusions and recommendations of the Conference on the development of higher education in Africa (Tananarive, 3–12 September 1962) Paris, 1963.

B. Semi-official and unofficial surveys on African education.

World Missionary Conference, 1910. 9 vols. Edinburgh, 1910. [Vol. III. Education in relation to the christianisation of national life: report of Commission III.]

Phelps-Stokes Fund. Education in Africa: a study of West, South, and Equatorial Africa by the African Education Commission under the auspices of the Phelps-Stokes Fund and Foreign Mission Societies of N. America and Europe. Report prepared by Thomas Jesse Jones. New York, 1922.

Phelps-Stokes Fund. Education in East Africa: a study of East, Central and South Africa by the second African Education Commission under the auspices of the Phelps-Stokes Fund, in cooperation with the International Education Board, Report prepared by Thomas Jesse Jones. New York, 1925.

Nuffield foundation and colonial office. African education: a study of educational policy and practice in British tropical Africa. Oxford, 1953.

C. Writing and discussion on current problems of higher education.

1 Universities in Britain, Europe and America.

Benda, Julien. La trahison des clercs (Cahiers verts, 2, vi). Paris, 1927.

Herklots, H. G. G. The new universities, an external examination. London, 1928.

Flexner, Abraham. Universities: American, English, German. London 1930.

Robertson, Sir Charles Grant. The British universities. London, 1930.

Barker, Ernest. 'Universities in Great Britain', in *Universities in a changing world, ed.* W. M. Kotschnig and E. Prys. London, 1932.

Hutchins, R. M. The higher learning in America. New Haven, 1936.

Löwe, Adolf. The universities in transformation. London, 1941.

Truscot, Bruce, *pseud.* [i.e. Edgar Allison Peers] Redbrick university. London, 1943.

— Redbrick and these vital days. London, 1945.

Harvard University. General education in a free society: report of the Harvard committee. Cambridge, Mass., 1945.

Ortega y Gasset, José. Mission of the university. London, 1946.

Kandel, I. L. and Oliver, R. A. C. 'American controversy on the philosophy of education', *Universities Quarterly*, II, No 2 (1947) 131–5.

Nuffield College, Oxford. The problem facing universities. Oxford, 1948.

Lindsay, A. D., *baron Lindsay of Birker.* 'The commission on German universities', *Universities Quarterly*, IV, No 1 (1949) 82–8.

McConnell, T. R. 'Impressions of British university education', *Universities Quarterly*, III, No 3 (1949) 656–64.

Moberly, Sir Walter. The crisis in the university. London, 1949.

'The mission of a university – a discussion', *Universities Quarterly*, IV, No 1 (1949) 15–81.

'The crisis in the university', *Report of the proceedings of the 1949 Conference of Great Britain and Northern Ireland.* Association of universities of the British Commonwealth. London, 1949.

2 Universities in Africa.

Horton, James A. B. Political economy of British Western Africa; with the requirements of the several colonies and settlements (the African view of the negro's place in nature); being an address to the African Aid Society. London, 1865.

— West African countries and peoples, British and native: with the requirements necessary for establishing that self government recommended by the committee of the house of commons, 1865; and a vindication of the African race. London, 1868.

Blyden, Edward W. The West African University: correspondence between Edward W. Blyden, M.A., and his excellency J. Pope Hennessy, C.M.G., administrator-in-chief of the West Africa settlements. Freetown, 1872.

— The aims and methods of a liberal education for Africans: inaugural address delivered by Edward Wilmot Blyden, LL.D., president of Liberia College, January 5, 1881. Cambridge, Mass., 1882.

— The Lagos Training College and Industrial Institute. Correspondence between Edward W. Blyden, LL.D., and his excellency Sir Gilbert T. Carter, K.C.M.G., governor and commander-in-chief of Lagos and its protectorates. Lagos, 1896.

Casely Hayford, J. E. Ethiopia unbound: studies in race emancipation. London, 1911.

National Congress of British West Africa. Resolutions of the Conference of Africans of British West Africa, held at Accra, Gold Coast, from 11th to 29th March 1920; Memorandum of the case of the National Congress of British West Africa for a memorial based upon the resolutions to be presented to his majesty the king emperor in council through the right honourable the secretary of state for the colonies. [1920]

Guggisberg, Sir Gordon. The keystone. London, 1924.

Guggisberg, Sir Gordon and Fraser, A. G. The future of the negro: some chapters in the development of a race. London, 1929.

Perham, Margery. 'The relation of the home universities to colonial universities and colleges', Conference of the Home Universities, 1946. University Bureau of the British Empire. London, 1946.

Balme, D. M. 'University aims in the Gold Coast', Universitas, I, iii (June 1954) 13–5.

Hodgkin, T. 'The idea of an African university', Universities Quarterly, XII (1958) 376–84.

Olubummo, Adegoke, and Ferguson, John. The emergent university, with special reference to Nigeria. London, 1960.

Saunders, J. T. and Dowuona, Modjaben, eds. The West African intellectual community: papers and discussions of an international seminar on inter-university cooperation in West Africa, held in Freetown, Sierra Leone, 11–16 December 1961. Ibadan, 1962.

Hanson, J. W. 'The land grant philosophy and African higher education', West African Journal of Education, VI (1962) 80–4.

Mellanby, Kenneth. 'Establishing a new university in Africa', Minerva, I, No 2 (1963) 149–58.

Hanson, J. W. Imagination and hallucination in African education. East Lansing, 1965.

3 University autonomy and academic freedom.

Polanyi, Michael. The foundations of academic freedom (Society for Freedom in Science, Occasional pamphlet No 6). Oxford, 1947.

Njoku, E. 'The relationship between university and society in Nigeria', in *The scholar and society* (Bulletin of the Committee on Science and Freedom, 13). Manchester, 1959. Pp. 82–6.

'Academic freedom', *Law and Contemporary Problems*, XXVIII (1963) 429–71.

Heron, D. B. 'Some reflections on academic freedom', *Makerere Journal*, 9 (1964) 33–43.

Perkins, J. A. 'The new conditions of autonomy' in Emerging patterns in American higher education, *ed*. Logan Wilson. Washington, 1965. P. 14.

D. Newspapers.

Daily Graphic (Accra), 1950–62.

Daily Times (Lagos), 1950–60.

The Ghanaian Times.

Ghana Today (London).

The Spark (Accra).

The Times (London).

Uganda Argus, 1955–62.

Uganda Herald, 1950–62.

E. University records.

1 Great Britain.

University of Durham. Calendars, 1877—.

University of London. Calendars, 1850—.

University of London. Schemes of special relation: regulations, 1952—.

2 Africa.

Universities and university colleges. Calendars and prospectuses.

University College of the Gold Coast (later, of Ghana, later University).

Reports by the principal; for 1948–52 [1953]—.

Notices, 1949–54.

University College [later University of Ghana] Reporter, 1954–.

University College of Ibadan (later, University).

Reports; for 1948–53 (1955)—.

F. Autobiography, memoirs, letters and speeches.

Awolowo, Obafemi. Awo: the autobiography of chief Obafemi Awolowo. Cambridge, 1960.

Azikiwe, Nnamdi. Zik: a selection from the speeches of Nnamdi Azikiwe. Cambridge, 1961.

Barker, W. H. 'The early days of the Accra Training Institution', *The Teachers' Journal*, I (1929) 136–40.

Bello, Sir Ahmadu. My life. Cambridge, 1962.

Burns, Sir Alan. Colonial civil servant. London, 1949.

Cameron, Sir Donald. My Tanganyika service and some Nigeria. London, 1939.

Casely Hayford, J. E. West African leadership: public speeches delivered by the Hon. J. E. Casely Hayford, *ed*. Magnus J. Sampson. Ilfracombe, [1949].

Hussey, E. R. J. Tropical Africa, 1908–1944: memoirs of a period. London, 1959.

Mitchell, Sir Philip. African afterthoughts. London, 1954.

Nkrumah, Kwame. The autobiography of Kwame Nkrumah. Edinburgh, 1957.

— I speak of freedom: a statement of African ideology. London, 1961.

Taha Husain. The stream of days: a student at the Azhar. Trans. Hilary Way-ment. 2nd edn. London, 1948.

G. Miscellaneous

Fyfe, Christopher. Sierra Leone inheritance. London, 1964.

Hodgkin, Thomas. Nigerian perspectives: an historical anthology. London, 1960.

Metcalfe, G. E. Great Britain and Ghana: documents of Ghana history, 1807–1957. London, 1964.

SECONDARY SOURCES

I *General*

Ahmed, Jamal Mohammed. The intellectual origins of Egyptian nationalism. London, 1960.

Burns, Sir Alan. History of Nigeria. 4th edn. London, 1948.

Diop, Cheikh Anta. L'Afrique noir pré-coloniale. Paris, 1960.

Dubois, F. Timbuctoo the mysterious. London, 1897.

Coleman, James S. Nigeria, background to nationalism. Berkeley, Cal., 1958.

Coleman, James S., *ed.* Education and political development. Princeton, 1965.

Ezera, Kalu. Constitutional developments in Nigeria. Cambridge, 1960.

Findlay, G. G. and Holdsworth, W. W. The history of the Wesleyan Methodist Missionary Society. 5 vols. London, 1921–4.

Fox, William. A brief history of the Wesleyan missions on the western coast of Africa. London, 1851.

Fyfe, Christopher. A history of Sierra Leone. London, 1962.

Groves, C. P. The planting of christianity in Africa. 4 vols. London, 1948–58.

Hailey, W. M., *baron Hailey.* An African survey: a study of problems arising in Africa south of the Sahara. London, 1938. Revd edn, 1957.

Hodgkin, Thomas. Nationalism in colonial Africa. London, 1956.

Kimble, David. A political history of Ghana: the rise of Gold Coast nationalism, 1850–1928. Oxford, 1963.

Oliver, Roland. The missionary factor in East Africa. London, 1952.

Padmore, G., *ed.* History of the Pan African Congress. London, 1947. 2nd edn, with new material, 1963.

Perham, Margery. The colonial reckoning (Reith lectures, 1961). London, 1961.

Post, Ken. The new states of West Africa. London, 1964.

Stock, Eugene. The history of the Church Missionary Society: its environment, its men and its work. 4 vols. London, 1889–1916.

II *Sociology*

Bascom, William R. and Herskovits, Melville, J., *eds.* Continuity and change in African cultures. Chicago, 1959.

Busia, K. A. The challenge of Africa. London, 1962.

Curle, Adam. Educational strategy for developing societies: a study of educational and social factors in relation to economic growth. London, 1963.

Forde, Daryll, *ed*. African worlds: studies in the cosmological ideas and social values of African peoples. London, 1954.

Fortes, M. and Evan-Pritchard, E. E., *eds*. African political systems. London, 1940.

Herskovits, Melville J. The human factor in changing Africa. New York, 1962.

Hunter, Guy. The new societies of tropical Africa: a selective study. London, 1962.

— Education for a developing region: a study in East Africa. London, 1963.

Malinowski, Bronislaw. The dynamics of culture change: an inquiry into race relations in Africa. *Ed*. Phyllis M. Kaberry. New Haven, 1945.

Mannoni, O. Prospero and Caliban: the psychology of colonization. London, 1956.

Mphahlele, Ezekiel. The African image. London, 1962.

Murray, A. Victor. The school in the bush: a critical study of the theory and practice of native education in Africa. London, 1929.

Okeke, U. Educational reconstruction in an independent Nigeria. Unpubd Ph.D. thesis, New York University, 1955.

Oldham, J. H. and Gibson, B. D. The remaking of man in Africa. London, 1931.

Read, Margaret. Education and social change in tropical areas. London, 1955.

— Education, culture and nationalism in Africa. London, 1961.

Smith, Edwin W. The golden stool: some aspects of the conflict of cultures in modern Africa. London, 1926.

Smythe, H. H. and Smythe, M. M. The new Nigerian élite. Stanford, 1960.

Southall, Aidan, *ed*. Social change in modern Africa: studies presented and discussed at the first international African seminar, Makerere College, Kampala, January 1959. London, 1961.

Westermann, Diedrich. The African today and tomorrow. 3rd edn. London, 1949.

III *History of education*

A. General.

Bartels, F. L. The provision and administration of education in the Gold Coast, 1765–1865. Unpubd M.A. thesis, Univ. of London, 1949.

Graham, Sonia F. A history of education in relation to the development of the protectorate of Northern Nigeria 1900–19, with special reference to the work of Hanns Vischer. Unpubd Ph.D. thesis, Univ. of London, 1955.

Hilliard, F. H. A short history of education in British West Africa. London, 1957.

Kitchen, Helen, *ed*. The educated African: a country-by-country survey of educational development in Africa. London, 1962.

Mason, R. J. British education in Africa. London, 1959.

McWilliam, H. O. A. The development of education in Ghana: an outline. London, 1959.

Mayhew, A. I. Education in the colonial empire. London, 1938.

Nduka, Otonti. Western education and the Nigerian cultural background. Ibadan, 1964.

Okongwu, N. J. History of education in Nigeria, 1842–1942. Unpubd Ph.D. thesis, New York University, 1955.

Sumner, D. L. Education in Sierra Leone. Freetown, 1964.

Wise, Colin G. A history of education in British West Africa. London, 1956.

B. Higher education.

Ashby, Sir Eric. African universities & western tradition (Godkin lectures, 1964). Cambridge, Mass., 1964.

Carr-Saunders, Sir Alexander M. New universities overseas. London, 1961.

[Denton, J.] 'History of Fourah Bay College', *Sierra Leone Messenger*, Nos 91, 92 (1915) 397–409, 429–41.

Heiser, F. B. 'Fourah Bay College', *Church Missionary Review*, LXXVII (1926) 60–72.

Macpherson, Margaret. They built for the future: a chronicle of Makerere University College, 1922–1962. Cambridge, 1964.

Mellanby, Kenneth. The birth of Nigeria's university. London, 1958.

Saunders, J. T. University college, Ibadan. Cambridge, 1960.

Tazi, Abdelhazi. Onze siècles à l'université Qarawiyin: 859–1960. Fez, 1960.

Thompson, Thomas J. The jubilee and centenary volume of Fourah Bay College, Freetown, Sierra Leone. Freetown, 1930.

Whiting, C. E. The University of Durham, 1832–1932. London, 1932.

Williams, C. Kingsley. Achimota: the early years, 1924–1948. Accra, 1962.

IV *Biography*

Perham, Margery. Lugard. I. The years of adventure; II. The years of authority. London, 1956, 60.

Sadleir, Michael [i.e. M. T. H. Sadler]. Michael Ernest Sadler (Sir Michael Ernest Sadler, K.C.S.I.) 1861–1943: a memoir by his son. London, 1949.

Sampson, Magnus J. Gold Coast men of affairs (past and present). London, 1937.

Smith, Edwin W. Aggrey of Africa: a study in black and white. London, 1929.

Ward, W. E. F. Fraser of Trinity and Achimota. Accra, 1965.

INDEX

Abbreviations used:

ACEC   Advisory committee on education in the colonies
ACNETA Advisory committee on native education in tropical Africa
IUC   Inter-university council
U   University
UC   University College

Page numbers in italics refer to the documentary appendix

a'Beckett, Sir William, 43
Abrahams, Lionel, 92, 103
Academic freedom: defined, 290–2;
  protection of, 293; distinguished
  from university autonomy, 293
— in African university institutions,
  292, 319, 320–1, 331–2, 333, 336. *See
  also* 'Bantu' colleges, and Dakar,
  Haile Sellassie I and Lovanium
  universities
— in British universities, 292–3
  See also Autonomy
Academic standards: confused with
  quality, 237, 259–60; need for
  setting, 272
— in African university institutions:
  concern for, in planning (1925–45),
  193, 194–5, 199, 201, 203, 204, 205,
  206–7, 208–10, 212, 215–20;
  character of, under special
  relationship, 234, 235; African zeal
  for (1950–60), 236–8; IUC emphasis
  on (1955), 259–60; discussed at
  Jamaica (1955), 260 and Makerere
  (1962), 285; proposal to set at lower
  level (1957), 260; new method of
  safeguarding, for U of E. Africa
  (1958), 262–3; Nigerian commission
  on, 271–3; at U of Nigeria, 280;
  Lockwood on, 287; proposals for N.

Rhodesia (1963) and Malawi (1964),
  287–9. *See also* 'Bantu' colleges, and
  Dakar, Haile Sellassie I and
  Lovanium universities
— in British universities: in mid 19th
  century, 20ff.; in mid 20th century,
  226ff.
— in Indian universities: proposed by
  Wood, 61, and Colvile committee,
  62–3; early disquiet over, at
  Calcutta, 65–6; verdict of Indian
  Education Commission, 66–7;
  modest level of, at Calcutta (1882),
  66–8; deterioration of, at Calcutta
  (1882–1902), 68–72; verdict of Simla
  educational conference (1901), 71,
  and Indian Universities Commission,
  389; remedial measures of Curzon,
  74–5, 77–8; proposals of Dacca
  University Committee, 97–102, and
  Sadler commission, 121–2, 125–31,
  137
  See also Concessional entry *and*
  Entrance standards
Achimota, Prince of Wales' College at:
  planning of, in Gold Coast (1919–24),
  188, and ACNETA (1925), 193; and
  Currie report, 194; and quinquennial
  inspection committee (1938), 201–3,
  W. African governors' conference